WORD BIBLICAL COMMENTARY

Volumes

1 Genesis 1–15 . . . . Gordon J. Wenham
2 Genesis 16–50 . . . . Gordon J. Wenham
3 Exodus. . . . . John I. Durham
4 Leviticus . . . . .John E. Hartley
5 Numbers . . . . Philip J. Budd
6a Deuteronomy 1:1–21:9, 2nd ed. . . Duane L. Christensen
6b Deuteronomy 21:10–34:12 . . . . . . Duane L. Christensen
7a Joshua 1-12, 2nd ed. . . . . Trent C. Butler
7b Joshua 13-24, 2nd ed. . . . . . . Trent C. Butler
8 Judges . . . . Trent C. Butler
9 Ruth–Esther . . . . Frederic W. Bush
10 1 Samuel, 2nd ed. . . . . Ralph W. Klein
11 2 Samuel . . . . A. A. Anderson
12 1 Kings, 2nd ed. . . . . Simon J. Devries
13 2 Kings. . . . . T. R. Hobbs
14 1 Chronicles . . . . .Roddy Braun
15 2 Chronicles . . . . Raymond B. Dillard
16 Ezra, Nehemiah . . . . . .H. G. M. Williamson
17 Job 1–20 . . . . David J. A. Clines
18a Job 21–37 . . . . David J. A. Clines
18b Job 38–42 . . . . David J. A. Clines
19 Psalms 1–50, 2nd ed. . . . . . Peter C. Craigie, Marvin E. Tate
20 Psalms 51–100 . . . . Marvin E. Tate
21 Psalms 101–150, rev. ed. . . . .Leslie C. Allen
22 Proverbs. . . . . Roland E. Murphy
23a Ecclesiastes . . . . Roland E. Murphy
23b Song of Songs/Lamentations . . . .Duane H. Garrett, Paul R. House
24 Isaiah 1–33, rev. ed. . . . . . .John D. W. Watts
25 Isaiah 34–66, rev. ed. . . . . .John D. W. Watts
26 Jeremiah 1–25 . . . . Peter C. Craigie, Page H. Kelley, Joel F. Drinkard Jr.
27 Jeremiah 26–52 . . . . Gerald L. Keown, Pamela J. Scalise, Thomas G. Smothers
28 Ezekiel 1–19. . . . . .Leslie C. Allen
29 Ezekiel 20–48 . . . . .Leslie C. Allen
30 Daniel . . . . John E. Goldingay
31 Hosea–Jonah** . . . . Douglas Stuart
32 Micah–Malachi**. . . . . Ralph L. Smith
33a Matthew 1–13. . . . . Donald A. Hagner
33b Matthew 14–28. . . . . Donald A. Hagner
34a Mark 1–8:26** . . . . .Robert A. Guelich
34b Mark 8:27–16:20 . . . . .Craig A. Evans
35a Luke 1–9:20 . . . . John Nolland
35b Luke 9:21–18:34. . . . . John Nolland
35c Luke 18:35–24:53. . . . . John Nolland
36 John, 2nd ed. . . . George R. Beasley-Murray
37a Acts 1–14* . . . . .Stephen J. Walton
37b Acts 15–28* . . . . .Stephen J. Walton
38a Romans 1–8 . . . . .James D. G. Dunn
38b Romans 9–16 . . . . .James D. G. Dunn
39 1 Corinthians* . . . . .Andrew D. Clarke
40 2 Corinthians, rev. ed. . . . . .Ralph P. Martin
41 Galatians . . . . Richard N. Longenecker
42 Ephesians . . . . Andrew T. Lincoln
43 Philippians, rev. ed. . . .Gerald F. Hawthorne, rev. by Ralph P. Martin
44 Colossians, Philemon** . . . Peter T. O'Brien
45 1 & 2 Thessalonians** . . . . F. F. Bruce
46 Pastoral Epistles . . . . . . William D. Mounce
47a Hebrews 1–8. . . . . William L. Lane
47b Hebrews 9–13. . . . . William L. Lane
48 James . . . . .Ralph P. Martin
49 1 Peter . . . . .J. Ramsey Michaels
50 Jude, 2 Peter** . . . . . . Richard J. Bauckham
51 1, 2, 3, John, rev. ed. . . . . Stephen S. Smalley
52a Revelation 1–5 . . . . .David E. Aune
52b Revelation 6–16 . . . . .David E. Aune
52c Revelation 17–22 . . . . .David E. Aune

**forthcoming as of 2014*
***in revision as of 2014*

6B WORD BIBLICAL COMMENTARY

Deuteronomy 21:10–34:12

DUANE L. CHRISTENSEN

ZONDERVAN ACADEMIC

ZONDERVAN

Deuteronomy 21:10-34:12, Volume 6B

Previously published as *Deuteronomy 21:10-34:12.*

Formerly published by Thomas Nelson, now published by Zondervan, a division of HarperCollins*Christian Publishing.*

Requests for information should be addressed to:
Zondervan, 3900 *Sparks Dr. SE, Grand Rapids, Michigan 49546*

This edition: ISBN 978-0-310-52212-6

The Library of Congress has cataloged the original edition as follows:
Library of Congress Control Number: 2005295211

The author's own translation of the Scripture text appears in italic type under the heading *Translation*.

The Graeca, Hebraica, and Semitica fonts used to print this work are available from Linguist's Software, Inc., P.O. Box 580, Edmonds, WA 98020-0580 USA; tel. (206) 775-1130.

Printed in the United States of America

22 23 24 25 26 27 28 29 30 31 32 33 /TRM/ 18 17 16 15 14 13 12 11 10 9 8 7 6 5 4 3

To

Casper J. Labuschagne,

colleague, friend, and modern סוֹפֵר*,*

for his work on the numerical

composition of the Bible

Contents

Editorial Preface

The launching of the Word Biblical Commentary brings to fulfillment an enterprise of several years' planning. The publishers and the members of the editorial board met in 1977 to explore the possibility of a new commentary on the books of the Bible that would incorporate several distinctive features. Prospective readers of these volumes are entitled to know what such features were intended to be; whether the aims of the commentary have been fully achieved time alone will tell.

First, we have tried to cast a wide net to include as contributors a number of scholars from around the world who not only share our aims but are in the main engaged in the ministry of teaching in university, college, and seminary. They represent a rich diversity of denominational allegiance. The broad stance of our contributors can rightly be called evangelical, and this term is to be understood in its positive, historic sense of a commitment to Scripture as divine revelation and the truth and power of the Christian gospel.

Then, the commentaries in our series are all commissioned and written for the purpose of inclusion in the Word Biblical Commentary. Unlike several of our distinguished counterparts in the field of commentary writing, there are no translated works, originally written in a non-English language. Also, our commentators were asked to prepare their own rendering of the original biblical text and to use those languages as the basis of their own comments and exegesis. What may be claimed as distinctive with this series is that it is based on the biblical languages, yet it seeks to make the technical and scholarly approach to the theological understanding of Scripture understandable by—and useful to—the fledgling student, the working minister, and colleagues in the guild of professional scholars and teachers as well.

Finally, a word must be said about the format of the series. The layout, in clearly defined sections, has been consciously devised to assist readers at different levels. Those wishing to learn about the textual witnesses on which the translation is offered are invited to consult the section headed *Notes*. If the readers' concern is with the state of modern scholarship on any given portion of Scripture, they should turn to the sections on *Bibliography* and *Form/Structure/Setting*. For a clear exposition of the passage's meaning and its relevance to the ongoing biblical revelation, the *Comment* and concluding *Explanation* are designed expressly to meet that need. There is therefore something for everyone who may pick up and use these volumes.

If these aims come anywhere near realization, the intention of the editors will have been met, and the labor of our team of contributors rewarded.

General Editors: *Bruce M. Metzger*
David A. Hubbard†
Glenn W. Barker†
Old Testament: *John D. W. Watts*
New Testament: *Ralph P. Martin*

Author's Preface

I am grateful to the publisher and editors of the Word Biblical Commentary for the decision to use this occasion to revise Volume 6A (Deut 1–11) and to publish the commentary in two volumes of equal length: Volume 6A (Deut 1:1–21:9) and Volume 6B (Deut 21:10–34:12). A special note of appreciation is expressed to Dr. John D. W. Watts, whose gentle but firm insistence and encouragement got me through difficult days in the process of completing this commentary, and to Dr. James W. Watts for his editorial assistance in the final stages of getting this manuscript ready for the copy-editing process. His suggestions did much to improve the format and content of this book at numerous points.

The outline for the entire commentary appears at the end of the Introduction in order to give the reader a clearer idea of the structure of the whole, which is arranged according to the eleven traditional lectionary readings ("weekly portions") of Jewish worship practice through the centuries.

In the preface to the first edition of Volume 6A in the Word Biblical Commentary (1991), I mentioned that my research for writing this commentary on the book of Deuteronomy forced me to rethink a number of presuppositions in my approach to understanding the Bible in the world of academia. The necessary process of growth and change led me down unfamiliar and lonely paths, as I made the choice to go with what I observed in the biblical text whether or not it fit comfortably within the established parameters of what my teachers had taught me in my graduate studies, or what my colleagues in the study of this pivotal book were saying. As a result, I found myself doing something a bit different with Deuteronomy.

Though I already knew that the accentual system of notation in the Hebrew text of Deuteronomy reflected some kind of musical performance of the text in antiquity and that the entire system of notation in the Masoretic tradition is remarkably well preserved, it was not until I got deeply into chaps. 21–25 that the details of that system became increasingly clear. It was the shorter passages in that section of the laws of Deuteronomy, the frequent use of the *sĕtûmā'* and *pĕtûḥā'* layout markers, and the systematic use of the so-called *Numeruswechsel* (change back and forth between second-person singular and plural pronouns) that finally enabled me to see what was going on from a prosodic-textual point of view. This in turn led to the discovery that the traditional lectionary cycle of "weekly portions" of readings from the book of Deuteronomy, as conveyed in the marginal notes of the text in various Jewish editions of the Hebrew Bible, in fact represent primary structural features for understanding the architectual design of the whole, something I did not know when the previous volume was published. In this commentary, I have followed closely the system of notation in the marginal notes of *The Leningrad Codex: A Facsimile Edition* (Grand Rapids, MI: Eerdmans, 1998). I am grateful to Professor Casper Labuschagne for the gift some years ago of a bound photocopy of the earlier facsimile edition of the book of Deuteronomy taken from this important manuscript, which he had obtained from the late Professor Claus Schedl.

When I worked through Calum Carmichael's book, *Law and Narrative in the Bible* (Ithaca, NY: Cornell UP, 1985), I found the key to unlock another door to new discoveries. Carmichael's work has played a significant role in shaping this commentary, though in a manner different from what he intended. His demonstration of the relationship between the laws of Deuteronomy and the narrative elsewhere in the Pentateuch and Former Prophets is accepted, but the direction of that influence appears to be the reverse of what Carmichael has found. Following the suggestions of his teacher David Daube, Carmichael argues that the laws of Deuteronomy have the character of "legal abstracts" derived from earlier narrative tradition that is preserved in the Torah and the Former Prophets. I take the direction of influence (from law to narratives) in precisely the opposite direction. The laws are primary, and are used to shape the narratives in question, as is most clearly seen in the law on distrained property in Deut 24:10–13. In short, the book of Deuteronomy illustrates in principle the subsequent midrashic approach to Scripture. The primary sacred text on which the book is based is the Ten Commandments, which are expanded in midrashic fashion to form the laws of Deut 12–25. These laws in turn are expanded in a similar manner in narrative form thoughout what D. N. Freedman has called "The Primary History" (Genesis through 2 Kings in the Masoretic tradition of the Hebrew Bible—that is, the Torah plus the Former Prophets within the Hebrew canon).

Four recent commentaries on Deuteronomy merit special attention here. The first volume of Moshe Weinfeld's commentary, *Deuteronomy 1–11,* AB 5 (Garden City, NY: Doubleday; 1991), appeared at the same time as my earlier volume of the same title in the Word Biblical Commentary. Weinfeld's commentary was particularly useful in updating the "List of Qumran Evidence Relating to Deuteronomy" below. Georg Braulik's commentary in Die Neue Echter Bibel (Würzburg: Echter) is now complete: *Deuteronomium 1–16,17* (1986) and *Deuteronomium 16,18–34,12* (1992). Though this work is intended primarily to expound the value of Deuteronomy for the church today, it remains an eminently useful reference tool for the scholar as well, particularly in the conciseness and clarity of thought in the organization of material throughout. Jeffrey Tigay's book, *Deuteronomy,* JPS Torah Commentary (Philadelphia: Jewish Publication Society, 1996), has proved invaluable as a point of reference in my own work. The fourth commentary of note is the monumental effort of Casper J. Labuschagne, *De Prediking van het Oude Testament: Deuteronomium* (Nijkerk: Uitgeverij G. F. Callenbach, 1990–97), which is now complete in four volumes. My limited understanding of the Dutch language has made it difficult to incorporate here the substance of this work, which sheds much light on the more recent stages of the canonical process in ancient Israel, in which the book of Deuteronomy played a central role. An English abridgment of Labuschagne's work would be most useful to students of Deuteronomy. As I worked my way through Deuteronomy, I became increasingly familiar with Labuschagne's method (*Logotechnische analyse*) and its value. For more information on this, see *Excursus:* "Deuteronomy as a Numerical Composition." I have attempted to incorporate Labuschagne's findings throughout the commentary at the end of the sections on *Form/Structure/Setting.*

Another work of importance in the writing of this commentary is the new translation of the Pentateuch by Everett Fox, *The Five Books of Moses,* Schocken

Bible 1 (New York: Schocken, 1997). Fox's approach to the text of the Hebrew Bible has much in common with my own. As he put it, "I have sought here primarily to echo the style of the original, believing that the Bible is best approached, at least at the beginning, on its own terms. So I have presented the text in English dress but with a Hebraic voice" (p. ix). That is my own goal as well.

My book, *Bible 101: God's Story in Human History* (North Richland Hills, TX: BIBAL Press, 1996), needed to be written before I was able to complete this commentary. This book approaches the study of the Bible from the perspective of the canonical process in ancient Israel and early Christianity and of the principle of intertextuality. It explores the formation of the entire canon of sacred Scripture as a very human process that was ultimately overseen by the Spirit of God. Patterns of symmetry are unfolded and substantiated in an introduction to the Bible that attempts to engage the reader at the experiential level and illuminate the mystery of God's revelation. My most recent book, *The Completed Tanakh: The Unity of the Bible within the Canonical Process,* 2nd ed.(Columbus, GA: TEC, 2001), carries this discussion much further. In addition to these two textbooks, I have written a series of study guides for the BIBAL Study Program: *The Torah, The Former Prophets, The Latter Prophets, The Hebrew Writings, Apostolic Writings I—The Four Gospels and the Book of Acts,* and *Apostolic Writings II—New Testament Epistles and the Revelation to John* (North Richland Hills, TX: BIBAL Press, 1996–2001). The process of writing these books sharpened my awareness of the concentric structural design of the Bible at all levels, enabling me to develop a systematic methodological approach to the analysis of the biblical text, which is evident in the *Form/Structure/Setting* sections throughout the whole of this commentary. The process led to an understanding of the macrostructure of the book of Deuteronomy that moves well beyond where I was at the time when the first edition of Volume 6A of this commentary was published (1991).

The fundamental building block in the canonical process is a simple chiasm with a structural center, in the pattern a-b-x-b′-a′. In the book of Deuteronomy, this structure is often expanded by adding an additional frame to form what C. J. Labuschagne has appropriately called a "menorah pattern" (a seven-part concentric structure: a-b-c-x-c′-b′-a′).

In the first edition of Volume 6A, three different fonts were used in the English translation of Deuteronomy in an attempt to convey certain information that is easily observed in the Hebrew text but not easy to convey in English. That system is simplified here to the use of two different fonts in order to convey at a glance the phenomenon called the *Numeruswechsel*—the frequent change in the use of the second-person singular and plural forms in verbs and pronominal suffixes. Since modern English makes no distinction between the singular and plural in the second person, there is no simple way to mark the changes in translation. Moreover, since the changes have no obvious effect on the meaning of the text, the matter is usually ignored by commentators as well.

A regular font is used wherever the text has second-person plural forms, until a change to second-person singular forms is encountered. At that point, the font is changed to italic and continues in that font until a form using the second-person plural form is encountered. It will be observed that most of these changes (i.e., the *Numeruswechsel*) appear at boundaries of prosodic units within the book of Deuteronomy, and occasionally in the center of such units. In short, the *Numeruswechsel* is an auditory signal of internal structure—used to convey information about the structure of the book to those who heard the book recited in antiquity. They would have picked up these changes as readily as we note incorrect grammatical usage today.

I would also take this opportunity to call the reader's attention to some of the volumes in the Stuttgarter biblische Aufsatzbände Altes Testament (SBAB) that make the published works of Georg Braulik and Norbert Lohfink more accessible (see vols. 4, 8, 12, 16, and 20 by Lohfink and vols. 2 and 24 by Braulik).

DUANE L. CHRISTENSEN

Rodeo, California
October 2001

Abbreviations

Periodicals, Serials, and Reference Works

AAAS	*Annales archéologiques arabes de Syrie*
AASOR	Annual of the American Schools of Oriental Research
AB	Anchor Bible
ABD	D. N. Freedman (ed.), *Anchor Bible Dictionary*, 6 vols. (New York: Doubleday, 1992)
AbLA	M. Noth, *Aufsätze zur biblischen Landes- und Altertumskunde*, ed. H. W. Wolff (Neukirchen-Vluyn: Neukirchener Verlag, 1991)
ABR	*Australian Biblical Review*
AcOr	*Acta orientalia*, Leiden
ActOr	*Acta Orientalia*, Copenhagen
AfO	*Archiv für Orientforschung*
AfOBei	Beihefte zur Archiv für Orientforschung
ÄgAT	Ägypten und Altes Testament
AHDO	*Archiv d'histoire du droit oriental*
AION	Annali dell'Istituto Orientale di Napoli
AJBI	Annual of the Japanese Biblical Institute
AJP	*American Journal of Philology*
AJSL	*American Journal of Semitic Languages and Literature*
AJSR	*Association for Jewish Studies Review*
AJT	*American Journal of Theology*
ALGHJ	Arbeiten zur Literatur und Geschichte des hellenistischen Judentums
ALUOS	Annual of Leeds University Oriental Society
AnBib	Analecta biblica
ANEP	J. B. Pritchard (ed.), *The Ancient Near East in Pictures*, 2nd ed. (Princeton: Princeton UP, 1969)
ANET	J. B. Pritchard (ed.), *Ancient Near Eastern Texts Relating to the Old Testament*, 3rd ed. (Princeton: Princeton UP, 1969)
AngTR	*Anglican Theological Review*
AnOr	Analecta orientalia
ANQ	*Andover Newton Quarterly*
AnSt	*Anatolian Studies*
AOAT	Alter Orient und Altes Testament
AOT	H. Gressman (ed.), *Altorientalische Texte und Bilder*
ArOr	*Archiv orientální*
ARw	*Archiv für Religionswissenschaft*
AS	Assyriological Studies
AsSeign	*Assemblées du Seigneur*
ASOR	American Schools of Oriental Research
ASTI	*Annual of the Swedish Theological Institute*
AsTJ	*Asbury Theological Journal*
ATAbh	Alttestamentliche Abhandlungen

ATANT	Abhandlung zur Theologie des Alten und Neuen Testaments
ATD	Das Alte Testament Deutsch
ATDan	Acta theologica Danica
ATSAT	Arbeiten zu Text und Sprache im Alten Testament
Aug	*Augustinianum* (Rome)
AUSS	*Andrews University Seminary Studies*
AVTRW	Aufsätze und Vorträge zur Theologie und Religionswissenschaft
AzT	Arbeiten zur Theologie
BA	*Biblical Archaeologist*
BARev	*Biblical Archaeology Review*
BASOR	Bulletin of the American Schools of Oriental Research
BAT	Die Botschaft des Alten Testaments
BB	Biblische Beiträge (Fribourg)
BBB	Bonner biblische Beiträge
BBC	*Broadman Bible Commentary*
BCPE	*Bulletin du Centre protestant d'études*
BDB	F. Brown, S. R. Driver, and C. A. Briggs, *Hebrew and English Lexicon of the OT* (Oxford: Clarendon, 1907)
BDBAT	Beiheft Dielheimer Blätter zum Alten Testament
BeO	*Bibbia e oriente*
BETL	Bibliotheca ephemeridum theologicarum lovaniensium
BEvT	Beiträge zur evangelischen Theologie
BFCT	Beiträge zur Förderung christlicher Theologie
BGBE	Beiträge zur Geschichte der biblischen Exegese
BHH	B. Reicke and L. Rost (eds.), *Biblisch-historisches Handwörterbuch*, 3 vols. (Göttingen: Vandenhoeck & Ruprecht, 1962–66)
BHK	R. Kittel, *Biblia hebraica*
BHS	*Biblia hebraica stuttgartensia*
BHT	Beiträge zur historischen Theologie
Bib	*Biblica*
BibBh	Bible Bhashyam
BibIll	*Biblical Illustrator*
BibOr	Biblica et orientalia
BIES	*Bulletin of the Israel Exploration Society* (= *Yediot*)
BJRL	*Bulletin of the John Rylands University Library of Manchester*
BJS	Brown Judaic Studies
BK	*Bibel und Kirche*
BLit	Bibel und Liturgie
BMS	BIBAL Monograph Series
BMik	*Beth Mikra*
BN	*Biblische Notizen*
BO	*Bibliotheca Orientalis* (Leiden)
BOr	*Beiträge zur Orientalistik*
BOT	De Boeken van het Oude Testament
BR	*Biblical Research*
BRev	*Bible Review*

BSac	*Bibliotheca Sacra*
BTB	*Biblical Theology Bulletin*
BWA(N)T	Beiträge zur Wissenschaft vom Alten (und Neuen) Testament
BZ	Biblische Zeitschrift
BZAW	Beihefte zur *ZAW*
CAD	The Assyrian Dictionary of the Oriental Institute of the University of Chicago
CahRB	Cahiers de la *Revue biblique*
CBC	Cambridge Biblical Commentary
CBib	The Cambridge Bible
CBQ	*Catholic Biblical Quarterly*
ChrJRel	*Christian and Jewish Relations*
ChW	*Christliche Welt*
CJ	*Concordia Journal*
CMHE	F. M. Cross, Jr., *Canaanite Myth and Hebrew Epic* (Cambridge: Harvard UP, 1973)
ColT	*Collectanea Theologica*
ConB	Coniectanea biblica
ConBas	*Concilium Baseliense*
Conc	*Concilium*
ConsJud	Conservative Judaism
CP	*Classical Philology*
CSCO	Corpus scriptorum christianorum orientalium
CT	*Christianity Today*
CTA	A. Herdner, *Corpus des tablettes en cunéiformes alphabétiques*, 2 vols. (Paris: Imprimerie Nationale, 1963)
CThM	Calwer theologische Monographien
CTM	*Concordia Theological Monthly*
CTQ	*Concordia Theological Quarterly*
CV	*Communio viatorum*
DA	Dissertation Abstracts
DD	*Dor le Dor*
DDS	M. Weinfeld, *Deuteronomy and the Deuteronomic School* (Oxford: Clarendon, 1972)
DiIs	*Dine Israel*
DJD	Discoveries in the Judaean Desert
EAEHL	M. Avi-Yonah and E. Stern (eds.), *Encyclopedia of Archaeological Excavations in the Holy Land,* 4 vols. (Englewood Cliffs, NJ: Prentice-Hall, 1975–78)
EchB	Echter Bibel
Ecout Bib	Écouter la Bible
EglT	*Eglise et Théologie*
EHS	Europäische Hochschulschriften
EI	*Ereṣ Israel*
EM	*'Entsiklopedyah Miqra'it* (Jerusalem: Mosad Bialik, 1950–88)
EncBrit	Encylcopaedia Brittanica

EncBib	T. Cheyne and J. Sutherland Black (eds.), *Encyclopaedia Biblica,* 4 vols. (New York Macmillan, 1899–1903)
EncBT	J. B. Bauer (ed.), *Encyclopedia of Biblical Theology* (1970)
EncJud	*Encyclopaedia Judaica,* 16 vols. (Jerusalem; New York: Keter, 1971–72)
EphC	Ephemerides Carmeliticae
ErFor	Erträge der Forschung
EstBib	*Estudios bíblicos*
EstEcl	*Estudios Eclesiásticos*
ETL	*Ephemerides theologicae lovanienses*
ETR	*Etudes théologiques et religieuses*
ETS	Erfurter theologische Studien
EvQ	*Evangelical Quarterly*
EvT	Evangelische Theologie
ExpTim	*Expository Times*
FAT	Forschungen zum Alten Testament
FB	Forschung zur Bibel (Echter)
FBM	E. Fox, *The Five Books of Moses,* Schocken Bible (New York: Schocken, 1997)
FolOr	Folia Orientalia
FRLANT	Forschungen zur Religion und Literatur des Alten und Neuen Testaments
FZPhTh	Freiburger Zeitschrift für Philosophie und Theologie
GeistLeb	*Geist und Leben* (Würzburg)
GKC	*Gesenius' Hebrew Grammar,* ed. E. Kautzsch, tr. A. E. Cowley (Oxford: Clarendon, 1910)
GLECS	*Comptes rendus du groupe linguistique d'études chamitosémitiques*
GOST	*Glasgow Oriental Society Transactions*
GSAT	*Gesammelte Studien zum Alten Testament* (G. von Rad, TBü 8 [1965] and 48 [1973]; M. Noth, TBü 6 [1966] and 39 [1969] [Munich: Kaiser])
GTA	Göttinger theologische Arbeiten
HAL	W. Baumgartner, *Hebräisches und aramäisches Lexicon zum Alten Testament,* rev. 3rd ed. of KB (Leiden: Brill, 1967)
HAR	*Hebrew Annual Review*
HAT	Handbuch zum Alten Testament
HBS	Herders biblische studien
HBT	*Horizons in Biblical Theology*
HDR	Harvard Dissertations in Religion
Hen	*Henoch*
Herm	*Hermathena*
HKAT	Handkommentar zum Alten Testament
HOTTP	D. Barthélemy et al. (eds.), *Preliminary and Interim Report on the Hebrew Old Testament Text Project: 1. Pentateuch,* 2nd rev. ed. (New York: United Bible Societies, 1979)
HR	History of Religions

HSM	Harvard Semitic Monographs
HS	Hebrew Studies
HSS	Harvard Semitic Studies
HTR	*Harvard Theological Review*
HTS	Harvard Theological Studies
HUCA	*Hebrew Union College Annual*
IB	*Interpreter's Bible*
IBHS	B. K. Waltke and M. O'Connor, *An Introduction to Biblical Hebrew Syntax* (Winona Lake, IN: Eisenbrauns, 1990)
IBS	*Irish Biblical Studies*
ICC	International Critical Commentary
IDB	G. A. Buttrick (ed.), *Interpreter's Dictionary of the Bible,* 4 vols. (Nashville: Abindgon, 1962)
IDBSup	K. Crim (ed.), Supplementary Volume to *IDB* (Nashville: Abingdon, 1976)
IEJ	*Israel Exploration Journal*
IKZ	Internationale kirchliche Zeitschrift
ILR	*Israel Law Review*
Int	*Interpretation*
IntDialZ	*Internationale dialog Zeitschrift*
IOS	*Israel Oriental Studies,* Tel Aviv University
IOSOT	International Organization for the Study of the Old Testament
ISBE	G. W. Bromiley (ed.), *International Standard Bible Encyclopedia,* 4 vols. (Grand Rapids: Eerdmans, 1979–88)
JAAR	*Journal of the American Academy of Religion*
JANESCU	*The Journal of the Ancient Near Eastern Society of Columbia University*
JAOS	*Journal of the American Oriental Society*
JAOSSup	Supplement to *JAOS*
JBC	R. E. Brown et al. (eds.), *The Jerome Biblical Commentary*
JBL	*Journal of Biblical Literature*
JBLMS	Journal of Biblical Literature Monograph Series
JBR	*Journal of Bible and Religion*
JBTh	Jahrbuch für biblische Theologie (Neukirchener Verlag)
JEA	*Journal of Egyptian Archaeology*
JEOL	*Jaarbericht van het Vooraziatisch-Egyptisch Genootschap Ex Oriente Lux*
JES	*Journal of Ecumenical Studies*
JESHO	*Journal of the Economic and Social History of the Orient*
JETS	*Journal of the Evangelical Theological Society*
JewEnc	I. Singer (ed.), *Jewish Encyclopaedia,* 12 vols. (New York: Funk and Wagnalls, 1916)
JHS	*Journal of Hellenic Studies*
JJS	*Journal of Jewish Studies*
JLA	Jewish Annual Law
JLASup	Jewish Law Annual Supplement
JLH	*Jahrbuch für Liturgik und Hymnologie*

JNES	*Journal of Near Eastern Studies*
JNSL	*Journal of Northwest Semitic Languages*
JPS	Jewish Publication Society
JQR	*Jewish Quarterly Review*
JRAS	*Journal of the Royal Asiatic Society*
JSJ	*Journal for the Study of Judaism in the Persian, Hellenistic, and Roman Period*
JSOT	*Journal for the Study of the Old Testament*
JSOTSup	JSOT Supplement Series
JSS	*Journal of Semitic Studies*
JTS	*Journal of Theological Studies*
JTSA	Journal of Theology for Southern Africa
Jud	*Judaica: Beiträge zum Verständnis . . .*
KAT	Kommentar zum Alten Testament
KatBl	*Katechetische Blätter*
KB	L. Koehler and W. Baumgartner, *Lexicon in Veteris Testamenti libros*, 2nd ed. (Leiden: Brill, 1958)
KD	*Kerygma und Dogma*
KeH	Kurzgefasstes exegetisches Handbuch zum Alten Testament
KHC	Kurzer Hand-Commentar zum Alten Testament
KlSchr	*Kleine Schriften* (A. Alt, 3 vols. [Munich: Beck, 1953–59]; O. Eissfeldt, 6 vols. [Tübingen: Mohr, 1962–79])
KT	Kaiser Traktate
KuI	Kirche und Israel
LAD	*Logotechnische analyse bij Deuteronomiu* (4 parts): published as inserts to C. J. Labuschagne, *Deuteronomium* (1987–97)
Lat	*Lateranum*
LB	*Linguistica Biblica*
LBC	The Layman's Bible Commentary
LD	Lectio divina
Leš	*Lešonénu*
LNB	C. Carmichael, *Law and Narrative in the Bible* (Ithaca: Cornell UP, 1985)
LQ	*Lutheran Quarterly*
LS	*Legendiger Seelsorge*
LSSt	Leipziger semitistische Studien
LTJ	*Lutheran Theological Journal*
LV	Lumìere et Vie
MANE	Monographs on the Ancient Near East (Leiden: Brill)
MBPR	Münchener Beiträge zur Papyrusforschung und antiken Rechtsgeschichte
MDB	*Le monde de la Bible*
MGWJ	*Monatsschrift für Geschichte und Wissenschaft des Judentums*
MHUC	Monographs of the Hebrew Union College

MThS	Münchener theologische Studien
MThSt	Marburger theologische Studien
MTZ	*Münchener theologische Zeitschrift*
Mus	*Le Muséon*
MVAG	*Mittelungen der vorderasiatisch-ägyptischen Gesellschaft*
NAWG	*Nachrichten der Akademie der Wissenschaften in Göttingen*
NCBC	New Century Bible Commentary
NEchB	Neue Echter Bibel
NedTTs	*Nederlands theologisch tijdschrift*
NGTT	*Nederduitse gereformeerde teologiese tydskrif*
NICOT	New International Commentary on the Old Testament
NKZ	*Neue kirchliche Zeitschrift*
NorTT	*Norsk Teologisk Tidsskrift*
NovT	*Novum Testamentum*
NovTSup	Novum Testamentum, Supplements
NRT	*La nouvelle revue théologique*
NThS	*Nieuwe theologische Studien*
NTOA	Novum Testamentum et Orbis Antiquus
NTS	*New Testament Studies*
OBO	Orbis biblicus et orientalis
OBT	Overtures to Biblical Theology
OCD	*Oxford Classical Dictionary*
OLP	*Orientalia lovaniensia periodica*
OLZ	*Orientalische Literaturzeitung*
Or	*Orientalia* (Rome)
OrAnt	*Oriens antiquus*
OTL	Old Testament Library
OTS	*Oudtestamentische Studiën*
OTWSA	*Die Ou Testamentiese Werkgemeenskap in Suid-Afrika* (Pretoria)
PAAJR	*Proceedings of the American Academy of Jewish Research*
PalCl	*Palestra del Clero*
ParVi	*Parole di Vita*
PEQ	*Palestine Exploration Quarterly*
PG	J.-P. Migne, *Patrologia graeca*
PIBA	*Proceedings of the Irish Biblical Association*
PJ	*Palästina-Jahrbuch*
PL	J.-P. Migne, *Patrologia latina*
POS	Pretoria Oriental Series
POT	De Prediking van het Oude Testament
POTT	D. J. Wiseman (ed.), *People of Old Testament Times* (Oxford: Clarendon, 1973)
PRS	*Perspectives in Religious Studies*
PRU	*Le Palais royal d'Ugarit*
PSB	*Princeton Seminary Bulletin*

PSBA	*Proceedings of the Society of Biblical Archaeology*
PW	Pauly-Wissowa, *Real-Encyclopädie der classischen Altertumswissenschaft* (Stuttgart: Metzler, 1893–1972)
QD	Quaestiones disputatae
RA	*Revue d'assyriologie et d'archéologie orientale*
RAI	Rencontre Assyriologique Internationale
RB	*Revue biblique*
RBibIt	*Rivista Biblica Italiana* (Brescia)
RechBib	Recherches bibliques
ResQ	*Restoration Quarterly*
RevExp	*Review and Expositor*
RevistB	*Revista bíblica*
RevQ	*Revue de Qumran*
RGG	K. Galling (ed.), *Religion in Geschichte und Gegenwart,* 3rd ed., 7 vols. (Tübingen: Mohr, 1957–65)
RHPR	*Revue d'histoire et de philosophie religieuses*
RHR	*Revue de l'histoire des religions*
RIDA	*Revue internationale des droites de l'antiquité*
RivB	*Rivista biblica*
RMP	*Rheinisches Museum für Philologie*
RRel	*Review for Religious*
RSEHA	*Revue sémitique d'épigraphie et d'histoire ancienne*
RSJB	*Recueils de la société Jean Bodin pour l'histoire comparative des institutions*
RSO	*Revista degli studi orientali*
RSP	L. R. Fisher and S. Rummel (eds.), *Ras Shamra Parallels,* AnOr 49-51 (Rome: Pontifical Biblical Institute, 1972–81)
RSPT	*Revue des sciences philosophiques et théologiques*
RSR	*Recherches de science religieuse*
RTQR	*Revue de théologie et de questions religieuses*
Salm	*Salmaticensis* (Salamanca)
SANT	Studien zum Alten und Neuen Testsament
SBAB	Stuttgarter biblische Aufsatzbände Altes Testament
SBEsp	Semana bíblica española
SBFLA	*Studii biblici franciscani liber annuus*
SBL	Society of Biblical Literature
SBLASP	SBL Abstracts and Seminar Papers
SBLDS	SBL Dissertation Series
SBLMS	SBL Monograph Series
SBLSCS	SBL Septuagint and Cognate Studies
SBLSP	Society of Biblical Literature Seminar Papers
SBM	Stuttgarter biblische Monographien
SBS	Stuttgarter Bibelstudien
SBT	Studies in Biblical Theology
SBTS 3	D. Christensen (ed.), *A Song of Power and the Power of Song,* Sources for Biblical and Theological Study 3 (Winona Lake, IN: Eisenbrauns, 1993)

ScEccl	*Sciences ecclésiastiques*
ScEs	*Science et esprit*
Schol	*Scholastik* (Freiburg)
ScrHier	Scripta hierosolymitana
SDHI	*Studi et documenta historiae et Iuris*
SEÅ	*Svensk exegetisk årsbok*
SEAJT	*South East Asia Journal of Theology*
Sem	*Semitica*
SFSHJ	South Florida Studies in the History of Judaism
SGKA	Studien zur Geschichte und Kultur des Altertums
SGKAO	Schriften zur Geschichte und Kultur des Alten Orients
SHR	Studies in the History of Religions
SJLA	Studies in Judaism in Late Antiquity
SJOT	*Scandinavian Journal of the Old Testament*
SJT	*Scottish Journal of Theology*
SKGG	Schriften der Königsberger Gelehrten Gesellschaft
SLR	*Stanford Law Review*
SR	*Studies in Religion/Sciences religieuses*
ST	*Studia theologica*
StMor	*Studia moralia*
StudBib	Studia Biblica
StudBT	*Studia biblica et theologica*
StZ	*Stimme der Zeit*
SUNT	Studien zur Umwelt des Neuen Testaments
SWBA	Social World of Biblical Antiquity
SWDS	*Scrolls from the Wilderness of the Dead Sea* (British Museum, 1965)
TBC	Torch Bible Commentaries
TBl	*Theologische Blätter*
TBT	*The Bible Today*
TBü	Theologische Bücherei
TD	*Theology Digest*
TDNT	G. Kittel and G. Friedrich (eds.), *Theological Dictionary of the New Testament,* tr. G. Bromiley, 9 vols. plus index vol. (Grand Rapids: Eerdmans, 1964–76)
TDOT	G. J. Botterweck, H. Ringgren, and H.-J. Fabry (eds.), *Theological Dictionary of the Old Testament,* tr. D. Green et al. (Grand Rapids: Eerdmans, 1974–)
TEH	Theologische Existenz heute
TGUOS	Transactions of the Glasgow University Oriental Society
ThA	Theologische Arbeiten
ThStud	Theologische Studiën
ThVers	*Theologische Versuche*
ThViat	*Theologia Viatorum* (Munich)
TLOT	E. Jenni and C. Westermann (eds.), *Theological Lexicon of the Old Testament,* tr. M. Biddle, 3 vols. (Peabody, MA: Hendrickson, 1997)
TLZ	*Theologische Literaturzeitung*

TOTC	Tyndale Old Testament Commentaries
TP	*Theologie und Philosophie*
TQ	*Theologische Quartalschrift* (Tübingen)
TRE	*Theologische Realenzyklopädie*
TRev	*Theologische Revue*
TRu	*Theologische Rundschau*
TS	*Theological Studies*
TSJTSA	Texts and Studies of the Jewish Theological Seminary of America
TSK	*Theologische Studien und Kritiken*
TsTNijm	*Tijdschrift voor Theologie* (Nijmegen)
TT	*Theologisch Tidsskrift*
TThSt	Trierer theologische Studien
TToday	*Theology Today*
TTZ	*Trierer theologische Zeitschrift*
TWAT	G. J. Botterweck, H. Ringgren, and H.-J. Fabry (eds.), *Theologisches Wörterbuch zum Alten Testament* (Stuttgart: Kohlhammer, 1970–)
TynBul	*Tyndale Bulletin*
TZ	*Theologische Zeitschrift* (Basel)
UCPNES	University of California Publications in Near Eastern Studies
UF	*Ugarit-Forschungen*
UT	C. H. Gordon, *Ugaritic Textbook,* AnOr 38 (Rome: Pontifical Biblical Institute, 1965)
VC	*Vigiliae christianae*
VD	*Verbum domini*
VetChr	*Vetera Christianorum*
VT	*Vetus Testamentum*
VTSup	*Vetus Testamentum,* Supplements
WBC	Word Biblical Commentary
WBT	Wiener Beiträge zur Theologie
WD	*Wort und Dienst*
WF	Wege der Forschung
WHJP	*World History of the Jewish People,* First Series: Ancient Times (in 4 divisions)
WHJP 1	E. A. Speiser, ed., *At the Dawn of Civilization: A Background of Biblical History*
WHJP 2	B. Mazar, ed., *Patariarchs*
WHJP 3	B. Mazar, ed., *Judges*
WHJP 4	A. Malamaat and I. Eph'al (eds.), *The Age of the Monarchies,* 2 vols.
WMANT	Wissenschaftliche Monographien zum Alten und Neuen Testament
WO	*Die Welt des Orients*

Wor	*Worship*
WoWa	*Wort und Wahrheit*
WTJ	*Westminster Theological Journal*
WUNT	Wissenschaftliche Untersuchungen zum Neuen Testament
YJS	Yale Judaica Series
ZA	*Zeitschrift für Assyriologie*
ZABR	*Zeitschrift für Altorientalische und Biblische Rechtsgeschichte*
ZAW	*Zeitschrift für die alttestamentliche Wissenschaft*
ZDMG	*Zeitschrift der deutschen morgenländischen Gesellschaft*
ZDPV	*Zeitschrift des deutschen Palästina-Vereins*
ZEE	*Zeitschrift für evangelische Ethik*
ZKT	*Zeitschrift für katholische Theologie*
ZTK	*Zeitschrift für Theologie und Kirche*
ZVS	*Zeitschrift für Völkerpsychologie und Sprachwissenschaft*
ZWT	*Zeitschrift für wissenschaftliche Theologie*
ZZ	*Zeichen der Zeit*

Texts, Versions, and Ancient Works

Akk.	Akkadian
Arab.	Arabic
Aram.	Aramaic
B	MT MS, edited by Jacob ben Chayim, Venice (1524/25)
Copt.	Coptic
DSS	Dead Sea Scrolls
Eng.	English
Eth.	Ethiopic
Fr.	French
Ger.	German
Gr.	Greek
Heb.	Hebrew
K	Kethib
L	MT MS, Leningrad Codex
LXX	Septuagint
LXX^{A}	LXX MS, Alexandrian Codex
LXX^{B}	LXX MS, Vatican Codex
LXX^{S*}	LXX MS, Sinai Codex, original reading
LXX^{Sc}	LXX MS, Sinai Codex, corrector
MT	Masoretic Text
Q	Qere
SP	Samaritan Pentateuch
SP^{W}	*Samaritan Pentateuch, London polyglot,* ed. B. Waltonii, vol. 1 (1654)
Syh	Syrohexaplaris
Syr.	Syriac
Tg.	Targum
Tg. Ps.-J.	*Targum Pseudo-Jonathan*
Ugar.	Ugaritic
Vg.	Vulgate
VSS	ancient versions
α′	Aquila
θ′	Theodotion
σ′	Symmachus

HEBREW GRAMMAR

abs.	absolute	impf.	imperfect
acc.	accusative	impv.	imperative
act.	active	ind.	indicative
adv.	adverb, adverbial	inf.	infinitive
c.	common	int.	interrogative
conj.	conjunction, conjunctive	juss.	jussive
consec.	consecutive	masc.	masculine
constr.	construct	niph.	niphal
def. art.	definite article	pass.	passive
disj.	disjunctive	pf.	perfect
du.	dual	pilp.	pilpel
fem.	feminine	pl.	plural
fut.	future	prep.	preposition
hiph.	hiphil	ptcp.	participle
hithp.	hithpael	sg.	singular
hoph.	hophal	suff.	suffix(es)

BIBLICAL AND APOCRYPHAL BOOKS

Gen	Genesis	Dan	Daniel
Exod	Exodus	Hos	Hosea
Lev	Leviticus	Joel	Joel
Num	Numbers	Amos	Amos
Deut	Deuteronomy	Obad	Obadiah
Josh	Joshua	Jonah	Jonah
Judg	Judges	Mic	Micah
Ruth	Ruth	Nah	Nahum
1–2 Sam	1–2 Samuel	Hab	Habakkuk
1–2 Kgs	1–2 Kings	Zeph	Zephaniah
1–2 Chr	1–2 Chronicles	Hag	Haggai
Ezra	Ezra	Zech	Zechariah
Neh	Nehemiah	Mal	Malachi
Esth	Esther		
Job	Job	1–4 Kgdms	1–4 Kingdoms
Ps(s)	Psalm(s)	1–2 Esdr	1–2 Esdras
Prov	Proverbs	Tob	Tobit
Eccl	Ecclesiastes	Jdt	Judith
Cant	Canticles, Song of Solomon	Add Esth	Additions to Esther
		4 Ezra	4 Ezra
Isa	Isaiah	Wis	Wisdom of Solomon
Jer	Jeremiah	Sir	Ecclesiasticus (Wisdom of Jesus the son of Sirach)
Lam	Lamentations		
Ezek	Ezekiel		

Bar	Baruch	1–2 Cor	1–2 Corinthians
Ep Jer	Epistle of Jeremiah	Gal	Galatians
S Th Ch	Song of the Three Children (or Young Men)	Eph	Ephesians
		Phil	Philippians
Sus	Susanna	Col	Colossians
Bel	Bel and the Dragon	1–2 Thess	1–2 Thessalonians
Pr Azar	Prayer of Azariah	1–2 Tim	1–2 Timothy
1–4 Macc	1–4 Maccabees	Titus	Titus
		Philem	Philemon
Matt	Matthew	Heb	Hebrews
Mark	Mark	Jas	James
Luke	Luke	1–2 Pet	1–2 Peter
John	John	1–2–3 John	1–2–3 John
Acts	Acts	Jude	Jude
Rom	Romans	Rev	Revelation

MISCELLANEOUS

ANE	Ancient Near East	n.	note
B.C.E.	Before Common Era, Before Christ	n.d.	no date
		NEB	New English Bible
ca.	circa	NIV	New International Version
C.E.	Common Era (A.D.)		
chap(s).	chapter(s)	NRSV	New Revised Standard Version
col(s).	column(s)		
diss.	dissertation	n.s.	new series
ed(s).	edition; edited by; editor(s)	NT	New Testament
		OT	Old Testament
esp.	especially	p(p).	page(s)
ET	English translation	repr.	reprint
FS	*Festschrift*	RSV	Revised Standard Version
JB	Jerusalem Bible		
KJV	King James Version	Sup	Supplement
l(l).	line(s)	tr.	translated by; translator
lit.	literally	Univ.	University
MOFFAT	J. Moffatt, *A New Translation of the Bible* (NT 1913)	UP	University Press
		v(v)	verse(s)
MS(S)	manuscript(s)	§	section/paragraph

Commentary Bibliography

In the text, references to works in this chronological bibliography of commentaries on Deuteronomy will be by author's last name and date. Pages are given when the reference does not obviously deal with a chapter and verse under discussion.

For a survey of works on Deuteronomy, see **L. B. Cross,** "Commentaries on Deuteronomy," *Theology* 64 (1961) 184–89; **H. D. Preuss,** *Deuteronomium,* ErFor 164 (Darmstadt: Wissenschaftliche Buchgesellschaft, 1982) 203–43.

The Church Fathers

Commentaries by the church fathers are listed here alphabetically with the date of the book or a date pertaining to the author in parentheses after the author's name: **Augustine** (354–430). *Locutiones. PL* 34, 531–38. ———. *Opus Quaestionum. PL* 34, 747–76. **Bede** (673–735). *PL* 91, 189–394. **Cyril of Alexandria** (441). *PG* 69, 643–78. **Diodorus of Tarsus** (394). *PG* 33, 1585–86; *PL* 50, 781–82 (only fragments remain). **Hieronymus** (Jerome) (410). *PG* 28, 451–504. **Isidore of Seville** (636). *PL* 83, 359–70. **Origen** (ca. 250). *Adnotationes. PG* 17, 23–36. ———. *Selecta. PG* 12, 805–18. **Paterius** (ca. 600). *PL* 79, 773–84. **Procopius of Gaza** (538). *PG* 87, 891–992. **Pseudo-Bede** (ca. 800). *PL* 93, 409–16. **Theodoretus of Cyrrhus** (457). *PG* 80, 401–56. **Walafrid Strabo** (849). *PL* 93, 67–506.

Early Jewish Commentators

In recent years there has been renewed interest in the study of early Jewish commentary on Deuteronomy. See in particular: **Basser, H. W.** *In the Margins of the Midrash: Sefre Ha'azinu Texts, Commentaries, and Reflections.* SFSHJ 11. Atlanta: Scholars Press, 1990. ———, ed. *Pseudo-Rabad: Commentary to Sifre Deuteronomy.* SFSHJ 92. Atlanta: Scholars Press, 1994. **Fraade, S. D.** *From Tradition to Commentary.* SUNY Series in Judaica. Albany: State Univ. of New York Press, 1991. **Hammer, R.,** ed. *Sifre: A Tannaitic Commentary on the Book of Deuteronomy.* YJS 24. New Haven, CT: Yale UP, 1986. **Isseroff, S. A.** *An Introduction to Rashi's Grammatical Explanations in the Book of Deuteronomy.* New York: M. P. Press, 1993. **Neusner, J.** *Sifre to Deuteronomy.* Vols. 1–2, *An Analytical Translation.* BJS 98, 101. Atlanta: Scholars Press, 1987. ———. *Sifre to Deuteronomy.* Vol. 3, *An Introduction to the Rhetorical, Logical, and Topical Program.* BJS 124. Atlanta: Scholars Press, 1987.

Medieval Jewish Scholars

Commentaries by medieval Jewish scholars primarily in France, Spain, and North Africa who wrote in Hebrew include: **Aaron ben Elijah (Aaron the Younger)** (1328–1369). **Aaron ben Joseph ha-Rofe (Aaron the Elder)** (1250–1320). **Abravanel (Isaac ben Judah)** (1437–1508). **Bahya ben Asher** (1291). **Bekhor Shor (Joseph ben Isaac)** (12th century). **Hizkuni (Hezekiah ben Manoah)** (13th century). **Ibn Ezra (Abraham ben Meir)** (1089–1164). **Ibn Janah (Jonah)** (ca. 1000–1050). **Judah ben Samuel he-Hasid** (1150–1217, Regensburg). **Radak (David Kimchi)** (1160–1235). **Ralbag (Levi ben Gershon** or **Gersonides)** (1288–1344). **Ramban (Moshe ben Nahman** or **Nahmanides)** (1194–1270). **Rashbam (Shemuel ben Meir)** (1080–1174). **Rashi (Solomon ben Isaac)** (1040–1105). **Saadia ben Joseph** (882–942). **Sforno (Obadiah ben Jacob)** (15th-century Italy).

Renewed scholarly interest is making some of this material more readily available for detailed study in such works as: **Bechor-Schor, J.** *Der Pentateuch-Kommentar des Joseph Bechor-Schor zum fünften Buche Moses.* Breslau: Koebnersche, 1914 (Heb.). **Ibn Ezra.** *Ibn Ezra's Commentary on the Pentateuch.* Tr. H. N. Strickmann and A. M. Silver. New York: Menorah, 1988. **Ramban (Nachmanides).** *Commentary on the Torah: Deuteronomy.* Tr. C. B. Chavel. New York: Shilo, 1976. ———. *Commentary to the Pentateuch.* Jerusalem: Makor (facsimile copy of 1470 ed.). **Rashbam.** *Der Pentateuch-Commentar des R. Samuel ben Meir* (Rashbam). Ed. D. Rosin. Breslau, 1881. **Rashi.** *The Commentary of Rashi on the Pentateuch by R. Shlomo Yitzhaki* (1040–1105). Berliners Edition and Sefer ha-Zikkaron, based on the first printed edition (Reggio de Calabria, 1475). Ed. M. R. Lehmann. New York: Manfred and Anne Lehmann Foundation, 1981. ———. *Pentateuch with Targum Onkelos, Haphtaroth and Prayers for Sabbath and Rashi's Commentary.* Tr. M. Rosenbaum and A. M. Silbermann. London: Shapiro, Vallentine, 1929–34. ———. *Sefer Debarim.* Amsterdam: Lob ben Moses Sussmans, 1768. **Sforno, O.** *Sforno Commentary on the Torah.* Tr. R. Pelcovitz. ArtScroll Mesora Series 2. Brooklyn: Mesora, 1989. See also the commentary by **S. Fisch** (1972).

Christian Scholars in the Middle Ages

Commentaries by Christian scholars in the Middle Ages include: **Bruno of Astensis** (1032–1101). *PL* 164, 505–50. **Denis le Chartreux** (Dionysius the Carthusian) (1402–71). In *Opera Omnia.* Montreuil, 1896. 2:519–721. **Hugh of St. Victor** (1096–1141). *PL* 175, 29–86. **Nicholas of Lyra** (1270–1349). *Postilla Super Totam Bibliam, I.* Strassburg, 1492. Repr. Frankfurt am Main: Minerva GmbH., 1971. **Peter the Chanter** (1197) (see Dahan, G. "Les interprétations juives dans les commentaires du pentateuque de Pierre le Chantre." In *The Bible in the Medieval World: Essays in Memory of Beryl Smalley.* Ed. K. Walsh and D. Wood. Studies in Church History, Subsidia 4. Oxford: Blackwell, 1985. 131–55). **Peter Damian** (1007–72). *PL* 145, 1063–1070. **Rupert of Deutz** (1070–1129). *PL* 167, 917–1000.

Protestant Reformers

Among Protestant Reformers who returned the church to an emphasis on the Bible, see: **Calvin, J.** *Commentaries on the Four Last Books of Moses Arranged in the Form of a Harmony.* Tr. C. W. Bingham. 2 vols. Grand Rapids, MI: Eerdmans, 1950. ———. *Commentarii Ioannis Calvini in Quinque Libros Mosis.* Geneva: Gaspar, 1573. ———. *Sermons upon Deuteronomie.* Tr. A. Golding. Folio, 1583. **Luther, M.** *Deuteronomion Mose cum Annotationibus.* Wittenberg: Hans Luft, 1525 (See *Lectures on Deuteronomy.* Luther's Works. Vol. 9. St. Louis: Concordia, 1960.). ———. *Vorlesung über das Deuteronomium.* 1523–24.

Roman Catholic Scholars

Roman Catholic scholars who wrote commentaries on Deuteronomy in the century after the Council of Trent include: **Bonfrère, J.** (Antwerp, 1625). **Calmet, A.** (Paris, 1707) (See *Commentarius Literalis in omnes Libros Veteris Testamenti.* Ed. J. D. Mansi. Wirceburgi Sumtibus Publicis, 1789. 2:524–839). **Cornelius a Lapide** (Antwerp, 1623) (See "Commentaria in Deuteronomium." In *Commentarii in Scripturam Sacram.* Vol. 1. Paris: J. P. Pelagaud et Socios, 1854. 959–1147. See also "In Deuteronomium Commentarium." In *Scripturae Sacrae Cursus Completus.* Vol. 7. Paris: J.-P Migne, 1861. 125–498). **Jansenius, C.** (Leuven, 1641). **Malvenda, T.** (Lyon, 1650). **Mansi, I. D.** (Venice, 1754). **Menochius, G. S.** (Lyon, 1627). **Sanctis Pagnini** (1470–1541) (See *Commentario in Mosi Pentateuchum.* Ed. Hieronymus ab Oleastro. Antwerp, 1568). **Tirin, J.** (Lyon, 1632) (See *Universam S. Scripturam Commentarius.* Ed. P. Zachariae and P. J. Brunengo. Taurini: Eq. Petri Marietti, 1882. 1:676–752).

Other Scholars before 1800

Other commentaries before 1800 include: **Anonymous.** *Explication de cinq chapitres du Deutéronome; et des prophéties d'Habacuc, et de Jonas* (Deut 29–33). Paris: Babuty, 1734. **Ainsworth, H.** *Annotations upon the Five Bookes of Moses.* London: M. Parsons, 1639. **Arguiti, Y. B.** (1773). *Debarim.* 3 vols. In *MeAm Lóez.* The Torah Anthology. Vols. 15–17 (Deut 1:1–21:9). Tr. A. Kaplan and S. Yerushalmi. New York; Jerusalem: Maznaim, 1984–85. **Bar Hebraeus, G. A.** (1226–85). *A Commentary to Deuteronomy.* Ed. G. Kerber. Chicago: Univ. of Chicago Press, 1897. **Bugenhagen, J.** *Annotationes ab ipso iam emissae: In Deuteronomium.* Basil: Petri, 1524. **Drusius, J.** *Ad loca difficiliora Pentateuchi, Quinque liborum Mosis commentarius Conscriptus.* Franekerae Frisiorum, 1617. **Frassen, C.** *Disquisitiones Biblicae in universum Pentateuchum.* Paris: P. Witte, 1705. **Gerhard, J.** (1634). *Commentarius super Deuteronomium.* Jena, 1657. **Guillemin, P.** *Commentaire littéral abrégé sur les livres de l'ancien et du nouveau Testament.* Paris: Emery, 1721. **Henry, M.** (1662–1714). *An Exposition of the Five Books of Moses.* Edinburgh: Lunisden & Robertson, 1757. **Kidder, R.** *A Commentary on the Five Books of Moses.* London: J. Heptinstall, 1694. **Leclerc, J.** *Mosis prophetae libri quatuor: Exodus, Leviticus, Numeri, et Deuteronomium.* Amstelodami: Wetstenium, 1696. **Le Maistre, I. L.** *Le Deuteronome.* Paris: G. Desprez, 1685. **Lorini, J.** *Commentarii in Deuteronomium.* Lugduni: Cardon, 1629. **Marius, L.** *Commentariorum . . . in universam S. Scripturam.* Dvsseldorpffii: Coloniae Agrippinae, 1621. **Michaelis, J. H.** (1717–91) (See *Commentaries on the Laws of Moses.* Tr. A. Smith. London: Rivington, 1814.). **Parker, S.,** ed. *Bibliotheca biblica: Being a Commentary upon . . . the Old and New Testament.* Oxford, 1720. **Patrick, S.** *Commentary on the Pentateuch.* London, 1727. **Pelargi, C.** *In Deuteronomium Sacrum; sive, Quintum librum Mosis commentarius.* Leipzig: Lambergi, 1608. **Pellicanus, C.** (1478–1556). *In Pentateuchum, sive Quinque libros Mosis . . . commentarii.* Tigvri: Christophorvs Froschovervs, 1582. **Piscator, J.** *Commentarius in Deuteronomium.* Herbornae Nassov, 1615. **Rabani Mavri.** *Commentaria, antehac nunquam typis excusa.* Mense Martio, 1532. **Spangenberg, C.** *In sacri Mosis Pentateuchum.* Basil, 1564. **Teller, R.** *Die Heilige Schrift des Alten und Neuen Testaments, nebst einer vollständigen Erklärung derselben.* Leipzig: Bernhard Christoph Breitkopf, 1750. 2:659–1013. **Wesley, J.** (1765–66) (See *Wesley's Notes on the Bible.* Grand Rapids, MI: Zondervan, 1987. 134–51.).

Nineteenth and Twentieth Centuries

For purposes of convenience, the writing of commentaries on Deuteronomy in the nineteenth and twentieth centuries may be divided into four phases: 1805–1894, 1894–1943, 1943–1963, and 1963–1999. Each phase is introduced by a major breakthrough in critical study: Phase 1—W. L. de Wette's 1805 dissertation on Deuteronomy, which laid the cornerstone for the edifice of Pentateuchal literary criticism; Phase 2—the simultaneous, but independent, publications of C. Steuernagel and W. Staerk in 1894, which introduced redaction-critical study of Deuteronomy based primarily on the so-called *Numeruswechsel* (see *Excursus:* "The *Numeruswechsel* in Deuteronomy"); Phase 3—the publication of M. Noth's theory that ties the study of Deuteronomy to the so-called Deuteronomic (or Deuteronomistic) History (Joshua through 2 Kings), which eventually led to what today is called canonical criticism; and Phase 4—N. Lohfink's "stylistic" analysis of Deut 5–11 in 1963, which suggests unity of authorship and opens the door to new models for understanding the canonical process in ancient Israel.

Phase One (1805–94)

Amat, D. F. "Libro del Deuteronomio." In *La Sagrada Biblia Nuevamente Traducida de la Vulgata al Español.* Madrid: Don Leon Amarita, 1824. 2:3–102. **Baumgarten, M.** *Theologischer Commentar zum Pentateuch: Erste Hälfte, Vom Anfang bis zum Gesetz.* 1843. ———. *Theologischer Commentar zum Pentateuch: Zweite Hälfte, Gesetzgebung.* Kiel: Universitätsbuchhandlung, 1843–44. **Bellamy, J.** *The Holy Bible, Newly Translated . . . with Notes, Critical and Explanatory.* London: Longman, 1818 (includes Pentateuch only). **Benson, J.** (1815). "Critical, Explanatory, and Practical Notes." In *The Holy Bible.* New York: G. Lane & C. B. Tippett, 1846. 483–587. **Brentano, D. von.** *Die Heilige Schrift des Alten Testament.* 1. Theils dritter Band, welcher das 5, *Buch Mosis entahalt.* Frankfurt am Main: Varrentrapp, 1832. **Clarke, A.** (1811–16). "The Fifth Book of Moses Called Deuteronomy." In *The Holy Bible: With a Commentary and Critical Notes.* Nashville: Abingdon, n.d. 1:734–848. **Dillman, A.** *Die Bücher Numeri, Deuteronomium und Josua.* KeH 13. 2nd ed. rev. Leipzig: S. Hirzel, 1886. **Du Clot, M.** "Notes sur le Deutéronome." In *La Sainte Bible vengée des attaques de l'incrédulité.* Paris: Librairie de Louis Vivès, 1875. 2:352–71. **Feilchenfeld, W.** *Die zwei letzten Abschnitte des Pentateuchs übersetzt und erklärt.* Düsseldorf: W. de Haen, 1866. **Felipe, D. scio de San Miguel.** "El Deuteronomio." In *La Biblia Vulgata Latina Traducida en Español, y Anotada Confrome al sentido de los Santos Padres y Espositores Católicos.* Mégico: En Casa de Cornelio C. Sebring, 1831. 2:323–478. **Fillion, L.** *Biblia Sacra, juxta Vulgatae exemplaria et correctoria romana.* Paris: Letouzey et Ané, 1887. **Henry, M.** *An Exposition of the Old and New Testament.* Vol. 1. Philadelphia: Towar & Hogan, 1828. **Jamieson, R.** "The Fifth Book of Moses, Called Deuteronomy." In *The Critical and Explanatory Pocket Bible.* Glasgow: William Collins, 1870. 1:131–58. ———, **Faussett, A. R.,** and **Brown, D.** (ca. 1875). "The Fifth Book of Moses, Called Deuteronomy." In *A Commentary: Critical, Experimental and Practical on the Old and New Testaments.* Grand Rapids, MI: Eerdmans, 1948. 1:620–715. **Kalisch, M.** *A Historical and Critical Commentary on the Old Testament.* London: Longman, 1855. **Keil, C. F.** *Biblischer Commentar über das Alte Testament.* 2 vols. Leipzig: Dörffling und Franke, 1865 (2nd ed. 1870; ET: *Biblical Commentary on the Old Testament.* Tr. J. Martin. Edinburgh: Clark, 1864–65). **Knobel, A. W.** *Die Bücher Numeri, Deuteronomium und Josua: Nebst einer Kritik des Pentateuchs und Josua.* KeH 13. Leipzig: S. Hirzel, 1861. **Lees, R. L.,** and **Burns, D.** "The Book of Deuteronomy." In *The Temperance Bible-Commentary.* 3rd ed. London: S. W. Partridge & Co., 1872 (2nd ed. 1868). **Lindsay, J. W.** *Deuteronomy.* Commentary on the Old Testament. Ed. D. D. Whedon. New York: Eaton, 1891. **M[ackintosh], C. H.** *Notes on the Book of Deuteronomy.* 2 vols. Chicago: Revell, 1880. **Maurer, F. J. V. D.** "Deuteronomium." In *Commentarius Grammaticus Criticus in Vetus Testamentum.* Leipzig: Fridericus Volckmar, 1835. 1:74–97. **Montet, F.** *Le Deutéronome et la question de l'Hexateuque: Étude critique et exégétique sous form de'introduction et de commentaire du Deutéronome considéré dans ses rapports avec les quatre premiers livres Pentateuque et Josué.* Paris, 1891. **Oettli, S.** *Das Deuteronomium und die Bücher Josua und Richter.* Kurzgefasster Kommentar zu den heiligen Schriften Alten und Neuen Testaments. Munich: Beck, 1893. **Rosenmüller, E. F. K.** *Scholia in Vetus Testamentum.* Vol. 2, *Leviticus, Numeri, Deuteronomion.* Leipzig: J. A. Bartius, 1821. **Schroeder, F. W. J.** *Das Deuteronomium oder das Fünfte Buch Mose.* Theologisch-homiletisches Bibelwerk. Bielefeld: Velhagen & Klasing, 1866 (ET enlarged by A. Gosman. *Deuteronomy or the Fifth Book of Moses.* New York: Scribner's Sons, 1879). **Schultz, Fr. W.** *Das Deuteronomium erklärt.* Berlin: Schlawitz, 1859. **Scott, T.** *The Holy Bible Containing the Old and New Testaments.* 5 vols. Boston: Samuel T. Armstrong, 1823. 1:488–585. **Trochon, C.** *Introduction a l'étude de l'Écriture Sainte d'aprés "La Sainte Bible avec commentaires."* Paris: P. Lethielleux, 1889. **Vater, J. S.** *Commentar über den Pentateuch.* Vol. 3, *Deuteronomium.* Halle: Verlag der Waisenhaus-Buchhandlung, 1805. **Waller, C. H.** *The Fifth Book of Moses, Called Deuteronomy.* Ed. C. J. Ellicott. Handy Commentary on the Old Testament 5. London: Cassell, n.d. [188–?]. **Weill, A.** *Le cinq livres de Moïse.* Paris, 1890–91. **Westphal, A.** *Le Deutéronome.* Toulouse, 1891.

Phase Two (1894–1943)

Anonymous. "Deuteronomy." In *The Sermon Bible.* New York: Funk & Wagnalls, 1919. 1.1:303–56. **André, M. T.** "Le Deutéronome." In *La Bible du Centenaire: La Sainte Bible: Traduction nouvelle d'aprés les meilleurs textes avec introduction et notes.* Paris: Société Biblique de Paris, 1936. 237–90. **Bertholet, A.** *Deuteronomium.* KHC 5. Tübingen: Mohr, 1899. **Betteridge, W. R.** *The Book of Deuteronomy.* American Commentary on the OT 2. Philadelphia: American Baptist Publication Society, 1915. **Clamer, A.,** ed. *Lévitiqué, Nombres, Deutéronome.* La Sainte Bible 2. Paris: Letouzey et Ané, 1940. **Driver, S. R.** *A Critical and Exegetical Commentary on Deuteronomy.* ICC. Edinburgh: T. & T. Clark, 1895. **Dummelow, J. R.,** ed. "Deuteronomy." In *A Commentary on the Holy Bible.* New York: Macmillan, 1909. 121–40. **Eerdmans, B. D.** *Deuteronomy.* London: Griffin & Co., 1927. **Espin, T. E.** "Deuteronomy." In *The Holy Bible with an Explanatory and Critical Commentary.* Ed. F. C. Cook. New York: Charles Scribner's Sons, 1895. 1.1:790–928. **Girdlestone, R. B.** *The Student's Deuteronomy.* London; New York: Eyre and Spottiswoode, 1899. **Gray, J. C.,** and **Adams, G. M.** "The Book of Deuteronomy." In *The Biblical Encyclopedia.* Cleveland: F. M. Barton, 1903. 1:457–553. **Gressmann, H.** *Die Schriften des Alten Testament.* Göttingen: Vandenhoeck & Ruprecht, 1910 (2nd ed. 1922). **Halley, H. H.** "Deuteronomy." In *Pocket Bible Handbook.* Chicago: Henry H. Halley, 1924 (20th ed. in 1955 as *Bible Handbook*). 142–47. **Harford, J. B.** *Deuteronomy.* New Commentary on the Holy Scripture. London, 1928. **Harper, A.** *The Book of Deuteronomy.* Expositor's Bible. London: Hodder & Stoughton, 1895. **Hastings, J.,** ed. "The Book of Deuteronomy." In *The Speaker's Bible.* Aberdeen: The 'Speakers' Bible' Offices, 1924. 3:1–192. **Hertz, J. H.,** ed. *Deuteronomy.* The Pentateuch and the Haftorahs 5. London: Oxford UP, 1936. **Hoberg, G.** *Exegetisches Handbuch zum Pentateuch mit hebräischem Text und lateinischen Text.* Freiburg: Herder, 1908. **Hoffmann, D.** *Das Buch Deuteronomium: Erster Halbband, Deut. I-XX, 9.* Berlin, 1913. ———. *Das Buch Deuteronomium: Zweiter Halbband, Deut. XXI, 16–XXXI.* Berlin: Poppelauer, 1922. **Hummelauer, F. von.** *Commentarius in Deuteronomium.* Cursus Scripturae Sacrae 3:2. Paris: Sumptibus P. Lethielleux, 1901. **Irwin, C. H.** "The Book of Deuteronomy." In *Irwin's Bible Commentary.* Chicago: John C. Winston, 1928. 59–68. **Jordan, W. G.** *Commentary on the Book of Deuteronomy.* New York: Macmillan, 1911. **Junker, H.** *Das Buch Deuteronomium.* Die Heilige Schrift des Alten Testament. Bonn: P. Hanstein, 1933. **König, E.** *Das Deuteronomium.* KAT 3. Leipzig: A. Deichert, 1917. **Kretzmann, P. E.** "The Book of Deuteronomy." In *Popular Commentary of the Bible.* St. Louis, MO: Concordia Publishing House, 1923. 1:303–62. **Maclagan, H.** *The Book of Deuteronomy Intepreted and Explained.* Paisley: Gardner, 1914. **Maclaren, A.** "The Book of Deuteronomy." In *Expositions of Holy Scripture.* Grand Rapids, MI: Eerdmans, 1938. 2:1–86. **Marti, K.** "Das fünfte Buch Moses oder Deuteronomium." In *Die Heilige Schrift des Alten Testament.* Ed. E. F. Kautzsch and A. Bertholet. 4th ed. Tübingen: Mohr, 1922. 258–327. **Moulton, R. G.** *Deuteronomy.* Modern Reader's Bible. New York: Macmillan, 1896. **Reider, J.** *Deuteronomy: The Holy Scriptures with Commentary.* Philadelphia: Jewish Publication Society, 1937. **Robinson, H. W.** *Deuteronomy and Joshua.* New Century Bible. Oxford: Oxford UP, 1907. **Scott, D. R.** "Deuteronomy." In *Abingdon Bible Commentary.* Ed. F. C. Eiselen, E. Lewis, and D. G. Downey. New York: Abingdon, 1929. 318–44. **Smith, G. A.** *The Book of Deuteronomy.* CBib. Cambridge: Cambridge UP, 1918. **Steuernagel, C.** *Das Deuteronomium.* HAT 1.3. Göttingen: Vandenhoeck & Ruprecht, 1898 (2nd ed. 1923). ———. *Übersetzung und Erklärung der Bücher Deuteronomium und Josua und allgemeine Einleitung in den Hexateuch.* HKAT 1.3. Göttingen: Vandenhoeck & Ruprecht, 1900 (2nd ed. 1923). **Wilkins, G.** *The Fifth Book of Moses, Called Deuteronomy.* Temple Bible 5. London; Philadelphia: J. B. Lippincott, 1902. **Witton, D. T.** "Deuteronomy." In *Peake's Commentary on the Bible.* London: T. C. & E. C. Jack, 1920. 231–43.

Phase Three (1943–63)

Cazelles, H. *Le Deutéronome.* La Sainte Bible. Paris: Cerf, 1950 (3rd ed. 1966). **Clarke, W. K. L.** "Deuteronomy." In *Concise Bible Commentary.* London: S.P.C.K., 1952. 383–93. **Cohen, A.**, ed. *The Soncino Chumash: The Five Books of Moses with Haphtaroth.* Hindhead: Soncino, 1947. **Colunga, A.**, and **García Cordero, M.** *Biblia Comentada. I. Pentateuco: Deuteronomio.* Madrid: Editorial Catolica, 1960. 908–1057. **Cooper, C. M.** "The Book of Deuteronomy." In *Old Testament Commentary.* Ed. H. C. Alleman and E. E. Flack. Philadelphia: Muhlenberg, 1948. 300–328. **Crichton, T. S.** *Deuteronomy.* Books of the Bible Series 5. Edinburgh: Church of Scotland Youth Committee, 1951. **Cunliffe-Jones, H.** "The Book of Deuteronomy." In *The Twentieth Century Bible Commentary.* Ed. G. H. Davies, A. Richardson, and C. L. Wallis. New York: Harper, 1955. 150–57. ———. "Deuteronomy." TBC. London: SCM Press, 1951. **Davies, G. H.** "Deuteronomy." In *Peake's Commentary on the Bible.* Ed. M. Black. London: Nelson, 1962. 269–88. **Dhorme, E.** *La Bible.* Paris: Gillimard, 1956. **Erdman, C. R.** *The Book of Deuteronomy: An Exposition.* Westwood, NJ: Revell, 1953. **Glanzman, G. S.** *The Book of Deuteronomy.* Pamphlet Bible Series 9. New York: Paulist, 1960. **Haratom, E. S.** *Sefer Debarim.* Tel Aviv: Yavneh, 1956 (Heb.). **Hirsch, S. R.** *The Pentateuch.* Vol. 5. London, 1962. **Holwerda, B.** *Oudtestamentische voordrachten: Deel III, Exegese Oude Testament (Deuteronomium) (gehouden in de collegejaren 1946–1952).* Kampen: Copiëerinrichtin, v.d. Berg, 1957. **Junker, H.** *Das Buch Deuteronomium.* Das Alte Testament. Zweites bis fünftes Buch Moses. Echter Bibel. Würzburg: Echter, 1952. **Keil, C. F.**, and **Delitzsch, F.** *The Pentateuch.* Vol. 3 of *Biblical Commentary on the Old Testament.* Tr. J. Martin. 25 vols. 1866. Repr. Grand Rapids: Eerdmans, 1956. **Krämer, K. F.** *Numeri und Deuteronomium.* Herders Bibelkommentar 2.1. Freiburg: Herder, 1955. **Kuhn, H. B.** "Deuteronomy." In *The Biblical Expositor.* Ed. C. F. H. Henry. Philadelphia: A. J. Holman, 1960. 1:184–208. **MacKenzie, R. A. F.** "Deuteronomy." In *A Catholic Commentary on Holy Scripture.* Ed. B. Orchard et al. London: Nelson, 1953. 261–72. **Manley, G. T.** "Deuteronomy." In *The New Bible Commentary.* Ed. F. Davidson. Grand Rapids, MI: Eerdmans, 1953 (2nd ed. 1954). 195–222. **Moraldi, L.** "Deuteronomio." In *La Sacra Bibbia.* Turin: Marietti, 1960. 395–467. **Morgan, G. C.** "Deuteronomy." In *An Exposition of the Whole Bible.* Westwood, NJ: Revell, 1959. 77–91. **Neil, W.** "Deuteronomy." In *Harper's Bible Commentary.* London: Hodder & Stoughton, 1962. 131–41. **Nichol, F. D.**, ed. "The Fifth Book of Moses Called Deuteronomy." In *The Seventh-Day Adventist Bible Commentary.* Washington, DC: Review and Herald Publishing Association, 1953. 1:951–1077. **Rabinowitz, C. D.** *Da'at Sofrim.* Jerusalem, Da'at Yisrael, 1957 (Heb.). ———. *Sefer Debarim.* In Samaritan characters. Tel Aviv: Nezach, 1959 (Heb. tr. from German). **Ridderbos, J.** *Het boek Deuteronomium, opnieuw uit den grondtekst vertaald en verklaard.* Korte verklaring der Heilige Schrift, met nieuwe vertaling. Kampen: Kok, 1950 (ET: *Deuteronomy.* Tr. M. van der Maas. Grand Rapids, MI: Regency Reference Libarary, 1984). **Shires, H. H.**, and **Parker, P.** "Deuteronomy: Exposition." *IB.* 12 vols. Nashville: Abingdon, 1953. 2:331–537. **Steinmann, J.** *Deutéronome: Texte français par Jean Steinmann: Introduction et commentaires par une équipe biblique du centre d'études Notre-Dame.* Connaître la Bible. Brussels, 1961. **Wright, G. E.** "The Book of Deuteronomy." *IB.* 12 vols. Nashville: Abingdon, 1953. 2:311–537.

Phase Four (1963–1999)

Achtemeier, E. *Deuteronomy, Jeremiah.* Proclamation Commentaries. Philadelphia: Fortress, 1979. **Ackland, D. F.** "Deuteronomy." In *The Teacher's Bible Commentary.* Ed. H. F. Paschall. Nashville: Broadman, 1972. 115–36. **Alonso Schökel, L.** *Deuteronomio.* Los Libros Sagrados 1.2. Madrid: Ediciones Cristianidad, 1970. 257–404. **Blair, E. P.** *The Book of Deuteronomy; The Book of Joshua.* LBC 5. Richmond: John Knox, 1964. **Blenkinsopp, J.** "Deuteronomy."

In *Jerome Biblical Commentary*. Englewood Cliffs, NJ: Prentice-Hall, 1968. 101–22. ———. "Deuteronomy." In *The New Jerome Biblical Commentary*. Ed. R. E. Brown, J. Fitzmyer, and R. Murphy. Englewood Cliffs, NJ: Prentice-Hall, 1990. 94–109. **Braulik, G.** *Das Testament des Mose: Das Buch Deuteronomium*. Stuttgarter kleiner Kommentar Altes Testament 4. Stuttgart: Katholisches Bibelwerk, 1976. ———. *Deuteronomium 1–16, 17*. NEchB. Würzburg: Echter, 1986. ———. *Deuteronomium 16, 18–34, 12*. NEchB. Würzburg: Echter, 1992. **Brown, R. E.** *The Message of Deuteronomy: Not by Bread Alone*. Downers Grove, IL: InterVarsity Press, 1993. **Brown, R. E., S.S.** *The Book of Deuteronomy*. OT Reading Guide 10. Collegeville: Liturgical Press, 1965. **Buis, P.**, and **Leclercq, J.** *Le Deutéronome*. Sources bibliques. Paris: Gabalda, 1963. ———. *Le Deutéronome*. Verbum Salutis: Ancien Testament 4. Paris: Beauchesne, 1969. **Cairns, I.** *Word and Presence: A Commentary on the Book of Deuteronomy*. International Theological Commentary. Grand Rapids, MI: Eerdmans, 1992. **Chouraqui, A.** *Paroles (Deutéronome)*. La Bible traduite et présentée 5. Paris: Desclée de Brouwer, 1974. ———. *L'Univers de la Bible*. Vol. 2. Paris: Lidis, 1983. **Clements, R. E.** "Deuteronomy." In *The New Interpreter's Bible*. Vol. 2. Nashville: Abingdon, 1998. 269–538. **Clifford, R.** *Deuteronomy, with an Excursus on Covenant and Law*. OT Message, A Biblical-Theological Commentary 4. Wilmington, DE: Glazier, 1982. **Coffman, J. B.** *Commentary on Deuteronomy: The Fifth Book of Moses*. Abilene, TX: Abilene Christian UP, 1988. **Cousins, P. E.** "Deuteronomy." In *The International Bible Commentary*. Ed. F. F. Bruce. Rev. ed. Grand Rapids, MI: Zondervan, 1986 (1st ed. 1979). 256–82. **Craigie, P. C.** *The Book of Deuteronomy*. NICOT. Grand Rapids, MI: Eerdmans, 1976. **Criado, R.** *Deuteronomio: La Sagrada Biblia*. Vol. 1. Madrid: Editorial Catolica, 1967. **Cunliffe-Jones, H.** *Deuteronomy*. TBC. London: SCM Press, 1964. **Drubbel, A.** *Numeri uit de grondtekst vertaald en uitgelegd*. BOT 2.2. Roermond en Maaseik: Romen & Zonen, 1963. **Fisch, S.** *Midrash ha-Gadol: Deuteronomy*. Jerusalem: Mosad ha-Rav Kuk, 1972 (Heb.). **Francisco, C. T.** *The Book of Deuteronomy*. Shield Bible Study Series. Grand Rapids, MI: Baker, 1964. **Gilchrist, P. R.** "Deuteronomy." In *The Evangelical Commentary on the Bible*. Ed. W. A. Elwell. Grand Rapids, MI: Baker, 1989. 107–30. **Gottwald, N. K.** "The Book of Deuteronomy." In *The Interpreter's One-Volume Commentary on the Bible*. Ed. C. M. Laymon. Nashville: Abingdon, 1971. 100–121. **Hamilton, V. P.** *Handbook on the Pentateuch*. Grand Rapids, MI: Baker, 1982. 375–474. **Hanke, H. A.** "The Book of Deuteronomy." In *The Wesleyen Bible Commentary*. Ed. C. W. Carter and W. R. Thompson. Grand Rapids, MI: Eerdmans, 1967. 1.1:467–50. **Hirsch, S. R.** *Deuteronomy*. In *The Pentateuch, V.* Tr. I. Levy. 2nd ed. (completely revised). London: Bloch, 1966. **Hoppe, L.** "Deuteronomy." In *The Collegeville Bible Commentary*. Ed. D. Bergant and R. J. Karris. Collegeville: Liturgical Press, 1989. 196–228. **Kaplan, A.** "Deuteronomy: Translation with Notes." In *The Living Torah*. New York: Moznaim, 1981. **Kline, M. G.** *Treaty of the Great King: The Covenant Structure of Deuteronomy: Studies and Commentary*. Grand Rapids, MI: Eerdmans, 1963. **Labuschagne, C. J.** *Deuteronomium*. Vols. 1A and 1B. POT. Nijkerk: Uitgeverij Callenbach, 1987. ———. *Deuteronomium*. Vol. 2. POT. Nijkerk: Uitgeverij Callenbach, 1990. ———. *Deuteronomium*. Vol. 3. POT. Nijkerk: Uitgeverij Callenbach, 1997. **Laconi, M.** *Deuteronomio*. Nuovissima Versione della Bibbia dai Test Originale 5. Rome: Paoline, 1970. **Lamparter, H.** *Der Aufruf zum Gehorsam: Das 5. Buch Mose*. BAT 9. Stuttgart: Calwer, 1977. **Lamsa, G. M.** *Old Testament Light: A Scriptural Commentary Based on the Aramaic of the Ancient Peshitta Text*. Englewood Cliffs, NJ: Prentice-Hall, 1964. **Malbim, M. L.** *Rabbenu Meir Leibush ben Yechiel Michel: Commentary on the Torah*. Tr. with notes by Z. Faier. Jerusalem: Hillel Press, 1978. **Manley, G. T.**, and **Harrison, R. K.** "Deuteronomy." In *New Bible Commentary*. Ed. D. Guthrie and J. A. Motyer. Rev. 3rd ed. Grand Rapids, MI: Eerdmans, 1970. 201–29. **Mann, T.** *Deuteronomy*. Ed. P. D. Miller and D. L. Bartlett. Westminster Bible Companion. Louisville: Westminster John Knox, 1995. **Maxwell, J. C.** *Deuteronomy*. Communicator's Commentary. Waco, TX: Word, 1987. **Mayes, A. D. H.** *Deuteronomy*. NCBC. Grand Rapids, MI: Eerdmans, 1981. **Merrill, E. H.** *Deuteronomy*. New American Commentary. Nashville: Broadman & Holman, 1994. **Miller, P. D.** *Deuteronomy*. Interpretation: A Bible Commentary for Teaching and Preaching. Louisville: John Knox, 1990.

Moraldi, L. *Introduzione alla Bibbia; corso sistematico di studi biblici.* Turin: Marietti, 1964. **Moran, W. L.** "Deuteronomy." In *A New Catholic Commentary on Holy Scripture.* Ed. R. C. Fuller, L. Johnston, and C. Kearns. New and fully rev. ed. London: Nelson, 1969. **Munk, E.** קול התורה: *La Voix de la Thora* 5. Paris: Fondation Samuel et Odette Levy, 1969 (2nd ed. 1978). **Nelson, R. D.** "Deuteronomy." In *Harper's Bible Commentary.* Ed. J. L. Mays et al. San Francisco: Harper & Row, 1988. 209–34. **Nielsen, E.** *Deuteronomium.* HAT 6. Tübingen: Mohr (Siebeck), 1995. **North, G.** *Inheritance and Dominion: An Economic Commentary on Deuteronomy.* Tyler, TX: Institute for Christan Economics, 1999 (electronic edition available at www.freebooks.com). **Payne, D. F.** *Deuteronomy.* Daily Study Bible. Philadelphia: Westminster, 1985. **Penna, A.** *Deuteronomio.* La Sacra Bibbia. Turin: Marietti, 1976. **Phillips, A.** *Deuteronomy.* CBC. Cambridge: Cambridge UP, 1973. **Plaut, W. G.** *Deuteronomy.* The Torah: A Modern Commentary 5. New York: Union of American Hebrew Congregations, 1974. **Polzin, R.** "Deuteronomy." In *The Literary Guide to the Bible.* Ed. R. Alter and F. Kermode. Cambridge: Harvard UP, 1987. 92–101. **Rad, G. von.** *Deuteronomy.* Tr. D. Barton. OTL. Philadelphia: Westminster, 1966. **Rennes, J.** *Le Deutéronome: Traduction et commentaire.* Geneva: Labor et Fides, 1967. **Ridderbos, J.** *Het Boek Deuteronomium: Opnieuw uit de grontekst vertaald en verklaard.* Kampen: Kok, 1963–64. **Rose, M.** *5. Mose.* Zürcher Bibelkommentare. AT 5. Zurich: Theologischer Verlag, 1994. **Sanders, J. A.** "Deuteronomy." In *The Books of the Bible.* Ed. B. W. Anderson. New York: Charles Scribner's Sons, 1989. 1:89–102. **Schultz, S. J.** *Deuteronomy: The Gospel of Love.* Everyman's Bible Commentary. Chicago: Moody Press, 1971. **Thompson, J. A.** *Deuteronomy.* TOTC. Downers Grove, IL: InterVarsity Press, 1974. **Tigay, J. H.** *Deuteronomy.* JPS Torah Commentary. Philadelphia: Jewish Publication Society, 1996. **Unger, M. F.** "Deuteronomy." In *Unger's Commentary on the Old Testament.* Chicago: Moody Press, 1981. 1:233–78. **Watts, J. D. W.** "Deuteronomy." In *BBC.* Ed. C. J. Allen. Nashville: Broadman, 1970. 2:175–296. **Weinfeld, M.** *Deuteronomy 1–11.* AB 5. New York: Doubleday, 1991. **Wijngaards, J.** *Deuteronomium.* BOT 2.3. Roermond en Maaseik: Romen & Zonen, 1971. **Wright, C. J. H.** *Deuteronomy.* New International Biblical Commentary. Peabody, MA: Hendrickson, 1996.

General Bibliography

Selected Books and Monographs

The list that follows is given in alphabetical order within chronological blocks of time, beginning with the seminal work of W. M. L. de Wette in 1805, which marks the beginning of the modern critical era in the study of Deuteronomy. Monographs on specific passages or portions are noted in the chapter bibliographies.

1805–39

Wette, W. M. L. de. *Beiträge zur Einleitung in das Alte Testament.* 2 vols. Halle, 1806–1807. Repr. Hildesheim, NY: Olms, 1971. ———. *Dissertatio critica qua Deuteronomium a prioribus Pentateuchi libris diversum alius cuiusdam recentioris auctoris opus esse monstratur.* Jena, 1805.

1840–89

Bertheau, E. *Die sieben Gruppen mosaischer Gesetz in den drei mittleren büchern des Pentateuchs: Ein Beitrag zur Kritik des Pentateuchs.* Göttingen: Vandenhoeck & Ruprecht, 1840. **Colenso, J. W.** *The Pentateuch and the Book of Joshua Critically Examined.* Part 3, *The Book of Deuteronomy.* London: Longman, 1863. **Dahler, J.** *Jérémie et le Deutéronome.* Strasbourg, 1872. **Kayser, A.** *Das vorexilische Buch der Urgeschichte Israels und seine Erweiterungen: Ein Beitrag zur Pentateuchkritik.* Strassburg: Schmidt, 1874. **Kleinert, P.** *Das Deuteronomium und der Deuteronomiker: Untersuchungen zur alttestamentliche Rechts- und Literaturgeschichte.* Bielefeld; Leipzig: Velhagen & Klasing. 1872. **Kübel, R.** *Das alttestamentliche Gesetz und seine Urkunde.* Stuttgart: Steinkopf, 1867. **Maine, H.** *Ancient Law.* London: Murray, 1870. **Riehm, E.** *Die Gesetzgebung Mosis im Lande Moab: Ein Beitrag zur Einleitung in's alte Testament.* Gotha: Perthes, 1854. **Saalschütz, J. L.** *Das Mosaische Recht.* Part 2. Berlin: Cotteymann, 1853–54. **Schoebel, C.** *Demonstration critique de l'authenticité Mosaique du Deutéronome.* Paris, 1868. **Sime, J.** *Deuteronomy, the People's Book: Its Origin and Nature.* London: Daldy, Isbister, 1877. **Stähelin, J. J.** *Kritische Untersuchungen über den Pentateuch, die Bücher Josua, Richter, Samuels und der Könige.* Berlin: G. Reimers, 1843.

1890–99

Addis, W. E. *The Documents of the Hexateuch Translated and Arranged in Chronological Order with Introduction and Notes.* London: Putnam, 1898. **Girdlestone, R. B.** *The Student's Deuteronomy.* London: Eyre and Spottiswoode, 1899. **Hartmann, A. T.** *Historisch-kritische Forschungen über die Bildung, das Zeitalter und den Plan der fünf Bücher Moses.* Rostock-Gustrow, 1893. **Klostermann, A.** *Der Pentateuch: Beiträge zu seinem Verständnis und seiner Entstehungsgeschichte.* 2 vols. Leipzig: A. Deichert, 1893, 1907. **König, J. L.** *Alttestamentliche Studien: Zweites Heft, Das Deuteronomium und der Prophet Jeremiah, gegen Bohlen, nebst anderen Beiträgen zur Authentie des Deuteronomiums.* Berlin: G. Reimer, 1893. **Kraetzschmar, R.** *Die Bundesvorstellung im Alten Testament in ihrer geschichtlichen Entwicklung untersucht und dargestellt.* Marburg: Elwert, 1896. **MacDill, D.** *Mosaic Authorship of the Book of Deuteronomy.* Dayton: W. J. Shuey, 1896. **Montet, F.** *La composition de l'Hexateuque, de Juges, de Samuel et des*

Rois: Étude critique biblique. Basel, 1894. **Moor, F. de.** *La Date de la Composition du Deutéronome.* Amien, 1891. **Muir, W.** *The Authorship of Deuteronomy.* Tr. G. J. Metzger. London, 1896. **Naumann, O.** *Das Deuteronomium: Das prophetische Staatsgesetz des theokratischen Königtums mit seinen Eingangs- und Schlussworten, aus der prophetischen Geschichte und Theologie erläutert.* Gütersloh, 1897. **Preiss, H.** *Zum Deuteronomium.* Schulprogramme Progress no. 55. Berlin, 1892. **Reuss, E.** *Das Alte Testament: III, Die Heilige Geschichte und das Gesetz: Der Pentateuch und Josua.* Braunschweig: Schwetschke, 1893 (French ed. 1879). **Staerk, W.** *Beiträge zur Kritik des Deuteronomiums.* Leipzig: Pries, 1894. ———. *Das Deuteronomium: Sein Inhalt und seine literarische Form: Eine kritische Studie.* Leipzig: Hinrich, 1894. **Steuernagel, C.** *Die Entstehung des deuteronomischen Gesetzes.* Halle: J. Krause, 1896. ———. *Der Rahmen des Deuteronomiums: Literarcritische Untersuchung über seine Zusammensetzung und Entstehung.* Halle: J. Krause, 1894. **Weill, A.** *Les cinq Livres (Mosaïstes) de Moïse: Cinquiéme Livre, Deutéronome.* Paris, 1891. **Wellhausen, J.** *Die Composition des Hexateuchs und der historischen Bücher des Alten Testament.* Berlin: de Gruyter, 1894 (3rd ed. 1899). **Zahn, A.** *Das Deuteronomium: Eine Schutzschrift wider modernkritisches Unwesen.* Gütersloh: Bertelsmann, 1890.

1900–1909

Bruston, C. *L'Histoire sacerdotale et le Deutéronome primitif.* Paris: Fischbacher, 1906. **Carpenter, J. E.** *The Composition of the Hexateuch: An Introduction with Select Lists of Words and Phrases and an Appendix on Laws and Institutions by G. Harford.* London: Longmans, 1902. **Cullen, J.** *The Book of the Covenant in Moab: A Critical Inquiry into the Original Form of Deuteronomy.* Glasgow: Maclehose and Sons, 1903. **Erbt, W.** *Die Sicherstellung des Monotheismus durch die Gesetzgebung im vorexilischen Juda.* Göttingen: Vandenhoeck & Ruprecht, 1903. **Fries, D. S. A.** *Die Gesetzesschrift des Königs Josia: Eine kritische Untersuchung.* Leipzig: A. Deichert, 1903. **Grimme, H.** *Das Gesetz Hammurabis und Moses.* Cologne: Backem, 1903 (ET: *The Law of Hammurabi and Moses.* London, 1907). **Halévy, J.** "Recherches bibliques: Le Deutéronome." *RSEHA* 7 (1899) 313–32; 8 (1900) 1–8, 97–114, 193–216. **Harper, A.** *The Book of Deuteronomy.* New York: Armstrong, 1901. **McGarvey, J. W.** *The Authorship of the Book of Deuteronomy.* Cincinnati: Standard Publishing Co., 1902. **Merx, A.** *Die Bücher Moses und Josua.* Tübingen: Mohr, 1907. **Müller, D. H.** *Die Gesetze Hammurabis und ihr Verhältnis zur mosaischen Gesetzgebung sowie zu den XII Tafeln.* Vienna: A. Hölder, 1903. **Smith, W. R.** *Kinship and Marriage in Early Arabia.* Boston: Beacon, 1903. **Sternberg, G.** *Die Ethik des Deuteronomiums: Inaugural-Dissertation.* Berlin: Trowitzsch, 1908. **Wiener, H.** *Essays in Pentateuchal Criticism.* Oberlin: Bibliotheca Sacra, 1909.

1910–19

Euringer, S. *Der Streit um das Deuteronomium: Biblische Zeitfragen 4,8.* Münster: Aschendorff, 1911. **Griffiths, J. S.** *The Problem of Deuteronomy.* London, 1911. **Hempel, J.** *Die Schichten des Deuteronomiums: Ein Beitrag zur israelitischen Literatur- und Rechtsgeschichte.* Leipzig: R. Voigtländer, 1914. **Jordan, W. G.** *Deuteronomy.* New York: Macmillan, 1911. **McNeile, A. H.** *Deuteronomy: Its Place in Revelation.* London: Longmans, 1912. **Naville, E.** *The Discovery of the Book of the Law under King Josiah.* Tr. M. L. McClure. London: S.P.C.K., 1911. **Oestreicher, T.** *Die josianische Reform: Das Reich Christi 12.* Berlin, 1911. **Pope, H.** *The Date of the Composition of Deuteronomy: A Critical Study.* Holy Apostolic See and the Sacred Congregation of Rites. Rome: Frederick Pustet, 1910. **Puukko, A. F.** *Das Deuteronomium: Eine literarkritische Untersuchung.* BWANT 5. Leipzig: Hinrichs, 1910. **Smend, R.** *Die Erzählung des Hexateuch: Auf ihre Quellen untersucht.* Berlin: G. Reimer, 1912. **Wiener, H. M.** *Pentateuchal Studies.* London: E. Stock, 1912.

1920–29

Bentzen, A. *Die josianische Reform und ihre Voraussetzungen.* Copenhagen: Haas & Söhne, 1926. **Bewer, J. A., Paton, L. B.,** and **Dahl, G.** "The Problem of Deuteronomy: A Symposium." *JBL* 47 (1928) 305–79. **Jirku, A.** *Das weltliche Recht im Alten Testament: Stilgeschichtliche und rechtsvergleichende Studien in den juristischen Gesetzen des Pentateuch.* Gütersloh: Bertelsmann, 1927. **Kennett, R. H.** *Deuteronomy and the Decalogue.* Cambridge: Cambridge UP, 1920. **Kittel, G.** *Sifre zu Deuteronomium.* Stuttgart: Kohlhammer, 1922. **Kugler, F. X.** *Untersuchungen zum Hexateuchsproblem.* BZAW 38. Giessen: Töpelmann, 1924. ———. *Von Moses zu Paulus.* Münster: Aschendorff, 1922. **Löhr, M.** *Das Deuteronomium: Untersuchungen zum Hexateuchproblem II.* SKGG 1.6. Berlin: Deutsche Verlagsgesellschaft, 1925. **Longacre, L. B.** *Deuteronomy, a Prophetic Lawbook.* New York: Methodist Book Concern, 1924. **Menes, A.** *Die vorexilschen Gesetze Israels.* BZAW 50. Berlin: Töpelmann, 1928. **Möller, W.** *Rückbeziehungen des 5. Buches Moses auf die vier ersten Bücher: Ein Beitrag zur Einleitung in den Pentateuch im Sinne seiner Einheit und Echtheit.* Lütjenburg, 1925. **Mowinckel, S.** *Femte Mosebok: Det Gamle Testament: I. Loven eller de Fem Moseböker.* Oslo, 1929. **Naville, E.** *Le Deutéronome, un livre Mosaique.* Fontenay-sous-Bois, 1924. **Oestreicher, T.** *Das deuteronomische Grundgesetz.* BFCT 27.4. Gütersloh: Bertelsmann, 1923. **Pedersen, J.** *Israel: Its Life and Culture.* 4 parts in 2 vols. London: Oxford UP, 1926–40. **Rad, G. von.** *Das Gottesvolk im Deuteronomium.* BWANT 47. Stuttgart: Kohlhammer, 1929. **Ring, E.** *Israels Rechtsleben in Lichte der neuentdeckten assyrischen und hethitischen Gesetzeurkunden.* Stockholm: V. Petterson; Leipzig: G. Fock, 1926. **Sanda, A.** *Moses und der Pentateuch.* ATAbh 9. Münster: Aschendorff, 1924. **Siebens, A.-R.** *L'origine du code deutéronomique: Examen historique et littéraire du sujet à la lumière de la critique contemporaine.* Paris: Leroux, 1929. **Staerk, W.** *Das Problem des Deuteronomiums: Ein Beitrag zur neuesten Pentateuchkritik.* BFCT 29.2. Gütersloh: Bertelsmann, 1924. **Welch, A. C.** *The Code of Deuteronomy: A New Theory of Its Origin.* London: Clarke, 1924; New York, 1925. **Wiener, H. M.** *Das Hauptproblem des Deuteronomiums.* Tr. M. Kegel. Gütersloh: Bertelsmann, 1924.

1930–39

Alt, A. *Die Ursprunge des Israelitischen Rechts: Berichte ber die Verhandlungen der Sächsischen Akademie der Wissenschaften zu Leipzig, Philologisch-historische Klasse 86/1.* Leipzig, 1934 (ET: "The Origins of Israelite Law." In *Essays on Old Testament History and Religion.* Tr. R. A. Wilson. Oxford: Blackwell, 1966. 79–132). **Auerbach, E.** *Wüste und Gelobtes Land II.* Berlin: Schocken, 1936. **Breit, H.** *Die Predigt des Deuteronomisten.* Munich: Kaiser, 1933. **Cadoux, C. J.** *The Book of Deuteronomy: Introduction and Translation.* London, 1932. **Granqvist, H.** *Marriage Conditions in a Palestinian Village.* 2 vols. Helsinki: Akademische Buchhandlung, 1931–35. **Horst, F.** *Das Privilegrecht Jahves: Rechtsgeschichtliche untersuchungen zum Deuteronomium.* FRLANT 45. Göttingen: Vandenhoeck & Ruprecht, 1930. Repr. in *Gottes Recht: Studien zum Recht im Alten Testament.* TBü 12. Munich: Kaiser, 1961. 17–154. **Hulst, A. R.** *Het Karakter van den Cultus in Deuteronomium.* Groningen: Wagingen, Veenman & Zonen, 1938. **Krause, H.-H.** *Das Deuteronomium in der wissenschaftlichen Bearbeitung des 19. und 20. Jahrhunderts.* Breslau: Guttmann, 1931. **Mackintosh, C. H.** *Deuteronomium: I. Vestaling.* The Hague, 1935. **Noth, M.** *Reichstempel und Ortsheiligtümer in Israel.* BFCT 33. Gütersloh: Bertelsmann, 1930. **Rad, G. von.** *Das Formgeschichtliche Problem des Hexateuch.* BWANT 4.26. Stuttgart: Kohlhammer, 1936 (ET, 1966). **Rudolph, W.** *Der "Elohist" von Exodus bis Jusua.* BZAW 68. Berlin: Töpelmann, 1938. **Siebens, A.-R.** *L'origine du code deutéronomique: Examen historique et littéraire du sujet à la lumière de la critique contemporaine.* Paris: Leroux, 1929. **Stoderl, W.** *Das Gesetz Israels nach Inhalt und Ursprung: I. Beiträge zur Einleitung ins Alte Testament.* Marienbad, 1933. **Welch, A. C.** *Deuteronomy: The Framework to the Code.* London: Oxford UP, 1932.

1940–49

Allis, O. T. *The Five Books of Moses.* Phillipsburg, NJ: Presbyterian and Reformed Publishing Co., 1943. **Brinker, R.** *The Influence of Sanctuaries in Early Israel.* Manchester: Manchester UP, 1946. **Cazelles, H.** *Études sur le code de l'alliance.* Paris: Letouzey, 1946. **Daube, D.** *Studies in Biblical Law.* Cambridge: Cambridge UP, 1947. **Hospers, J. H.** *De Numeruswisseling in het Boek Deuteronomium.* Utrecht: Kemink, 1947. **Leroy, J.** *Introduction à l'étude des anciens codes orientaux.* Paris: Maisonneuve, 1944. **Neufeld, E.** *Ancient Hebrew Marriage Laws.* London: Longmans, Green, 1944. **Noth, M.** *Die Gesetze im Pentateuch: Ihre Voraussetzungen und ihr Sinn.* SKGG, *Geisteswissenschaftliche Klasse 17, 2.* Halle: Niemeyer, 1940 (ET, 1966). ———. *Überlieferungsgeschichtliche Studien I: Die sammelnden und bearbeitenden Geschichtswerke im Alten Testament.* Tübingen: Niemeyer, 1943 (ET, 1981). **Östborn, G.** *Tōrā* in the Old Testament: A Semantic Study. Lund: Ohlssons Bookstore, 1945. **Pedersen J.** *Israel: Its Life and Culture.* London: Oxford UP, 1940. 3.4:580ff. **Rabast, K.** *Das apodiktische Recht im Deuteronomium und im Heiligkeitsgesetz.* Berlin: Heimatdienstverlag, 1948. **Rad, G. von.** *Deuteronomium-Studien.* FRLANT 40. Göttingen: Vandenhoeck & Ruprecht, 1947 (ET, 1953). **Winnett, F. V.** *The Mosaic Tradition.* Near and Middle East Series 1. Toronto: Univ. of Toronto Press, 1949.

1950–59

Althaus, P. *Gebot und Gesetz: Zum Thema "Gesetz und Evangelium."* BFCT 46.2. Gütersloh: Bertelsmann, 1952. **Cazelles, H.** *Le Deutéronomie: La Sainte Bible.* Paris: Cerf, 1958. **Diamond, A. S.** *The Evolution of Law and Order.* London: Watts, 1951. **Gray, J.** *The Legacy of Canaan.* VTSup 5. Leiden: Brill, 1957 (2nd ed. 1965). **Hempel, J.** *Der textkritische Wert des Konsonantentextes von Kairener Genizafragmenten in Cambridge und Oxford zum Deuteronomium.* Nachrichten der Akademie der Wissenschaften in Göttingen 1. Phil-Hist. Kl. no. 10, 1959. **Kraus, H.-J.** *Die prophetische Verkündigung des Rechts in Israel.* ThStud 51. Zollikon: Evangelischer Verlag, 1957. **Kuyper, L. J.** "The Book of Deuteronomy." *Int* 6 (1952) 321–40. **Lewy, I.** *The Growth of the Pentateuch: A Literary, Sociological, and Biographical Approach.* New York: Bookman Associates, 1955. **Manley, G. T.** *The Book of the Law: Studies in the Date of Deuteronomy.* London: Tyndale, 1957. **Mendenhall, G. E.** *Law and Covenant in Israel and the Ancient Near East.* Pittsburgh: Biblical Colloquium, 1955. **Rad, G. von.** *Studies in Deuteronomy.* Tr. D. Stalker. SBT 1.9. Chicago: Regnery, 1953 (German 2nd ed. 1948). **Robinson, D. W. B.** *Josiah's Reform and the Book of the Law.* London: Tyndale, 1951. **Smend, R.** *W. M. Leberecht de Wettes Arbeit zum Alten und am Neuen Testament.* Basel: Helbirg & Lichtenhahn, 1958. **Teeple, H. M.** *The Mosaic Eschatological Prophet.* JBLMS 10. Philadelphia: Society of Biblical Literature, 1957. **Wilson, J. A.,** et al. *Authority and Law in the Ancient Orient.* JAOSSup 17. New Haven, CT: American Oriental Society, 1954.

1960–69

Aharoni, Y. *The Land of the Bible: A Historical Geography.* Tr. A. F. Rainey. Philadelphia: Westminster, 1967 (rev. ed. 1979). **Albright, W. F.** *Yahweh and the Gods of Canaan.* London: Athlone, 1968. **Alt, A.** *Essays on Old Testament Religion.* Tr. R. A. Wilson. Oxford: Blackwell, 1966. **Bächli, O.** *Israel und die Völker: Eine Studie zum Deuteronomoium.* Zurich: Zwingli, 1962. **Baltzer, K.** *Das Bundesformular.* WMANT 4. Neukirchen: Verlag der Buchhandlung des Erziehungsvereins, 1960 (ET, 1971). **Barkun, M.** *Law without Sanctions.* New Haven, CT: Yale UP, 1968. **Becker, J.** *Gottesfurcht im Alten Testament.* Rome: Papstliches Bibelinstitut, 1965. **Boecker, H. J.** *Redeformen des Rechtslebens im Alten Testament.* WMANT 14. Neukirchen-Vluyn: Neukirchener Verlag, 1964 (2nd ed. 1984). **Brichto, H. C.** *The Problem of "Curse" in the Hebrew Bible.* JBLMS 13. Philadelphia: Society of Biblical Literature and

Exegesis, 1963. **Cazelles, H.**, ed. *Moses in Schrift und Uberlieferung.* Düsseldorf: Patmos, 1963. **Claburn, W. E.** "Deuteronomy and Collective Behavior." Diss., Princeton, 1968. **Clements, R. E.** *God's Chosen People: A Theological Interpretation of the Book of Deuteronomy.* London: SCM Press, 1968. ———. *Prophecy and Tradition.* Atlanta: John Knox; Oxford: Blackwell, 1975. **Coulton, P. E.** "Geographical Aspects in the Deuteronomistic History." Diss., Trinity College, Dublin, 1968–69. **Ellul, J.** *The Theological Foundation of Law.* Tr. M. Wieser. Garden City, NY: Doubleday, 1960. **Falk, Z. W.** *Hebrew Law in Biblical Times.* Jerusalem: Wahrmann Books, 1964. **Fenz, A. K.** *Auf Jahwes Stimme Hören.* WBT 6. Vienna: Herder, 1964. **Finkelstein, L.**, ed. *Sifre on Deuteronomy.* New York: Jewish Theological Seminary of America, 1969. **Gerstenberger, E.** *Wesen und Herkunft des apodiktischen Rechts.* WMANT 20. Neukirchen-Vluyn: Neukirchener Verlag, 1965. **Gunneweg, A. H. J.** *Leviten und Priester.* FRLANT 89. Göttingen: Vandenhoeck & Ruprecht, 1965. **Hillers, D. R.** *Covenant: The History of a Biblical Idea.* Baltimore: Johns Hopkins UP, 1969 (= *Int* 15 [January 1961] issue devoted to Deuteronomy). **Jocz, J.** *The Covenant: A Theology of Human Destiny.* Grand Rapids, MI: Eerdmans, 1968. **Kitchen, K. A.** *Ancient Orient and the Old Testament.* London: Tyndale, 1966. **LaBonnardière, A. M.** *Biblia Augustiniana Ancien Testament: la Deutéronome.* Paris: Études Augstiennes, 1967. **L'Hour, J.** *La morale de l'alliance.* Paris: Gabalda, 1966. **Loersch, S.** *Das Deuteronomium und seine Deutungen: Ein forschungsgeschichtlicher Überblick.* SBS 22. Stuttgart: Katholisches Bibelwerk, 1967. **Lohfink, N.** *Bibelauslegung im Wandel.* Frankfurt am Main: Knecht, 1967. ———. *Das Hauptgebot: Eine Untersuchung literarischer Einleitungsfragen zu Deuteronomium 5–11.* AnBib 20. Rome: Pontifical Biblical Institute, 1963. ———. *Höre Israel! Auslegung von Texten aus dem Buch Deuteronomium.* Die Welt der Bibel 18. Düsseldorf: Patmos, 1965. ———. *Die Landverheißung als Eid.* SBS 28. Stuttgart: Katholisches Bibelwerk, 1967. ———. "Lectures in Deuteronomy." Unpublished paper presented in Rome, 1968 (available in Graduate Theological Union Library, Berkeley, CA). **Maarsingh, B.** *Onderzoek naar de Ethiek van de Wetten in Deuteronomium.* Utrecht: Winterswijk, J. M. van Amstel, 1961. **McBride, S. D.** "The Deuteronomic Name Theology." Diss., Harvard, 1969. **McCarthy, D. J.** *Der Gottesbund im Alten Testament.* SBS 13. Stuttgart: Katholisches Bibelwerk, 1966. ———. *Treaty and Covenant: A Study in Form in the Ancient Oriental Documents and in the Old Testament.* AnBib 21. Rome: Biblical Institute Press, 1963. **McKay, J. W.** "Josiah's Reformation: Its Antecedents, Nature and Significance." Diss., Cambridge, 1966–67. **Merendino, R. P.** *Das deuteronomische Gesetz: Eine literarkritische, gattungs- und überlieferungsgeschichtliche Untersuchung zu Dt 12–26.* BBB 31. Bonn: Hanstein, 1969. **Nicholson, E. W.** *Deuteronomy and Tradition.* Oxford: Blackwell, 1967. **Noth, M.** *The Laws of the Pentateuch and Other Studies.* Tr. D. R. Ap-Thomas. Philadelphia: Fortress, 1966 (German ed., *GSAT,* 1960). **Ottoson, M.** *Gilead: Tradition and History.* ConBOT 3. Lund: Gleerup, 1969. **Peucker, H.** "Deuteronomium Kapitel 12–26 form- und rechtsgeschichtlich Untersucht." Diss., Greifswald, 1962. **Plöger, J. G.** *Literarkritische, formgeschichtliche und stilkritische Untersuchungen zum Deuteronomium.* BBB 26. Bonn: Hanstein, 1967. **Porter, J. R.** *Moses and Monarchy.* Oxford: Blackwell, 1963. **Poulssen, N.** *König und Tempel im Glaubenszeugnis des Alten Testament.* SBM 3. Stuttgart: Katholisches Bibelwerk, 1967. **Preuss, H. D.** *Jahweglaube und Zukunftserwartung.* BWANT 5.7. Stuttgart: Kohlhammer, 1968. **Rad, G. von.** *The Problem of the Hexateuch and Other Essays.* Tr. E. W. Trueman Dicken. New York: McGraw-Hill, 1966 (German ed., *GSAT,* 1958). **Richter, W.** *Recht und Ethos: Versuch einer Ortung des weisheitlichen Mahnspruchs.* SANT 15. Munich: Kosel, 1966. **Schmid, H.** *Moses: Überlieferung und Geschichte.* BZAW 110. Berlin: Töpelmann, 1968. **Segal, M. H.** *The Pentateuch: Its Composition and Authorship and Other Biblical Studies.* Jerusalem: Magnes, 1967. **Smend, R.** *Die Bundesformel.* ThStud 68. Zurich: EVZ-Verlag, 1963. **Thompson, J. A.** *The Ancient Near Eastern Treaties and the Old Testament.* Tyndale Lecture in Biblical Archaeology 1963. London: Tyndale, 1964. **Vaux, R. de.** *Ancient Israel.* Tr. J. McHugh. New York: Macmillan, 1961. ———. *Studies in Old Testament Sacrifice.* Tr. J. Bourke and R. Potter. Cardiff: Univ. of Wales Press, 1964. **Walkenhorst, K. H.** *Der Sinai im liturgischen Verständnis der deuternomistischen und priester-*

lichen Tradition. BBB 33. Bonn: Hanstein, 1969. **Welten, P.** *Die Königstempe: Ein Beitrag zur Militärpolitik unter Hiskia und Josia.* Wiesbaden: Harrassowitz, 1969. **Wenham, G. J.** "The Structure and Date of Deuteronomy." Diss., King's College, London, 1969. **Wijngaards, J. N. M.** *The Dramatization of Salvific History in the Deuteronomic Schools.* OTS 16. Leiden: Brill, 1969. ———. *The Formulas of the Deuteronomic Creed.* Tilburg: A. Reijnen, 1963; *Review and Expositor* (Fall 1964); *Southwestern Journal of Theology* (Fall 1964). **Yadin, Y.** *The Art of Warfare in Biblical Lands.* 2 vols. New York: McGraw-Hill, 1963.

1970–79

Baltzer, K. *The Covenant Formulary.* Tr. D. Green. Philadelphia: Fortress, 1971 (from German 2nd ed., 1964; 1st ed., 1960). **Barthélemy, D., Hulst, A. R., Lohfink, N., McHardy, W. D., Rüger, H. P.,** and **Sanders, J. A.** *Preliminary and Interim Report on the Hebrew Old Testament Text Project: I. The Pentateuch.* London: United Bible Societies, 1973. **Beegle, D. M.** *Moses, the Servant of Yahweh.* Grand Rapids, MI: Eerdmans, 1972. **Begg, C. T.** "Contributions to the Elucidation of the Composition of Deuteronomy with Special Attention to the Significance of the *Numeruswechsel.*" 5 vols. Diss., Univ. of Leuven, 1978. **Bellefontaine, E.** "A Study of Ancient Israelite Laws and Their Function as Covenant Stipulations." Diss., Univ. of Notre Dame, 1973. **Bergren, R. V.** *The Prophets and the Law.* MHUC 4. Cincinnati: Hebrew Union College–Jewish Institute of Religion, 1974. **Blenkinsopp, J.** *Prophecy and Canon.* Notre Dame, IN: Univ. of Notre Dame Press, 1977. **Braulik, G.** *Die Mittel deuteronomischer Rhetorik: Erhoben aus Deuteronomium 4,1–40.* AnBib 68. Rome: Biblical Institute Press, 1978. **Brekelmans, C.,** ed. *Questions disputées d'Ancien Testament: Méthode et théologie.* BETL 33. Leuven: Leuven UP, 1974. **Bright, J.** *Covenant and Promise.* Philadelphia: Westminster, 1976. **Broide, I.** "The Speeches in Deuteronomy." Diss., Univ. of Tel Aviv, 1970 (Heb.; Eng. abstract). **Brueggemann, W.** *The Land: Place as Gift, Promise, and Challenge in Biblical Faith.* OBT. Philadelphia: Fortress, 1977. **Buis, P.** *La notion d'alliance dans l'Ancien Testament.* LD 88. Paris: Cerf, 1976. **Carmichael, C. M.** *The Laws of Deuteronomy.* Ithaca, NY: Cornell UP, 1974. **Chołewinski, A.** *Heiligkeitsgesetz und Deuteronomium.* AnBib 66. Rome: Biblical Institute Press, 1976. **Cogan, M.** *Imperialism and Religion: Assyria, Judah and Israel in the Eighth and Seventh Centuries B.C.E.* SBLMS 19. Missoula, MT: Society of Biblical Literature, 1974. **Cohen, A.** *L'entrée en terre promise: Deutéronome, Josué, Juges, une lecture de la Bible.* Écouter la Bible 3. Paris: Desclée de Brouwer, 1977. **Cross, F. M.,** ed. *Symposia Celebrating the Seventy-fifth Anniversary of the Founding of the American Schools of Oriental Research (1900–1975).* Cambridge: ASOR, 1979. **Davies, G. I.** *The Way of the Wilderness.* Cambridge: Cambridge UP, 1979. **Diepold, P.** *Israels Land.* BWANT 95. Stuttgart; Berlin; Cologne; Mainz: Kohlhammer, 1972. **Dietrich, W.** *Israel und Kanaan: Vom Ringen zweier Gesellschaftssysteme.* SBS 94. Stuttgart: Katholisches Bibelwerk, 1979. **Floss, J. P.** *Jahwe dienen—Göttern dienen: Terminologische, literarische und semantische Untersuchung einer theologischen Aussage zum Gottesverhältnis im Alten Testament.* BBB 45. Cologne; Bonn: Hanstein, 1975. **Fritz, V.** *Israel in der Wüste: Traditionsgeschichtliche Untersuchung der Wüstenüberlieferung des Jahwisten.* MThSt 7. Marburg: Elwert, 1979. **Gilmer, H. W.** *The If-You Form in Israelite Law.* SBLDS 15. Missoula, MT: Scholars Press, 1975. **Greenberg, M.** "Mankind, Israel and the Nations in the Hebraic Heritage." In *No Man Is Alien: Essays on the Unity of Mankind.* Ed. J. R. Nelson. Leiden: Brill, 1971. **Gutmann, J.,** ed. *The Image and the Word: Confrontations in Judaism, Christianity and Islam.* Religion and the Arts 4. Missoula, MT: Scholars Press, 1975. **Hoppe, L.** "The Origins of Deuteronomy." Diss., Northwestern, 1978. **Jackson, B. S.** *Essays in Jewish and Comparative Legal History.* SJLA 10. Leiden: Brill, 1975. **Jüngling, H.-W.** *Das Gesetz der Wiedervergeltung und das Ideal der Versöhnung im Alten Testament.* Augsburg: Blasaditsch, 1975. **Kane, T. F.** *God Who Gives: A Verbal Study of the Actions Attributed to God in the "Deuteronomic School," with Special Attention to the Concept of God's Giving.* Universidad de Navarro Coleccion Teologica 7. Pamplona: Ediciones Universidad de Navarra, 1973. **Kline, M. G.** *The Structure of Biblical Authority.* Grand Rapids, MI: Eerdmans,

1972. **Köppel, U.** *Das deuteronomistiche Geschichtswerk und seine Quellen: Der Absicht der deuteronomistischen Geschichtsdarstellung aufgrund des Vergleichs zwischen Num 21,21–35 und Dtn 2,26–3,3.* EHS 23.122. Bern: Lang, 1979. **Kutsch, E.** *Gottes Zuspruch und Anspruch.* BETL 33. Gembloux: Duculot, 1974. ———. *Verheissung und Gesetz: Untersuchungen zum sogenannten 'Bund' im Alten Testament.* BZAW 131. Berlin: de Gruyter, 1973. **Levine, B. A.** *In the Presence of the Lord.* SJLA 5. Leiden: Brill, 1974. **Liedke, G.** *Gestalt und Bezeichnung alttestamentlicher Rechtssätze: Eine formgeschichtlich-terminologische Studie.* WMANT 39. Neukirchen-Vluyn: Neukirchener Verlag, 1971. **Lindblom, J.** *Erwägungen zur Herkunft der josianischen Tempelurkunde.* Lund: Gleerup, 1971. **Lohfink, N.** *Unsere grossen Wörter: Das Alte Testament zum Thema dieser Jahre.* Freiburg i. B.: Herder, 1977 (3rd ed.1985; ET, 1981). **Mann, T. W.** *Divine Presence and Guidance in Israelite Tradition.* Baltimore: Johns Hopkins UP, 1977. **McCarthy, D. J.** *Old Testament Covenant: A Survey of Current Opinion.* Richmond: John Knox, 1972. ———. *Treaty and Covenant.* AnBib 21A. Rome: Biblical Institute Press, 1978 (new ed., completely rewritten). **Milgrom, J.** *Cult and Conscience.* SJLA 18. Leiden: Brill, 1976. **Mittmann, S.** *Deuteronomium 1,1–6,3: Literarkritisch und traditionsgeschichtlich untersucht.* BZAW 139. Berlin: de Gruyter, 1975 (see G. Braulik, *Bib* 59 [1978] 351–83). **Morris, P. M. K.**, and **James, E.** *A Critical Word Book of Leviticus, Numbers, Deuteronomy.* The Computer Bible 8. Missoula, MT: Scholars Press, 1975. **Nebeling, G.** "Die Schichten des deuteronomischen Gesetzeskorpus." Diss., Münster, 1970. **Neumann, P. K.** *Hört das Wort Jahwäs: Ein Beitrag zur Komposition alttestamentlicher Schriften.* Schriften zur Stiftung Europa-Kolleg 30. Hamburg: Fundament-Verlag Sasse, 1975. **Otto, E.** *Das Mazzotfest in Gilgal.* BWANT 107. Stuttgart: Kohlhammer,1975. **Paul, S. M.** *Studies in the Book of the Covenant in the Light of Cuneiform and Biblical Law.* VTSup 18. Leiden: Brill, 1970. **Perlitt, L.** *Bundestheologie im Alten Testament.* WMANT 36. Neukirchen-Vluyn: Neukirchener Verlag, 1970. **Phillips, A.** *Ancient Israel's Criminal Law: A New Approach to the Decalogue.* Oxford: Blackwell, 1970. **Rofé, A.** *Introduction to the Book of Deuteronomy I: Cult-Unity and Anti-Idolatry Laws.* Jerusalem: Aqademon, 1975 (Heb.). **Rose, M.** *Der Ausschliesslichkeitsanspruch Jahwes: Deuteronomische Schultheologie und die Volksfrömmigkeit in der späten Königszeit.* BWANT 106. Stuttgart: Kohlhammer, 1975. **Rücker, H.** *Die Begründungen der Weisungen Jahwes im Pentateuch.* ETS 30. Leipzig: St. Benno, 1973. **Rupprecht, K.** *Der Temple von Jerusalem.* Ed. G. Fohrer. BZAW 144. Berlin: de Gruyter, 1976. **Schedl, C.** *Baupläne des Wortes: Einführung in die biblische Logotechnik.* Vienna: Herder, 1974. **Schmidt, W. H.** *Einführung in das Alte Testament: Das Deuteronomium.* Berlin: de Gruyter, 1979. **Schmitt, G.** *Du sollst keinen Frieden schliessen mit den Bewohnern des Landes: Die Wegweisung gegen die Kanaanäer in Israels Geschichte und Geschichtsschreibung.* BWANT 91. Stuttgart: Kohlhammer, 1970. **Schneider, B. N.** *Deuteronomy: A Favored Book of Jesus.* Grand Rapids, MI: B. M. H. Books, 1970. **Seitz, G.** *Redaktionsgeschichtliche Studien zum Deuteronomium.* BWANT 93. Stuttgart: Kohlhammer, 1971. **Skweres, D. E.** *Die Rückverweise im Buch Deuteronomium.* AnBib 79. Rome: Biblical Institute Press, 1979. **Speyer, W.** *Bucherfunde in der Glaubenswerbung der Antike.* Göttingen: Vandenhoeck & Ruprecht, 1970. **Terrien, S.** *The Elusive Presence: Toward a New Biblical Theology.* Religious Perspectives 26. New York: Harper and Row, 1978. **Thompson, R. J.** *Moses and the Law in a Century of Criticism since Graf.* VTSup 19. Leiden: Brill, 1970. **Tiffany, F. C.** "Parenesis and Deuteronomy 5–11 (Deut 4:45; 5:2–11:29): A Form Critical Study." Diss., School of Theology at Claremont, 1978. **Valentin, H.** *Aaron: Eine Studie zur vorpriesterschriftlichen Aaron-Überlieferung.* OBO 18. Göttingen: Vandenhoeck & Ruprecht, 1978. **Wagner, V.** *Rechtssätze in gebundener Sprache und Rechtssatzreihen im israelitischen Recht.* BZAW 127. Berlin: de Gruyter, 1972. **Weimar, P.** *Untersuchungen zur Redaktionsgeschichte des Pentateuch.* BZAW 146. Berlin: de Gruyter, 1977. **Weinfeld, M.** *Deuteronomy and the Deuteronomic School.* Oxford: Clarendon, 1972. ———. *Introduction to Deuteronomy, Part I.* Jerusalem, 1975 (Heb.). **Wevers, J. W.** *Text History of the Greek Deuteronomy.* Göttingen: Vandenhoeck & Ruprecht, 1978. **Whybray, R. N.** *The Intellectual Tradition in the Old Testament.* BZAW 135. Berlin: de Gruyter, 1974. **Wittstruck, T. K.** "The Greek Translation of Deuteronomy." Diss., Yale Univ., 1972.

1980–89

Auld, A. G. *Joshua, Moses and the Land: Tetrateuch—Pentateuch—Hexateuch in a Generation since 1938.* Edinburgh: T. & T. Clark, 1980. **Aurelius, E.** *Der Fürbitter Israels: Eine Studie zum Mosebild im Alten Testament.* Ed. T. N. D. Mettinger and M. Y. Ottoson. ConBOT 27. Lund: Almqvist & Wiksell, 1988. **Benjamin, D. C.** *Deuteronomy and City Life: A Form Criticism of Texts with the Word CITY (ir) in Deuteronomy 4:41–26:19.* Lanham, MD: Univ. Press of America, 1983. **Boling, R. G.** *The Early Biblical Community in Transjordan.* SWBA 6. Sheffield: Almond Press, 1988. **Bovati, P.** *Ristabilire la Giustizia: Procedure, Vocabulario, Orientamenti.* AnBib 110. Rome: Biblical Institute Press, 1986. **Braulik, G.** *Studien zur Theologie des Deuteronomiums.* SBAB 2. Stuttgart: Katholisches Bibelwerk, 1988. **Buchholz, J.** *Die ältesten Israels im Deuteronomium.* GTA 36. Göttingen: Vandenhoeck & Ruprecht, 1988. **Carmichael, C. M.** *Law and Narrative in the Bible: The Evidence of the Deuteronomic Laws and the Decalogue.* Ithaca, NY: Cornell UP, 1985. **Christensen, D. L.**, ed. *Experiencing the Exodus from Egypt.* Berkeley: BIBAL Press, 1988. **Clements, R. E.** *Deuteronomy.* Old Testament Guides. Sheffield: JSOT Press, 1989. **Coats, G. W.** *Moses: Heroic Man, Man of God.* JSOTSup 57. Sheffield: Sheffield Academic Press, 1988. **Duncan, J.** "A Critical Edition of Deuteronomy Manuscripts from Qumran Cave 4." Diss., Harvard Univ., 1989. **Epsztein, L.** *Social Justice in the Ancient Near East and the People of the Bible.* Tr. J. Bowden. London: SCM Press, 1986. **Eslinger, L.** *Into the Hands of the Living God.* JSOTSup 84. Bible and Literature Series 24. Sheffield: Almond Press, 1989. **Fishbane, M.** *Biblical Interpretation in Ancient Israel.* Oxford: Oxford UP, 1985. **Friedman, R. E.** *The Exile and Biblical Narrative: The Formation of the Deuteronomistic and Priestly Works.* HSM 22. Chico, CA: Scholars Press, 1981. **García Lopez, F.** *Le Deutéronome: Une loi prêchée.* Cahiers Evangile 63. Paris: Cerf, 1988. **Giesen, G.** *Die Wurzel* שבע *"schwören": Eine semasiologische Studie zum Eid im Alten Testament.* BBB 56. Bonn: Hanstein, 1981. **Ginsberg, H. L.** *The Israelian Heritage of Judaism.* Texts and Studies of the Jewish Theological Seminary of America 24. New York: Jewish Theological Seminary of America, 1982. **Gottfriedsen, C.** *Die Fruchtbarkeit von Israels Land.* EHS 23.267. Frankfurt: Peter Lang, 1985. **Ha, J.** *Genesis 15: A Theological Compendium of Pentateuchal History.* BZAW 181. Berlin: de Gruyter, 1989. **Haag, E.**, ed. *Gott der Einzige: Zur Entstehung des Monotheismus in Israel.* QD 104. Freiburg; Basel; Vienna: Herder, 1985. **Hoffmann, H.-D.** *Reform und Reformen: Untersuchungen zu einem Grundthema der deuteronomischen Geschichtsschreibung.* ATANT 66. Zurich: Theologischer Verlag, 1980. **Hofius, O.**, and **Stuhlmacher, P.**, eds. *"Gesetz" als Thema Biblischer Theologie.* JBTh 4. Neukirchen-Vluyn: Neukirchener Verlag, 1989. **Hossfeld, F.-L.**, ed. *Vom Sinai zum Horeb: Stationen alttestamentlicher Glaubensgeschichte.* Würzburg: Echter, 1989 (= *Int* 41 [July 1987] issue on Deuteronomy; *Int* 43.3 [1989] issue on the Decalogue). **Knapp, D.** *Deuteronomium 4: Literarische Analysen und theologische Interpretation.* GTA 35. Göttingen: Vandenhoeck & Ruprecht, 1987. **Koch, D.-A.** *Die Schrift als Zeuge des Evangeliums.* BHT 69. Tübingen: Mohr, 1986. **Lang, B.** *Der einzige Gott: Die Geburt des biblischen Monotheismus.* Munich: Kösel, 1981. **Leibowitz, N.** *Studies in Devarim.* Tr. A. Newman. Jerusalem: World Zionist Organization, 1980. **Lemaire, A.** *Les écoles et la formation de la Bible dans l'ancien Israel.* OBO 39. Göttingen: Vandenhoeck & Ruprecht, 1981. **Lewis, T. J.** *Cults of the Dead in Ancient Israel and Ugarit.* HSM 39. Atlanta: Scholars Press, 1989. **Lohfink, N.** *Great Themes from the Old Testament.* Tr. R. Walls. Chicago: Franciscan Herald Press, 1982 (German ed. 1977). ———. *Studien zum Pentateuch.* SBAB 4. Stuttgart: Katholisches Bibelwerk, 1988. ———. *Unsere neuen Fragen und das Alte Testament: Wiederendeckte Lebensweisung.* Freiburg: Herder, 1989. ———, ed. *Das Deuteronomium: Entstehung, Gestalt und Botschaft.* BETL 68. Leuven: Leuven UP, 1985. **McConville, J. G.** "Cultic Laws in Deuteronomy." Diss., Queen's Univ., Belfast, 1980. ———. *Law and Theology in Deuteronomy.* JSOTSup 33. Sheffield: JSOT Press, 1984. **Mettinger, T. N. D.** *The Dethronement of Sabaoth: Studies in the Shem and Kabod Theologies.* ConBOT 18. Lund: Gleerup, 1982. **Mulder, M. J.**, ed. *Mikra: Text, Translation, Reading and Interpretation of the*

Hebrew Bible in Ancient Judaism and Early Christianity. Compendia Rerum Iudaicarum ad Novum Testamentum. Assan; Maastricht: Van Gorcum, 1988. **Nelson, R. D.** *The Double Redaction of the Deuteronomistic History.* JSOTSup 18. Sheffield: JSOT Press, 1981. **Niehr, H.** *Rechtsprechung in Israel.* SBS 130. Stuttgart: Katholisches Bibelwerk, 1987. **Nielsen, E.** *Law, History, and Tradition: Selected Essays Issued by Friends and Colleagues.* Ed. N. Holm-Nielsen and O. Benedikt. Copenhagen: Gad, 1983. **Noth, M.** *The Deuteronomistic History.* Tr. J. Douall et al. JSOTSup 15. Sheffield: JSOT Press, 1981 (German ed. 1943). **Otto, E.** *Wandel der Rechtsbegründungen in der Gesellschaftsgeschichte des antiken Israel: Eine Rechtsgeschichte des "Bundesbuches" Ex XX 22—XXIII 13.* StudBib 3. Leiden: Brill, 1988. **Patrick, D.** *Old Testament Law.* Atlanta: Knox, 1985. **Peters, M.** *Critical Edition of the Coptic Pentateuch: Deuteronomy.* SBLSCS 15. Atlanta: Scholars Press, 1983. **Polzin, R.** *Moses and the Deuteronomist: A Literary Study of the Deuteronomic History.* Part 1, *Deuteronomy, Joshua, Judges.* New York: Seabury, 1980. **Preuss, H. D.** *Deuteronomium.* ErFor 164. Darmstadt: Wissenschaftliche Buchgesellschaft, 1982. **Regt, L. J. De.** *A Parametric Model for Syntactic Studies of a Textual Corpus, Demonstrated on the Hebrew of Deuteronomy 1–30.* Studia Semitica Neerlandica. Assen; Maastricht: Van Gorcum, 1988. **Ries, G.** *Prolog und Epilog in Gesetzen des Altertums.* MBPR 76. Munich: Beck, 1983. **Rifat, S.** *Motive Clauses in Hebrew Law: Biblical Forms and Near Eastern Parallels.* SBLDS 45. Missoula, MT: Scholars Press, 1980. **Rofé, A.** *Introduction to Deuteronomy: Part I and Further Chapters.* Jerusalem: Akademon Publishing House, 1988 (Heb.). **Rose, M.** *Deuteronomist und Jahwist: Untersuchung zu den Berührungspunkten beider Literaturwerke.* ATANT 67. Zurich: Theologische Verlag, 1981. **Rüterswörden, U.** *Von der politischen Gemeinschaft zur Gemeinde: Studien zu Dt 16,18–18,22.* BBB 65. Frankfurt am Main: Athenaum, 1987. **Sanmartín Ascaso, J.** *Las guerras de Josué: Estudio de Semiótica narrativa.* Institución San Jerónimo 14. Valencia: n.p., 1982. **Schulz, H.** *Leviten im vorstaatlichen Israel und im Mittleren Osten.* Munich: Kaiser, 1987. **Schuman, N. A.** *Deuteronomium; op weg naar hat land Utopia.* Kampen: VBG, 1983. **Sitarz, E.,** ed. *Höre, Israel! Jahwe ist einzig: Bausteine für eine Theologie des Alten Testament.* Biblische Basis Bücher 5. Stuttgart: Katholisches Bibelwerk, 1987. **Strecker, G.,** ed. *Das Land Israel in biblischer Zeit: Jerusalem Symposium 1981 der Hebräischen Universität und der Georg-August-Universität.* GTA 25. Göttingen: Vandenhoeck & Ruprecht, 1983. **Tan, C. W.** "A Comparative Study of the Concept of Election in the Book of Deuteronomy and the Book of Jonah and Its Implications for Bible Study in the Chinese Churches in South-East Asia Today." Diss., School of Theology at Claremont, 1983. **Tigay, J. J.** *You Shall Have No Other Gods: Israelite Religion in the Light of Hebrew Inscriptions.* HSS 31. Atlanta: Scholars Press, 1986. **Weinfeld, M.** *Justice and Righteousness in Israel and the Nations: Equality and Freedom in Ancient Israel in Light of Social Justice in the Ancient Near East.* Jerusalem: Magnes, 1985. **Wesel, U.** *Frühformen des Rechts in vorstaatlichen Gesellschaften.* Frankfurt: Suhrkamp, 1985. **Westbrook, R.** *Studies in Biblical and Cuneiform Law.* CahRB 26. Paris: Gabalda, 1988. **White, S.** "The Critical Edition of Seven Manuscripts of Deuteronomy." Diss., Harvard Univ., 1988. **Whybray, R. N.** *The Making of the Pentateuch: A Methodological Study.* JSOTSup 53. Sheffield: Sheffield Academic Press, 1987. **Wilms, F.-E.** *Freude vor Gott: Kult und Fest in Israel.* Schlüssel zur Bibel. Regensburg: Pustet, 1981.

1990–2000

Bell, R. H. *Provoked to Jealousy: The Origin and Purpose of the Jealousy Motif in Romans 9–11.* WUNT 2.63. Tübingen: Mohr (Siebeck), 1994. **Braulik, G.** *Die deuteronomischen Gesetze und der Dekalog: Studien zum Aufbau von Deuteronomium 12–26.* SBS 145. Stuttgart: Verlag Katholisches Bibelwerk, 1991. ———. *Studien zum Buch Deuteronomium.* SBAB 24. Stuttgart: Katholisches Bibelwerk, 1997. ———, ed. *Bundesdokument und Gesetz: Studien zum Deuteronomium.* Herders Biblische Studien 4. New York: Herder, 1995. **Christensen, D. L.,** ed. *A Song of Power and the Power of Song: Essays in Deuteronomy.* Winona Lake, IN: Eisenbrauns, 1991. **Dahmen, U.** *Leviten und Priester im Deuteronomium: Literarkritische und Redaktionsgeschechtliche Studien.* BBB 110. Bodenheim: Philo, 1996. **Dangl, O.** *Methoden im Widerstreit: Sprachwissenschaftliche Zugange zur deuteronomischen Rede von der Liebe Gottes.* Tübingen: Francke, 1993. **Eyre, S. D.** *Deuteronomy: Becoming Holy People.* London: Inter-Varsity Press, 1998. **Firmage, E. B., Weiss, B. G.,** and **Welch, J. W.** *Religion and Law: Biblical-Judaic and Islamic Perspectives.* Winona Lake, IN: Eisenbrauns, 1990. **Gertz, J. C.** *Die Gerichtsorganisation Israels im deuteronomischen Gesetz.* FRLANT 165. Göttingen: Vandenhoeck & Ruprecht, 1994. **Haïk-Vantoura, S.** *The Music of the Bible Revealed.* Tr. D. Weber. Ed. J. Wheeler. Berkeley: BIBAL Press, 1991 (= *Int* 44 [July 1990] issue on the figure of Moses). **Keller, M.** *Untersuchungen zur deuteronomisch-deuteronomistischen Namentheologie.* BBB 105. Weinheim: Belt Athenaum, 1996. **Kissling, P. J.** *Reliable Characters in the Primary History: Profiles of Moses, Joshua, Elijah, and Elisha.* JSOTSup 224. Sheffield: Sheffield Academic Press, 1996. **Labuschagne, C. J.** *Numerical Secrets of the Bible: Rediscovering the Bible Codes.* North Richland Hills, TX: BIBAL Press, 2000. **Levinson, B. M.** *Deuteronomy and the Hermeneutics of Legal Innovation.* New York: Oxford UP, 1997. **Lohfink, N.** *Studien zur biblischen Theologie.* SBAB 16. Stuttgart: Katholisches Bibelwerk, 1993. ———. *Studien zum Deuteronomium und zur deuteronomistischen Literatur I.* SBAB 8. Stuttgart: Katholisches Bibelwerk, 1990. ———. *Studien zum Deuteronomium und zur deuteronomistischen Literatur II.* SBAB 12. Stuttgart: Katholisches Bibelwerk, 1991. ———. *Studien zum Deuteronomium und zur deuteronomistischen Literatur III.* SBAB 20. Stuttgart: Katholisches Bibelwerk, 1995. ———. *Theology of the Pentateuch: Themes of the Priestly Narrative and Deuteronomy.* Tr. L. M. Maloney. Minneapolis: Fortress, 1994. ———. *Die Väter Israels im Deuternomium.* OBO 111. Göttingen: Vandenhoeck & Ruprecht, 1991. **Lubsczyk, H.** *Die Bundesurkunde: Ursprung und Wirkungsgeschichte des Deuteronomiums.* Weil-Bierbonnen: Gustav-Siewerth-Akademie, 1991. **McConville, J. G.** *Grace in the End: A Study in Deuteronomic Theology.* Studies in OT Biblical Theology. Grand Rapids, MI: Zondervan, 1993. ——— and **Millar, J. G.** *Time and Place in Deuteronomy.* JSOT Sup 179. Sheffield: Sheffield Academic Press, 1994. **Merwe, C. H. J. van der.** *The Old Hebrew Particle gam: A Syntactic-Semantic Description of gam in Gn–2Kg.* ATSAT 34. St. Ottilien: EOS, 1990. **Milgrom, J.** *Numbers.* JPS Torah Commentary. Philadelphia: Jewish Publication Society, 1990. **Morrow, W. S.** *Scribing the Center: Organization and Redaction in Deuteronomy 14:1–17:13.* SBLMS 49. Atlanta: Scholars Press, 1995. **Nohrnberg, J.** *Like unto Moses: The Constituting of an Interruption.* Bloomington: Indiana UP, 1995. **Olson, D. T.** *Deuteronomy and the Death of Moses: A Theological Reading.* OBT. Minneapolis: Fortress, 1994. **Perlitt, L.** *Deuteronomium Studien.* FAT 8. Tübingen: Mohr, 1994. **Pressler, C.** *The View of Women Found in the Deuteronomic Family Laws.* BZAW 216. Berlin: de Gruyter, 1993. **Reuter, E.** *Kultzentralization: Entstehung und Theologie von Dtn 12.* BBB 87. Frankfurt am Main: Anton Hain, 1993. **Romer, T.** *Israels Vater: Untersuchung zur Vaterthemnatik in Deuteronomium und in der deuteronomistischen Tradition.* OBO 99. Göttingen: Vandenhoeck & Ruprecht, 1990. **Sonnet, J.-P.** *The Book within the Book: Writing in Deuteronomy.* Biblical Interpretation Series 14. Leiden: Brill, 1997. **Veijola, T.,** ed. *Das Deuteronomium und seine Querbeziehungen.* Schriften der Finnischen exegetischen Gesellschaft 32. Göttingen: Vandenhoeck & Ruprecht, 1996. **Westbrook, R.** *Bundesdokument und Gesetz: Studien zum Deuteronomium.* Ed. G. Braulik. HBS 4. Freiburg: Herder, 1995. **Wilson, I.** *Out of the Midst of the Fire: Divine Presence in Deuteronomy.* SBLDS 151. Atlanta: Scholars Press, 1995. **Zobel, K.** *Prophetie und Deuteronomium: Die Rezeption prophetischer Theologie durch das Deuteronomium.* BZAW 199. Berlin; New York: de Gruyter, 1992.

FESTSCHRIFTEN (with significant articles on Deuteronomy)

A number of important articles on Deuteronomy appear in collections of essays presented in honor of various scholars. Such entries often have more than one editor and tend to take up considerable space when cited in full. Since

Festschriften are referred to numerous times throughout the commentary, they are listed here for reference in alphabetical order, according to the last name of the person honored in the *Festschrift,* and arranged in consecutive blocks of time. Citations of these works in the commentary will include both the name of the person honored and the date of publication.

1897–1949

Barth, K. *Theologische Aufsätze K. Barth zum 50. Geburstag.* Ed. E. Wolf. Munich: Kaiser, 1936. **Baudissin, W. W. G. von.** *Abhandlungen zur semitischen Religionskunde und Sprachwissenschaft.* Ed. W. Frankenberg. Giessen: Töpelmann, 1918. **Beer, G.** *FS für Georg Beer zum 70. Geburtstag.* Ed. A. Weiser. Stuttgart: Kohlhammer, 1935. **Gunkel, H.** Εὐχαριστηριόν. Ed. H. Schmidt. FRLANT 36. Göttingen: Vandenhoeck & Ruprecht, 1923. **Kohut, A.** *Semitic Studies in Memory of Rev. Dr. Alexander Kohut.* Ed. G. A. Kohut. Berlin, 1897. **Kohut, G. A.** *Jewish Studies in Memory of G. A. Kohut.* Ed. S. W. Baron, A. Marx, E. D. Coleman, and R. Marcus. New York: Alexander Kohut Memorial Foundation, 1935. **Marti, K.** *Vom Alten Testament.* Ed. K. Budde. Giessen: Töpelmann, 1925. **Sellin, E.** *Beiträge zur Religionsgeschichte und Archäologie Palästinas.* Leipzig: A. Deichert, 1927. **Visscher, F.** *Mélanges de Fernand Visscher* I. *RIDA* 2 (1949). **Wellhausen, J.** *Studien zur semitischen Philologie und Religionsgeschichte Julius Wellhausen zum siebzigsten Geburtstag.* BZAW 27. Geissen: Töpelmann, 1914.

1950–1969

Albright, W. F. *The Bible and the Ancient Near East.* Ed. G. E. Wright. Garden City, NY: Doubleday, 1961 (Anchor Book ed. 1965). ———. *EI.* Vol. 9. Ed. A. Malamat. Jerusalem: Israel Exploration Society, 1969. **Barth, K.** *Antwort: Karl Barth zum siebzigsten Geburtstag.* Zollikon-Zurich: Evangelischer Verlag, 1956. ———. *Parrhesia: K. Barth zum 80. Geburstag.* Zurich: EVZ-Verlag, 1966. **Baumgartner, W.** *Hebräische Wortforschung.* VTSup 16. Leiden: Brill, 1967. **Bertholet, A.** *FS Alfred Bertholet zum 80. Geburstag.* Ed. W. Baumgartner. Tübingen: Mohr, 1950. **Driver, G. R.** *Hebrew and Semitic Studies.* Ed. D. Winton Thomas and W. D. McHardy. Oxford: Clarendon, 1963. **Eissfeldt, O.** *Von Ugarit nach Qumran: Beiträge zur alttestamentlichen und altorientalischen Forschung.* Ed. J. Hemple and L. Rost. BZAW 77. Berlin: de Gruyter, 1958. **Elliger, W.** *Theologie und Kunst: Walter Elliger zum 65. Geburtstag.* Ed. S. Herrmann and O. Sohngen. Wittenberg: Luther, 1968. **Geiselmann, J. R.** *Kirche und Überlieferung.* Ed. J. Betz. Freiburg: Herder, 1960. **Gelin, A.** *A la Rencontre Dieu.* Bibliothèque de la Faculté Catholique de Théologie de Lyon 8. Le Puy: Mappus, 1961. **Goodenough, E. R.** *Religions in Antiquity.* Ed. J. Neusner. SHR 14. Leiden: Brill, 1968. **Hertzberg, H. W.** *Gottes Wort und Gottes Land.* Ed. H. Reventlow. Göttingen: Vandenhoeck & Ruprecht, 1965. **Junker, H.** *Lex Tua Veritas.* Ed. H. Gross and F. Mussner. Trier: Paulinus, 1961. **Klauser, T.** *Mullus.* Ed. A Stuiber and A. Herrmann. Jahrbuch für Antike und Christentum 1. Münster: Aschendorffsche Verlagsbuchhandlung, 1964. **Marx, A.** *Alexander Marx Jubilee Volume on the Occasion of His 70th Birthday.* New York: Jewish Theological Seminary of America, 1950. **Michel, O.** *Abraham Unser Vater.* Arbeiten zur Geschichte des Spätjudentums und Urchristentums 5. Leiden: Brill, 1963. **Muilenburg, J.** *Israel's Prophetic Heritage.* Ed. B. W. Anderson and W. Harrelson. New York: Harper & Row; London: SCM Press, 1962. **Quervain, A. de.** *Freude am Evangelium.* Ed. J. J. Stamm and E. Wolf. BEvT 44. Munich: Kaiser, 1966. **Rahner, K.** *Gott in Welt.* Vol. 1. Ed. J. B. Metz et al. Freiburg: Herder, 1964. **Rinaldi, G.** *Studi sull' oriente e la Bibbia.* Ed. G. Buccellati. Gênes: Studio e Vita, 1967. **Robinson, T. H.** *Studies in Old Testament Prophecy.* Ed. H. H. Rowley. Edinburgh: T. & T. Clark, 1950. **Rost, L.** *Das ferne und nahe Wort.* Ed. F. Maass. BZAW 105. Berlin: Töpelmann, 1967. **Rudolph, W.** *Verbannung und Heimkehr: Beitrage zur Geschichte und Theologie Israels im*

6. und 5. Jahrhundert v. Chr. Ed. A. Kuschke. Tübingen: Mohr, 1961. **Thielicke, H.** *Leben Angesichts des Todes.* Tübingen: Mohr, 1968. **Thomas, D. W.** *Words and Meanings.* Ed. P. Ackroyd and B. Lindars. Cambridge: Cambridge UP, 1968. **Vriezen, T. C.** *Studia Biblica et Semitica.* Ed. W. van Unnik and A. van der Woude. Wageningen: Veenman, 1966.

1970–79

Albright, W. F. *Near Eastern Studies in Honor of W. F. Albright.* Ed. H. Goedicke. Baltimore: Johns Hopkins UP, 1971. **Botterweck, G. J.** *Bausteine biblischer Theologie.* Ed. H.-J. Fabry. BBB 50. Cologne; Bonn: Hanstein, 1977. **Daube, D.** *Daube Noster: Essays in Legal History for D. Daube.* Ed. A. Watson. Edinburgh; London: Chatto and Windus, 1974. **Davies, G. H.** *Proclamation and Presence.* Ed. and tr. J. I. Durham and J. R. Porter. 1970. Repr. Macon, GA: Mercer UP, 1983. **Davies, W. D.** *Jews, Greeks and Christians: Religious Cultures in Late Antiquity.* Ed. R. Hammerton-Kelly and R. Scroggs. SJLA 21. Leiden: Brill, 1976. **Doerne, M.** *Fides et Communicatio.* Ed. D. Rössler et al. Göttingen: Vandenhoeck & Ruprecht, 1970. **Dupont-Sommer, A.** *Hommages à Andre Dupont-Sommer.* Paris: Adrien-Maisenneuve, 1971. **Elliger, K.** *Wort und Geschichte.* Ed. H. Gese and H. Rüger. AOAT 18. Neukirken-Vluyn: Neukirchener Verlag; Kevealer: Butzon & Berker, 1973. **Finkelstein, J. J.** *Essays on the Ancient Near East.* Memoirs of the Connecticut Academy of Arts and Sciences 19. Hamden, CT: Archon, 1977. **Friedrich, G.** *Das Wort und die Wörter.* Stuttgart: Kohlhammer, 1973. **Gaster, T. H.** *JANESCU* 5. Ed. M. David. New York: Columbia UP, 1973. **Glueck, N.** *Near Eastern Archaeology in the Twentieth Century.* Ed. J. A. Sanders. Garden City, NY: Doubleday, 1970. **Gordon, C. H.** *Orient and Occident.* Ed. H. A. Hoffner. AOAT 22. Neukirken-Vluyn: Neukirchener; Kevelaer: Butzon & Bercker, 1973. **Höffner, J.** *Die Kirche im Wandel der Zeit.* Ed. F. Groner. Cologne: Bachem, 1971. **Hyatt, J. P.** *Essays in Old Testament Ethics.* Ed. J. L. Crenshaw and J. T. Willis. New York: Ktav, 1974. **Jepsen, A.** *Schalom: Studien zu Glaube und Geschichte Israels.* Ed. K. Bernhardt. AzT 1. Stuttgart: Calwer, 1971. **Kempf, W.** *Testimonium Veritati.* Ed. H. Wolter. Frankfurter theologische Studien 7. Frankfurt am Main: Knecht, 1971. **Kornfeld, W.** *Studien zum Pentateuch.* Ed. G. Braulik. Vienna: Herder, 1977. **Kuyper, L. J.** *Grace upon Grace.* Ed. J. I. Cook. Grand Rapids, MI: Eerdmans, 1975. **LaSor, W. S.** *Biblical and Near Eastern Studies.* Ed. G. A. Tuttle. Grand Rapids, MI: Eerdmans, 1978. **Liagre Böhl, F. M. T. de.** *Symbolae Biblicae et Mesopotamicae.* Ed. M. A. Beek et al. Leiden: Brill, 1973. **Loewenstamm, E.** *Studies in Bible and Ancient Near East.* Ed. Y. Avishur and J. Blau. Jerusalem: Rubenstein, 1978. **McKenzie, J. L.** *No Famine in the Land.* Ed. J. W. Flanagan and A. W. Robinson. Missoula, MT: Scholars Press, 1975. **Myers, J. M.** *A Light unto My Path.* Ed. H. Bream. Philadelphia: Temple UP, 1974. **Rad, G. von.** *Probleme biblischer Theologie.* Ed. H. W. Wolff. Munich: Kaiser, 1971. **Schelkle, K. H.** *Wort Gottes in der Zeit.* Ed. H. Feld and S. Nolte. Düsseldorf: Patmos, 1973. **Schlier, H.** *Die Zeit Jesu.* Ed. G. Bornkamm and K. Rahner. Freiburg: Herder, 1970. **Selms, A. van.** *De Fructu Oris Sui.* Ed. I. H. Eybers et al. POS 9. Leiden: Brill, 1971. **Stanley, D. M.** *Word and Spirit.* Ed. J. Plevnik. Willowdale, Ont.: Regis College Press, 1975. **Volterra, E.** *Studi in Onore di Edoardo Volterra.* Pubblicazioni della Facolta di Giurisprudenza dell'Universita di Roma 45. Milan: Giuffré, 1971. **Wright, G. E.** *Magnalia Dei: The Mighty Acts of God: Essays on the Bible and Archaeology.* Ed. F. M. Cross et al. Garden City, NY: Doubleday, 1976. **Ziegler, J.** *Wort, Lied und Gottesspruch: Festschrift für Joseph Ziegler.* Ed. J. Schreiner. FB 1–2. Würzburg: Echter, 1972. **Zimmerli, W.** *Beiträge zur alttestamentlichen Theologie.* Ed. H. Donner et al. Göttingen: Vandenhoeck & Ruprecht, 1977.

1980–89

Abramsky, S. *Beer Sheva.* Vol. 2. Ed. M. Cogan. Studies by the Department of Bible and the Ancient Near East. Jerusalem: Magnes, 1985. **Ahlström, G. W.** *In the Shelter of Elyon: Essays* *on Ancient Palestinian Life and Literature.* Ed. W. B. Barrick and J. R. Spencer. JSOTSup 31. Sheffield: JSOT Press, 1984. **Alonso Díaz, J.** *Palabra y Vida.* Ed. A. Vargas-Machuca and G. Ruiz. Publicaciones de la Universidad Pontificia Comillas de Madrid 1.28. Madrid: Universidad Comillas, 1984. **Alonso Schökel, L.** *El Misterio de la Palabra.* Ed. V. Collado and E. Zurro. Madrid: Cristiandad, 1983. **Barthélemy, D.** *Mélanges D. Barthélemy: Études bibliques.* Ed. P. Casetti, O. Keel, and A. Schenker. OBO 38. Fribourg: Universitaires, 1981. **Bornkamm, G.** *Kirche: Festschrift für Gunther Bornkamm zum 75. Geburtstag.* Ed. D. Lührmann and G. Strecker. Tübingen: Mohr, 1980. **Brelich, A.** *Religioni e Civiltà 3.* Ed. V. Lanternari and M. Massenzio. Bari: Dedalolibri, 1982. **Brunner, H.** *Fontes agque Pontes.* Ed. M. Görg. ÄgAT 5. Wiesbaden: Harrassowitz, 1983. **Cazelles, M. H.** *De la Torah au Messie.* Ed. M. Carrez, J. Doré, and P. Grelot. Paris: Desclée, 1981. ———. *Mélanges bibliques et orientaux en l'honneur de M. Henri Cazelles.* Ed. A. Caquot and M. Delcor. AOAT 212. Neukirchen-Vluyn: Neukirchener; Kevelaer: Butzon & Bercker, 1981. **Craigie, P. C.** *Ascribe to the Lord: Biblical and Other Studies.* Ed. L. Eslinger and G. Taylor. JSOTSup 67. Sheffield: JSOT Press, 1988. **Cross, F. M.** *Ancient Israelite Religion.* Ed. P. Miller, P. Hanson, and S. McBride. Philadelphia: Fortress, 1987. ———. *Tradition and Transformation: Turning Points in Biblical Faith.* Ed. B. Halpern and J. Levenson. Winona Lake, IN: Eisenbrauns, 1981. **Delcor, M.** *Mélanges biblique et orientaux.* AOAT 215. Neukirchen-Vluyn: Neukirchener Verlag; Kevelaer: Butzon & Bercker, 1985. **Diakonoff, I. M.** *Societies and Languages of the Ancient Near East.* Ed. M. A. Dandamayev. Warminster: Aris & Phillips, 1982. **Freedman, D. N.** *The Word of the Lord Shall Go Forth.* Ed. C. Meyers and M. O'Connor. ASOR: Special Volume Series 1. Winona Lake, IN: Eisenbrauns, 1983. **Gordon, C. H.** *The Bible World.* Ed. G. Rendsburg et al. New York: Ktav, 1980. **Harrelson, W.** *Justice and the Holy.* Ed. D. A. Knight and P. J. Paris. Atlanta: Scholars Press, 1989. **Harrison, R. K.** *Israel's Apostasy and Restoration.* Ed. A. Gileadi. Grand Rapids, MI: Baker, 1988. **Hofmann, A.** *Diener in eurer Mitte.* Ed. R. Beer et al. Schriften der Universität Passau, Reihe Katholische Theologie 5. Passau: Passavia Universitätsverlag, 1984. **Hospers, J. H.** *Scripta Signa Vocis.* Ed. H. L. J. Vanstiphout. Groningen: Egbert Forsten, 1986. **Kaiser, O.** *Prophet und Prophetenbuch.* Ed. V. Fritz. BZAW 185. Berlin: de Gruyter, 1989. **Kraus, H.-J.** *"Wenn Nicht Jetzt, Wann Dann?"* Ed. H.-G. Geyer et al. Neukirchen-Vluyn: Neukirchener Verlag, 1983. **Krause, G.** *Vom Amt des Laien in Kirche und Theologie.* Ed. H. Schröer and G. Müller. Theologische Bibliothek Töpelmann 39. Berlin: de Gruyter, 1982. **Lohfink, N.** *BN* 43 (1988). **Martin-Achard, R.** *Hommage à Robert Martin-Achard.* Ed. M. Faessler. Bulletin du Centre Protestant d'Études 36. Geneva: Centre Protestant d'Études. 1984. **Mendenhall, G. E.** *The Quest for the Kingdom of God.* Ed. H. Huffmon, F. Spina, and A. Green. Winona Lake, IN: Eisenbrauns, 1983. **Molin, G.** *Meqor Hajjim.* Ed. I. Seybold. Graz: Akademische Druck und Verlagsanstalt, 1983. **Möller, J.** *Im Gespräch, der Mensch: Ein interdisziplinarer Dialog: Joseph Möller zum 65. Geburtstag.* Ed. H. Gauly et al. Düsseldorf: Patmos, 1981. **Ploeg, J. P. M. van der.** *Vonn Kanaan bis Kerala.* Ed. W. C. Delsman et al. AOAT 211. Kevelaer: Butzon & Bercker, 1982. **Plöger, J. G.** *Freude am Gottesdienst: Aspekte ursprünglicher Liturgie.* Ed. J. Schreiner. Stuttgart: Katholisches Bibelwerk, 1983. **Polotsky, H. J.** *Studies Presented to Hans Jakob Polotsky.* Ed. D. W. Young. East Gloucester, MA: Pirtle & Polson, 1981. **Pope, M. H.** *Love and Death in the Ancient Near East.* Ed. J. H. Marks and R. M. Good. Guilford, CT: Four Quarters Publishing Co., 1987. **Reicke, B.** *The New Testament Age.* Vol. 2. Ed. W. C. Weinrich. Macon, GA: Mercer UP, 1984. **Rosenthal, E. I. J.** *Interpreting the Hebrew Bible.* Ed. J. A. Emerton and S. C. Reif. Univ. of Cambridge Oriental Publications 32. Cambridge: Cambridge UP, 1982. **Scharbert, J.** *Die Väter Israels: Beiträge zur Theologie der Patriarchenüberlieferungen im Alten Testament.* Ed. M. Görg. Stuttgart: Katholisches Bibelwerk, 1989. **Schnackenburg, R.** *Neues Testament und Ethik.* Ed. H. Merklein. Freiberg: Herder, 1989. **Seeligmann, I. L.** *Essays on the Bible and the Ancient World.* Ed. A. Rofé and Y. Zakovitch. 3 vols. Jerusalem: Rubinstein, 1983. **Smalley, B.** *The Bible in the Medieval World.* Ed. K. Walsh and D. Wood. Studies in Church History, Subsidia 4. Oxford: Blackwell, 1985. **Steiger, L.** *Theologische Brosamen für Lothar Steiger zu* *seinem 50. Geburtstag.* Ed. E. Stegemann. BDBAT 5. Heidelberg, 1985. **Vajda, G.** *Études d'histoire et de pensée juives.* Ed. G. Nahon and C. Touati. Louvain-la-Neuve: Peeters, 1980. **Voigt, F. G.** *Das lebendige Wort: Beiträge zur kirchlichen Verkündigung.* Ed. H. Seidel and K.-H. Bieritz. Berlin: Evangelische Verlagsanstalt, 1982. **Westermann, C.** *Werden und Wirken des Alten Testaments: FS C. Westermann.* Ed. R. Albertz et al. Göttingen: Vandenhoeck & Ruprecht, 1980. **Wevers, J. W.** *De Septuaginta.* Ed. A. Pietersma and C. Cox. Mississauga, Ont.: Benben, 1984. **Wolff, H. W.** *Die Botschaft und die Boten.* Ed. J. Jeremias and L. Perlitt. Neukirchen-Vluyn: Neukirchener Verlag, 1981. **Yadin, Y.** *JJS* 33 (1982) (repr. as *Essays in Honor of Yigael Yadin.* Ed. G. Vermes and J. Neusner. Totowa, NJ: Allanheld, Osmun, 1983).

1990–99

Assfalg, J. *Lingua Restituta Orientalis.* Ed. R. Schulz and M. Görg. ÄgAT 20. Wiesbaden: Harrassowitz, 1990. **Brekelmans, C. H. W.** *Deuteronomy and Deuteronomic Literature.* Ed. M. Vervenne and J. Lust. BETL 133. Leuven: Leuven UP, 1997. **Füglister, N.** *Ein Gott, eine Offenbarung: Beiträge zur biblischen Exegese, Theologie und Spiritualität.* Ed. V. Reiterer. Würzburg: Echter, 1991. **Greenberg, M.** *Tehillah le-Moshe: Biblical and Judaic Studies in Honor of Moshe Greenberg.* Ed. M. Cogan, B. Eichler, and J. Tigay. Winona Lake, IN: Eisenbrauns, 1997. **Greenfield, J.** *Solving Riddles and Untying Knots: Studies in Honor of Jonas C. Greenfield.* Ed. Z. Zevit, S. Gitin, and M. Sokoloff. Winona Lake, IN: Eisenbrauns, 1995. **Haran, M.** *Texts, Temples, and Traditions: A Tribute to Menahem Haran.* Ed. M. V. Fox et al. Winona Lake, IN: Eisenbrauns, 1996. **Labuschagne, C. J.** *Studies in Deuteronomy.* Ed. F. García et al. VTSup 53. Leiden: Brill, 1994. **Lohfink, N.** *Biblische Theologie und gesellschaftlicher Wandel.* Ed. G. Braulik, W. Gross, and S. McEvenue. Freiburg; Basel; Vienna: Herder, 1993. **Milgrom, J.** *Pomegranates and Golden Bells: Studies in Biblical, Jewish, and Near Eastern Ritual, Law, and Literature.* Ed. D. P. Wright, D. N. Freedman, and A. Hurwitz. Winona Lake, IN: Eisenbrauns, 1995. **Nejanc, F.** *The Four Gospels 1992: FS Frans Nejanc.* Vol. 1. Ed. F. Van Segbroeck et al. BETL 100. Leuven: Leuven UP, 1992. **Reinelt, H.** *Die alttestamentliche Botshaft als Wegweisung.* Ed. J. Zmijewski. Stuttgart: Katholisches Bibelwerk, 1990. **Rendtorff, R.** *Die hebräische Bibel und ihre zweifache Nachgeschichte: FS für Rolf Rendtorff zum 65. Geburtstag.* Ed. E. Blum. Neukirchen-Vluyn: Neukirchener Verlag, 1990. **Sanders, J. A.** *The Quest for Meaning: Studies in Biblical Intertextuality in Honor of James A. Sanders.* Ed. C. A. Evans and S. Talmon. Biblical Interpretation Series 28. Leiden: Brill, 1997. **Tadmor, H.** *Ah, Assyria: Studies in History and Ancient Near Eastern Historiography: FS H. Tadmor.* Ed. M. Cogan and I. Eph'al. Jerusalem: Magnes, 1991.

Deuteronomy 21:10–34:12

Reading 6: Laws on Human Affairs in Relation to Others (21:10–25:19)

Bibliography

Braulik, G. "Die Abfolge der Gesetze in Deuteronomium 12–26 und der Dekalog." In *Das Deuteronomium.* Ed. N. Lohfink. 1985. 252–72 (= *Studien zur Theologie des Deuteronomiums.* Ed. G. Braulik. 1988. 231–55). ———. "Die dekalogische Redaktion der deuteronomischen Gesetze: Ihre Abhängigkeit von Levitikus 19 am Beispiel von Deuteronomium 22,1–12; 24,10–22; 25,13–16." In *Bundesdokument und Gesetz: Studien zum Deuteronomium.* Ed. G. Braulik. HBS 4. Freiburg: Herder, 1995. 1–25 (= *Studien zum Buch Deuteronomium.* Ed. G. Braulik. 1997. 147–82). ———. "Weitere Beobachtungen zur Beziehung zwischen dem Heiligkeitsgesetz und Deuteronomium 19–25." In *Studien zum Buch Deuteronomium.* Ed. G. Braulik. 1997. 183–223. **Bultmann, C.** *Der Fremde im antiken Juda: Eine Untersuchung zum sozialen Typenbegriff "ger" und seinem Bedeutungswandel in der alttestamentlichen Gesetzgebung.* FRLANT 153. Göttingen: Vandenhoeck & Ruprecht, 1992. **Carmichael, C. M.** "A Common Element in Five Supposedly Disparate Laws." *VT* 29 (1979) 129–42. ———. "A Time for War and a Time for Peace: The Influence of the Distinction upon Some Legal and Literary Material in Deuteronomy." *JJS* 25 (1974) 50–64. ———. "Uncovering a Major Source of Mosaic Law: The Evidence of Deut 21:15–22:5." *JBL* 101 (1982) 505–20. ———. *Women, Law and the Genesis Traditions.* Edinburgh: Univ. of Edinburgh Press, 1979. **Carrière, J.-M.** "L'organisation des lois en Dt 19–26: Les lois sur le mariage." *NRT* 114 (1992) 519–32. **Gertz, J. C.** *Die Gerichtsorganisation Israels im deuteronomischen Gesetz.* FRLANT 165. Göttingen: Vandenhoeck & Ruprecht, 1994. **Greenberg, M.** "Some Postulates of Biblical Criminal Law" (1960). Repr. in SBTS 3:17–20. **Houten, C. van.** *The Alien in Israelite Law.* JSOTSup 107. Sheffield: JSOT Press, 1991. **Kaufman, S. A.** "The Structure of the Deuteronomic Law." *MAARAV* 1.2 (1978–79) 105–58. **Lohfink, N.** "Das deuteronomische Gesetz in der Endgestalt—Entwurf einer Gesellschaft ohne marginale Gruppen." In *Studien zum Deuteronomium III.* Ed. N. Lohfink. 1995. 205–18. **Merendino, R. P.** *Das deuteronomische Gesetz.* 1969. **Otto, E.** "Aspects of Legal Reforms and Reformulations in Ancient Cuneiform and Israelite Law." In *Theory and Method in Biblical and Cuneiform Law.* Ed. B. Levinson. JSOTSup 181. Sheffield: Sheffield Academic Press, 1994. 160–96. ———. "Soziale Verantwortung in Deuteronomium 19–25." In *Kontinuum und Proprium: Studien zur Sozial- und Rechtsgeschichte des Alten Orients und des Alten Testaments.* Orientalia Biblica et Christiana 8. Wiesbaden: Harrassowitz, 1996. 123–38. ———. "Soziale Verantwortung und Reinheit des Landes: Zur Redaktion der kasuistischen Rechstssätze in Deuteronomium 19–25." In *Prophetie und geschichtliche Wirklichkeit im alten Israel: FS S. Herrmann.* Ed. R. Liwak and S. Wagner. Stuttgart: Kohlhammer, 1991. 290–306. ———. "Vom Bundesbuch zum Deuteronomium." In *FS N. Lohfink.* 1992. 260–78. **Rofé, A.** "Family and Sex Laws in Deuteronomy and the Book of the Covenant." *Hen* 9 (1987) 131–59. **Wenham, G. J.,** and **McConville, J. G.** "Drafting Techniques in Some Deuteronomic Laws." *VT* 30 (1980) 248–52. **Westbrook, R.** "Biblical and Cuneiform Law Codes." *RevistBib* 92 (1985) 247–64. ———. "Riddles in Deuteronomic Law." In *Bundesdokument und Gesetz.* 1995. 159–74. **Yaron, R.** "Biblical Law: Prolegomena." In *Jewish Law in History and the Modern World.* Ed. B. S. Jackson. JLASup 2. Leiden: Brill, 1980. 27–44, esp. 33–34.

Introduction

The sixth of the eleven weekly portions in the lectionary cycle of Torah readings from Deuteronomy, which is known as כי תצא, "when you go forth," from its opening words, extends from 21:10 through 25:19 and coincides with the fourth major section in my outline of Deut 12–26.

A	Public worship at the central sanctuary and in local towns	12:1–14:21
B	Laws on human affairs in relation to God—sacred	14:22–16:17
X	Laws on leadership and authority—executive and judicial	16:18–21:9
B′	Laws on human affairs in relation to others—secular	21:10–25:19
A′	Public worship at the central sanctuary and in local towns	26:1–19

Within the so-called central core of Deuteronomy (chaps. 12–26), the weekly portions in the assigned Torah readings agree with the book's literary structure on the basis of the prosodic-textual analysis presented here, except that the fourth of the weekly portions (11:26–16:17) covers two sections of my outline, and the seventh (26:1–29:8 [9]) extends well into the next major section of the book (Deut 27–30).

Commentators almost always describe the laws in 21:10–25:19 as "miscellaneous laws," with the implication that there is little if any discernible structure in the arrangement of these forty-three laws. As we will see in the discussion below, the ordering of the laws is concentric in nature and the primary structural markers are a sequence of laws on the subjects of marriage and war (24:10–14; 23:1 [Eng. 22:30]; 24:1–5; 25:17–19), which correspond with the sixth and seventh commandments (prohibiting murder and adultery). Within this structure, most of the laws here deal with matters of social ethics in laws that correspond with the eighth, ninth, and tenth commandments (on theft, false testimony, and coveting).

As was the case for each of the previous three major sections of the central core of Deuteronomy, the forty-three laws in 21:10–25:19 may be outlined in a five-part concentric structural design:

A	Marriage with a woman captured in war	21:10–14
B	Eighteen laws on "true religion" and illicit mixtures	21:15–22:29
X	Prohibition of marrying one's father's wife	23:1
B′	Seven laws on "true religion"	23:2–26
A′	Sixteen laws on marriage, war, and "true religion"	24:1–25:19

In this reading the primary structural markers are two laws dealing with both marriage and war (21:10–14 and 24:1–4), which make up the first half of the outer frame (21:10–14) and the opening law in its second half (24:1–25:19). The inner frame is made up of twenty-five laws in two complex sections whose primary themes are what I have called "true religion" and the subject of illicit mixtures (21:15–22:29 and 23:2–26). By "true religion" I mean with the letter of James, "Religion that is pure and undefiled before God and the Father is this: to visit orphans and widows in their affliction, and to keep oneself unstained from the world" (Jas 1:27). These laws on matters of humanitarian concern are extended to the animal world as well. In the center of the above structure is a distinctive and enigmatic law prohibiting marriage to one's father's wife, which in a polygamous society includes one's father's concubines, as we will see.

The forty-three laws in this section are distributed in a combination of seventeen plus twenty-six, the two sacred numbers that C. J. Labuschagne has discussed in "The Secret of the Hidden Sacred Numbers 17 and 26," in *Numerical Secrets of the Bible* [1999] 75–104). The twenty-six laws in the center (21:15–25:16) are framed by laws on the subjects of marriage and war (21:10–14 and 24:1–5), which are among seventeen in the outer frame: the initial law on marriage and war (21:10–14), and sixteen laws in 24:1–25:19 that are framed by a law on marriage and war (24:1–5) and another on holy war (25:17–19). The last is the concluding exhortation to remember the Amalekite aggression in the days of the exodus from Egypt.

The sixteen laws in 24:1–25:19, which I take up in detail later in this commentary, may be outlined in a menorah pattern:

A	Forbidden remarriage and military deferral of a new husband	24:1–5
B	Eight laws on social ethics and humanitarian concerns	24:6–22
C	Limits on flogging and not muzzling the ox	25:1–4
X	Levirate marriage	25:5–10
C′	Improper intervention in a fight	25:11–12
B′	Social ethics: honest weights and measures	25:13–16
A′	Remembering Amalekite aggression (holy war)	25:17–19

The framework in this construction (A, X, A′) is made up of two laws on marriage (24:1–4; 25:5–12) and two on war (24:5; 25:17–19). The law on levirate marriage in the center (25:5–12) is framed by three laws dealing with humanitarian issues: laws setting limits on flogging (25:1–3) and a law that prohibits the muzzling of an ox as it threshes grain (25:4). These laws are set over against the curious law on improper intervention on the part of a woman in behalf of her husband, in which she grabs his opponent by the genitals (25:11–12). The remaining frame moves from a series of eight laws on matters of social ethics and humanitarian concerns (24:6–22), to a single law on social ethics in the matter of honest weights and measures (25:13–16).

Another way of looking at the structural unity of 21:10–25:19 as a whole is to examine the relationship between the individual laws within a more elaborate concentric structural design:

A	Marriage with a woman captured in war	21:10–14
B	Social justice: right of firstborn in polygamous marriage	21:15–17
C	Family law: insubordinate son	21:18–21
D	Humanism: treatment of executed criminal's body	21:22–23
E	Social ethics: helping with lost and fallen animals	22:1–4
F	Humanism: releasing a mother bird; parapet on the roof	22:6–8
G	Sex: adultery and other illicit mixtures prohibited	22:9–22:29
H	Prohibition of marrying one's father's former wife	23:1
I	Restrictions on entry into the assembly of YHWH	23:2–9
X	Sanctity of the military camp	23:10–15
I′	Asylum for escaped slaves	23:16–17
H′	Prohibition of prostitution [+ 23:20–26]	23:18–19
G′	Sex: forbidden remarriage	24:1–4

F′	Humanism: deferral of new husband from the army	24:5
E′	Social ethics: taking care of poor and vulnerable	24:6–22
D′	Humanism: limits on flogging and not muzzling the ox	25:1–4
C′	Family law: levirate marriage	25:5–12
B′	Social justice: honest weights and measures	25:13–16
A′	Remembering Amalekite aggression (holy war)	25:17–19

The structural design of the whole appears to be shaped around four central issues: warfare, marriage (sex and family), social ethics (care of the poor and vulnerable), and humanitarian concerns. These four general subjects are extensions of commandments six through ten of the Ten Commandments: on homicide (warfare), adultery (illicit mixtures), theft (property), false testimony (social and economic justice), and coveting (humanitarian issues). Matters of warfare, though limited to only four short laws, play a dominant role in the structure of the whole as observed here, appearing at the beginning (21:10–14), in the middle (23:10–17), and at the end (25:17–19). The second major concern is that of marriage and obligations in the area of sexual behavior and family life. The third concern of primary importance centers on the matter of social ethics, and the care of the widow, orphan, and alien in particular. The fourth concern is humanitarian in nature, with laws on the treatment of the body of an executed criminal (21:22–23), limits to flogging (25:1–3), not muzzling an ox while it threshes (25:4), and not taking the mother bird with her young (or eggs) (22:6–7). In almost all cases, the laws in which these four concerns are expressed are arranged in a carefully balanced manner in palindromic manner. These laws are often also arranged in a pattern of three plus one, with a single law in one part of the structure set over against a group of three, which are usually more closely related with one other in some way. The reason most commentators have concluded that the laws in this section of Deuteronomy are miscellaneous in nature is that they have failed to observe the concentric structural design of the whole and of its parts, at all levels of analysis.

Each half of the inner frame in the five-part concentric design of 21:10–23:1 and 23:2–25:19 may in turn be outlined within parallel five-part structures:

A	Marriage with a woman captured in war	21:10–14
B	Family law: right of firstborn, insubordinate son	21:15–21
X	Laws on "true religion" and illicit mixtures	21:22–22:12
B′	Family law: premarital unchastity, adultery, and rape	22:13–29
A′	Prohibition of marrying one's father's wife	23:1

A	On admission to the assembly of YHWH in the future	23:2–9
B	War and sex: a frame around caring for the poor and vulnerable	23:10–24:5
X	Laws on "true religion"—protecting the poor and vulnerable	24:6–25:4
B′	Levirate marriage, improper fighting, weights and measures	25:5–16
A′	Remembering Amalekite aggression in times past	25:17–19

The focus of interest in the first half (21:10–23:1) is marriage, family law, and illicit mixtures. The primary concern of the second half (23:2–25:19) is social and business ethics, focused primarily on care for the poor and vulnerable, symbolized in the familiar Deuteronomic trio of the widow, orphan, and resident alien. Within these parallel structures, each section displays a similar pattern, which I take up in detail in the commentary below.

The key to understanding the literary structure of 21:10–25:19 is found in a close look at the laws dealing with war and marriage. As I have shown in the general introduction to the laws of 16:18–21:9, the subject of war corresponds with the sixth commandment, the prohibition of murder (5:17). The subject of marriage and family law corresponds with the seventh commandment, the prohibition of adultery (5:18). Deut 21:10–25:19 opens with a law that touches on both marriage and war: the law on marriage with a woman captured in war (21:10–14). It closes with a brief passage on holy war in the exhortation to remember the aggression of the Amalekites in the days of the exodus from Egypt (25:17–19). The second law on marriage per se, the prohibition of marrying one's father's wife (23:1), functions as the second half of an envelope that marks the end of the first major subsection (21:10–23:1), which is essentially a commentary on the seventh commandment.

The law in 23:1 plays a double role, for it is also the initial part of a structural frame for the laws of 23:1–24:4, forming an inclusion with the law forbidding remarriage if a man's former wife has remarried in the interim (24:1–4). The laws on social ethics in 23:2–26 open with a group of laws on who is permitted to be included in the assembly of YHWH (23:2–9) and the second of the four laws on matters of war, the sanctity of the military camp (23:10–15). As shown in the discussion below, the laws in 23:1–24:4 are essentially a commentary on the sixth through the tenth commandments, in relation to commandments one through three on the matter of true religion, a topic that was already introduced in the previous subsection (21:22–22:4; 22:6–8; and in 22:12 by way of a riddle of sorts on the meaning of wearing tassels on garments). The vertical aspect of true religion in 23:2–24:4, in terms of the relationship between the worshiper and God, moves from the opening demand for holiness in the military camp (23:10–15) to the prohibition of "holy prostitution" (23:18–19) and then to the law on timely fulfillment of vows made to YHWH (23:22–24).

The horizontal aspect of true religion is introduced in the previous section of laws dealing with marriage and family and illicit mixtures (Deut 21:10–23:1) in the three subunits designated here as "true religion." The subject is expanded in 23:2–24:4 with a law on asylum for escaped slaves (23:16–17) and three laws dealing with the protection of the poor and vulnerable in 23:20–26. What is presented here is expanded in the concluding major subsection of the sixth weekly portion of Torah readings in Deuteronomy (24:5–25:19), which has in its center a summation of the matter: "You shall not pervert justice to the alien or the orphan and you shall not take in pledge a widow's garment" (24:17). This is essentially what James described as "true religion": "to care for orphans and widows in their need, and to keep oneself unstained by the world" (Jas 1:27).

The concluding section in 24:5–25:19 spells out in detail what it means to protect the poor and the vulnerable, within a framework that moves from the last of the four laws on marriage (21:10–14; 23:1; 24:1–4; 24:5), to the last of the four laws on war (21:10–14; 23:10–15; 24:5; 25:17–19). The law on deferral of a new husband from military service in 24:5 and the concluding admonition to remember Amalekite aggression in 25:17–19 form an envelope around what is essentially a grand conclusion to the collection of laws in Deut 12–25. In short, to keep the Torah as taught by Moses is to "fear God" and to love your neighbor as yourself (Matt 22:37–39).

The twenty laws in 21:10–23:1 are essentially an expansion of the seventh commandment prohibiting adultery (5:18), which include six laws on what I have called "true religion." The laws are grouped in four general categories that are arranged in a concentric pattern:

A *On marriage*—with a woman captured in war (21:10–14)
B *Family laws:* on children (21:15–21)
Right of firstborn in a polygamous family (21:15–17)
Punishment of an insubordinate son (21:18–21)
C *True religion* (21:22–22:4)
Treatment of the corpse of an executed criminal (21:22–23)
Returning lost animals (22:1–3)
Assisting fallen animals (22:4)
D *Illicit Mixtures* (22:5)
Not wearing clothing of the opposite sex (22:5)
X *True Religion* (22:6–8)
Not capturing a mother bird with her young (22:6–7)
Building a parapet around the roof of one's house (22:8)
D′ *Illicit Mixtures* (22:9–11)
Forbidden combinations of seed (22:9)
Forbidden combinations of animals in plowing: ox and ass (22:10)
Forbidden combinations in textiles (22:11)
C′ *True religion* (22:12)
Tassels on garments (22:12)
B′ *Family laws*: marital and sexual misconduct (22:13–29)
False accusations of premarital unchastity (22:13–19)
True accusations of premarital unchastity (22:20–21)
Adultery with a married woman or engaged virgin (22:22–24)
Rape of an engaged virgin (22:25–27)
Rape of an unengaged virgin (22:28–29)
A′ *On marriage*—prohibition of taking one's father's wife (23:1)

Two laws on marriage function as the outer frame in this structure (21:10–14 and 23:1), whereas the next level in the nesting of parallel laws extends the concept of "family law" to children (21:15–21) and to the central issue of marital and sexual misconduct (22:13–29). Within this last group of five laws, we find explicit repetition of the law prohibiting adultery (22:22), of which the larger structure is a literary expansion. The aspect of adultery as an illicit mixture is expanded in a law pertaining to human beings (not wearing clothing of the opposite sex, 22:5) that is set over against three laws pertaining to the nonhuman aspect of the created order: forbidden combinations in seed, plow animals (the ox and the ass together), and textiles (the combination of wool and linen). On either side of these laws on illicit mixtures are a series of laws I have designated as "true religion." In the first such frame are three laws pertaining to either human beings (the corpse of an executed criminal, 21:22–23) or animals (lost or fallen, 22:1–4) and a fourth dealing with the wearing of tassels on garments (22:12). In the center are two peculiar laws on "true religion" in relation to the nonhuman aspect of the created order (not capturing a mother bird with her young, 22:6–7) and the human aspect as well (building a parapet around the edge of the roof of one's house, 22:8). The message presented within this structural arrangement is profound: in the world of ecology, as well as in human relations, we are entrusted with responsibility under God to exercise our "dominion over everything that has the breath of life" (Gen 1:30).

A series of four distinctive laws on matters pertaining to marriage and war is used as a structuring framework within which to organize the laws in 21:10–25:19. The law on marriage with a woman captured in war (21:10–14) is the first of these four laws, which form a chiastic framework around seven laws on matters of social ethics (23:2–26), which may be outlined as follows:

A	Marriage with a woman captured in war	21:10–14
B	Prohibition of marrying one's father's wife	23:1
X	Seven laws on matters of social ethics	23:2–26
B′	Prohibition of remarriage if former wife has remarried	24:1–4
A′	Deferral of new husband from military service	24:5

The pair of laws in the outer frame of this structure deal with the subjects of both marriage and war (21:10–14 and 24:5). The two laws in the inner frame both deal with circumstances in which marriage is prohibited (23:1 and 24:1–4). The seven laws in the center of this structure may be outlined in a menorah pattern:

A	Admission to the assembly of YHWH	23:2–9
B	Sanctity of the military camp	23:10–15
C	Asylum for escaped slaves	23:16–17
X	Prohibition of "holy prostitution"	23:18–19
C′	Prohibition of lending at interest	23:20–21
B′	Timely fulfillment of vows to YHWH	23:22–24
A′	Right to eat from a neighbor's unharvested crops	23:25–26

The central law within the seven laws on matters of social ethics in this structure is the curious law on "holy prostitution" (23:18–19), which has the quality of a "riddle at the middle" that we have seen elsewhere. The framework in this structure (A, X, A′) moves from a law concerning those who are excluded from the assembly of YHWH (including Ammonites and Moabites) and the inclusion of the Edomites, "for he is your brother" (v 8), and the Egyptians (23:2–9), to a law on the right to eat from a neighbor's unharvested crops (23:25–26). As we will see in the detailed discussion of this law below, it was used to shape narrative tradition elsewhere about the "unbrotherly conduct" of the Edomites. In the center of this structure we find the riddle of "holy prostitution" (23:18–19). The outermost frame in this structure moves from the law on the sanctity of the military camp (23:10–15), where "YHWH your God" walks in the midst of the camp (v 15), to a law on the timely fulfillment of vows to YHWH (23:22–24). The innermost frame moves from a law on asylum for escaped slaves (23:18–19) to a law prohibiting lending at interest "to your brother" (v 20), who as a fellow Israelite has the heritage of being an escaped slave (23:20–21).

The structures outlined here suggest that the law prohibiting "holy prostitution" in its center (23:18–19) is to be interpreted within the context of the other six laws on marriage and war as the center of another menorah pattern:

A	Marriage and war—marriage with a woman captured in war	21:10–14
B	Marriage—prohibition of marrying one's father's wife	23:1
C	War—sanctity of the military camp	23:10–15
X	Prohibition of "holy prostitution"	23:18–19
C′	Marriage—prohibition of remarriage if former wife remarried	24:1–4
B′	Marriage and war—deferral of new husband from military service	24:5
A′	YHWH's Holy War—remembering Amalekite aggression	25:17–19

The framework in this structure (A, X, A′) moves from the first of two laws dealing with both marriage and war (21:10–14) to the concluding reminder to remember Amalekite aggression at the outset of YHWH's Holy War in times past (25:17–19), with the curious law on the prohibition of "holy prostitution" in the center (23:18–19). The outermost frame moves from a law prohibiting marriage to one's father's wife (23:1) to the second law that deals with both marriage and war—the deferral of a new husband from military service (24:5). The innermost frame moves from a law on war, the sanctity of the military camp (23:10–15), to a law on marriage, the prohibition of remarriage if one's former wife has remarried in the interim (24:1–4). Once again, the careful arrangement of these individual laws on marriage and war within the structural design of the whole of 21:10–25:19 is evident.

Another way of looking at the structure of the laws of 21:10–25:19 within the framework of laws dealing with matters of sex and war is to include all of the laws in a menorah pattern:

A	Marriage with a woman captured in war	21:10–14
B	Family laws, true religion, and illicit mixtures (17 laws)	21:15–22:29
C	Marriage and war (3 laws)	23:1–15
X	Laws on social ethics (5 laws)	23:16–26
C′	Marriage and war (2 laws)	24:1–5
B′	Protecting the poor and vulnerable (12 laws)	24:6–25:16
A′	Remembering Amalekite aggression (YHWH's Holy War)	25:17–19

The framework in this structure (A, X, A′) moves from a law on marriage with a woman captured in war (21:10–14), to the concluding reminder to remember to hate the Amalekites because of their military aggression at the outset of YHWH's Holy War in the exodus from Egypt (25:17–19), with a group of five laws on matters of social ethics in the center (23:16–26). The outermost frame moves from a collection of seventeen laws on matters of social ethics (21:15–22:29), to another collection of twelve laws protecting the poor and vulnerable (24:6–25:16). Both of these substructures are in turn concentric in nature with laws on true religion at their centers, laws that mean concern for both the mother bird with her young (22:6–7) and fellow human beings (22:8), and in particular with the protection of sojourners, orphans, and widows in our midst (24:17–22).

The evidence for the use of the divine-name numbers according to Labuschagne for Reading 6 (21:10–25:19) as a whole reveals the following:

Words:	before ʾatnāḥ			after ʾatnāḥ				
21:14	11		+	6		=	17	
21:10–14	39		+	31		=	70	
21:10–23	133		+	85	(= 5 × 17)	=	218	
22:1–12	109		+	61		=	170	(= 10 × 17)
22:13–29	170	(= 10 × 17)	+	97		=	267	
23:1–26	182	(= 7 × 26)	+	157		=	339	
24:1–9	78	(= 3 × 26)	+	75		=	153	(= 9 × 17)
24:10–18	65		+	54		=	119	(= 7 × 17)
24:19–22	32		+	23		=	55	
25:1–19	160		+	100		=	260	(= 10 × 26)
21:10–25:19	929		+	652		=	1,581	(= 93 × 17)

The divine-name numbers 17 and 26 are carefully woven into the fabric of the Hebrew text throughout the sixth reading of the lectionary cycle (21:10–25:19) in a variety of ways.

A. Three Laws on Marriage and Family(21:10–21)

1. Marriage with a Woman Captured in War (21:10–14)

Bibliography

Alt, A. "Zu *hit ʿammer.*" *VT* 2 (1952) 153–59. **Batto, B.** *Studies on Women at Mari.* Baltimore: Johns Hopkins UP, 1974. 83–84. **Buit, M. du.** "Quelques contacts bibliques dans les Archives Royales de Mari." *RB* 66 (1959) 576–81. **Cassuto, U.** *The Goddess Anath.* Tr. I. Abrahams. Jerusalem: Magnes, 1971. 45. **Cohen, S. J. D.** "Conversion to Judaism in Historical Perspective: From Biblical Israel to Postbiblical Judaism." *ConsJud* 36 (1982–83) 31–45. **David, M.** "*Hit ʿammer.*" *VT* 1 (1951) 219–21. **Eph'al,** I. "Lexical Notes on Some Ancient Military Terms." *EI* 20 (1989) 115. **Gelb, I. J.** "Prisoners of War in Early Mesopotamia." *JNES* 32 (1973) 70–98 **Hallo, W. W.** *The Book of the People.* Atlanta: Scholars Press, 1991. 97. **Horst, F.** "Zwei Begriffe für Eigentum (Besitz)." *FS W. Rudolph.* 1961. 135–56. **Hulst, A. R.** *Old Testament Translation Problems.* Helps for Translators 1. Leiden: Brill, 1960. 16. **Kippenberg, H. G.** *Religion und Klassenbildung im antiken Judäa: Eine religionssoziologische Studie zum Verhältnis von Tradition und gesellschaftlicher Entwicklung.* 2nd ed. SUNT 14. Göttingen: Vandenhoeck & Ruprecht, 1982. 27. **Lipiński, E.** "Sale, Transfer and Delivery in Ancient Semitic Terminology." In *Gesellschaft und Kultur im Alten Vorderasien.* Ed. H. Klengel. SGKAO 15. Berlin: Akademie-Verlag, 1982. 173–85. **Merendino, R. P.** *Das* *deuteronomische Gesetz*. 1969. 243–44. **Smith, W. R.** *Kinship and Marriage in Early Arabia*. 1903. 89–92. **Tigay, J. H.** "Conversion and Marriage." In *Deuteronomy*. 1996. 479–80.

Translation and Prosodic Analysis

Marriage with a Woman Captured in War [(6:7):(6:6):(7:6)]

10 *When you go forth to war / against your enemies*[a] *//*	18	2
and YHWH your God / gives him / into your hand[b] */*	19	3
and you take captive his captives //	9	1_
11 *And you see /* [a]*among the female captives /*	11	2
a woman[a] */ beautiful in appearance //*	8	2
and you desire her /	7	1
[b]*and you would take her*[b] *to yourself / as a wife //*	11	2_
12 *You are to bring her / into your house //*	13	2
[a]*And she shall shave*[a] */ her head /*	10	2
[b]*and she shall pare*[b] */ her nails //*	12	2_
13 *And she*[a] *shall put off her / captive's garb /*	20	2
and she shall dwell\[b] *in your house /*	11	1
and she shall mourn / her father and mother / a full month //	24	3_
And after that / you may come in to her /	14	2
and you shall marry her /	6	1
And she shall be / your wife //	11	2
14 *and it shall be / if you no longer have delight in her /*	14	2_
Then you shall release her\[a] *outright /*	9	1
[b]*and you shall surely not sell her*[b] */ for money //*	17	2
[c]*You shall not treat her as merchandise*[c] */*	8	1
since / you have humbled her // ס	9	2_

Notes

10.a. One Heb. MS, printed editions, and Cairo Geniza fragments read איבך, "your enemy," for MT איביך, "your enemies."

10.b. A few Heb. MSS, Cairo Geniza fragments, and Syr. read בידיך, "into your hands," for MT בידך, "into your hand."

11.a-a. SP reads בשביו אשה, "among his captives a woman," for MT בשביה אשה, "among the female captives a woman."

11.b-b. One Heb. MS, SP, LXX, Syr., and Tg. read וּלְקַחְתָּהּ, "and you shall take her," for MT וְלָקַחְתָּ, "and you shall take."

12.a-a. LXX reads 2 sg., "you shall shove," for MT וגלחה, "and she shall shove."

12.b-b. LXX reads 2 sg., "you shall do [i.e., pare]," for MT ועשתה, "and she shall do [i.e., pare]."

13.a. LXX reads 2 sg.

13.b. Reading *paštāʾ* followed by *zāqēp qāṭôn* as conj.

14.a. Reading *paštāʾ* followed by *zāqēp qāṭôn* as conj.

14.b-b. LXX reads πραθήσεται (= תִּמָּכֵר), "she shall be sold."

14.c-c. LXX reads ἀθετήσεις (= תֵעָמֵר), "you shall treat contemptuously."

Form/Structure/Setting

Though the opening law in the series here deals with warfare, which is the subject of the laws in Deut 20, its primary focus is on marital relations, not the war in which the woman was captured. It is one of two laws that deal with both marriage and war, the other being the deferral of a new husband from military service in 24:5. The sequence of laws on the subjects of marriage and war play a primary role as markers in the literary structure of 21:10–25:19 as a whole. The law on marriage with a woman captured in war (21:10–14) also serves as an introduction to a series of three laws on the subject of marriage and family, which include the laws on the right of the firstborn in a polygamous family (21:15–17) and the punishment of an insubordinate son (21:18–21).

The boundaries of the passage in 21:10–14 are marked by the *sĕtûmāʾ* layout markers after vv 9 and 14. Though no further indications of internal structure are given, the law on marriage with a woman captured in war (21:10–14) may be outlined on the basis of content:

A	When you see among the female captives a beautiful woman	21:10–11a
B	And you desire to take her to yourself as a wife	21:11b
X	Shave her head, pare her nails, and keep her for a full month	21:12–13a
B′	Then you may take her as your wife	21:13b
A′	If she no longer pleases you, you must release her outright	21:14

The outer frame in this structure moves from an initial desire on the part of a soldier to take to wife a beautiful woman from among the female captives (vv 10–11a) to a ruling regarding the woman's future should the man change his mind at some later date (v 14). The inner frame moves from a statement of the man's desire to marry the woman (v 11b) to the granting of permission to do so (v 13b). The focus of attention at the center is the actual treatment the prospective bride is to receive. The woman is to be taken into the man's house for a "trial" month, during which time her physical beauty is minimalized by shaving her head, cutting her nails short, and having her "mourn her father and mother a full month" (vv 12–13a). If the man can live with a wailing and relatively unattractive woman for a month and still want her as his wife, perhaps the marriage will last.

Carmichael interprets the law of the female captive here in relation to the narrative of Laban's pursuit of Jacob in Gen 31:25–50. He argues that there was hostility between Jacob and Laban, "as evidenced by Laban's cheating Jacob and the latter's response" (*LNB,* 140). When Laban caught up with Jacob and his family at Mizpah, he compared Jacob's actions to the taking of women captives in war: "What have you done, that you have cheated me, and carried away my daughters like captives of the sword?" (Gen 31:26). "The remarkable reference about the Israelite's beholding among the captives a woman 'beautiful in form' (יפת תאר) has someone like Rachel in mind" (Carmichael, *LNB,* 141). Moreover, this expression is found only twice in the Pentateuch: in Gen 29:17 (of Rachel) and the law here in Deut 21:11. Rachel's theft of her father's household gods may have something to do with the law's demands that the woman sever contact with her past—shave her head, pare her nails, put off her captive's garb, and bewail her parents for a month. For a parallel in the Mari texts, in which hair and clothing were removed during a rite symbolizing severance from homeland, see du Buit, *RB* 66 (1959) 576–77 (cited by Carmichael, *LNB,* 141 n. 5).

A further indication that details in the story of Jacob and the daughters of Laban were shaped by the content of the law in Deut 22:10–14 is the consideration given to the possibility of separation, as Carmichael has shown (*LNB*, 141–42). Laban pressed Jacob to agree that in their life in the land of Canaan his daughters would not be "humbled" (עִנָּה). He did not want Jacob to take any wives in addition to Rachel and Leah (Gen 31:50). As the law states, Laban did not want the "captive women" to be "humbled" (עִנָּה) should their Israelite husband "no longer have delight in them" and seek to rid himself of them.

The evidence of the use of the divine-name numbers from Labuschagne's "logotechnische analyse" reveals little for 21:10–14 other than the fact that v 14 is made up of 17 words.

Comment

12–13 The acts of "shaving her head, paring her nails, and putting off her captive's garb" are usually interpreted as part of the woman's mourning process. "The shaving of the head and putting off of the clothes is referred to in the Mari texts where it has the purpose of getting rid of everything that would remind the captive of home" (Mayes [1981] 303; cf. du Buit, *RB* 66 [1959] 576–77). Rabbi Akiba thought they were intended to make the woman less attractive to her captor (*Sifre* 212; see Tigay [1996] 194, 381 n. 29). The "captive's garb" (שׂמלת שבי־ה) is simply the clothes the woman was wearing when taken captive. The woman is to "mourn her father and mother a full month," which in the lunar calendar of ancient Israel was thirty days (cf. the thirty days mourning for the death of Aaron in Num 20:29 and Moses in Deut 34:8).

14 The verb שׁלח, "to send (away)," is used of freeing slaves (15:12) and for divorce (22:19, 29). The translation "treat her as merchandise" (תתעמר) explains the previous clause, "you shall surely not sell her" (מכר לא־תמכרנה). The traditional translation of תתעמר as "to enslave" is an ancient conjecture. The term appears only here and in 24:7. The piel of the verb עמר appears in Ps 129:7 with the meaning "to bind sheaves," from עמיר, "row of fallen grain." The precise meaning of the verb התעמר remains uncertain. Alt has argued from a cognate noun in the Ugaritic texts, which designates a group of people liable for military service, that it means the action of one who claims unlimited power of disposal over others (*VT* 2 [1952] 153–59). The translation here follows that of David (*VT* 1 [1951] 219–21) and Hulst (*Old Testament Translation Problems*, 16). The piel verbal form עִנָּה, which is translated here as "you have humbled her," carries the sense of "doing violence to" in sexual matters (cf. 22:24, 29). The woman is brought low by the circumstances of the forceful loss of her family and her former way of life.

Explanation

The law on marriage with a woman captured in war (21:10–14), like the law that grants military deferral to a new husband (24:5), combines matters pertaining to war and sex. The law here concerns the matter of a captive female from a distant city, according to the rule in 20:10–15, not to marriage with a Canaanite woman, which is forbidden. The reasoning behind the specific terms of the law in 21:10–14 is not spelled out.

With her head shaved and nails pared (v 12), her "captive's garb" was discarded and the woman was to "mourn her father and her mother a full month," after which the man was permitted to marry her (v 13). Reasons for these actions have been conjectured through the years, as illustrated by the comments of Thomas Scott long ago: "Considering things thus coolly, we may perhaps before it be too late, have our admiration changed into disgust, and many fatal consequences may be prevented. . . . Irregular indulgences frequently end in dislike and ill-treatment of the very object that was inordinately loved!" (*Holy Bible* [1823] 539). The shaving of the head, the paring of the nails, and the changing of clothing signified a change in status and the taking on of a new life in another culture. But even this is not enough to assure a lasting union.

The concluding note about the man no longer having delight in the woman with the command to "release her outright" (v 14) is easily misinterpreted. A surface reading suggests that a husband, at least in some circumstances, can get rid of his wife for trivial reasons. In light of the sanctity of marriage, as taught elsewhere in the Bible, we know that this is not a proper conclusion to draw from this text. Maxwell states that he prefers "to think that the phrase "*if you have no delight in her*" refers to the new wife's refusal to accept her husband's spiritual values . . . since her previous culture and religion have been foreign to Israel" ([1987] 251). Though there is some truth in this opinion, it moves beyond the evidence in the text itself, which presents no reasons for the change in the man's attitude. The law focuses on the rights of the woman by stating that the man who marries a female prisoner of war and subsequently becomes dissatisfied with her, for whatever reasons, is not permitted to reduce her to slavery. Such a woman had legal rights in ancient Israel, and moral obligations ensue from the fact that the man initiated a sexual relationship with her. Perhaps the most significant conclusion to draw from this text is the respect for the personhood of a captured woman. A primary concern in the laws of Deut 21–25 is for protecting the poor and vulnerable in society from exploitation on the part of the powerful.

In ancient Jewish practice, a formal procedure was introduced in which the woman in such circumstances agreed to convert to Judaism. Even so, the rabbis discouraged such marriages, notes Tigay, regarding "such unions as motivated by lust and [they] considered the present law as a concession to the likelihood that they would take place whether permitted or not. In their view, verses 12–13 are designed to delay and, ideally, discourage such a marriage by making the woman unattractive" ([1996] 194).

One of the lessons to be learned from the law on marriage with a woman captured in war is the importance of a husband and wife sharing common spiritual values as the proper basis of a lasting union. We would do well to follow the example here in deliberately delaying commitment in marriage for a period of time to assure that the decision to marry is not based primarily on physical lust.

2. *Right of the Firstborn Son in a Polygamous Family (21:15–17)*

Bibliography

Albertz. R. "Das Überleben der Familie Sichern." *Lutherische Monatshefte* 25 (1986) 401–5. **Carmichael, C. M.** "A Ceremonial Crux: Removing a Man's Sandals as a Female Gesture of Contempt." *JBL* 96 (1977) 321–36, esp. 325. ———. *LNB.* 142–50. ———. "Uncovering a Major Source of Mosaic Law: The Evidence of Deut 21:15–22:5." *JBL* 101 (1982) 505–20, esp. 506–11. ———. *Women, Law, and the Genesis Traditions.* Edinburgh: Univ. of Edinburgh Press, 1979. 22–30. **Causse, A.** "L'Idéal politique et social du Deutéronome: La fraternité d'Israel." *RHPR* 13 (1933) 289–323. **Daube, D.** *Studies in Biblical Law.* 1947. 5–7. ———. "The Culture of Deuteronomy." *Orita* 3 (1969) 41–43. **Eybers, I. H.** "Some Examples of Hyperbole in Biblical Hebrew." *Semitics* 1 (1970) 38–49. **Fohrer, G.** "Twofold Aspects of Hebrew Words." In *FS D. Winton Thomas.* 1968. 99. **Goetze, A.** "Number Idioms in Old Babylonian." *JNES* 5 (1946) 202. **Goodenough, E. R.** *The Jurisprudence of the Jewish Courts in Egypt.* 1929. Repr. Amsterdam: Philo Press, 1968. 56–67. **Granqvist, H.** *Marriage Conditions.* 1931–35. 2:194. **Henninger, J.** "Zum Erstgeborenenrecht bei den Semiten." In *Festschrift Werner Caskel zum siebzigsten Geburtslag.* Ed. E. Gräf. Leiden: Brill, 1968. 162–83. **Horst, F.** "Zwei Begriffe für Eigentum (Besitz)." In *FS W. Rudolph.* 1961. 135–56. **Kippenberg, H. G.** *Religion und Klassenbildung im antiken Judäa.* 2nd ed. Göttingen: Vandenhoeck & Ruprecht, 1982. 26. **Mendelsohn, I.** "On the Preferential Status of the Eldest Son." *BASOR* 156 (1959) 38–40. **Milgrom, J.** "Firstborn." *IDBSup.* 337–38. **Neufeld, E.** *Ancient Hebrew Marriage Laws.* London; New York: Longmans, Green, 1944. 263. **Rabinowitz, J. J.** "Marriage Contracts in Ancient Egypt in the Light of Jewish Sources." *HTR* 46 (1953) 91–97. **Rubin, N.** "On the Social Significance of the *bekhor* in the Bible." *BMik* 33 (1988) 162–63 (Heb.). **Skaist, A. J.** "Inheritance Laws and Their Social Background." *JAOS* 95 (1975) 424–47. **Snaith, N. H.** "The Daughters of Zelophehad." *VT* 16 (1966) 124–27. **Vaux, R. de.** *The Early History of Israel.* Tr. D. Smith. Philadelphia: Westminster, 1978. 250–51. **Watson, P.** "A Note on the 'Double Portion' of Deut 21,17 and 2 Ki 2,9." *ResQ* 8 (1965) 70–75. **Yaron, R.** "On Divorce in Old Testament Times." *RIDA* 4 (1957) 117–28.

Translation and Prosodic Analysis

Right of the Firstborn in a Polygamous Family [(4:6):(5:5):(6:4)]

15 *When a man has / two wives /* 15 2
the[a] one loved / and the[a] other hated / 19 2_
And they both have borne him sons / 12 1
the loved one / and the hated one // 14 2
and it happens / the firstborn is the son / of the hated one[b] // 18 3_
16 *And it shall be / on the day /* 8 2
he gives as inheritance to his sons / what he / has // 18 3_
He must not / 5 1
treat as firstborn / the son of the loved one / 13 2
in the presence of the son of the hated one / the firstborn // 15 2_

[17] *Rather / the firstborn son of the hated one he shall recognize /* [17 2
by giving him / 5 1
a double portion / of all that belongs / to him // 17 3
For he / is the first issue of his procreative power / [12 2
[a]*to him / belongs the right of the firstborn //* ס 10 2

Notes

15.a. One Heb. MS and SP read אחת and ואחת for MT האחת, "the one," and והאחת, "and the (other) one," omitting the def. art.

15.b. SP reads לשנואה for MT לשניאה, "the hated one," with no change in meaning.

17.a. The *waw*-conj. is added in SP, LXX, Syr., and Vg.

Form/Structure/Setting

In the larger literary structure of 21:10–23:1, the two laws on children (21:15–21) are set over against five laws on marital and sexual misconduct (22:13–29). The two laws on children have to do with inheritance rights on the part of the firstborn in a polygamous family (21:15–17) and the punishment of an insubordinate son (21:18–21). The first, dealing with inheritance rights and the subject of property, corresponds with the eighth commandment, prohibiting stealing. The second, the matter of the insubordinate son, has to do with the fifth commandment, requiring parental respect.

The boundaries of the law on the inheritance right of the firstborn son in a polygamous family (21:15–17) are marked by the *sĕtûmâ'* layout markers after vv 14 and 17. The law may be outlined on the basis of its content:

A A man has sons of two wives, one loved and one unloved 21:15
B When he assigns his property to his sons 21:16a
X He is not permitted to ignore the one who is firstborn 21:16b
B′ The firstborn is to receive a double portion 21:17a
A′ To the eldest son belongs the right of the firstborn 21:17b

The legal situation is presented in the outer frame: when a man has sons by two wives (v 15), the right of the firstborn belongs to the eldest son (v 17b). The situation is complicated, however, by the fact that the man loves one of his wives more than the other. The inner frame expands the legal situation by spelling out what the law entails. When a man assigns his property to his sons (v 16a), he must give a double portion to the firstborn (v 17b). The point is reinforced in the center of the structure (v 16b): the man is not permitted to ignore the rights of the firstborn, even if he has a favorite son by the wife he loves the most whom he desires to recognize as his primary heir.

Though Carmichael has argued that the laws in Deuteronomy were written later than the narratives of the Torah and the Former Prophets and were shaped by that very tradition (*LNB*, 16–17), the evidence here points in the opposite direction. The laws of Deuteronomy were foundational, and the narrative tradition appears to be shaped by what is later called midrash. They are stories intended to elucidate a sacred "canonical" text, in this case the collection of laws in Deut 12–26, which in turn were written as a midrash of sorts on the Ten Commandments. What God revealed to Moses on Mount Sinai was the "acorn," which contained the genetic code, as it were, that enabled it to grow in the course of time so as to become the "mighty oak tree" we know as the Bible.

Though Jacob's transfer of the birthright from his eldest son Reuben to his favorite son Joseph portrays Jacob denying the right of the firstborn, Carmichael argues that the story of Jacob and Esau brings out the issue more clearly (*LNB*, 142–45), for Jacob "steals" the birthright from his elder brother Esau, with the connivance of his mother Rachel. The story in Genesis then moves on to broach another question: When does a son deserve to be cut off by his parents? (*LNB*, 146–50). This is the subject of the second of the two family laws in Deut 21:18–21, the punishment of a rebellious son. It is his mother's favoritism toward his brother Jacob that unjustly deprived Esau of his birthright. But the story moves on as Esau's situation turned into an offense comparable to that of Reuben's sin with his father's concubines, for Esau married two Hittite wives, who "made life bitter for Isaac and Rebekah" (Gen 26:35).

The story of Jacob's problem with his firstborn son Reuben in Gen 29:31–32; 35:22; and 49:3–4 illustrates the law in matters of detail, as Carmichael has shown (*LNB*, 142–45). Jacob had two wives—Rachel, the loved wife, and Leah, the unloved. Reuben was the firstborn son of Leah. Rachel's firstborn, Joseph, was Jacob's eleventh son; and six of Joseph's older brothers were the sons of Leah, the unloved wife. Reuben forfeited his firstborn status by lying with his father's concubine (35:22). In his final blessing of his twelve sons, Jacob acknowledged Reuben as his firstborn (49:3); but he gave the chief blessing to Joseph (49:22–26).

Though we can see why Reuben forfeited the right of the firstborn in this instance, the question remains as to why the other brothers were passed over. If there were extenuating circumstances, the account in Genesis does not record them. As Jacob himself attained his brother's birthright fraudulently, he passed on the birthright of his own firstborn son in an improper manner to the son of his favored wife. Here Deuteronomy declares that his action was contrary to God's law.

Though Labuschagne's "logotechnische analyse" for 21:15–17 reveals no evidence on the use of the divine-name numbers 17 and 26, the pattern within its larger context in 21:10–23 may be summarized as follows:

Words:	before *ʾatnāḥ*		after *ʾatnāḥ*		
21:15–17	37	+	22	=	59
21:18	12	+	5	=	17
21:18–23	57	+	32	=	89
21:10–23	133	+	85 (= 5 × 17)	=	218

It is only when vv 15–17 are taken within its larger context that the use of the divine-name number 17 becomes clear, for there are a total of 85 (= 5 × 17) words after *ʾatnāḥ* in 21:10–23. There are also 17 words in v 18 and a total of 32 words after *ʾatnāḥ* in vv 18–23. Since 32 is the numerical value of כבוד, "glory," the presence of 32 and 17 here signifies the "glory of YHWH."

Comment

15 The expression "the one loved and the other unloved" (lit. the "loved" [אהובה] and the "hated" [שׂנואה]) as an idiom for the favored and the unfavored wife is found in Arabic (Granqvist, *Marriage Conditions,* 2:194), Egyptian (A. Erman, cited by Rabinowitz, *HTR* 46 [1953] 94 n. 12), and Akkadian (*Gilgamesh Epic* 12:23–26, 42–45; see Tigay [1996] 382 n. 39). Biblical examples include Jacob's wives Rachel and Leah (Gen 29:30–31) and Elkanah's wives Hannah and Peninah (1 Sam 1:5).

16–17 The phrase לא יוכל functions as a rhythmic bridge connecting the two halves of v 16. When read with what precedes it, the meaning is essentially "he must not prevail" (cf. Gen 30:8) by exerting his own will contrary to the law. When read with what follows, it is translated "He must not treat as firstborn . . ." by assigning him "a double portion" (פי שׁנים, lit. "two mouths"). The assigning of this right of the firstborn has been interpreted in different ways. The early versions and Ben Sira (Sir 12:5; 18:32) took this to mean "double portion," but as Tigay has shown ([1996] 195–96, 382 n. 43), this may reflect postbiblical exegesis. The estate was divided into shares equal to the number of sons plus one, in Assyria, Nuzi, and Ptolemaic Egypt (see Tigay [1996] 382 n. 4; Mendelsohn, *BASOR* 156 [1959] 38–40; and Milgrom, *IDBSup,* 337–38). It should also be noted that in Zech 13:8 the phrase פי שׁנים has the meaning "two-thirds" (cf. also 2 Kgs 2:9), and in Egyptian "two mouths" means "two-thirds" (A. Gardiner, *Egyptian Grammar,* 3rd ed. [London: Oxford UP, 1957] 197, 452). Thus the law here may have meant that the firstborn is to inherit two-thirds. Tigay ([1996] 196) cites an adoption contract from Mari that stipulates that the chief heir would receive two-thirds of the estate no matter how many other heirs there might be (ARM 8:1; cf. *ANET,* 545, no. 13, where J. J. Finkelstein translates "double share"). As Tigay has noted, this is still more generous to younger sons than was the case in medieval England, where the chief heir received the entire estate ([1996] 196). Similar laws in Scandinavia were responsible for the Vikings of the eighth to tenth centuries C.E. who were primarily "younger sons" who were obliged to find their "inheritance" abroad as pirates.

The verb יכיר, "he shall recognize," is a technical term for legal acknowledgment (Daube, *Studies in Biblical Law,* 5–7). The phrase "first issue of his procreative power" (ראשׁית אנו) appears elsewhere as a description of the firstborn (Gen 49:3 [Reuben], Pss 78:51; 105:36 [firstborn of Egypt]). The translation "procreative power" rather than "strength" follows Fohrer (*FS D. Winton Thomas,* 99) and Craigie ([1976] 283 n. 20). In the Bible the preferential treatment of the firstborn is also referred to as "the right of the firstborn" (הבכרה), which means literally "primogeniture" (Rubin, *BMik* 33 [1988] 162–63). "The purpose of granting one son a preferential share may have been to enable him to bear additional responsibilities as head of the family, such as managing the estate on behalf of all the survivors, providing for survivors who were minors, bearing the costs of burying and mourning for deceased parents, or simply to enable him to carry on his father's name in dignity" (Tigay [1996] 196).

Explanation

Although polygamy was practiced in ancient Israel, without exception it is also depicted as an occasion for family trouble. The law of the right of the firstborn (Deut 21:15–17) was given to limit the extent of that trouble. The story of Adam and Eve presents monogamy as the divine ideal for marriage (Gen 2:20–24). In sharp contrast, the story of Jacob and his two wives illustrates the problem of polygamy: "So Jacob went into Rachel also, and he loved Rachel more than Leah" (Gen 29:30). Jacob's preference here reflects the human condition, for rivalry between the wives in such a polygamous relationship is inevitable.

This rivalry extends to the children in a polygamous family as well, particularly in the matter of the disposition of property. The law on the right of the firstborn (21:15–17) prohibits disinheriting the eldest son without just cause. When a man settles his estate, a child must not fare the worse for his mother's unhappiness in being the less favored wife. This principle regarding favoritism within the family applies in monogamous relationship today as well, in the sense that parents should give their children what is due them without showing partiality. Parents should show no more differentiation in dispensing affections among their children than God makes in dispensing his grace among his children.

The reference to a "double portion" of the inheritance (v 17) is not an instance of favoritism but a legal right. The same phrase appears in 2 Kgs 2:9, when Elisha asks Elijah, "Please let me inherit a double share of your spirit." Elisha is asking Elijah to declare him to be his spiritual heir and successor in terms of the law of the right of inheritance in a polygamous family. By law the firstborn receives a more generous portion of the inheritance in ancient Israel, however one interprets the specific meaning of the Hebrew words פי שנים of 21:17, which are rendered here as "double portion."

3. The Punishment of an Insubordinate Son (21:18–21)

Bibliography

Bellefontaine, E. "Deuteronomy 21:18–21: Reviewing the Case of the Rebellious Son." *JSOT* 13 (1979) 13–31. **Benjamin, D. C.** *Deuteronomy and City Life.* 1983. **Buchholz, J.** *Die ältesten Israels im Deuteronomium.* 1988. **Callaway, P. R.** "Deut 21:18–21: Proverbial Wisdom and Law." *JBL* 103 (1984) 341–52. **Carroll, R. P.** "Rebellion and Dissent in Ancient Israelite Society." *ZAW* 89 (1977) 176–204. **Daube, D.** "Consortium in Roman and Hebrew Law." *Juridical Review* 62 (1950) 73–77. **Falk, Z. W.** "Sociological Notes on Deuteronomy." *DiIs* 3 (1972) 41. **Fensham, F. C.** "Aspects of Family Law in the Covenant Code in Light of Ancient Near Eastern Parallels." *DiIs* 1 (1969) v–xix, esp. xv. **Good, E. M.** "Capital Punishment and Its Alternatives in Ancient Near Eastern Law." *SLR* 19 (1967) 965–66. **Hirzel, R.** "Die Strafe der Steinigung." *Abhandlungen der philologisch-historischen Klasse der königlich sächsischen Gesellschaft der Wissenschaften* 27 (1909) 223–66, esp. 243. **Hoppe, L. J.** "Elders and Deuteronomoy: A Proposal." *EglT* 14 (1983) 259–72, esp. 262. **Klíma, F.** "La *Patria Potestas* dans les nouveaux fragments législatifs sumériens." In *Symbolae Iuridicae et historicae Martino David Dedicatae.* 2 vols. Ed. J. A. Ankum et al. Leiden: Brill, 1968. 2:1–8. **Lohfink, N.** "Die ältesten Israels und der Bund zum Zusammenhang von Dtn 5,23; 26,17–19; 27,1.9f und 31,9." *BN* 67 (1993) 26–42. **Marcus, D.** "Juvenile Delinquency in the Bible and the Ancient Near East." *JANESCU* 13 (1981) 31–52. **Perlitt, L.** "Der Vater im Alten Testament." In *Das Vaterbild in Mythos und Geschichte.* Ed. H. Tellenbach. Stuttgart: Kohlhammer, 1976. 76–78. **Reviv, H.** *The Elders in Ancient Israel: A Study of a Biblical Institution.* Jerusalem: Magnes, 1989. **Rofé, A.** "Family and Sex Laws in Deuteronomy and the Book of the Covenant." *BMik* 22 (1976/77) 19–36 (Heb.; Eng. summary, 155–56).

Translation and Prosodic Analysis

Punishment of an Insubordinate Son [(5:4):(5:5):(4:5)]

18 *When a man has / a son / who is rebellious and defiant*[a] /	18	3
who does not obey /	10	1
the voice of his father /	7	1
Or the voice of his mother // though they chastise him /	17	2
indeed[b] *he does not listen / to them //*	9	2
19 *His father and his mother / shall seize him //*	16	2
and they shall bring him /	11	1
to the elders of his city / [a]*at the gates*[b] *of his place //*	17	2
20 *And they shall say / to the elders*[a] *of his city /*	14	2
"This son of ours \\[b] *is rebellious and defiant*[c] /	15	1
he does not listen / to our voice //	17	2
He is a glutton / and a drunkard" //	9	2
21 *and all*[a] *the men of his city / shall stone him with stones /*	23	2
And he shall die /	4	1
and you shall purge the evil / from your[b] *midst //*	14	2
and [c]*all Israel*[c] */ shall hear (of it) and they shall fear //* ס	17	2

Notes

18.a. SP[MSS] read ומרא, "and fat, well-fed," for MT ומרה, "and defiant."
18.b. The *waw*-conj. is read here as emphatic.
19.a. A few Heb. MSS and SP omit *waw*-conj.
19.b. Tg. and *Tg. Ps.-J.* add *byt dyn.* Prosodic analysis favors MT.
20.a. SP and LXX (τοῖς ἀνδράσιν) read אל־אנשי, "to the men."
20.b. Reading *paštā'* followed by *zāqēp parvum* at conj.
20.c. SP[MSS] read ומרא, "and fat, well-fed," for MT ומרה, "and defiant."
21.a. LXX[-L] omits כל, "all."
21.b. LXX, Syr., *Tg. Ps.-J.*, and Vg. read 2 pl.
21.c-c. LXX reads καὶ οἱ ἐπίλοιποι, "and the rest (of them)" (= והנשארים) with 19:20 for MT וכל־ישראל, "and all Israel."

Form/Structure/Setting

The boundaries of the law on the punishment of an insubordinate son (Deut 21:18–21) are marked with *sĕtûmā'* layout markers at the beginning and the end, and by the distinctive summary command to "purge the evil from your midst," which is repeated elsewhere in similar contexts. This law may be outlined on the basis of its content:

A	A man has a rebellious son who "does not listen"	21:18
B	His parents shall bring him before the elders of his city	21:19
X	They shall declare: "He is a glutton and a drunkard"	21:20
B′	All the men of his city shall stone him to death	21:21a
A′	You shall purge the evil from your midst	21:21b

In this structure the outer frame moves from a presentation of the legal situation in which "a man has a son who is rebellious and defiant, who does not obey the voice of his father or the voice of his mother" (v 18), to a summary command to "purge the evil from your midst" (v 21b). The inner frame presents the legal procedure to be followed: the parents shall bring their son before the elders of the city for judgment at the gates of the city (v 19); and, if he is found guilty, "all the men of the city shall stone him to death" (v 21a). The declaration of guilt stands in the structural center: "he is a glutton and a drunkard" (v 20b).

Within rabbinic Judaism, the law of the rebellious son was interpreted so narrowly that it was virtually impossible for it to be carried out, as Tigay's summary of the halakic reading suggests: "the law applies for only the three months after a son turns thirteen and only if he has ravenously eaten semi-cooked meat and drunk partially mixed wine, in the company of a group that does not include one decent person, and not on a religious occasion; paying for the food with money misappropriated from his father; only if both parents are living and are not deaf, mute, blind, lame, or maimed in the hand; and only if both agree to prosecute him" ([1996] 382 n. 52).

Carmichael calls attention to Esau's ravenous appetite for meat in the story of Jacob and Esau (*LNB*, 146–50). Though Esau is certainly not presented as the rebellious and defiant son of Deut 21:18–21, Carmichael argues that he had the potential for that disreputable state. Esau stands as an example of a wayward son who changed his ways, for he decided not to marry another Canaanite woman and sought out an Ishmaelite instead in an effort to please his parents (Gen 28:6–9).

D. N. Freedman has written a significant book (*The Nine Commandments: Uncovering the Hidden Pattern of Crime and Punishment in the Hebrew Bible* [New York: Doubleday, 2000]) that demonstrates that a master editor compiled what Freedman calls the Primary History (the Torah and the Former Prophets). Evidence for this conclusion is found in a series of episodes distributed book by book through eight successive books in the Hebrew Bible that chart the violation of the first nine commandments one by one. The series starts with the sin of national apostasy (worship of the golden calf, Exod 32), which violates the first and second commandments, and concludes with the sin of bearing false witness (the ninth commandment) in the story of Naboth in 1 Kgs 21. Because covetousness lies behind all the crimes committed, each act implicitly breaks the tenth commandment as well. The Ten Commandments constitute the essence of the covenant relationship established between God and the people of Israel at Mount Sinai. The pattern of defiance of that covenant with God led inexorably to the downfall of the nation of Israel, the destruction of the temple, and the banishment of survivors from the promised land. The message is clear to a community in the Babylonian exile that their fate is not the result of God's abandoning them but a consequence of their abandonment of God. The true people of God are those who maintain the covenant commitment to God by observing the Ten Commandments.

Genesis does not include an episode in this series because the covenant at Mount Sinai, in which the stone tablets with the Ten Commandments are given to Moses, takes place later—in the book of Exodus. The commandments and their violations within the Primary History are as follows:

Commandment	*Text*	*Episode*
1. Do not worship other gods	Exod 32	Golden-calf incident
2 Worship no idols	Exod 32	Golden-calf incident
3 Do not take YHWH's name in vain	Lev 24:10–17	Stoning to death for sin of blasphemy
4 Keep the Sabbath	Num 15:32–36	Stoning to death for violating the Sabbath
5 Honor your parents	Deut 21:18–21	Stoning to death of stubborn and rebellious son
6 You shall not steal	Josh 7:20–26	Stoning to death of Achan and his family for theft
7 You shall not murder	Judg 20:34–48	Murder of Levite's concubine
8 You shall not commit adultery	2 Sam 11	David and Bathsheba
9 You shall not bear false witness	1 Kgs 21	Ahab, Jezebel, and Naboth's vineyard

The implications of Freedman's study, so far as the canonical process in ancient Isreal is concerned, are profound. The law of punishment of an insubordinate son (Deut 21:18–21) is an essential element in this series of episodes that extends through eight successive books in the canon of the Hebrew Bible (including Deuteronomy). Since Freedman argues that these episodes appear to be the work of a single editorial hand, this raises interesting questions. The fact that Labuschagne found little of interest in the text of Deut 21:18–21 in his numerical analysis lends some support to the possibility of this particular law being a subsequent editorial insertion. On the other hand, the grand totals for the numbers in Reading 6 (Deut 21:10–25:19) and in the book of Deuteronomy as a whole represent figures determined by the divine-name numbers 17 and 26. This fact indicates that the process of adjusting the text to achieve this remarkable phenomenon continued after the initial work of Freedman's "master editor." If that editor is to be identified with Baruch in the time of the prophet Jeremiah, as Freedman suggests (*Nine Commandments,* 93–97, 168), the editorial process continued well into the period of the Babylonian exile (ca. 587–538 B.C.E.) and perhaps the subsequent Persian era as well. One of the persons involved in the earlier period of this process may be Baruch's brother Seraiah, who apparently went to Babylon with Jeremiah's writings in ca. 593 B.C.E. (Jer 51:59–64). The circle of scribes ("counters") in Babylon who labored in the canonical process within ancient Israel probably included the prophet Ezekiel as well.

Comment

18 On the "rebellious and defiant" child, see Marcus, *JANESCU* 13 (1981) 31–52. The discipline the parents inflict on their rebellious son is translated here in the general sense of "chastise him" (ויסרו אתו). It could also be rendered "they flog him," following both rabbinic interpretation and the meaning in 22:18.

19 The text states that both "his father and his mother shall seize him," which indicates that the two must agree to this action. According to Josephus (*Ant.* 16.11.2 §§365–66), Herod I used this law as a pretext for killing two of his sons (see Tigay [1996] 382 n. 55). On the city gates as a place for litigation, see the *Comment* on 17:8.

20 The charge that the son "is a glutton and a drunkard" appears to be proverbial in nature, as a typical example of insubordination (cf. Prov 23:20–21; 28:7).

21 The statement that "all the men of his city shall stone him with stones" does not mention the parents, perhaps to demonstrate that they do not have the power of life and death over their children (so Tigay [1996] 197). The verb רגם, "to stone," does not appear elsewhere in Deuteronomy, though it is used elsewhere in the Torah (Lev 20:2, 27; 24:14, 23; Num 15:35) and in Josh 7:25 of the stoning of Achan and his household (cf. 13:10, where סקל, "to stone," is used instead). On "purge the evil from your midst," see the *Comment* on 13:6.

Explanation

Since there is no record in the Bible that the law of the insubordinate son (Deut 21:15–17) was ever enforced, it is safe to conclude that the primary purpose of this law was pedagogical—that "all Israel shall hear and fear" (v 21). Maxwell observes that "when a person is confronted with his own disobedience to biblical commands, he or she is more likely to 'hear and sneer' than to 'hear and fear.' Why? The church body lacks discipline. The greatest deterrent to sin in a society is that the people love God and fear (reverence) Him by obeying His commands. Love without fear is mush. Fear without love is legalism. Only the two together in proper balance will bring about the obedience required by God" ([1987] 253).

Respect for and obedience to parents were of vital importance in ancient Israel. In the Book of the Covenant, a son who strikes his father or mother, or who curses them, "shall be put to death" (Exod 21:15, 17; cf. also Lev 20:9); and the covenant curses of Deut 27:16 include "anyone who dishonors father or mother." The law here concerns a completely hardened and worthless son.

In his comments on this law some three hundred years ago, Matthew Henry said of the insolent son, "If he carry himself proudly and insolently toward his parents, contemn their authority, slight their reproofs and admonitions, disobey the express commands they give him for his own good, hate to be reformed by the correction they give him, shame their family, grieve their hearts, waste their substance, and threaten to ruin their estate by riotous living; this is a *stubborn and rebellious son*" (*Exposition of the Old and New Testament* [1828] 659). This description shares some of the tendencies of the halakic reading of the law in rabbinic Judaism (see *Form/Structure/Setting* above), and shows why there is no record of this law ever being enforced.

The concluding sentence in the indictment of the insubordinate son, that "he is a glutton and a drunkard" (v 20), bears further reflection in applying the meaning of this text in a modern setting. Few evils can match the pervasive power of drunkenness, particularly if this phenomenon is extended to include addiction to drugs other than alcohol. The modern parent of such an insubordinate son may have specific evils in mind quite different from those faced by parents in antiquity. In the words of King Lemuel's mother, "It is not for kings to drink wine, or . . . to desire strong drink; lest they drink and forget what has been decreed" (Prov 31:4–5). In principle these words apply to anyone, not just to kings. Drunkenness, whether induced by alcohol or other substance abuse, leads inevitably to disobeying God's law—with all its necessary consequences.

Though the parents are the prosecutors in this instance, they are not themselves permitted to put their children to death. Unlike the law concerning transgression of the covenant in Deut 17:2–7, where "the hand of the witnesses shall be on them as the first to kill them" (v 7), it is "the men of his city" alone who are commanded to stone the insubordinate son (21:21). No mention is made of the participation of the parents in the execution itself. Parents do not have the power of life and death over their children, as was the case in ancient Roman law. Judaism and Christianity do not condone such practices, though neither condemns the occasional parent who is forced to seek civil help in restraining willful children.

At the heart of the legislation here lies the need for the stability of the family. Sound family life requires the authority of the parents, upheld by respect for the law. Like disrespect for parents, disrespect for the law breeds contempt for discipline in general, whether divine or human, and the ultimate breakdown of society itself. At the same time, we do well to remember that the restraint of laws can never be so effective in the inculcation of parental respect as conversion of the heart, and the lovingkindness that comes from the enabling Spirit of God within.

B. *Ten Laws on "True Religion" and Illicit Mixtures (21:22–22:12)*

1. *Treatment of the Body of an Executed Criminal (21:22–23)*

Bibliography

Armstrong, G. T. "The Cross in the Old Testament according to Athanasius, Cyril of Jerusalem and the Cappadocian Fathers." In *Theologia Crucis, Signum Crucis: FS E. Dinkler.* Ed. C. Andresen and G. Klein. Tübingen: Mohr (Siebeck), 1979. 17–38. **Bernstein, M. J.** "כי קללת אלהים תלוי: A Study in Early Jewish Exegesis." *JQR* 74 (1983) 21–45. **Betz, O.** "Die Bedeutung der Qumranschriften für die Evangelien des Neuen Testaments." *BK* 40

(1985) 54–64. **Brichto, H. C.** *The Problem of "Curse" in the Hebrew Bible.* 1963. 191–95. **Fish, T.** "War and Religion in Ancient Mesopotamia." *BJRL* 23 (1939) 397. **Greenberg, M.** "Hanging." *IDB* 1:522. **Hengel, M.** *Crucifixion in the Ancient World and the Folly of the Message of the Cross.* Tr. J. Bowden. Philadelphia: Fortress; London: SCM Press, 1977. **Holzmeister, U.** "De Christi Crucifixione quid e Deut 21,22s. et Gal 3,13 Consequatur." *Bib* 27 (1946) 18–29. **Jacob, E.** "Die altassyrischen Gesetze und ihr Verhältnis zu den Gesetzen des Pentateuch." *Zeitschrift für vergleichende Rechtswissenschaft* 41 (1925) 384–86. **Koch, D.-A.** *Die Schrift als Zeuge des Evangeliums.* BHT 69. Tübingen: Mohr (Siebeck), 1986. 120–26. **Kooy, V. H.** "Impalement." *IDB* 2:690. **Kuhn, H.-W.** "Jesus als Gekreuzigter in der Frühchristlichen Verkündigung bis zur Mitte der 2. Jahrhunderts." *ZTK* 72 (1975) 33–35. **Lewis, T. J.** *Cults of the Dead in Ancient Israel and Ugarit.* 1989. 49–51. **Mendenhall, G. E.** *The Tenth Generation.* Baltimore: Johns Hopkins UP, 1974. 119–21. **Phillips, A.** *Ancient Israel's Criminal Law.* 1970. 25–26. **Rosso, L.** "Dt 21,22: Contributo del Rotolo del Tempio alla Valutazione di una Variante Medievale dei Settante." *RevQ* 34 (1977) 231–36. **Saggs, H. W. F.** "Assyrian Warfare in the Sargonid Period." *Iraq* 25 (1963) 149–50. **Schwartz, D. R.** "Two Pauline Allusions to the Redemptive Mechanism of the Crucifixion." *JBL* 102 (1983) 259–68. **Tuckett, C. M.** "Deuteronomy 21,23 and Paul's Conversion." In *L'Apôtre Paul.* Ed. A. Vanhoye. BETL 73. Leuven: Leuven UP, 1986. 345–50. **Unnik, W. C. van.** "Der Fluch des Gekreuzigten: Deut 21,23 in der Deutung Justinus des Märtyrers." In *Theologia Crucis, Signum Crucis: FS E. Dinkler.* Ed. C. Andresen and G. Klein. Tübingen: Mohr (Siebeck), 1979. 483–99. **Wilcox, M.** "'Upon the Tree'—Deut 21:22–23 in the New Testament." *JBL* 96 (1977) 85–99.

Translation and Prosodic Analysis

Treatment of the Body of an Executed Criminal [(4:4):(4:4)]

22 *And*[a] *when it happens that a man*\[b] *is guilty /* 10 1
of a capital offense\[c] *and he is put to death //* 10 1
and you hang him up / on a[d] *gibbet //* 13 2<u> </u>
23 *His body shall not remain overnight / on the*[a] *gibbet /* 16 2
but you shall surely bury him / on that day / <u>17</u> 2<u> </u>
For [b]*accursed of God / is a hanging person*[b] *//* 13 2
and [c]you shall not so defile[c] / your soil / 13 2
that / YHWH [ ][d] / *is giving you / as an inheritance //* [?] <u>15</u> 4<u> </u>

Notes

22.a. One Heb. MS, SP, LXX[N], and Vg. omit *waw*-conj.

22.b. Replacing *rĕbîaʿ* with a conj. accent to achieve prosodic balance in terms of the distribution of accentual stress units.

22.c. Reading *ṭip̄ḥāʾ* as conj. because of misplaced *ʾatnāḥ*.

22.d. One Heb. MS, SP, LXX[min], Tg., and *Tg. Ps.-J.* read העץ, "the tree," for MT עץ, "a tree [i.e., gibbet]."

23.a. One Heb. MS and LXX[-min] read עץ, "a tree," for MT העץ, "the tree [i.e., gibbet]."

23.b-b. SP reads תלאי for MT תלוי, "a hanged (man)," with no change in meaning. LXX reads πᾶς κρεμάμενος ἐπὶ ξύλου (= כל תלוי על עץ, "all who are hanged on a tree"). The addition may have been caused by the need to compensate in terms of prosodic balance for the secondary addition of the word אלהיך, "your God," in the second half of this verse. See discussion below under *Form/Structure/Setting.*

23.c-c. Reading 2 pl. with LXX and *Tg. Ps.-J.* as *lectio difficilior* for MT תטמא, "you [sg.] shall (not) defile."

23.d. Reading אלהיך, "your God," as a secondary expansion of the text (see discussion under *Form/Structure/Setting*).

Form/Structure/Setting

From a law on the inheritance rights of the firstborn son and one in which a son loses his rights because his conduct requires his execution, Moses moves on to an aspect of the death penalty itself. If the sentence has been carried out and the body has been exposed for public view, so that "all Israel shall hear and fear" YHWH (21:21), the corpse must be removed and buried before nightfall. Failure to do this will "defile the land that YHWH your God is giving to you as an inheritance" (v 23).

Having raised a humanitarian issue in the treatment of the corpse of an executed criminal, attention shifts to the more general issue of lost livestock (22:1–3), then to a lost garment, and then "any lost thing of your brother's" (v 3). From there the focus broadens to include coming to the assistance of an animal in need, an ass or an ox that has "fallen on the road" under the burden of its load (v 4). This focus outward "to love your neighbor [including his pack animals] as yourself" is subsequently broadened even further in laws concerning a mother bird and her young (vv 6–7), before shifting back to human beings in risk of injury by falling from a roof without a protective parapet (v 8), and finally to a concluding "riddle" in the law on making tassels "at the four corners of your cloak" (v 12).

The boundaries of the law on the hanging corpse (21:22–23) are marked with *sĕtûmā'* layout markers at the beginning and the end, and the *Numeruswechsel* in v 23 as restored from LXX and *Tg. Ps.-J.* In terms of prosodic structure, the law is in three parts, each of which has six accentual stress units. The law, which is the first of three successive laws dealing with humanitarian issues, may be outlined as follows:

A	When a man is put to death and his body hanged on a tree	21:22
B	You shall not leave the body hanging on the tree	21:23a
X	You shall bury him on that same day	21:23b
B′	For accursed by God is a hanging man	21:23c
A′	You shall not defile the land God is giving you	21:23d

The law stipulates that the corpse of an executed criminal must be buried on the same day as the execution (v 23b). The inner frame declares that his body is not to be left hanging on a tree (v 23a), for a hanged man is accursed by God (v 23c). The outer frame states the problem in plain words: when a corpse is left hanging on a tree (v 22), the land itself is defiled (v 23d).

Carmichael sees a connection between this law and the narratives of Joshua and the corpse of the king of Ai, who was "hanged . . . on a tree until evening" (Josh 8:29), and the story of the execution of Saul's sons by the Gibeonites in 2 Sam 21:1–14, when the seven corpses were not buried according to the law (*LNB*, 150–55). At the outset in the book of Joshua the focus of the eisodus is on the conquest of Jericho and Ai. After the conquest of Ai, and immediately before the renewal of the covenant at Shechem on Mount Ebal, Joshua "hanged the king of

Ai on a tree until evening; and at sunset Joshua commanded, and they took his body down from the tree, threw it down at the entrance of the gate of the city, and raised over it a great heap of stones, which stands there to this day" (Josh 8:29 NRSV). Immediately following, Joshua built an altar on Mount Ebal and erected plastered stones on which a copy of the laws of Deuteronomy were displayed for the people of Israel to read (Josh 8:30–32; cf. Deut 27:2–4). A bit later in the narrative in Joshua we read of the defeat of the five Canaanite kings who hid themselves in the cave at Makkedah (Josh 10:16). Joshua "put them to death, and he hung them on five trees. And they hung on the trees until evening. At sunset Joshua commanded, and they took them down from the trees and threw them into the cave where they had hidden themselves; they set large stones against the mouth of the cave, which remain to this very day" (Josh 10:26–27 NRSV).

In between these two accounts of Joshua and the law of "the hanging corpse" we find the story of the Gibeonites, who tricked Israel into making a covenant treaty with them (Josh 9). Much later, after King Saul "put the Gibeonites to death" (2 Sam 21:1), King David sought to make atonement for Saul's sin with those who remained in Gibeon. In response to their request, David delivered seven of Saul's sons (some were grandsons) "into the hands of the Gibeonites, and they hanged them on the mountain before the LORD" (2 Sam 21:9). But in this instance the bodies were not buried according to the law of Deuteronomy. Thus, according to the laws of Deuteronomy, the land was defiled.

Much as the law of an insubordinate son was used in the subsequent literary development of the narrative story of the Torah and Former Prophets to anticipate a surprisingly negative view of "Israel," so the law of the hanging corpse was used to portray a surprisingly negative assessment of the kingdom of David (Carmichael, *LNB*, 146–55).

At first glance, the evidence assembled by Labuschagne on the use of the divine-name numbers in 21:22–23 reveals very little. But when the text is modified in light of the prosodic analysis by omitting the word אלהיך, "your God," in the second half of v 23, fascinating results emerge that may be summarized as follows:

Words:	before *'atnāḥ*		after *'atnāḥ*				
21:18	12	+	5		=	17	
21:20–21	20	+	6		=	26	
21:22–23	21	+	13		=	34	(= 2 × 17)
21:18–23	57	+	32		=	89	
21:10–23	133	+	85	(= 5 × 17)	=	218	
21:10–25:19	929	+	652		=	1,581	(= 93 × 17)

In the previous law on the punishment of an insubordinate son (21:18–21), Labuschagne observed that both of the divine-name numbers appear with a total of 17 words in v 18 and 26 words in vv 20–21. When this law is combined with the law on the treatment of the body of an executed criminal (21:22–23) to form a literary unit, we find 32 words after *'atnāḥ*, signifying the numerical value of the Hebrew כבוד, "glory" (= 20 + 2 + 6 + 4 = 32). In the larger literary context we now find a total of 85 (= 5 × 17) words after *'atnāḥ* in 21:10–23. But of greater significance, we find a total of 1,581 (= 93 × 17) words in the whole of the sixth weekly portion in the lectionary cycle of readings in Deuteronomy (21:10–25:19). In their "commentary" on the Ten Commandments, the scribes ("counters") of ancient Israel carefully counted the words and arranged them in a manner to bear witness to the divine name YHWH—to the glory of God.

Comment

22 The phrase "hang him up on a gibbet" refers to exposing the body of the executed for public display (cf. Gen 40:19; Josh 10:26; Esth 9:6–14). The body of an executed criminal was sometimes impaled or hanged for public display on a tree or wooden post, as a deterrent to warn others of the consequence of their actions. Though it is common to interpret the action as impaling the body on a stake (so JPS *Tanakh*), Tigay has shown that this is probably not what is meant: "According to the Mishnah a gibbet (a pole with a horizontal beam) was erected and the dead man's hands were bound and slung over the beam, leaving his body suspended" ([1996] 198). See the account of the execution of the sons of Rizpah who were hanged on a mountain, with their bodies left exposed for "the birds of the air to come upon them by day, or the beasts of the field by night" (2 Sam 21:10).

23 The text restricts the practice of exposing the bodies of executed criminals: "His body shall not remain all night on the gibbet; for you shall surely bury him on that day." *Antigone,* the classical tragedy by Sophocles (ca. 440 B.C.E.), represents a parallel in the literature of ancient Greece on the seriousness of the curse of being denied a proper burial. The daughter of Oedipus and Jocasta defied her Uncle Creon's decree and performed the forbidden funeral rites for her dead brother, Polynices, at the cost of her own life. (For Mesopotamian evidence, see Epic of Gilgamesh 12:151–52 [*ANET,* 99a]; Code of Hammurabi §153 [*ANET,* 172b]; Middle Assyrian Laws §53 [*ANET,* 185a]; Prism of Sennacherib ii.37–iii.49 [*ANET,* 288a]; and Annals of Ashurbanipal iv.65–82 [*ANET,* 288b]. On other parallels in the Greco-Roman world, see *Iliad* 23.72–74 and *Aeneid* 6.324–30.) The translation of the phrase "accursed of God" (קללה אלהים) has produced comment and speculation through the years. Phillips has rendered it "repudiation of God" (*Ancient Israel's Criminal Law,* 25–26), and Fox translates it as "an insult to God" (*FBM,* 945). It is better to follow the traditional interpretation "accursed of God," as read by the apostle Paul (see Gal 3:13). Craigie put it well: "The body was not accursed of God because it was hanging on a tree; it was hanging on the tree because it was accursed of God." Death by execution "was a formal and terminal separation from the community of God's people. Hence the use of this verse in Paul's Epistle to the Galatians is very forceful. Christ took upon himself the curse of the law, the penalty of death, thereby redeeming us from the curse of the law. . . . His separation from the family of God made possible our admission to the family of God, because the curse of the broken law—which would have permanently barred admission—had been removed" ([1976] 285–86).

That the term אלהים alone is used in the laws of Deuteronomy as a reference to God only here and in 25:18 led Sforno to conclude that it does not mean "God" here but rather the "spirit of the dead man that is affronted by the impaled body" (see Tigay [1996] 198). The meaning of the verb תטמא<ו> shifts from "you shall become ceremonially unclean" to "you shall pollute" as the reader/hearer moves on to the words "your soil" (את־אדמתך), which introduce the final clause: "that YHWH your God is giving you as an inheritance." The statement "you shall not so defile the soil" refers to the fact that a dead body is a source of pollution in terms of ritual uncleanness. Allowing the body to decompose and to be scattered by birds and beasts would spread the impurity.

Explanation

The hanging of persons by the neck until dead was not practiced in ancient Israel, but it was common to display the corpse of an executed criminal upon a post or a tree as a spectacle for all to see, so as to strike terror in others. What is prescribed here is that no matter what time of day bodies were so displayed, they must be taken down at sunset and buried, lest the land itself be defiled. According to the law, touching a dead body was defiling; therefore dead bodies must not be left hanging, because, by this same rule, that would defile the land.

The statement that "accursed by God is a hanged man" (v 23) is taken up by Paul in reference to the death of Jesus Christ (Gal 3:13), who has "redeemed us from the curse of the law, having become a curse for us." Though Moses used the words in reference to the ignominious treatment of an executed criminal, he said more than he knew. As Bishop Patrick observed long ago, "this passage is applied to the death of Christ, not only because he bare our sins and was exposed to shame, as these malefactors were that were accursed of God, but because he was in the evening taken down from the accursed tree and buried, (and that by the particular care of the Jews, with an eye to this law, John 19:31) in token that now, the guilt being removed, the law was satisfied, as it was when the malefactor had hanged till sunset; it demanded no more. Then he ceased to be a curse, and those that are his. And as the land of Israel was pure and clean, when the dead body was buried, so the church is washed and cleansed by the complete satisfaction which thus Christ made" (quoted by Matthew Henry, *An Exposition of the Old and New Testament* [1828] 660).

2. Three Laws on "True Religion"—Loving Your Neighbor as Yourself (22:1–5)

Bibliography for 22:1–4

Barbiero, G. *L'Asino del Nemico: Rinuncia alla vendetta e amore del nemico nella legislatione dell'Antico Testamento (Es 23,4–5; Dt 22,1–4; Lv 19,17–18)*. AnBib 128. Rome: Pontifical Biblical Institute, 1991. 131–202, 340–42. **Braulik, G.** "Die dekalogische Redaktion der deuteronomischen Gesetze: Ihre Abhängigkeit von Levitikus 19 am Beispiel von

Deuteronomium 22,1–12; 24,10–22; 25,13–16." In *Studien zum Buch Deuteronomium.* Ed. G. Braulik. 1997. 147–82, esp. 160–61. **Canaan, T.** "The Palestinian Arab House." *JPOS* 13 (1933) 41–42, 70. **Daube, D.** "The Culture of Deuteronomy." *Orita* 3 (1969) 41–43. **Dempster, S.** "The Deuteronomic Formula *kî yimmāṣē'* in the Light of Biblical and Ancient Near Eastern Law: An Evaluation of David Daube's Theory." *RB* 91 (1984) 188–211. **Fishbane, M.** *Biblical Interpretation in Ancient Israel.* 1985. 177–79. **Haase, R.** "Zur Anzeigepflicht des Finders nach Hethitischem Recht." *WO* 12 (1957) 378–81. **Huffmon, H. B.** "Exodus 23:4–5: A Comparative Study." In *FS J. M. Myers.* 1974. 271–78. **Lang, B.** "Persönlicher Gott und Ortsgott: Über Elementarformen der persönlichen Frömmigkeit in Israel." In *FS H. Brunner.* 1983. 282–89. **Lewy, I.** "Dating of Covenant Code Sections on Humaneness and Righteousness (Ex xxii 20–26; xxiii 1–9)." *VT* 7 (1957) 322–26. **Stager, L.** "The Archaeology of the Family in Ancient Israel." *BASOR* 260 (1985) 12–15. **Tigay, J. H.** "Some Archaeological Notes on Deuteronomy." In *FS J. Milgrom.* 1995. 373–74.

Bibliography for 22:5

Epstein, L. M. *Sex Laws and Customs in Judaism.* New York: Bloch, 1948. 64–67, 75–78. **Fichtner, J.** "Die Bewältigung heidnischer Vorstellungen und Praktiken in der Welt des Alten Testaments." In *FS F. Baumgärtel.* Ed. L. Rost. Erlanger Forschungen A.10. Erlangen: Universitätsbibliothek, 1959. 32. **Gaster, T. H.** *Myth, Legend, and Custom in the Old Testament.* New York: Harper & Row, 1969. 316–18. **Good, E. M.** "Capital Punishment and Its Alternatives in Ancient Near Eastern Law." *SLR* 19 (1967) 960. **Gordon, C. H.** "A Note on the Tenth Commandment." *JBR* 31 (1963) 208–9. **Hoffner, H. A.** "Some Contributions of Hittitology to Old Testament Study." *TynBul* 20 (1969) 48–51. ———. "Symbols for Masculinity and Femininity." *JBL* 85 (1966) 326–34. **Lambert, W. G.** *Babylonian Wisdom Literature.* Oxford: Clarendon, 1960. 226–30. **Licht, H.** *Sexual Life in Ancient Greece.* London: Routledge and Kegan Paul, 1932. 124–25, 128, 500. **Paschen, W.** *Rein und Unrein: Untersuchungen zur biblischen Wortgeschichte.* SANT 24. Munich: Kösel, 1970. 55. **Römer, W. H. P.** "Randbemerkungen zur Travestie von Deut. 22,5." In *Travels in the World of the Old Testament: FS M. A. Beek.* Ed. M. Heerma van Voss, P. Houwink ten Cate, and N. van Uchelen. Studia Semitica Neerlandica 16. Assen: Van Gorcum, 1974. 217–22.

Translation and Prosodic Analysis

Returning Lost Animals and Other Property [(8:5):(5:8)]

1 *You are not to see your brother's ox /*	13	1
or / his sheep[a] */ go astray / and hide yourself / from them //*	21	5
you shall take them back / to your brother //	15	2_
2 *And if your brother is not near / you /*	18	2
and you do not know him //	7	1
you shall bring it / into the midst of your house /	12	2_
And it is to remain with you / until your brother claims / it[a] */*	21	3
and you shall return it\[b] *to him //*	10	1
3 *and*[a] *thus you shall do with his ass /*	12	1_
And thus you shall do / with his garment /	12	2
and thus you shall do /	6	1
with any lost thing of your brother's /	11	1
That is lost by him / and you find it //	16	2
you are not allowed / to hide yourself // ס	10	2_

Assisting Your Neighbor with Fallen Pack Animals [3:4]

4 *If you see your brother's ass / or*[a] *his ox /* 19 2
fallen on the road // 8 1
You shall not withhold your help / from them // 9 2
you shall help him / lift them up // ס 11 2

Not Wearing Clothing of the Opposite Sex [4:3]

5 *Things pertaining to a man shall not be worn / by a woman /* 13 2
and a man shall not wear / a woman's garment // 12 2
For it is an abomination / to YHWH your God / 15 2
anyone doing these things // פ 8 1

Notes

1.a. The accent here is read as the conj. *mahpāk.* SP adds או את כל בהמתו, "or any of his animals." Prosodic analysis supports MT.

2.a. SP adds מעמך, "from your people." Prosodic analysis favors MT.

2.b. Reading *ṭip̱ḥāʾ* as conj. because of misplaced *sillûq.*

3.a. The *waw*-conj. is omitted in a few Heb. MSS, SP, Syr., and Vg.

4.a. Three Heb. MSS, SP, and Tg.[MS] add את.

Form/Structure/Setting

The humanitarian concern introduced by the previous law on the treatment of the corpse of an executed criminal is here extended to living human beings and their lost property or fallen pack animals. The five laws in 22:1–8 may be outlined in a five-part concentric structure:

A	Returning your brother's lost property	22:1–3
B	Assisting fallen animals	22:4
X	Not wearing clothing of the opposite sex	22:5
B′	Not capturing a mother bird with her young	22:6–7
A′	Building a parapet around the roof of one's house	22:8

The outer frame in this structure moves from a law on returning a neighbor's lost property (vv 1–3), to a law regarding one's own property to protect the welfare of a neighbor by building a protective wall around the edge of the roof of one's house (v 8). The inner frame here moves from a law expressing concern for the welfare of domestic animals, by assisting a fallen ass or ox (v 4), to a parallel law expressing concern for the welfare of a mother bird in the wild (vv 6–7). In the center we find, once again, an enigmatic law on not wearing the clothing of the opposite sex, which law poses a riddle of sorts (v 5).

The topic of adultery, on which the larger literary unit of 21:10–23:1 is based, is extended to include illicit mixtures in general in a series of four laws, the first of which (22:5) applies to human beings and the other three (22:9–11) to seeds, plow animals, and textiles. Like the law of the insubordinate son (21:18–21), all four of these laws have produced much comment, reflection, and modification in subsequent Jewish tradition.

The boundaries of the three laws on returning lost animals and other items (22:1–3), assisting fallen pack animals (22:4), and not wearing clothing of the opposite sex (22:5) are marked with *sĕtûmāʾ* layout markers after 21:23 and 22:3 and 4 and the *pĕtûḥāʾ* layout marker after 22:5. On the basis of content, 22:1–4 may be outlined as follows:

A	If your brother's ox or sheep goes astray, lend him your help	22:1
B	If the owner is not known, take care of it as your own	22:2abc
X	When your brother claims it, give it back to him	22:2d
B′	Do the same for his ass, garment, or any lost thing	22:3
A′	If your brother's ass or ox falls in the way, help him	22:4

The outer frame presents two parallel situations of need: an ox or sheep of one's neighbor that has strayed (v 1), and an ass or an ox that has fallen under its load (v 4). In both instances the person is commanded to come to his neighbor's aid. The inner frame extends the situation into more complex situations: where the owner is not known, the person is to take care of the animal until it is claimed (v 2); and the principle extends to other animals, even clothing, or anything that is lost (v 3). When such lost items are claimed by the rightful owner, they are to be returned (v 2d).

In *BHS* and *BHK* the boundary separating the brief law on assisting a brother with fallen pack animals (v 4) from the law forbidding the wearing of clothing of the opposite sex (v 5) is a bit misleading. L has a major indentation at the beginning of v 4, much the same as for 21:22; 22:1, 9, 11, and 12; but there is no major break at the end of the verse. Here the situation is similar to that of 22:8, 10, and 13, with a break in the middle of the line. There is a difference, however, in that the upper tail of the *lamed* in the next line fills up most of the blank space such that at first glance there appears to be no major break indicated at all. According to Tigay, SP indicates a significant break between vv 5 and 6, but not between vv 4 and 5 ([1996] 383 n. 1).

The manner in which the text is laid out in L suggests that vv 4 and 5 are to be connected as a literary unit in two parts. Such a reading lends support to the suggestion by Carmichael (*LNB*, 160–64), who interprets both laws within the context of the wars in Transjordan in which the tribes of Reuben and Gad received their tribal allotment in the days of Moses. He suggests that the Hebrew phrase כלי־גבר is a "type of deliberate confusion in the context of war." For him, "a transvestite ruse constitutes an example of secret sinning in this context of avoiding military service and would, in the words of the law, be properly described as 'an abomination to Yahweh'" (*LNB*, 162). Moses is thus warning the Reubenites and Gadites that they should not seek to avoid their obligation by the men disguising themselves in women's clothing, so as to remain behind, nor should the women choose to accompany their husbands by taking up the military paraphernalia of men.

The laws of returning lost animals and assisting fallen ones (Deut 22:1–4) have their narrative analogue in the cattle of the Reubenites and the Gadites in Carmichael's reading (*LNB*, 155–59). As Carmichael put it, the tradition in Num 32 brings out "the need for brother Israelites to help one another out, to reciprocate so that a brother's inheritance is made secure. The Reubenites and

Gadites did go to help out their fellow Israelites, and hence it was reasonable to imagine how Moses could have raised the question as to when a reciprocal service might be rendered to them in the future. In that they possessed many animals their brothers could help in protecting them" (*LNB*, 158).

Labuschagne's study of the use of the divine-name numbers in 22:1–5 lends support to the two-part structure that emerged in the prosodic analysis:

Words:	before *ʾatnāḥ*		after *ʾatnāḥ*		
22:1–3	33	+	18	=	51 (= 3 × 17)
22:4–5	22	+	10	=	32

The divine-name number 17 is intensified in the first subsection, with its total word count of 51 (= 3 × 17). The 32 words in the second subsection signify the "glory" of YHWH, since this is the numerical value of the word כבוד, "glory."

Comment

1 The reference to "your brother," which appears five times in vv 1–4, emphasizes kinship with the person in need in the broadest sense of being a fellow Israelite. In the parallel passage of Exod 23:4–5, one must help even one's enemy in such circumstances. The command not to "hide yourself from them" (והתעלמת מהם) refers to open and active help in circumstances of a neighbor in need. Quiescence is expressly forbidden. Craigie translated the verb התעלם as "take no notice," arguing that it demonstrates "the spirit of the Hebrew law. Unlike Babylonian law, it is not concerned primarily with a criminal act . . . rather it deals with shouldering responsibility as a member of the covenant community" ([1976] 287).

2–3 Even if the owner is unknown—"you do not know him"—the responsibility stands. The finder is to bring the animal to his own home and keep it there, provide for it as if it were his own, "until your brother claims it." The list of what is included in this law is inclusive: livestock (ox and sheep), major beast of burden (ass), clothing, and "any (other) lost thing of your brother's." On the statement "you are not allowed to hide yourself," see the discussion in v 1. To fulfill the demands of the law here "requires an inner attitude which makes such activity cheerfully possible" (G. E. Wright, *IB* 2:464).

4 The "ass" (חמור) and the "ox" (שור) were common beasts of burden, which on occasion collapsed under their load and lay there "fallen in the road" (cf. Exod 23:5).

5 The law on transvestism (22:5) is brief and enigmatic. Some scholars have noted that here the term כלי־גבר, "things pertaining to a man," could just as well be translated as the "gear of a warrior." As K.-M. Beyse has noted (*TDOT* 7:173), the term כלי in reference to clothing occurs only in legal texts, but the sole text he cites without qualification to demonstrate its use in this manner is Deut 22:5, and then only on the basis of the fact that the verse includes a parallel line that forbids men to wear female clothing (שמלת אשה). The use of the word in 1:41 in the phrase כלי מלחמתו, "his weapons of war," is illustrative, for the word גבר always "contains the element of strength, especially in a general sense" (H. Kosmala,

TDOT 2:377). The use of the term in the Song of Deborah (Judg 5:30), where the RSV reads, "a maiden [womb] or two for every man [גבר]," represents the coarse language of soldiers according to *HAL*. Though such actions are described as "an abomination to YHWH," it is not clear what the reasons for this law were. Römer has collected interesting examples of transvestism and related matters from Mesopotamian sources (*FS M. A. Beek*, 217–22). For references to transvestism in the Greco-Roman period, see Driver ([1895] 250). Craigie presents an interesting quotation that merits repetition: "Again, in some religions, it has been the custom for priests to assume a quasi-female or even completely female garb, and . . . this usually occurred when the deity was a goddess rather than a god" (Craigie [1976] 288 n. 5, citing C. Allen, *A Textbook of Psychosexual Disorders* [London: Oxford UP, 1962] 243).

Explanation

Though the original meaning of the term "brother" in the law of returning lost animals (22:1–3) and assisting fallen ones (22:4) referred to fellow Israelites, it applies to any human being in need, as Jesus demonstrated in his definition of the term "neighbor" in the parable of the good Samaritan (Luke 10:29–37). The law here is essentially that of the Golden Rule to do to others what we would have them do to us. Moreover, we ought not to let trouble and expense prevent us from doing a kind action to a neighbor in need; nor are we permitted to retain lost property we have found when there is a possibility of finding the rightful owner.

If a merciful person is to assist another's lost or fallen beast of burden, how much more should we hasten to the relief of a neighbor who has fallen into distress or poverty? The dangerous days in which we live have caused some to ignore the needs of those we meet. Stories of those who have been victimized by stopping to help others enable us to rationalize why it is wiser not to get involved, and so we pass on by—as did the priest and the Levite in Jesus' story of the good Samaritan. We do well to remember that our neighbor is anyone in true need, whether friend or foe.

The law in 22:5 has been the source of considerable debate and difference of opinion in both Jewish and Christian circles. At first glance it appears to forbid the practice of transvestism, a form of sexual behavior characterized by wearing clothing appropriate to the opposite sex. The law is without parallel in the Torah, and the Hebrew words translated "things pertaining to a man" (כלי גבר) do not refer specifically to male clothing, but to ornaments, weapons, and other items as well.

Craigie has called attention to two possibilities, either of which might help to explain the remark that the behavior in question is an abomination to YHWH. "First, transvestism tends to be associated with certain forms of homosexuality; second, in the ancient world, it is probable that transvestite practices were associated with the cults of certain deities" ([1976] 288). In either case transvestism would be "an abomination to YHWH your God" (cf. Lev 18:22; 20:13 and Deut 7:25; 18:12).

But we have no certainty as to what lay behind this particular law. The folly in taking a hard stand on a surface reading of the text is well illustrated in older commentaries, such as that of Thomas Scott: "Let stage-players and others of similar occupations well consider, (among many other and great evils connected with their line of life,) how they will answer to God, for their continual violation of this express commandment. . . . and let young people remember that this change of apparel is not to be considered as a frolic, but as an act of rebellion against God" (*Holy Bible* [1823] 1:540). In this regard, the portrayal of Mrs. Doubtfire by Robin Williams in the movie of that name or Tootsie by Dustin Hoffman would be considered a glaring abomination to YHWH.

However one chooses to interpret the specific meaning of this prohibition against wearing clothing of the opposite sex, it is difficult to make a case against transvestism in matters of detail on the basis of this one isolated text, the purpose of which within the culture of ancient Israel remains enigmatic.

3. Not Capturing a Mother Bird along with Her Young (22:6–7)

Bibliography

Carmichael, C. M. "Forbidden Mixtures." *VT* 32 (1982) 395–415. ———. *The Laws of Deuteronomy.* 1974. 151–56. **Daube, D.** "Direct and Indirect Causation in Biblical Law." *VT* 11 (1961) 251. 283–94, esp. 286. **Haran, M.** "Biblical Studies: The Kid in Its Mother's Milk and the Kid Who Sucks Its Mother's Milk." *Tarbiz* 52 (1982/83) 371–92 (Heb.). **Henry, M.-L.** *Das Tier im religiösen Bewusstsein des alttestamentlichen Menschen.* Sammlung gemeinverständlicher Vorträge und Schriften aus dem Gebiet der Theologie und Religionsgeschichte 220/221. Tübingen: Mohr, 1958. **Johnston, R. M.** "The Least of the Commandments: Deuteronomy 22:6–7 in Rabbinic Judaism and Early Christianity." *AUSS* 20 (1982) 205–15. **Keel, O.** *Das Böcklein in der Milch seiner Mutter und Verwandtes im Lichte eines altorientalischen Bildmotivs.* OBO 33. Freiburg: Universitätsverlag, 1980. **Nielsen, E.** "'You Shall Not Muzzle an Ox While It Is Treading out the Corn,' Dt. 25,4." In *Law, History and Tradition.* 1983. 94–105. **Peacock, H. F.** "Deut 22,7." *BT* 27 (1976) 246–47. **Toeg, A.** "שלוח הקן." *EM* 7:634–36.

Translation and Prosodic Analysis

Not Capturing a Mother Bird along with Her Young [(6:4):(4:6)]

6 *When you chance upon a bird's nest / before you /* 17 2
in the way / in any tree / 7 2
or on the ground / with fledglings \[a] *or eggs /* 19 2
And the mother is sitting / on the fledglings / 17 2
or / on the eggs // 8 2
You shall not take away the mother / with the young ones // 14 2

7 *you shall surely release / the mother /* 12 2
And the young ones / you may take for yourself // 11 2
that / it may go well with you / 8 2
and you may prolong / your days // ס 9 2_

Notes

6.a. Reading *paštā'* followed by *zāqēp qāṭôn* as conj.

Form/Structure/Setting

As noted above in the discussion of 21:22–22:4, the laws on not capturing a mother bird with her young (22:6–7) and building a parapet around the roof of one's house (22:8) are part of a series of six laws that are placed under the general topic of what I have called "true religion." They stand at the structural center of the larger literary unit of 21:10–23:1.

The law on sparing a mother bird extends the principle of humanitarian concern beyond that of domestic animals that are the property of human beings to animal life in general. God's people are commanded to carry the principle of protecting and providing for the poor and vulnerable in need even to insignificant animals that are part of the normal food supply. In the law of the parapet (22:8) the focus returns to the human sphere, where the concern is to prevent a person from having a fatal accident.

The law of the mother bird (22:6–7) is often compared to the laws of Lev 22:27–28, "When a bull or sheep or goat is born, it shall remain seven days with its mother. . . . And whether the mother is a cow or a ewe, you shall not kill both her and her young in one day." It is argued that the reverence for the parent-child relationship is extended to animals. The same motive is often used to explain the prohibition of boiling a kid in its mother's milk (14:21). It should be noted, however, that the law of the mother bird is in the center of a concentric structure and that the rule of the "riddle at the middle" applies to its interpretation.

The boundaries of the law of the mother bird (22:6–7) are marked with the *sětûmā'* layout markers at the beginning and the end. At the same time, it should be noted that L appears to make a structural connection between vv 7 and 8. Though the prosodic analysis presented above scans vv 6–7 as a 6:4:4:6 prosodic unit, in terms of syntactic accentual stress units, it is also possible to read vv 6–8 as a 7:6:6:7 rhythmic unit in which the *zāqēp qāṭôn*, which was read as a conjunctive accent in v 6, is read as disjunctive. Moreover, such a reading corresponds exactly with the versification in *BHS:*

6 When you chance upon a bird's nest / before you / in the way / 20 3
in any tree / or on the ground / with fledglings / 17 3
or eggs / 6 1_
And the mother is sitting / on the fledglings / or / the eggs // 25 4
you shall not take the mother / with the young ones // 14 2_
7 You shall surely release / the mother / 12 2
and the young ones \ you may take for yourself // 11 1
that / it may go well with you / and you may live long // 18 3_

8 When you build / a new house /	10	2
you shall make a parapet / for your roof //	13	2
that you do not bring bloodguilt / on your house /	16	2
if anyone should fall from it //	<u>14</u>	1_

This particular prosodic analysis suggests that the two very different laws in vv 6–7 and 8 belong together to form a single literary unit, at least in one particular reading. At the same time, it should be noted that v 8 is also closely tied to v 9 and the following section on illicit mixtures. In other words, v 8 forms a rhythmic bridge connecting vv 6–7 with 9–12.

The relationship of vv 6–7 to v 8 may be outlined within a concentric structure that extends from v 5 through v 11:

A	Illicit mixtures: transvestism	22:5
B	If you find a bird's nest, release the mother and keep the young	22:6–7a
X	That it may go well with you and you may prolong your life	22:7b
B′	When you build a new house, make a parapet for the roof	22:8
A′	Three laws on illicit mixtures: seed, plow animals, and textiles	22:9–11

A brief quotation taken from the fifth commandment to honor one's parents (5:16) stands at the center of this structure. The inner frame presents two parallel actions that will serve to achieve the blessing in the center. On the one hand, we find the release of the mother bird (vv 6–7); and on the other we find the building of the parapet around the edge of the roof of one's house (v 8). Both acts are humanitarian in nature: one toward the animal world, and the other toward human beings. The outer frame moves from the first law of illicit mixtures, which pertains to human beings (v 5), to a set of three laws on illicit mixtures, which concern the nonhuman world (vv 9–11).

Carmichael argues that the conventional interpretations of the law on sparing the mother bird leave many questions unanswered. "The law is manifestly interested in the question of what to kill and what not to kill; in particular, the view is that killing in a selective way means that an important life is preserved" (*LNB*, 166).

A close reading of the language of the law itself has led Carmichael to an interesting series of texts to explain the meaning of this law. The niphal use of the verb קרא at the outset appears elsewhere of hostile encounters, as D. Daube has shown (*Suddenness and Awe in Scripture* [London: Robert Waley Cohen Memorial Lecture, Council of Christians and Jews, 1963] 6–10). For instance, when Absalom "met" (וַיִּקָּרֵא) the servants of David (2 Sam 18:9), violence was anticipated.

The mention of "the mother with the children" has parallels in two other contexts that involve violent confrontation. In the story of Jacob's return to the land of Canaan, just before his encounter with Esau and his four hundred men, Jacob's prayer for deliverance includes these words in Gen 32:12 (Eng. 32:11): "for I am afraid of him; he may come and kill us all, the mothers with the children [אם על־הבנים]" (NRSV). See also Hos 10:14. The same image appears in Greek literature, as Carmichael has observed (*LNB,* 167 n. 6; Apollodorus, *Epitome* 3.15; Homer, *Iliad* 2.299–330).

The most instructive parallel discussed by Carmichael is found in two stories of David in which cities are compared to a mother, and its inhabitants to her children, where the central issue is the question of whom to kill and whom not to kill (see also D. M. Gunn, *The Story of King David,* JSOTSup 6 [Sheffield: Sheffield UP, 1978] 39–40). In the story of Sheba's rebellion (2 Sam 20:1–22), the wise woman of Abel of Beth-maacah makes a curious reference to "a city that is a mother in Israel" (v 19 NRSV). Sheba had taken refuge within that city and Joab had come to get him. The woman's response to Joab's request that Sheba alone be given over to him was forthright: "His head shall be thrown over the wall to you" (v 21 NRSV). The second incident involves another wise woman, Abigail, the wife of Nabal (1 Sam 25). David's intended attack on Nabal's household was primarily to obtain food, which Abigail supplied to forestall bloodshed. For Carmichael, "Such a desirable consequence is the aim of the law on the bird's nest, just as it is for the following law about blood on a new house" (*LNB,* 173).

It would appear that those who composed the stories of David made use of the law of the sparing of the mother bird as a structuring motif. The law on the treatment of the body of an executed criminal (Deut 21:22–23) was used to structure the movement of the narrative from the conquest of Ai to the renewal of the covenant at Shechem. But when David gave up the seven sons of Saul to the Gibeonites, the law was violated and consequently the land was defiled. In short, the law on not capturing a mother bird with her young was used to structure the account of David's military activity.

According to Carmichael (*LNB,* 176–80), the law of the parapet is connected with the narrative of the transition from the kingdom of David to that of his son Solomon. When David was on his deathbed, he ordered his son Solomon to execute Joab for the murder of Amasa (1 Kgs 2:5–6) and of Shimei for cursing David at the time of Abasalom's rebellion (1 Kigs 2:8–9). The death of Joab was justified on the grounds that he had murdered Abner and Amasa, "retaliating in time of peace for blood that had been shed in war, and putting the blood of war on the belt around his waist, and on the sandals on his feet" (1 Kgs 2:5 NRSV). The law requiring an Israelite to build a parapet on the roof of his new house in the new land was used to shape the story of David and Solomon. The blood shed by Joab "remained a problem for David's house (in a symbolic sense), and [its] removal was vital for the establishment of Solomon's house (both symbolic and actual)" (*LNB,* 180).

The law of the bird's nest with its interest in "mother with children" was used to shape the traditions relating to David and the establishment of his dynasty; whereas the law on the new house was used to shape the tradition about the succession of Solomon and the building of his new house. The purpose of the parapet was "that you may not bring the guilt of blood upon your house" (Deut 22:8). Solomon justified the execution of Joab with these words: "and thus take away from me and from my father's house the guilt for the blood which Joab shed without cause" (1 Kgs 2:31).

The evidence from Labuschagne's "logotechnische analyse" for 22:6–7 is as follows:

Words:	before *ʾatnāḥ*		after *ʾatnāḥ*		
22:6	21	+	5	=	26
22:6–7	29	+	10	=	39

There are 26 words in v 6. Moreover, the total of 39 words in vv 6–7 is divided into 26 words in main clauses and 13 words in subordinate clauses. Once again, the divine-name number 26 is carefully woven into the fabric of the Hebrew text.

Comment

6–7 The term "fledglings" (אפרחים) appears also in Job 39:30 (of fledgling birds of prey) and Ps 84:4 (Eng. 3) (of the young of a sparrow and a swallow). The phrase "the mother with the young ones" (האם על־בנים) is also used in contexts of war (Hos 10:14) and of Jacob's fear of what Esau might do to his family on his return to the land of Canaan (Gen 32:12 [11]). It appears to have been a common expression for wanton killing. The expression "you shall surely release [שלח תשלח] the mother" has been interpreted as meaning either "release" or "chase away," so that the mother would not see her young taken away (Maimonides, *Guide* 3.48; citation from Tigay [1996] 383 n. 17). The clause "that it may go well with you and you may prolong your life" appears earlier in the conclusion of the fifth commandment to honor one's parents (Deut 5:16), but in reverse order. "Inversion of clauses often indicates an intentional allusion to earlier passages in biblical literature. This allusion calls attention to the fact that the present command is likewise an aspect of respecting a parent" (Tigay [1996] 201). In his expression, "exchanging a long-term profit for an immediate gain," Craigie ([1976] 289) used language from the commercial world to say what some of the Jewish sages noted in times past. To kill the mother removes a capital asset, a future means of supplying more food.

Explanation

The law fosters reverence for the parent-child relationship even among the animals. As Matthew Henry put it, "The remembrance of this may, perhaps, some time or other, keep us from doing a hard or unkind thing to those whom we have at our mercy" (*An Exposition of the Old and New Testament* [1828] 661).

An entirely different kind of meaning is found in this law when interpreted along the lines that Carmichael has proposed: killing in a selective way means that an important life is preserved. When the high priest Caiaphas said "it is better for you to have one man die for the people than to have the whole nation destroyed" (John 11:50 NRSV), he spoke to the same issue. According to the Gospel account, Jesus died that we might live.

4. *Five Laws on "True Religion" and Illicit Mixtures (22:8–12)*

Bibliography

Ahituv, S. "*sha'atnez.*" *EM.* 8:228–29. **Boecker, H. J.** "'Du sollst dem Ochsen, der da drischt, das Maul nicht verbinden': Überlegungen zur Wertung der Natur im Alten Testament." In *FS F. Lang.* 1978. 72–89. **Braulik, G.** "Die dekalogische Redaktion der deuteronomischen Gesetze: Ihre Abhängigkeit von Levitikus 19 am Beispiel von Deuteronomium 22,1–12; 24, 10–22; 25,13–16." In *Studien zum Buch Deuteronomium.* Ed. G. Braulik. 1997. 147–82, esp. 153–60. **Dommen, A. J.** *Innovation in African Agriculture.* Boulder, CO: Westview, 1988 (see "intercropping" in index). **Douglas, M.** *Purity and Danger.* London: Routledge and Kegan Paul, 1980. **Fensham, F. C.** "Liability in Case of Negligence in the Old Testament Covenant Code and Ancient Legal Traditions." In *Acta Juridica 1976: FS B. Beinart.* Cape Town: Juta, 1978. 283–94. **Goldziher, I.** "Zu Šaaṭnêz." *ZAW* 20 (1900) 36–37. **Görg, M.** "Eine rätselhafte Textilbezeichnung im Alten Testament." *BN* 12 (1980) 13–17. **Greenstein, E. L.** "Biblical Law." In *Back to the Sources: Reading the Classic Jewish Texts.* Ed. B. W. Holtz. New York: Summit, 1984. 83–103. **Haran, M.** *Temples and Temple Service.* Oxford: Clarendon, 1978. 160–62, 212. **Hopkins, D. C.** *Highlands of Canaan.* SWBA 3. Sheffield: Almond, 1985. 284–85. **Houtman, C.** "Another Look at Forbidden Mixtures." *VT* 34 (1984) 226–28. **Lambdin, T. O.** "Egyptian Loan Words in the Old Testament." *JAOS* 73 (1953) 145–55. **Loss, N. M.** "A Proposito di Lev 19,19b e di Deut 22,10." *RBiblt* 6 (1959) 361–64. **Milgrom, J.** "Excursus 38: The Tassels 'Tsitsit.'" In *Numbers.* 1990. 410–14. **Noonan, J. T.** "The Muzzled Ox." *JQR* 70 (1979) 172–75. **Paschen, W.** *Rein und Unrein.* Munich: Kosel, 1970. 55. **Rüterswörden, U.** "צמד." *TWAT* 6:1072–75. **Sheffer, A.** "The Textiles." In *Kuntillet Ajrud.* Ed. Z. Meshel. Jerusalem: Israel Museum, 1978.

Translation and Prosodic Analysis

Building a Parapet on the Roof of One's House [5]

8 *When you build*\\[a] *a new house /* 10 1
you shall make a parapet\\[b] *for your roof //* 13 1
that you do not bring bloodguilt / on your house / 16 2
if anyone should fall from it // ס 14 1

Not Sowing Mixed Seed in Your Vineyard [6]

9 *You shall not sow your vineyard / with a second kind of seed //* 12 2
lest [a]*you forfeit as holy*[a] */* 3 1
the crop from the seed\\[b] *you have sown /* 14 1
and the produce / of the vineyard // ס 10 2

Not Mixing the Ox and the Ass as Plow Animals [2]

10 *You shall not plow*[a] *with an ox and an ass / together //* ס 18 2

Not Mixing Wool and Linen in Clothing [4]

11 *You shall not put on / the finery of a prostitute /* 8 2
wool and linen / woven together // ס 10 2_

True Religion: Wearing Tassels on Garments [5]

12 *Tassels / you shall make for yourselves //* 10 2
at the four / corners of your cloak / 10 2
with which you cover[a] *yourself //* ס 7 1_

Notes

8.a. Reading *paštā'* followed by *zāqēp qāṭôn* as conj.
8.b. Reading *ṭipḥā'* as conj. because of misplaced *'atnāḥ*.
9.a-a. SP reads תקדיש for MT תקדש, "you shall forfeit as holy," with no change in meaning.
9.b. Reading *paštā'* followed by *zāqēp qāṭôn* as conj.
10.a. SP reads תחריש for MT תחרש, "you shall plow," with no change in meaning.
12.a. Syr. appears to be reading תִּתְכַּסֶּה, "you shall cover yourself," for MT תכסה, "you shall cover."

Form/Structure/Setting

The five laws in this section include three on forbidden combinations of seed, plow animals, and the mixing of wool and linen in woven textiles (the finery of a prostitute), which, together with the law on transvestism (22:5), complete the list of four laws on illicit mixtures. The three laws here are framed by two transitional ones, from a literary point of view, which fall under the general category of what I have called "true religion" (on humanitarian issues): the law on building a parapet around the roof of one's house (22:8) and the law requiring tassels on garments (22:12). The first two laws are tied together in a balanced rhythmic structure, as are the last three. Moreover, the last two are also connected in terms of content, moving from the prohibition of combining wool and linen in the same woven fabric (v 11) to the law requiring tassels, which are made by combining these very materials (v 12).

The laws in 22:8–12 are divided into five parts with *sĕtûmā'* layout markers after each verse. On the basis of prosodic analysis it becomes clear that the five laws are in a single prosodic structure that scans 5:6:6:5 in terms of syntactic accentual stress units.

From a prosodic point of view, the law on building a parapet on the roof of one's house (22:8) appears to function as a rhythmic bridge connected with both vv 6–7 on the release of the mother bird, and with v 9 on sowing two kinds of seed in one's vineyard. The structural tie between v 8 and vv 9–12 may be shown in the following outline, which should be compared with the one in the previous section of this commentary for vv 5–11:

A	Build a parapet on the roof of your house	22:8
B	Do not sow your vineyard with two kinds of seeds	22:9
X	Do not plow with an ox and an ass together	22:10
B′	Do not wear cloth of wool and linen woven together	22:11
A′	Make tassels at the four corners of your cloak	22:12

The focus of attention in this reading is on the law that forbids plowing with the ox and the ass together (v 10), which is also the shortest of the five laws. That this verse does not have an *ʾatnāḥ* to divide it in two parts suggests that vv 10 and 11 constitute a single verset in terms of the rhythmic structure of 22:8–12 as a whole. The inner frame moves from the law forbidding the sowing of two kinds of seed in one's vineyard (v 9) to the law on not mixing wool and linen in clothing (v 11). The outer frame moves from the injunction to build a parapet on the roof of one's house (v 8) to that of wearing tassels on garments (v 12). The outer frame is expressed in positive terms, stating what a person is to do; whereas the three laws inside this frame are expressed negatively, stating what is forbidden so far as "mixtures" are concerned. The whole of this literary unit is permeated with enigma so far as actual meaning is concerned.

The placing of the law against plowing with the ox and the ass together in the center of this structure serves to tie the entire structural unit of vv 9–12 to the law about returning lost animals (vv 1–4), which also mentions the ox and the ass. The structure of the whole section of nine domestic laws in 22:1–12 may be outlined in concentric fashion:

A	Returning lost animals and raising fallen ones (ox and ass)	22:1–4
B	Illicit mixtures: wearing clothing of the opposite sex	22:5
X	Humanitarian concern: mother bird with her young and parapet	22:6–8
B′	Illicit mixtures: seeds, plowing with ox and ass, textiles	22:9–11
A′	Put tassels on the corners of your cloak	22:12

The inner frame in this structure continues the focus on laws associated with the seventh commandment prohibiting adultery, in the law on transvestism (v 5), which is set over against three other laws on forbidden combinations: mixed seed (v 9), plowing with an ox and an ass together (v 10), and mixing wool and linen in the same woven fabric (v 11). The outer frame, with its focus on humanitarian concerns, moves from two laws on the treatment of lost and fallen animals (vv 1–4) to the curious law prescribing tassels on garments (v 12).

The phrase "the mother with her children" (האם על־הבנים) in the law of the bird's nest (22:6–7) took Carmichael from the story of Jacob in Gen 32 to two stories of David (1 Sam 25 [Abigail] and 2 Sam 20 [the wise woman of Abel of Beth-maacah]; *LNB*, 165–76). The law of the parapet (22:8) carried the story to the execution of Joab in the beginning of Solomon's reign (1 Kgs 2; *LNB*, 176–80). The law of the mixing of seed (22:9) takes him from Solomon back to the stories of Judah and his sons in Genesis (*LNB*, 185–93). Solomon belonged to the tribe of Judah, and his son Rehoboam was king of Judah, not of the Northern Kingdom (Israel). Thus the focus shifts back to Solomon's ancestor Judah and a series of stories in Genesis. The mention of only one son of Solomon parallels the plight of Judah, after the death of Er and Onan, both of whom were slain by YHWH (Gen 38:7–10). As Carmichael has noted, both Solomon and Judah produced children of mixed seed (*LNB*, 182). It is interesting to note that Solomon and Judah are juxtaposed for genealogical purposes in 1 Chr 3:10–4:1.

The three laws that follow on sowing mixed seed in a vineyard (v 9), plowing with an ox and ass together (v 10), and mixing wool and linen in the same fabric are all in the form of proverbs, expanded in story form in the narrative literature of the Pentateuch and the Former Prophets (Carmichael, *LNB*, 185–97). "By way of illuminating events in the human world, proverbs often refer to activity in the plant and animal one" (*LNB*, 183–84), as is the case here in the laws of illicit mixtures.

If the law prohibiting the sowing of "a second kind of seed" (כִּלְאָיִם) in a vineyard is taken literally, it raises puzzling questions. Indeed, as Carmichael has noted, there is evidence "that it might have been the normal, and one might add the sensible, thing to do" (*LNB*, 187). The use of the dual form, כִּלְאָיִם, rather than the plural, raises questions, as does the simple fact that a vineyard presupposes grapevines. If the vineyard is not a new one, then it might be possible to interpret the text as referring to two other kinds of seed; but the second half of the verse makes specific reference to "the crop from the seed you have sown and the produce of the vineyard." Israel, which is Jacob's family in the widest sense, is God's vineyard (see Ps 80:9, 15 [Eng. 8, 14]; Isa 5:2; Jer 2:21, 6:9; Hos 10:1; and elsewhere).

The story of Judah having sons through his daughter-in-law Tamar in Gen 38 is structured in terms of the law on sowing mixed seed. The vine here is interpreted as Jacob/Israel, who indeed was a fruitful vine with twelve sons. The situation with his son Judah, however, was not the same. The two elder of Judah's three sons, Er and Onan, died in their attempt to continue the family line through Tamar. When Jacob, on his deathbed, referred to Judah's binding first one and then another ass to the vine (Gen 49:11), he was alluding to the story of Er and Onan. Jacob continued: "he washes his garments in wine and his vesture in the blood of grapes." This is a symbolic act, as Carmichael has shown: "The reference to Judah's washing it [the man's garment—i.e., his wife] by treading upon it in the juice of the grapes alludes not just to the deaths of Er and Onan in association with the Israelite vine, but to their origin from Judah's union with the daughter of Shuah. They constituted a branch of his father's vine. To wash one's garment in the juice of grapes is to acknowledge that the 'grapes' produced by one's wife have perished" (*LNB*, 189).

When Judah would not give Shelah to Tamar, so as to perform the levirate duty, she took matters into her own hand and seduced Judah, her father-in-law, by whom she bore twins: Perez and Zerah. These two constitute the "mixed seed" (כלאים), thus the dual form—in reference to Er and Onan, on the one hand, and to Perez and Zerah, on the other.

The ambiguity about the relationship between the double seed and the vine is clarified by the story. Er and Onan constituted the half-Israelite vine. When Judah had them give of their seed to the Israelite vineyard (the line of Abraham, Isaac, Jacob, and Judah) through union with Tamar, neither the seed that was sown nor the existing vine produced anything. The vineyard itself, however, continued to exist because Judah himself sowed the seed in Tamar that produced the surviving "mixed seed" (כלאים) in the twins that were born of that union. "It is just possible that the breach birth that Tamar eventually experienced, and that was intended to be remembered in the name Perez, signified either to the narrator of the story, or to later thinkers, the precarious nature of the union between Judah, who would be regarded as pure vine, and Tamar, the palm tree" (Carmichael, *LNB*, 192).

The law on plowing with an ox and an ass (v 10) carries the proverbial motif further. "The plowing and cultivation of a field is a natural figure for sexual intercourse" (M. Pope, *Song of Songs,* AB 7C [Garden City, NY: Doubleday, 1977] 323). The ass refers to the Canaanite aspect, and the ox to the Israelite. In the story of the action taken by Simeon and Levi to the so-called rape of Dinah on the part of Shechem, the imagery of the ox and the ass becomes explicit: Jacob complains that "in their anger they slay men, and in their wantonness they hamstring oxen" (Gen 49:6). The man killed is Hamor ("ass"), and the parallel reference to the ox that still lives but is hamstrung is Jacob's family, as presented in the story of Gen 34. On the imagery of the ox in relation to Israel see Deut 33:17; Num 22:4; 1 Kgs 22:11; Amos 6:12–13.

From a prosodic point of view, v 12 belongs with vv 8–11 as the final part of a rhythmic unit that is scanned 5:6:6:5 in terms of syntactic accentual stress units. It should be noted that vv 10–12 are symmetrically balanced in terms of mora count: 26 + 10 + 27; and that the clause in the center of this structure, "wool and linen woven together," functions as a rhythmic bridge connecting the two versets. It is the key to interpreting the meaning as well.

The requirement of tassels on garments is discussed in Num 15:37–41, where they are called "fringes" (ציצית). In traditional Jewish interpretation, they are understood to be reminders to keep all of God's commandments so as to be a holy people. According to Num 15:38, a blue cord is to be tied "on the fringe at each corner." Tigay notes that "according to early rabbinic sources, the blue cord is made of wool while the other cords are linen. In other words, the tassels are made of *sha'atnez,* the combination of fabrics forbidden in verse 11. This interpretation most likely stems from biblical times, since it is highly unlikely that the rabbis would have initiated a practice contradicting a biblical prohibition" (Tigay [1996] 203).

Once again, a look beneath the surface of the text to its symbolic meaning within the context of the stories in Genesis is instructive, as Carmichael has shown (*LNB,* 198–205). The law is to be understood figuratively in relation to the story of Judah and Tamar in Gen 38. Judah faced a major problem in perpetuating his line through his half-Israelite, half-Canaanite sons (the "mixed seed" of v 9); and his own marriage to a Canaanite woman is essentially the "plowing of an ox and an ass together," which is an extension of the earlier problem of intermarriage between his father Jacob's family and that of Hamor (the "ass"). The focus now shifts to Judah's intercourse with his daughter-in-law Tamar, who was disguised as an attractively dressed prostitute at Enaim that Judah encountered on his way to a sheep-shearing festival.

Numerous commentators have noted the problems in a literal interpretation of the law here. Priestly garments such as the girdle, robe, breastpiece, and ephod all call for mixing wool and linen. Only the priestly turban, breeches, and coat were to be made of linen alone (L. Bellinger, "Cloth," *IDB* 1:654). Moreover, in its present context the law about tassels on garments follows laws concerning the sexual activity of Judah's sons Simeon and Levi and Jacob's daughter Dinah (vv 9–11) and is followed by a series of laws dealing with marital and sexual misconduct (vv 13–29) within a larger unit that is essentially a "commentary" on the seventh commandment prohibiting adultery (21:10–23:1 [Eng. 22:30]). The law of tassels on garments in 22:12 forms an inclusion with the law of levirate marriage in 25:5–10, which reflects the story of Tamar's problem in Gen 38.

The first thing to note in the story of Judah and Tamar is the emphasis on her clothing. She put off her "widow's garments" (בגדי אלמנותה) and dressed herself as a prostitute, presumably garments made of linen because of its luxurious quality. She used her clothing to conceal her identity and to attract Judah, who was on his way to gather his annual supply of wool. The sexual union was a violation of the law, an illicit mixture (Carmichael, *LNB*, 199).

Clothes have symbolic meaning in the Bible. To spread a garment over a woman to cover her nakedness refers to sexual union and symbolizes spiritual union, as the prophet Ezekiel expressed vividly in describing the relationship between God and his faithless bride: "I spread the edge of my cloak over you, and covered your nakedness. . . . I clothed you with embroidered cloth and with sandals of fine leather; I bound you in fine linen and covered you with rich fabric. . . . You took some of your garments, and made for yourself colorful shrines, and on them played the whore" (Ezek 16:8–16 NRSV). In describing the marriage relationship, the man is portrayed as putting on the woman as his new garment in an action that will cover his own nakedness. See the words of Ruth to Boaz in Ruth 3:10. "She is suggesting that she will become his new garment, that is, his wife, just as her action of uncovering his feet and lying at them conveys the similar sexual suggestion of becoming his new 'shoes' to be put on his genital 'feet'" (Carmichael, *LNB*, 198; see also idem, *ZAW* 92 [1980] 248–66).

The interpretation of the three laws on illicit mixtures in vv 9–11 provides the occasion for a fresh look at the earlier fourth such law on not wearing clothing of the opposite sex (v 5). "The transvestite law prohibits a man's disguising himself in a woman's clothing. . . . Tamar's disguise and Judah's subsequent intercourse with her combine to suggest the notion of Judah's covering himself with her 'clothing.' This idea is also suggested by the fact that Tamar would not have removed her clothes when giving herself to Judah. It is also interesting to observe that from Tamar's side she required a male of Judah's family to 'spread his skirt' over her because she had a legitimate claim to it" (Carmichael, *LNB*, 202). The law of v 5 has to do with the story of Judah and Tamar in Gen 38, more even than it does to the shaping of the tradition about the tribes of Reuben and Gad as noted above in the discussion of 12:5.

Carmichael notes that clothing continues to be a dominant motif as the reader moves on from the story of Judah and Tamar (Gen 38) to the story of Joseph and his brothers (Gen 39–50). Joseph's special coat, a symbol of his father Jacob's favoritism, was eventually stripped from him, dipped in blood, and used as evidence of his death. Joseph was not dead, however, and a garment again becomes a central motif in the story of Joseph and Potiphar's wife. Unlike his brother Judah, Joseph resisted sexual temptation; but his garment was used as evidence against him. Potiphar's wife used that garment to send Joseph to prison for twelve years, in spite of his innocence. He was condemned because a woman possessed his garment. Carmichael has argued that "the tassels are to be put upon an Israelite's garment precisely for this purpose, to remind him that like Joseph he should be virtuous in matters of sexual morality, that he 'should not follow after his heart and eyes to commit fornication,' as Judah did in possessing the *šaʿaṭnēz* Tamar" (*LNB*, 208). He also calls our attention to the interesting story in *b. Men.* 44a of the disciple who was about to have intercourse with a prostitute but was stopped by the tassels on his garment, which miraculously struck him in the face. The prostitute was so impressed she became a proselyte and married him (*LNB*, 208 n. 2).

An interesting parallel expression that serves to connect the law on the tassels (22:12) and the contrasting stories of Judah and Joseph in matters of sexual desire was noted by Carmichael in the story of Abraham passing his wife off as his sister to Abimelech, king of Gerar, in Gen 20. Though Abimelech rightly avowed his innocence of any sexual impropriety, he did pay Abraham a substantial amount of money as "a covering of the eyes" (כסות עינים) in Gen 38:15. The term כסות is the word used here for "garment," and the term for "eyes" (עינים) is also the name of the town (Enaim) where Tamar seduced Judah (38:14). Further evidence that the language of Gen 38 was influenced by the law on tassels is that the expression "to cover oneself with" (the piel of כסה with the prep. ב) is found only in Gen 38:14 and Deut 22:12 (with the possible exception of Jonah 3:6).

Labuschagne's study of the use of the divine-name numbers in 22:8–12 and its immediate context may be summarized as follows:

Words:	before *ʾatnāḥ*			after *ʾatnāḥ*				
22:8–12	54		+	34	(= 2 × 17)	=	88	
22:9–10	9		+	8		=	17	
22:9–11	15		+	8		=	23	
22:7–11	30		+	21		=	51	(= 3 × 17)
21:22–22:12	130	(= 5 × 26)	+	75		=	205	
22:1–12	109		+	61		=	170	(= 10 × 17)

Labuschagne has also shown that the 170 (= 10 × 17) words in 22:1–12 are divided into 102 (= 6 × 17) words in main clauses and 68 (= 4 × 17) words in subordinate clauses. The numerical composition gives important insight into the literary structure, as perceived by the scribes ("counters") in ancient Israel. The whole of 21:22–22:12 is a literary unit, as I have found on independent grounds through the prosodic analysis presented here. In the outline of Deuteronomy in the Introduction, I have called this unit "Ten Laws on 'True Religion' and Illicit Mixtures." Within this structure, 22:1–12 is also a literary unit, as the chapter division in MT bears witness. Moreover, 22:8–12 is a distinct literary subunit, which I have also shown in the prosodic analysis presented here.

Comment

8 A "parapet" (מעקה) is a low wall built around the edge of the roof as a safety precaution. The reference to "bring bloodguilt on your house" suggests that failure to provide a parapet amounts to criminal negligence (on "bloodguilt" see also the *Comment* on 19:10).

9 Sowing a "vineyard with a second kind of seed" (כלאים) refers to "mixed cropping" or "intercropping," a common practice in subsistence farming on limited amounts of agricultural land. The space between the vines is used for other crops. Scholars have suggested various reasons for the prohibition of mixed cropping. The law may "have originated in a desire to avoid foreign practices which had some magical or cultic associations; it may have a utilitarian reason in the inappropriate and wasteful use of crops and land," as Mayes ([1981] 307–8) and others have suggested. The rendering "lest you forfeit" (פן־תקדש) is an attempt to interpret a technical phrase: literally "lest you make sacrosanct," which implies that it would not be available for common use. Taken literally, the terms rendered as "the crop from the seed" (המלאה הזרע) could be rendered "the fullness of the seed," or the whole yield.

10 The command not "to plow with an ox and an ass together" may have been intended to protect animals of unequal strength. At the same time, however, it should be noted that on occasion an ass and an ox were yoked together in plowing, as Driver has shown ([1895] 253). Craigie ([1976] 290) has also called attention to the fact that the ox was "clean" and the ass "unclean" according to 14:1–8.

11 The prohibition against wearing "mixed material [שעטנז], wool and linen woven together," does not forbid combining wool and linen as such, but only wearing a garment of cloth made from that combination. The rabbis in Jewish tradition could find no explanation for this prohibition (Tigay [1996] 203). Josephus suggested that the prohibition applies only to the laity, because officiating priests did wear garments made of such mixtures (Josephus *Ant.* 4.8.11 §208; see Tigay [1996] 384 n. 35). The term שעטנז appears to be Egyptian (Lambdin, *JAOS* 73 [1953] 145–55; see Craigie [1976] 290 n. 13). Craigie suggested the possibility that the reason for the prohibition comes from Egypt, which during the Eighteenth Dynasty imported various pattern weaves, perhaps from Syria ([1976] 290, citing J. R. Harris, ed., *The Legacy of Egypt,* 2nd ed. [Oxford: Clarendon, 1971] 92).

Here in v 11, however, Hebrew שעטנז apparently refers not to mixed materials as such but to a luxurious linen garment that a prostitute might wear (T. O. Lambdin, *JAOS* 73 [1953] 155). The interpretation "mixed stuff" in most translations comes from a surface reading of its use in a context of illicit mixtures. Carmichael's translation is more apropros: "Thou [Judah/Israel] shalt not put on *šaʿaṭnēz* [a prostitute], wool [the Israelite] and linen [the prostitute] together" (*LNB,* 201).

12 "Tassels" (גדלים) were twisted braids of thread that were attached "at the four corners" (כנפות) of the "cloak" (כסות). According to Tigay ([1996] 203), "The four corners (lit., 'wings' or 'extremities') were probably either the points on scalloped hems or the places at which vertical bands of embroidery met the hems. Both styles, sometimes with tassels attached, are visible in ancient Near Eastern murals." The cloak served both as a coat for daytime use and as a blanket at night. Carmichael's suggestions in regard to the meaning of the term גדלים, "tassels," merit comment (*LNB,* 210 n. 4). The term has cognates in Aramaic and Arabic that denote plaited cords or hair. Nonetheless, he associates the term with the root גדל, "to become strong," in the sense of mature sexually (cf. use of the verb גדל in Gen 38:11, 14). See the observations of G. R. Driver ("L'interprétation du text masorétique à la lumière de la lexiocographie hébraïque," *ETL* 26 [1950] 343), who connects the meaning of "strong" and "twisting." In traditional usage, the blue cord (which according to Num 15:38 must be attached to each tassel) was made of wool while the other cords were linen. According to Milgrom, the reason for this exception to the law of "mixed materials" was that the שעטנז characterized priestly garments; and thus wearing tassels reminds every Israelite to strive for holiness like the priests, to become a "kingdom of priests" and a "holy nation" (Exod 19:6) (Milgrom, *Numbers* [1990] 410–14). In Jewish tradition the tassels were made of four white threads folded double (hence eight thread ends), each with five double knots. The numerical value of the word ציצית ("tassels" in Num 15:37 = גדלים here in Deuteronomy) is 600 (= 90 + 10 + 90 + 10 + 400), since צ = 90, י = 10, and ת = 400. Adding these numbers (600 + 8 + 5) yields 613, the traditional number of commandments in the Torah.

Explanation

Houses in the ancient Near East had flat roofs that were used for various purposes. According to Tigay, in traditional Jewish interpretation, the law on building a parapet (22:8) is taken "as an example of an obligation to block or remove anything on one's property that is capable of causing death, such as a pit, a faulty ladder, or a vicious dog; and to personally avoid potentially harmful food and drink." The law has also been used in recent years "to support a ban on smoking" ([1996] 201). The law reminds us that each member of society is responsible for the safety of others. We are our brother's keeper.

The three laws on illicit mixtures in Deut 22:9–11 have their parallel in Lev 19:19 (NRSV): "You shall not let your animals breed with a different kind; you shall not sow your field with two kinds of seed; nor shall you put on a garment made of two different materials." The reasons for these laws are not clear. In this regard, the comments of the medieval Jewish exegete Rashi are worthy of note; he argued that these laws belong among the sovereign decrees of God, for which no reason need be given (Rashi, at Lev 19:19; see Tigay [1996] 202 and 384 n. 25). In other words, we ought not to press the matter trying to find explanations for the law.

The prohibition of mixing the ox and ass as plow animals (v 10) has been explained in various ways, usually as an attempt to protect draught animals. But once again, the reasoning of the exegetes from presumed parallels in the practice of ancient Roman agriculture are less than convincing. It seems more likely that a symbolic meaning is the primary reason for these laws, perhaps along the lines of what Carmichael has suggested in terms of relating the words of the law itself to the larger narrative tradition within the Torah and the Former Prophets—and to set the stage for the following law on wearing tassels on garments, which are expressly made of the forbidden mixture of textiles in 22:11. The ancient rabbis could find no explanation for the prohibition of mixing wool and linen in clothing (v 11), and like Rashi, considered the commandment to be one for which there is no apparent reason. Tigay refers to the observations made by Josephus (*Ant.* 4.8.11 §208): "the prohibition applies to the laity, because the priests, when they officiate, do wear garments made of such mixtures. The status of such garments is thus comparable to that of the sacred anointing oil and the incense that is used in the sanctuary and may not be made or used by laypersons, as stated in Exodus 30:22–37" ([1996] 203).

The law on the tassels takes on the form of a riddle that, with proper instruction and guidance, invites the reader into the complex world of the commandments in the Torah in relation to the biblical narrative with its many layers of meanings. The primary meaning, however, is clear: we are reminded of the need to keep God's commandments.

C. Seven Laws on Marriage and Sexual Misconduct (22:13–23:1 [Eng. 22:30])

1. Two Laws on Premarital Unchastity (22:13–21)

2. Two Laws on Adultery (22:22–24)

3. Two Laws on Rape (22:25–29)

Bibliography for 22:13–29

Amran, D. W. *The Jewish Law of Divorce according to Bible and Talmud.* New York: Hermon Press, 1969. 1–31. **Boschi, B. G.** "Problemi della Famiglia nella Bibbia." *Sacra Doctrina* 20 (1975) 395–417. **Burrows, M.** *The Basis of Israelite Marriage.* American Oriental Series 15. 1938. Repr. New York: Kraus, 1970. **Eberharter, A.** *Das Ehe- und Familienrecht der Hebräer mit Rücksicht auf die ethnologische Forschung.* ATAbh 5.1–2. Münster: Aschendorff, 1914. **Epstein, L. M.** *Marriage Laws in the Bible and the Talmud.* HSS 12. Cambridge: Harvard UP, 1942. ———. *Sex Laws and Customs in Judaism.* New York: Ktav, 1967. 165, 206. **Fensham, F. C.** "Aspects of Family Law in the Covenant Code in the Light of Ancient Near Eastern Parallels." *DiIs* 1. (1969) v–xix. **Finkelstein, J. J.** "The Laws of Ur-Nammu." *JCS* 22 (1968–69) 73. ———. "Sex Offenses in Sumerian Laws." *JAOS* 86 (1966) 355–72, esp. 368–69. **Friedman, M. A.** *Jewish Marriage in Palestine: A Cairo Geniza Study.* Tel Aviv: Tel Aviv Univ., 1980. **Granqvist, H. N.** *Marriage Conditions.* 1931–35. 2:127–30. **Greenberg, M.** "More Reflections on Biblical Criminal Law." In *Studies in Bible.* Ed. S. Japhet. Jerusalem: Magnes, 1986. 1–4. ———. "Some Postulates of Biblical Criminal Law." In SBTS 3:283–300, esp. 288–89. **MacDonald, E. M.** *The Position of Women as Reflected in Semitic Codes of Law.* University of Toronto Studies, Oriental Series 1. Toronto: Univ. of Toronto Press, 1931. **MacDonald, J.** "The Status and Role of the Naʿar in Israelite Society." *JNES* 35 (1976) 147–70. **Mace, D. R.** *Hebrew Marriage: A Sociological Study.* London: Epworth, 1953. **Malul, M.** "SUSAPINNU: The Mesopotamian Paranymph and His Role." *JESHO* 32 (1989) 264. **Neufeld, E.** *Ancient Hebrew Marriage Laws.* London: Longmans, Green, 1944. **Otto, E.** "Aspects of Legal Reforms and Reformulations in Ancient Cuneiform and Israelite Law." In *Theory and Method in Biblical and Cuneiform Law.* Ed. B. Levinson. JSOTSup 181. Sheffield: Sheffield Academic Press, 1994. 160–96, esp. 189–92. ———. "Das Eherecht im Mittelassyrischen Kodex und im Deuteronomium: Tradition und Redaktion in den 12–16 der Tafel A des Mittelassyrischen Kodex und in Dtn 22,22–29." In *Mesopotamica, Ugaritica, Biblica: FS K. Bergerhof.* Ed. M. Dietrich and O. Loretz. AOAT 232. Kevelaer: Butzon & Bercker, 1993. 259–81. ———. *Wandel der Rechtsbegründungen in der Gesellschaftsgeschichte des antiken Israel: Eine Rechtsgeschichte des 'Bundesbuches' Ex XX 22-XXIII 13.* StudBib 3. Leiden: Brill, 1988. 9–56. **Praag, A. van.** *Droit matrimonial assyro-babylonien.* Allard Pierson Stichting Archaeologisch-Historische Bijdragen 12. Amsterdam: Noord-Hollandsche Uitgevers Maatschappij, 1945. **Rauh, S.** "Hebräisches Familienrecht in vorprophetischer Zeit." Diss., Berlin, 1907. **Reintjens, H.** *Die soziale Stellung der Frau bei den nordarabischen Beduinen unter besonderer Berücksichtigung ihrer Ehe- und Familienverhältnisse.* Bonner orientalistische Studien, n.s. 30. Bonn: Selbstverlag des Orientalisches Seminars der Universität Bonn, 1975. **Roth, M.** "Age at Marriage and the Household: A Study of Neo-Babylonian and Neo-Assyrian

Forms." In *Comparative Studies in Society and History* 29 (1987) 715–47. **Schereschewsky, B.** "Child Marriage." *EncJud* 5:423–26. **Selms, A. van.** *Marriage and Family Life in Ugaritic Literature.* POS 1. London: Luzac, 1954. **Stuhlman, L.** "Sex and Familial Crimes in the D Code: A Witness to Mores in Transition." *JSOT* 53 (1992) 58–60. **Weiss, D. H.** "A Note on אשר לא ארשה." *JBL* 81 (1962) 67–69. **Wenham, G. J.,** and **McConville, J. G.** "Drafting Techniques in Some Deuteronomic Laws." *VT* 30 (1980) 248–52. **Westbrook, R.** "Riddles in Deuteronomic Law." In *Bundesdokument und Gesetz.* 1995. 159–74.

Bibliography for 22:13–21

Branson, R. D. "A Study of the Hebrew Term שׂנא." Diss., Boston Univ., 1976. Ann Arbor, MI: UMI Order No. 76–21272. **Buchholz, J.** *Die Ältesten Israels im Deuteronomium.* 1988. **Burrows, M.** "Levirate Marriage in Israel." *JBL* 59 (1940) 23–33, esp. 29. **Cassin, E.** "Pouvoirs de la Femme et Structures Familiales." *RA* 63 (1969) 121–48. **Ceresko, A. R.** "The Function of Antanaclasis (*mṣʾ* 'to find' // *mṣʾ* 'to reach, overtake, grasp') in Hebrew Poetry, Especially in the Book of Qoheleth." *CBQ* 44 (1982) 551–69. **Collins, O. E.** "The Stem *znh* and Prostitution in the Hebrew Bible." Diss., Brandeis Univ., 1977. Ann Arbor, MI: UMI Order No. 77–13364. **Cruveilhier, P.** "Le droit de la femme dans la Genèse et dans le recueil de lois assyriennes." *RB* 36 (1927) 350–76. **Dempster, S.** "The Deuteronomic Formula *kî yimmāṣēʾ* in the Light of Biblical and Ancient Near Eastern Law: An Evaluation of David Daube's Theory." *RB* 91 (1984) 188–211. **D'Ercole, G.** "La Struttura Giuridica di Israele." In *Studia et Documenta Historiae et Iuris* 31 (1965) 246–304, esp. 250–55. **Derrett, J. D. M.** "The Disposal of Virgins." *Man* 9 (1974) 23–30. **Gelb, I. J.** "Household and Family in Early Mesopotamia." In *State and Temple Economy in the Ancient Near East: Proceedings of the International Conference Organized by the Katholieke Universiteit Leuven 10.–14.4.1978.* Ed. E. Lipiński. Orientalia Lovaniensia Analecta 5.6. Leuven: Peeters, 1979. 1–97. **Gerleman, G.** "Die Nicht-Mensch: Erwägungen zur hebräischen Wurzel *NBL.*" *VT* 24 (1974) 147–58. **Hallo, W. W.** "The Slandered Bride." In *Studies Presented to A. Leo Oppenheim.* Ed. R. D. Biggs and J. A. Brinkman. Chicago: Univ. of Chicago Press, 1964. 95–105. **Hirzel, R.** "Die Strafe der Steinigung." *Abhandlungen der philologisch-historischen Klasse der königlich sächsischen Gesellschaft der Wissenschaften* 27 (1909) 223–66, esp. 245. **Jakobson, V. A.** "Studies in Neo-Assyrian Law: 1. Matrimonial Law." *Altorientalische Forschungen* 1 (1974) 115–21. **Lipiński, E.** "The Wife's Right to Divorce in the Light of an Ancient Near Eastern Tradition." *JLA* 4 (1981) 9–27. **Locher, C.** "Deuteronomium 22,13–21: Vom Prozeßprotokoll zum kasuistischen Gesetz." In *Das Deuteronomium.* Ed. N. Lohfink. 1985. 298–303. ———. *Die Ehre einer Frau in Israel: Exegetische und rechtsvergleichende Studien zu Deuteronomium 22, 13–21.* Ed. O. Keel. OBO 70. Freiburg: Universitätsverlag, 1986. **Lohfink, N.** "Die Ältesten Israels und der Bund: Zum Zusammenhang von Dtn 5,23; 26,17–19; 27,1.9f und 31,9." *BN* 37 (1993) 26–42. **Marx, V.** "Die Stellung der Frauen in Babylonien gemäss den kontrakten aus der Zeit von Nebukadnezar bis Darius (604–485)." *Beiträge zur Assyriologie* 4 (1902) 1–77. **Miller, C. M.** "Maidenhood and Virginity in Ancient Israel." *ResQ* 22 (1979) 242–46. **Neubauer, J.** *Beiträge zur Geschichte des biblische-talmudischen Eheschliessungsrechts: Eine rechtsvergleichend-historische Studie.* MVAG 24–25. Leipzig: Hinrichs, 1920. **Neufeld, E.** "Inalienability of Mobile and Immobile Pledges in the Laws of the Bible." *RIDA* 9 (1962) 42. **Piattelli, D.** "The Marriage Contract and Bill of Divorce in Ancient Hebrew Law." *JLA* 4 (1981) 66–78. **Phillips, A.** "*Nebalah*—A Term for Serious Disorderly and Unruly Conduct." *VT* 25 (1975) 237–42. **Preuss, J.** *Biblical and Talmudic Medicine.* Tr. F. Rosner. New York: Sanhedrin Press, 1978. 477–79. **Reviv, H.** *The Elders in Ancient Israel: A Study of a Biblical Institution.* Jerusalem: Magnes, 1989. **Rofé, A.** "Family and Sex Laws in Deuteronomy and the Book of Covenant." *Hen* 9 (1987) 131–59. ———. *Mavoʾ le-sefer Devarim.* Jerusalem: Akademon, 1988. 147–50 (Heb.). **Scharbert, J.** "Ehe und Eheschließung in der

Rechtssprache des Pentateuch und beim Chronisten." In *FS W. Kornfeld*. 1977. 213–25. **Skaist, A. J.** "Studies in Ancient Mesopotamian Family Law Pertaining to Marriage and Divorce." Ph.D. diss., Univ. of Pennsylvania, 1963. Ann Arbor, MI: UMI Order No. 63–7087. **Tigay, J.** "Examination of the Accused Bride in 4Q159: Forensic Medicine at Qumran." In *Comparative Studies in Honor of Yohanan Muffs*. Ed. E. L. Greenstein and D. Marcus. *JANESCU* 22 (1993) 129–34. ———. "Excursus 20: Accusations of Premarital Unchastity." In *Deuteronomy*. 1996. 476–77. **Tosato, A.** "Il Linguaggio Matrimoniale Veterotestamentario: Stato degli Studi." *AION* 43 (1983) 135–60. **Wenham, G. J.** "Bᵉtûlāh—A Girl of Marriageable Age." *VT* 22 (1972) 326–48. **Westbrook, R.** "Old Babylonian Marriage Law." 2 vols. Ph.D. diss., Yale Univ., 1982. Ann Arbor, MI: UMI Order No. 82–21763. **Westermarck, E.** *Marriage Ceremonies in Morocco*. London: Macmillan, 1914. 159, 228–29, 246. **Yaron, R.** "On Divorce in Old Testament Times." *RIDA* 4 (1957) 117–28.

Bibliography for 22:22–24

Daube, D. "Concerning Methods of Bible Criticism: Late Law in Early Narratives." *ArOr* 17.1 (1949) 88–89. ———. "To Be Found Doing Wrong." In *FS E. Volterra*. 1971. 3–13. **David, M.** "Overspel volgens Deuteronomium 22,22ss." *JEOL* 8 (1942) 650–54. **Dempster, S.** "The Deuteronomic Formula *kî yimmāṣēʾ* in the Light of Biblical and Ancient Near Eastern Law: An Evaluation of David Daube's Theory." *RB* 91 (1984) 188–211. **Dion, P. E.** "Tu feras disparaitre le mal du milieu de toi." *RB* 87 (1980) 321–49, esp. 333. **Good, E. M.** "Capital Punishment and Its Alternatives in Ancient Near Eastern Law." *SLR* 19 (1967) 957–58. **Labuschagne, C. J.** "The Emphasizing Particle *gam* and Its Connotations." In *FS Th. C. Vriezen*. 1966. 193–203. **Locher, C.** "Wie Einzigartig war das altisraelitische Recht?" *Jud* 38 (1982) 130–40. **McKeating, H.** "A Response to Dr. Phillips." *JSOT* 20 (1981) 25–26. ———. "Sanctions against Adultery in Ancient Israelite Society, with Some Reflections on Methodology in the Study of Old Testament Ethics." *JSOT* 11 (1979) 57–72. **Mezger, F.** "The Origin of a Specific Rule on Adultery in the Germanic Laws." *JAOS* 68 (1948) 145–48. **Phillips, A.** "Another Example of Family Law." *VT* 30 (1980) 240–45. ———. "Another Look at Adultery." *JSOT* 20 (1981) 3–25. ———. "A Response to Dr. McKeating [*JSOT* 20 (1981) 25–26]." *JSOT* 22 (1981) 142–43. ———. "Some Aspects of Family Law in Pre-Exilic Israel." *VT* 23 (1973) 349–61; 25 (1975) 237–41. **Tigay, J.** "Adultery." *EncJud* 2:313–15. **Westbrook, R.** "Adultery in Ancient Near Eastern Law." *RB* 97 (1990) 542–80.

Bibliography for 22:25–29

Boyce, R. N. *The Cry to God in the Old Testament*. SBLDS 103. Atlanta: Scholars Press, 1988. **Fishbane, M.** *Biblical Interpretation in Ancient Israel*. 1985. 217–20. **Hiebert, R. J. V.** "Deuteronomy 22:28–29 and Its Premishnaic Interpretations." *CBQ* 56 (1994) 203–20. **Otto, E.** "Zur Stellung der Frau in den ältesten Rechtstexten des Alten Testamentes (Ex 20,14; 22,15f.)—Wider die hermeneutische Naivität im Umgang mit dem Alten Testament." *ZEE* 26 (1982) 279–305. **Weiss, D. H.** "A Note on אשר לא־ארשה." *JBL* 81 (1962) 67–69.

Translation and Prosodic Analysis

False Accusation of Premarital Unchastity—The Man Is Fined
[(6:8):(6:6):(6:6):(8:6)]

13 *When a man takes / a woman //* 9 2
and he goes in to her / and then he hates her // 16 2
14 *and he makes baseless charges / against her /* 15 2_

And he brings on her / a bad name // and he says /	19	3
"This woman / I have taken as a wife /	14	2
and when I came to her / I found she / was not a virgin" //	25	3_
15 *And the father of the girl / and her mother\[a] shall take //*	16	2
and they shall bring out / evidence of the girl's virginity /	18	2
to the elders of the city / at the gate[b] //	14	2_
16 *And the father of the girl / shall say\[a] to the elders //*	19	2
"I gave / my daughter[b] / to this man / as a wife /	19	4_
And he hates her //	7	1
17 *and behold he / has made up[a] baseless charges / saying /*	22	3
'I did not find your daughter / to be a virgin' /	17	2_
But here is / evidence of the virginity of my daughter" //	12	2
and <he>[b] shall spread out / the garment /	9	2
before / the elders of the city //	10	2_
18 *And the elders of that city / shall take\[a] the man[b] //*	21	2
and they shall flog / him //	9	2
19 *And they shall fine him / a hundred pieces of silver /*	16	2
and they shall give it / to the father of the girl /	16	2_
For he has brought / an evil name / on\[a] a virgin in Israel //	20	3
and she shall be his wife /	9	1
he may not [b]divorce her[b] / all his days // ס	15	2_

True Accusation of Premarital Unchastity—The Woman Shall Die [7:7]

20 *But if / this[a]\[b] charge is true //*	15	2
the girl was found / not to have been a virgin //	16	2
21 *Then they shall bring out the girl /*	13	1
to the entrance of her father's house /	11	1
and [a]the men of her city[a] shall stone her with stones /	23	1_
And she shall die / for she has done folly / in Israel /	24	3
[b]committing fornication[b] / in her father's house //	10	2
and you shall purge the evil / from your[c] midst // ס	13	2_

Adultery with a Married Woman—Both Parties Shall Die [4:5]

22 *When a man is found / lying\[a] with the wife of another man /*	23	2
then both of them / shall die /	11	2_
The man / who lay with the woman / and the woman //	21	3
and you shall purge the evil / from Israel // ס	15	2_

Adultery with a Betrothed Virgin—Both Parties Shall Die [(5:5):(5:4)]

23 *When there is / a virgin / who is betrothed\[a] to a man //*	23	3
and a man finds her / in the city /	13	2_
And he lies with her //	7	1
24 then you shall bring them both / to the gate / of that city /	21	3
and you shall stone them with stones /	16	1_

And they shall die / 6 1
the maiden / because / she did not cry out in the city / 22 3
and the man / 6 1_
Because he humbled / his neighbor's wife // 18 2
and *you shall purge the evil / from your midst //* ס 14 2_

Rape of an Engaged Virgin—The Man Shall Die [(9:6):(5:5)]

25 *But if it is in the field /* 6 1
where the man finds / the girl[a] *who is betrothed /* 21 2
and the man seizes her / 11 1_
And he lies with her by force // 7 1
then he shall die / the man / who slept with her / he alone // 20 4_
26 *And to the girl / you*[a] *shall do nothing /* 15 2
[b]*the girl did not commit / a mortal sin //* 12 2
for this / is like a man who attacks his neighbor / 18 2_
And he murders him / so / is this matter // 18 3
27 *for in the field / he found her //* 11 2_
The betrothed / girl / cried out / 18 3
but there was no one / to save her // ס 10 2_

Rape of an Unengaged Virgin—The Man Is Fined [6:9]

28 *When a man finds / a virgin /* 16 2
who has never been betrothed / and he seizes her / 17 2
and he lies with her by force // and they[a] *are found //* 13 2_
29 *Then the man who lay with her / shall give /* 16 2
to the father of the girl / fifty pieces of silver // 16 2
And she shall be his wife / because / he has humbled her / 16 3
he may not [a]*divorce her*[a] / *all his days //* ס 14 2_

Notes

15.a. Reading the *tipḥā'* as conj. because of misplaced *'atnāḥ*.

15.b. Tg. and *Tg. Ps.-J.* add *byt dyn*, "house of judgment." Prosodic analysis favors MT.

16.a. Reading the *tipḥā'* as conj. because of misplaced *'atnāḥ*.

16.b. LXX adds ταύτην (= הזאת, "this"). Prosodic analysis favors MT.

17.a. A few Heb. MSS, Cairo Geniza fragments, and LXX add לָהּ, "to her."

17.b. Reading 3 sg with SP for MT ופרשו, "and they shall spread out." It should be noted that this emendation does not add an additional word in the Hebrew text.

18.a. Reading *tipḥā'* as conj. because of misplaced *'atnāḥ*.

18.b. One Heb. MS, SP, and LXX add ההוא, "that." Prosodic analysis favors MT.

19.a. Reading *tipḥā'* as conj. because of misplaced *'atnāḥ*.

19.b-b. One Heb. MS and SP read שלחה (without the prepositional prefix) for MT לשלחה, "to send her (away)." Prosodic analysis favors MT.

20.a. One Heb. MS and LXX[MS] omit הזה, "this." Prosodic analysis favors MT.

20.b. Reading *tipḥā'* as conj. because of misplaced *'atnāḥ*.

21.a-a. Omitted in LXX[B]; many Heb. MSS, Cairo Geniza fragments, and Tg.[MS] add כל, "all." Prosodic analysis favors MT.

21.b-b. SP and LXX read להזנות for MT לזנות, "to commit fornication," with no change in meaning.

21.c. LXX, Syr., and *Tg. Ps.-J.* read 2 pl. Codex MSS of Vg. read *de medio Israel,* "in the midst of Israel" (= מקרב ישראל).

22.a. Reading *mûnāḥ* with *pāsēq* as conj.

23.a. Reading *ṭip̄ḥā'* as conj. because of misplaced *'atnāḥ.*

25.a. Reading *pašṭā'* followed by *zāqēp̄ qāṭôn* as conj.

26.a. SP, LXX, Syr., and *Tg. Ps.-J.* read תַעֲשׂוּ, "you [pl.] shall do," for MT תַעֲשֶׂה, "you [sg.] shall do"; LXX[A] reads ποιήσεται, "it shall be done," i.e., "she shall suffer (nothing)" (= תֵעָשֶׂה).

26.b. Two Heb. MSS, LXX[MS], and Syr. add כִּי, "for."

28.a. LXX reads 3 sg.

29.a-a. Some Heb. MSS and Vg. read לשלחה, "to send her (away)," for MT שלחה, "send her (away)."

Form/Structure/Setting

The six laws in 22:13–29 are sharply focused on the overt meaning of the seventh commandment forbidding adultery, with the command itself repeated at the center of a concentric structural design:

A	False accusation of premarital unchastity—man fined, no divorce	22:13–19
B	True accusation of premarital unchastity—woman dies	22:20–21
X	Adultery with a married woman or betrothed virgin—both die	22:22–24
B′	Rape of betrothed virgin in the field—man dies	22:25–27
A′	Rape of unbetrothed virgin—man fined, marriage, no divorce	22:28–29

On one side of the central law on adultery with a married woman or a betrothed virgin (vv 22–24), we have two laws on the matter of premarital unchastity: one in which the charges brought by the man are false and he is flogged and fined one hundred pieces of silver (vv 13–19), and the other where the charges are true and the woman is executed by stoning (vv 20–21). On the other side of the center, we find two laws on the matter of rape: one where the man only is condemned to death, in the case of rape of a betrothed virgin in the field (vv 25–27), and the other where the man is required to pay fifty pieces of silver to the girl's father and marry the woman without the possibility of divorce (vv 28–29).

The internal symmetry in terms of punishment is remarkable in the above concentric structure. In each section of the outer frame (vv 13–19 and 28–29), the man is fined and "he may not divorce her all his days" (vv 19 and 29). In the first half of the inner frame the woman only is executed, because "she did not cry out" for help (vv 20–21); whereas in the second half it is the man only who is executed, because the woman did cry out and there was no one there to hear her (vv 25–27). In the center, both parties are executed for committing adultery (vv 22–24). All of these laws are expanded in story form within the book of Genesis, as Carmichael has shown (*LNB,* 210–20).

In terms of rhetorical markers within the MT, the laws in 22:13–29 are divided into six sections, each of which ends with the *sĕtûmā'* layout marker: vv 13–19, 20–21, 22, 23–24, 25–27, and 28–29. Further indications of overall structure are present in the two occurrences of the *Numeruswechsel* in v 24. The first two occurrences of second singular forms of the verb and pronominal suffixes appear in the formulaic expression "you shall purge the evil from your midst" at the end of vv 21 and 22. The rest of the material in vv 13–22 is in the third person, except for quotation of direct speech in the first person in vv 14 and 16–17. The two occurrences of second plural verbal forms in v 24 (והוצאתם and וסקלתם) mark the center of the larger structure of vv 13–29 as a whole. The shift back to second singular forms at the end of v 24 occurs again within the same formulaic expression "you shall purge the evil from your midst," which appears here for the third and final time within vv 13–29.

The issue at hand in the first law is an accusation of premarital unchastity on the part of the husband of a new bride. In terms of internal symmetry, the content of this literary unit may be outlined as follows:

A	A man attempts to put aside his wife on baseless charges	22:13–14
B	The girl's parents present evidence to the elders	22:15
X	The girl's father states his case	22:16–17a
B′	The girl's father presents evidence before the elders	22:17b
A′	The man is flogged, fined, and may never divorce the woman	22:18–19

The central point in this structure is the statement of the case itself by the girl's father: "I gave my daughter to this man as a wife; and he hates her, and behold he has made up baseless charges saying, 'I did not find your daughter to be a virgin'" (vv 16–17a). The inner frame concerns the evidence produced by the parents that the charges are false (vv 15 and 17b), whereas the outer frame moves from a description of the legal issue (vv 13–14) to the decision rendered by the elders in such a case (vv 18–19). The second layout (vv 20–21) deals with what is to be done if the charges are substantiated.

There are puzzling features about this law that lend substance to the symbolic reading proposed by Carmichael. First, the bride's parents are to present the so-called wedding night cloth and could fake it. "Talmudic sources report that in some places the bride was searched to make certain that she did not bring an already stained cloth into the nuptial chamber (the groom was likewise searched to ensure that he did not bring a clean cloth to switch with the legitimately stained one in order to detroy the evidence of virginity . . . (Tosef. Ket. 1:4ff.; TJ Ket. 1:1, 25a; 4:4, 28c; and Ket. 12a)" (Tigay [1996] 539 n. 1).

The statement that the absence of the bloodstained cloth is sufficient evidence to convict the bride appears to be contrary to the normal requirement of two witnesses to a crime involving capital punishment (17:2; 19:15). "It also overlooks the fact that not all virgins have intact hymens or bleed the first time they have sexual relations, a fact also recognized in talmudic sources" (Tigay [1996] 476). Moreover, the law seems to be in contradiction to others that indicate that such sexual misconduct calls for execution only if the girl in question is betrothed at the time (see vv 23–24 and Exod 22:15–16).

In short, the law as stated is not practicable. "Even the avowedly literalistic Karaite exegesis agrees that the matter cannot hinge on the cloth alone and that witnesses (attendants who examined the cloth or the bride at the time of the marriage) are required. A fragmentary paraphrase of this law from Qumran states that the matter is to be determined on the basis of a physical examination of the bride by trustworthy women shortly after consummation of the marriage" (Tigay [1996] 476).

Driver and Miles have suggested that in comparable laws in ancient Mesopotamia "the penalties are only inserted *in terrorem* and will never be inflicted" (*The Babylonian Laws*, 2 vols. [Oxford: Clarendon, 1952–55] 1:204 n. 3).

This view is similar to rabbinic interpretation of the law about the insubordinate son, which was for educational purposes and not to be enforced. The purpose of the law would then be rhetorical as a means of condemning premarital sex and deterring girls from such activity. "It would provide ammunition for parents to use in warning their daughters against unchastity, much as they could have used 21:18–21 in warning sons against insubordination" (Tigay [1996] 477).

Otto has noted what he calls a concentrically arranged redaction of 22:23–27, which may be outlined as follows ("Aspects of Legal Reforms," 190 n. 99):

A "When a virgin is betrothed. . ." כי יהיה נער בתולה מארשה לאיש 22:23
B "(a man) finds her" מצאה 22:23
C "in the city" בעיר 22:23
X Stone them with stones to purge the evil from your midst 22:24
C′ "in the field" בשדה 22:25
B′ "(where the man) finds her" מצאה 22:25
A′ "(where) the man finds the betrothed girl" את־הנער המארשה 22:25

The center of this structure is marked by the *Numeruswechsel* at the beginning and end of v 24. "This concentric structure precludes a traditio-historical claim that 22.25–27 is a later addition to an original unit in 22.23–24" (Otto, "Aspects of Legal Reforms," 190 n. 99, against Stuhlman, *JSOT* 53 [1992] 58–60).

The two laws on adultery with a married woman (v 22) or a betrothed virgin (vv 23–24) form a literary subunit that may be outlined as follows:

A If a man has sex with another man's wife, "purge the evil" 22:22
B If a man has sex with a betrothed virgin in the city 22:23
X Bring them both to the city gate and stone them to death 22:24a
B′ The woman because she did not cry out, and the man 22:24b
A′ Because he "humbled" his neighbor's wife—"purge the evil" 22:24c

The central issue in this reading is the death penalty itself, which is imposed on both the man and woman guilty of adultery, whether the woman is the wife of another man (v 22) or betrothed to another man (23). Both the man and the woman are to be stoned to death, to purge the evil from the midst of Israel.

The law on the rape of a betrothed virgin in 22:25–27 may also be outlined in concentric fashion:

A If a man finds a betrothed girl in the field and rapes her 22:25a
B Only the man shall be put to death 22:25b
X Do nothing to the girl, for she did not commit a mortal sin 22:26a
B′ It is like the case of a man who murders his neighbor 22:26b
A′ The man found her in the field—there was no one to save her 22:27

The focus of attention in this structure is on the woman, for she did not commit a mortal sin and so should not be punished (v 26a). When the man found her in the field and raped her, there was no one to save her (vv 25a and 27). Thus only the man is to be put to death (v 25b), because the situation is comparable to the case where a man murders his neighbor (v 26b).

According to Carmichael (*LNB*, 210–14), the law of the wedding-night cloth (vv 13–21) stands in sharp contrast with what happened to Joseph. Joseph's garment in the hands of Potiphar's wife falsely condemned him to prison for a sexual crime he did not commit. The case of the slandered bride points us back to Jacob's marriage to Leah instead of Rachel (Gen 29:15–31), which took place on the wedding night when Jacob was to marry Rachel. As in the law, Jacob after his wedding night does not wish to marry his new bride.

A second story that appears to be shaped, at least in part, by the laws of marital and sexual misconduct of Deut 22:13–29 is that of Dina and the Canaanite prince Shechem, son of Hamor, in Gen 34 (see Carmichael, *LNB,* 213–14). The same phrase used to condemn Shechem for his misconduct with Dinah is applied to the woman's premarital activity in the law: the girl "has done folly in Israel committing fornication in her father's house" (Deut 22:21; cf. Gen 34:7). Moreover, the Genesis story describes Shechem's offense as treating Dinah like a harlot (Gen 34:31).

The law about adultery in v 22 appears to have shaped, at least in part, the stories about Sarah's relationship with both the pharaoh and Abimelech (Carmichael, *LNB,* 214–16). It is noteworthy that the technical designation of "a man's wife" (בעלת בעל) occurs within the Hebrew Bible only in Gen 20:3 and Deut 22:22, in the context of references to capital punishment.

The law of the seduction of a betrothed woman (Deut 22:23–27) plays a role in the shaping of the story of Joseph and Potiphar's wife (Carmichael, *LNB,* 217–18). For Potiphar's wife to be in the clear, if the story is shaped by the law here in Deuteronomy, she must either cry out for help or be sufficiently distant from human habitation to make such cries futile (v 25). The analogy of the man who is murdered in a remote setting (v 26) also applies to the larger story of Joseph, who was almost murdered in such a setting before his brothers changed their minds and sold him into slavery instead (Gen 37:17–20).

The law of the seduction of an unbetrothed woman (Deut 22:28–29) points us once again to the story of Dinah's plight at the hands of Shechem (Gen 34; see Carmichael, *LNB,* 218–20). Dinah was not with her own people when the incident occurred, and hence a cry from her would not have been heard by her brothers. She had gone "to visit the women of the land" (Gen 34:1). Shechem "humbled" (ענה) Dinah, treating her as a harlot (Gen 34:31). The same verb ענה appears in the law of Deut 22:29.

The evidence assembled by Labuschagne on the use of the divine-name numbers in 22:13–29 may be summarized as follows:

Words:	before *ʾatnāḥ*		after *ʾatnāḥ*		
22:13–21	78 (= 3 × 26)	+	51 (= 3 × 17)	=	129
22:22	16	+	3	=	19
22:23–29	76	+	43 (= 17 + 26)	=	119 (= 7 × 17)
22:13–14	12	+	14	=	26
22:13–17	34 (= 2 × 17)	+	34 (= 2 × 17)	=	68 (= 4 × 17)
22:18–21	44	+	17	=	61
22:22–27	73	+	34 (= 2 × 17)	=	107
22:23–24	34 (= 2 × 17)	+	8	=	42
22:25–27	23	+	23	=	46 (= 2 × 23)
22:1–12	109	+	61	=	170 (= 10 × 17)
22:13–29	170 (= 10 × 17)	+	97	=	267

The laws on marriage and sexual misconduct in 22:13–29 are carefully arranged in two major sections (vv 13–21 and 23–29), with the basic citation of the seventh commandment (forbidding adultery) in the center (v 22). In the first half of this mathematical composition there are 78 (= 3 × 26) words before *ʾatnāḥ* and 51 (= 3 × 17) words after *ʾatnāḥ*, an arrangement that symbolically intensifies the divine presence in this text. The total number of words in the second half (vv 23–29) comes to 119 (= 7 × 17), which reinforces this intensification. Moreover, there are 43 (= 17 + 26) words after *ʾatnāḥ* here to communicate the same message yet a third time.

Within the body of the text we find six subunits that correspond, for the most part, with the prosodic subunits found in the prosodic analysis here on independent grounds. There are 26 words in vv 13–14, which presents the false accusation of premarital unchastity. When this text is combined with the following subsection that presents the case for the defense on the part of the parents of the accused girl (vv 15–17), we have 34 (= 2 × 17) words before and after *ʾatnāḥ*. When these two subunits are combined with the decision on the part of the elders before whom the case was brought (vv 18–19), we find that the total number of 98 words is divided so as to have 26 words in the subordinate clauses of 22:13–19. Moreover, the law on false accusation of premarital unchastity (22:13–19) is tied together with the law on true accusation of premarital unchastity (22:20–21) by the fact that vv 18–21 have 17 words after *ʾatnāḥ*.

The law prohibiting adultery with a betrothed virgin (vv 23–24), which has 34 (= 2 × 17) words before *ʾatnāḥ*, is tied together with what follows by the fact that there are 34 words after *ʾatnāḥ* in 22:22–27. The law on rape of an engaged virgin (vv 25–27) has 23 words before and after *ʾatnāḥ*, an arrangement that signifies that all this hidden information on the use of the two divine-name numbers was done to the "glory" (כבוד = 11 + 2 + 6 + 4 = 32) of God.

When chap. 22 is examined as a whole, in terms of the use of the divine-name numbers, we find that there are 170 (= 10 × 17) words in vv 1–12 and the same number of words before *ʾatnāḥ* in vv 13–29. The message here seems to be a reminder that we are dealing with the Ten Commandments, which is the very word of God that Moses received at the beginning.

Comment

13–14 The situation here is one in which a man's feelings toward his new wife have changed and "he hates her" (ושׂנאה) to the extent that "he makes baseless charges against her" by bringing "on her a bad name," that is, he makes public the charge that she was not a virgin at the time of the consummation of the marriage. The phrase עלילת דברים, translated here as "baseless charges," has been translated in different ways. LXX, Vg., Ibn Ezra, and also KJV ("occasions") interpret the word עלילת from Aramaic עילה, "circumstance," "occasion." Mayes has noted ([1981] 309–10) that this sense is not otherwise attested for the root עלל in biblical Hebrew, where the hithpael has the meaning "to act wantonly" or "to act ruthlessly" (cf. Num 22:29; Judg 19:25; 1 Sam 6:6; 31:4). The RSV thus translates the word as "shameful conduct," and the NRSV paraphrases to read "slandering her." The translation here follows Craigie ([1976] 291) in the sense of "wantonness of words," or baseless accusations. Tigay has drawn attention to a parallel situation in Arab culture: "if a groom found his bride not to have been a virgin, he turned her out immediately, and if her family refunded the bride-price, he was obligated to keep quiet. If, however, he spoke out, the girl was examined. If she was found guilty, irrespective of whether she lost her virginity long before or recently, she was executed, but if she was innocent, the groom was executed" ([1996] 204; see A. Musil, *Arabia Petraea,* 3 vols. [Vienna: Hoelder, 1908] 3:208). Translated literally, "I did not find her to be a virgin" would be "I did not find virginity [בתולים] in her," that is, her hymen was not intact or she did not bleed (see v 17 below). Wenham interprets the word בתולים as referring to proof of menstruation immediately before marriage, meaning the bride is not already pregnant (*VT* 22 [1972] 331–33). This interpretation is necessary, as Mayes has observed ([1981] 310), if Wenham's interpretation of the related word בתולה, "virgin," is correct (see the *Comment* on v 23).

15–17 Since the legal responsibility for defending the young woman rested on the parents, "the girl's father and her mother shall . . . bring out evidence of the girl's virginity," which is "the garment" (השמלה), or the cloth spotted by the girl's blood when her hymen was broken. It was not uncommon within Jewish and Arab communities in the Middle East, until recent times, for the "wedding cloth" to be displayed by the proud parents of the bride (Westermarck, *Marriage Ceremonies in Morocco,* 159, 228; Granqvist, *Marriage Conditions,* 2:127–30; I. Ben-Ami and D. Noy, eds., *Studies in Marriage Customs* [Jerusalem: Magnes, 1974] 54, 174, 260, 262; and Karaite sources cited by Malul, *JESHO* 32 [1989] 264; all cited by Tigay [1996] 384 n. 47). The "wedding cloth" (השמלה), which was normally an outer garment that was also used as a cover while sleeping (cf. 24:13), was "spread out . . . before the elders of the city," which is another instance in which the elders exercised jurisdiction in matters of family law. On the meaning of "at the gate" see the *Comment* on 17:5. "The custom that virgins wed on Wednesdays arose because courts held session on Thursdays; thus a man who suspected his bride of premarital unchastity could press charges immediately (Mish. Ket. 1:1; Tosef. Ket. 1:1)" (Tigay [1996] 384 n. 48).

18–19 The husband receives a triple punishment: "they shall flog him," "they shall fine him a hundred pieces of silver," and "he may not divorce her all his days," which provides her the needed economic protection for survival. It should be noted with Mayes ([1981] 310) that the translation "they shall flog him" (ויסרו אתו) is not certain, even though the ancient versions understood it in this way. Apart from this passage, and possibly 21:18, the verbal root יסר has the meaning of "admonish" or "discipline" more generally. Mayes suggests the translation "punish him," with the following verse prescribing the nature of the punishment: the fine of "a hundred pieces of silver," which is normally interpreted as double the bride-price for a virgin (however, see v 29 below and Exod 22:16). It should be noted with Mayes that it is the father's reputation that is at stake here ([1981] 310), even though it is the woman who has been slandered. The father is implicitly charged with deceitfully passing off his daughter as a virgin. The concluding statement that the man "has brought an evil name on a virgin of Israel" suggests that his accusation would raise doubts about the character of all Israelite girls, as the *Sifre* indicates (Tigay [1996] 205).

20–21 If the accusation turns out to be correct, "the girl was found not to have been a virgin," the girl was to be taken "to the entrance of her father's house," since she is guilty of "committing fornication in her father's house."

Such action would also be a form of communal judgment against the father. Tigay cites an interesting parallel from the Code of Hammurabi (§21): "where a man who breaks into a house is to be executed in front of the breach that he made" ([1996] 206). Execution by stoning ("the men of her city shall stone her with stones") was also required in the law of the insubordinate son (see the *Comment* on 21:21 and 13:11). On the statement "you shall purge the evil" see the *Comment* on 13:6.

22 The prohibition of adultery is the seventh of the Ten Commandments (see 5:17). In such cases, "both of them shall die—the man who lay with the woman and the woman." According to Tigay ([1996] 206–7), other law collections from the ancient Near East also prescribe capital punishment for adultery (Code of Hammurabi, §129; Middle Assyrian Laws, A §§14–16; Hittite Laws, §§197–98). But in these other cultures the offense is considered to be one that is done against the husband of the woman, who may choose to spare his wife, and her lover, by imposing a lesser penalty. There is no clear evidence that adulterers were actually executed in ancient Israel, though that is clearly the implication of the story of the woman taken in adultery as presented in John 8:1–11. The story of Judah and Tamar, in which her death was ordered for what was thought to be adultery, may simply be a story form of the law in question, as Carmichael's research suggests. The warning in Prov 6:32–35 implies the right of a husband to accept a financial payment from an adulterer, even if his normal inclination might be otherwise. Once again, as in the case of the law of the insubordinate son (21:18–21) and the accused bride (22:13–21), we appear to be dealing with a law that was seldom, if ever, put in practice (see Greenberg, "More Reflections on Biblical Criminal Law," 1–4; McKeating, *JSOT* 11 [1979] 57–72; Phillips, *JSOT* 20 [1981] 3–26; Westbrook, *RB* 97 [1990] 542–80; and Tigay, *EncJud* 2:313–15).

23–24 Wenham has argued that the word translated here as "virgin" (בתולה) should be rendered "girl of marriageable age" (*VT* 22 [1972] 326–48). The laws on premarital unchastity in 22:13–21, however, imply the subject of virginity in the laws that follow in vv 25–29 as well, which are to be read over against vv 13–21 in the concentric structural design of the seven laws on marriage and sexual misconduct in 22:13–23:1. In cases where a man has sexual intercourse with "a virgin who is betrothed . . . in the city," both parties are to be brought "to the gate of that city, and you shall stone them with stones." The woman's guilt in the matter is determined on the basis of whether she was a willing partner. Again, we have a law that is difficult actually to apply. Philo, Josephus, and early rabbinic sources broaden the law, as Tigay has noted: "whether in town or in the country, evidence that there was no one who could have saved her, that she resisted, or that her life was threatened if she resisted, would establish innocence; evidence to the contrary would establish guilt" ([1996] 207).

25–27 If the girl is raped in the open country and the man lies with her by force, then only the man shall die who slept with her. In such cases, the girl is a victim and not a participant—"the girl did not commit a mortal sin," for she "cried out, but there was no one to save her." A text from among the Dead Sea Scrolls at Qumran (11QTemple 66:4–5) attempts to clarify the situation by adding: "in a far-away place, hidden from the city." In subsequent Jewish tradition, the statement "to the girl you shall do nothing" became the basis for the principle that one who violates the law under compulsion is not liable (*b. Ned.*

27a; *Sefer Ha-Ḥinnukh,* no. 573; cited by Tigay [1996] 385 n. 67). Fishbane has interpreted v 26 as an exegesis of 19:2–13 (*Biblical Interpretation,* 217–20).

28–29 Though sexual intercourse with an unbetrothed virgin is against the law, it is not a capital offense. The translation "who has never been betrothed" (אשר לא־ארשה) is that of Weiss (*JBL* 81 [1962] 67–69), who noted the use of the passive perfect here rather than the passive participle of vv 23, 25, and 27. The compensation to the father is for loss in the expected bride price he would normally receive. In such cases, "the man who lay with her shall give to the father of the girl fifty pieces of silver," often interpreted as the normal bride-price for a virgin (cf. also Exod 22:15–16). Tigay has argued convincingly, however, that "if the seducer of Exodus 22:16 is required to pay an average bride-price, the fifty pieces of silver paid by the rapist represents a combination of an average bride-price [thirty pieces of silver] plus punitive damages." It should be noted that the law here deals only with a girl for whom a bride-price has never been paid. The law concludes with the statement that the rapist must marry the girl and that "he may not divorce her all his days." Once again, we have a law that runs contrary to common practice, for in subsequent Jewish tradition, in cases of both seduction and rape, both the girl and her father can refuse the marriage. Tigay has noted parallels in Middle Assyrian Laws ([1996] 209), where "the rapist must pay triple the normal bride-price and marry the girl (if the father is willing) without right of divorce. If the rapist has a wife, a typically Mesopotamian measure-for-measure punishment is added: the girl's father can have the rapist's wife raped and then keep her" (Middle Assyrian Laws, A §55).

Explanation

Three situations are addressed in the laws on marital and sexual misconduct in 22:13–29, each of which is in two parts. The first situation concerns a husband's accusation of premarital unchastity on the part of the woman (vv 13–21). If the charges are proved false, the man is to be flogged and fined one hundred pieces of silver (vv 13–19). If the charges are proved true, the woman is to be stoned to death at "the entrance of her father's house" (vv 20–21). The specific location of the execution indicates parental responsibility for the sexual behavior of their children. The instruction that execution be carried out by "men of her city" indicates that the entire community is involved in the incident. Sexual misconduct is not simply a private affair. The community also suffers as a consequence. As John Maxwell put it, "There is no such thing as a 'casual affair.' One need only read the statistics concerning abortions, sexually transmitted diseases, and government assistance for unwed mothers to realize that private sexual sins quickly become public matters of concern" (*Deuteronomy* [1987] 262–63). The law here encourages premarital sexual purity and the value of sexual abstinence prior to marriage.

The second situation addressed is the matter of adultery, which includes sexual intercourse with a betrothed virgin as well as with another man's wife. Both parties are to be executed. Though the means of execution is not indicated in the matter of adultery with a married woman (v 22), it was presumably by stoning as in the case of adultery with a betrothed virgin (v 24). This is clearly the method of execution indicated for the woman caught in adultery in John 8:5.

The third situation addressed is the matter of rape. If a man rapes a betrothed virgin in the open country, the man alone is to be executed, since the screams of the woman would not have been heard (vv 25–27). If a man rapes an unbetrothed woman in the city, it is considered seduction, requiring marriage and paying the girl's father fifty pieces of silver (vv 28–29), as a dowry.

In light of what is often called the modern sexual revolution, the laws on premarital sex in this text seem quaint to some and certainly out of touch with reality. Nonetheless, this law teaches that parents are to be concerned with the actions of their children in matters of sexual conduct. In the teaching of Jesus the ideals reach greater heights, equating lust with the act of adultery itself (Matt 5:27–28). Paul argued that the human body is to be considered the temple of the Holy Spirit and treated accordingly (Eph 5:32).

4. Prohibition of Marrying One's Father's Wife (23:1 [Eng. 22:30])

Bibliography

Baker, D. W. "Further Examples of the *Waw Explicativum.*" *VT* 30 (1980) 129–36. **Carmichael, C. M.** "A Ceremonial Crux: Removing a Man's Sandals as a Female Gesture of Contempt." *JBL* 96 (1977) 321–36, esp. 326, 333. ———. "Forbidden Mixtures." *VT* 32 (1982) 395–415, esp. 396. ———. "'Treading' in the Book of Ruth." *ZAW* 92 (1980) 248–66 (259). **Dahan, G.** "Les interprétations juives dans les commentaires du Pentateuque de Pierre le Chantre." In *FS B. Smalley.* 1985. 131–55. **Daniel, C.** "Esséniens et Eunuques." *RevQ* 6 (1967/68) 353–90. **Daube, D.** "The Culture of Deuteronomy." *Orita* 3 (1969) 31. **Halévy, J.** "Recherches bibliques: Le Deutéronome." *RSEHA* 8 (1900) 107. **Hoffner, H. A.** "Incest, Sodomy and Bestiality in the Ancient Near East." In *FS C. H. Gordon.* 1973. 81–90. **Phillips, A.** "Uncovering the Father's Skirt." *VT* 30 (1980) 38–43. **Smith, W. R.** *Kinship and Marriage in Early Arabia.* 1903. 104–11. **Tsevat, M.** "Marriage and Monarchical Legitimacy in Ugarit and Israel." *JSS* 3 (1958) 237–43.

Translation and Prosodic Analysis

Prohibition of Marrying One's Father's Wife [2:2]

23:1 (22:30) *A man shall not take / his father's wife //*	14	2
and he shall not remove / his father's garment // ס	<u>12</u>	2

Form/Structure/Setting

The law prohibiting marriage to one's father's wife (23:1) functions as a literary bridge connecting two larger groups of laws on matters of social ethics (21:10–22:29 and 23:2–26 [Eng. 23:1–25]). It is also in parallel with a somewhat similar law prohibiting remarriage if one's former wife has remarried (24:1–4), which functions in the same manner connecting the laws of 23:2–26 and 24:5–25:19, as the following outline indicates:

A	Marriage/war, true religion, and illicit mixtures	21:10–22:29
B	Prohibition of marrying one's father's wife	23:1
X	Laws on social ethics (true religion)	23:2–26
B′	Prohibition of remarriage if one's former wife has remarried	24:1–4
A′	Marriage/war and true religion (on the poor and vulnerable)	24:5–25:19

Within this structure, 23:1 serves as an inclusion with the law on marriage with a woman captured in war (21:10–14) and as an introduction to the laws on the assembly of YHWH and the sanctity of the military camp (23:2–15). By the term "true religion" I mean concern for the protection of the poor and vulnerable, as the letter of James put it: "Religion that is pure and undefiled before God, the Father, is this: to care for orphans and widows in their distress, and to keep oneself unstained by the world" (Jas 1:27 NRSV).

The law in 23:1 is also part of a series of seven laws (21:10–14; 22:13–23:1) that function as a "commentary" on the seventh commandment (5:18; prohibiting adultery) within another concentric structure (21:10–23:1), which may be outlined as follows:

A	Marriage with a woman captured in war	21:10–14
B	Two family laws pertaining to children	21:15–21
X	Ten laws on true religion and illicit mixtures	21:22–22:12
B′	Five family laws on marital and sexual misconduct	22:13–29
A′	Prohibition of marrying one's father's wife	23:1

Two of the seven laws on matters pertaining to the seventh commandment (prohibiting adultery) make up the outer frame (21:10–14 and 23:1) of this structure, and the other five are in the second half of the inner frame, the five family laws on marital and sexual misconduct (22:13–29).

Another way of looking at the structure of 21:10–23:1, which is shaped by the seventh commandment (5:18), is to place that very law as it appears in 22:22–24 at the center of the outline:

A	Marriage with a woman captured in war (+ 12 laws [21:15–22:12])	21:10–14
B	Two laws regarding accusations of premarital unchastity	22:13–21
X	Adultery with a married woman or a betrothed virgin	22:22–24
B′	Two laws on the rape of a virgin	22:25–29
A′	Prohibition of marrying one's father's wife	23:1

The seventh commandment (5:18) in the center of this structure applies to a betrothed virgin as well as a woman who is married to another man. The inner frame moves from two laws on premarital unchastity (22:13–19), to two laws on rape (22:25–29). The outer frame is made up of two laws on marriage, which are part of a series of four such laws on marriage functioning as a framework around seven laws on matters of social ethics (23:2–26), as the following outline shows:

A Marriage with a woman captured in war (+ 17 laws on social ethics [21:15–22:29]) 21:10–14
B Prohibition of marrying one's father's wife 23:1
X Seven laws on matters of social ethics ("true religion") 23:2–26
B′ Prohibition of remarriage if one's former wife has remarried 24:1–4
A′ Deferral of new husband from military service 24:5

The two laws in the outer frame of this structure deal with both marriage and war (i.e., commandments six and seven). The two laws in the inner frame of this structure (23:1 and 24:1–4) function as bridges connecting two larger structures and belonging to both of them.

The seven laws in the center of the previous structure may be outlined within the larger literary structure of Deut 23–25:

A From forbidden marriage to sanctity of the military camp 23:1–15
B Law protecting the poor and vulnerable: asylum for escaped slaves 23:16–17
X Prohibition of "holy" prostitution 23:18–19
B′ Three laws protecting the poor and vulnerable 23:20–26
A′ From forbidden remarriage to Holy War (war with Amalek) 24:1–25:19

The outer frame in this structure opens with the law prohibiting marriage to one's father's wife (23:1), which introduces a lesser structure that concludes with a law pertaining to the sanctity of the military camp (23:10–15). It continues with a law prohibiting remarriage to a former wife who has remarried (25:1–4), which introduces a group of fourteen laws, concluding with one on YHWH's Holy War (25:17–19, which is a command to remember Amalekite aggression in the exodus from Egypt). The inner frame is made up of four laws protecting the poor and vulnerable (true religion), in the familiar three-plus-one structural pattern of Jungian psychology. The center of this structure has the character of a "riddle at the middle" in the prohibition of "holy" prostitution (23:18–19).

In terms of prosodic structural units, vv 13–29 are divided into four sections: vv 13–19, 20–21, 22–24, and 25–29. This suggests the possibility of reading 23:1 as the fifth part of a literary unit in a five-part concentric structure; 23:1 forms an inclusion with the law on attempting to put aside one's wife on false charges (22:13–19). The concentric design of 22:13–23:1 in this reading may be outlined as follows:

A Attempt to put away one's wife on false charges—man fined 22:13–19
B Premarital unchastity—woman dies 22:20–21
X Adultery with a married or a betrothed woman—both die 22:22–24
B′ Rape of betrothed or unbetrothed virgin—man dies or is fined 22:25–29
A′ Prohibition of marrying one's father's wife 23:1

The law on adultery (with a married woman, v 22; or a betrothed woman, vv 23–24) remains in the center. The inner frame has the law on premarital unchastity, in which the woman is executed (vv 20–21), set over against the two laws on rape, in which the man is executed (vv 25–27) or fined (vv 28–29). Further evidence for this reading is the manner in which 22:13 and 23:1 form an inclusion around the whole with repetition of specific words and phrases: כי־יקח איש אשה,

"When a man takes a woman," in 22:13 and לא־יקח איש את־אשת אביו, "A man shall not take his father's wife," in 23:1. Moreover, the attempt to make these parallel lines virtually identical helps to explain the peculiar wording of 23:1, which is translated "former wife" in the new JPS *Tanakh* (1988), though it is not so qualified in the Hebrew text.

Following the series of five laws on marital and sexual misconduct (22:13–29), the law forbidding a sexual relationship with one's father's wife (23:1) takes the reader back to the story of Reuben and his father's concubine (Gen 35:22; 49:4), and the law of inheritance rights of the firstborn son (21:15–17), to form an inclusion with the beginning of the larger section of laws in 21:10–23:1. The association of the previous law with the story of Dinah, Jacob's first and only daughter (Gen 34), is easy to understand, for Reuben is Jacob's firstborn son.

The first part of the law here, which prohibits a man from taking his father's wife, includes the taking and possessing of his father's concubine(s) in a formal legal relationship. The prohibition against removing his father's garment in the second half of the verse resorts to figurative language. According to Carmichael, it focuses on Reuben's intercourse with Bilhah. In his discussion of what he calls the law on "a forbidden relationship with a father's wife," Carmichael says: "In the law, a man's wife is his skirt, and for a son to lie with her means that figuratively he has removed his father's covering and put it on himself. In a literal sense he uncovers his stepmother's nakedness, in a figurative sense, his father's" (*LNB,* 222). Furthermore, he calls attention to the "double nature of this law." The general prohibition of taking one's father's wife, presumably after his death, is followed by a specific condemnation of a son having intercourse with his father's concubine while the father is still alive, as Reuben did with Bilhah (Gen 35:22).

Comment

1 The phrase אשת אביו, "wife of his father," here must refer to a father's former wife or concubine; for one's own mother see Lev 18:7–8 and 27:20 below. Craigie interpreted this verse as prohibiting adultery with a man's stepmother. It is more likely that the law "precludes a man from marrying a woman divorced by his father and inheriting or marrying his father's wives and concubines after his death," as Tigay has argued ([1996] 209). If the law were interpreted broadly so as to include concubines as well as wives, it would prohibit the action taken by Absalom (2 Sam 16:21–22). The phrase "remove his father's garment" (יגלה כנף אביו), like "seeing [or 'uncovering'] someone's nakedness," means having sexual relations with that person (Lev 18:7–8; 20:11; see also Lev 18:10, 14, 16; 20:20, 21; Nah 3:5). "The point seems to be either that one sees nakedness that is reserved for his father or that the act is tantamount to having sexual relations with *him*" (Tigay [1996] 209). On the basis of Ruth 3:9 and Ezek 16:8, Mayes interpreted the phrase "to cover with the skirt" as meaning "to marry": "to uncover the skirt" would mean "to invade the privacy of the father's marriage relationship" (Mayes [1981] 313).

Explanation

The law in Deut 23:1 prohibits sexual relations with one's father's wife, as in the parallel passages of Lev 18:8 and 20:11 (see also Deut 27:20). It is clear that the text here refers to a woman who is not one's own mother since a separate law in Lev 18:6–7 deals with that situation. In ancient Israel, girls married at a young age, often in their early teens. In the case of a later wife (for whatever reason), it was sometimes the case that the woman would be the same age as, if not younger than, the man's son by an earlier wife. Their presence together in the same house would sometimes create enticing situations, along the lines of what transpired between the slave Joseph and Potiphar's wife (Gen 39). Tigay ([1996] 209) calls attention to Middle Assyrian Laws (Mal A, §46) allowing a man to marry his father's former wife; and in pre-Islamic Arab culture an heir inherited a man's wives and concubines along with the rest of his property (W. R. Smith, *Kinship and Marriage in Early Arabia* [1903] 104–11).

The specific wording of the law here shapes details in the story in the book of Genesis about Reuben, who had sexual relations with Bilhah, his father's concubine (see Gen 35:22). In that instance we have a polygamous household in which Jacob's wife Leah was Reuben's mother (Gen 29:32). Bilhah was the slave of Jacob's other wife, Rachel (Gen 30:2–5). Reuben was subsequently cursed by his father, Jacob, for his sexual relationship with Bilhah (Gen 49:4).

Tsevat argues that the taking of a ruler's wives or concubines was a way of asserting or strengthening the claim to royalty on the part of a would-be usurper to the throne ("Marriage and Monarchical Legitimacy in Ugarit and Israel," *JSS* 3 [1958] 237–43). Thus Adonijah's request for David's concubine Abishag led to his execution by Solomon (1 Kgs 2:13–25). Earlier in the narrative story of David's reign, Absalom publicly consorted with David's concubines in his aborted *coup d'état* (2 Sam 16:21–22). Such action violates the law that prohibits marriage to one's father's wife. The tenth commandment declares that a man is not to covet his neighbor's wife (Deut 5:21). This applies even in specific situations where that "neighbor" is one's own father, who may be the king—particularly in the question of succession to the throne.

D. Seven Laws on "True Religion" (23:1–26 [Eng. 22:30–23:25])

1. Admission to the Assembly of YHWH (23:1–9 [Eng. 22:30–23:8])

Bibliography

Bertholet, A. *Die Stellung der Israeliten und Juden zu den Fremden.* Leipzig, 1896. 173. **Blenkinsopp, J.** "Second Isaiah—Prophet of Universalism." *JSOT* 41 (1988) 83–103. **Brichto, H. C.** *The Problem of "Curse" in the Hebrew Bible.* 1963. 195–96. **Carmichael, C. M.** *LNB.* 228–31. ———. "A New View of the Origin of the Deuteronomic Credo." *VT* 19 (1969) 287–88. ———. *Women, Law and the Genesis Traditions.* Edinburgh: Edinburgh UP, 1979.

Christensen, D. L. "A New Israel: The Righteous from among All Nations." In *FS R. K. Harrison*. 1988. 251–59. **Cohen, S.** "Conversion to Judaism in Historical Perspective: From Biblical Israel to Postbiblical Judaism." *ConsJud* 36 (1982–83) 31–45. **Daube, D.** "The Culture of Deuteronomy." *Orita* 3 (1969) 31. **Eerdmans, B. D.** *Deuteronomy*. 1927. 77–84. **Falk, Z. W.** "Those Excluded from the Congregation." *BMik* 20 (1975) 342–51, 438 (Heb.). **Feigin, S.** "Etymological Notes." *AJSL* 43 (1926/27) 53–60. **Fishbane, M.** *Biblical Interpretation in Ancient Israel*. 1988. 114–43. ———. "The Treaty Background of Amos 1:11 and Related Matters." *JBL* 89 (1970) 313–18. **Freund, J.** "'Do Not Abhor the Edomite, for He Is Your Brother' (Deut 23,8)." *BMik* 11 (1965–66) 117–21 (Heb.). **Galling, K.** "Das Gemeindegesetz in Deuteronomium 23." In *FS A. Bertholet*. 1950. 176–91. **Gevaryahu, H.** "Thou Shalt Not Abhor an Egyptian." *DD* 3 (1974) 6–9 (Heb.). **Glueck, N.** "Deut 23:8, 9." In *The Mordecai M. Kaplan Jubilee Volumes*. Ed. M. Davis. 2 vols. New York: Jewish Theological Seminary of America, 1953. 2:261–62. **Gordis, R.** "Primitive Democracy in Ancient Israel." In *Poets, Prophets, and Sages*. Bloomington: Indiana UP, 1971. 45–60. **Greenberg, M.** "Mankind, Israel and the Nations in the Hebraic Heritage." In *No Man Is Alien: Essays on the Unity of Mankind*. Ed. J. R. Nelson. Leiden: Brill, 1971. 15–40, esp. 28–29. **Hillers, D. R.** "A Note on Some Treaty Terminology in the Old Testament." *BASOR* 176 (1964) 46–47. **Hossfeld, F.-L.** "Volk Gottes als 'Versammlung.'" In *Unterwegs zur Kirche—Alttestamentliche Konzeptionen*. Ed. J. Schreiner. QD 110. Freiburg im Breisgau: Herder, 1987. 123–42. **Hulst, A. R.** "Het Woord *kahal* in Deuteronomium." *NThS* 22 (1939) 159–66. ———. "Der Name 'Israel' im Deuteronomium." *OTS* 9 (1951) 65–106. **Kaufmann, Y.** *History of the Religion of Israel: From the Babylonian Captivity to the End of Prophecy*. Tr. C. W. Efroymson. New York: Ktav, 1977. 136–39, 331–49, 384–85. ———. *The Religion of Israel*. Tr. M. Greenberg. Chicago: Univ. of Chicago Press, 1960. 206, 300–301, 449, 451. **Kellermann, U.** "Erwägungen zum deuteronomischen Gemeindegesetz Dt 23,2–9." *BN* 2 (1977) 33–47. **Klein, H.** "Die Aufnahme Fremder in die Gemeinde des Alten und des Neuen Bundes." *Theologische Beiträge* 12 (1981) 21–35. **Kritzinger, J. D. W.** *Qehal Jahwe: Wat dit es en wie daaraan mag behoort*. Kampen: Kok, 1957. **McCarthy, D. J.** "Ebla, ὅρμια τέμνειν, *ṭb*, *šlm*: Addenda to *Treaty and Covenant*[2]." *Bib* 60 (1979) 247–53. **Milgrom, J.** "Religious Conversion and the Revolt Model for the Formation of Israel." *JBL* 101 (1982) 169–76, esp. 173–74. ———. *Studies in Cultic Theology and Terminology*. SJLA 36. Leiden: Brill, 1983. 1–17. **Moran, W. L.** "A Note on the Treaty Terminology of the Sefire Stelas." *JNES* 22 (1963) 173–76. **Mowinckel, S.** "Zu Dt 23,2–9." *ActOr* 1 (1923) 81–104. **Neufeld, E.** *Ancient Hebrew Marriage Laws*. 1944. 224–27. ———. "The Prohibition against Loans at Interest in Ancient Hebrew Laws." *HUCA* 26 (1955) 355–412. **Ohana, M.** "Prosélytisme et Targum palestinien: Données nouvelles pour la datation de Néofiti 1." *Bib* 55 (1974) 317–32. **Rouillard, H.** *La Péricope de Balaam (Nombers 22–24)*. Fondation Singer-Polignac. Etudes bibliques. Paris: Gabalda, 1985. **Saggs, H. W. F.** *The Greatness That Was Babylon*. London: Sidgwick & Jackson, 1988. 332. **Stamm, J. J.** "Hebräische Frauennamen." In *FS W. Baumgartner*. 1967. 301–39. **Sumner, W. A.** "Israel's Encounters with Edom, Moab, Ammon, Sihon, and Og according to the Deuteronomist." *VT* 18 (1968) 216–28. **Tadmor, H.** "Was the Biblical *saris* a Eunuch?" In *FS J. Greenfield*. 1995. 317–25. **Tadmor, H.,** and **Cogan, M.** "Ahaz and Tiglath-Pileser in the Book of Kings: Historiographic Considerations." *Bib* 60 (1979) 491–508. **Tigay, J.** "Excursus 21: The Background and Development of the Regulations about Admission to the Assembly of the Lord." In *Deuteronomy*. 1996. 477–80. **Weinfeld, M.** "Congregation." *EncJud* 5:893–96. **Welch, A. C.** *Deuteronomy: The Framework to the Code*. 1932. 200. **Wiseman, D. J.** "'Is It Peace?'—Covenant and Diplomacy." *VT* 32 (1982) 311–26, esp. 313.

Bibliography for 23:4–9

Bartlett, J. R. "The Brotherhood of Edom." *JSOT* 4 (1977) 2–27. ———. "The Land of Seir and the Brotherhood of Edom." *JTS* 20 (1969) 1–20. ———. "The Moabites and

Edomites." In *POTT.* 229–58. **Coats, G. W.** "Balaam: Sinner or Saint?" *BR* 17 (1973) 1–9. **Coogan, M. D.** "Canaanite Origins and Lineage: Reflections on the Religion of Ancient Israel." In *FS F. M. Cross.* 1987. 115–24, esp. 116. **Donner, H.** "Balaam Pseudopropheta." In *FS W. Zimmerli.* 1977. 112–23, esp. 121–23. **Finkelstein, J. J.** "Mesopotamia." *JNES* 21 (1962) 73–92. **Hackett, J.** "Religious Tradition in Israelite Transjordan." In *FS F. M. Cross.* 1987. 125–36, esp. 127. **Luria, B. Z.** "The Curse That Has Come upon Ammon and Moab." *BMik* 27 (1981/82) 191–94 (Heb.). **Milgrom, J.** "Excursus 1: Some Political Institutions of Early Israel"; and "Excursus 60: Balaam and the Deir 'Alla Inscription." In *Numbers.* 1990. 335–36, 473–76. **Müller, H.-P.** "Die aramäischen Inschrift von Deir 'Allā und die älteren Bileamsprüche." *ZAW* 94 (1982) 214–44. ———. "Der neu gefundene Bileam-Text aus Deir 'Allā." *ZDMG Sup* 4 (1980) 129–33. **O'Callaghan, R. T.** *Aram Naharaim.* AnOr 26. Rome: Pontifical Biblical Institute, 1948.

Translation and Prosodic Analysis

Restrictions on Entry into the Assembly of YHWH [6] [6]

23:1(22:30) *A man shall not take*\[a] *his father's wife* //	14	1
and he shall not remove / his father's garment // ס	12	2
2(1) *No one with crushed*[a] *testicles / or whose penis is cut off* /	13	2
shall enter the assembly of YHWH // ס	13	1_
3(2) *No one "misbegotten" shall enter / the assembly of YHWH* //	14	2
[a]*even / to the tenth generation* /	8	2
his descendants shall not enter / the assembly of YHWH[a] // ס	13	2_

Exclusion of the Ammonites and Moabites [5:6] [8:8]

4(3) *No Ammonite / or Moabite / shall enter the assembly of YHWH* //	24	3
even[a] / *to the tenth generation* /	8	2_
None of them shall enter / the assembly of YHWH\[b] *forever* //	19	2
5(4) *because / they did not meet* you \[a] with bread and water /	21	2
on the road / when you came out from Egypt //	13	2_
And because he[b] hired against *you* /	11	1
Balaam son of Beor / from Pethor[c] /	12	2
of Aram-naharaim / to curse you //	11	2
6(5) *and YHWH your God / did not consent / to hear Balaam* /	24	3_
And YHWH your God turned for you / the curse / into a blessing //	28	3
for YHWH your God / loved you //	16	2
7(6) *You shall not seek their peace*\[a] *and their good* //	17	1
all your days / forever // ס	10	2_

Inclusion of the Edomites and the Egyptians [6:5]

8(7) *You shall not abhor an Edomite / for he is / your brother* // ס	19	3
[a]*you shall not abhor an Egyptian / for you were* /	13	2
a sojourner in his land //	9	1_
9(8) *Children / born to them / of the third generation* //	22	3
may enter / the assembly of YHWH // ס	12	2_

Notes

1.a. Reading *ṭiphā'* as conj. because when 23:1 is read with the following verse as a prosodic unit, the *'atnāḥ* is displaced.

2.a. Many Heb. MSS and printed editions, Cairo Geniza fragments, and SP read דכה for MT דכא, "crushed." The two verbal roots have the same meaning, though דכה is found in Scripture only in the book of Psalms.

3.a-a. Omitted in LXX. Prosodic analysis supports MT.

4.a. Omitted in LXX^{MS}.

4.b. Reading *ṭiphā'* as conj. because of misplaced *sillûq*.

5.a. Reading *pašṭā'* followed by *zāqēp qāṭôn* as conj.

5.b. LXX and Vg. read pl. Prosodic analysis favors MT.

5.c. SP reads פתרה for MT פתור, "Pethor."

7.a. Reading *ṭiphā'* as conj. because of misplaced *'atnāḥ*.

8.a. A number of Heb. MSS, SP, and Syr. add *waw*-conj.

Form/Structure/Setting

The second major section of laws in the sixth of the eleven weekly portions in the lectionary cycle of Torah readings from Deuteronomy (21:10–25:19) moves from the prohibition of marrying one's father's wife (23:1) to the prohibition of remarriage if one's former wife has remarried in the interim (24:1–4), which is followed by the law on deferral of a new husband from military service (24:5).

The opening words of 23:1, לא־יקח איש את־אשת אביו, "a man shall not take his father's wife," form an inclusion with the opening words of 22:13, כי־יקח איש אשה, "when a man takes a wife," on accusations of premarital unchastity, which in turn are identical with the opening words of 24:1 and 24:5. The arrangement of the laws from 22:13–23:1 may be outlined as follows:

A	False accusation of premarital unchastity (כי־יקח איש אשה)	22:13–19
B	Premarital unchastity—woman dies	22:20–21
X	Adultery with married woman or betrothed virgin—both die	22:22–24
B′	Rape of betrothed or unbetrothed virgin man dies or is fined	22:25–29
A′	Marrying a father's wife prohibited (לא־יקח איש את־אשת אביו)	23:1

The focus of attention in this structure is on the seventh commandment, which prohibits adultery, where both parties face the death penalty (22:22–24). The inner frame moves from the mortal sin of a woman in sexual matters (premarital unchastity, 22:20–21) to that of a man (rape of a betrothed virgin, 22:25–29). The outer frame moves from a specific action on the part of a man who falsely accuses his wife of premarital unchastity (22:13–19) to a general prohibition against a man marrying his father's wife (23:1). Both of these laws are introduced by the words "when a man takes a woman" (22:13; 23:1).

In addition to its role in the above structure, 23:1 also functions as the introduction to another literary unit that may be outlined as follows:

A	Laws on marriage and war (לא־יקח איש את־אשת אביו in 23:1)	23:1–15
B	The law of asylum for the fugitive slave	23:16–17
X	The law prohibiting "holy prostitution"	23:18–19
B′	Laws on the protection of the poor and vulnerable	23:20–26
A′	Laws on marriage and war (כי־יקח איש אשה in 24:1 and 5)	24:1–5

The center in this structure associates the seventh commandment, the prohibition of adultery, with the worship of YHWH (commandments 1–3) in what I call here "holy prostitution," and thus forms an inclusion of sorts with the whole of the collection of laws in 12:1–14:21 ("Right Worship—Relationship to God") as well. The outer frame moves from laws that link war and marriage (23:1–15) to another shorter series on the same topic (24:1–4). As was the case for the laws in 22:13–23:1, both of these sections are introduced by the words "when a man takes a woman" (23:1; 25:1) with repetition of the same words in 25:4. The theme of marriage in both instances is expanded into that of war, moving from the law on the sanctification of the military camp (23:10–15) to the deferral of a new husband from military service (24:5). The inner frame picks up another central theme, which is expanded in depth in the thirteen laws in 24:5–25:19 on the protection of the poor and vulnerable in the society of ancient Israel (23:16–17; 23:20–26).

Having raised the issue of the relationship between the prohibition of adultery and the worship of YHWH within the larger structural design of 23:2–24:4 as a whole, the author's attention focuses first on the assembly of YHWH and the question of membership. The regulations in vv 2–9 bar specific types or groups of people from entering the assembly of YHWH: certain individuals, on the basis of physical impairment of the means of procreation or the questionable nature of their birth in relation to the matter of "holy prostitution" (vv 2–3); and certain aliens—Ammonites and Moabites (vv 4–7), and, at least temporarily, Edomites and Egyptians (vv 8–9).

From a prosodic perspective, 23:1 functions as a rhythmic bridge. When read as a 2:2 unit by itself (in terms of syntactic accentual stress units), it concludes the previous section of laws pertaining to marital and sexual misconduct (22:13–23:1). But when read with what follows, it becomes an integral part of a transitional 6:6 rhythmic unit, which introduces a section of laws on social ethics (23:1–24:5). Within this context, it is closely tied to vv 18–19 (the prohibition of "holy prostitution") and to 24:1–5, which begins and ends with repetition of the opening words of 22:13 (which are modified slightly at the beginning of 23:1): "when a man takes a woman."

The place of the laws on admission to the assembly of YHWH in 23:2–9 within the larger structure of 23:2–26 may be outlined as follows:

A	The assembly of YHWH	23:2–9
B	Sanctity of the military camp	23:10–15
X	Protection of poor and vulnerable: asylum for escaped slaves	23:16–17
B′	Prohibition of "holy prostitution"	23:18–19
A′	Three laws on protection of the poor and vulnerable	23:20–26

If there is substance in this structural outline, the outer frame suggests that the assembly of YHWH (23:2–9) includes the poor and the vulnerable as a primary category. The center of this structure defines the assembly of YHWH in relation to escaped slaves who find asylum in the promised land (23:16–17). The inner frame explores another dimension of the assembly of YHWH in the image of the military camp (23:10–15), the sanctity of which is in some way related to the law prohibiting "holy prostitution." This larger structural design provides the basis for a fresh look at the laws on "misbegotten folk" who are excluded from the assembly of YHWH in 23:2–3.

Though the MT of 23:1–9 contains six *sĕtûmā'* layout markers (after vv 1, 2, 3, 7, 8a, and 9), the passage is in five parts in terms of its prosodic structure, which may be outlined as follows:

A	No one who abuses procreative powers is allowed in the assembly	23:1–2
B	No one "misbegotten" in the assembly—to the tenth generation	23:3a
X	Their descendants are excluded from the assembly of YHWH	23:3b
B′	No Ammonite or Moabite in the assembly—to the tenth generation	23:4–7
A′	Edomites and Egyptians may enter the assembly in the third generation	23:8–9

The break between vv 5a and 5b is marked with the *Numeruswechsel* (change from second sg. to second pl. forms and back again to second sg.). The central aspect of YHWH's promised blessing to Abraham, Isaac, and Jacob is that of fertility. Consequently those who abuse their procreative powers, or who are unable to participate in the blessing itself, are barred from membership in the assembly of YHWH. In particular this means Ammonites and Moabites, who are presented in Genesis as the incestuous offspring of Abraham's nephew Lot. In spite of immediate hostility on the part of Edom and Egypt in the generation of the exodus from Egypt, these nations are presented as "brothers" (Esau/Edom) and friends. As such they are welcome in the assembly of YHWH.

After the opening verse (23:1), which also functions as the conclusion to the previous section of laws on marital and sexual misconduct (22:13–23:1), the transitional list of restrictions on entry into the assembly of YHWH and the exclusion of the Ammonites and Moabites in vv 2–4 are marked with a fourfold repetition of the words "he shall not enter" (לא־יבא) at the beginning of each line in the Hebrew text, in the familiar pattern of three plus one in Jungian psychology: eunuchs, "misbegotten ones" (ממזר), and the "children of Lot," followed by a general reference: "none of them shall enter the assembly of YHWH forever" (v 4c).

Another way of looking at the structure of this section is to examine in detail the exclusion of the "sons of Lot" and the inclusion of the "sons of Esau" (Edomites) and Egyptians in vv 4–9, which may be outlined as follows:

A	No Ammonite or Moabite in the assembly to the tenth generation	23:4
B	They opposed you when you came up out of Egypt—hiring Balaam	23:5
X	YHWH turned the curse to a blessing—do not seek their peace	23:6–7
B′	Edom is your brother and you were a sojourner in Egypt	23:8
A′	No Edomite or Egyptian in the assembly—to the third generation	23:9

The focus of attention in this reading shifts from that of the exclusion of the descendants of the "misbegotten folk" from the assembly of YHWH (vv 1–9) to the fact that YHWH has turned Balaam's curse into a blessing (vv 6–7). One wonders if this is not a subtle anticipation of a future change, as God once again turns a curse into a blessing—when the "sons of Lot" are included in the assembly of YHWH in the book of Ruth.

Carmichael has shown that there is a specific link between the laws of Deuteronomy and the narrative in Genesis (esp. in *LNB*). Since Deuteronomy is essentially the farewell address of Moses to the assembly of the children of Israel, it is not surprising to find a link between it and Jacob's (Israel's) parting words to his twelve sons in Gen 49. There is also a link between Jacob's poetic words of blessing and the narrative stories that precede it in Genesis. What is important to note here, as we move from the sex laws of 22:13–23:1 to the laws in 23:2–9 about who is to be admitted into and who is to be excluded from the assembly of YHWH, is Israel's place among the nations.

In the narratives of Genesis, the change of Jacob's name to that of Israel is recorded twice within a concentric structural design:

A	Story of Jacob's family begins: Jacob returns from Aram	32:1–3
B	Jacob sends presents to appease Esau (Edom)	32:4–22
C	Jacob and a "man" at the Jabbok—name changed to Israel	32:23–33
D	Jacob/Israel and Esau/Edom are reconciled	33:1–17
X	Jacob/Israel erects an altar at Shechem	33:18–20
D′	Jacob/Israel and the Hivites are alienated: rape of Dinah	34:1–24
C′	Jacob and an "angel" at Bethel—name changed to Israel	35:1–15
B′	The descendants of Esau (Edom): genealogical lists	36:1–43
A′	Story of Jacob's family resumes: Joseph sold into Egypt	37:1–36

As shown in the discussion below, the narrative structure outlined here is an expansion of the laws in Deut 23:1–24:4. It is also the same as the overall structure of the story of Abram/Abraham in Gen 12:

A	Abram leaves Mesopotamia for the land of Canaan	12:1–4
B	Abram arrives in the land of Canaan with his household	12:5
X	Abram erects an altar to YHWH at Shechem	12:6–8
B′	Abram journeys from the Negev to Egypt in time of famine	12:9–16
A′	Abram leaves Egypt after YHWH afflicts Egypt with plagues	12:17–20

The story moves from Mesopotamia (32:1–3) to Egypt (Gen 37), with the erection of an altar for the worship of YHWH at Shechem in the land of Canaan at its center. This altar is "the place that YHWH has chosen to make his name dwell there"—the site of the central sanctuary in Deuteronomy (see Deut 26–27). In the inmost frame we find Israel and Edom reconciled (Gen 33:1–17), and Israel and the Hivites in the land of Canaan alienated (Gen 34). The next frame contains the parallel accounts of the change of Jacob's name to that of Israel (32:23–33 and chap. 35). The next frame focuses on Edom, Israel's "twin brother" (32:4–22 and chap. 36). The outer frame moves from Laban's departure from his son-in-law Jacob in the land of Aram (32:1–3) to Joseph's arrival in Egypt as a slave in the house of Potiphar (chap. 37).

The second account of the change in Jacob's name to Israel includes the repetition of the blessing originally given to Abraham (Gen 15 and 17), in which he is told to "be fruitful and multiply; a nation and a company of nations shall come from you, and kings shall spring from you" (35:11). This statement and the narratives that follow in Genesis on the matter of maintaining the family line are an expansion of the law that "no one with crushed testicles or whose penis is cut off shall enter the assembly of YHWH" (Deut 23:2). The concern of the law is that of procreation so as to "be fruitful and multiply" as God commanded.

Carmichael argues that "Reuben was Jacob's firstborn, the one through whom the line of descendants should have proved most prominent. He was the first fruit of his father's virility (Gen 49:3)" (*LNB*, 226). But Reuben misused his sexual potency in lying with his father's concubine Bilhah; in so doing he took "his father's wife" and he "remove(d) his father's garment" (Deut 23:1). This is why Moses had so little to say about Reuben in his own blessing in 33:6.

The law on the exclusion of eunuchs from YHWH's assembly in 23:2 carries the matter a significant step further. The man whose testicles are crushed or whose penis is cut off cannot produce offspring and thus is unable to participate in YHWH's blessing upon the line of Jacob/Israel. Jacob's pronouncement on Reuben is followed immediately by harsh words concerning his brothers Simeon and Levi and their actions recorded in Gen 34, where the Hivites attempted to associate with Jacob and his sons by means of marriage and commercial transactions. Simeon and Levi were opposed to this idea of "mixed seed," so they tricked the Hivites into becoming circumcised and then killed all the males. The Hivite wives and children, however, were absorbed into the family line of Jacob/Israel. Circumcision ordinarily indicates inclusion in the community of Israel; "but in this instance it was used to facilitate forcible exclusion from it" (Carmichael, *LNB*, 227). The primary reason for excluding "eunuchs" from the assembly of YHWH is that such people cannot participate in God's blessing of fertility bestowed on Abraham (Gen 15, 17, 22), Isaac (Gen 26), and Jacob/Israel (Gen 35).

The capacity to reproduce, however, is not sufficient reason to be included in the assembly of YHWH. The manner of conception renders some unacceptable; this is what is meant by the law of the "misbegotten" (ממזר) in 23:3. Though the term ממזר may refer to the offspring of those who are dedicated to the service of another deity such as the prophet Balaam of vv 5–6, it is more interesting to observe how the law was expanded in the narrative tradition of Genesis as the basis for understanding the subsequent exclusion of the Ammonites and Moabites.

If the law of Deut 23:1 was interpreted by Genesis as condemning Reuben for "removing his father's garment," that is, lying with his father's wife, so it implicitly condemned Lot's daughters for "uncovering their father's nakedness" in Gen 19:30–38 so as to "preserve offspring through [their] father" (19:34). The result of this incestuous union was the birth of Moab and his brother Ben-ammi, the father of the Ammonites (19:37–38). "It is also noteworthy that just as Simeon and Levi caused the Hivites to be off their guard by encouraging them to undergo circumcision, so Lot's daughters achieved a similar result by getting him drunk. In each instance, someone resorts to a ruse, and each time the ruse's focus is genital" (Carmichael, *LNB*, 229). The law here that excludes the "misbegotten" products of an incestuous union indicates "that some increases are incompatible with the legal and moral conditions under which this blessing operates" (*LNB*, 230). Two specific historical arguments are added to underscore the decision to exclude future generations of Ammonites and Moabites. They did not come through with provisions of bread and water when Israel traveled from Egypt, and they hired Balaam to curse Israel.

The law excluding Ammonites and Moabites from the assembly of YHWH in 23:4–5 may be related to the narrative in 1 Kings on David and his grandson

Rehoboam, as Milgrom has suggested (*JBL* 101 [1982] 173–74). He sees the law as a polemic against these two Judean monarchs who were born, respectively, of Moabite (Ruth 4:18–22) and Ammonite (1 Kgs 14:31) ancestry. From the perspective of a writer in the Northern Kingdom of Israel this lineage demonstrates the illegitimacy of Judah, whose founding kings are thus both "misbegotten" (ממזר) and should have been excluded from the assembly of YHWH's people.

The law that admits Edomites and Egyptians to the assembly of YHWH "in their third generation" (Deut 23:8–9) leads us back to the narrative structure of Gen 32–37. The Edomites are to be included because Edom "is your brother" (v 8). The narrative structure in Genesis spells out in detail what this means when Jacob/Israel and Esau/Edom are reconciled (Gen 32–33) and Edom participates in the blessing of YHWH, as the genealogies of Esau in Gen 36 demonstrate. Jacob/Israel was well received by his brother Esau, in spite of the fact that Jacob had cheated him out of his birthright. Contrary to Jacob's fears as he crossed the Jabbok on his return to the land of Canaan, Esau proved to be friendly and helpful. "He even suggested that some of his people might join Jacob's to help out (Gen 33:15). In other words, the narrative itself mentions the incorporation of the Edomites into Jacob's assembly" (Carmichael, *LNB,* 233).

The Egyptians are to be included because "you were a sojourner in his land" (v 8); thus the narrative story of Jacob's family continues in Gen 37 by quickly moving Joseph from the land of Canaan to the household of Potiphar in the land of Egypt. After an interlude with the story of Judah and Tamar (Gen 38), the story resumes with Jacob's entire family moving to Egypt (45:16–20) and prospering.

The evidence from Labuschagne's study on the use of the divine-name numbers 17 and 26 in 23:1–26 may be summarized as follows:

Words:	before *'atnāḥ*		after *'atnāḥ*		
23:1–9	66	+	51 (= 3 × 17)	=	117
23:10–15	43 (= 17 + 26)	+	37	=	80
23:16–17	15	+	7	=	22
23:18–24	43 (= 17 + 26)	+	51 (= 3 × 17)	=	94
23:18–26	58	+	61	=	119 (= 7 × 17)
23:1–26	182 (= 7 × 26)	+	156 (= 6 × 26)	=	338 (= 13 × 26)
23:11–15	38	+	34 (= 2 × 17)	=	72
23:14–15	18	+	16	=	34 (= 2 × 17)
23:16–18	20	+	12	=	32 (= כבוד, "glory")
23:19	11	+	6	=	17
23:22	8	+	9	=	17

The prohibition of marrying one's father's wife in 23:1, which is structurally part of the previous section as well, and the seven laws on true religion in 23:2–26 are carefully constructed on the basis of the divine-name numbers. In the opening section (vv 1–9), which deals with those who are restricted from admission to the assembly of YHWH, there are 51 (= 3 × 17) words after *'atnāḥ*. The law on the sanctity of the military camp (vv 10–15) has 43 (= 17 + 26) words before *'atnāḥ*.

Though the law on asylum for fugitive slaves (vv 16–17) shows no evidence of the divine-name numbers, the next three laws fall together in vv 18–24 with 43 (= 17 + 26) words before *ʾatnāḥ* and 51 (= 3 × 17) words after *ʾatnāḥ*. When these three verses are joined with the law on the right to eat from a neighbor's unharvested crop (vv 25–26), the total number of words in vv 18–26 comes to 119 (= 7 × 17). Moreover, we find a grand total of 338 (= 13 × 26) words in the chapter as a whole (23:1–26), with 182 (= 7 × 26) words before *ʾatnāḥ* and 156 (= 6 × 26) words after *ʾatnāḥ*. In short, the mathematical composition of this passage presents further evidence of the incredible labor of love on the part of ancient scribes ("counters") in Israel who produced a carefully constructed literary work of art in which God's name is woven into the fabric of the Hebrew text.

Comment

1 See previous section, "Prohibition of Marrying One's Father's Wife (23:1 [Eng 22:30])."

2 Two types of emasculation are presented here: "crushed testicles" (פצוע־דכא) and those "whose penis is cut off" (וכרות שפכה). Either condition excludes the person from membership in "the assembly of YHWH" (קהל יהוה). Though Tigay maintains that "it is not known which part of the genitals the noun *shofkha,* from a root meaning 'pour,' refers to" ([1996] 386 n. 23), it would appear that it is the male organ, the penis. The prohibition was probably not aimed at those emasculated by accident or illness, as Craigie has noted ([1976] 296–97), for Isa 56:3–5 makes reference to eunuchs as among YHWH's people. On eunuchs see H. Tadmor, "Rab-saris and Rab-shakeh in 2 Kings 18," in *FS D. N. Freedman* [1983] 279–85; idem, "Was the Biblical *saris* a Eunuch?" On ritual self-castration, see Lucian of Samosata, *The Syrian Goddess (De dea Syria),* tr. H. W. Attridge and R. Oden, Texts and Translations 9 (Missoula, MT: Scholars Press, 1976) 55, §51.

3 The term ממזר, translated here as "misbegotten" with JPS *Tanakh,* appears to derive from the root מזר, "be bad" (of eggs), or "be foul" (corrupt, rotten). The term appears only twice in the OT, here and in Zech 9:6. Craigie suggested that the term refers to children born to cult prostitutes (see vv 18–19 below), and supports his case with the following etymology: *mamzēr* < *manzēr* (hiph. ptcp. of נזר, "dedicate, consecrate"). "The ממזר would thus be a child 'dedicated' to a foreign god, by reason of its conception during some kind of temple fertility ritual" ([1976] 297 n. 8). The larger literary structure of the laws in 23:1–24:4, as discussed in the introduction to this section of the commentary, lends some support to Craigie's interpretation; for the text here is to be read in relation to the law on "holy prostitution" in 23:18–19. The reference to "the tenth generation" here probably means "forever," as it does in v 4. That the story of Ruth challenges the permanent exclusion of Moabites suggests that liberalization is in order on this point as well, and seems to reflect the outlook of the author of Isa 56:3–5, at least in regard to eunuchs and the community of faith.

4–7 "Ammonite(s)" and "Moabite(s)" are permanently excluded from the "assembly of YHWH—even to the tenth generation," which is explained in poetic parallelism to mean "forever." As Keil and Delitzsch put it, the ten here "is the number of complete exclusion" (*Pentateuch* [1956]. 414). The reason for their exclusion is based on specific historical experiences: "they did not meet you with bread and water on the road when you came out from Egypt." Moreover, the king of Moab hired "Balaam son of Beor from Pethor of Aram-naharaim to curse you" (see Num 22–24). On the specific territory covered by the term "Aram-naharaim" in northern Mesopotamia, see W. Pitard in *ABD* 1:341. In light of this past experience the people of Israel are told not to establish a friendly relationship with these peoples: "you shall not seek their peace [שלום] and their good [טובה]," in the sense of seeking a political alliance. Craigie ([1976] 298) argued that seeking "peace, friendship" reflects the terminology of Near Eastern political treaties (cf. Moran, *JNES* 22 [1963] 173–76; and Hillers, *BASOR* 176 [1964] 46–47). King David eventually subdued them and incorporated the Ammonites, Moabites, and Edomites into his empire (2 Sam 8:2–12).

8–9 The "Edomite(s)" and the "Egyptian(s)" are treated here with much greater leniency in a temporary exclusion from entering "the assembly of YHWH"—"children born to them of the third generation" qualify for inclusion. The designation of Edom as "your brother" (אחיך) stems from the story of Esau, twin brother of Jacob (Israel), in Gen 36. Glueck considered the verb "abhor" (תתעב) to be precisely the opposite of "lovingkindness" (חסד; *Mordecai Kaplan Jubilee Volume,* 261–62). In spite of their experience as slaves in Egypt, the people of Israel are reminded that "you were a sojourner [גר] in his land." The reference to "the third generation" is counting from the first generation that arrived in the land of Israel, much the same as the term "third-generation American" is used today, that is, the grandchildren of the original immigrant.

Explanation

The reasoning behind the laws restricting entry into the assembly of YHWH in 23:2–9 suggests the principle that only those who are perfect physically and not the product of some unnatural union should be members of the covenant community in ancient Israel. The situation is somewhat similar to a superficial reading of the words of Jesus in the Sermon on the Mount: "You, therefore, must be perfect, as your heavenly Father is perfect" (Matt 5:48). The holiness of God demands perfection in those who would approach his presence. In the gospel of the NT, this perfection is found in Christ, who provides the means of access to God for all people, regardless of their imperfections, whether moral, physical, or spiritual. The follower of Jesus stands in God's presence as perfect—clothed in the perfection of Jesus himself.

Though the people of Israel believed that God was not pleased or honored with bodily mutilation of any kind, they did come to realize that God's mercy extends even to eunuchs who faithfully keep his commandments (Isa 56:4–5; cf. also the story of the conversion of the Ethiopian eunuch under the ministry of Philip in Acts 8:27–39).

Tigay sees the "assembly" mentioned here as "the national governing body of the Israelites, that is, the entire people, or all the adult males, meeting in plenary session, and perhaps sometimes to their representatives acting as an executive committee. This Assembly convenes to conduct public business such as war, crowning a king, adjudicating legal cases, distributing land, and worship. It is synonomous with *ʿedah,* 'community,' which likewise refers to the entire nation, to the adult males (especially those bearing arms), and perhaps to the tribal leaders acting as an executive on behalf of the nation" ([1996] 210). He compares the assembly with similar popular assemblies in the ancient world, such as the *ekklesia* in Athens and the *puḫrum* in the cities of Mesopotamia. The point here in vv 2–9 is that certain types of people, within the national entity itself (vv 2–3) and among neighboring peoples (vv 4–9), are not permitted to become members of this governing assembly.

It should be noted that Deuteronomy presents a more complicated picture than what Tigay has described in terms of the city-state models found in ancient Greece and Mesopotamia. There were two types of "assemblies" in premonarchic Israel: that of the central sanctuary at the pilgrimage festivals and in times of national crisis, and local assemblies within the structure of the Levitical cities (particularly the six cities of refuge). The assembly of YHWH (קהל יהוה) probably includes both levels in this religio-political structure. The point of the law here seems to be that certain individuals and groups of people are excluded from "citizenship" within these gatherings that took place every seven weeks in the עצרת, "sacred assemblies," some of which were held locally and others at "the place God chooses to cause his name to dwell," that is, at the central sanctuary.

Whatever the assembly was in the society of ancient Israel, the people of YHWH as envisioned in the Latter Prophets, the Writings of the Hebrew Bible, and in the NT of the Christian Bible took on a different character. See D. Christensen, "Nations," *ABD* 4:1037–49; idem, *FS R. K. Harrison,* 251–59.

2. *Sanctity of the Military Camp (23:10–15 [Eng. 9–14])*

Bibliography

Tigay, J. "Excursus 3: The Concept of War in Deuteronomy." In *Deuteronomy.* 1996. 430. **Vaux, R. de.** "Une hachette essénienne?" *VT* 9 (1959) 399–407. **Yadin, Y.** *The Scroll of the War of the Sons of Light against the Sons of Darkness.* Tr. B. Rabin and C. Rabin. London: Oxford UP, 1962. 73 n. 3.

See also *Bibliography* for 20:1–20.

Translation and Prosodic Analysis

The Sanctity of the Military Camp [(4:8):(5:4):(4:5):(8:4)]

10(9) *When you go forth as an army camp*\\[a] *against your enemies //* 16 1
then you must be on guard / against any / evil thing // 14 3
11(10) *When there is among you*\\[a] *a man /* [8 1
who / is not clean / because of an event in the night // 18 3

Then he shall go outside / the camp /	13	2
[b]*he shall not come into the midst / of the camp //*	14	2_
12(11)[a]*And it shall be toward evening / he is to bathe in water //*	16	2
and at sundown / he may come / into [the midst of][a] *the camp*[b] *//*	17	3
13(12)*and you shall have / a latrine*[a] */ outside / the camp //*	14	4_
And you shall go to that place / outside[b] *//*	12	2
14(13)*and you shall have / a trowel*[a] *among your implements*[b] *//*	15	2
So that / when you squat outside[c] */ you may dig a hole with it /*	19	3
and you shall turn / and you shall cover your excrement //	15	2_
15(14)*For YHWH your God / walks about / in the midst of your camp*[a] */*	22	3
to deliver you /	6	1
And to hand over your enemies[b] */ before you /*	17	2
so your camp[c] *must be / holy //*	13	2_
And let him not find among you / a naked thing /	12	2
that he should turn away / from you // ס	10	2_

Notes

10.a. Reading *tiphā'* as conj. because of misplaced *'atnāḥ*.
11.a. Reading *paštā'* followed by *zāqēp qāṭôn* as conj.
11.b. Some Heb. MSS, LXX[-N], Syr., and Vg. add *waw*-conj.
12.a-a. Deleting תוך, "midst," with one Heb. MS, SP, and Vg. SP reads כי אם רחץ בשרו במים ובא השמש ואחרי כן יבוא אל המחנה, "for if he washes his flesh in water and the sun sets, then afterward he may enter the camp." The omission of this one word achieves perfect word counts—before *'atnāḥ*, after *'atnāḥ*, and in the grand total for 23:1–26 as a whole. All are divisible by the divine-name number 26.
12.b. Omitted in one Heb. MS, SP, and Vg. Prosodic analysis favors MT.
13.a. LXX reads καὶ τόπος, "and (there shall be) a place," which may be an interpretation of the unusual use of the word יד, "hand," here. On the use of the word יד as a euphemism for phallus, see Isa 57:8 (יד חזית, "a phallus you behold," according to a number of commentators; see BDB, 390). The use of יד with the meaning of "side" (= "place") appears also in Num 2:17 and Jer 6:3. The "place" here is taken as a euphemism for "latrine."
13.b. SP reads החוצה for MT חוץ, "outside."
14.a. Reading *tiphā'* as conj. because of misplaced *'atnāḥ*.
14.b. Reading אזנך, "your [sg.] implement(s)," as collective. A number of Heb. MSS and Cairo Geniza fragments read אזניך, "your implements"; LXX reads ἐπὶ τῆς ζώνης σου, "your girdle," or warrior's waistcloth (= אזרך).
14.c. SP reads החוצה for MT חוץ, "outside." Prosodic analysis favors MT.
15.a. Many Heb. MSS, Cairo Geniza fragments, and SP[MSS] read מחניך, "your camps," for MT מחנך, "your camp"; *Tg. Ps.-J.* has 2 pl.
15.b. LXX reads sg. איבך, "your enemy," for MT איביך, "your enemies."
15.c. Reading מחנך, "your camp," for MT מחניך, "your camps," with many Heb. MSS, Cairo Geniza fragments, SP, LXX, Syr., and Tg. Prosodic analysis favors the emendation, which improves the balance in terms of mora count.

Form/Structure/Setting

The concept of the assembly of YHWH in ancient Israel as a military camp in which "YHWH your God walks about in the midst of your camp to deliver you and to hand over your enemies before you" (v 15) points to what I have earlier described as "Holy War as Celebrated Event" (see *Excursus:* "Holy War as Celebrated Event in Ancient Israel"). Impurity is incompatible with the presence of God and must be removed: "Thus you shall keep the people of Israel separate from their uncleanness, lest they die in their uncleanness by defiling my tabernacle that is in their midst" (Lev 15:31; see J. Milgrom, "Excursus 49: The Effect of the Sinner upon the Sanctuary," in *Numbers,* JPS Torah Commentary [Philadelphia: Jewish Publication Society, 1990] 444–47).

A man who experienced a nocturnal emission within the military camp was considered unclean and was ordered to leave the camp in order to purify himself before reentering the camp at sundown (vv 11–12). Though the routine act of defecation is not described as something that makes a person ritually unclean in the same manner as a nocturnal emission of semen, specific instructions are given to make sure that excrement is properly disposed of outside the boundaries of the camp.

The two key words in this passage are the noun מחנה, "army camp," which appears seven times in six verses, and the verb יצא, "to go forth," which appears four times, in the following sequences:

מחנה → למהנה → המחנה (twice) → למחנה → מחנך (twice)
תצא → ויצא → ויצאת → צאתך

In the first instance, it is "an army" (מחנה) that "goes forth" (תצא) against "your enemies" (v 10). The second occurrence presents a specific case when an individual soldier is required to leave the camp because of a certain "event in the night" (v 11). Having stated the matter in the third person for this particular case, the focus shifts to a general command in the second person: a latrine is to be located outside the camp (מחוץ למחנה) to which "you must go" (ויצאת, v 13) and there you must cover up what "goes forth from you" (צאתך), "your excrement" (v 14). YHWH himself "walks about in the midst of your camp" (מתהלך בקרב מחנך, v 15), as he did in the garden of Eden (cf. Gen 3:8; cf. also התהלך as used of both Enoch and Noah in Gen 5:22, 24, and 6:9, where it denotes intimacy). Therefore "your camp" (מחנך) must be kept holy (v 15). Otherwise YHWH might soil himself by stepping in your mess as he walks with you in the battle camp.

Those who object to such an anthropomorphic portrayal of God need to recognize that the language here is poetic and symbolic, even metaphorical in nature—much like the language of Gen 1–11. R. Norman Whybray (*Introduction to the Pentateuch* [Grand Rapids: Eerdmans, 1995] 33–34) saw the same phenomenon in his reading of Gen 1–11 when he wrote:

> One may say that the author [of Gen 1–11] presents the reader with a rather unexpected portrait of God. Despite the assurance at the beginning (1:31) that when God surveyed his creative actions he concluded that the result was wholly good, God appears quite soon to be somewhat nervous about what he has done and, in particular, concerned about his own supremacy over his creatures. He sets conditions to mankind's freedom (2:17) and threatens immediate death as a consequence of disobedience, a threat that the snake—quite correctly, as it turns out—flatly rejects, calling God a liar. When the act of disobedience has been committed, God betrays nervousness about the possibility that mankind may now go further and seize the immortality which properly belongs only to God (3:22). The same anxiety betrays itself in the final episode of these chapters (11:6), when God fears that mankind may succeed in wresting unlimited (i.e., divine) power for themselves. In both cases God takes steps to forestall such ambitions. Meanwhile the mysterious incident of the union of the "sons of God" with the daughters of men (6:1–2) also seems to have been regarded

by God as containing a threat of immortality human or semi-divine (compare 3:22), which needed to be suppressed.

This startling portrayal of the character of God appears to be shaped, at least in part, by the poetic language of the law on sanctity of the military camp in Deut 23:15 (Eng. 23:14).

The boundaries of the law on the sanctity of the military camp in 23:10–15 are marked with the *sĕtûmâ'* layout markers after vv 9 and 15. The words translated "evil thing" (דבר רע, v 10) and "naked thing" (ערות דבר, v 15b) function as an inclusion within which further repetition of words and phrases appear in a nested concentric structure:

A	"Be on guard against any evil thing"	ונשמרת מכל דבר רע	23:10
B	"He shall go forth"	ויצא	23:11
C	"outside the camp"	אל־מחוץ למחנה	
D	"He shall not reenter the camp"	לא יבא אל־תוך המחנה	
X	"He shall bathe in water . . ."	ירחץ במים	23:12
D′	"He shall reenter the camp"	יבא אל־תוך המחנה	
C′	"for you outside the camp"	. . . לך מחוץ למחנה	23:13a
B′	"He shall go forth outside"	ויצאת שמה חוץ	23:13b–14
A′	"Let him not find . . . a naked thing"	ולא־יראה בך ערות דבר	23:15

Taking v 12 as the center, one may outline the content of the law in 23:10–15 in a concentric structural design:

A	When in the camp, be on guard against any evil thing (דבר רע)	23:10
B	When an event in the night occurs, a man must leave the camp	23:11
X	After purification, he may reenter the camp at sundown	23:12
B′	You shall defecate outside the camp and cover your excrement	23:13–14
A′	YHWH is in the camp; let him not find a naked thing (ערות דבר)	23:15

The focus of attention in this structure is on the sanctity of the military camp and the ritual purification required of those who are temporarily unclean (v 12). The outer frame moves from an injunction to be on guard against any "evil thing" that may lead to defilement (v 10), for YHWH himself walks in your midst as the camp goes forth against your enemies to deliver you: "your camp must be holy; and let him not find among you a naked thing that he should turn away from you" (v 15). The inner frame moves from a somewhat enigmatic reference to some "event in the night" that makes a person unclean (v 11), to specific instructions regarding defecating outside the camp and covering one's excrement (vv 13–14). The "naked thing" (ערות דבר) is something exposed for all to see that ought not to be exposed, such as excrement that one might inadvertently step in.

The previous law about the inclusion of Edomites and Egyptians in the assembly of YHWH suggests the possibility that people may be excluded from the community for a while and then be readmitted to the "camp." This idea is taken up in the law of the army camp, for a man may be excluded temporarily because of impurity.

The law on cleanliness in the army camp (23:10–15) is expanded in story form in Gen 32 (see Carmichael, *LNB*, 234–37). The passage begins with a note in Gen 32:2–3 (Eng. 1–2) in which Jacob encounters angels of God (מלאכי אלהים) at a place called Mahanaim (מחנים, "two army camps"). When Jacob saw the angels of God (מלאכי אלהים), he said, "This is God's army!" (Gen 32:2–3). In the fascinating story of what took place later "that same night" (32:23), Jacob wrestled with a man who "touched the hollow of his thigh" (32:24) and crippled him in a manner that disqualified him temporarily for inclusion "within the camp."

In the law of Deut 23:10–15, the warrior who is made unclean by virtue of a nocturnal emission must leave the camp and remain outside until evening, and then return only after performing the appropriate ablutions. Jacob's experience is different, as Carmichael has noted (*LNB*, 237): "he remains in camp and receives a divine blessing, followed next morning by success in the face of Esau's expected enmity."

According to the law, the army camp is sacred space, "for YHWH your God walks about in the midst of your camp to deliver you and to hand over your enemies before you" (v 15). The implications are clear: the assembly of YHWH is to be understood in the imagery of a military camp and YHWH himself is the Divine Warrior, "so your camp must be holy" (v 15).

Comment

10 On the translation "army camp" for מחנה see Gen 32:2. The reference to "when you go forth as an army camp against your enemies" probably refers to more than normal military situations, however, for the people of Israel envisioned themselves as the "hosts of YHWH" with God himself as a Divine Warrior. In the context of the pilgrimage festivals, particularly in the Feast of Unleavened Bread and Passover as observed at Gilgal near Jericho (see Josh 1–6), the people pitched camp in "battle array" with the ark of the covenant in the tabernacle in the midst of the camp. This tradition was still alive in the community of the Dead Sea Scrolls at Qumran (see Yadin, 73 n. 3, regarding the Scroll of the Sons of Light against the Sons of Darkness). In the camp "you must be on guard against any evil thing" (כל דבר רע). See Deut 17:1, where the phrase כל דבר רע refers to bodily defects in sacrificial animals that disqualify their use. Here it forms an inclusion with the phrase "a naked thing" (ערות דבר) of v 15.

11 The "event in the night" (מקרה־לילה) is defined concretely in the parallel text in Lev 15:16: "And if a man has an emission of semen, he shall bathe his whole body in water, and be unclean until the evening." The elusive terminology here lends itself well to the symbolic reading of the text proposed by Carmichael in relation to Jacob's unusual "events in the night" with mysterious visitors sent from God at Bethel (Gen 28) and at the Jabbok (Gen 32).

12–14 The phrase "toward evening" refers to the Hebrew concept of the beginning of a new day at sunset. On the translation "latrine" (יד) see *Note* 13.a above. Though human excrement was not usually described as impure, extreme steps are taken here because of the unusual sanctity of the military camp. "Josephus thought it notable that although defecation is a natural function, the Essenes washed themselves afterward 'as if defiled'" (Tigay [1996] 214, referring to *J.W.* 2.8.9 §149). Most commentators have rendered the term יד here as "monument" or "sign" (see Craigie [1976] 299). Though this is possible, the more likely interpretation is that of a euphemism for "latrine," in the sense of a place designated for such use in a military bivouac area. See the *Comment* on 11:10, where רגל, "foot," is so used as a euphemism for the penis. The translation "trowel [יתד] among your implements [אזנך]" is an attempt to interpret the term יתד, which is a pointed digging tool of some sort "like a dibble" (Tigay). The modern traveler in southern Europe (and other places as well) who has puzzled over what to do in moments of distress at certain "public toilets," which are sometimes nothing more than a hole in the concrete floor, knows what is intended here in the translation "when you squat outside." As I have observed in rural Egypt, this is much more easily done in the loosely fitting attire of peasants in Middle Eastern countries, where undergarments are often omitted.

15 On the translation of מתהלך as "walks" or "travels," see Gen 3:8; 1 Sam 30:31; 2 Sam 7:6–7; and Ps 105:13. Tigay ([1969] 214) argues that YHWH as Divine Warrior "walks in the midst of your camp" in the sense of marching with his troops to battle, not that he is "walking about within the camp" (cf. NIV, "God moves about in your camp"). See also 20:4, "YHWH [your God] is the one going with you to fight for you against your enemies to save you." This is the language of Holy War (see *Excursus:* "Holy War as Celebrated Event in Ancient Israel"). On the imagery of the Divine Warrior marching in the vanguard of his hosts to war, see the archaic poetry of Deut 33:2; Ps 68:8 (Eng. 7); Hab 3:3–9; and D. L. Christensen, "Num 21:14–15 and the Book of the Wars of YHWH," *CBQ* 36 (1974) 359–60; idem, "The March of Conquest in Isaiah x 27c–34," *VT* 26 (1976) 385–99. On what it means to "be holy," see Lev 19:2 and the discussion of B. Levine, "Excursus 6: Biblical Concepts of Holiness (chap. 19)," in *Leviticus,* JPS Torah Commentary (Philadelphia: Jewish Publication Society, 1989) 256–57. Levine's concluding remarks merit quotation: "The command to achieve holiness, to become holy, envisions a time when life would be consecrated in its fullness and when all nations would worship God in holiness. What began as a process of separating the sacred from the profane was to end as the unification of human experience, the harmonizing of man with his universe, and of man with God" (p. 257). True holiness is a gift from God, not a human achievement. As noted above in the *Comment* on v 10, the phrase translated "a naked thing" (ערות דבר), in the sense of something exposed or out in the open to be seen by all, forms an inclusion with "any bad thing" (דבר רע). The repetition of the words and sounds ר ע // ע ר in chiastic fashion is surely intentional: דבר רע // ערות דבר. The use of the same words in 24:1, and the parallel expression ערות הארץ, "nakedness of the land," in Gen 42:9 suggests an idiom of some sort, perhaps analogous to the English expression "caught with one's pants down." The "naked thing" in this instance is essentially the female genitals (cf. also Lam 1:8, of the personified city of Jerusalem), such that it may be understood as "caught with her pudenda exposed," an idiom for something shameful and offensive. See the discussion of 24:1.

Explanation

The motivation for cleanliness in the army camp is the holiness of God, who marches with his troops to battle. Though the laws on sanctity of the military camp in 23:10–15 applied specifically to those times when Israel actually went forth to fight against enemy nations, they were also operative in annual pilgrimage festivals when the people gathered to reenact YHWH's Holy War and pitched their tents in battle formation about the ark of the covenant and the portable tent shrine, which was set up in the midst of the camp, particularly during the spring celebration of Passover and the Feast of Unleavened Bread in the vicinity of Jericho in premonarchic Israel.

The people of Israel were commanded to keep their camp pure from all forms of pollution. The individual soldiers were to be "on guard against any evil thing" (v 10). In executing their commission they must keep themselves from moral pollution in terms of overt sin or contact with idols and the accursed things found in the camps they plundered. They must also keep themselves from ceremonial and natural pollution of all sorts, such as an "event in the night," which is normally understood to be an involuntary nocturnal emission of semen (cf. Lev 15:16–18). If this were to occur at home, a man needed only to wash himself; but in the army he must "leave the camp" and remain outside until after sundown so as to maintain ritual purity (vv 11–12). Since the camp of YHWH must have nothing offensive in it, even the latrine was to be located "outside the camp" (vv 13–14).

3. Two Laws on "True Religion" (23:16–19 [Eng. 15–18])

Bibliography

Bialik, E., and **Beinart, H.** "*Keleb.*" *EM* 4:113. **Bird, P.** "The Place of Women in the Israelite Cultus." In *FS F. M. Cross.* 1987. 397–19, esp. 404–6. **Donner, H.,** and **Röllig, W.** *KAI.* 1:82; 2:54–55 (no. 37). **Feliks, Y.** *The Animal World of the Bible.* Tel Aviv: Sinai, 1962. 34. **Goodfriend, E. A.** "Could *keleb* in Deuteronomy 23:19 Actually Refer to a Canine?" In *FS J. Milgrom.* 1995. 381–97. **Greenfield, J. C.** "Asylum at Aleppo: A Note on Sefire III, 4–7." In *FS H. Tadmor.* 1991. 272–78. **Gruber, M.** "Hebrew *qĕdēšāh* and Her Canaanite and Akkadian Cognates." *UF* 18 (1986) 133–47. ———. "The Qadesh in the Book of Kings and Elsewhere." *Tarbiz* 52 (1983) 167–76. ———. "The *qedeshah*: What Was Her Function?" *Beer-Sheva* 3 (1988) 45–51. **Gwaltney, W. C.** "The *Qadištum* and *Išaritum* in Mesopotamian Society." Ph.D. diss., Hebrew Union College, 1964. **Hooks, S.** "Sacred Prostitution in Israel and the Ancient Near East." Ph.D. diss., Hebrew Union College, 1985. **Licht, H.** *Sexual Life in Ancient Greece.* London: Routledge and Kegan Paul, 1932. 350, 356, 404, 436–40. **Liver, J.** "*Kālēb.*" *EM* 4:109–10. **Margalith, O.** "*Keleb:* Homonym or Metaphor?" *VT* 33 (1983) 491–94. **McCullough, W. S.** "Dog." *IDB* 1:862. **Miller, P. D.** "Israel as Host to Strangers." In *Today's Immigrants and Refugees: A Christian Understanding.* Washington, DC: U.S. Catholic Conference, Inc., 1988. 1–19. **Reviv, H.** "The Escaped Slaves of Shimei ben Gera." In *Galut 'Aḥar Golah: Studies in the History of the Jewish People Presented to Professor Haim Beinart.* (Heb.) Ed. A. Mirsky et al. Jerusalem: Makhon Ben-Zvi, 1988. 32–39. **Soden, W. von.** "Zur Stellung des 'Geweiten' (*qdš*) in Ugarit." *UF* 2 (1970) 329–30. **Stager, L.** "Why Were Hundreds of Dogs Buried at Ashkelon?" *BAR* 17.3 (1991) 27–42. **Thomas, D. W.** "*KELEBH* 'Dog': Its Origin and Some Usages of It in the Old Testament." *VT* 10 (1960) 410–27. **Toorn, K. van der.** "Female Prostitution in Payment of Vows in Ancient Israel." *JBL* 108 (1989) 193–205, esp.

201. **Westermann, W.** *The Slave Systems of Greek and Roman Antiquity.* Philadelphia: American Philosophical Society, 1955. 17–18, 38–39, 40–41.

Translation and Prosodic Analysis

Asylum for Fugitive Slaves [4:7]

16(15) *You shall not deliver up a slave / to his master //*	[13	2
who has escaped to you / from his master //	20	2_
17(16) *With you / he shall dwell* [a] *in your midst /*	11	2
in the place that he will choose / in one[b] *of your towns*[a] */*	[18	2
wherever it pleases him // you shall not / oppress him // ס	12	3_

Prohibition of "Holy Prostitution" [4:7]

18(17) *There shall be no "holy prostitute" / among Israel's daughters //*	[18	2
and there shall be no "pagan priest" / among Israel's sons //	18	2_
19(18) *You shall not bring a harlot's fee / or the price of a dog /*	19	2
to the house / of YHWH your God\\[a] *in payment for any vow //*	[15	2
for an abomination / to YHWH your God / are both of them // ס	20	3_

Notes

17.a-a. LXX[B] reads ἐν ὑμῖν· κατοικήσει οὗ ἐὰν ἀρέσῃ αὐτῳ, "with you, he shall dwell where he shall please."

17.b. SP reads באחת, "in one of," for MT באחד, "in one of."

19.a. Reading *tiphā'* as conj. because of misplaced *'atnāḥ*.

Form/Structure/Setting

The law of asylum for escaped slaves (23:16–17) and the law prohibiting "holy prostitution" (23:18–19) are closely connected in terms of prosodic structure and belong together as a single literary unit, which stands at the center of a concentric structural pattern:

A	Prohibition of marrying one's father's wife	23:1
B	The assembly of YHWH and sanctity of the military camp	23:2–15
X	The fugitive slave and "holy prostitution"	23:16–19
B′	Three laws on protecting the poor and vulnerable	23:20–26
A′	Prohibition of remarriage if one's former wife has remarried	24:1–4

The outer frame in this structure is made up of two parallel laws on forbidden marriages (23:1 and 24:1–4). The seven laws contained within this frame (23:2–26) are arranged in three subgroups, with the laws on the fugitive slave and "holy prostitution" in the center (23:16–19). The inner frame in this structure moves from two laws on the nature of YHWH's assembly as a military camp (23:2–15) to three specific laws that deal with ways in which the people are called on to be good "neighbors" to those who are part of YHWH's assembly (23:20–26).

The seven laws of 23:2–26 should also be studied in relation to each other, for they form a nested menorah pattern:

A	The assembly of YHWH	23:2–9
B	The sanctity of the military camp	23:10–15
C	Asylum for escaped slaves	23:16–17
X	Prohibition of "holy prostitution"	23:18–19
C′	Prohibition of lending at interest	23:20–21
B′	Timely fulfillment of vows made to YHWH	23:22–24
A′	Right to eat from a neighbor's unharvested crops	23:25–26

The law prohibiting "holy prostitution" (23:18–19) is the structural center in this particular reading of Deut 23. The innermost frame is made up of two parallel laws on what it means to be a "neighbor" to those who are exploited economically: the law of asylum for escaped slaves (vv 16–17), and the law prohibiting lending at interest (vv 20–21). The next frame moves from the law on cleanliness and purity within the military camp (vv 10–15) to the law demanding the timely fulfillment of vows made to YHWH (vv 22–24). The outer frame moves from the laws regarding the assembly of YHWH, which raise the question as to who is to be considered one's "neighbor" (vv 2–9), to the law on the right to eat from a neighbor's unharvested crops (vv 25–26). It does not take much imagination to realize that there are powerful lessons to be learned in this section of Deuteronomy, lessons that call for careful reflection and proclamation.

Although the two laws discussed here appear at first glance to be disparate in nature, they are connected in prosodic structure, and together they shape the content of narrative stories in Gen 32–38. The boundaries of the two laws are marked by *sĕtûmāʾ* layout markers after vv 15, 17, and 19. The law of the fugitive slave (vv 16–17) may be outlined as follows:

A	You shall not deliver up an escaped slave to his master	23:16
B	He shall dwell in your midst	23:17a
X	In the place that he will choose in one of your towns	23:17b
B′	Wherever it pleases him	23:17c
A′	You shall not oppress him	23:17d

The focus of the law is on the fact that the former slave is to be given the right of asylum in the promised land. He is to settle anywhere he chooses: "wherever it pleases him." He is not to be extradited to his former master; nor is he to be oppressed by continuing his former status in his new homeland.

Like the preceding law on the sanctity of the military camp (23:10–15), the law of the fugitive slave influenced the shape and content of the story of Jacob in Gen 32 (see Carmichael, *LNB*, 238–40). Having first been delivered from Laban's hostile intent in Aram-naharaim, Jacob now faces his estranged brother Esau. He describes himself to Esau as a fugitive slave who is on his way to serve a new master, instructing his messengers to speak as follows: "Thus you shall say to my lord Esau: Thus says your servant Jacob, 'I have sojourned with Laban, and stayed there until now . . . and I have sent to tell my lord, in order that I may find favor in your sight'" (Gen 32:3–5). Carmichael points out that Esau "did not treat the suppliant as a slave but rather left him free to do as he wished, to settle wherever he chose" (*LNB,* 239)—exactly as the law in Deut 23:16–17 says he should do. Since Jacob/Israel, presented as a מחנה, "army camp," in Gen 33:8, was well received by Esau/Edom, the Edomite is "your brother" (v 8) and is thus a welcome member in the assembly of YHWH.

The law as stated is a form of social idealism, which is used to shape the narrative story of the brothers Jacob/Israel and Esau/Edom and the assembly of YHWH in the promised land in Gen 32–38. When read in this manner, there is no need to limit the law with Tigay ([1996] 215) to a statement about "foreign" slaves nor to ponder "the absence of a comparable law dealing with Israelite slaves."

The law on "holy prostitution" in 23:18–19 may be outlined as a circular sentence in somewhat similar fashion:

A	There shall be no "holy prostitute" or "pagan priest" in Israel	23:18
B	You shall not bring a "harlot's fee" or the "price of a dog"	23:19a
X	To the house of YHWH	23:19b
B′	In payment for any vow	23:19c
A′	For both of these are abhorrent to YHWH your God	23:19d

Prostitution and religious activity in the service of pagan gods is abhorrent to YHWH. Payments received from those engaged in such practices are not to be brought to the house of YHWH.

In terms of prosodic structure, the law of asylum for escaped slaves in 23:16–17 is connected with the following law on "holy prostitution" in 23:18–19. The two laws are scanned together as a 7:4:7:4 rhythmic structure (which can also be canted to a 6:5:5:6 pattern in syntactic accentual stress units with a mora count of 44 + 30 = 74 and 37 + 35 = 72, with v 18a functioning as a rhythmic bridge connecting these two units); and the architectural design of the whole may be outlined as follows:

A	You shall not deliver up an escaped slave to his master	23:16
B	The slave shall dwell where he chooses; do not oppress him	23:17
X	There shall be no "holy prostitute" among Israel's children	23:18
B′	You shall bring no fees of "holy prostitution" to God's house	23:19a
A′	Both of these are abhorrent to YHWH your God	23:19b

In this reading, the focus of interest is on the prohibition of a קדשה, "holy prostitute," among Israel's daughters or a קדש, "pagan priest," among Israel's sons (v 18). The outer frame in the above structure moves from the prohibition of extraditing an escaped slave (v 16) to the prohibition of bringing fees in the form of votive offerings derived from "holy prostitution" (v 19).

It should be noted that the law of "holy prostitution" (23:18–19) is an instructive example of what I have elsewhere (*The Writings: A Study Guide* [North Richland Hills, TX: BIBAL Press, 1998] 69) called the "riddle at the middle" in the structure of the literature of the Bible. As we saw at the beginning of the section of the laws of 23:1–24:5, the prohibition of "holy prostitution" stands at the center of a concentric structure:

A	Laws on marriage and war	23:1–15
B	The law of the fugitive slave	23:16–17
X	The law prohibiting "holy prostitution"	23:18–19
B′	Laws on the protection of the poor and vulnerable	23:20–26
A′	Laws on marriage and war	24:1–5

The beginning, middle, and concluding sections of this structure all have something to do with the seventh commandment prohibiting adultery or illicit mixtures, particularly in sexual matters. The inner frame has to do with humanitarian issues that are expanded in the laws of 24:6–25:16, as shown below. The center is enigmatic in meaning, so that the situation from a literary perspective is somewhat analogous to that of Gen 6:3, which functions as a "riddle at the middle" in the curious passage on "the sons of God" (בני אלהים) and "the daughters of human beings" (בנות האדם). See D. L. Christensen, "Janus Parallelism in Genesis 6:3," *HS* 27 (1986) 20–24.

The section of laws on social ethics in 23:2–24:4 began with a law excluding "eunuchs" from the assembly of YHWH in 23:2, which was used to shape the story of Simeon and Levi's treacherous response to the so-called rape of Dinah in Gen 34. The law on "holy prostitution" in 23:18–19 returns to that same story to form an inclusion with 23:2–7 for the first half of the collection of laws on social ethics, as the following outline suggests:

A	Those excluded from YHWH's assembly—"misbegotten folk"	23:2–7
B	Edom and Egypt are included in YHWH's assembly	23:8–9
X	Sanctity of the military camp: Jacob at the Jabbok	23:10–15
B′	Asylum for the fugitive slave: Israel and Edom in Canaan	23:16–17
A′	Israel and the Hivites—prohibition of "holy prostitution"	23:18–19

Though the "misbegotten folk" of 23:3 may originally have been the children of prostitutes, as Craigie ([1976] 297) has suggested, the concept was expanded in 23:4–5 to include the incestuous "children of Lot"—the Ammonites and the Moabites, who share the distinction of being excluded from the assembly of YHWH "even to the tenth generation." This is what the outer frame of this structure is about. The inner frame focuses attention on Edom, presented as Israel's "brother," who is to be included in the assembly of YHWH. The center of this structure focuses on the moment when Jacob/Israel crossed over the Jabbok from a sojourn of twenty years in the foreign land of Aram-naharaim to take up residence again in the promised land alongside his brother Esau/Edom.

Together with the earlier law on the exclusion of eunuchs from the assembly of YHWH in 23:2, the law prohibiting "holy prostitution" (23:18–19) plays a formative role in shaping the story of Simeon and Levi and the violence they did to the Hivites in response to the so-called rape of Dinah in Gen 34 (cf. Carmichael, *LNB*, 240–43). In the eyes of Simeon and Levi, the Canaanite prince Shechem had treated their sister Dinah as a harlot (Gen 34:31); thus the first attempt to forge a link between the Israelites and the Canaanites in the promised land ended in violence with the mass slaughter of all the newly circumcised male Hivites.

The next chapter has Jacob removing foreign gods from his own household before fulfilling his vow to YHWH (Gen 35:1–7). Carmichael says this story "is specifically concerned with payment to God's house in connection with the fulfillment of a vow and recognizes that impure worship, service to foreign gods, is incompatible with such payment" (*LNB*, 242). The subject of "holy prostitution" is used to tie this incident to other aspects of the larger story in Genesis. Tamar seduced her father-in-law in order to continue the family line through Judah (Gen 38). Jacob's own involvement with Canaanite women and their religious practices took place just after his separation from his brother Esau (Gen 34). Judah actually called Tamar "the holy prostitute" (הקדשה) when he sought to pay Tamar for her services (38:21). "In paying for her services as a cult prostitute (his description of her), he was in effect paying for the increase in Israel's family numbers, an outcome that would ordinarily warrant tangible thanks to Yahweh" (Carmichael, *LNB*, 242).

Thus the story of Jacob/Israel is that of an Israelite paying into the house of God the gains from "holy prostitution" in the form of a tenth of the wealth God has given him. In so doing he has violated the law of Deut 23:18–19, which appears to be a deliberately ambiguous invitation for an able teacher to discuss and amplify each of its words, so as to guide the curious into "a more fantastic country"—the literary world of the Bible, and the book of Genesis in particular.

Comment

16–17 "You shall not deliver up a slave to his master." This command runs contrary to all known ancient Near Eastern law codes, which forbade the harboring of runaway slaves. In particular, note the words of an Aramaic treaty text known as Sefire III (*KAI*, no. 224; *ANET*, 660), which expresses the opposite of the words that appear here: "he shall dwell in your midst, in the place that he will choose in one of your towns, wherever it pleases him."

18–19 The words קדשה and קדש, which are translated here in a general collective sense as "holy prostitution," may be euphemisms. It is best to avoid the terms "cultic prostitute" and "temple prostitute" (BDB, 873) altogether, however, because of the misinformation these expressions communicate. The description "holy prostitution" in this commentary is an attempt to draw the reader's attention to the use of the root קדש, "to be holy," in reference to both female and male cultic activity in the service of pagan deities in this passage. The phrase "harlot's fee" (אתנן זונה) refers to income received by prostitutes for their services; they were sometimes paid in kind, such as "a kid from the flock" (Gen 38:17). The "price of a dog" (ומחיר כלב) refers either to the "barter of a canine" in traditional Jewish interpretation or to income received by "pagan priests" (men functioning in behalf of pagan deities) for their illicit religious activities. The word כלב, "dog," in this context is generally interpreted as a male prostitute, and has been rendered as "sodomite" (KJV, ASV) or "catamite" (J. Moffatt, *A New Translation of the Bible* [New York: Harper & Row, 1954] 226; a catamite is a boy kept for pederastic purposes). It should be noted, however, that כלב in the Hebrew Bible is not "an opprobrious term for a male prostitute" (*The Jerusalem Bible* [Garden City, NY: Doubleday, 1966] 247 n. 23.d). That Joshua's compatriot Caleb (כלב) is so named is evidence to the contrary. Goodfriend has argued convincingly that we need to take a closer look at traditional Jewish interpretation, which renders כלב literally as a canine (*FS J. Milgrom*, 381–97). See also the discussion of Winton

Thomas (*VT* 10 [1960] 410–27), and note the association of dogs (כלבים) and prostitutes (זנות) in 1 Kgs 22:38. Gruber sees קדשה and קדש as two separate and wholly distinct kinds of professionals (*UF* 18 [1986] 133–47). The קדשה was the equivalent of the זונה, "harlot." The קדש, however, was a priest or diviner in a heterodox, non-Yahwistic cult. The association of the two terms here is poetic in the sense that it is based primarily on association of sounds and the common verbal root, not on the identification of the two professionals in terms of social role or function in society. The recent discovery of a huge dog cemetery from the Persian period at Ashkelon in Israel raises new questions about the possible significance of dogs in certain pagan cults, perhaps in relation to gods of healing, which may help to explain the objection to "the price of a dog" here (Stager, *BAR* 17.3 [1991] 26–42).

Explanation

Though virtually all commentators have interpreted the law of the fugitive slave (23:16–17) as referring to a slave who comes to Israel from a foreign country, it is also possible to see Jacob/Israel as the slave who has left a foreign master in another country to find asylum in the land of Canaan. What the law bans, then, is precisely what parallel laws in the ancient Near East enjoin: the extradition of the fugitive slave. "The only thing remotely close to this biblical law in the ancient world is the practice at certain temples of granting asylum to slaves fleeing harsh treatment by their masters" (Tigay [1996] 215). Even in these cases, the asylum was only temporary, designed to protect the slave until he could come to terms with his former master or be sold to another master. (See Greenfield, *FS H. Tadmor,* 272–78; see also W. Westermann, *Slave Systems,* 17–18, 38–39, 40–41; citations from Tigay [1996] 387, n. 59.)

The law of asylum for escaped slaves was intended to remind the people of Israel that they had been slaves in Egypt. Those who have known firsthand the degradation of human slavery understand; we too are in a position to begin to understand why Israel's policy against extradition flies in the face of other law codes produced by the powerful nations responsible for inflicting slavery on subject peoples.

A good example of the application of the law of asylum for escaped slaves has emerged in recent years in Thailand, where World Vision International has established youth camps as places of asylum for young girls who have been sold into "sex slavery" by their own parents in what is surely one of the vilest examples of human exploitation known. It is estimated that more than a million girls are enslaved in this manner at this point in time, and that such "sex slaves" have been exported to the United States, the United Kingdom, Germany, Australia, and elsewhere. It is our responsibility under God's law to provide asylum for such innocent victims of slavery, and to take positive collective action to stamp out such evils at their source.

The law on prostitution in Deut 23:18–19 is the source of much of the confusion on the subject of "cultic prostitution" because the Hebrew words used here for a female prostitute (קדשה) and a male "pagan priest" (קדש) come from the verbal root קדש, "to be holy," with the idea of being set apart, or consecrated, to God. Thus the idea of a "temple prostitute" was an obvious way to interpret the primary words in an elusive text. I have chosen to translate the combination of the two terms קדשׁה and קדשׁ as "holy prostitution," in a general sense, in order to draw the reader's attention to the root meaning of קדשׁ and to the fact that the individuals in question, so far as the law and related narratives are concerned, are indeed engaged in prostitution (as females) and illicit religious activity in the service of a pagan deity (as males).

One of the products of the feminist movement of recent years has been the reassessment of the role of women past and present. Few subjects illustrate the positive contributions of this movement as well as what is often called "cultic prostitution." "There is no subject in the field of ancient Near Eastern religion on which more has been written, with so much confidence, on the basis of so little explicit evidence. . . . There is, in fact, no evidence available to show that ritual intercourse was ever performed by laymen anywhere in the ancient Near East, nor that sacred marriage . . . was practiced in or near Israel during the biblical period" (Tigay [1996] 481)—the vivid and persuasive description of James Michener notwithstanding (see *The Source* [New York: Random House, 1965], chap. 3, "Level XIV: Of Death and Life").

Physical prostitution is a gross evil, one that usually results in a form of sex slavery and premature death. But the metaphor of prostitution in the form of the activities of a "pagan priest" raises deeper issues. The "pagan priest" is one who traffics in the service of some god other than YHWH and who salves his conscience by using the proceeds of such activity to present gifts "to the house of YHWH." In the metaphorical sense, this too is a form of prostitution, with the same evil consequences at the end of the road: slavery and death.

4. Three More Laws on "True Religion" (23:20–26 [Eng. 19–25])

Bibliography

Borowski, O. *Agriculture in Iron Age Israel.* Winona Lake, IN: Eisenbrauns, 1987. 58–59. **Cohn, H. H.** "Usury." *EncJud* 16:30–32. **Eichler, B. L.** *Indenture at Nuzi.* New Haven: Yale UP, 1973. **Ellis, E. E.** "Vow." *New Bible Dictionary.* Ed. J. D. Douglas. Downers Grove, IL: InterVarsity Press, 1962. 1313. **Gamoran, H.** "The Biblical Law against Loans on Interest." *JNES* 30 (1971) 127–34. **Ginsberg, H. L.** "Psalms and Inscriptions of Petition and Acknowledgment." In *Louis Ginzberg Jubilee Volume.* Ed. A. Marx et al. 2 vols. New York: American Academy for Jewish Research, 1945. 1:163–64. **Greenberg, M.** "On the Refinement of the Conception of Prayer in Hebrew Scriptures." *AJSR* 1 (1976) 78–81. ———. "Religion: Stability and Ferment." In *WHJP* 4/2 (1979). 91. **Haran, M.** "The Yearly Family Sacrifice." In *Temples and Temple Service in Ancient Israel.* 1978. Repr. Winona Lake, IN: Eisenbrauns, 1985. 304–16. **Lipiński, E.** "*Nešek* and *Tarbit* in the Light of Epigraphic Evidence." *OLP* 10 (1979) 133–41. **Milgrom, J.** "Excursus 66: "Oaths, Vows, and Dedications." In *Numbers.* JPS Torah Commentary. Philadelphia: Jewish Publication Society, 1990. 488–90. **Neufeld, E.** "The Prohibition against Loans at Interest in Ancient Hebrew Laws." *HUCA* 26 (1955) 355–57. **Porten, B.** *Archives from Elephantine.* Berkeley: Univ. of California Press, 1968. 77.

Silver, M. *Prophets and Markets.* Boston: Kluwer-Nijhoff, 1983. 65–66, 237. **Stein, S.** "The Laws on Interest in the Old Testament." *JTS* 4 (1953) 161–70. **Tigay, J.** "On Some Aspects of Prayer in the Bible." *AJSR* 1 (1976) 372. **Toorn, K. van der.** "Female Prostitution in Payment of Vows in Ancient Israel." *JBL* 108 (1989) 196. **Veenhof, K. R.** "An Ancient Anatolian Money-Lender: His Loans, Securities, and Debt-Slaves." In *FS Lubor Matouš.* Ed. B. Hruška and G. Komoróczy. Budapest: Eotvos Lorand Univ., 1978. 282–84.

Translation and Prosodic Analysis

Prohibition of Lending at Interest [8:7]

20(19) *You shall not lend on interest to your brother /*	11	1
interest on money\[a] *interest on food //*	9	1
[b]*interest / on anything / that is lent*[c] *//*	12	3
21(20) *To the foreigner you may lend on interest /*	7	1
but to your brother / you shall not lend on interest //	13	2_
In order that YHWH your God / may bless you /	17	2
in all / [a]*you undertake*[a] */ upon the land /*	15	3
that you are entering / to take possession of it // ס	15	2_

Timely Fulfillment of Vows [(4:5):(5:4)]

22(21)[a] *When you vow a vow / to YHWH your God /*	17	2
you shall not put off / paying it //	11	2_
For YHWH your God / will surely require it / of you //	25	3
and it will be a sin / in you //	9	2_
23(22) *And*[a] *if you refrain*\[b] *from making a vow //*	7	1
it will not be a sin / in you //	8	2
24(23) *the things passing your lips / you shall be careful to do //*	20	2_
What you vow / [a]*to YHWH your God*[a]\[b] *is a freewill offering /*	23	2
that you have promised / with your own mouth // ס	10	2_

The Right to Eat from a Neighbor's Unharvested Crops [7] [8]

25(24) *When you enter / your neighbor's vineyard /*	13	2
you may eat grapes / freely / until you are satisfied //	17	3
but into your container / you shall not put them // ס	10	2_
26(25) *When you enter / your neighbor's standing grain /*	14	2
you may pluck off ears / in your hand[a] *//*	16	2
But a sickle / you may not wield /	10	2
on / your neighbor's standing grain // ס	8	2_

Notes

20.a. Reading *tiphā'* as conj. because of misplaced *'atnāh.*
20.b. LXX adds *waw*-conj.
20.c. LXX^{ML} add τῷ ἀδελφῷ σου, "to your brothers" (= לאחיך). Prosodic analysis favors MT.

21.a-a. Many Heb. MSS and SP read משלח ידיך, "extending of your hands," for MT משלח ידך, "extending of your hand"; LXX reads τοῖς ἔργοις σου, "your deeds" (= מעשיך).

22.a. One Heb. MS and Syr. add *waw*-conj.

23.a. One Heb. MS, Syr.[MSS], and Vg. omit *waw*-conj.

23.b. Reading *ṭipḥā'* as conj. because of misplaced *'atnāḥ*.

24.a-a. LXX[Bmin] and OL read τῷ θεῷ (σου), "to (your) God," for MT ליהוה אלהיך, "to YHWH your God." Prosodic analysis favors MT.

24.b. Reading *paštā'* followed by *zāqēp qāṭôn* as conj.

26.a. A few Heb. MSS and LXX read בידיך, "in your hands," for MT בידך, "in your hand."

Form/Structure/Setting

The three laws on protecting the poor and vulnerable in the society of ancient Israel (23:20–26) are framed by two parallel laws on prohibited sexual union: prostitution (23:18–19) and remarriage to one's former wife who has remarried in the interim (24:1–4). Both of these situations are considered to violate the seventh commandment (prohibiting adultery), as shown above in the laws on marital and sexual misconduct in 22:13–29.

A	Prohibition of "holy prostitution"	23:18–19
B	Prohibition of lending at interest	23:20–21
X	Timely fulfillment of vows made to YHWH	23:22–24
B′	Right to eat from a neighbor's unharvested crops	23:25–26
A′	Prohibition of remarriage if one's former wife has remarried	24:1–4

The inner frame in this structure presents parallel laws on specific ways in which a member of the covenant community in ancient Israel is to demonstrate that he loves his neighbor: by not lending at interest to those in need (23:20–21), and by observing the right that members of the covenant community have to eat from a neighbor's unharvested crops (23:25–26). In the center of this structure we find a law on the timely fulfillment of vows made to YHWH (23:22–24), which forms an inclusion with the law in the first half of the outer frame prohibiting the use of income from "holy prostitution" to pay vows made to YHWH (23:19). The prohibition of prostitution itself in 23:18 forms an inclusion with the second half of the outer frame, the forbidden remarriage in 24:1–4. In short, the arrangement of the laws here is carefully worked out to form another "wheel within a wheel" in the architectural design of Deuteronomy.

Though 23:20–26 is a single literary unit from the point of view of its prosodic structure, it is divided into four parts with *sĕtûmā'* layout markers at the end of vv 21, 24, 25, and 26. It also contains three separate laws that differ in subject matter. The content of the literary unit as a whole may be outlined as follows:

A	You shall not lend on interest anything to your brother	23:20
B	You may lend on interest to the foreigner in your midst	23:21
X	When you make a vow to YHWH, do not put off fulfilling it	23:22–24
B′	When you enter your neighbor's vineyard, you may eat grapes	23:25
A′	When you enter his standing grain, you may pluck ears to eat	23:26

The focus of attention in such a reading is on the timely fulfillment of vows made to YHWH (vv 22–24). On one side of this center we have two laws regarding charging interest on loans (vv 20–21) that are set over against two laws to eat freely from a neighbor's unharvested crops of grapes (v 25) and grain (v 26).

The law on the timely fulfillment of vows to YHWH may in turn be outlined in the same manner, as Seitz has observed (*Redaktionsgeschichtliche Studien* [1971] 177–78):

A	When you make a vow to YHWH, do not put off fulfilling it	23:22a
B	YHWH will require it of you and you will incur guilt	23:22b
X	If you do not make a vow, you incur no guilt	23:23
B′	The things passing your lips you shall be careful to do	23:24a
A′	Your vow to YHWH is a freewill offering you have promised	23:24b

In this reading, the focus shifts to the voluntary aspect of making vows to YHWH. There is nothing wrong with a decision not to make a vow. Guilt is incurred only when a vow is made and a person fails to fulfill it in a timely manner.

According to Carmichael's analysis (*LNB*, 243–53), the three laws regarding care for the poor and vulnerable in 23:20–26, like the earlier law of the fugitive slave in 23:16–17, are used to shape the stories about Jacob in the land of Canaan after the crossing of the Jabbok in Gen 32. The first law in this brief series, which concerns loans on interest (Deut 23:20–21), is applied to the story of Jacob's growing wealth (Gen 28–34).

As we take a closer look at the details in this story we see how the law prohibiting the lending at interest to a brother was used to shape the content of the narrative in Genesis. "Esau wanted to give Jacob some of his men to help him look after his possessions. This offer was given freely and carried no obligation on Jacob's part to pay for the service. It was a fine brotherly example of lending without interest" (Carmichael, *LNB*, 244). But Esau's descendants, the Edomites, acted differently when the Israelites asked permission to pass through their territory, in spite of the Israelites' promise to keep out of their fields and vineyards, and despite the law on the right to eat from a neighbor's unharvested crops in vv 25–26, which suggests that this was normal hospitality among "brothers." Esau's example of hospitality was also shaped in part by the law of the fugitive slave (vv 16–17), as we have already seen. In this regard Carmichael has made the interesting observation that "a returning slave in most instances, if not in Jacob's, would need loans without interest to enable him to live a free life back in his homeland" (*LNB*, 245).

The second part of the law on loans (vv 20–21), which grants permission to lend with interest to foreigners, plays a role in shaping the story about Jacob in relation to the Hivites in Gen 34. As things turned out, Israel gained much population and property at their expense: their men were killed, but the women and children joined Israel's ranks. Carmichael has shown that the story in Genesis focuses on extraordinary events, whereas Deuteronomy describes normal Israelite relations with approved foreign groups in which gain accrues to Israel from straightforward business transactions.

The second law on the timely fulfillment of vows carries the reader back again to Gen 28, when Jacob's original vow was made to YHWH. From there it moves to Gen 35, when that vow was fulfilled, in a timely manner. In giving a vow, however unnecessary it may actually be, a person promises to give back to "the sanctuary" (see Milgrom, *Numbers,* 488, and *Comment* on vv 2–24) something in exchange for God's blessing, and the law requires its prompt fulfillment. "This aspect of the law contrasts with lending on interest where a delayed payment is of the essence of the transaction. The law about cultic prostitution, which comes just before the lending law, is related in that it specifically concerns the kind of payment that might be made to the deity by way of fulfilling a vow" (Carmichael, *LNB,* 247).

The law about the permission to eat from a neighbor's unharvested crops (vv 25–26) shapes the manner in which the story of the relation between Israel and Edom is picked up in the more recent past, from the perspective of Moses as law-giver. In the words of Moses to the king of Edom, "Thus says your brother Israel: You know all the adversity that has befallen us. . . . Now let us pass through your land. We will not pass through field or vineyard, neither will we drink water from a well; we will go along the King's Highway, we will not turn aside to the right hand or to the left, until we have passed through your territory" (Num 20:14–17). Yet even refusing the right granted by this law did not alter the Edomites' hostility.

Comment

20 To "lend on interest" (תשיך נשך) suggests a money economy, which is somewhat misleading. The loans in question are primarily charitable loans "to your brothers" (לאחיך). Though Silver has made a case for the existence of interest-bearing commercial loans in ancient Israel (*Prophets and Markets,* 65ff., 327), the consensus of scholarly opinion is still reflected by Tigay: "There is no evidence that there was a money market of any significance, or that solvent Israelites commonly borrowed for commercial or other purposes, though a couple of passages imply that not all borrowers were poor (Exod. 22:24; Deut. 24:12)" ([1996] 217). This prohibition has no parallel in the laws of the ancient Near East, where rates of interest were ruinous: 20–25 percent for silver and 30–50 percent for grain, and sometimes higher (G. R. Driver and J. C. Miles, *Babylonian Laws,* 2 vols. [1952–55], 1:173–77; Tigay [1996] 217).

The term נשך, which is here translated as "interest," is sometimes interpreted as "advance interest" in the sense of money deducted from the loan at the outset, because the verbal root נשך means "to bite." Ezek 18:8 refers to "lending at interest" (נשך) and "collecting increase" (תרבית).

21 "To the foreigner you may lend on interest" (cf. 15:3). The "foreigner" in ancient Israel was usually a businessman traveling for purposes of profit, not subsistence living. There is no moral obligation to forgo interest in such cases. It should be noted, as Mayes has observed ([1981] 321), that only Deuteronomy explicitly allows lending on interest to a foreigner.

22–24 The content of these verses has no parallel in the Book of the Covenant (Exod 20:22–23:33). Its parallel in Eccl 5:3–4 (Eng. 4–5) suggests that we have here a wisdom saying (C. Brekelmans, "Wisdom Influence in Deuteronomy," in SBTS 3:123–34). The making of "a vow to YHWH your God" was a normal expression of worship in ancient Israel. "All vows in the Bible are dedications to the sanctuary," according to Milgrom (*Numbers,* 488). Hannah's vow is illustrative: "O Lord of hosts, if only you will look on the misery of your servant, and remember me, and . . . give to your servant a male child, then I will set him before you . . . until the day of his death" (1 Sam 1:11 NRSV). When such a vow is made, the law states: "you shall not put off paying it." The text does not specify, however, what a reasonable time is for fulfilling vows made to YHWH. The rule of thumb that emerged in Judaism is that in most circumstances, the vow was to be fulfilled at the occasion of the next pilgrimage festival. In subsequent Jewish tradition, it was not considered late until after three festivals (*Sifre* 63; Tigay [1996] 219). Hannah took the child to the central sanctuary at Shiloh after she had weaned him (1 Sam 1:24), which was certainly more than a single calendar year. If a person fails to fulfill the law in a reasonable time, the law states that "it will be a sin in you." This same warning appears again in 24:14–15 in regard to delayed payment of wages due. The statement "if you refrain from making a vow it will not be a sin in you" indicates that making vows is a voluntary act. There is no penalty for not making a vow, but there is for failure to keep the vow once it is made—"the things passing your lips you shall be careful to do." The word נדבה, translated as "freewill offering," appears also in 12:6.

25–26 "When you enter your neighbor's vineyard" or his field of "standing grain," a person was permitted to eat on the spot sufficient to satisfy one's hunger, but no more.

Explanation

Paying interest on loans is so much a part of daily life in the modern world that the casual reader would be surprised at the law prohibiting lending at interest in 23:20–21. What motivated this law was the desire to prohibit exploitation of the poor.

The law on the timely fulfillment of vows made to YHWH (23:22–24) raises significant issues. To make a vow to YHWH and not to follow through is contrary to the very spirit of the covenant made between God and his people.

The law establishing the right to eat from a neighbor's unharvested crops (23:25–26) provided an interesting occasion for a dispute between Jesus and certain Pharisees in Matt 12:1–8. The issue was not that of stealing when his disciples plucked someone else's grain, for that plucking was permitted under this law. The issue was that the incident took place on the Sabbath, and thus they were falsely accused of violating the fourth commandment (Deut 5:12–15).

The combining of the three laws in 23:20–26 on matters concerning care for the poor and the vulnerable in that society within a single prosodic structure suggests that we are primarily dealing with humanitarian issues here; and that the reading of these laws in relation to the associated narratives in Genesis is of greater worth than mere comparative study of ancient legal traditions. The individual laws, as recorded here, were introductory to telling stories based on those laws, the stories being the essence of the Torah.

E. Sixteen Laws on Marriage, War, and "True Religion" (24:1–25:19)

1–2. Forbidden Remarriage and Military Deferral of a New Husband (24:1–5)

Bibliography

Amran, D. W. *The Jewish Law of Divorce according to Bible and Talmud.* New York: Hermon, 1969. 1–31. **Anderson, G.** *A Time to Mourn, a Time to Dance.* University Park, PA: Pennsylvania State UP, 1991. 27–37, 55–57. **Boschi, B. G.** "Problemi della Famiglia nella Bibbia." *Sacra Doctrina* 20 (1975) 395–417. **Daube, D.** "Concerning Methods of Bible-Criticism: Late Law in Early Narratives." *ArOr* 17.1 (1949) 89–99. ———. "The Culture of Deuteronomy." *Orita* 3 (1969) 40–43. **Epstein, L. M.** *Marriage Laws in the Bible and the Talmud.* HSS 12. Cambridge: Harvard UP, 1942. **Fensham, F. C.** "Widow, Orphan, and the Poor in Ancient Near Eastern Legal and Wisdom Literature." *JNES* 21 (1962) 129–39. **Finkelstein, J. J.** "Cutting the *sissiktu* in Divorce Proceedings." *WO* 8 (1976) 236–40. ———. "Sex Offenses in Sumerian Laws." *JAOS* 86 (1966) 362–63. **Fishbane, M.** *Biblical Interpretation in Ancient Israel.* 1988. 307–12. ———. "Torah and Tradition." In *Tradition and Theology in the Old Testament.* Ed. D. A. Knight. Philadelphia: Fortress, 1977. 275–300. **Fisher, L. R.** "An International Judgment." In *The Claremont Ras Shamra Tablets.* Ed. L. R. Fisher. AnOr 48. Rome: Pontifical Biblical Institute, 1972. 14–19. **Friedman, M.** "Divorce upon the Wife's Demand as Reflected in Manuscripts from the Cairo Geniza." *JLA* 4 (1981) 103–27. ———. "Israel's Response in Hosea 2:17b: 'You Are My Husband.'" *JBL* 99 (1980) 199–204, esp. 199 n. 1. ———. "Termination of the Marriage upon the Wife's Request: A Palestinian Ketubba Stipulation." *PAAJR* 37 (1969) 29–55. **Friedman, S.** "The Case of the Woman with Two Husbands in Talmudic and Near Eastern Law." *ILR* 15 (1980) 530–58. **Geller, M. J.** "The Elephantine Papyri and Hosea 2:3." *JSJ* 8 (1977) 139–48. **Granqvist, H.** *Marriage Conditions.* 1931–35. 2:281–82. **Greengus, S.** "A Textbook Case of Adultery in Ancient Mesopotamia." *HUCA* 40–41 (1969–70) 33–44. **Gurewicz, S.** "Divorce in Jewish Law." *Res Iudicatae* 7 (1956) 357–62. **Hobbes, T. R.** "Jeremiah 3,1–5 and Deuteronomy 24,1–4." *ZAW* 86 (1974) 23–29. **Hunt, H. B.** "Attitudes toward Divorce in Post-Exilic Judaism." *BibIll* 12 (1986) 62–65. **Kysar, M.,** and **Kysar, R.** *The Asundered.* Atlanta: John Knox, 1978. **Lehmann, M. R.** "Gen 2,24 as the Basis for Divorce in Halakhah and New Testament." *ZAW* 72 (1960) 263–67. **L'Hour, J.** "Une législation criminelle dans le Deutéronome." *Bib* 44 (1963) 1–28, esp. 24. **Lipiński, E.** "The Wife's Right to Divorce in the Light of an Ancient Near Eastern Tradition." *JLA* 4 (1981) 9–27. **Lloret, V. J. A.** "El Pacado en el Deuteronomio." *EstBib* 29 (1970) 267–85, esp. 272–74. **Malul, M.** "'*Sissiktu'* and '*sikku*'—Their Meaning and Function." *BO* 43 (1986) 19–36. **Martin, J. D.** "The Forensic Background to Jeremiah iii 1." *VT* 19 (1969) 82–92. **Marucci, C.** *Parole di Gesù sul Divorzio.* Aloisiana 16. Naples: Morcelliana, 1982. **Moran, W. L.** "The Scandal of the 'Great Sin' at Ugarit." *JNES* 18 (1959) 280–81. **Müller, H.-P.,** and **Raming, I.** "Women and Judaism." *TD* 34 (1987) 216–18. **Nembach, U.** "Ehescheidung nach alttestamentlichem und jüduschem Recht." *TZ* 26 (1970) 161–71. **Neudecker, R.** "Das 'Ehescheidungsgesetz' von Dtn 24,1–4 nach altjüdischer Auslegung." *Bib* 75 (1994) 350–87. ———. *Frührabbinisches Ehescheidungsrecht.* BibOr 39. Rome: Biblical Institute Press, 1982. **Neufeld, E.** *Ancient Hebrew Marriage Laws.* 1944. 244. **Otto, E.** "Das Verbot der Wiederherstellung einer geschiedenen Ehe: Deuteronomium 24,1–4 im Kontext des israelitische und judäischen Eherechts." *UF* 24 (1993) 301–10. **Pardee, D.** "A New Ugaritic Letter." *BO* 34 (1977) 3–20. **Phillips, A.** "Another Example of Family Law." *VT* 30 (1980) 240–45. ———. "Another Look at Adultery." *JSOT* 20 (1981) 3–25. **Praag, A. van.** *Droit matrimonial assyro-babylonien.* Allard Pierson Stichting Archaeologisch-Historische Bijdragen 12. Amsterdam: Noord-Hollandsche Uitgevers Maatschappij, 1945. **Rabinowitz, J. J.** "The Great Sin in Ancient Egyptian Marriage Contracts." *JNES* 18 (1959) 73. ———. "Marriage Contracts in Ancient Egypt in the Light of Jewish Sources." *HTR* 46 (1953) 91–97. **Rowley, H. H.** "The Prophet Jeremiah and the Book of Deuteronomy." In *FS T. H. Robinson.* 1950. 157–74. **Toeg, A.** "Does Deuteronomy 24:1–4 Incorporate a General Law on Divorce?" *DiIs* 2 (1970) v–xxiv. **Wambacq, B. N.** "De Libello Repudii." *VD* 33 (1955) 331–35. **Westbrook, R.** "The Prohibition on Restoration of Marriage in Deuteronomy 24:1–4." In *Studies in Bible.* Ed. S. Japhet. ScrHier 31. Jerusalem: Magnes, 1986. 399–403. **Yaron, R.** "Biblical Law: Prolegomena." In *Jewish Law in History and the Modern World.* Ed. B. S. Jackson. JLA Sup 2. Leiden: Brill, 1980. 27–44, esp. 37. ———. "On Divorce in Old Testament Times." *RIDA* 4 (1957) 117–28. ———. "The Restoration of Marriage." *JJS* 17 (1966) 1–11. **Zakovitch, Y.** "The Woman's Rights in the Biblical Law of Divorce." *JLA* 4 (1981) 28–46, esp. 40.

Translation and Prosodic Analysis

On Restoring a Marriage If One's Former Wife Has Remarried [(7:5):(7:7):(5:7)]

1 *When a man takes / a woman*[a] */ and marries her //*	16	3
and it shall be / if she does not find favor in his eyes /	18	2
because he finds in her / "a naked thing" /	13	2_
And he writes for her / a bill of divorce /	15	2
and he puts it in her hand /	9	1
and he sends her out / from his house //	10	2_
2 *And she goes forth* \[a] [b]*from his house //*	11	1
and she proceeds[b] */ to become the wife of another man //*	18	2
3 *And the latter husband / hates her /*	17	2
and he writes her / a bill of divorce /	14	2_
And he puts it in her hand /	9	1
and he sends her out / from his house //	9	2
Or if the [a]*latter man*[b] */ dies /*	18	2
who took her to himself / to be his wife[a] *//*	13	2_
4 *Her former husband who divorced her is not permitted /*	19	1
to turn to take her again / to be his wife /	17	2
after / she has been defiled /	12	2_
For that is an abomination \[a] *before YHWH*[b] *//*	16	1
and you[c] shall not bring sin / to the land /	13	2
that / YHWH *your God / gives you / for an inheritance //* ס	20	4_

Deferral of a New Husband from Military Service [6:6]

5 *When a man takes / a new wife /*	14	2
he shall not / go forth / with the army /	11	3
and he shall not be assigned to it /	11	1_

In[a] *every instance // there is exemption*[b] *from obligations /* 10 2
he shall remain at home / one year / 14 2
[c]*to bring happiness*[c] */ to his wife whom he has taken //* ס 13 2

Notes

1.a. SP adds ובא אליה, "and he comes to her." Prosodic analysis supports MT.
2.a. Reading *ṭipḥāʾ* as disj. because of misplaced *ʾatnāḥ*.
2.b-b. LXX omits. Prosodic analysis supports MT.
3.a-a. Vg. omits. Prosodic analysis supports MT.
3.b. SP reads בעלה, "her husband," for MT האיש, "the man"; some LXX witnesses add αὐτῆς, "her."
4.a. Reading *ṭipḥāʾ* as disj. because of misplaced *ʾatnāḥ*.
4.b. LXX adds τοῦ θεοῦ (= אלהיך, "your God"). Prosodic analysis supports MT.
4.c. Reading 2 pl. with SP and LXX as *lectio difficilior.* It is more difficult to explain the appearance of the *Numeruswechsel* here in SP and LXX, if it is not original, than to explain its omission in MT.
5.a. A few Heb. MSS, LXX, Tg.[MS], and *Tg. Ps.-J.* read כל for MT לכל, "to all" or "in every (instance)."
5.b. SP reads נקיא, "innocent," for MT נקי, "exempt" (cf. Jonah 1:14 for the same confusion of these two terms).
5.c-c. Syr. reads *wnḥdʾ* (= וְשָׂמַח) for MT וְשִׂמַּח, "and he shall cause to rejoice." Prosodic analysis favors MT slightly with a mora count of three rather than four.

Form/Structure/Setting

In terms of the prosodic analysis presented in this commentary, the laws in the sixth of the eleven weekly portions in the lectionary cycle of Torah readings from Deuteronomy (21:10–25:19) are in three major parts: 21:10–23:1; 23:1–24:4; and 24:5–25:19. The law prohibiting marrying one's father's wife (23:1) functions as a bridge connecting the first and second section. The situation is somewhat similar in regard to the two laws in 24:1–5, which also serve to connect the second and third sections in a more complex manner.

From a literary point of view, the laws of 24:1–5 are transitional in nature, completing the previous section (23:1–24:4) and introducing what follows in the rest of Deut 24:

A	Forbidden remarriage and one-year deferral for new husband	24:1–5
B	Taking a millstone as distrained property and kidnapping	24:6–7
X	Dealing with "leprosy"	24:8–9
B′	Taking and holding distrained property	24:10–13
A′	Humanitarian concerns: care for the poor and vulnerable	24:14–22

Details within this structure, and its place within the design of the larger group of laws protecting the poor and vulnerable in 24:5–25:19, are discussed below. Here it is sufficient to note that the laws on renovating a marriage (vv 1–4) and military deferral of a new husband (v 5) function as a single literary unit from a prosodic point of view, which is set over against three laws aimed at protecting the poor and the vulnerable in Israelite society: timely payment of wages (vv 14–15), prohibition of transgenerational punishment (v 16), and the law protecting sojourners, orphans, and widows (vv 17–22). The central law on dealing with "leprosy" (vv 8–9), which displays the familiar quality of the "riddle at the middle," is framed by three laws with much in common: the taking of a millstone as pledge (v 6) and the theft of a fellow Israelite (v 7), both of which are set over against a law that sets limits in regard to taking and holding property taken in pledge on a loan (vv 10–13).

The laws in 21:10–23:1, which are structured in relation to the seventh commandment (prohibition of adultery), deal primarily with family laws (including a group of six laws on marital and sexual misconduct in 22:13–29) and certain "illicit mixtures" (22:5, 9–11). Though the laws in 23:2–24:4, which deal with matters of social ethics, are structured in relation to the seventh commandment (particularly in regard to three laws that include the expression "When a man takes a woman" in 23:1 and 24:1, 5), they include laws corresponding to the first three of the Ten Commandments (on our relationship with God) and the last three of the Ten Commandments (on theft, false witnesses, and coveting) as well, including ones that pertain to worship (23:22–24), war (23:10–15; 24:5), and the protection of the poor and vulnerable (23:20–26).

The third and final section of laws (24:5–25:19) in the sixth of the weekly portions in the lectionary cycle (21:10–25:19) includes thirteen laws dealing with humanitarian issues (24:6–25:16), which are framed by two laws on war (24:5 and 25:17–19), with a law on marriage in the center (25:5–10). The section as a whole may be outlined in a menorah pattern:

A	Deferral of a new husband from military service	24:5
B	Eight laws protecting the poor and vulnerable	24:6–22
C	Limits on flogging; not muzzling an ox	25:1–4
X	Levirate marriage	25:5–10
C′	Immodest intervention in a fight	25:11–13
B′	Honest weights and measures	25:13–16
A′	Remembering the Amalekite aggression	25:17–19

The outer frame in this structure moves from a transitional law that deals with both marriage and war (24:5), to the law on levirate marriage in the center (25:5–10), to a final law dealing with YHWH's Holy War (25:17–19). The outermost frame moves from a series of seven laws on ruinous actions against a fellow Israelite (24:6–22), which is set over against a single law on a similar subject: honest weights and measures (25:13–16). The innermost frame in this structure contains three laws: limits on flogging and an injunction not to muzzle an ox when it threshes (25:1–4). This law is set over against the curious law on immodest intervention in a fight on the part of a man's wife (25:11–12). In the center is the law on levirate marriage (25:5–10), which marks the conclusion of a series of five laws on marriage (21:10–14; 23:1; 24:1–4; 24:5; 25:5–10).

The preceding laws on matters of social ethics in 23:1–26 were used to shape the narrative in Genesis that concerns Israel's interaction with foreign peoples: Ammon and Moab (Gen 19), Aram (Gen 28–31), Edom (Gen 32–36), the Hivites in the land of Canaan (Gen 34), and Egypt (Gen 37–50). In terms of the narrative stories in Genesis, the focus was on the person of Jacob in relation to his brother Esau (Edom) and on Jacob's children, the twelve tribes of Israel. Deut 23 began with a law that was used to shape the story of Abraham's kinship with Lot's descendants, the Ammonites and the Moabites. Deut 24 begins with laws that shape the stories of Abraham himself.

The previous law on the right to eat from a neighbor's unharvested crops functioned in a transitional manner in shaping the narrative stories within the Torah by shifting attention from Jacob and Esau in Genesis to that of Israel and Edom in the more recent past, from the perspective of Moses—namely the incident when messengers were sent from Kadesh to the king of Edom with the request that the Israelites be given permission to pass through his land (Num 20:14–17). Carmichael's observations are apropos (*LNB*, 255): "At an earlier period in time, Israel's renowned ancestor, Abraham, was likewise traveling near Kadesh and sojourned in Gerar (Genesis 20). He too anticipated enmity from the ruler of that region, Abimelech, king of Gerar." As we observed in the discussion of 23:2–9, the narrative structure of the story of Abram in Gen 12 mirrors that of the larger structure of the story of Jacob/Israel (Gen 32–37), while anticipating the story of Jacob's descent into Egypt and the exodus from Egypt under Moses as well.

The laws of 23:5–25:19 were used to shape the narrative of Genesis (Gen 21:9–12; 24; 31:4–42; 34; 37–47, esp. 38) and other passages (Exod 16; 17:1–14; Num 12:1–14). The relation between the individual laws and the narrative stories are explored in detail below. In anticipation of that discussion, it is useful to outline the larger structural design of the narrative in Genesis, Exodus, and Numbers against Deut 24–25:

A	Gen 21:9–12: Isaac and Ishmael—millstone as pledge	24:5–6
B	Gen 37:26–28: sale of Joseph—theft of a fellow Israelite	24:7
C	Num 12:1–14: Miriam's leprosy—dealing with "leprosy"	24:8–9
D	Gen 24 (Gen 15): a wife for Isaac—distrained property	24:10–13
E	Gen 31:4–42: Jacob and Laban—the hired servant	24:14–15
F	Gen 34: Hamor and his son—fathers and sons	24:16
X	Gen 37–47: Joseph in Egypt—protecting the vulnerable	24:17–22
F′	Gen 37–47: Joseph in Egypt—limits on flogging	25:1–3
E′	Gen 38: Judah and Tamar—unmuzzled ox	25:4
D′	Gen 38: Judah and Tamar—levirate marriage	25:5–10
C′	Gen 38: Judah and Tamar—immodest intervention in fight	25:11–12
B′	Gen 42–44; Exod 16: Joseph and manna—honest weights and measures	25:13–16
A′	Exod 17:1–14: Amalek's attack—extermination of Amalekites	25:17–19

The focus of the laws in 24:5–25:19, so far as the narrative in Genesis is concerned, is on the stories of Jacob's twelve sons (the tribes of Israel) in Gen 37–50. Jacob's descent into Egypt is introduced at the outset (in the law on the "theft" of a fellow Israelite in Deut 24:7), which is set over against the stories of Joseph in Egypt in Gen 42–44 and the law of honest weights and measures (Deut 24:13–16). The second half of the structure expands the laws with stories about Joseph and Judah, using a series of three successive laws in each case. The Genesis narrative in the first half of the above structure, which corresponds with the laws in Deut 24:5–16, completes a series of three laws that pertain to stories of Abraham (24:1–6), including the birth of his son Isaac (24:5) and his marriage to Rebekah (24:6); and moves on to the marriage of Isaac (24:10–13), along with a brief review of the stories about his son Jacob with Laban in Aram-naharaim (24:14–15), and Hamor with his sons in Canaan (24:16), which stories were the focus of attention for the laws in the previous section (23:1–24:4).

It is useful at this point to examine some of the more prominent literary structures in Genesis that reflect the sequence of laws here in Deut 24–25. The narrative tradition of Gen 37–50 may be outlined as follows:

A	Joseph and his dreams	Gen 37
B	Judah and Tamar: Judah begets Perez and Zerah	Gen 38
X	Joseph in Egypt: his rise to power by interpreting dreams	Gen 39:1–44:17
B′	Judah's speech: "Keep me in place of the lad Benjamin"	Gen 44:18–34
A′	Fulfillment of Joseph's dreams: Jacob's family in Egypt	Gen 45–50

As we will see in the discussion below, these stories are shaped, at least in part, by the individual laws in Deut 24:7–25:16. In this narrative structure the focus of attention is on Joseph in Egypt, reflecting the laws on protecting the vulnerable in 24:17–25:3. Attention then shifts to the person of Judah in the land of Canaan, as reflected in the laws of 25:5–12. The corresponding narrative tradition in Genesis may be outlined as follows:

A	Judah persuades his brothers to sell Joseph into slavery	Gen 37:26–28
B	The brothers deceive Jacob into believing Joseph is dead	Gen 37:29–36
X	Judah and Tamar: Judah begets Perez and Zerah	Gen 38
B′	Joseph's rise to power in Egypt—he deceives his brothers	Gen 39:1–44:17
A′	Judah's speech: "Keep me in place of Benjamin"	Gen 44:18–34

The order and content of the laws in Deut 24–25 are an invitation to teach the meaning and content of Genesis, primarily as it relates to the two most prominent sons (or tribes) of Israel: Joseph and Judah.

The laws in 24:17–25:16 form a literary unit in five parts, from a prosodic point of view, which may be outlined as follows:

A	Protecting aliens, orphans, and widows	(Joseph in Egypt)	24:17–22
B	Limits on flogging and unmuzzled ox	(Joseph and Judah)	25:1–4
X	Levirate marriage	(Tamar and Judah)	25:5–10
B′	Improper intervention in a fight	(Judah and Joseph)	25:11–13
A′	Honest weights and measures	(Israel in the wilderness)	25:13–16

The outer frame in this structure has two parallel laws on the protection of the poor and vulnerable (24:17–22 and 25:13–16) that are used to shape the narrative content of the story of Joseph in Gen 37 and 45–50 and God's provision for the people of Israel in the wilderness en route to Mount Sinai (Exod 14–18). The first half of the inner frame picks up on the same theme in the law that sets limits on flogging (25:1–3), but then moves to another topic in the law on not muzzling the ox (25:4). As will be shown in the discussion below, the second half of the inner frame with the curious law on improper intervention in a fight (25:11–13) is also used to shape the narrative stories of both Judah and Joseph. Together with the central law concerning levirate marriage (25:5–10), these three laws shape the narrative of Judah and Tamar (Gen 38) and the story of the twelve sons of Jacob/Israel in the land of Egypt (Gen 39–50), with a focus on the person of Joseph and Judah.

The two-part structure of the laws on marriage and war in 24:1–5 is indicated in *BHS* with *sĕtûmā'* layout markers at the end of vv 4 and 5. The break between the two subsections is also marked with the *Numeruswechsel* at the end of v 4, as restored from SP and LXX. Moreover, the prosodic analysis reveals that the two laws are distinct literary units. The law on the deferral of a new husband from military service in 24:5 functions as a rhythmic literary bridge, much like 23:1 in the previous chapter. From the point of view of overall structure, it completes one major unit (23:1–24:5), begins another (24:5–25:19), and belongs to both.

Phrases that combine the verb לקח, "to take," and its object אשה, "a woman," appear three times, as the outer frame in a concentric structure of repeated words and phrases, which are nested as follows:

A	"When a man takes a woman"	כי־יקח איש אשה	24:1a
B	"he shall write a bill of divorce . . ."	וכתב לה ספר כריתת ונתן בידה	24:1b
X	"and she goes forth from his house . . ."	ויצאה מביתו והלכה	24:2b–3a
B′	"he shall write a bill of divorce . . ."	וכתב לה ספר כריתת ונתן בידה	24:3a
A′	"who took her as his wife . . ."	אשר־לקחה לו לאשה . . .	24:3b–4a
	"to take her again as his wife"	לקחתה להיות לו לאשה	

The outer frame in this structure moves from the original marriage, "when a man takes a woman" (v 1a), to the situation where that husband is not permitted to take the woman a second time to be his wife (vv 3b–4a). The center of this structure focuses attention on the legal situation itself, as the woman marries a second time only to find that her second husband "hates her" and wants a divorce (v 3). The inner frame in this structure is the exact repetition of a three-part clause: "and he writes her a bill of divorce and he puts it in her hand and he sends her out from his house" (vv 1 and 3).

The content of the two laws in 24:1–5 itself may be outlined in a five-part concentric structure:

A	When a man takes a woman, he is permitted to divorce her	24:1
B	If she then becomes another man's wife	24:2
X	And the new husband divorces her or dies	24:3
B′	The former husband cannot take her again as wife	24:4
A′	When a man takes a woman, he receives a military deferral	24:5

In this reading, the structural center remains much the same: a divorced woman, who has remarried, faces the loss of her new husband (24:3). Can she remarry her original husband, if he wants to take her back? According to the law (24:4), he cannot; however, in the story of Gen 20, which is shaped by this law, Abraham did take Sarah back from the king of Gerar—but one wonders, at what cost in terms of their subsequent relationship?

Setting the permission for the man to divorce his wife in the first place (24:1) over against the law of deferral from military service, with its injunction that the man is responsible "to bring happiness to his wife whom he has taken" (24:5), the outer frame in this structure raises the question as to why the possibility of remarriage in this instance is denied. Perhaps, once again, we are dealing with a law intended primarily as a teaching device on the deterrence of divorce in the first place—somewhat like the law of the insubordinate son (21:18–21) and the woman guilty of premarital unchastity (22:13–21). A contract for remarriage of a

Jewish couple in the year 124 C.E. was found in a cave at Wadi Murabba'at near Qumran (DJD 2:243ff.; see Tigay [1996] 222, who also cites a later such contract for remarriage in A. Gulak, *'Otsar Ha-Shetarot* [Jerusalem: Defus Ha-Po'alim, 1926] 42, no. 37 [reference courtesy of J. C. Greenfield]). Tigay notes that Islamic law prescribes exactly the opposite of what we find here: "if a man has irrevocably divorced his wife, he may not remarry her unless she *has* been married in the interim. When a couple wishes to reunite, a beggar is hired to marry the woman and consort with her for one night, after which he divorces her and frees her to reunite with her husband. Wives understandably find this repulsive, and some Muslims permit a sacrifice to be offered in place of the intervening marriage" ([1996] 222, citing Quran 2:229–30, with commentary of Abdullah Yusuf Ali, *The Holy Qur 'an* [Washington, DC: American International Printing, 1946]; Granqvist, *Marriage Conditions,* 2:281–82; Neufeld, *Ancient Hebrew Marriage Laws,* 244).

The words "when a man takes a woman" (כי־יקח איש אשה) are used as the primary rhetorical marker to indicate the structure of 24:1–5 and its relation to 21:11 and to 22:13–23:1, where the same expression is used as an inclusion to mark the beginning and ending of a parallel prosodic unit—what I have called the laws on marital and sexual misconduct in 22:13–29 (see also 21:11 in the law on marriage with a woman captured in war, where the expression is first introduced). Here the words are used to mark the beginning of each of the major subunits (vv 1–4 and 5) and the ending of v 5 as well, in modified chiastic form: את־אשתו אשר־לקח, "his wife whom he has taken." The phrase thus appears eight times (within a seven-part concentric structure) in the sixth of the eleven weekly portions in the lectionary cycle of Torah readings (21:10–25:19):

A	Beginning of sequence (21:10–14)	ולקחת לך לאשה	21:11
B	Beginning: marriage and sex laws (22:13–29)	כי־יקח איש אשה	22:13
C	Beginning: marrying one's father's wife	לא־יקח איש את־אשת	23:1
X	Beginning: renovation of marriage (24:1–4)	כי־יקח איש אשה	24:1
C′	Beginning of inner frame within same law	אשר־לקחה לו לאשה	24:3
	End of frame within same law	לקחתה להיות לו לאשה	24:4
B′	Beginning: deferral of new husband	כי־יקח איש אשה	24:5
A′	End of sequence	את־אשתו אשר־לקח	24:5

The piling up of this formulaic expression in 24:1–5 indicates that we have reached the end of the larger section of laws on the seventh commandment, the prohibition of adultery. What follows in 24:6–25:16 focuses primarily on humanitarian concerns (commandments eight through ten, on theft, false witness, and coveting), within a framework on matters of "love and war" (commandments six and seven, prohibiting murder and adultery) in 24:5 (on military deferral for a new husband) and 25:17–19 (on Holy War—remember to "hate" the Amalekites).

It is interesting to note how the story about Abraham, Sarah, and Abimelech begins in Gen 20. After Abimelech sent and took Sarah into his household (Gen 20:2), God appeared to him in a dream with these words (20:3): "You are a dead man because the woman you have taken is another man's wife." The story picks up where the above sequence of formulaic expressions left off in Deut 24:5. It should be noted that the phrase "another man's wife" (בעלת בעל) appears only twice in the Hebrew Bible: in Gen 20:3 and Deut 22:22, which repeats the law forbidding adultery at the structural center of the collection of laws on marital and sexual misconduct (22:13–23:1). These laws are framed by repetition of the formula "when a man takes a woman." It should be noted that God's words to Abimelech, "You are a dead man" (הנך מת), which immediately precede the formulaic expression in question in Gen 20:3, are similar to the words that immediately precede the twofold repetition of the same formula in Deut 24:3–4, כי ימות האיש, "for the man shall die."

In the shift to Abraham at this point in the use of the laws in Deuteronomy to shape the Genesis narrative, we learn that the problems involving offspring and the increase in numbers, which are part of the promises to the fathers, were there from the beginning. The subsequent story of Abraham and Sarah, in regard to the birth of their son Isaac, is shaped by the law about exemption from military service in 24:5.

Abraham did not technically divorce Sarah, nor did Abimelech consummate a marriage with her, so obviously he could not divorce her in a legal sense. Nonetheless, Abraham did set her free to the point that she was taken into Abimelech's house as his spouse. Abimelech did subsequently "divorce" her, a second time, as it were; and in this instance Abraham "remarried" his former wife, an act, of course, contrary to the law of Moses. One gets the impression that the storyteller is taking delight in the subtle manner in which he is able to show how the fathers in Genesis appear to violate the laws in Deuteronomy. But, after all, that would be permissible, since in the time of Abraham, Isaac, and Jacob, the law of Moses had not yet been given. Moreover, it should be noted that Abraham's strategem encouraged Sarah's adultery. She has been "defiled" (הֻטַּמָּאָה, Deut 24:4). Carmichael notes that God declared to Abimelech that his offense was that of adultery, "an abomination to Yahweh" (*LNB*, 257).

The law of giving pleasure to a new wife in 24:5 is used to carry the story of Abraham and Sarah a significant step further. "Apart from his fear that a foreign potentate might take his wife and kill him, Abraham was also faced with the prospect that should he die he would have no heir by his chief wife Sarah" (Carmichael, *LNB*, 258). But God himself had promised Abraham a son by Sarah. It is the story of the birth of this son, Isaac, that is shaped by the law of military deferral in Deut 24:5.

The law grants a newly married man a year's exemption from military duty so that "he should bring happiness to his wife whom he has taken" (ושמח את־אשתו אשר־לקח). The purpose of the original law may have been to provide the occasion for the couple to enjoy the birth of their first child. But the narrative story of Genesis emphasizes the notion of giving pleasure to the woman. The birth of Isaac was to take place within the course of "one year," as the following words indicate: "I will surely return to you in the spring, and Sarah your wife shall have a son" (Gen 18:10). Sarah's response was shaped by the law in Deut 24:5: "After I have grown old, and my husband is old, shall I have pleasure?" (Gen 18:12). The use of the word "pleasure" (עֶדְנָה), which appears in the feminine form only here in the Hebrew Bible, points the reader to the story of creation in Gen 2–3 and the garden of Eden (עֵדֶן), the proverbial source of pleasure for the first man

(Adam) in the creation of the first woman (Eve). Moreover, the story that unfolds in the life and progeny of the promised son, Isaac, is an event of parallel magnitude in God's special creation of his own people, the children of Israel.

The evidence from Labuschagne's "logotechnische analyse" for 24:1–5 may be summarized as follows:

Words:	before *ʾatnāḥ*		after *ʾatnāḥ*		
24:1–3	18	+	32	= 50	
24:2–3	13	+	13	= 26	
24:2–5	45	+	33	= 78	(= 3 × 26)
24:3–4	30	+	19	= 49	(= 23 + 26)
24:4–5	32	+	20	= 52	(= 2 × 26)
24:5	13	+	10	= 23	
24:1–5	50	+	52 (= 2 × 26)	= 102	(= 6 × 17)
24:6–9	28	+	23	= 51	(= 3 × 17)
24:1–9	78 (= 3 × 26)	+	75	= 153	(= 9 × 17)

In the numerical composition of the text it appears that the primary literary unit is 24:1–9, which includes five laws. The total number of words in these nine verses comes to 153 (= 9 × 17), which is also the sum of the digits 1 through 17. Within these verses there are 78 (= 3 × 26) words before *ʾatnāḥ*. This unit is divided in two main parts: vv 1–5, with its total of 102 (= 6 × 17) words, in which there are 52 (= 2 × 26) words after *ʾatnāḥ*; and vv 6–9, with its total of 51 (= 3 × 17) words, in which there are 23 words after *ʾatnāḥ*. Within vv 1–5 there are a series of overlapping structures based on the divine-name number 26 and the numbers 32 and 23 (the two ways of counting the numerical value of כבוד, "glory").

Comment

1–4 I have translated the expression ערות דבר as "a naked thing" (BDB, 789; see the *Comment* on 23:15). It is possible to interpret the phrase as something like "pudenda exposed" in an attempt to draw the reader's attention to the riddle-like quality of the words. Since these words in 23:15 are used to form an inclusion with "any bad thing" (כל דבר רע), it is clear that the interpretation "something indecent, obnoxious, or shameful" is not far off the mark as an interpretive comment. Such a rendering does not communicate the terse quality of the original Hebrew expression, however, which defies concrete objective definition. The word ערוה comes from the root ערה, "to be naked," and is commonly used with the meaning "nakedness" or "genitals" (particularly of a woman). Incest is described in Leviticus as uncovering a relative's ערוה. Though most translators and commentators agree that the phrase refers to sexually indecent behavior, it is clear that it does not mean adultery, because the biblical punishment for adultery is execution. The phrase is taken here as an idiom, perhaps analogous to the English expression "caught with one's pants down." The "naked thing" here is essentially the woman's genitals (cf. also Lam 1:8, of the personified city of Jerusalem). The interpretation "pudenda exposed" attempts to convey the idiomatic quality of the phrase in a manner that raises questions for the reader rather than simply supplying a definitive answer. The phrase means that the issue at hand, whatever it is, is out in the open for all to see—the woman "is caught with her pudenda exposed."

As stated here, "a bill of divorce" (ספר כריתת) was written by the husband. The term כריתת means literally "severance." It is possible that the term originally referred to the symbolic act of cutting the wife's hem or garment, which is the ceremonial act of divorce in ancient Mesopotamia, according to Tigay ([1996] 221–22). The phrase "she has been defiled" (הטמאה) refers to the woman in relation to her first husband and not a general state brought about by her remarriage. The reference to "an abomination before YHWH" can be interpreted in two ways, as Mayes has observed ([1981] 323): either the act of remarriage itself (with Craigie, [1976] 305, who compares the situation with the law on adultery in Lev 18:20), or the woman herself. It is the action of the woman that is "an abomination to YHWH," rather than the effect of that action on the land (cf. Jer 3:1). On the relation between the law here and its parallel in Jer 3:1–5, see Hobbes, *ZAW* 86 (1974) 23–29.

5 The phrase "a new wife" (אשה חדשה) refers to one who has never been married, or to a second marriage, but not to one's ex-wife. Otherwise some men might seek to gain deferral from military service by divorcing and remarrying their wives. The man is to "remain at home one year," presumably to conceive a child. According to Tigay Hebrew וְשִׂמַּח, "bring happiness," could also be translated "gratify" in the sense of giving the wife conjugal pleasure ([1996] 223). The concern for the woman's feelings is also expressed in 21:10–14 (marriage with a woman captured in war). See also the earlier law on military deferral in the context of preparing the army for battle (20:6–8). Some Hebrew texts read וְשָׂמַח, which would mean "he shall have happiness with his bride," in the sense that the two rejoice equally, or that he rejoices over her. Craigie cited a parallel in the Ugaritic texts (*CTA* 14.II.100–102 = *UT* Krt 100–102) where the practice was suspended because war was being undertaken to acquire a new wife for King Keret ([1976] 306 n. 5).

Explanation

The biblical teaching on divorce has been a matter of debate in times past as well as in current discussions within both the church and the synagogue. In short, as R. Wall has put it, "Matthew's exception clause becomes an ironical reminder that one's character is formed by a God whose will is for indissoluble monogamy (19:6). Clearly, the sum of the synoptic tradition argues that Jesus' teaching intended to create among his disciples an intolerance for divorce even though Jewish law tolerated it" (*ABD* 2:218).

It is important to note that there are no laws on divorce as such in the Torah. Some would argue that such laws were common knowledge in ancient Israel, and that the law here presupposes such divorce proceedings as normal legal action in that society. Though this is probably true, it seems that the issue at hand is not so much the matter of divorce per se as it is the meaning of marriage, with a profound reflection on "the great evil" (דבר רע) that is present wherever divorce is experienced. Divorce wreaks havoc in the lives of all concerned. The original intent of the Torah in matters concerning marriage is that of an inviolable union. The man's responsibility in this relationship is "to bring happiness to the woman he has taken" (24:5); but in some instances this may not be possible.

The law as stated in 24:1–5 and expanded in the narrative of Gen 20 recognizes the consequences of divorce for all concerned, because of its finality. Divorce is a form of death, the only difference being the simple fact that the corpses are still walking around! Life presents moments of ultimate decision, and the matter of divorce is one of those "moments." Divorce provides an ending, without the possibility of returning to what may have been, at least within the limitations of life in this present world. The matter is a bit like the profound story of the "man of God" in 1 Kgs 13 killed by the lion of Judah, who stood guard over his corpse without mauling the body. The man died because he ate bread and drank water in Bethel, contrary to what God had demanded of him. But God also commanded him not to "return by the way that you came" (1 Kgs 13:9). There is a reason why the laws of Deuteronomy have linked the subjects of "love and death" (i.e., marriage and war). To go home by a different way in the matter of remarriage means to step out into the unknown, into unfamiliar territory, on a new journey of faith. To attempt to go home by the way that one has come is contrary to the law of 24:1–4, because in almost all cases it is the way of death itself. The time to work through marital differences is before divorce, not in a second marriage to a former spouse.

3–4. Taking a Millstone in Pledge and Theft of a Fellow Israelite (24:6–7)

Bibliography

Alt, A. "Zu *hit 'ammer.*" *VT* 2 (1952) 153–59. **Amiran, R.** "The Millstone and the Potter's Wheel." *EI* 4 (1956) 46–49 (Heb.). **Baudissin, W. W. G.** "Die alttestamentliche Religion und die Armen." *Preussische Jahrbücher* 149 (1912) 193–231. **Cathcart, K. J.** " *Trkb qm* in the Arad Ostracon and Biblical Hebrew *Rekeb,* 'Upper Millstone.'" *VT* 19 (1969) 121–23. **Daube, D.** "To Be Found Doing Wrong." In *FS E. Volterra.* 1971. 3–13, esp. 4–10. **David, M.** "Deux anciens termes bibliques pour le gage." *OTS* 2 (1943) 79–86. **Dietrich, W.** ". . . den Arment das Evangelium zu Verkünden." *TZ* 41 (1985) 31–43. **Eichler, B. L.** *Indenture at Nuzi.* New Haven, CT: Yale UP, 1973. 88–89. ———. "Loan." In *Harper's Bible Dictionary.* Ed. P. Achtemeier. San Francisco: Harper & Row, 1985. 571–72. **Falk, Z.** *Hebrew Law in Biblical Times.* Jerusalem: Wahrmann, 1964. 101. **Finet, A.** "Le 'gage' et la 'sujétion' (*nipûtum* et *kiššatum*) dans les textes de Mari et le Code de Hammurabi." *Akkadica* 8 (1978) 12–18. **Good, E. M.** "Capital Punishment and Its Alternatives in Ancient Near Eastern Law." *SLR* 19 (1967) 953. **Greenberg, M.** "Mankind, Israel and the Nations." 1971. 15–40, esp. 29. **Lieberman, S.** "[Grain] Mills and Those Who Work Them." *Tarbiz* 50 (1980/81) 126–35 (Heb.). **Lipiński, E.** "Sale, Transfer and Delivery in Ancient Semitic Terminology." In *Gesellschaft und Kultur in alten Vorderasien.* Ed. H. Klengel. SGKAO 15. Berlin: Akademie-Verlag, 1982. 173–85. **Lisowsky, G.** "Dtn 25,4. לא־תחסם שור בדישו Du Sollst dem Rind bei seinem Dreschen Nicht das Maul verbinden: In religionsgeschichtlicher und ethischer

Sicht erläutert." In *FS L. Rost.* 1967. 144–52. **Mendelsohn, I.** "Samuel's Denunciation of Kingship (1 Sam 8:4–17) in the Light of the Akkadian Documents from Ugarit." *BASOR* 143 (1956) 17–22, esp. 20–22. **Milgrom, J.** *Cult and Conscience.* 1976. 94–104. **Moritz, L. A.** *Grain-mills and Flour in Classical Antiquity.* London: Oxford UP, 1958. **Neufeld, E.** "Inalienability of Mobile and Immobile Pledges in the Laws of the Bible." *RIDA* 9 (1962) 33–44. ———. "*Ius redemptionis* in Ancient Hebrew Law." *RIDA* 8 (1961) 29–40. **Richardson, H. N.** "Mill, Millstone." *IDB* 3:380–81 (with photo). **Stager, L.** "The Archaeology of the Family in Ancient Israel." *BASOR* 260 (1985) 12–15. **Tigay, J. H.** "Some Archaeological Notes on Deuteronomy." In *FS J. Milgrom.* 1995. 373–80, esp. 374–76. **Toorn, K. van der.** "Judges xvi 21 in the Light of the Akkadian Sources." *VT* 36 (1986) 248–53. ———. "Mill, Millstone." *ABD* 4:831–32.

Translation and Prosodic Analysis

Taking a Millstone as Distrained Property [6:6]

6 *No one* [a]*shall take in pledge a handmill /*	10	1
or an upper millstone //	5	1
for that would be taking a life / in pledge // ס	10	2

Theft of a Fellow Israelite

7 *When a man is found / stealing a person from his brothers /*	20	2_
from the sons of Israel /	9	1
and he treats him[a] *as merchandise / and he sells him //*	13	2
Then that thief\[b] *shall die /*	11	1
and you shall purge the evil / from your[c] midst //	13	2_

Notes

6.a. LXX reads ἐνεχυράσεις (= תחבל), "you shall take in pledge," for MT יחבל, "he shall take in pledge."

7.a. Sebire reads בָּה, "(he treats) her," for MT בו, "(he treats) him."

7.b. Reading *paštā'* followed by *zāqēp qāṭôn* as conj.

7.c. Reading 2 pl. with LXX and Syr. as *lectio difficilior* (cf. *Note* 24:4.c), which is another instance of the so-called *Numeruswechsel.* This might help to explain the absence of the *sĕtûmā'* paragraph marker in MT as redundant.

Form/Structure/Setting

As shown in the previous section, 24:5 functions as a bridge, serving as the conclusion to 23:2–24:5 and the introduction to what follows in 24:5–25:19. The six laws in 24:5–13 are closely connected in terms of their prosodic structure, which may be outlined in five rhythmic units:

A	Deferral of a new husband from military service	[6:6]	24:5
B	On taking ruinous action against a fellow Israelite	[6:6]	24:6–7
X	Dealing with "leprosy"	[6:6]	24:8–9
B′	Entering your neighbor's house to take a pledge	[6:6]	24:10–11
A′	Returning a poor man's pledge at sundown	[6:6]	24:12–13

Each of the five parts in this structure has twelve syntactic accentual stress units, which may be scanned in identical 6:6 rhythmic units. To do this, however, it should be noted that the phenomenon of enjambment occurs in vv 6–7, in which the thought runs across the verse division in a somewhat surprising manner. See further below.

The center of the above structure focuses attention on the enigmatic law on dealing with "leprosy" (vv 8–9). The inner frame is made up of parallel laws on matters pertaining to ruinous action against a fellow Israelite by "stealing a person" (vv 6–7), and by entering a neighbor's house to take his pledge on a loan (vv 10–13). The outer frame moves from one specific instance of showing humanitarian concern to another: from deferral of a new husband from military service (v 5) to the return of a neighbor's pledge at sundown (vv 12–13).

The seven laws on ruinous action against a fellow Israelite in 24:6–22 may be outlined in a menorah pattern as well, to form another "wheel within a wheel" in the architectural design of the laws in Deuteronomy:

A	Taking a millstone as pledge (distrained property)	24:6
B	Theft of a fellow Israelite (kidnapping)	24:7
C	Dealing with "leprosy"	24:8–9
X	Taking and holding distrained property	24:10–13
C′	Timely payment of wages	24:14–15
B′	Transgenerational punishment	24:16
A′	Protecting aliens, the fatherless, and widows	24:17–22

The framework in this structure moves from a specific law on the taking of distrained property (a millstone, v 6), to another more detailed law on the subject of distrained property in the structural center (vv 10–13), to a general statement of concern for protecting the poor and vulnerable in society (vv 17–22). The outermost pair of laws within this framework moves from a law on the theft of a fellow Israelite (kidnapping, v 7) to a law prohibiting transgenerational punishment (v 16). The inmost pair of laws concern the matter of "leprosy" (vv 8–9) and the timely payment of wages due (vv 14–15).

Another way of looking at the structure of the laws in 24:5–25:19 is to outline the whole collection in a concentric structural design:

A	Deferral of a new husband from military service	24:5
B	Taking a millstone as pledge	24:6
C	Theft of a fellow Israelite (kidnapping)	24:7
D	Dealing with "leprosy"	24:8–9
E	Taking and holding distrained property	24:10–13
F	Timely payment of wages	24:14–15
G	Transgenerational punishment	24:16
X	Protecting aliens, the fatherless, and widows	24:17–18
G′	Gleanings for the poor	25:19–22
F′	Limits on flogging	25:1–3
E′	Not muzzling the ox	25:4
D′	Levirate marriage	25:5–10
C′	Immodest intervention in a fight	25:11–13
B′	Honest weights and measures	25:13–16
A′	Remembering the Amalekite aggression	25:17–19

The outer frame in this structure moves from a law on warfare, which grants military deferral (24:5), to the concluding injunction to hate the Amalekites because of their enmity in the first war the people of Israel faced when they went out from the land of Egypt (25:17–19). Within this framework are a series of twelve laws, arranged so as to place the summary law on protecting the symbolic trio of poor and vulnerable folk (resident alien, orphan, and widow) in the structural center (24:17–22). All the other laws in 24:6–25:16, which are framed by the two laws on matters of warfare, explore humanitarian issues that pertain primarily to commandments eight through ten (prohibition of theft, false witnesses, and coveting).

The two laws in 24:6–7 are of unequal length, and the boundary between them is marked with a *sĕtûmāʾ* paragraph marker after v 6; but there is no such marker at the end of v 7. Indeed, the space left in *BHS* is conjecture on the part of the editor. No space was left at this point in L, though the *Numeruswechsel* is present, as restored from LXX and Syr.

In light of the prosodic analysis, the clause at the beginning of v 7 could be read in two different ways. The first reading is determined by the *sĕtûmāʾ* marker that divides the two verses into separate literary units and two distinct laws. A second reading, however, is also possible, and indeed is dictated by the rhythmic structure of the whole. Repetition of the word נפש, "life," ties the clause to what precedes by the phenomenon of enjambment. The matter of "taking a life in pledge" (v 6) is explained as "stealing a person [life] from his brothers" (v 7). The rhythmic unit that follows, then, begins with further definition in terms of the meaning of "his brothers," namely the "sons of Israel" who "treat him as merchandise and sell him." The allusion to the story of Joseph and his brothers in Genesis is transparent, as Carmichael has observed (*LNB*, 261–62). See further below.

It is interesting to note that the proverblike wording of the law on the taking of a millstone as a pledge in 24:6 also lends itself to a concentric reading, in which the term חבל, "pledge," functions as an inclusion:

A	"He shall not take in pledge"	לא־יחבל
B	"a mill"	רחים
X	"or an upper millstone"	ורכב
B′	"for that would be taking a life"	כי־נפש
A′	"in pledge"	הוא חבל

It is the portable upper millstone "rider" (רכב) in the center of this structure that would be taken away in pledge by the creditor. The inner frame states the issue in the symbolic language of a proverb: the mill(stone) in the home is a matter of life and death, so do not take it in pledge. To take an essential household item as collateral in order to pressure repayment of a loan is regarded as so oppressive that it is equivalent to "taking a life in pledge."

Referring to Sarah's exclusion of Hagar and Ishmael from the family (Gen 21), Carmichael says: "It is . . . accurate to paraphrase Abraham's agreement to Sarah's request by stating that it constituted his promise to give Isaac the prime inheritance because she had granted him the benefit of this son. By so agreeing, a life (Ishmael's and perhaps Hagar's too) was literally at stake" (*LNB*, 260). The illustration that was selected to accompany Richardson's article, "Mill, Millstone" (*IDB* 3:380), of a statuette of a woman grinding grain with a millstone, from Gizeh, is essentially a portrait of Hagar, the Egyptian handmaid of Sarah; that would have been one of her daily tasks. Taking "a mill or an upper millstone" in pledge could easily lead to starvation within a family. Note also how the issue of starvation itself arises in the story.

It is a short step from the idea of "taking a life in pledge" of the previous law to that of forcibly acquiring a person, enslaving them, or selling them into slavery. It is also a short step so far as the narrative in Genesis is concerned to move ahead to the selling of Joseph into slavery in Gen 37:26–28. Of all the connections between a specific law in Deuteronomy and its narrative counterpart in Genesis, this is the most transparent.

The sale of Joseph to Ishmaelites connects this law with the previous one and its links with Hagar, the mother of Ishmael. "Oppression characterizes each story. Hagar and Ishmael were cast out from their home and family; so too was Joseph. Each time the cruelty arose within the family; each time material gain was involved. Sarah acquired the prime inheritance for Isaac, and Joseph's brothers received money from the Ishmaelites" (Carmichael, *LNB,* 262). Moreover, in contrast with Isaac, when his mother Sarah ousted his older brother, Ishmael, Judah lost out in his attempts to oust his younger brother Joseph from his position as his father's favorite son (Gen 37:26; 38; 49:8–12).

It should be noted that the term התעמר, "to treat (someone) as merchandise," occurs only here and in the law legislating against the bad treatment of a captive woman (21:10–14), linked to Laban's rebuke of Jacob for running off with his two daughters. "From Laban's perspective Jacob had wrongfully removed them ('like captives of the sword') from their homeland, Aram (Gen 31:25–50). Joseph too was removed from his homeland" (Carmichael, *LNB,* 262).

Once again, it is interesting to read the law in 24:7 itself as a concentric structure, which may be outlined as follows:

A If a man is found stealing one of his brothers
B   And he treats him as merchandise
X   And he sells him
B′   That thief shall die
A′ Purge the evil from your midst

The focus of the law is that a man has stolen one of his brothers, whom he has sold into slavery. That evil must be purged "from your midst." If a man treats his brother as merchandise and sells him, that man must die.

Comment

6 "A handmill or an upper millstone" (רחים ורכב), a necessary item in food preparation, was made of basalt or other hard stone able to withstand constant rubbing (for photo see *ANEP,* no. 149; and *IDB* 3:380 [Egyptian woman using a mill]). Millstone sets were used to make flour for bread and thus were part of the necessary "kitchen utensils" in every home. To dispossess a family of its grain mill would amount to taking away its means of sustenance. It would appear that creditors took only the upper stone, which usually weighed about four or five pounds (Tigay [1996] 223; cf. idem, *FS J. Milgrom,* 374–76). To "take in pledge" (חבל) refers to distraint to compel repayment of a loan. The phrase "taking a life" means that the item is a necessary means of survival. "Items necessary for producing food . . . were often called 'life' in Mesopotamian, Egyptian, and postbiblical Jewish literature" (Tigay [1996] 224, who gives further references).

7 According to Craigie ([1976] 307), the law here is essentially a restatement of the eighth commandment in which the crime of "stealing" is in fact kidnapping (5:19). Unlike its parallel in Exod 21:16, which forbids kidnapping in general, the law here forbids a man from "stealing a person from his brothers from the sons of Israel." The interpretation of the law in terms of the story of the sale of Joseph by his brothers helps to explain this anomalous feature. On the meaning of והתעמר as "he treats him as merchandise," see the *Comment* on 21:14. The term appears in the Hebrew Bible only in these two places, where the Targums interpret it in this manner. The penalty is severe—"that thief shall die"—because the crime is essentially that of "social murder," to use the words of Craigie ([1976] 307). The same penalty applies in the Code of Hammurabi (*ANET,* 166, §14).

Explanation

All too often throughout history wealth has been garnered at the expense of others, sometimes by exploitation that reduces people to subsistence levels of living and premature death. In the world of antiquity, the millstone was an absolute necessity of life. It was needed daily to reduce grain to groats, meal, or flour. The sound of the grinding of the millstones was as characteristic of the common home as the light of the lamp (Jer 25:10). To dispossess a family of their millstone was to take from them the means of sustenance. Thus the law declares that there are limits to what a person may take from another in payment for a loan that is due. No matter what the circumstances may be, we do not have the moral right to take from another person their means of livelihood, however much they may owe us for loans made in times past.

In like manner, no one has the right to "steal a person [life]" by treating a fellow human being as merchandise. Though the text here refers directly to the circumstance of kidnapping, the principle applies to the matter of selling someone into slavery as well. In either case the culprit was condemned to death in ancient Israel. We do well to remember that there are many ways to "enslave" a fellow human being. Those who traffic in addicting drugs, including tobacco and alcoholic beverages, or encourage other addictions such as gambling, pornography, and illicit sex, are often guilty of stealing the life of a fellow human being. In biblical law there is no comparison between those who would steal livestock, or property of any sort, and those who would "steal" a human life. The punishment for the latter was death.

5. Dealing with "Leprosy" (24:8–9)

Bibliography

Caplice, R. "An Apotropaion against Fungus." *JNES* 33 (1974) 345–49. **Dols, M. W.** "The Leper in Medieval Islamic Society." *Speculum* 58 (1983) 891–916. ———. "Leprosy in Medieval Arabic Medicine." *Journal of the History of Medicine and Allied Sciences* 36 (1979) 314–33. **Douglas, M.** *Purity and Danger.* New York: Praeger, 1966. **Görg, M.** "'Ausschlag' an Häusern: Zu einem problematischen Lexem in Lev 14, 37." *BN* 14 (1981) 20–25. **Hulse, E. V.** "The Nature of Biblical 'Leprosy' and the Use of Alternative Medical Terms in Modern Translations of the Bible." *PEQ* 107 (1975) 87–105. **Kinnier-Wilson, J.** "Leprosy in Ancient Mesopotamia." *RA* 60 (1966) 47–58. ———. "Medicine in the Land and Times of the Old Testament." In *Studies in the Period of David and Solomon.* Ed. T. Ishida. Winona Lake, IN: Eisenbrauns, 1982. 337–65. **Lowe, J.** "Comments on the History of Leprosy." *Leprosy Review* 18 (1947) 54–64. **Meier, S.** "House Fungus: Mesopotamia and Israel." *RB* 96 (1989) 184–92. **Moller-Christensen, V.** "Evidence of Leprosy in Earlier People." In *Diseases in Antiquity.* Ed. D. Brothwell and A. T. Sandison. Springfield, IL: C. C. Thomas, 1967. 295–306. **Pilch, J. J.** "Biblical Leprosy and Body Symbolism." *BTB* 11 (1981) 108–13. **Sawyer, J. F. A.** "A Note on the Etymology of *Ṣaraʿat.*" *VT* 26 (1976) 241–45. **Seidl, T.** *Tora für den "Aussatz"-Fall: Literarische Schichten und syntaktische Strukturen in Levitikus 13 und 14.* ATSAT 18. St. Ottilien: EOS, 1982. **Skinsnes, O. K.** "Leprosy in Society." *Leprosy Review* 35 (1964) 21–35, 106–22, 175–82. **Sussman, M.** "Diseases in the Bible and the Talmud." In *Diseases in Antiquity.* Ed. D. Brothwell and A. T. Sandison. Springfield, IL: C. C. Thomas, 1967. 209–21. **Wilkinson, J.** "Leprosy and Leviticus: A Problem of Semantics and Translation." *SJT* 31 (1978) 153–66. ———. "Leprosy and Leviticus: The Problem of Description and Identification." *SJT* 30 (1977) 153–69. **Wright, D. P.** *The Disposal of Impurity: Elimination Rites in the Bible and in Hittite and Mesopotamian Literature.* SBLDS 101. Atlanta: Scholars Press, 1987. **Wright, D. P.,** and **Jones, R. N.** "Leprosy." *ABD* 4:277–82.

Translation and Prosodic Analysis

Dealing with "Leprosy" [6:6]

8 *Be careful in an attack of leprosy /*	12	1
to be very diligent \[a] *indeed*[b] *to do //*	11	1
according to all[c] *they shall teach* you /	11	1
(Namely) the Levitical[d] priests /	10	1
just as I commanded them / you shall be careful to do // ס	15	2
9 Remember / what he did /	12	2
(what) YHWH *your God (did) / to Miriam //*	13	2
in the way / [a]*in* your going out from Egypt[a] // ס	13	2

Notes

8.a. Reading *ṭiphā'* as conj. because of misplaced *'atnāḥ.*

8.b. Two Heb. MSS, SP, and LXX omit *waw*-conj., which is read here as emphatic (M. Dahood, *Psalms III: 101–150,* AB 17A [Garden City, NY: Doubleday, 1970] 400–402).

8.c. SP and LXX add התורה, "the Torah"; Syr. omits כל. Prosodic analysis favors MT.

8.d. Syr. reads והלוים, "and the Levites," for MT הלוים, "the Levites."
9.a-a. Vg. reads 2 sg. בצאתך for MT בצאתכם, "in your [pl.] going out."

Form/Structure/Setting

The law on leprosy in 24:8–9 is enigmatic because of its brevity. The people are commanded to "be careful in an attack of leprosy to be very diligent indeed to do according to all [the Levitical priests] shall teach you" (v 8); but the details of that teaching are not spelled out. Instead the subject shifts abruptly to what appears at first glance to be another law commanding the people to "remember what . . . YHWH your God (did) to Miriam in the way in your going out from Egypt" (v 9), for the two verses are separated by the *sĕtûmāʾ* paragraph marker. Knowledge of the detailed teaching on the subject of "leprosy," as preserved in Lev 13–14, is assumed, as is the incident of Miriam challenging Moses' unique relation to God in Num 12 and her punishment as she became "leprous, as white as snow" (Num 12:9).

When the law on leprosy (24:8–9) is examined in its larger context within Deut 24, its function becomes evident as a "riddle at the middle" in the following concentric structure:

A	Deferral of a new husband from military service	24:5
B	Taking a millstone and theft of a fellow Israelite	24:6–7
X	Dealing with "leprosy"	24:8–9
B′	Taking and holding distrained property	24:10–13
A′	Three laws on protecting the poor and vulnerable	24:14–22

The inner frame in this structure moves from a specific law on the matter of taking a millstone as distrained property, which is structurally tied to the law on kidnapping (24:6–7), to a more general law on taking and holding distrained property from a poor debtor (24:10–13). The outer frame is another example of the familiar three-plus-one pattern in Jungian psychology, with three laws on protecting the poor and vulnerable in society (24:14–22) set over against a single law granting military deferral to a new husband (24:5). The center of this structure (24:8–9) raises the question as to the meaning and significance of the "riddle at the middle."

The *sĕtûmāʾ* layout markers as given in *BHS* are misleading. There is no space after v 7 in L, though there is space at the end of one line and the beginning of the next to mark the end of v 8 (as is the case at the end of vv 6 and 13). The frequency of the *Numeruswechsel,* which appears four times in three verses (at the end of vv 7 and 8, and twice in v 9), suggests that we are dealing here with a pivotal passage in terms of prosodic structure.

A concentric reading of the law in question (vv 8–9) is instructive, as the following outline indicates:

A Be careful in an attack of leprosy
B Be very diligent indeed to do
X   According to all that the Levitical priests shall teach you
B′ As I commanded them, you shall be careful to do
A′ Remember what God did to Miriam after you left Egypt

The teaching of the Levitical priests is central in this reading and the people are instructed to follow that teaching, in any "attack of leprosy." In a symbolic sense, leprosy is associated here with God's punishment of those who fail to recognize proper authority.

In the larger concentric structure of the laws of 24:5–25:19 taken as a whole, the text on the "leprosy" of Miriam is to be read over against the law on the woman who intervenes inappropriately in a fight (25:11–12). In that instance we are also dealing with a transitional law from a literary point of view, in which the narrative is moving to a law associated with Joseph (25:13–16, honest weights and measures), whereas in the present context the narrative is moving in the opposite direction: *from* a law associated with Joseph (24:7, the theft of a fellow Israelite).

The issue at hand appears to be the matter of Moses' authority over the Levitical priests. In the narrative of Num 12, Aaron was the first to recant and acknowledge that Moses was God's appointed leader. Aaron was also the one who requested that Miriam be healed. In short, "Moses emerges as the key authority in the incident, and in that Aaron as the head of the Levitical priests is made to recognize this, the lawgiver infers that their instructions were the ones to be followed in curing leprosy" (Carmichael, *LNB*, 264).

Labuschagne's study of the use of the divine-name numbers in 24:8–9, within the larger context of 24:1–9, may be summarized as follows:

Words:	before *ʾatnāḥ*		after *ʾatnāḥ*		
24:8–9	13	+	13	=	26
24:1–5	50	+	52 (= 2 × 26)	=	102 (= 6 × 17)
24:6–9	28	+	23	=	51 (= 3 × 17)
24:7–9	24	+	19	=	43 (= 17 + 26)
24:1–9	78 (= 3 × 26)	+	75	=	153 (= 9 × 17)

The law dealing with "leprosy" in 24:8–9 is a single literary subunit made up of 26 words. It is closely related to what precedes and follows in the subunit 24:7–9, with its 43 (= 17 + 26) words. The larger literary context is 24:1–9, with 78 (= 3 × 26) words before *ʾatnāḥ* and its total of 153 (= 9 × 17) words, which is also the sum of the digits 1 through 17.

Comment

8 צרעת, translated "leprosy" here, describes a rather wide range of conditions referred to in the Bible—conditions on the skin, in cloth fabric, and on walls. In reference to skin disease, the term does not necessarily refer to leprosy (Hansen's disease) as defined by modern medicine. Lev 13–14 contains instructions for the priests, who observed and diagnosed the symptoms. "The exhortation at this point assumes that the legislation on leprosy is known to the audience, and Moses simply exhorts the people to be diligent in their observation of that legislation" (Craigie [1976] 308). The individual is instructed "to do according to all [the Levitical priests] shall teach you." On הכהנים הלוים, translated here as "Levitical priests," see the *Comment* on 18:1–2.

9 The instruction to "remember what . . . YHWH . . . (did) to Miriam" calls attention to the incident related in Num 12:10–15. Milgrom has noted that Miriam received special treatment in this instance, since she was isolated only one week instead of two (*Numbers* [1990] 98). The point seems to be "that nobody is immune, so that people wouldn't assume 'it can't happen to me' and fail to consult a priest regarding a potentially 'leprous' skin affliction" (Tigay [1996] 225).

Explanation

The leprosy of Miriam was inflicted by God for her hubris in challenging Moses' unique role in ancient Israel as covenant mediator and leader of the people. It should be noted that Miriam was also a spiritual leader (see Exod 15:20; Mic 6:4). She is one of five women in the Hebrew Bible who are designated as a "prophetess" (נביאה, Exod 15:20), the others being Deborah (Judg 4:4), Huldah (2 Kgs 22:14; 2 Chr 34:22), the wife of Isaiah (Isa 8:3), and Noadiah (Neh 6:14). In spite of her rank and character as presented in the book of Exodus, Miriam was excluded from the camp for seven days and restored only when she submitted to the authority of Moses.

Though we cannot identify the precise nature of the skin disease with which Miriam was afflicted, it is clear that her "leprosy" was a divine punishment that brought pollution into the midst of God's people. She was ritually unclean and had to undergo certain rites of purification before she could resume her place in that community.

There is a significant lesson here for anyone who would presume to challenge the role of a leader God has raised up within a given community. Such action is sinful and brings pollution in its wake that must be dealt with. No one in leadership, however high the rank or position, is immune from the danger of committing Miriam's sin of hubris. When such a matter occurs, the law is clear: God himself will bring punishment in the form of "leprosy"—a symbolic way of saying that a contaminating disease will become evident on that person, and that disease must be dealt with according to God's own instructions. The afflicted person is to be excluded from the "camp" for a season, until such time as the proper rites of purification have removed the pollution, and the guilty party submits once again to proper authority under God.

6. Taking and Holding Distrained Property (24:10–13)

Bibliography

Baudissin, W. W. G. "Die alttestmentliche Religion und die Armen." *Preussische Jahrbücher* 149 (1912) 193–231. **Botterweck, G. J.** "Die soziale Kritik des Propheten Amos." In *FS J. Höffner.* 1971. 39–58. **Braulik, G.** "Die Enstehung der Rechtfertigungslehre in den Bearbeitungsschichten des Buches Deuteronomium." *TP* 64 (1989) 321–33, esp. 140–42. **Carmichael, C. M.** *LNB.* 263–64. **Cazelles, H.** "De l'idéologie royale." In *FS T. H. Gaster.* 1973. 59–73. **Daube, D.** "The Culture of Deuteronomy." *Orita* 3 (1969) 33–34. **David, M.** "Deux anciens termes bibliques pour le gage." *OTS* 2 (1943) 79–86. **Finet, A.** "Le 'gage' et la 'sujétion' (*nipûtum et kiššatum*) dans les textes de Mari et le Code de Hammurabi." *Akkadica* 8 (1978) 12–18. **Kippenberg, H. G.** *Religion und Klassenbildung im antiken Judäa.* 2nd ed. SUNT 14. Göttingen: Vandenhoeck & Ruprecht, 1982. 27. **Lewy, I.** "Dating of Covenant Code Sections on Humaneness and Righteousness (Ex xxii 20–26; xxiii 1–9)." *VT* 7 (1957) 322–26. **Milgrom, J.** *Cult and Conscience.* 1976. 102–4. **Naveh, J.** "A Hebrew Letter from the Seventh Century B.C." *IEJ* 10 (1960) 129–39. **Neufeld, E.** "Inalienability of Mobile and Immobile Pledges in the Laws of the Bible." *RIDA* 9 (1962) 33–47. ———. "The Rate of Interest and the Text of Nehemiah 5.11." *JQR* 44 (1953/54) 194–204. **Ploeg, J. van der.** "Les pauvres d'Israel et leur piété." *OTS* 7 (1950) 236–70. **Tigay, J.** *Empirical Models for Biblical Criticism.* Philadelphia: Univ. of Pennsylvania Press, 1985. 168. ———. "A Talmudic Parallel to the Petition from Yavneh-Yam." In *Minḥah le-Naḥum: FS N. Sarna.* Ed. M. Brettler and M. Fishbane. JSOTSup 154. Sheffield: JSOT Press, 1993. 328–33. **Vogt, E.** "Ostracon Hebraicum saec. 7 A.C." *Bib* 41 (1960) 183–84. **Weil, H. M.** "Gage et cautionnement dans la Bible." *AHDO* 2 (1938) 171–241.

Translation and Prosodic Analysis

Taking and Holding Distrained Property [(6:6):(6:6)]

[10]When [a]*you make a loan*[a] *to your neighbor* |[b] *a loan of any sort //*	14	2
you shall not enter his house / to take his pledge //	20	2
[11] *outside / you shall stand //*	7	2
And the man / to whom / [a]*you make the loan*[a] */*	15	3
[b]*he shall bring to you*[b] */ the pledge / outside //*	18	3
[12]*And if he is / a poor man //*	10	2
you shall not sleep / in his pledge //	10	2
[13]*You shall surely return the pledge*[a] *to him /*	15	1
when the sun goes down /	6	1
That he may sleep in his garment[b] */ and he shall bless you //*	17	2
and it shall be counted as righteousness[c] */ for you /*	11	2
before / YHWH your God // ס	12	2

Notes

10.a-a. One Heb. MS and SP read חשא for MT חשה, "you make a loan," with no change in meaning.
10.b. Reading disj. accent *ṭiphā'* here with most Heb. MSS and printed editions, including Letteris.
11.a-a. Two Heb. MSS and SP read חשא for MT חשה, "you make a loan," with no change in meaning.
11.b-b. DSS and SP read יוצא for MT יוציא, "he shall bring," with no change in meaning.
13.a. Many Heb. MSS and DSS read העבט for MT העבוט, "the pledge," with no change in meaning.
13.b. SP[W] reads בְּשִׂמְלָתוֹ for MT בְּשַׂלְמָתוֹ, "in his garment," with no change in meaning.
13.c. On a parallel use of צדקה, "righteousness," see 6:25.

Form/Structure/Setting

As noted in the previous section of this commentary, the laws on taking and holding distrained property in Deut 24 are in two parts (24:6, on taking a millstone in pledge; and 24:10–13), which form a frame around the law dealing with "leprosy" (24:8–9). Another way of looking at the function of 24:10–13 within the structure of Deut 24 is to outline the whole, in relation to the corresponding narrative stories in Genesis, within a menorah pattern:

A	Taking a millstone as pledge	(Isaac and Ishmael)	24:6
B	Theft of a fellow Israelite	(Joseph and brothers)	24:7
C	Dealing with "leprosy"	(Miriam [and Moses])	24:8–9
X	Taking and holding distrained property	(Isaac and Rebekah)	24:10–13
C′	Timely payment of wages	(Jacob and Laban)	24:14–15
B′	Transgenerational punishment forbidden	(Hamor and Shechem)	24:16
A′	Protecting aliens, orphans, and widows	(Joseph in Egypt)	24:17–22

The framework in this structure moves from a specific law on taking a millstone in pledge (24:6), to a more general law on the taking of distrained property in the center (vv 10–13), and back to a specific law on the taking of a widow's garment in pledge at the end (vv 17–22). When one examines the narrative stories in Genesis that are shaped by these three laws, the story begins with the conflict between Isaac and Ishmael, as sons of Abraham, concerning who will be the primary heir (Gen 21:9–12), to the marriage between Isaac and Rebekah (Gen 24, with a flashback to God's covenant with Abraham in 15:5–21), and concludes with the expanded story of Isaac's grandson Joseph in Egypt (Gen 37–47). Within this framework, the first pair of laws moves from that of kidnapping (Deut 24:7) to the prohibition of transgenerational punishment (24:16). In this instance the corresponding narrative stories are the sale of Joseph into slavery by his brothers (Gen 37:26–28) and the plight of the Canaanite king Hamor and his son Shechem (Gen 34). The next frame moves from the law on leprosy (Deut 24:8–9) to the law on timely payment of wages (24:14–15). The corresponding narratives here are the stories about Miriam's sin (Num 12:1–14) and Jacob as the hired servant of Laban (Gen 31:4–42).

The boundaries of the law on taking and holding distrained property in Deut 24:10–13 are marked with *sĕtûmā'* layout markers at the end of vv 9 and 13. The key words in this passage are the noun עבוט, "pledge," which appears four times here and nowhere else in the Hebrew Bible, and the word חוץ, "outside." These terms appear nested in a concentric structure:

A	"you shall not enter . . . to take his pledge"	לא־תבא . . . לעבט עבטו	24:10b
B	"outside you shall stand"	בחוץ תעמד	24:11a
X	"the man . . . shall bring to you the pledge"	יוציא אליך את־העבוט	24:11b
B′	"outside"	החוצה	24:11c
A′	"you shall not sleep in his pledge"	לא תשכב בעבטו	24:12b
	"you shall surely return the pledge to him"	השב תשיב לו את־העבוט	24:13a
	"that he may sleep in his garment"	ושכב בשלמתו	24:13b

The structure focuses on the moment when the man to whom the loan is made brings forth the pledge outside (v 11b). In the outer frame, the man who made the loan is instructed not to enter "his house" (v 10b) and not to sleep in his pledge, but to return it at sundown so that "he may sleep in his garment" (v 13). The inner frame focuses on the place where the man who made the loan is to stand, namely, "outside" (v 11a, c).

The concluding section of the above structure may in turn be outlined in concentric fashion to show further nesting of the key word "pledge" (עבוט):

A	"you shall not sleep in his pledge"	לא תשכב בעבטו	24:12b
B	"you shall surely return to him"	השב תשיב לו	24:13a
X	"the pledge"	את־העבוט	24:13b
B′	"when the sun goes down"	כבא השמש	24:13c
A′	"that he may sleep in his garment"	ושכב בשלמתו	24:13d

The center of this structure focuses attention on the "pledge" itself. The inner frame makes the command explicit: you shall surely return it to the man at sundown (v 13). In the outer frame we see that the man who made the loan is not to sleep in "his pledge" (v 12b) but to return it so that the other man may sleep in "his garment" (v 13d).

The law on taking and holding distrained property in 24:10–13 may be outlined as follows:

A	Do not enter your neighbor's house to take his pledge	24:10
B	Outside you shall stand, and he shall bring it to you outside	24:11
X	If he is a "poor man," you shall not sleep in his pledge	24:12
B′	You shall surely return the pledge when the sun goes down	24:13a
A′	It shall be counted righteousness for you before God	24:13b

In this reading, the focus of the law is the prohibition of sleeping in the pledge of a poor man (v 12). By refusing to enter a neighbor's house to take his pledge (v 10), the individual receives "righteousness" before God (v 13b). The inner frame contains the "midrashic kernel" that shaped the stories in both Gen 24 and Gen 15: the person is to stand outside the house of his neighbor (v 11). This statement is set over against the statement that, "You shall surely return the pledge to him when the sun goes down" (v 13a).

It is also possible to read v 11 as a concentric sentence, which moves from a man standing outside a house to the pledge brought to him there outside:

A	"Outside you shall stand"	בחוץ תעמד
B	"and the man"	והאיש
X	"to whom you make the loan"	אשר אתה נשה בו
B′	"he shall bring to you"	יוציא אליך
A′	"the pledge outside"	את־העבוט החוצה

In this circular sentence, in which the content is much the same as the larger whole (vv 10–13), the word חוץ, "outside," functions as an inclusion.

If the law prohibiting the theft of a fellow Israelite in 24:7 is the most transparent in terms of the relationship between an individual law in Deuteronomy and the narrative associated with it in Genesis (i.e., the sale of Joseph into slavery in Gen 37:26–28), the law on distrained property in Deut 24:10–13 may be the most opaque, and Carmichael missed it in his study. It is also the most detailed in terms of its subsequent expansion in the story of Isaac obtaining Rebekah as his wife (Gen 24:1–67), and to a lesser degree the story of God's covenant with Abram in Gen 15:5–21. Almost every word in Deut 24:10–13 takes on fresh meaning within the narrative stories.

In the story of Gen 24, the "pledge" (עבוט) is Rebekah, who is obtained by an unnamed servant, described as "the oldest of *his house*" (ביתו, v 2; cf. Deut 24:10).

When this man, who has been sent to obtain the "pledge" from the house of Laban, arrives at his destination, Rebekah asks, "Why do you stand outside?" (תעמד בחוץ, v 31; cf. Deut 24:11). In one sense it is Isaac, the servant's master, who is "standing outside" the land of Aram-naharaim waiting at "his house" in Canaan for his servant to return to him (cf. "he shall surely return to him," השב תשיב לו, in Deut 24:13) with the "pledge"—his bride-to-be. Isaac went out to meditate in the field "in the evening" (לפנות ערב)in Gen 24:63, shortly before "the going down of the sun" (כבא השמש) of Deut 24:13. And the words "that he may sleep in his garment" take on fresh meaning in relation to the following words of the Genesis narrative: "and [Isaac] took Rebekah and she became his wife" (Gen 24:67), which should be compared with the same expression in Deut 21:11; 22:13; 23:1; 24:1–5 (five times). Moreover, the words "he shall bless you" (וברכך) in Deut 24:13 become ויברכו, "and they blessed," in Gen 24:60 to introduce the blessing pronounced by the men of Laban's house on Rebekah: "Our sister, be the mother of thousands of ten thousands; and may your descendants possess the gate of those who hate them!"

At this point, the hearer is reminded of a similar blessing to Abraham in times past, for the very next phrase in the law, "it shall be counted as righteousness" (ולך תהיה צדקה), takes us back to the narrative of God's covenant with Abram in Gen 15, when God "brought him outside" (ויוצא אתו החוצה) and said, "Look toward heaven and number the stars, if you are able. . . . So shall your descendants be" (Gen 15:5). And Abraham believed God, who "reckoned it to him as righteousness" (ויחשבה לו צדקה, v 6). A few verses later: "As the sun was going down [ויהי השמש לבוא], a deep sleep [תרדמה] fell on Abram; and lo, a dread and great darkness fell upon him. Then the Lord said to Abram, 'Know of a surety that your descendants will be . . . oppressed for four hundred years. . . . As for yourself, you shall go to your fathers [אבתיך] in peace; you shall be buried in a good old age. And *they shall come back here in the fourth generation. . . .*' When the sun had gone down [ויהי השמש באה] and it was dark . . . on that day the Lord made a covenant with Abram" (Gen 15:12–18).

The statement "they shall come back here in the fourth generation" takes on new meaning in this reading, for that is what we have just now done in following the syllabus of the laws in Deuteronomy to read the narrative in Genesis. The four generations are: Abraham, Isaac, Jacob/Israel, and Jacob's twelve sons (the tribes of Israel), with the focus narrowing to the persons of Joseph (Deut 24:7, 17–22; 25:1–3, 13–16) and Judah (25:4–12) in that fourth generation. The moment the sale of Joseph by his brothers is introduced in 24:7 (in the law prohibiting such a theft of a fellow Israelite) our attention is first directed to Miriam's "leprosy" (24:8–9) in the era of the exodus from Egypt and the "present," from the perspective of Deuteronomy. But the next law (24:10–13) takes us back three generations to Isaac's quest for a wife in Gen 24:1–67, which then takes us back still further, one more generation, to the original story of Abram, who had already outlined all that was to follow in a brief prophecy, which concludes with the curious words that "they will come back here in the fourth generation" (ודור רביעי ישובו הנה). And that is what we have done in this reading of Genesis through the lens of the laws of Deuteronomy.

The content of Gen 15:12–18, which is framed by repetition of words expanding the phrase כבא השמש, "when the sun goes down," of Deut 24:13, may be outlined as follows:

A	As the sun was going down, a deep sleep fell on Abram	15:12
B	After 400 years of oppression your descendants will come out	15:13–14
X	As for you, you shall go to your fathers (אבתיך) in peace	15:15
B′	And they shall come back here in the fourth generation	15:16
A′	When the sun had gone down, YHWH made a covenant with Abram	15:17–18

The inner frame in this structure pairs the four hundred years of oppression in Egypt with the "coming back in the fourth generation," in the form of poetic speech. In the center we find the key to unlock the puzzle of the repeated use of the word עֲבוֹט, "pledge," in Deut 24:10–13. The word was chosen because of its similarity in sound to the word אָבוֹת as used in Gen 15:15. Here the reference is to the death of Abram, who would go to be with his *fathers* "in a good old age" (בשיבה טובה). Rebekah, who is the עבוט in the story of Gen 24, is also related to the אבות of Gen 15:15 in that she, like Sarah before her, is the "mother of the fathers," as it were; for her two sons are Jacob, the father of the twelve tribes of Israel, and Esau, whose lineage includes the chiefs of Edom, one of whom will take center stage in another time and place within the biblical narrative—in the land of Uz, where Job lives to see "his sons, and his son's sons, four generations." Like his "brother" Abram, Job "died, an old man and full of days" (Job 42:16–17).

In Labuschagne's "logotechnische analyse" of Deut 24:10–13, he found 17 words in secondary clauses and a total of 46 words. Though this could be interpreted as 2 × 23 (the numerical value of כבוד, "glory"), Labuschagne found deeper significance in the fact that the numerical value of the key word צדקה in v 13 is also 46 (= [צ = 18] + [ד = 4] + [ק = 19] + [ה = 5]), and the numerical value of another key word, משפט, "justice," is 60. The reasons for these conclusions become clear when the evidence for the whole of 24:10–18 is examined:

Words:	before *ʾatnāḥ*		after *ʾatnāḥ*		
24:10–13	21	+	25	=	46 (= צדקה)
24:10–18	65	+	54	=	119 (= 7 × 17)
24:14–15, 17–18	34 (= 2 × 17)	+	26	=	60 (= משפט)
24:14–15	20	+	14	=	34 (= 2 × 17)
24:14–16	30	+	17	=	47
24:17–18	14	+	12	=	26
24:18	9	+	8	=	17

It is clear that the primary literary unit here is 24:10–18, which has a total of 119 (= 7 × 17) words. Within this larger unit, the major subunits are vv 10–13, 14–15, and 17–18. The prohibition of transgenerational punishment in v 16 was treated somewhat differently by the ancient scribes, who connected it with vv 14–15 so as to have 17 words after *ʾatnāḥ* in vv 14–16. The compositional formula 34 + 26 = 60 represents the distribution of words between main clauses and subordinate clauses, as well as the number of words before and after *ʾatnāḥ* in vv 14–15 + 17–18. In their numerical composition, the scribes of ancient Israel appear to be associating God, as signified by the divine-name numbers, with the concepts of צדקה, "righteousness," and משפט, "justice."

Comment

10 "When you make a loan [תשה] to your neighbor, a loan of any sort," you are not permitted to "enter his house [בא אל־ביתו] to take his pledge [עבטו]." Mayes says the law here is influenced by its parallel in Exod 22:26–27, which also uses the expression רעך, "your neighbor," instead of the expected word אח, "brother" ([1981] 325). The term used for making a loan is the verbal root נשה, "to lend, become a creditor." The verb תשה was sometimes read as תשא, from the root נשא, which also means "to lend on interest." The reason the creditor is not permitted to enter the debtor's home to distrain property is usually interpreted to mean that "the debtor and his family would be humiliated by another man acting as master in the debtor's domain, and the confrontation could lead to a fight" (Tigay [1996] 225). Reasoning along these lines, subsequent Jewish interpreters of the law determined that distraint by force of any kind was oppressive, such that distraint was permitted only with permission of the court. The same reasoning is reflected in the Laws of Hammurabi that penalized a creditor who distrains grain forcefully from a debtor, as Tigay has observed ([1996] 389 n. 42, citing Code of Hammurabi §113). A different interpretation of the law emerges in light of the use of the unusual word הָעֲבוֹט, "the pledge," from the root עבט, "to take or give a pledge." The term עֲבוֹט used as a noun appears four times in vv 10–13 and nowhere else in the Hebrew Bible. Its use as a verb is limited to four occurrences as well, all in Deuteronomy: 15:6 (twice); 15:8; and here in 24:10 (in Joel 2:7 the root עבט appears with an altogether different meaning). Moreover, the synonym חבל appears in vv 6 and 17, which has led Milgrom (*Cult and Conscience,* 102–4) and others (Tigay, *Empirical Models,* 168) to argue that we have evidence here for conflation. It is more likely that a new word is introduced because of the play on sounds the author wishes to convey (see discussion above in *Form/Structure/Setting*).

11 The phrase בחוץ תעמד, "outside you shall stand," appears in reverse order in Gen 24:31 (תעמד בחוץ), and nowhere else in the Hebrew Bible (the phrase לעמוד בחוץ in Ezra 10:13 being the only other time the two lexical items appear together). The instruction to bring the pledge outside to the man who is receiving that pledge takes on deeper meaning in the story of Rebekah becoming the wife of Isaac in Gen 24.

12 The phrase איש עני, which I render here as "he is a poor man," could also be interpreted as "a man of the poor [עני, or perhaps ענו]," where, in a metaphorical sense, the second term refers to "Israel" itself as the poor, afflicted, or pious one (as it frequently does in the Psalms and elsewhere; cf. Pss 10:17; 22:27 [Eng. 26]; 25:9 [twice]; 34:3 [Eng. 2]; 37:11; 69:33 [Eng. 32]; etc.). In a Hebrew letter from the seventh century B.C.E. found at Yavneh-Yam a man asks for the return of a garment that was wrongfully seized (cited by Craigie [1976] 308 n. 15; see *ANET,* 568; and Tigay, *FS N. Sarna,* 328–33). The words "sleep in his garment [pledge]" (שכב בעבט) take on a deeper meaning when "the pledge" (העבוט) becomes Rebekah, who is taken to the man "standing outside" (first to Isaac's unnamed servant in Aram-naharaim, and then to Isaac himself).

13 The statement "you shall surely return the pledge to him when the sun goes down" takes on concrete meaning as one reads: "And Isaac went out to meditate in the field *in the evening;* and he lifted up his eyes and looked, and behold, there were camels coming. And Rebekah lifted up her eyes, and when she saw Isaac, she alighted from the camel" (Gen 24:63–64). Moreover, the words ושכב בשלמתו, "he shall sleep in his garment," also take on new meaning in light of what we have already learned from other laws: that a man's wife is his garment. As the law in Deut 23:1 clearly states, for a son to lie with his father's wife (or concubine) means figuratively that he has removed his father's covering and put it on himself. The statement "and he shall bless you" (וברכך) evokes a comparison with the blessing (ויברכו) that Rebekah received when she departed from her brother Laban's house: "Our sister, be the mother of thousands of ten thousands; and may your descendants possess the gate of those who hate them!" (Gen 24:60). It would appear that the new term עֲבוֹט, "pledge," was chosen so that, in the telling of the story, the people would also hear the word אָבוֹת, "fathers"; for Rebekah, like Sarah before her, is indeed the mother of the fathers in ancient Israel, through both of her twin sons, Jacob/Israel and Esau/Edom. The law concludes: ולך תהיה צדקה, "it shall be counted as righteousness for you," which carries the reader's attention back to the story of God's covenant with Abram in Gen 15 (see the discussion under *Form/Structure/Setting,* and cf. also the use of צדקה in Deut 6:25 [וצדקה תהיה לנו] and 9:4–6 [three times, and the reference there to Abraham, Isaac, and Jacob]).

Explanation

The older version of the law on taking and holding distrained property in Exod 22:25–27 makes no mention of not entering the house of the debtor to take what he has pledged in security. If the debtor is poor, the article pledged (usually an item of clothing) must be returned that same day, before sundown, "for that is his only covering, it is his mantle for his body; in what else shall he sleep?" (Exod 22:26). Deuteronomy adds an injunction that prohibits the creditor from entering the debtor's home to remove the pledge. As shown in the discussion above, this addition plays a substantive role in shaping the narrative stories in Gen 24 and 15, which reflect the wording of this law.

As Matthew Henry put it long ago, the law in Deuteronomy forbids the taking of anything for a pledge "by want of which a man was in danger of being undone. Consonant to this is the ancient common law of England, which provides, That no man can be distrained of the utensils or instruments of his trade or profession, as the axe of a carpenter, or the books of a scholar, or beasts belonging to the plough, as long as there are other beasts, of which distress may be made" (*Exposition of the Old and New Testament* [1828] 668).

The law concludes with the remark that the debtor "shall bless you, and it shall be counted for righteousness for you before YHWH your God" (v 13), when you refrain from withholding distrained property. Even within the covenant community, where God's blessing is bestowed, there will still be those who are disadvantaged and poor. It is our responsibility, under God, to alleviate their hardship.

7. Mistreatment of a Hired Servant— Timely Payment of Wages Due (24:14–15)

Bibliography

Bienert, W. *Die Arbeit nach der Lehre der Bibel.* Stuttgart: Evangelisches Verlagswerk, 1954. **Botterweck, G. J.** "Die soziale Kritik des Propheten Amos." In *FS J. Höffner.* 1971. 39–58. **Fuchs, K.** *Die alttestamentliche Arbeitergesetzgebung im Vergleich zum Codex Hammurabi, zum altassyrischen und hethitischen Recht.* Heidelberg: Evangelischer Verlag, 1935. **Kim, Y.** "The Vocabulary of Oppression in the Old Testament: *'sq, ynh, lhs,* and Congeners." Diss., Drew Univ., 1981. Order No. 8119746. DA 42 (1981/82) 1213-A. **Klengel, H.** "Soziale Aspekte der altbabylonischen Dienstmiete." In *Beiträge zur sozialen Struktur des alten Vorderasien.* Ed. H. Klengel. SGKAO 1. Berlin: Akademie-Verlag, 1971. 39–52. **Milgrom, J.** *Cult and Conscience.* 1976. 95–96, 98–102. **Pons, J.** *L'Oppression dans l'Ancien Testament.* Paris: Letouzey, 1981. **Talmon, S.** "Double Readings in the Massoretic Text." *Textus* 1 (1960) 154. **Wolff, H. W.** "Herren und Knechte: Anstösse zur Überwindung der Klassengegensätze im Alten Testament." *TTZ* 81 (1972) 129–39.

Translation and Prosodic Analysis

Mistreatment of a Hired Servant—Timely Payment of Wages Due [(4:4):(4:4)]

14 *You shall not withhold the wage*[a] / *of a poor and needy one* //	16	2
among your brothers / *or among* your[b] sojourners /	13	2_
Whoever is [c]in your land[c] / in your[d] towns //	12	2
15 on the same day you shall give him his wages /	13	1
before the sun goes down /	14	1_
For he is \[a] poor /	8	1
and upon it / he lifts / his life breath //	15	3_
That he not call out against *you* / *to YHWH* /	14	2
and it becomes in you / *a sin* // ס	8	2_

Notes

14.a. Reading שְׂכַר as the constr. with Craigie ([1976] 309 n. 16). Some Heb. MSS, including DSS (1Q5, frg. 8, in DJD 1:58), read שׂכר, "wages," for MT שׂכיר, "laborer" or "hireling." The revocalization improves the balance in mora count.

14.b. Reading 2 pl. with SP[Mss], LXX, and *Tg. Ps.-J.* as *lectio difficilior* (cf. *Notes* 24:4.c and 24:7.c).

14.c-c. Omitted in two Heb. MSS, LXX[-O], and Syr.

14.d. Cairo Geniza fragments read 2 sg.

15.a. Reading *pašṭa'* followed by *zāqēp parvum* as conj.

Form/Structure/Setting

The first of three laws on protecting the poor and vulnerable in 24:14–22 deals with the matter of mistreating a hired servant by not paying wages due in a timely manner (24:14–15). The place and function of this law within the larger structure of 24:5–25:19 (the third major subsection within the sixth of the eleven weekly portions of Torah readings in Deuteronomy) as a whole may be outlined in a menorah pattern:

A	Deferral of a new husband from military service	24:5
B	Four laws on distrained property, kidnapping, and "leprosy"	24:6–13
C	Mistreating a hired servant—timely payment of wages	24:14–15
X	Transgenerational punishment on fathers and sons	24:16
C′	Protecting the sojourner, orphan, and widow	24:17–22
B′	Five laws on humanitarian and social issues	25:1–16
A′	Remembering Amalekite aggression	25:17–19

This structure should be compared with the one presented above in the introduction to the section on the laws of 24:6–25:16, in which specific interest was focused on the first of four laws on humanitarian and social issues in 24:6–13, with the law on levirate marriage (25:5–10) in the center of a menorah pattern. The outer frame remains the same, as we move from one law on matters of Holy War, in which a new husband is deferred from military service (24:5), to another law on YHWH's Holy War (25:17–19). The series of twelve laws on matters of social ethics within this frame are arranged in a symmetrical pattern, with three laws dealing with the protection of the poor and vulnerable in the center (24:14–22). It should be noted in passing that the symmetry between sections B and B′ in this outline is greater than appears at first glance; for the laws on limits to flogging (25:1–3) and not muzzling an ox (25:4) are combined in a single literary unit, which is set over against three laws dealing with sexual matters or with sexual allusions (25:5–16), including the law on honest weights and measures, as we will see. In sections B and B′, the four literary subunits are arranged in simple chiasms, which also display the familiar three-plus-one structuring pattern, though in a somewhat surprising manner (see the detailed discussion of these laws below). The relation between these laws may be outlined as follows:

A	Taking a millstone as pledge (distrained property)	24:6
B	Theft of a fellow Israelite (kidnapping)	24:7
B′	Dealing with "leprosy"	24:8–9
A′	Taking and holding distrained property	24:10–13

A	Humanitarian concern for human beings and draft animals	25:1–4
B	Levirate marriage	25:5–10
B′	An immodest lady wrestler (assisting her husband in a fight)	25:11–12
A′	Honest weights and measures	25:13–16

In the first of these structures (24:6–13), we find a pair of laws on taking and holding distrained property (v 6 and vv 10–13) functioning as a frame around a pair of laws on kidnapping (v 7) and "leprosy" (vv 8–9). It is the law on "leprosy" that stands apart as separate from the other three, which have to do with similar humanitarian concerns: taking or "stealing a person [life]" (v 7) from among those who are one's brothers (v 7) or neighbors (v 10). The second of these structures (25:1–16) displays a similar pattern; most translators and commentators miss the double entendre of 25:13. See the detailed discussion of these laws below.

The innermost frame in the concentric structural design of 24:5–25:19 moves from a law protecting the hired servant from mistreatment (24:14–15) to a more general law on the protection of the sojourner, orphan, and widow (24:17–22). It should be noted that the term גר, "sojourner," appears in both of these laws (vv 14 and 17). Once again it is easy to see the familiar three-plus-one patterning of Jungian psychology in the trio of sojourner, orphan, and widow (vv 17–22) set over against the law of the hired servant (vv 14–15), who is designated "a laborer who is poor and needy among your brothers or among your sojourners" (v 14).

Both boundaries of the law in 24:14–15 are marked with the *Numeruswechsel* as well as *sĕtûmā'* layout markers. The law in between (vv 10–13) is thus singled out as the center of another structural unit, perhaps as follows:

A	Taking a millstone as pledge	(Isaac and Ishmael)	24:5–6
B	Theft of a fellow Israelite	(Joseph enslaved in Egypt)	24:7
C	Dealing with "leprosy"	(Miriam vs. Moses)	24:8–9
X	Law on distrained property	(Isaac/Rebekah and Abraham)	24:10–13
C′	Mistreating a hired servant	(Jacob vs. Laban)	24:14–15
B′	Transgenerational punishment	(Israel and the Hivites)	24:16
A′	On the widow, orphan, and alien	(Joseph and his brothers)	24:17–22

In this reading the story of the conflict between Jacob and Laban (as shaped by the law on the mistreatment of a hired servant in 24:14–15) is to be read over against the story of conflict between Moses and his sister Miriam (and his brother Aaron as well) in 24:8–9.

The structure of the law in 24:14–15 may be outlined as follows:

A	You shall not oppress a laborer who is poor and needy	24:14a
B	among your brothers or sojourners in your town	24:14b
X	Pay his wages on the same day, before the sun goes down	24:15a
B′	for he is poor and depends on it	24:15b
A′	Lest he cry out against you to YHWH and it be sin in you	24:15c

In the center is the law requiring the timely payment of wages due "before the sun goes down" (v 15a). The outer frame puts that law in a more general context by adding a motive clause: you shall not oppress a laborer who is poor and needy, lest he cry out against you to YHWH and it be sin in you (vv 14a, 15c). In the inner frame we see that the law applies to anyone who is poor and dependent on wages that are timely paid (v 15b), whether that person is an Israelite brother or a sojourner in your towns (v 14b).

When Carmichael read the law on timely payment of wages (24:14–15) in relation to the narrative in Genesis (*LNB,* 268–70), he found himself once again dealing with the stories of Jacob and Laban (see the law of the fugitive slave in 23:15–16)—and in the story of Jacob's flight from Haran in particular (Gen 31:4–7; 40–42). "All the concerns that are mentioned in the law about mistreating a hired servant—he is poor and needy, he may be a brother Israelite or a sojourner, his hire should be given him on the day he earns it—show up in Laban's treatment of Jacob" (Carmichael, *LNB,* 269).

In the words of Deut 24:14–15, Laban oppressed his servant after seven years by not paying the wages he had promised, namely Rachel. Though Jacob later received Rachel as well, Jacob still complained to Laban: "These twenty years I have been in your house; I served you fourteen years for your two daughters, and six years for your flock, and you have changed my wages ten times. If the God of my father, the God of Abraham and the Fear of Isaac, had not been on my side, surely now you would have sent me away empty-handed" (Gen 31:41–42). The law makes reference to the downtrodden servant crying out against his employer to God, who intervenes in his behalf. In short, the story of Jacob and Laban is an expansion of the law in Deut 24:14–15, almost phrase by phrase.

In his "logotechnische analyse" of the law in Deut 24:14–15, Labuschagne found the 34 (= 2 × 17) words in these two verses distributed before and after *'atnāḥ* and between main clauses and subordinate clauses to be identical (20 + 14). On the relationship of these two verses to their larger context in 24:10–18, see the discussion in the previous section on 24:10–13.

Comment

14 "You shall not oppress [תעשק] a laborer." The term עשק refers to cheating someone out of their belongings. On a "laborer" (שכיר) cf. Matt 20:1–16, the parable of Jesus and the hiring of such laborers at different times in the same day for the same wage.

15 The words rendered "upon it he lifts his life breath" mean "he is counting on it" (Tigay [1996] 227). Though the worker may be unable to force his employer to pay him on time, he can "call out against you to YHWH," who will intervene (cf. Exod 22:21–23; Deut 15:9). "Some of the prayers of Jeremiah, and a number of Psalms, are cries against mistreatment" (Tigay [1996] 227; on 390 n. 52 he refers to Jer 11:20; 20:12; Ps 109; and B. Porten, *Archives from Elephantine* [Berkeley: Univ. of California Press, 1968] 157–58, 315–16). On the matter of incurring guilt, i.e., "and it becomes in you a sin," see also 23:22 above.

Explanation

The employer-employee relationship is addressed in the law on mistreatment of a hired servant (24:14–15), which law focuses its interest primarily on the matter of timely payment of wages due. For Craigie, "the use of this legislation in the NT (Jas. 5:4) makes clear that it protects not only the poor, but also the rich; the rich men, fulfilling their obligations to their poor laborers, maintain the integrity of the community. But failure to deal honestly in transactions of this sort brings severe condemnation (Jas. 5:1–6)" ([1976] 309).

The parable of Jesus on the laborers in the vineyard (Matt 20:1–16) picks up on these words in the statement that "when evening came" (Matt 20:8) the owner of the vineyard paid them their wages. In this particular instance, however, the wages received were the same for each person regardless of how many hours they had worked. Thus the question of just payment for their labor was raised by the ones who had worked longest and were the last to be paid, for they expected to receive more than the others, who had not "borne the burden of the day and the scorching heat" as they had (Matt 20:12). The owner's response was forthright: "I am doing you no wrong; did you not agree with me for a denarius [the usual daily wage]?" (Matt 20:13). So long as the employer pays what is due to those he has employed, he remains free to do what he chooses with what belongs to him (Matt 20:15). Jesus concludes his parable with a riddle: "So the last will be first, and the first last" (Matt 20:16).

There is an important spiritual lesson here. With God as the "owner of the vineyard," we have an "employer" who is both just and merciful. We do well to pattern our own lives accordingly; for the deepest and most satisfying experiences in life are not found through self-centered acquisition of wealth and power achieved through exploitation of others, or even by the exercise of "justice" alone to those under us. Charles Dickens saw this principle with remarkable clarity in the portrayal of Ebenezer Scrooge in his classic work, *A Christmas Carol*, as did Frank Capra in his timeless film, *It's a Wonderful Life.*

8. *Transgenerational Punishment Forbidden (24:16)*

Bibliography

Ahuis, F. *Autorität im Umbruch: Ein forgeschichtlicher Beitrag zur Klärung der literarischen Schichtung und der zeitgeschichtlichen Bezüge von Num 16 und 17.* CThM A.13. Stuttgart: Calwer, 1983. **Callaway, P. R.** "Deut 21:18–21: Proverbial Wisdom and Law." *JBL* 103 (1984) 341–52, esp. 351 n. 42. **Cazelles, H.** "Les origines du Décalogue." *EI* 9 (1969) 14–19, esp. 15. **Daube, D.** "Concerning Methods of Bible-Criticism: Late Law in Early Narratives." *ArOr* 17.1 (1949) 88–99, esp. 96. **Furlani, G.** "Familienhaftung." *Reallexikon der Assyriologie.* Ed. E. Ebeling et al. Berlin: de Gruyter, 1928ff. 3:19. **Gammie. J. G.** "The Theology of Retribution in the Book of Deuteronomy." *CBQ* 32 (1970) 1–12. **Greenberg, M.** "Some Postulates of Biblical Criminal Law" (1960). In SBTS 3:295–300. **Jacob, E.** "Die altassyrischen Gesetze und ihr Verhältnis zu den Gesetzen des Pentateuch." *Zeitschrift für vergleichende Rechtswissenschaft* 41 (1925) 319–87. **Leibowitz, N.** *Studies in Devarim.* Jerusalem: World Zionist Organization, 1986. 238–39. **Verdam, P. J.** "'On ne fera mourir les enfants pour les pères' en droit biblique." *RIDA* 3 (1949) 393–416. **Yaron, R.** "Biblical Law: Prolegomena." In *Jewish Law in History and the Modern World.* Ed. B. S. Jackson. JLA Sup 2. Leiden: Brill, 1980. 27–44, esp. 34–36. **Yeivin, S.** "Social, Religious and Cultural Trends in Jerusalem under the Davidic Dynasty." *VT* 3 (1953) 149–66.

Translation and Prosodic Analysis

Transgenerational Punishment Forbidden [3:3]

16 *Fathers shall not* [a]*be put to death*[a] */ for children /* [17 2
and as for the children / 6 1
They shall not [b]*be put to death*[b] *for fathers //* [12 1
each one for his own sin / shall [c]*be put to death*[c] *//* ס 10 2

Notes

16.a-a. SP[MSS], LXX, Syr., and Tg. read יָמוּתוּ, "they will die"; two Heb. MSS read ימותו(ן), "they will die," for MT יוּמְתוּ, "they shall be put to death."

16.b-b. Same as previous note with an additional Heb. MS reading ימתו, "they shall die."

16.c-c. One Heb. MS and SP read יומת, "he will be put to death"; another Heb MS, DSS, LXX, Syr., and Vg. read ימות, "he will die."

Form/Structure/Setting

Like a number of other laws in the sixth of the eleven weekly portions of Torah readings from Deuteronomy (21:10–25:19), the brief law prohibiting transgenerational punishment in 24:16 functions in more than one role from a structural point of view. In one reading, it is the center of the collection of laws on matters of social ethics in 24:5–25:19, for it stands between the two laws on protecting the poor and the vulnerable (24:14–15 and 24:17–22) in the center of the menorah pattern discussed in the previous section of this commentary. At the same time, however, it completes a major subsection in a group of five laws on humanitarian issues within the larger architectural design of Deut 24–25 as a whole, which may be outlined as follows:

A	Two laws on marriage and war	24:1–5
B	Laws on humanitarian concerns and social ethics	24:6–16
a	Taking a millstone in pledge and kidnapping	24:6–7
b	Dealing with "leprosy"	24:8–9
x	Taking and holding distrained property	24:10–13
b′	Mistreating a hired servant—timely payment of wages	24:14–15
a′	Transgenerational punishment forbidden	24:16
X	Law protecting the sojourner, orphan, and widow	24:17–22
B′	Laws on humanitarian concerns and social ethics	25:1–16
a	Limits on flogging	25:1–3
b	Not muzzling the ox	25:4
x	Levirate marriage	25:5–10
b′	Wife's immodest intervention in a fight	25:11–12
a′	Honest weights and measures	25:13–16
A′	Remembering Amalekite aggression (YHWH's Holy War)	25:17–19

The framework of this structure (A, X, A′) is made up of three laws on marriage and war (24:1–5 and 25:17–19), which are set over against the summary law on protecting the sojourner, orphan, and widow (24:17–22) in the center. The outer frame in this structure moves from a law on forbidden marriage in 24:1–4 (corresponding with the seventh commandment on adultery) and a law on both war and marriage in 24:5 (sixth and seventh commandments) to a law on YHWH's Holy War in 25:17–19 (sixth commandment on murder/war, with overtones on matters of worship in the first, second, and third commandments in terms of YHWH's Holy War as celebrated event in ancient Israel; see *Excursus:* "Holy War as Celebrated Event in Ancient Israel"). The inner frame is made up of two parallel five-part concentric substructures with laws on matters of social ethics and humanitarian concerns dealing primarily with the eighth, ninth, and tenth commandments (on stealing, bearing false witness, and coveting what belongs to one's neighbor). The laws on taking and holding distrained property (24:10–13) and the levirate marriage (25:5–10) appear in the center of the two concentric subsections; this structure directs attention once again to commandments seven through ten of the Decalogue.

Once again, the brief law itself in 24:16 is circular in its structural design—in the form of a circular sentence—with the term יומתו, "they shall be put to death," appearing at the beginning, middle, and end.

A	"Fathers shall not be put to death"	לא־יומתו אבות
B	"for (their) children"	על־בנים
X	"and children shall not be put to death"	ובנים לא־יומתו
B′	"for (their) fathers"	על־אבות
A′	"each one for his own sin shall be put to death"	איש בחטאו יומתו

Three of the nine lexical items in this sentence are the word יומתו, which appears in both parts of the outer frame and in the center of this structure. The inner frame has the pairing of אבות, "fathers," and בנים, "children" in the context of judicial procedure in regard to capital punishment. This simple structure has profound ramifications for theological reflection within the context of the narrative in Genesis and beyond.

Though the narrative of the rape of Dinah (Gen 34) was shaped in part by both the law of illicit mixtures on plowing with an ox and an ass together (22:10) and the law on the rape of an unengaged virgin (22:28–29), its literary structure is shaped by the law of transgenerational punishment in 24:16 as well. "It is this story . . . that provides an instance (the only one in biblical literature) of a father's being put to death because of his son's misdeed, namely, Shechem's seduction of Dinah" (Carmichael, *LNB,* 271–72). In the story both the father (Hamor) and the son (Shechem) died. It should be noted that Jacob complains that his own life (as father) was endangered by the sin of his sons (Gen 34:30).

The shaping of the narrative of Gen 34 in terms of the law in Deut 24:16 is evident from the anlysis of its content, which may be outlined as follows:

A	Shechem (son of Hamor) seduced Dinah (daughter of Israel)	Gen 34:1–4
B	Jacob's response: he held his peace until his sons came	Gen 34:5
C	Hamor (father of Shechem) negotiates with Jacob	Gen 34:6–12
X	Jacob's sons plot revenge—death of father and son	Gen 34:13–25
C′	Hamor and his son Shechem are slain by Simeon and Levi	Gen 34:26–29
B′	Jacob's response: "I shall be destroyed, both I and my household"	Gen 34:30
A′	The sons' response: "Should he treat our sister as a harlot?"	Gen 34:31

The center of this structure (34:6–29) corresponds with the law of Deut 24:16 and the issue of transgenerational punishment. The outermost frame sets the sin of Shechem (son of Hamor) in Gen 34:1–4 over against the angry response of Dinah's brothers, who are incensed with what Shechem has done (34:31). The second frame presents the plight of the father Jacob/Israel, whose life is jeopardized by the rash immoral action of his sons (vv 5, 30). In the innermost frame Hamor negotiates with Jacob (vv 6–12), but dies because of the sin of his son Shechem (vv 26–29). It would appear, according to this story, that fathers are put to death for the sins of their children.

Comment

16 The word יומתו, "they shall (not) be put to death," appears three times in this verse and elsewhere only in reference to human execution, rather than divine punishment. The law is quoted in 2 Kgs 14:6 to explain Amaziah's conduct when he became king of Israel. For parallels in ancient Near Eastern law, where members of a man's family were considered extensions of his personal property rather than individuals as such, see Code of Hammurabi §§116, 209–10, 230; Middle Assyrian Laws §§50, 55; Hittite Instructions, *ANET,* 207–8 (see Tigay [1996] 390 n. 55). See also Exod 21:31, in the law of the goring ox, which does not include the provision that the owner's child is to be punished if the victim is a child, as might be the case elsewhere in the ancient Near East where such *lex talionis* was carried out—that is, a person being punished by the same harm done to a member of his own family, often the corresponding member. On the proverbial maxim "The fathers have eaten sour grapes and the children's teeth are set on edge," see Jer 31:29–30 and Ezek 18:2. Mayes ([1979] 326) has called attention to "a catchword connection with the previous verse" in the use of the word בחטאו, "for his own sin," which corresponds with the word חטא, "sin," there. Craigie called attention to an interesting parallel in Middle Assyrian Law (*ANET,* 180, A §2) where "a woman convicted of blasphemy was to bear the penalty of her crime, but her husband and children were not to be punished" ([1976] 310 n. 17). Craigie also noted that the law here must be held in balance with that of 5:9, where "the iniquity of the fathers is visited on their children to the third and fourth generations," for a father's criminal act inevitably affects the lives of his children. On the one hand, a person is criminally responsible under the law for his or her own behavior. On the other hand, a criminal act carries with it consequences that affect the children of that guilty person.

Explanation

The law prohibiting transgenerational punishment in 24:16 stands out in even a cursory reading of the text of Deut 24–25 because it alone addresses the issue of capital punishment. Though some have argued that a law such as this is superfluous in modern society, we do well to recall the ballad of "The Martins and the Coys" in our own folk tradition, and other similar portrayals of vengeance in the name of the family in which children die for the sins of their parents and vice versa.

The law was apparently overriden in ancient Israel in matters of Holy War, for Achan's entire family was executed, including "his sons and daughters" (Josh 7:24), for the sin of the father in violating the ban on taking booty during the destruction of Jericho (see Josh 7:6–26). The law was violated in other contexts as well throughout the history of ancient Israel. King David surrendered seven sons (including grandsons) of Saul to be executed by the Gibeonites for the sin of Saul (2 Sam 21:1–9); and King Baasha slew "all the house of Jeroboam" when he usurped the throne of the Northern Kingdom (1 Kgs 15:29–30), with Zimri after him doing the same to the house of Baasha (1 Kgs 16:11–13), and Jehu after him to the sons of Ahab (2 Kgs 10:6–7). It should be noted, however, that King Amaziah spared the children of his father's murderers on the basis of the law here in Deuteronomy, which is cited: it "is written in the book of the law of Moses . . . 'fathers shall not be put to death for the children, or the children be put to death for the fathers, but every man shall die for his own sin'" (2 Kgs 14:6).

A deeper theological issue emerges as we reflect on the meaning of atonement for sin. Some have suggested that when David surrendered the "seven of [Saul's] sons" (2 Sam 21:6) to the Gibeonites to be executed for the sin of Saul, "they died rather as sacrifices than as malefactors" (M. Henry, *Exposition of the Old and New Testament* [1828] 669). Be that as it may, it is clear that the doctrine of the "original sin" of Adam and the atoning death of Jesus Christ as the "second Adam" (Rom 5:14; 1 Cor 15:22, 45) is understood in Christian theology in terms of a reversal of the law as stated here—the transgenerational guilt of "original sin" is countered with transgenerational blessing. The children of Adam do suffer for the sin of their father; and the atoning death of Jesus, as the incarnation of God the Father, applies to all of God's "family," for all time and eternity.

9–10. Taking a Widow's Garment in Pledge and Gleanings for the Poor (24:17–22)

Bibliography

Borowski, O. *Agriculture in Iron Age Israel.* Winona Lake, IN: Eisenbrauns, 1987. **Canaan, T.** "Plant-Lore in Palestine Superstition." *JPOS* 8 (1928) 140–41. **Carmichael, C. M.** "The Law of the Forgotten Sheaf." In *SBLSP* 20. Chico, CA: Scholars Press, 1981. 35–37. **Dahood, M.** "Eblaite and Biblical Hebrew." *CBQ* 44 (1982) 1–24, esp. 15–16. **Epstein, L. M.** *Sex Laws and Customs in Judaism.* New York: Bloch, 1948. 64–67, 75–78. **Fensham, F. C.** "Aspects of Family Law in the Covenant Code in Light of Ancient Near Eastern Parallels." *DiIs* 1 (1969) v–xix. ———. "Widow, Orphan, and the Poor in Ancient Near Eastern Legal and Wisdom Literataure." *JNES* 21 (1962) 129–39. **Fichtner, J.** "Die Bewältigung heidnischer Vorstellungen und Praktiken in der Welt des Alten Testaments." In *FS Friedrich Baumgärtel.* Ed. L. Rost. Erlanger Forschungen 10. Erlangen, 1959. 24–40. **Haran, M.** "Das Böcklein in der Milch seiner Mutter und das säugende Muttertier." *TZ* 41 (1985) 135–59, esp. 150. **Heaton, E. W.** "Sojourners in Egypt." *ExpTim* 58 (1946) 80–82. **Houton, C. van.** *The Alien in Israelite Law.* JSOTSup 107. Sheffield: JSOT Press, 1991. **Hvidberg-Hansen, O.** "Die Vernichtung des goldenen Kalbes und der ugaritische Ernteritus: Der rituelle Hintergrund für Exod. 32,20 und andere alttestamentliche Berichte über die Vernichtung von Götterbildern." *AcOr* 33 (1971) 5–46, esp. 14–15. **Kellermann, D.** "גּוּר *gûr.*" *TDOT* 2:439–49. **Lohfink, N.** *Option for the Poor.* Tr. L. M. Maloney. 2nd ed. N. Richland Hills, TX: BIBAL Press, 1995. **Mauch, T. M.** "Sojourner." *IDB* 4:397–99. **Meek, T. J.** "The Translation of *Ger* in the Hexateuch and Its Bearing on the Documentary Hypothesis." *JBL* 49 (1930) 172–80. **Melamed, A.** "Break-up of Stereotype Phrases as an Artistic Device in Biblical Poetry." In *Studies in the Bible.* Ed. C. Rabin. ScrHier 8. Jerusalem: Magnes, 1961. 115–53. **Merendino, R. P.** *Das deuteronomische Gesetz.* 1969. 307–8. **Miller, P. D.** "Studies in Hebrew Word Patterns." *HTR* 73 (1980) 79–89. **Montet, P.** *Everyday Life in Egypt.* Tr. A. R. Maxwell-Hyslop and M. S. Drower. Philadelphia: Univ. of Pennsylvania Press, 1981. 116. **Muntingh, L. M.** "Die Begrip 'Gēr' in die Ou Testament." *NGTT* 3 (1962) 534–58. **Nielsen, E.** "You Shall Not Muzzle an Ox While It Is Treading out the Corn." In *Law, History and Tradition.*

1983. 94–105. **Ogletree, T. W.** *Hospitality to the Stranger.* Philadelphia: Fortress, 1985. **Peckham, B.** "Phoenicia and the Religion of Israel." In *FS F. M. Cross.* 1987. 79–99, esp. 81. **Pedersen, J.** *Israel: Its Life and Culture.* 2 vols. London: Oxford UP, 1926–40. 1:39–46. **Rothschild, M. M.** "Aliens and Israelites." *DD* 9 (1981) 196–202; 10 (1981–82) 118–21; 11 (1982) 35–39. **Scaria, K. J.** "Social Justice in the Old Testament." *BibBh* 4 (1978) 163–92. **Schmidt, K. L., Schmidt, M. A.,** and **Meyer, R.** " Πάροικος." *TDNT* 5:841–53. **Smith, D. L.** *The Religion of the Landless.* Bloomington, IN: Meyer Stone, 1989. **Spencer, J. R.** "Sojourner." *ABD* 6:103–4. **Spina, F. A.** "Israelites as *gērîm,* 'Sojourners,' in Social and Historical Context." In *FS D. N. Freedman.* 1983. 321–35. **Sulzberger, M.** *The Status of Labor in Ancient Israel.* Philadelphia: Dropsie College, 1923. **Wolff, H. W.** "Herren und Knechte: Anstösse zur Überwindung der Klassengegensätze im Alten Testament." *TTZ* 81 (1972) 129–39. **Yaron, R.** "Biblical Law: Prolegomena." In *Jewish Law in History and the Modern World.* Ed. B. S. Jackson. JLA Sup 2. Leiden: Brill, 1980. 27–44, esp. 34–36. **Yeivin, S.** "Social, Religious and Cultural Trends in Jerusalem under the Davidic Dynasty." *VT* 3 (1953) 149–66, esp. 153.

Translation and Prosodic Analysis

Taking a Widow's Garment in Pledge [8:7]

17 *You shall not pervert / justice / to the alien or*[a] *the orphan //*	13	3
and you shall not take in pledge / a widow's / garment //	14	3
18 *and you shall remember / that you were a slave*\[a] *in Egypt*[b] */*	19	2_
And YHWH your God / redeemed you\[c] [d]*from there*[d] *//*	17	2
therefore / I command you / to do / this / thing // ס	25	5_

Gleanings for the Poor [7:4:7] [7:8]

19 *When you reap your harvest in your field /*	15	1
and you overlook a sheaf in the field /	13	1
You shall not return / to take it[a] */*	10	2
to the alien / [b]*to the orphan and*[c] *widow / it shall go //*	18	3_
In order that YHWH your God / may bless you /	17	2
in all / the work of your[d] *hands //*	12	2_
20 *When you beat / your olive tree /*	8	2
you shall not gather again / after you //	11	2
[a]*to the alien /* [b]*to the orphan and*[c] *widow / it shall go //* ס	18	3_
21 *When you gather / from your vines /*	8	2
you shall not glean / after you //	12	2
[a]*to the alien /* [b]*to the orphan and widow / it shall go //*	18	3_
22 *And you shall remember /*	6	1
that you were a slave / in the land of Egypt //	17	2
therefore / I command you / to do / this / thing // ס	25	5_

Notes

17.a. Three Heb. MSS, LXX[-MS], Syr., Tg.[MSS], *Tg. Ps.-J.*, and Vg. add *waw*-conj.; LXX adds καὶ χήρας, "and widow."

18.a. Reading *pašṭā'* followed by *zāqēp qāṭôn* as conj.

18.b. Some Heb. MSS, LXX[-MS], and *Tg. Ps.-J.* read בארץ מצרים, "in the land of Egypt," for MT במצרים, "in Egypt." Prosodic analysis favors MT.
18.c. Reading *ṭipḥāʾ* as conj. because of misplaced *ʾatnāḥ*.
18.d-d. Omitted in one Heb. MS and SP. Prosodic analysis favors MT.
19.a. LXX[-Bmin] adds τῷ πτωχῷ καί (= לאביון ו), "to the poor and." Prosodic analysis favors MT.
19.b. Two Heb. MSS, LXX, Syr., and Vg. add *waw*-conj.
19.c. One Heb. MS and LXX[MS] omit *waw*-conj.
19.d. Many Heb. MSS read ידך, "your hand," for MT ידיך, "your hands." Although *BHS* has a space after this word, L does not.
20.a. LXX adds τῷ πτωχῷ καί (= לאביון ו), "to the poor and."
20.b. A few Heb. MSS, LXX, Syr., and Vg.[MSS] add *waw*-conj.
20.c. One Heb. MS omits *waw*-conj.
21.a. LXX adds τῷ πτωχῷ καί (= לאביון ו), "to the poor and."
21.b. LXX[-MS] and Syr. add *waw*-conj.

Form/Structure/Setting

The law here is in two parts, which serve as a frame around one more instance of a law on distraining property: "you shall not take in pledge a widow's garment" (24:17b). The function of this clause appears to be that of forming a menorah pattern around the structural theme of distraint:

A	Taking a millstone in pledge	24:6
B	Theft of a fellow Israelite (kidnapping)	24:7
C	Dealing with "leprosy"	24:8–9
X	Taking and holding distrained property	24:10–13
C′	Mistreating a hired servant—timely payment of wages	24:14–15
B′	Transgenerational punishment forbidden	24:16
A′	Taking a widow's garment in pledge	24:17–18

Within a framework on the subject of distraint (A, X, A′), four laws on humanitarian concerns and social ethics are arranged in two pairs. The relationship between these four laws is easily seen in the narratives shaped by them. The outer pair concerns conflict within the members of a given family: the theft of Joseph, who was sold into slavery by his brothers (Gen 37; cf. Deut 24:7), which is set over against the conflict between two of Joseph's brothers (Simeon and Levi) and the Hivite King Hamor and his son Shechem (Gen 34; cf. Deut 24:16). The inner pair moves from the problem of "leprosy" in the conflict between Moses and his sister Miriam in the wilderness (Num 12; cf. Deut 24:8–9), and the conflict between Jacob and Laban in Mesopotamia (Gen 31; cf. Deut 24:14–15).

Though Tigay ([1996] 228–29) divides vv 17–22 into two laws, prosodic analysis supports Craigie ([1976] 310) and others who see a single literary unit here. That unit is divided into three parts with *sĕtûmāʾ* layout markers after vv 18, 20, and 22. *BHS* incorrectly divides the section into four parts, with spaces following vv 18, 19, 20, and 22. What appears as *sĕtûmāʾ* layout markers in *BHS* are actually blank spaces in L, and there is no space whatsoever left between vv 19 and 20 in that manuscript. The reason for difficulties in determining the subsections in vv 17–22 is that the prosodic structure of vv 19–20 is somewhat anomalous, with all of v 19b ("In order that YHWH your God may bless you in all the work of your hands") functioning as a rhythmic bridge in a 7:4:7 unit in terms of accentual stress units. This central unit is also precisely in the center of the larger literary structure that extends from 24:5 through 25:19.

The concentric structural design of 24:17–22 as a whole may be outlined as follows:

A	Do not pervert justice to the alien, orphan, and widow . . .	24:17–18
B	Leave some of your grain for the alien, orphan, and widow	24:19a
X	So that YHWH may bless you in all you do	24:19b
B′	Leave some of your olives for the alien, orphan, and widow	24:20
A′	Leave some of your grapes for the alien, orphan, and widow . . .	24:21–22

There is a great deal of repetition in these verses. Both sections of both the inner and outer frames make specific reference to the alien, the orphan, and the widow (vv 17, 19, 20, 22). Moreover, the statement "and you shall remember that you were a slave in Egypt . . . therefore I command you to do this thing" appears in both parts of the inner frame (vv 18, 22). The source of God's blessing is clear in this structure. It comes from protecting the aliens, orphans, and widows in our midst. As Jesus once put it, the second greatest commandment is this: "Love your neighbor as yourself" (Matt 22:39). That is the substance of the law, especially in Deut 24:6–25:16.

Carmichael has noted a number of connections between the law as expressed here and the story of Joseph, the most obvious being the repeated statement to "remember that you were a slave in Egypt" (vv 18, 22). "A blatant example of a perversion of justice was Joseph's imprisonment for an offense he never committed, namely, lying with Potiphar's wife. Joseph, moreover, was at this time a slave in Egypt (Potiphar's wife refers to him as the 'Hebrew servant' [Gen 39:17])" (*LNB,* 280). Joseph is also comparable to the sojourner in the law. Though the topic of the widow's garment taken in pledge has fewer clear parallels in the Joseph narrative, it should be noted that his garment was the key piece of evidence for the injustice done to him in the incident with Potiphar's wife. Moreover, the Hebrew word בגד, "garment," appears in both Gen 39:12 and Deut 24:17. The connection between the widow's garment taken in pledge in the law and the narrative tradition in Genesis is much easier to see in the story of Tamar's seduction of Judah in Gen 38. "Judah in effect forced her to put away her widow's garment in order to obtain what should have already been given to her, namely, seed that she would then return to him in the form of a child to continue the family line" (Carmichael, *LNB,* 281).

The law of the forgotten sheaf (Deut 24:19) differs markedly from its counterparts in Lev 19:9 and 23:22, which indicate that specific parts of the field are to be left unharvested for the poor: "When you reap the harvest of your land, you shall not reap your field to its very border, neither shall you gather the gleanings after your harvest." This rule is much more systematic than that in Deut 24:19 concerning a sheaf that is "overlooked" or "forgotten" (ושכחת).

Carmichael makes a strong case for relating the laws of 24:17–25:3 with the story of Joseph in Gen 37–47 (*LNB,* 278–91). He notes that the sheaf plays a central role in the Joseph story, as does an emphasis on remembering (Gen 40:14, 23; 41:9). The verb זכר, "remember," occurs twice in the law, both times in the statement, "You shall remember that you were a slave in Egypt" (vv 18, 22). And the sheaf of v 19 is described with the verb שכח, "forget." The emphasis on grain for the needy shapes the story of Joseph's rule in Egypt. "As overseer of the harvest Joseph saved everyone from starvation. His high position—in figurative terms he is the dominant sheaf—and the supply to needy people of sheaves of grain (in the literal sense) are intimately linked" (Carmichael, *LNB,* 286).

The evidence assembled by Labuschagne on the use of the divine-name numbers in 24:17–22 may be summarized as follows:

Words:	before *'atnāḥ*		after *'atnāḥ*		
24:17–18	14	+	12	=	26
24:19–22	32	+	23	=	55
24:18	9	+	8	=	17
24:19–21	26	+	15	=	41

The law on protecting the sojourner, orphan, and widow in vv 17–18 has a total of 26 words, and the law on gleanings for the poor in vv 19–22 is an example of what Schedl called the "minor tetraktys" 32 + 23 = 55 (see *Excursus:* "Deuteronomy as a Numerical Composition"). The two parts in this construction, 23 and 32, are the alternate numerical values of Hebrew כבוד, "glory," with כ counted as either 11 or 20.

Comment

17–18 For a parallel law in the Pentateuch, see Exod 22:21–24. To "pervert justice" (חטה משפט) is to judge unfairly in legal matters (see 16:19). *Tg. Pseudo-Jonathan* and ancient rabbinic sources suggest that the reason the widow is shown greater solicitude than aliens and orphans has to do with the fact that holding her garment during the day would "lead to unchastity or to rumors harmful to her reputation" (Tigay [1996] 228, and sources cited on 390 n. 65). On the treatment of the familiar phrase "alien, orphan, and widow" in two separate parts, see also 10:18, the discussion of Melamed (*Studies in Bible,* 115–53), and the comments on the resultant menorah pattern in *Form/Structure/Setting* above.

19–22 See Ruth 2 and cf. Lev 19:9–10; 23:22, Exod 23:10–11; and Lev 25:2–7. Mayes notes that the phrase "in all the work of your hands" normally appears as a concluding formula ([1981] 327). In this particular law it appears precisely in the middle of the two laws in 24:17–22, which concern the protection of the rights and privileges of the sojourner, the orphan, and the widow in ancient Israel. Moreover, from a prosodic perspective, v 19b functions as a rhythmic bridge connecting vv 19a and 20, which may be read in two different ways in terms of total mora count: (28 + 28 + 29):(19 + 18) or (28 + 28):(29 + 8 + 29).

Explanation

The story of Ruth was shaped with this law in view, for she was at the same time an alien, an orphan (she left all her family behind in Moab), and a widow. The fields, olive trees, and vineyards were not to be picked clean. Landowners were obliged to leave a portion of food behind so that those in need could glean from them; and Boaz actually ordered his workers to leave handfuls of grain for Ruth to gather (Ruth 2:16). Such a practice kept the needy from the humiliation of begging for subsistence. The poor were thus able to maintain their dignity by working for their own food, though the owner of the field did not profit directly from their labors.

The law itself is framed by parallel references to the motivation for the concern for the poor and vulnerable in ancient Israel: "remember that you were a slave in (the land of) Egypt" (vv 18, 22).

A	Remember that you were a slave in Egypt	24:18
B	The overlooked grain is for the alien, orphan, and widow	24:19
X	The overlooked olives are for the alien, orphan, and widow	24:20
B′	The overlooked grapes are for the alien, orphan, and widow	24:21
A′	Remember that you were a slave in the land of Egypt	24:22

The phrase "the alien, the orphan, and the widow" appears four times in this law (vv 17, 19, 20, 21). The image here is one of the most picturesque of all the laws of Deuteronomy and continued to influence customs within Christianity for centuries to come, as illustrated by Millet's famous painting, *The Gleaners.*

11–12. Limits on Flogging and Not Muzzling the Ox (25:1–4)

Bibliography for 25:1–3

Allgeier, A. "Dt. 25, 1–3 im Manchester-Papyrus (PRG 458)." *Bib* 19 (1938) 1–18. **Cohn, H. H.** "Flogging." *EncJud* 6:1348–49. **Glanville, S. R. K.,** ed. *The Legacy of Egypt.* Oxford: Clarendon, 1942. 204. **Hofbauer, J.** "Zu den Textfamilien der Septuaginta im Deuteronomium zu Dt 25,1–3 nach PRG 458." *ZKT* 62 (1938) 385–89. **Hoffner, H. A.** "Some Contributions of Hittitology to Old Testament Study." *TynBul* 20 (1969) 27–55. **Roscher, W. H.** "Die Zahl 40 im Glauben, Brauch und Schrifttum der Semiten." *Abhandlungen der philologisch-historische Klasse der königlich sächsischen Gesellschaft der Wissenschaften* 27 (1909) 93–138. **Tigay, J. H.** "Some Archaeological Notes on Deuteronomy." In *FS J. Milgrom.* 1995. 377. **Wilkinson, J. G.** *The Manners and Customs of the Ancient Egyptians.* 3 vols. Ed. S. Birch. London: John Murray, 1878. 1:305–8.

Bibliography for 25:4

Boecker, H. J. "'Du sollst dem Ochsen, der da drischt, das Maul nicht verbinden.' Überlegungen zur Wertung der Natur im Alten Testament." In *Fs F. Lang.* 1978. 72–89. **Borowski, O.** *Agriculture in Iron Age Israel.* Winona Lake, IN: Eisenbrauns, 1987. 63–65. **Carmichael, C. M.** "'Treading' in the Book of Ruth." *ZAW* 92 (1980) 248–66, esp. 250–52. **Eslinger, L.** "More Drafting Techniques in Deuteronomic Laws." *VT* 34 (1984) 221–26. **Finkelstein, J. J.** *The Ox That Gored.* Transactions of the American Philosophical Society 71. Philadelphia: American Philosophical Society, 1981. **Haran, M.** "Das Böcklein in der

Milch seiner Mutter und das säugende Muttertier." *TZ* 41 (1985) 135–59, esp. 153. **Henry, M.-L.** *Das Tier im religiösen Bewusstsein des alttestamentlichen Menschen.* Sammlung Gemeinverständlicher Vorträger und Schriften aus dem Gebiet der Theologie und Religionsgeschichte 220–221. Tübingen: Mohr, 1958. **Jacob, E.** "Die altassyrische Gesetze und ihr Verhältnis zu den Gesetzen des Pentateuch." *Zeitschrift für vergleichende Rechtswissenschaft* 41 (1925) 319–87, esp. 385–86. **Kaiser, W. C.** "The Current Crisis in Exegesis and the Apostolic Use of Deuteronomy 25:4 in 1 Corinthians 9:8–10." *JETS* 21 (1978) 3–18. **Lisowsky, G.** "Dtn 25,4." In *FS L. Rost.* 1967. 144–52. **Miller, M. S.,** and **Miller, J. L.** *Harper's Encyclopedia of Bible Life.* 3rd ed. New York: Harper & Row, 1971. 180–81 and illustration 70. **Nielsen, E.** "'You Shall Not Muzzle an Ox While It Is Treading out the Corn,' Dt. 25,4." In *Law, History and Tradition.* 1983. 94–105. **Noonan, J. T.** "The Muzzled Ox." *JQR* 70 (1979) 172–75. **Pangritz, W.** *Das Tier in der Bibel.* Munich; Basel: Reinhardt, 1963. **Weippert, H.** "Dreschen und Worfeln." *BRL.* 63–64. **Yaron, R.** "The Goring Ox in Near Eastern Laws." *ILR* 1 (1966) 396–406.

Translation and Prosodic Analysis

Limits on Flogging [(6:5):(5:6)]

1 *When there is a dispute / between men /*	13	2
and they take it to court / [a]and they render a decision[a] //	16	2
and they declare one / righteous /	11	2_
And they declare the other / guilty //	13	2
2 *and it shall be / if the guilty one / is to be flogged //*	16	3_
[a] *The magistrate shall have him lie down /*	11	1
and he shall be given lashes in his presence[a] /	11	1
[b]*According to his guilt*[b] \\[c] *by number //*	12	1
3 *forty times he may be stricken / but not more //*	15	2_
Lest being flogged further than this / to excess /	21	2
your brother is degraded[a] / in your eyes // ס	13	2

Not Muzzling the Ox

4 *You shall not muzzle an ox / while it is threshing //* ס	12	2_

Notes

1.a-a. Omitted in LXX[B]. Prosodic analysis supports MT.

2.a-a. LXX[B] reads καθιεῖς αὐτὸν ἐναντίον αὐτῶν (= הִפַּלְתּוֹ לִפְנֵיהֶם, "you shall lay him down before them") for MT והפילו השפט והכהו לפניו. Prosodic analysis supports MT.

2.b-b. Omitted in LXX[B].

2.c. Reading *ṭiphā'* as conj. because of misplaced *sillûq.*

3.a. SP[MSS] reads ונקל, "he is lightly esteemed," for MT ונקלה, "and he is degraded."

Form/Structure/Setting

The laws in Deut 25 are in two parts of unequal length: a group of five laws on humanitarian concerns and social ethics (vv 1–16) and the concluding injunction to remember to hate the Amalekites (vv 17–19) for their aggression against the people of Israel in the wilderness, as recorded in Exod 17:8–15. Though the first two of these laws, putting limits on flogging (vv 1–3) and not muzzling an ox when it threshes grain (v 4), make up a single literary unit from a prosodic point of view, they are also separate laws within a five-part concentric structure:

A	Limits on flogging	(Joseph sold into slavery)	25:1–3
B	Not muzzling an ox	(Joseph in Egypt)	25:4
X	Levirate marriage	(Judah and Tamar)	25:5–10
B′	Immodest intervention in a fight	(Joseph in Egypt)	25:11–12
A′	Honest weights and measures	(Israel in the wilderness)	25:13–16

The relationship between these laws in this structure is more easily seen by examining the stories in Genesis that are shaped by them. The outer frame in this structure moves from the law limiting flogging to forty lashes (Deut 25:1–3), which is used to shape the story of Joseph and his brothers in Gen 37, to the law on honest weights and measures (Deut 25:13–16), which shapes the story of Israel in the wilderness en route to Mount Sinai immediately following the exodus from Egypt in Exod 16. The inner frame is made up of two laws (Deut 25:4, 11–12), both of which are used to shape aspects of the stories of Joseph in Egypt in Gen 37–45. These two laws form a frame around the law of the levirate marriage in the center (Deut 25:5–10), which is used to shape the story of Judah and Tamar in Gen 38.

Though the MT of Deut 25:1–4 is divided in two parts with *sĕtûmā'* layout markers after vv 3 and 4, it is a single literary unit from a prosodic point of view (scanning 6:5:5:6 in accentual stress units). The brief law on not muzzling an ox while it threshes (v 4) functions as a transitional element to move from the Joseph story (Gen 37, 39–50) to that of the episode with Judah and Tamar (Gen 38). The two laws together may be outlined in concentric structural fashion:

A	When the decision is rendered that a man is to be flogged	25:1–2a
B	He shall be flogged by count as his guilt warrants	25:2b
X	Forty lashes he may be given, but not more	25:3a
B′	The man shall not be humiliated by being flogged to excess	25:3b
A′	You shall not muzzle an ox while it is threshing	25:4

In this reading, the law on not muzzling the ox (v 4) is the second half of the outer frame and is to be read over against the account of the decision that a man should be flogged (vv 1–2a). The inner frame spells out the manner in which the sentence is to be carried out and sets specific limits so that the person is not humbled unduly. Forty lashes are the limit, and no more.

The manner in which the story is told in Gen 37 suggests that the writer is aware that "only an impartial inquiry, such as would be found in a court, could get to the heart of the matter and decide where to fix the blame" (*LNB*, 289–90). We learn at the outset that "Joseph brought an ill report of [his brothers] to their father" (Gen 37:2), but we are not told the details. All his brothers found fault with him. Moreover, as Carmichael observed, Reuben pleaded with his brothers at one point not to take his life (Gen 37:21).

Carmichael called attention to another significant feature in the narrative of Gen 45. After Joseph had given his brothers grain, he instructed them: "Do not quarrel on the way" (Gen 45:24). "These words recall the quarrel between Joseph and his brothers and one major cause of it, namely, his dream about himself as the upright sheaf standing before the other prostrate ones. At this point in the narrative Joseph the forgotten sheaf has come into his own and can command his brothers" (Carmichael, *LNB*, 291).

The law of the unmuzzled ox is made up of only four words in the Hebrew text (v 4). Carmichael's arguments for interpreting the verse in a figurative sense, rather than the literal one usually given to it, are convincing; for "from a practical point of view the animal should be muzzled and, having done its work, then be fed. In typical proverbial fashion the impracticality of the injunction catches the hearer's attention in order to direct it to another meaning" (*LNB*, 292).

The figurative nuance of the forgotten sheaf in the previous law, where Joseph himself becomes the sheaf of grain forgotten for awhile and then remembered, is carried over into the law about the ox as well. An Israelite hearer would have puzzled over the requirement as it applies to a treading ox, for if a treading ox is not muzzled or driven by a whip, it will merely consume the seed it is supposed to be producing in the process of treading. "The oddness of a literal reading of the requirement is the clue that the meaning is to be displaced. In switching from one reading to the other, it is crucial to observe that a third party will have to be involved in getting the unmuzzled ox to produce seed. . . . A man, left to himself like the ox with the grain, dies without producing offspring. As with the unmuzzled ox, a third party has to be involved. A relative, like the person responsible for attending to the ox, is under an obligation to ensure that seed [progeny] is forthcoming" (Carmichael, *LNB*, 294).

The evidence assembled by Labuschagne on the use of the divine-name numbers in 25:4 and its larger literary context may be summarized as follows:

Words:	before *ʾatnāḥ*		after *ʾatnāḥ*		
25:1–4	22	+	23	=	45
25:5–12	70	+	52 (= 2 × 26)	=	122
25:13–19	68 (= 4 × 17)	+	25	=	93
25:1–19	160	+	100	=	260 (= 10 × 26)
25:11–19	85 (= 5 × 17)	+	32	=	117
25:13–16	29	+	17	=	46 (= 2 × 23)
25:17–18	17	+	6	=	23
24:10–25:4	119 (= 7 × 17)	+	100	=	219
21:10–25:19	929	+	652	=	1,581 (= 93 × 17)

The Hebrew text of the sixth weekly portion in the lectionary cycle of Torah readings from Deuteronomy (21:10–25:19) is indeed a numerical composition from beginning to end, in which the divine-name numbers are carefully woven into the fabric of the text in a variety of ways.

Comment

1–3 In this instance a ריב, "dispute," refers to a matter of litigation that is taken "to court" (אל־המשפט). Here "the guilty one" (הרשע) is sentenced "to be flogged" (בן הכות; lit. he is "a son of the striking"). Flogging was also prescribed as the punishment for a man who falsely accused his bride of not being a virgin at the time of their marriage (22:18). Though we are not informed of other circumstances in Israel in which offenses were punished in this way, we do know from ancient Mesopotamian law that flogging was imposed "for such offenses as destroying someone's house, encroaching on a neighbor's land, selling persons whom one has distrained because of a debt, defrauding creditors, theft, and changing brands on sheep" (Tigay [1996] 230). The statement כדי רשעתו במספר, "in a number according to his guilt," goes with the following words, "forty times he may be stricken but not more." As Mayes noted ([1981] 327), "forty" is also the amount of punishment in some Middle Assyrian laws (*ANET,* 181, A §18), while others range from five to one hundred (for specific citations see Tigay [1996] 390 n. 2). On "lest . . . your brother is degraded in your eyes," Tigay says, "Perhaps the person being flogged would humiliate himself further by crying or begging hysterically for mercy, or by soiling himself from fright or from the severity of the beating" ([1996] 230).

4 This brief law relating to the ox consists of only three lexical items in the Hebrew text, and there is no *ʾatnāḥ*. From a prosodic point of view, it is closely related to vv 1–3, in spite of the sharp difference in content. Oxen "threshed" the grain by trampling the stalks or pulling a threshing sledge over them. Farmers would sometimes "muzzle an ox" to keep it from stopping to eat. The alternative was to freely administer a whip to goad the animal on in its work.

Explanation

In the Torah many crimes are mentioned for which no specific punishment is specified. It is supposed that scourging was used at the discretion of the magistrates in these cases. The punishment was administered in open court, under the inspection of the magistrate, and without respect to the rank of the criminal. If some crimes were punished in this manner today, as with judicial caning in Singapore, and capital punishment eliminated, as is the case in numerous other countries, it might be effective in our own nation in curbing flagrant violations of the law. At the same time, it must be remembered that to punish persons commensurate with their crimes does not dishonor them; but to beat them excessively in public does not demonstrate the respect due a fellow human being. In ancient Israel, at least within the context of the laws in Deuteronomy, beating was to be given as punishment in certain cases, and the punishment must be proportionate to the crime committed.

The law on not muzzling an ox while it threshes grain is cited in 1 Cor 9:9 and 1 Tim 5:18 as meaning "the laborer deserves his wages" in reference to compensation for those in the ministry: "those who proclaim the gospel should get their living by the gospel" (1 Cor 9:14). At the same time, it should be noted that Paul chose not to exercise this right: "we have not made use of this right, but we endure anything rather than put an obstacle in the way of the gospel of Christ" (1 Cor 9:12). Matthew Henry summed up the matter well, long ago, when he said the law in 25:4 teaches us that we must "not only be just, but kind, to all who are employed for our good, not only to maintain but to encourage them, especially those that labour among us in the word and doctrine, and so are employed for the good of our better part" (*Exposition of the Old and New Testament* 1:670).

13. Levirate Marriage (25:5–10)

Bibliography

Ahroni, R. "The Levirate and Human Rights." In *Jewish Law and Current Legal Problems.* Ed. N. Rakober. Jerusalem: Library of Jewish Law, 1984. 67–76. **Bayliss, M.** "The Cult of the Dead Kin in Assyria and Babylonia." *Iraq* 35 (1973) 115–25. **Belkin, S.** "Levirate and Agnate Marriage in Rabbinic and Cognate Literature." *JQR* 60 (1970) 275–329. **Bloch-Smith, E.** "The Cult of the Dead in Judah: Interpreting the Material Remains." *JBL* 111 (1992) 213–24. **Brichto, H. C.** "Kin, Land, Cult, and Afterlife—A Biblical Complex." *HUCA* 44 (1973) 1–54. **Burrows, M.** "The Ancient Oriental Background of Hebrew Levirate Marriage." *BASOR* 77 (1940) 2–15. ———. "Levirate Marriage in Israel." *JBL* 59 (1940) 23–33. **Campbell, E. F.** *Ruth.* AB 7. Garden City, NY: Doubleday, 1975. 160–61. **Cardascia, G.** "L'Adoption matrimoniale à Babylone et à Nuzi." *Revue historique de droit Français et étranger* 37 (1959) 1–16. **Carmichael, C.** "A Ceremonial Crux: Removing a Man's Sandal as a Female Gesture of Contempt." *JBL* 96 (1977) 321–36. ———. *Women, Law, and the Genesis Traditions.* Edinburgh: Univ. of Edinburgh Press, 1979. 65–70. **Cruveilhier, P.** "Le lévirat chez les hébreux et chez les assyriens." *RB* 34 (1925) 524–46. **Dahood, M.** "Northwest Semitic Philology and Job." In *The Bible and Current Catholic Thought.* Ed. J. L. McKenzie. New York: Herder, 1962. 55–74, esp. 70. **Daube, D.** "Consortium in Roman and Hebrew Law." *Juridical Review* 62 (1950) 72–74. ———. "The Culture of Deuteronomy." *Orita* 3 (1969) 35–36. ———. "To Be Found Doing Wrong." In *FS E. Volterra.* 1971. 3–13, esp. 8. **Davies, E. W.** "Inheritance Rights and the Hebrew Levirate Marriage." *VT* 31 (1981) 138–44, 257–68. **Donner, H.** "Adoption oder Legitimation?" *OrAnt* 8 (1969) 87–119. **Emerton, J.** "Some Problems in Genesis XXXVIII." *VT* 25 (1975) 357–60. **Epstein, L. M.** *Marriage Laws in the Bible and the Talmud.* Cambridge: Harvard UP, 1942. **Falk, Z.** *Hebrew Law in Biblical Times.* Jerusalem: Wahrmann, 1964. 88, 159. **Fensham, F. C.** "Widow, Orphan, and Poor in Ancient Near Eastern Legal and Wisdom Literature." *JNES* 21 (1962) 129–39. **Gordis, R.** "Love, Marriage, and Business in the Book of Ruth." In *FS J. M. Myers.* 1974. 241–64. **Huehnergard, J.** "Biblical Notes on Some New Akkadian Texts from Emar (Syria)." *CBQ* 47 (1985) 428–34. **Katz, J.** "Levirate Marriage (*yibbum*) and *haliẓiah* in Post-Talmudic Times." *Tarbiz* 51 (1981) 59–106 (Heb.). **Kirwen, M. C.** *African Widows.* Maryknoll, NY: Orbis, 1979. **Koch, D.-A.** *Die Schrift als Zeuge des Evangelium.* BHT 69. Tübingen: Mohr, 1986. 203–4. **Koschaker, P.** "Fratriarchat, Hausgemeinschaft, und Mutterrecht in Keilschriftrechten." *ZA* 41 (1933) 76–80. ———. "Zum Levirat nach hethitischem Recht." *RHA* 2.10 (1933) 77–89. **Legget, D. A.** *The Levirate and Goel Institutions in the Old Testament with Special Attention in the Book of Ruth.* Cherry Hill, NY: Mack, 1974. **Lehmann, M. R.** "Biblical Oaths." *ZAW* 81 (1969) 74–92. **Lewis, T. J.** *Cults of the Dead.* 1989. **Manor, D. W.** "A Brief History of Levirate Marriage as It Relates to the Bible." *ResQ* 27 (1984) 129–42. **Mittelmann, J.** *Der altisraelitische Levirat.* Leipzig: A. Teicher, 1934. **Neufeld, E.** *Ancient Hebrew Marriage Laws.* 1944. 23–55. **Neusner, J.** *A History of the Mishnaic Law of Women.* 5 vols. SJLA 33. Leiden: Brill, 1980. **Niditch, S.** "Legends of Wise Heroes and Heroines." In *The Hebrew Bible and Its Modern Interpreters.* Ed. D. A. Knight and G. M. Tucker. Chico, CA: Scholars Press, 1985. 451–63. ———. "The Wrong Woman Righted: An Analysis of Genesis 38." *HTR* 72 (1979) 143–49. **Patai, R.** *Sitte und Sippe in Bibel und Orient.* Frankfurt am Main: Ner-Tamid, 1962. 97–104. **Pedersen, J.** *Israel: Its Life and Culture.* 1926–40. 1:91–96. **Phillips, A.** "Another Example of Family Law." *VT* 30 (1980) 240–45. ———. "Some Aspects of Family Law in Pre-Exilic Israel." *VT* 23 (1973) 359–61. **Pope, M.** "The Cult of the Dead at Ugarit." In *Ugarit in Retrospect.* Ed. G. D. Young. Winona Lake, IN: Eisenbrauns, 1981. 159–79. **Praag, A. van.** *Droit matrimonial assyro-babylonien.* Allard

Pierson Stichting Archaeologisch-historische Bijdragen 12. Amsterdam, Noord-Hollandsche Uitg. Mij., 1945. **Price, I. M.** "The So-called Levirate-Marriage in Hittite and Assyrian Laws." In *Oriental Studies: FS Paul Haupt*. Ed. C. Adler. Baltimore: Johns Hopkins UP, 1926. 268–71. **Puuko, A. F.** "Die Leviratsehe in den altorientalischen Gesetzen." *ArOr* 17.2 (1949) 296–99. **Rabinowitz, L. I.** "Levirate Marriage and Ḥaliṣah." *EncJud* 11:125. **Rengstorf, K. H.** *Die Re-Investitur des Verlorenen Sohnes in der Gleichniserzählung Jesu Lk 15,11–32*. Arbeitsgemeinschaft für Forschung des Landes Nordrhein-Westfalen 137. Cologne: Westdeutscher Verlag, 1967. **Richter, H.-F.** "Zum Levirat im Buch Ruth." *ZAW* 95 (1983) 123–26. **Rowley, H. H.** "The Marriage of Ruth." In *The Servant of the Lord and Other Essays on the Old Testament*. Oxford: Blackwell, 1952. 171–94. **Snaith, N. H.** "The Daughters of Zelophehad." *VT* 16 (1966) 126–27. **Thompson, T.**, and **Thompson, D.** "Some Legal Problems in the Book of Ruth." *VT* 18 (1968) 79–99. **Tigay, J. H.** "Excursus 23: Levirate Marriage." In *Deuteronomy*. 1996. 482–83. **Tsevat, M.** "Marriage and Monarchical Legitimacy in Ugarit and Israel." *JSS* 3 (1958) 237–43. **Vaux, R. de.** *Ancient Israel*. Tr. J. McHugh. New York: McGraw-Hill, 1961. 37–38. **Wegner, J. R.** "Chattel or Person? The Status of Women in the System of the Mishnah." Diss., Brown Univ., 1986. **Westbrook, R.** "The Law of the Biblical Levirate." *RIDA* 24 (1977) 65–87. ———. "The Law of the Biblical Levirate." In *Property and the Family in Biblical Law*. JSOTSup 113. Sheffield: JSOT Press, 1991. 69–89. **Yaron, R.** "Biblical Law: Prolegomena." In *Jewish Law in History and the Modern World*. Ed. B. S. Jackson. JLA Sup 2. Leiden: Brill, 1980. 27–44, esp. 28–29.

Translation and Prosodic Analysis

Levirate Marriage [(4:5):(6:5):(6:6):(5:6):(5:4)]

5 *When brothers dwell / together /*	13	2
and one of them dies / and he has no son /	17	2_
The dead man's wife shall not / go outside / to a stranger //	18	3
her husband's brother / shall go [a]*in to her*[a] */*	14	2_
And he shall take her as his / wife /	13	2
and he shall perform the brother-in-law's duty //	9	1
6 *And it shall be / in regard to the firstborn*[a] */*	9	2
whom she bears /	6	1_
He will be established / under the name of his dead / brother //	14	3
that his name may not be blotted out / from Israel //	16	2_
7 *And if the man / does not wish / to take / his brother's wife //*	20	4
his brother's wife shall go out to the gate / to the elders /	21	2_
And she shall say / "My husband's brother refuses[a] */*	15	2
to establish his brother's name / in Israel /	18	2
[b]*he will not perform / a brother-in-law's duty by me" //*	10	2_
8 *And the elders of his city shall summon him /*	15	1
and they shall speak to him //	9	1
But if he stands firm and he says /	8	1
"I do not wish / to take her" //	19	2_
9 *Then his brother's wife shall approach him /*	12	1
in the sight of the elders /	11	1
And she shall remove his sandal / from his foot /	15	2
and she shall spit / before his face //	11	2_
And she shall declare / and she shall say /	12	2
*"Thus *[a] *let it be done to the man /*	13	1
who will not build up / his brother's house" //	13	2_

[10]*And his name shall be called / in Israel //*	13	2
the "house / of the unsandaled one" // ס	9	2_

Notes

5.a-a. SP reads אליה, "to her," for MT עליה, "to her."

6.a. SP reads reads הבן הבכור, "the firstborn son"; LXX[L] reads τὸ παιδίον τὸ πρωτότοκον, "the firstborn son."

7.a. Reading מֵאֵן, "he refuses," with most Heb. MSS and printed editions, rather than L מֵאֵין.

7.b. Some Heb. MSS, SP[MS], LXX[N], Syr., and Vg. add *waw*-conj. Prosodic analysis favors MT.

9.a. Reading *paštāʾ* followed by *zāqēp qāṭôn* as conj.

Form/Structure/Setting

The phrase "levirate marriage" comes from Latin *levir,* "husband's brother." The verb יבם means to do the duty of a יָבָם, "husband's brother." When a man died childless, his brother was to marry the widow. The first son born to them was considered the son of the deceased man from a legal point of view. If the brother refused to do this, he was submitted to a public procedure called "removal of the sandal," and the woman was free to marry outside the family. The matter is taken up in two other biblical texts: Gen 38 and Ruth 4 (which involves a more distant relative than the brother-in-law).

The law on levirate marriage is in the middle of a concentric structural design of the final sixteen laws in the Deuteronomic collection (24:1–25:19), which may be outlined as follows:

A	Forbidden remarriage and one-year deferral for new husband	24:1–5
B	Eight laws protecting the poor and vulnerable	24:6–22
C	Limits on flogging and not muzzling an ox while threshing	25:1–4
X	Levirate marriage	25:5–10
C′	Improper intervention in a fight	25:11–12
B′	Honest weights and measures	25:13–16
A′	Remember to hate the Amalekites (YHWH's Holy War)	25:17–19

The framework in this menorah pattern (A, X, A′) moves from a pair of laws on marriage and war (24:1–5) to a concluding note on YHWH's Holy War at the time of the exodus from Egypt (25:17–19), with the law on levirate marriage in the center (25:5–10). These four laws display the familiar three-plus-one pattern, in which the concluding reminder to "hate the Amalekites" stands in opposition to the other three laws on specific matters of war and marriage. The remaining twelve laws in this concentric structure move from ten laws on specific matters of social ethics (24:6–25:4) to two symbolic laws (25:11–16), which direct the reader's attention to the beginning and end of what we have called the first phase of YHWH's Holy War, the exodus from Egypt, with Joseph in Egypt (25:11–13) and the nation of Israel in Sinai en route to the promised land (25:13–16). See further below, particularly the pivotal role played by the curious verse on having two "stones" of different size in one's "pouch" (25:13), which verse belongs to both these laws.

The law of the levirate marriage in 25:5–10 has no internal structural indicators, other than the *sĕtûmāʾ* layout marker at the end of v 10 and three instances of direct speech: twice on the part of the woman (vv 7b, 9b), and once on the part of the dead husband's brother (v 8). Nonetheless, it can be divided into five parts in terms of its prosodic structure:

A	When a widow has no son, her husband's brother must take her	25:5a
B	The firstborn shall be accounted to the dead brother	25:5b–6
X	If the man refuses, she announces it at the city gate	25:7
B′	Ritual of removing the sandal at the city gate	25:8–9a
A′	His name shall be called "house of the unsandaled one"	25:9b–10

In this reading, the outside frame presents the situation: if a widow has no son, her husband's brother is obliged to father a son in his dead brother's name, or his own name shall be called "house of the unsandaled one." If the man refuses to do the duty of the levir, the woman is to make a public declaration at the city gate and to perform there the ritual of removing the sandal.

The nouns יָבָם, "brother-in-law," and יְבֵמָה, "sister-in-law," and the verb יבם, "do the duty of a יָבָם," appear a total of seven times in 25:5–10 within the following concentric structure:

A	"Her brother-in-law shall go in to her"	יבמה יבא עליה	25:5b
B	"He shall take her and do the levir's duty"	ולקחה לו לאשה ויבמה	25:5c
C	"He does not wish to take his sister-in-law"	לא יחפץ... לקחת את־יבמתו	25:7a
X	"His sister-in-law shall go to the gate"	ועלתה יבמתו השערה	25:7b
C′	"My brother-in-law refuses"	מאן יבמי להקים... שם	25:7c
B′	"He will not perform the levir's duty"	לא אבה יבמי	25:7d
A′	"His sister-in-law shall go up to him . . ."	ונגשה יבמתו אליו	25:9a

The outer frame in this structure moves from a presentation of the legal duty of the יָבָם, "husband's brother," in v 5 to that of the יְבֵמָה, "sister-in-law," in vv 9–10. The man's responsibility is to take his brother's wife and father a child in his name. If he refuses to do this, the woman's duty is to appear before the elders at the city gate to perform the symbolic act of "removing the sandal" (v 7). The innermost frame presents the refusal on the part of the husband's brother to take his "sister-in-law" (יְבֵמָה) in v 7a, which refusal is set over against the declaration on her part in v 7c that her "brother-in-law" (יָבָם) has refused to do his duty as a levir. The next frame contains the two occurrences of the verb יבם (both in the piel, vv 5c, 7d). The only other occurrence of this verb in the Hebrew Bible is in Gen 38:8, the narrative that presents this law in story form.

The key words אח, "brother," and שם, "name," are also nested in a carefully constructed concentric pattern:

A	"When brothers dwell together"	כי־ישבו אחים יחדו	25:5a
B	"He shall establish his dead brother's name"	יקום על־שם אחיו המת	25:6a
X	"That his name is not blotted out in Israel"	ולא־ימחה שמו מישראל	25:6b
B′	"To establish his brother's name in Israel"	להקים לאחיו שם בישראל	25:7b
A′	"He who will not build up his brother's house"	אשר לא־יבנה את־בית אחיו	25:9b

The outer frame in this structure moves from the opening introduction of the story about certain brothers who live together, one of whom dies without a son (v 5), to the conclusion in which the wife of the dead brother makes her declaration about her husband's brother: "'Let it be done to the man who will not build up his brother's house [את־בית אחיו]'; and his name shall be called in Israel the 'house of the unsandaled one'" (vv 9b–10). The inner frame includes both of the key words as we move from an account of the levir's duty to establish a name for his dead brother (v 6a), to the woman's announcement that he has refused "to establish his brother's name in Israel" (v 7b). The center of the structure states the purpose of the law: "that his name may not be blotted out from Israel" (v 6b).

The word "Israel" appears three times in 25:5–10; these occurrences form a framework within which the levir repeats his desire not to fulfill his duty:

A	"That his name not be blotted out from Israel"	ולא־ימחה שמו מישראל	25:6b
B	"He does not wish to take his sister-in-law"	לא יחפץ . . . לקחת את־יבמתו	25:7a
X	"To establish his brother's name in Israel"	להקים לאחיו שם בישראל	25:7b
B′	"He declares: 'I do not wish to take her'"	ואמר לא חפצתי לקחתה	25:8b
A′	"His name shall be called in Israel . . ."	ונקרא שמו בישראל	25:10

The outer frame in this construction moves from a statement of the purpose of the law, that a man's name not be blotted out in Israel (v 6b), to a new name given to the man who refused to do his duty: the "unsandaled one" (v 10). The inner frame places the man's refusal as reported by the woman (v 7a) over against a reiteration of that refusal on the part of the man himself (v 8b). In the center again we find the purpose of the law: to establish his brother's name in Israel (v 7b). The connection between the law of the levirate marriage (25:5–10) and the story of Judah and his daughter-in-law Tamar in Gen 38 is obvious. Onan refused to do the duty of a levir and was punished by death. His motivation for going through the motions but "spilling his seed to the ground" is presumably greed, as Carmichael has noted, for in the circumstances he would retain his dead brother's portion of the estate (*LNB*, 296).

According to the law, if the brother refuses, the widow takes off his sandal, spits "before his face"—that is, on the ground in front of him—and declares, "Thus let it be done to the man who will not build up his brother's house." The description of Onan "spilling his semen on the ground" is a graphic interpretation of "before his face" (לפניו) in 25:9, for "the shoe represents the female genitals, the foot the male organ, and the spitting semen" (Carmichael, *LNB*, 296). The verb חלץ (v 9) is taken with the sense of "to loose, withdraw," in this instance from sexual intercourse. Carmichael also links the law with the preceding figurative law about not muzzling an "ox" in its "sexual treading": "for without a shoe the man cannot tread in order to produce seed for his brother" (*LNB*, 297).

The evidence assembled by Labuschagne on the use of the divine-name numbers in 25:5–10 may be summarized as follows:

Words:	before *ʾatnāḥ*		after *ʾatnāḥ*		
25:5	17	+	7	=	24
25:5–6	26	+	11	=	37
25:5–7	33	+	26	=	59
25:7–10	27	+	34 (= 2 × 17)	=	61

There are 17 words before *ʾatnāḥ* in the opening verse presenting the legal situation: a man's brother dies without leaving an heir (v 5). The basic law is completed by adding a description of the law's purpose to provide an heir "under the name of his dead brother" (v 6). The numerical composition is carried out with 26 words before *ʾatnāḥ* in vv 5–6. The problem arising should the brother choose not to exercise his duty is presented in v 7 in such a manner that there are 26 words after *ʾatnāḥ* in vv 5–7. The ceremony carried out in the case of such a refusal is described in vv 8–10 in a carefully constructed manner so that there are now 34 (= 2 × 17) words after *ʾatnāḥ* in vv 7–10. Once again, the ancient scribes have woven the divine name into the very fabric of the Hebrew text in their numerical composition, this time in the form of a simple chiasm: 17 (v 5) / 26 (vv 5–6) / 26 (vv 5–7) / 17 (vv 7–10).

Comment

5 On the basis of Gen 13:6 and 36:7, Tigay says "dwelling together" means living close enough to share the same pastureland, and that "this may mean that in biblical times the marriage was obligatory only if the levir's home, where the widow and her future child would reside, was close to that property" ([1996] 231). Subsequent Jewish tradition (including LXX, which rendered בן as "offspring") interpreted the words "he has no son" to mean children of either sex because of the law on the inheritance rights of Zelophehad's daughters in Num 27:1–11. The purpose of levirate marriage was to avoid the loss of property to the family. The injunction "he shall take her as his wife" appears to contradict texts in Lev 18:16 and 20:21, which prohibit marriage between a brother- and sister-in-law. The ancient rabbis argued that Leviticus states the general principle and the law in Deuteronomy applies only when a married man dies without children. Tigay maintains that this conclusion has support in parallel texts of ancient Hittite laws, which place the prohibition of relations with one's brother's wife and the levirate law adjacent to each other, showing that the latter is the exception to the former ([1996] 232).

6 The statement that "the firstborn . . . will be established under the name of his dead brother" means that the child is legally the son and heir of the deceased. "According to Sefer Ha-Ḥinnukh, the offspring of the levirate marriage can even be thought of as the biological offspring of the deceased man, since, when the child's mother married the deceased man she had become 'bone of his bones and flesh of his flesh' (Gen. 2:23), and since the husband's brother is also partly his brother's flesh" (Tigay [1996] 232).

7 The man may not "wish to take his sister-in-law" as wife for personal, familial, or financial reasons. The text in Gen 38:9 states simply that "since Onan knew that the offspring would not be his, he spilled his semen on the ground whenever he went in to his brother's wife, so that he would not give offspring to his brother." To "establish a name for his brother" means to sire an heir (cf. Gen 38:8: "raise up offspring for your brother").

8–10 The significance of the details of the symbolic action are not explained. Tigay cites a parallel practice "among the ancient Germans, who symbolized the giving up of property and heritable rights by removing the shoe" ([1996] 233). The woman "shall remove his sandal from his foot, and she shall spit before his face." The meaning of the term בפניו, translated here "before his face," is ambiguous. Some translate it "in his face," and others interpret it as spitting on the ground in front of the man. Support for the latter reading is found in

Carmichael's conclusion: "The shoe represents the female genitals, the foot the male organ, and the spitting semen" (*LNB,* 296), for Onan spilled his semen on the ground. The name "house of the unsandaled one" is a pejorative title to degrade the brother.

Explanation

The purpose of the law was to keep the inheritance separate and to preserve the genealogies distinct, as well as to provide for the destitute widow when the estate devolved on the next heir. Though the Sadducees cited their law to Jesus in a dispute about resurrection (Matt 22:23–33), the law of the levirate marriage concerns matters of social and economic justice in this world brought on by premature death, not in relationships in another world beyond death.

14. Improper Intervention in a Fight (25:11–13)

Bibliography

Carmichael, C. M. "Forbidden Mixtures." *VT* 32 (1982) 395–415. ———. "On Separating Life and Death: An Explanation of Some Biblical Laws." *HTR* 69 (1976) 1–7. **Dahood, M.** "Hebrew-Ugaritic Lexicography I." *Bib* 44 (1963) 289–303. **Eslinger, L.** "The Case of an Immodest Lady Wrestler in Deuteronomy xxv 11–12." *VT* 31 (1981) 269–81. **Goodfriend, E.** "Could *Keleb* in Deuteronomy 23:19 Actually Refer to Canine?" In *FS J. Milgrom.* 1995. 381–97. **Gordon, C. H.** "A New Akkadian Parallel to Dt 25, 11–12." *JPOS* 15 (1935) 29–34. **Kaufman, S. A.** "The Structure of the Deuteronomic Law." *MAARAV* 1.2 (1979) 105–58. **Lieberman, S.** *Texts and Studies.* New York: Ktav, 1974. 37–43. **Paul, S. M.** "Biblical Analogues to Middle Assyrian Laws." In *Religion and Law.* 1990. 336–37. **Phillips, A.** *Ancient Israel's Criminal Law.* 1970. 94. **Rendsburg, G.** "Late Biblical Hebrew and the Date of 'P.'" *JANESCU* 12 (1980) 65–80, esp. 68. **Roth, E.** "Does the Tora Punish Impudence? A Note to Dt 25,11s." In *Études Orientales à la memoire de Paul Hirschler.* Ed. O. Komlos. Budapest, 1950. 116–21. **Saggs, H. W. F.** *The Greatness That Was Babylon.* London: Sidgwick & Jackson, 1962. 282. **Tigay, J. H.** "Excursus 24: Improper Intervention in a Fight." In *Deuteronomy.* 1996. 484–86. **Weinfeld, M.** *DDS.* 292–93.

Translation and Prosodic Analysis

Improper Intervention in a Fight [6:6] [5]

11 *When men get into a fight together / a man and his brother /* [22 2
and the wife of one / comes near / to rescue her husband / 23 3
from the power of his assailant // 7 1
And she stretches forth her hand / [10] 1
and she seizes him / [a]by his genitals[a] // 12 2
12 *Then you shall cut off\[a] her hand //* [10] 1
[b]your eyes[b] / shall show no pity // ס 11 2

[13] *You shall not have / in your "pouch" /*	11	2
"two stones" /	[7	1
a large one / and a small one // ס	11	2

Notes

11.a-a. SP reads בבשרו, "in his flesh," for MT במבשיו, lit. "by that which excites shame."

12.a. Reading *ṭip̄ḥā'* as conj. because of misplaced *'atnāḥ*.

12.b-b. A few Heb. MSS, Cairo Geniza fragments, and LXX read עיניך, "your eyes," for MT עינך, "your eye"; *Tg. Ps.-J.* reads עיניכם, "your [pl.] eyes"; LXX adds ἐπ' αὐτῇ (= עליה), "on her." The *Numeruswechsel* is restored here with *Tg. Ps.-J.* as *lectio difficilior.*

Form/Structure/Setting

Prosodic analysis reveals that v 13 functions as a rhythmic bridge connecting this law with the law on honest weights and measures that follows and belongs to both of them. Moreover, the content of this verse displays the quality of what is elsewhere called "Janus parallelism," in that the meaning shifts as the reader moves from one context to the other.

In terms of prosodic structure, the content of Deut 25 as a whole may be outlined in a concentric structure:

A	Limits on flogging and not muzzling the ox	(Joseph in Egypt)	25:1–4
B	Levirate marriage	(Judah and Tamar)	25:5–10
X	Improper intervention in a fight	(Joseph in Egypt)	25:11–13
B′	Honest weights and measures	(Israel in Sinai)	25:13–16
A′	Remembering Amalekite aggression	(YHWH's Holy War)	25:17–19

In this reading the narrative stories associated with the framework of the laws in the above structure (A, X, A′) move from the "prelude" to the epic story of YHWH's Holy War in which Joseph is sold into slavery in Egypt by his brothers (25:1–4), to a reflection on a still further meaning of כיס, "pouch," of v 13—read as כוס, "cup," in the narrative of the dream of Pharaoh's cupbearer in Gen 40:11–21—and the beginning of the episode that will bring Joseph's brothers to Egypt as well, and then to the first battle of YHWH's Holy War in the wilderness of Sinai against the Amalekites (25:17–19). The focus of the inner frame of this structure, in this particular reading, associates the law of the levirate marriage (25:5–10) with the law on honest weights and measures (25:13–16). Since the imagery of the second of these two laws evokes that of God's provision for his people in their flight from Egypt to Mount Sinai in Exod 14–18 (remembered in the Festival of Passover), it is not difficult to see how the beautiful story of Ruth was eventually shaped by the law of the levirate marriage in Deut 25:5–10 to explore God's provision for "his people" (now enlarged to include Moab) in the annual celebration of the Feast of Weeks. The inclusion of the "enemy" nations within the "assembly of YHWH," at the level of allusion in the story of Ruth, anticipates the eschatological assembly of the nations in Jerusalem at the Festival of Booths (Sukkoth). The story of YHWH's Holy War thus moves through the three major moments in the festal calendar: from the Festival of Unleavened Bread and Passover (and the exodus from slavery in Egypt; 25:1–4), to the Festival of Weeks (25:5–10 and the book of Ruth), to the Festival of Booths (by way of theological anticipation, when the nations are gathered with Israel in Jerusalem, the city of David).

The boundaries of 25:11–13 are marked by *sĕtûmāʾ* layout markers (after vv 12 and 13) and the *Numeruswechsel* in v 12, which is restored on the basis of *Tg. Pseudo-Jonathan* in v 12b. A further indication of structure is the appearance of the second singular verbal form at the beginning of v 12, which has been absent since 25:4 (on not muzzling the ox). The prosodic analysis suggests that v 13 belongs with vv 11–12, though it is also an essential part of the following law on honest weights and measures (vv 13–16).

It seems best to interpret v 13 as an example of Janus parallelism: the verse takes on a different meaning when read with what precedes it than when read with what follows (for an instructive example of this phenomenon elsewhere in the Pentateuch, see D. L. Christensen, "Janus Parallelism in Gen. 6:3," *HS* 27 [1986] 20–24). When read with vv 11–12, the "stones" become the testes of the man in v 11, in parallel with the statement: "she seizes him by his genitals," as suggested by Goodfriend (*FS J. Milgrom* [1995] 394). When read with vv 14–15, the meaning shifts sharply as the "stones" become weights, in parallel with the two kinds of measures of v 14. On the phenomenon of a verse functioning as a bridge connecting two sections and belonging to both, see also 23:1 and 24:5.

A number of other reasons for juxtaposing vv 11–12 and 13 have been suggested. Goodfriend cites one of her students, Shannon Gordon, who noted "that the common feature of the two situations described is the unfair advantage taken of the injured parties, the combatant who is taken by surprise by the wife of his fellow and the person who trades with the user of unjust weights." Goodfriend's discussion of Jacob ben Asher's suggestion in his commentary *Baʿal ha-Ṭurim* is also worthy of note: "he derives the teachings that one should not look at one's own nakedness, and alternatively, that one should not be too preoccupied with money, i.e., the contents of one's pockets. He also suggests that the placing of the laws together offers proof for the rabbinic position that monetary compensation (inferred from the reference to pockets and weights), and not mutilation, was the intention of v. 12" (*FS J. Milgrom,* 394 n. 58). Kaufman (*MAARAV* 1.2 [1979] 142–43) suggests that the law in vv 11–12 is connected with the first part of the tenth commandment, concerning the coveting of one's neighbor's wife (5:21a), whereas v 13 is concerned with the second part of that commandment, concerned with coveting a neighbor's property (5:21b).

The law of improper intervention in a fight, as it appears in 25:11–13, may be outlined as follows:

A	If two brothers are fighting and she approaches	25:11a
B	The wife of one of them comes to deliver her husband	25:11b
X	And she seizes the man by his genitals	25:11c
B′	You shall cut off her hand, your eye shall show no pity	25:12
A′	You shall not have "two stones" in your "pouch"	25:13

The issue at hand is the specific action taken by the woman in seizing the man by his genitals in her attempt to come to her husband's assistance in the fight (v 11c). The outer frame moves from the situation at the outset in which two brothers are engaged in a fight (v 11a), and concludes with a double entendre on the "two stones in a pouch" (v 13). For this shameful action, she is to suffer corporal punishment by having the offensive hand cut off (v 12a). The severity of the punishment invites a symbolic interpretation along the lines suggested by Carmichael (*LNB* [1985] 297–99): the startling shift in imagery also marks a corresponding shift in the narrative associated with this law, as we move from the stories of Joseph and Judah in Gen 37–50 to stories of Israel's experiences in the wilderness en route from Egypt to Mount Sinai in the days of Moses as recorded in Exod 17:8–15 and the battle with the Amalekites (which is shaped by the law in Deut 25:17–19 to hate the Amalekites).

The law of 25:11–13 was used to shape certain details of the narrative in Gen 38 of the episode with Judah and Tamar. "Her mode of action requires that she pursue him sexually; in crude terms, she goes after his genitals" (Carmichael, *LNB,* 299). The severity of the punishment in the law is mirrored in Judah's order: "Bring her out, and let her be burned" (Gen 38:24). The presence of the *sĕtûmā'* layout marker and the *Numeruswechsel* at this point in the law of Deut 25:11–13 serves a disjunctive function, which mirrors that of the narrative in Genesis as well, as we move from Gen 38 to Gen 39–44.

The connection between Deut 25:13 and the corresponding narrative in Gen 42:25–35 and 44:1–13 may be shown by the story about the sacks (שקו, "his sack," in Gen 42:25, 27, 35) of grain in which Joseph twice returned his brothers' money, and Benjamin's "sack" (אמתחת) in which his own silver cup was placed (Carmichael, *LNB,* 299–303). The word for "pouch" in the law of Deut 25:13 is כיס, which appears nowhere else in the Pentateuch. The word שק, "sack," which appears four times in Gen 42:25–35 and also in 37:34 in reference to the "sackcloth" that Jacob put on in his grief over the "death" of Joseph as reported by his brothers after they had sold him into slavery. The words in the Genesis narrative that correspond to the "bag" of the law in Deut 25:13 are apparently used with precision. A connection was apparently intended between the consonants in כיס and שק in the form of a chiasm: ס כ // ק ש. Moreover, it is interesting to note the distribution of the term אמתחת, "sack," which appears twice in Gen 42:27–28 and seven times in Gen 44:1–12, but nowhere else in the Hebrew Bible. The distribution of the seven occurrences of אמתחת in 44:1–12 are as follows:

A	"Fill their sacks"	אמתחת האנשים	Gen 44:1
B	"Money in each sack" + "my cup in Benjamin's"	אמתחת + אמתחתו	44:1–2
X	"We found money in our sacks"	אמתחתינו	44:8
B′	"Money in each sack" / "each opened his sack"	אמתחתו / אמתחתו	44:11
A′	"Cup found in Benjamin's sack"	באמתחת בנימן	44:12

The outer frame moves from the words of Joseph, "Fill the men's sacks with food" (v 1), to the search in which Joseph's "cup was found in Benjamin's sack" (v 12). In the center is the use of the word with the first-person plural suffix, in reference to their first trip to purchase food in Egypt (v 8). The inner frame contains four occurrences of the word אמתחת, three of which have the third singular suffix and the fourth, אמתחת הקטן, refers to Benjamin, "the smallest." It should be noted that the concluding word of the law in Deut 25:13 is וקטנה, "and small."

The evidence assembled by Labuschagne on the use of the divine-name numbers in 25:11–13, which is to read within the larger literary structure of 25:5–13, may be summarized as follows:

Words:	before *'atnāḥ*		after *'atnāḥ*		
25:5–10	53	+	45	=	98
25:11–12	17	+	7	=	24
25:11–13	23	+	9	=	32
25:5–13	76	+	54	=	130 (= 5 × 26)
25:5–12	70	+	52 (= 2 × 26)	=	122
25:9–12	31	+	21	=	52 (= 2 × 26)

There are 17 words before *'atnāḥ* in vv 11–12, the law on improper intervention on the part of a woman in the defense of her husband. When these verses are combined with the verse on the "two stones" in the "pouch" (v 13), vv 11–13 total 32 words, and 23 words before *'atnāḥ*—the two alternative numbers for the word כבוד, "glory." And the total number of words in vv 5–13 comes to 130 (= 5 × 26). Moreover, the divine-name number 26 is woven into the text in two additional ways when vv 11–12 are combined with the preceding law on levirate marriage (25:5–10): there are 52 (= 2 × 26) words after *'atnāḥ* in vv 5–12, and a total of 52 (= 2 × 26) words in vv 9–12

Comment

11–12 Though the law on improper intervention in a fight complements the laws of Exod 21:18–19, 22–25, which also deal with injuries caused by men fighting, it is without any real parallel. Though a Middle Assyrian law (*ANET,* 181, A §8, quoted by Tigay [1996] 485) is often cited as a parallel to this law, important factors make the law in Deuteronomy unique and puzzling. The Assyrian law speaks of a brawl in which the woman injures a man by crushing his testicle(s). In the biblical account the fight involves two brothers, one of whom is the husband of the woman. The woman seizes the other man by his genitals in an attempt to save her husband from the power of his assailant. Moreover, nothing is said as to the nature of any injury inflicted by the woman. Weinfeld argues that a second text from Nuzi, which C. H. Gordon presented as a parallel (*JPOS* 15 [1935] 29–34), is not clear enough to draw any conclusions (*DDS,* 293).

The expression "a man and his brother" indicates that both parties in this conflict are Israelites. The wife of one of them seeks "to rescue her husband" by grasping the opponent במבשיו, "by his genitals," literally "by what excites shame." The punishment, "you shall cut off her hand," is severe and without parallel in the Bible for mandating mutilation as punishment apart from the law of talion. It may be that the principle of *lex talionis* is in play here in a figurative sense, for the word יד seems to have been used as a euphemism for the male sexual organ in Isa 57:8 (and other texts, e.g., Cant 5:4 [see M. Pope, *Song of Songs* (1977) 523]; 1QS 7:13; *CTA* 23.33-35, 46-47). "It may be that this very particular piece of casuistic law is intended as an example of how *lex talionis* was able to be interpreted when it could not be applied literally" (Craigie [1976] 316). The peculiar nature of the crime and the severity of its punishment led to attempts within traditional Jewish circles to mitigate the punishment by interpreting "cut off the hand" to mean the presumed amount of the fine, that is, the value of the woman's hand (Tigay [1996] 234). Cutting off the hand remains a common punishment for certain crimes in Saudi Arabia and other parts of the Arab world.

13 The phrase אבן ואבן is read as "two stones," one of which is larger than the other—that is, a description of the male testes (Goodfriend, *FS J. Milgrom,* 394). As one hears the content of v 14, however, which is in perfect poetic parallelism, the imagery shifts quickly to that of business ethics with two kinds of weights and measures.

Explanation

Like the law of the insubordinate son (21:18–21) and the law on premarital unchastity (22:20–21), there is little evidence that the law on improper intervention in a fight was ever enforced. Once again, we probably have here a law that was primarily pedagogical in its intent, though perhaps more in terms of symbolic meaning in relation to the reading of related narrative material in Genesis than a warning *in terrorem* to shape specific behavior. In this respect the close relationship between the law itself and v 13 on the "pouch" with its two stones, one large and the other small, merits reflection and comment.

When understood within the larger context of the telling of YHWH's Holy War within the context of the festivals of ancient Israel, the law on improper intervention in a fight takes on deeper meaning. If Israel is taken as the wife, and her husband (YHWH) is seen to be engaged in mortal combat with the Enemy in the realm of spiritual warfare, an important lesson emerges. YHWH does not need our assistance in that combat. Moreover, insistence on our part to get involved in the struggle will result in great pain and suffering on our part, which will leave us permanently maimed. The battle belongs to YHWH; and we must learn to trust him and remain as an observer to that conflict, even when the immediate course of the titanic struggle appears to be going against our self-centered interests.

15. Honest Weights and Measures (25:13–16)

Bibliography

Aharoni, Y. "A 40-Shekel Weight with a Hieratic Numeral." *BASOR* 201 (1971) 35–36. ———. "The Use of Hieratic Numerals in Hebrew Ostraca and the Shekel Weights." *BASOR* 184 (1966) 13–19. **Briend, J.** "Bible et archéologie." *MDB* 75 (1992) 38, fig. 34. **Cazelles, H.** "De l'idéologie royale." In *FS T. H. Gaster.* 1973. 59–73, esp. 63. **Dahood, M.** "Hebrew-Ugaritic Lexicography I." *Bib* 44 (1963) 289–303, esp. 291. **Diringer, D.** "The Early Hebrew Weights Found at Lachish." *PEQ* (1942–43) 85–86. ———. "Weights." In *DOTT.* 227–30. **Goodfriend, E. A.** "Could *Keleb* in Deuteronomy 23:19 Actually Refer to a Canine?" In *FS J. Milgrom.* 1995. 394–95. **Kerkhof, V. I.** "An Inscribed Weight from

Shechem." *BASOR* 184 (1966) 20–21. **Petrie, W. M. F.** "Balance." In *Dictionary of the Bible.* Ed. J. Hastings. 5 vols. New York: Scribner, 1902–4. 1:234. **Pilcher, E. J.** "Hebrew Weights in the Book of Samuel." *PEQ* 48 (1916) 77–85. ———. "Weights of Ancient Palestine." *PEQ* 44 (1912) 178–95. **Powell, M. A.** "Weights and Measures." *ABD* 6:897–908. **Pritchard, J. B.** "Inscribed Weight." In *Hebrew Inscriptions and Stamps from Gibeon.* Philadelphia: University Museum, University of Pennsylvania, 1959. 29–30. **Rendsburg, G.** "Late Biblical Hebrew and the Date of 'P.'" *JANESCU* 12 (1980) 65–80 (68). **Scott, R. B. Y.** "The NṢP Weights from Judah." *BASOR* 200 (1970) 62–66. ———. "The Scale Weights from Ophel." *PEQ* 97 (1965) 128–39. ———. "Weights and Measures in the Bible." *BA* 22 (1959) 22–40. **Sellers, O. R.** "Balances." *IDB* 1:342–43. **Spaer, A.** "A Group of Iron Age Stone Weights." *IEJ* 32 (1982) 251. **Stern, E.** "Weights and Measures." *EncJud* 16:376–88. **Vaux, R. de.** *Ancient Israel.* 1961. 199. **Wambacq, B. N.** "De Mensuris in S. Scriptura." *VD* 32 (1954) 266–74, 325–34. ———. "De Ponderibus in S. Scriptura." *VD* 29 (1951) 341–50.

Translation and Prosodic Analysis

Honest Weights and Measures [(5:5):5:(5:5)]

13 *You shall not have / in your bag / two kinds of weights //*	[18	3
larger / and smaller // ס	11	2_
14 *You shall not have / in your house / two kinds of measures //*	[20	3
larger / and smaller //	11	2_
15 *A full and honest weight / you shall keep /*	15	2
a full / and honest measure / you shall keep //	17	3_
In order that your days may be long /	[14	1
in / the land / that YHWH your God /	19	3
is giving you //	6	1
16 *For an abomination / to YHWH* [a]*your God*[a] */*	[15	2
is anyone doing these things //	8]	1
anyone / doing injustice // ס	9	2_

Notes

16.a-a. The term אלהיך, "your God," is omitted here in some Heb. MSS, Cairo Geniza fragments, and OL texts.

Form/Structure/Setting

The law on honest weights and measures (25:13–16) completes the second of two five-part groups of laws on humanitarian and social ethics (24:6–16 and 25:1–16). As shown in the discussion above, the laws of Deut 24–25 may be outlined in a simple five-part concentric structure:

A	Framework: laws on marriage and war	24:1–5
B	Laws on humanitarian concerns and social ethics, part one	24:6–16
X	Summary law on protecting the sojourner, orphan, and widow	24:17–22
B′	Laws on humanitarian concerns and social ethics, part two	25:1–16
A′	Framework: law on YHWH's Holy War (Amalekite aggression)	25:17–19

Within this structure, the second group of laws on humanitarian and social ethics (25:1–16) was outlined above in *Form/Structure/Setting* on Deut 25:1–4.

The law in Deut 25:13–16 focuses on business ethics, at least in terms of the plain meaning of the text. At the same time, it should be noted that the narrative in Exod 16, which is shaped by this law, is transitional in nature, with its focus on the people of Israel moving from the crossing of the Red Sea (Exod 14–15), in the exodus from slavery in Egypt, en route to Mount Sinai and to receiving the Ten Commandments (Exod 19–20).

The law on honest weights and measures (25:13–16) is divided into two parts by means of *sĕtûmāʾ* layout markers after vv 13 and 16, a situation that does not seem to match the content; for vv 13 and 14 are in perfect parallelism from a poetic point of view. Moreover, the prosodic analysis reveals an unusual pattern, somewhat like the 7:4:7 accentual stress unit in 24:19–20, in that the law in 25:13–16 can also be scanned (5:5):5:(5:5), with v 15a functioning as a bridge between two subunits. But this would necessitate ignoring the *sĕtûmāʾ* marker after v 13, which normally indicates a significant structural break.

As I suggested in the discussion of the law on improper intervention in a fight (25:11–13), v 13 belongs with what both precedes it and follows it. Moreover, when vv 11–13 and 14–16 are read as parallel rhythmic structures, the total mora counts are 124 and 128, respectively. In other words, 25:11–16 is carefully arranged in two parallel structural units, which are virtually equal in length from a prosodic point of view. At the same time, v 13 certainly belongs with what follows, and vv 13–15a can also be scanned as three parallel units in terms of both mora count (29 + 31 + 32) and content. In short, 25:13 is a rhythmic bridge connecting the two laws and belonging to both of them, much like 23:1 and 24:5.

When the law in Deut 25:13–16 is outlined in concentric fashion, we are able to see more clearly the relationship between the law and the narrative:

A	You shall not have two kinds of weights in your bag	25:13
B	You shall not have two kinds of measures in your house	25:14
X	You shall keep honest weights and measures (איפה שלמה וצדק)	25:15a
B′	In order that your days may be long in the land	25:15b
A′	Doing injustice is an abomination to YHWH	25:16

The outer frame in this structure sets the issue of "two kinds of weights in your bag" (בכיסך) in v 13 over against the concluding phrase, "anyone doing injustice" (כל עשה עול, v 16). The inner frame is in the form of an extended poetic line: You shall not keep two kinds of measures (v 14), if you want your days to be long in the land (v 15b). In the center of the above structure (v 15a) is a summary statement in poetic parallelism:

A full and honest "weight" (אבן) you shall keep;
a full and honest "measure" (איפה) you shall keep.

Carmichael argued that this couplet is related to the narrative of Exod 16, when God provided bread for the wilderness in the form of the mysterious manna (*LNB*, 302). The term איפה, "ephah," provides the key, for the narrative of the manna concludes with the comment: "An omer is the tenth part of an ephah"

(Exod 16:36). In this story it made no difference whether the measure was an honest one: "The people of Israel did so; they gathered, some more, some less" (16:17). God saw to it that the people kept "a full and honest measure"—namely, an "omer" (עמר)—a tenth of an "ephah" (איפה, 16:36).

The evidence assembled by Labuschagne on the use of the divine-name numbers in Deut 25:13–16, within its larger literary context in 25:1–19, may be summarized as follows:

Words:	before *ʾatnāḥ*			after *ʾatnāḥ*				
25:1–4	22		+	23		=	45	
25:5–6	26		+	11		=	37	
25:7–10	27		+	34	(= 2 × 17)	=	61	
25:11–19	85	(= 5 × 17)	+	32		=	117	
25:1–19	160		+	100		=	260	(= 10 × 26)
25:11–12	17		+	7		=	24	
25:13–16	29		+	17		=	46	(= 2 × 23)
25:11–16	46	(= 2 × 23)	+	24		=	70	
25:13–19	68	(= 4 × 17)	+	25		=	93	

There are 17 words after *ʾatnāḥ* in 25:13–16 (the law on honest weights and measures) and a total of 46 (= 2 × 23) words, numbers that suggest that the ancient scribes made their numerical composition to the "glory" (כבוד = 23) of YHWH (יהוה = 17 or 26). The law on improper intervention in a fight (25:11–12), which has 17 words before *ʾatnāḥ*, was attached. In 25:11–16 there are 46 (= 2 × 23) words before *ʾatnāḥ*. The concluding reminder to remember to "hate the Amalekites" in 25:17–19 was appended to the law on honest weights and measures (vv 13–16) to give a larger literary structure (vv 13–19), which has 68 (= 4 × 17) words before *ʾatnāḥ*. These laws were integrated into the still larger literary context of 25:1–19, which has a total of 260 (= 10 × 26) words, a fitting number for this concluding section of the literary expansion on the Ten Commandments in 11:26–25:19.

Comment

13 See the *Comment* on 25:11–13. For parallel legislation on weights and measures, see Lev 19:35–37 and the sixteenth chapter of the "Instructions of Amenemope" (*ANET*, 423). On parallels in Mesopotamia, see H. W. F. Saggs, *The Greatness That Was Babylon* (New York: Praeger, 1969) 282 (cited in Craigie [1976] 316 n. 16).

14–16 The phrase "two kinds of measures" interprets Hebrew איפה ואיפה. An איפה was a unit of capacity in vessels designed to hold grain. The positioning of the phrase "a full and honest weight/measure" at the beginning of each of the parallel lines in v 15a is for emphasis. The motive clause "in order that your days may be long in the land" is essentially the same as the motive clause in the center of the Ten Commandments in 5:16b. Long life is the reward God grants to those who obey his commandments. The statement that "an abomination to YHWH your God is anyone doing these things" concludes the civil and criminal laws of Deuteronomy (12:1–25:16). Attention now shifts back to the subject of proper worship, following a brief digression on matters of Holy War (25:17–19).

Explanation

The law on honest weights and measures (25:13–16) is the final law dealing with matters of civil law in Deut 12–25, and its parallel in Lev 19:35–36 functions as the conclusion to the laws of holiness in Lev 19 in a similar manner. Amos also scorned those who "make the ephah small and the shekel great, and deal deceitfully with false balances" (Amos 8:5; cf. also Mic 6:11; Hos 12:7; Prov 11:1; 16:11; 20:10, 23). Jesus spoke to the same issue in his emphasis on honesty in the sense of utter sincerity as the hallmark of character: "Let what you say be simply 'Yes' or 'No'; anything more than this comes from the evil one" (Matt 5:37).

The motivation behind this law is transparent. Justice and equity lead toward God's blessing, "that your days may be long in the land that YHWH your God is giving you" (v 15). By contrast, deceitful actions on our part are "an abomination to YHWH your God" (v 16), and thus expose us to God's curse.

16. Remember to Hate the Amalekites (25:17–19)

Bibliography

Abramsky, S. "Amalekites." *EncJud* 2:787–91. **Braulik, G.** "Some Remarks on the Deuteronomistic Conception of Freedom and Peace." In *The Theology of Deuteronomy.* Tr. U. Lindblad. N. Richland Hills, TX: BIBAL Press, 1994. 87–98. **Brueggemann, W.** "Weariness, Exile and Chaos (A Motif in Royal Theology)." *CBQ* 34 (1972) 19–38 (22). **Carmichael, C. M.** "A New View of the Origin of the Deuteronomic Credo." *VT* 19 (1969) 273–89 (278). **Christensen, D. L.** *Prophecy and War in Ancient Israel.* Berkeley: BIBAL Press, 1989. **Coats, G. W.** "Moses Versus Amalek: Aetiology and Legend in Exodus 17:8–16." In *Congress Volume, Edinburgh 1974.* VTSup 28. Leiden: Brill, 1975. 29–41. **Dahan, G.** "Les interprétations juives dans les commentaires du Pentateuque de Pierre le Chantre." In *FS B. Smalley.* 1985. 131–55. **Foresti, F.** *The Rejection of Saul in the Perspective of the Deuteronomistic School: A Study of 1 Sam 15 and Related Texts.* Studia Theologica-Teresianum 5. Rome: Edizioni del Teresianum, 1984. **Grønbaek, J. H.** "Juda und Amalek: Überlieferungsgeschichtliche Erwägungen zu Exodus 17,8–16." *ST* 18 (1964) 26–45, esp. 40–42. **Hostetter, E. C.** *Nations Mightier and More Numerous: The Biblical View of Palestine's Pre-Israelite Peoples.* BIBAL Diss. Series 3. N. Richland Hills, TX: BIBAL Press, 1995. 85–89. **L'Hour, J.** "Les interdits *To'eba* dans le Deutéronome." *RB* 71 (1964) 481–503, esp. 499. **Robinson, B. P.** "Israel and Amalek: The Context of Exodus 17.8–16." *JSOT* 32 (1985) 15–22. **Roth, W.** "The Deuteronomic Rest Theology: A Redaction-Critical Study." *BR* 21 (1976) 5–14. **Sarna, N.** "The Battle with the Amalekites." In *Exploring Exodus: The Heritage of Biblical Israel.* New York: Schocken, 1986. 120–26. **Schuil, A.** *Amalek: Onderzoek naar oorsprong en ontwikkeling van Amaleks rol in het Oude Testament.* Zoetermeer: Uitgeverij Boekencentrum, 1997. **Stern, P. D.** "A Window on Ancient Israel's Religious Experience: The

Ḥerem Re-investigated and Re-interpreted." Ph.D. diss., New York Univ., 1989. 102–3. **Waldman, N. M.** "The Sin of Amalek in Bible and Midrash." *DD* 11 (1982–83) 77–81. **Weinfeld, M.** "The Fear of God." In *DDS.* 274–81, esp. 274–75.

Translation and Prosodic Analysis

Remember to Hate the Amalekites [(8:6):(6:8)]

17 *Remember / what / Amalek / did to you //*	18	4
on the way / when you[a] went forth from Egypt //	13	2
18 how he encountered *you / on the way /*	9	2
And he smote the hindmost of you /	7	1
all the stragglers behind you /	13	1
And you / were famished and weary //	14	2
and he did not fear / God[a] //	12	2
19 *And it shall be / when YHWH your God grants rest /*	20	2
to you / from all your enemies / round about / in the land /	20	4
That YHWH your God /	11	1
is giving to you as an inheritance / to possess it /	14	2
You shall blot out / the remembrance of Amalek /	12	2
from under\\[a] *heaven // you shall not / forget //* ס	13	3

Notes

17.a. LXX[L] and Vg. read 2 sg. Note the use of the *Numeruswechsel* here, which helps to explain the variant reading.

18.a. Syr. adds אלהיך, "your God"; LXX[A] reads τὸν κύριον (= יהוה) for MT אלהים, "God."

19.a. Reading *ṭip̄ḥā'* as conj. because of misplaced *'atnāḥ*.

Form/Structure/Setting

In biblical tradition the war against the Amalekites of Exod 17:8–15 marks the beginning of an enmity that continues throughout the whole canonical process in ancient Israel. The initial war with Amalek is marked by the figure of Moses, with his hands held aloft by Aaron and Hur—"one on one side, and the other on the other side; so his hands were steady until the sun set" (Exod 17:12)—for as long as his hands were upraised, Israel prevailed over the Amalekites. The story contains the fragment of an archaic war poem, which has been reconstructed as follows (see Christensen, *Prophecy and War,* 48):

> For the hand is on Yahweh's banner;
> the battle belongs to Yahweh,
> against Amalek from generation to generation. (Exod 17:16)

The conflict with Amalek is the starting point in the account of YHWH's Holy War, as the Divine Warrior brought his people from the land of Egypt to their home in the land of Canaan.

King Saul's rejection by the prophet Samuel is tied to the fact that he violated the law of Deut 25:17–19 by failing to observe the terms of YHWH's Holy War against Amalek, when "he took Agag the king of the Amalekites alive, but utterly destroyed all the people with the edge of the sword" (1 Sam 15:8). Centuries later, in the story of Esther, the wicked Haman, who plotted the destruction of the Jews, is introduced as "the Agagite, the son of Hammedatha" (Esth 3:1), to draw the observant reader's attention to the story of Saul and Agag of times past. Mordecai, the cousin of Esther, who plays such a pivotal role in the story, is introduced as "the son of Jair, son of Shimei, son of Kish, a Benjaminite" (Esth 2:5), that is, a descendant of King Saul. Thus at the end of the story of ancient Israel within the canon of sacred Scripture, we return to the beginning of that epic story in the exodus from Egypt and to the injunction to "remember what Amalek did to you" (Deut 25:17). Esther remembered, and the Jews finally fulfilled the words of Moses: "the ten sons of Haman the son of Hammedatha, the enemy of the Jews [were hanged]; but they laid no hand on the plunder" (Esth 9:10). Thus the law of Deuteronomy was fulfilled, "You shall blot out the remembrance of Amalek from under heaven; you shall not forget" (Deut 25:17–19).

The presence of the *Numeruswechsel* at the beginning of this final literary unit in the sixth of the eleven weekly portion of Torah readings from Deuteronomy (21:10–25:19) suggests that it is to be separated somewhat from the preceding law. In fact, it forms an inclusion with the law on marriage to a woman captured in war (21:10–14), a law that introduced the larger literary structure. It also forms a more immediate inclusion with the law on the deferral of a new husband from military service in 24:5, which frames the third major subsection in the larger structure, 24:5–25:19.

Though the law of 25:17–19 differs from what precedes it in this section of Deuteronomy, to the point that some have questioned whether it should even be called a law in the formal sense, it shares the same structural design, which may be outlined as follows:

A	"Remember what Amalek did to you"	זכור את אשר־עשה לך עמלק	25:17a
B	"when you went forth from Egypt"	בדרך בצאתכם ממצרים	25:17b–18a
X	"And he did not fear God"	ולא ירא אלהים	25:18b
B′	"When YHWH grants rest . . . in the land"	והיה בהניח . . . לך נחלה	25:19a
A′	"Blot out the remembrance of Amalek . . . do not forget"	תמחה את־זכר עמלק . . . לא תשכח	25:19b

In the center of this structure we find the simple statement that Amalek did not fear God (v 18b). The "fear of God" in wisdom literature is synonymous with wisdom (Prov 1:7; 9:10; 15:33; Job 28:28; Ps 111:10). In light of Deut 10:12, we know what it means to fear YHWH—it means to love him and to walk in his ways. The inner frame moves from a description of the experience of the people of Israel when they "went forth from Egypt" and faced the treachery of Amalek "on the way" (vv 17b–18a) to a glimpse into the future when YHWH grants them rest and they possess their inheritance in the promised land (v 19a). The outer frame reminds the people to remember what Amalek did in times past (v 17a) and to blot out the remembrance of Amalek from under heaven in times to come: "you shall not forget!" (v 19b).

In the discussion of the previous law on honest weights and measures (25:13–16), the influence over narrative elsewhere in the Pentateuch moved from Gen 42–44 to Exod 16 (cf. Carmichael, *LNB*, 299–303). The law on remembering Amalekite aggression (Deut 25:17–19) moves from the tradition in Exod 16 to Exod 17:7 (Carmichael, *LNB*, 304). This attack was made on the weak and vulnerable among the people of Israel, which is the reason their action is judged so severely.

The evidence assembled by Labuschagne on the use of the divine-name numbers in 25:17–19 and its larger literary context may be summarized as follows:

Words:	before *ʾatnāḥ*		after *ʾatnāḥ*		
25:17–18	17	+	6	=	23
25:13–19	68 (= 4 × 17)	+	25	=	93
25:11–19	85 (= 5 × 17)	+	32	=	117 (= 10^2 + 17)
21:10–25:19	929	+	652	=	1,581 (= 93 × 17)

Once again, we find the divine-name number 17 carefully woven into the fabric of the Hebrew text in different ways. Vv 17–18 have 17 words before *ʾatnāḥ* and a total of 23 words (the numerical value of כבוד, "glory"), signifying the "glory of YHWH." V 19 is constructed in a manner that ties 25:17–19 to its immediate literary context, with 68 (= 4 × 17) words before *ʾatnāḥ* in 25:13–19 and 85 (= 5 × 17) words before *ʾatnāḥ* in 25:11–19. The most striking figure, however, is the total achieved for the words in the sixth of the eleven weekly readings in the lectionary cycle taken as a whole (21:10–25:19), for there are a grand total of 1,581 (= 93 × 17). The tedious and laborious task of achieving these figures was done to the glory of YHWH.

Comment

17–18 "Amalek" was a grandson of Esau and one of the six sons of Eliphaz (Gen 36:11–12), who is linked with the land of Edom. As the first nation to attack Israel at Rephidim shortly after the exodus from Egypt (Exod 17:8–16), the Amalekites subsequently take their place as the enemy par excellence in biblical tradition. Details of their aggression emerge here that are not found elsewhere. In a surprise attack, they "launched an assault . . . against the stragglers [נחשלים] . . . [who] were famished [עיף] and weary [יגע]." The "stragglers behind" were those who were too weak to keep up with the others on their march through the wilderness. The word עיף, translated here as "famished," carries the meaning of "thirsty" or "hungry" more than "tired" (normally יעף), though the two words are sometimes used interchangeably (Tigay [1996] 392 n. 56). Within the traditions of YHWH's Holy War, the Amalekites became a familiar subject for later generations as they remembered the exodus-eisodus events in cultic celebration (see *Excursus:* "Holy War as Celebrated Event in Ancient Israel"). The absence of extrabiblical information about this people should remind us that we are dealing with traditions of holy war in which the Amalekites play a central role symbolically—as the archenemy of God's people—and the first enemy defeated by the Divine Warrior, after the "Crossing of the Sea." The reference to the fact that the Amalekites "did not fear God" indicates that they had no fear of divine punishment. Sarna has noted that reference to the "fear of God" (יראת אלהים) often appears in connection with situations that invoke norms of moral and ethical conduct (*Exploring Exodus,* 25–26, 120). On the "fear of God" see Gen 20:11 (Abraham); Gen 42:18 (Joseph); Exod 1:17 (Hebrew midwives); Lev 19:14, 32 (laws of holiness); and Job 1:1, 8 (Job). From a historical point of view, it appears that the Amalekites ceased to exist as a nation in the days of Hezekiah, when "five hundred men of the Simeonites . . . destroyed the remnant of the Amalekites" (1 Chr 4:42–43). The concept of the Amalekites as the enemy par excellence was alive as late as the book of Esther, where Haman is described as an Agagite (Esth 3:1,10; 8:3,5; 9:24) so as to relate him to Agag, the Amalekite enemy of King Saul (1 Sam 15).

19 The words "remember" and "do not forget" form an envelope around 25:17–19. The people are to remember what Amalek did, and they are to remember what Moses has commanded them to do about it—"you shall blot out the name of Amalek from under heaven." In Jewish tradition the injunction to "remember the Amalekites" is carried out by reading the words of Deut 25:17–19 in public worship on the Sabbath immediately before the Feast of Purim (when the book of Esther is read), which is celebrated one month before Passover (Tigay [1996] 236). To "blot out the name" means to "wipe them out." The account of the war with Amalek in Exod 17:8–15 closes with the command that YHWH gave to Moses: "Write this as a reminder in a book and recite it in the hearing of Joshua: I will utterly blot out the remembrance of Amalek from under heaven" (Exod 17:14 NRSV). Moses then adds these words: "The LORD will have war with Amalek from generation to generation" (Exod 17:15 NRSV). On Exod 17:16 as a fragment of an archaic war poem appended to the narrative, and the war with Amalek as the first of a series of wars that, together with the defeat of the Egyptians at the Red Sea, constitute YHWH's Holy War par excellence, see my earlier discussion (*Prophecy and War,* 48–49). The first recorded attempt to eliminate the Amalekites appears in the Former Prophets, when Samuel commanded Saul to "go and smite Amalek, and utterly destroy all that they have; do not spare them, but kill both man and woman, infant and suckling, ox and sheep, camel and ass" (1 Sam 15:3). The canonical process for the Hebrew Bible concludes with the inclusion of the book of Esther, when the ten sons of Haman the Agagite (Esth 3:1) were hanged on the gallows their father had built to execute Mordecai (Esth 9:13–14).

Explanation

The language of holy war, as presented here in the injunction to remember to hate the Amalekites, has been the occasion of great mischief through the centuries within both Judaism and Christianity. Many scholars, like H. H. Shires and P. Parker, have concluded that "the antagonism which was felt toward foreigners . . . in the form in which it appears here, . . . sinks far below the lofty heights elsewhere to be seen in this book. . . . Like the chauvinists and totalitarians of our own generation, the author felt that hatred of another people would help to unify the nation" (see their "Exposition of the Book of Deuteronomy," *IB* 2:482).

Such a teaching is contrary to that of the apostle Paul when he quoted Jesus' words: "If your enemies are hungry, feed them; if they are thirsty, give them something to drink; for by doing this you will heap burning coals on their heads"

(Rom 12:20 NRSV). It is also contrary to the teaching of Deuteronomy itself, when properly understood and interpreted.

The war with Amalek in Exod 17 is the first in a series of wars that, together with the defeat of the Egyptians at the Red Sea, constitute YHWH's Holy War par excellence, as celebrated event in ancient Israel. Further battles in this series include the war with the Canaanite kings of Arad (Num 21:1–3), the wars with Amorite kings Sihon and Og (Num 21:21–35), and the war against Midian (Num 31:1–54)—all under the leadership of Moses. After Moses' death, Joshua led the people of Israel across the Jordan River to the second phase of YHWH's Holy War against Jericho, Ai, and the Canaanite inhabitants of the promised land. What we are dealing with here is the presentation of Egypt and Amalek as paradigmatic enemies within the canonical process.

Seven other traditional enemies appear, alongside Amalek, in Deuteronomic tradition, namely the "seven nations greater and mightier than [Israel]"—the Hittites, Girgashites, Amorites, Canaanites, Perizzites, Hivites, and Jebusites (Deut 7:1; Josh 3:10; 24:11). Though some of these "nations" are identifiable, the Perizzites and the Girgashites remain obscure. Detailed study of the occurrences of these seven names within the biblical tradition suggests that the complete listing of seven nations is traditional in nature. Within the Holy War materials of the Deuteronomic tradition, these seven nations constitute a roll call of enemies within some sort of cultic context, in which Amalek was considered the archenemy par excellence.

Though the book of Esther continues that ancient tradition and brings it to a fitting conclusion in the death of Haman and his ten sons, the Latter Prophets and the Writings together present a remarkable transformation of teachings about Israel's enemies. Egypt becomes "the rod of [YHWH's] anger" in Isa 10:5, which is to be understood in terms of the great "march of conquest" portrayed in Isa 10:27c–34 (D. Christensen, "The March of Conquest in Isaiah 10:27c–34," *VT* 26 [1976] 385–99). In this passage it is the Divine Warrior himself who threatens daughter Zion with destruction. The vision continues across the chapter division. In spite of the hewing down of "the thickets of the forest" (Isa 10:34), a shoot from the stump of Jesse will become an ensign to the nations (11:1,10) for an eschatological contest. Although the focus in these passages is on the remnant of Israel, it is clear that YHWH is Lord of the nations. He will use, however unwittingly, even wicked Assyria to pave the way for a "new eisodus" (11:12–16) that will establish his people in a "new kingdom" described in messianic terms (11:1–9). The image is carried even further within Isaiah's subsequent oracles against Egypt (Isa 19:24–25): "In that day Israel will be the third with Egypt and Assyria, a blessing in the midst of the earth, whom the LORD of hosts has blessed, saying: 'Blessed be Egypt my people, Assyria the work of my hands, and Israel my heritage.'"

Along with the seven paradigmatic enemies of ancient Israel, Amalek faced annihilation in the ancient traditions of YHWH's Holy War. Subsequent enemy nations, however, were treated very differently within the canonical process. Cultic gatherings at the temple in Jerusalem became anticipations of all nations gathering to worship YHWH. Kings from Egypt, Ethiopia, and all the kingdoms of the earth, bearing gifts for the temple and singing praises to God, join the procession of the tribes of Israel to the temple in Ps 68.

In Isa 40–55 the descendants of Israel return to Zion from exile, in contexts that suggest that the "survivors of the nations" are reckoned among these descendants (44:1–5; 45:22–25; 49:12–20; 53:10). When, as a result of the suffering and mission of the servant, the peoples at the ends of the earth are waiting for YHWH's rule, their survivors join themselves to Israel to converge on Jerusalem (55:5). People from nations "of every tongue" join the returning Jews (Zech 8:21–23), and the alienation of the enemy nations is removed when YHWH changes "the speech of the peoples to a pure speech" so that they may call on his name (Zeph 3:9). Kings lead their nations in a great procession (Isa 60:3, 11), which extends "from sea to sea and from mountain to mountain (Mic 7:12), bringing the wealth of the nations on camels (Isa 60:5–6), driving before them animals for sacrifice, and carrying the sons and daughters of Israel in their arms (v 4). They join themselves to YHWH and become his people (Zech 2:11) and go up every year to the great fall festival in Jerusalem (Zech 14:16)—where they assemble to hear the words of Deuteronomy recited "every seventh year, in the set time, the year of release, at the Festival of Booths, when all Israel comes to appear before YHWH your God in the place that he will choose" (Deut 31:10–11).

Reading 7. Public Worship and Covenant Renewal (26:1–29:8 [Eng. 9])

Introduction

The seventh of the weekly portions in the cycle of Torah readings from Deuteronomy (26:1–29:8) is known as כי תבוא, "when you come," from its opening words. Its first segment, with its two liturgies for use in the annual pilgrimage festivals (26:1–15), functions as a transitional passage tying together the stipulations of the covenant as spelled out in the laws of the central core (chaps. 12–26) with the covenant ceremony that follows in 27:1–29:8 (Eng. 9) and the appeal for covenant loyalty in 29:9 (Eng. 10)–30:20.

Deut 26 functions as the conclusion to the collection of laws in the central core, as shown in the following outline:

A	Public worship at the central sanctuary and in local towns	12:1–14:21
B	Laws on human affairs in relation to God	14:22–16:17
X	Laws on leadership and authority—executive and judicial	16:18–21:9
B′	Laws on human affairs in relation to others	21:10–25:19
A′	Public worship at the central sanctuary and in local towns	26:1–19

In this structure the whole of 26:1–19 is read over against the section on proper worship at the central sanctuary ("the place YHWH chooses to make his name dwell there") in 12:1–14:21.

Deut 26 is also to be read in relation to 14:22–16:17, for the subject of the special triennial tithe in ancient Israel appears in 14:28–29 and here in 26:12–15, but nowhere else in the Torah. Moreover, the fourth of the weekly portions of the Torah readings from Deuteronomy in 11:27–16:17 concludes with a section on the three pilgrimage festivals (16:1–17) where the liturgy of 26:5–9 had its *Sitz im Cultus*. The relationship between 16:1–17 and 26:1–19 may be outlined as follows:

A	The Passover sacrifice and the Feast of Unleavened Bread	16:1–8
B	The Feast of Weeks and the Feast of Booths	16:9–15
X	Do not appear empty-handed at the three festivals	16:16–17
B′	The liturgy of firstfruits and the triennial tithe	26:1–15
A′	Mutual commitments between God and Israel in covenant renewal	26:16–19

The presentation of the pilgrimage festivals in Deut 16 follows the agricultural year, beginning in the spring with Passover and the Feast of Unleavened Bread and moving on to the Feast of Weeks (Pentecost), seven weeks later in early summer, and then to the Feast of Booths (Sukkoth) in the fall. The section concludes with a summary command that every male is to appear at the central sanctuary ("the place God will choose") "three times in the year . . . at the Feast of Unleavened Bread and at the Feast of Weeks and at the Feast of Booths; and they shall not appear before YHWH empty-handed" (16:16). The declaration in 26:5–9 (and vv 12–15) is what each individual worshiper was commanded to say as he placed his offerings (and tithes) before YHWH in public worship at the central sanctuary.

The above outline suggests that the ceremony of covenant renewal, with its mutual commitments made between God and Israel, was celebrated in conjunction with the spring festival of Passover and Unleavened Bread. The Feast of Weeks (at the culmination of grain harvest) and the Feast of Booths (on completion of the agricultural year as a whole) were the occasions for the liturgy of firstfruits and the presentation of the annual tithes. The special triennial tithe was apparently stored locally in the towns, or perhaps in the nearest Levitical city, as provision for the needs of the Levites, resident aliens, orphans, and widows—and perhaps for use in the context of local assemblies every fifty days within the towns throughout the country, except on the occasions of the three pilgrimages to the central sanctuary (see *Excursus:* "The Triennial Cycle of Torah Readings in Palestinian Judaism"). The injunction not to appear at these three festivals empty-handed is the focus of attention, for the entire system in terms of the religious establishment (priests and Levites) and social welfare (provision for the needs of resident aliens, orphans, and widows) was dependent on this income.

Though Deut 26 is in three parts, with the boundaries of each section marked by *sĕtûmâʾ* layout markers after vv 11, 15, and 19, careful prosodic analysis reveals five major rhythmic structures:

A	Worship by offering God the firstfruits	26:1–4
B	Liturgy—declaration at the central sanctuary	26:5–9
X	Worship in providing for human need—Levites and aliens	26:10–11
B′	Liturgy—declaration at local sanctuaries	26:12–15
A′	Worship and mutual commitments between God and his people	26:16–19

The literary structure alternates between third-person description of worship and first-person liturgical declaration, which constitutes the inner frame in this particular structure. The concluding subunit in 26:16–19, which serves as a connecting link between 11:26–32 and 27:1–10, is itself in two parts (vv 16–17 and 18–19), in which mutual commitments are made between God and Israel in covenant renewal—in anticipation of the covenant ceremony itself, which follows in Deut 27–30.

A close reading of Deut 27–30 reveals a mixture of two covenant ceremonies: one on the plains of Moab, in the days of Moses, and another to be observed in the future at Shechem under Joshua. The most useful approach for our purposes here is to examine in detail the whole of Deut 26–30, the seventh and eighth of the weekly readings from Deuteronomy in the lectionary cycle, which may be outlined as follows:

A	Public worship at the annual festivals in the promised land	26:1–19
B	The renewal of the covenant at Shechem	27:1–26
X	Blessings and curses of covenant renewal in Moab	28:1–69
B′	Appeal for covenant faithfulness in the future	29:1–28
A′	Call to decision: life and blessing or death and cursing	30:1–20

The outer frame in this structure moves from the presentation of liturgies for public worship within the context of the pilgrimage festivals in the promised land (26:1–19) to the great summons to decision—to choose life and the blessing of the covenant rather than death and its curses (30:1–20). The inner frame moves from the account of the renewal of the covenant at Shechem in the days of Joshua (27:1–26) to an appeal for covenant faithfulness addressed to future generations (29:1–28). The center of this structure is the blessings and curses of the covenant itself (28:1–69 [Eng. 28:1–29:1]), which includes the ponderous and depressing reiteration of the details of future disaster if the terms of the covenant are not observed (28:20–68).

The next step in our analysis of the structure of Deut 26–30 is to outline each of the two weekly portions in the same manner:

Outline of Reading 7: Public Worship and Covenant Renewal (26:1–29:8 [Eng. 29:9])

A	Public worship at the annual festivals in the promised land	26:1–19
B	Renewal of the covenant at Shechem	27:1–26
X	Covenant blessings for obedience and curses for disobedience	28:1–19
B′	Warning of future disaster for breaking the covenant	28:20–69
A′	Remembering the past: the basis of the covenant spelled out	29:1–8

Outline of Reading 8: Appeal for Covenant Loyalty (29:9 [Eng. 10]–30:20)

A	Covenant ceremony in Moab under Moses	29:9–20
B	Aftermath of punishment—conclusion to Moses' warning	29:21–28
X	Conclusion: observe the words of this Torah	29:28
B′	The possibility of restoration	30:1–10
A′	Conclusion of the summons to the covenant	30:11–20

The two centers in this reading of Deut 26–30 focus attention on the covenant blessings and curses (28:1–19), and the summary command to observe the words of this Torah, which is presented in the form of a riddle: "The secret things belong to YHWH our God, and the revealed things to us and to our children forever—to do all the words of this Torah" (29:28). The plain meaning of the text refers to its immediate context, which speaks of national disaster as a consequence of disobedience to YHWH's commandments. But at the same time, as Labuschagne has shown, "it has another message: the concealed things, the esoteric knowledge with regard to the written text of the law, the sacred numerical structures, are for the benefit of God, to his glory, but the text of the law in its straight, plain language is for the benefit of the people. It is a coded message to the ordinary people, to the uninitiated, who do not know the hidden intricacies of the text, to obey the law in its plain meaning" ("Divine Speech in Deuteronomy," in SBTS 3:388–89). The content of that revealed truth is what is contained in the Deuteronomic code of law (Deut 12–26), or what I have called here the "central core" of Deuteronomy.

Another way of reading this section of Deuteronomy is to divide each of these halves in half, to find "four wheels of the same likeness" with another single summary verse (28:69) at the center:

A	Public Worship at the Festivals in the Promised Land	26:1–19
a	Worship by offering God the firstfruits	26:1–4
b	Liturgy declaration at presentation of firstfruits	26:5–9
x	True religion providing for Levites, aliens, etc.	26:10–11
b′	Liturgy declaration at presentation of triennial tithe	26:12–15
a′	Worship and mutual commitments between God and his people	26:16–19
B	The Covenant Blessings and Curses	27:1–28:68
a	Renewal of the covenant at Shechem	27:1–26
b	Covenant blessings and curses	28:1–19
x	First expanded description of future disasters	28:20–37
b′	Second expanded description of future disasters	28:38–57
a′	Undoing of blessings—final reversal of Israel's history	28:58–68
X	Summation: "These are the words of the covenant"	28:69
B′	The Covenant Is for Future Generations Too	29:1–28
a	Moses reviews the basis of the covenant	29:1–8
b	Moses reminds the people of the purpose of the assembly	29:9–12
x	The covenant is for future generations as well	29:13–14
b′	Moses warns of consequences for breaking the covenant	29:15–27
a′	Conclusion: "Do all the words of this Torah!"	29:28
A′	The Terms of the Covenant Are Doable	30:1–20
a	The possibility of restoration is there	30:1–5
b	When you seek to purify yourselves you will receive help	30:6–10
c	This instruction is not beyond your reach	30:11
b′	God's requirements are known, understandable, and doable	30:12–14
a′	Call to decision: life and blessing or death and cursing	30:15–20

The four centers, together with the summary statement in 28:69, that emerge in this reading tell the basic story of Deut 26–30. A brief summary of the nature of "true religion" in the promised land, in which the needs of "the Levite and the sojourner in your midst" are met (26:10–11), is set over against the assurance that "this commandment that I command you today is not too hard for you" (30:11)—this instruction is not beyond your reach, it is doable. The words of the covenant are the words that YHWH commanded Moses in the land of Moab, in addition to the covenant he made with them at Mount Sinai (28:69). The centers of sections B and B′ move from an expanded description of future disasters in the wake of covenant violation (28:20–37) to the declaration that the terms of the covenant apply for future generations as well (29:13–14).

The implication is clear: the terms of YHWH's covenant stand for all time—including the covenant renewal celebration under Joshua at Shechem (with YHWH's altar on Mount Ebal), and in the more distant future on Mount Zion. Though Israel and their king will ultimately suffer exile from the promised land for disobedience (28:36–37), the covenant stands forever: "I am making this covenant, sworn by an oath, not only with you who stand here with us today before YHWH our God, but also with those who are not here with us today" (29:13–14).

A. Preview: Two Liturgies for Worship in the Promised Land (26:1–15)

1. Liturgy of Firstfruits at the Central Sanctuary (26:1–11)

Bibliography

Bartlett, J. R. "The Brotherhood of Edom." *JSOT* 4 (1977) 2–27. **Beauchamp, P.** "Propositions sur l'alliance de l'Ancien Testament comme structure centrale." *RSR* 58 (1970) 161–93. **Beek, M. A.** "Das Problem des Aramäischen Stammvaters (Dt 26,5)." *OTS* 8 (1950) 193–212. **Braulik, G.** *Sage, was du glaubst: Das älteste Credo der Bibel—Impuls in neuester Zeit.* Stuttgart: Katholische Bibelwerk, 1979. ———. "Wie aus Erzählung ein Bekenntnis wird; das Credo Israels—Eine Kurzformel des Glaubens." *Entschluss* 38 (1983) 15, 24–26. **Brekelmans, C. H. W.** "Het 'Historische Credo' van Israel." *Tijdschrift voor Theologie* 3 (1963) 1–11. **Buber, M.** "The Prayer of the First Fruits." In *On the Bible.* Ed. N. Glatzer. New York: Schocken, 1968. 122–30. **Buck, H. M.** "Story and Celebration." In *Scripture in History and Theology: FS J. C. Rylaarsdam.* Ed. A. L. Merrill and T. W. Overholt. PTMS 17. Pittsburgh: Pickwick, 1977. 357–72. **Carmichael, C. M.** "Climactic Ceremony of First Fruits and the Historical Credo." In *Laws of Deuteronomy.* 1974. 246–54. ———. "A New View of the Origin of the Deuteronomic Credo." *VT* 19 (1969) 273–89. **Childs, B. S.** "Deuteronomic Formulae of the Exodus Traditions." In *FS W. Baumgartner.* 1967. 30–39. **Danker, W.** *Creeds in the Bible.* Saint Louis: Concordia Publishing House, 1966. **Dreyfus, F.** "'L'Araméen voulait tuer mon père': L'actualisation de Dt 26,5 dans la tradition juive et la tradition chrétienne." In *De la Tôrah au Messie: FS H. Cazelles.* 1981. 147–61. **Gibson, J. C. L.** "Observations on Some Important Ethnic Terms in the Pentateuch." *JNES* 20 (1961) 217–38. **Giesen, G.** *Die Wurzel* שבע. 1981. 276–78. **Gross, W.** "Syntaktische Erscheinungen am Anfang althebräischer Erzählungen: Hintergrund und Vordergrund." In *Congress Volume, Vienna 1980.* Ed. J. Emerton. VTSup 32. Leiden: Brill, 1981. 131–45. **Gutmann, Y.** "פרשת הביכורים." In *FS Y. Kaufmann.* 1960. 43–53 (Heb.). **Haag, H.** "'Offenbaren' in der hebräischen Bibel." In *Das Buch des Bundes: Aufsätze zur Bibel und ihrer Welt.* Ed. B. Lang. Düsseldorf: Patmos, 1980. 73–78. **Halévy, J.** "Recherches bibliques: Le Deutéronome." *RSEHA* 8 (1900) 113–14, 193–94. **Hammershaimb, E.** "History and Cult in the Old Testament." In *Near Eastern Studies: FS W. F. Albright.* 1971. 269–82. **Haran, M.** "Priestertum, Tempeldienst und Gebet." In *Das Land Israel in biblischer Zeit: Jerusalem-Symposium 1981 der Hebräischen Universität und der Georg-August-Universität.* Ed. G. Strecker. Göttingen: Vandenhoeck & Ruprecht, 1983. 141–53. **Harner, P. B.** "Exodus, Sinai, and Hittite Prologues." *JBL* 85 (1966) 233–36. **Huffmon, H. B.** "The Exodus, Sinai and the Credo." *CBQ* 27 (1965) 101–13. **Hyatt, J. P.** "Were There an Ancient Historical Credo in Israel and an Independent Sinai Tradition?" In *Translating and Understanding the Old Testament: FS H. G. May.* Ed. H. Frank and W. Reed. Nashville: Abingdon, 1970. 152–70. **Jenni, E.** "Faktitiv und Kausativ von *'bd* 'Zugrunde Gehen.'" In *FS W. Baumgartner.* 1967. 143–57. **Kadushin, M.** *Worship and Ethics.* Evanston: Northwestern UP, 1964. 71–81. **Kliesch, K.** *Das heilsgeschichtliche Credo in den Reden der Apostelgeschichte.* BBB 44. Cologne; Bonn: Hanstein, 1975. **Lang, B.** "Glaubensbekenntnisse im Alten und Neuen Testament." *Conc* 14 (1978) 499–503. **Larcher, C.** "La profession de foi dans l'Ancien Testament." *LV* 2 (1952) 15–38. **Lohfink, G.** "Dtn 26,5–9: Ein Beispiel altisraeltischer Geschichtstheologie" (1976). Repr.

in *Studien zum Deuteronomium.* 1990. 1:291–303. ———. "Die Gattung der 'historischen Kurzgeschichte' in den letzen Jahren von Juda und in der Zeit des babylonischen Exils" (1978). Repr. in *Studien zum Deuteronomium.* 1991. 2:55–86. ———. *Option for the Poor.* Berkeley: BIBAL Press, 1986. 35. ———. "Zum 'kleinen geschichtlichen Credo' Dtn 26,5–9." *TP* 46 (1971) 19–39. **Luckenbill, D. D.** "The 'Wandering Aramean.'" *AJSL* 36 (1919/20) 244–45. **Marti, M.** "Das erste officielle Bekenntnis." *ZTK* 2 (1892) 29–73. **McCarthy, D. J.** "What Was Israel's Historical Creed?" *Lexington Theological Quarterly* 4 (1969) 46–53. **McNamara, M.** "De Populi Aramaeorum Primordiis." *VD* 35 (1957) 129–42. **Millard, A. R.** "A Wandering Aramean." *JNES* 39 (1980) 153–55. **Moriarty, F. L.** "My Father Was a Wandering Aramean." *TBT* 1 (1962) 97–108. **Pedersen, J.** *Israel.* 2:299–307. **Richter, W.** "Beobachtungen zur theologischen Systembildung in der alttestamentlichen Literatur anhand des 'kleinen geschichtlichen Credo.'" In *Wahrheit und Verkündigung: FS M. Schmaus.* Ed. L. Scheffczyk et al. 2 vols. Paderborn: Schöningh, 1967. 1:175–212. **Rinaldi, G.** "*Ṭene*" in Deut 26,2.4." *BeO* 12 (1970) 104. **Rost, L.** "Das kleine geschichtliche Credo." In *Das kleine Credo.* Heidelberg: Quelle & Meyer, 1965. 11–25. **Schreiner, J.** "Die Entwicklung des israelitischen 'Credo.'" *Conc* 2 (1966) 757–62. **Seebass, H.** *Der Erzvater Israel und die Einführung der Jahweverehrung in Kanaan.* BZAW 98. Berlin: Töpelmann, 1966. **Thompson, J. A.** "The Cultic Credo and the Sinai Tradition." *Reformed Theological Review* 27 (1968) 53–64. **Tigay, J.** "On Some Aspects of Prayer in the Bible." *AJSR* 1 (1976) 377–78. **Vriezen, T. C.** "The Credo in the Old Testament." *OTWSA* 6 (1963) 5–17. **Wassermann, G.** "Das kleine geschichtliche Credo (Deut 26,5ff.) und seine deuteronomische Übermalung." In *Theologische Versuche* 2. Ed. J. Rogge and G. Schille. Berlin: Evangelische Verlagsanstalt, 1970. 27–46. **Weinfeld, M.** "The Liturgical Oration." In *DSS.* 32–45. **Weippert, M.** "Fragen des israelitischen Geschichtsbewußtseins." *VT* 23 (1973) 414–42. **Wijngaards, J. N. M.** *The Formulas of the Deuteronomic Creed (Dt. 6/20–23: 26/5–9).* Tilburg: A. Reijnen, 1963. **Zang-Embolo, P.** "Histoire et accès au sens dans le petit crédo historique (Dt xxvi,1–15) ou les présupposés d'une herméneutique." Diss., Freiburg Univ., Theol. Fak., 1983.

Translation and Prosodic Analysis

Liturgy of Firstfruits at the Central Sanctuary [(7:7):(5:5):(7:7)]
[(5:3):6:(5:5):(4:4):(5:5):6:(3:5)]

1 *And it shall be / when you come into the land /*	17	2
that\[a] YHWH your God / is giving you / as an inheritance //	21	3
and you possess it / and you dwell in it //	13	2_
2 *And you shall take /*	6	1
from the first / of [all][a] the fruit of the ground /	16	2
[b]that you shall bring from your land[b] /	11	1
That YHWH your God / is giving to you /	17	2
and you shall put it in a basket //	7	1_
And you shall go\[c] to the place /	12	1
that YHWH your God / chooses /	13	2
to make his name dwell / there //	9	2_
3 *And you shall come / to the priest /*	12	2
who is there / in those days //	13	2
and you shall say to him /	10	1_
"I declare TODAY / to YHWH <my>[a] God /	16	2
that I have entered / the land /	12	2
that YHWH <my God />[b] swore to our fathers / to give to us" //	27	3_

[4] *And the priest shall receive / the basket / from your hand<s>*[a] *//*	18	3
and he shall put it / before / the altar / of YHWH your God //	20	4_
[5] *And you shall answer and say / before / YHWH your God /*	23	3
[a] *"A wandering*[a] *Aramean / was my father /*	12	2
And he went down to Egypt /	8	1
and he sojourned there / few in number //	13	2_
And there he became / a great nation /	13	2
<indeed>[b] *mighty* [c]*and populous*[c] *//*	9	1
[6] *And the Egyptians / treated us badly /*	17	2
and they afflicted us //	7	1_
And they imposed upon us / hard servitude //	20	2
[7] *and we cried out / to YHWH / God of our fathers //*	19	3
And YHWH heard / our voice /	13	2
and he saw our affliction / and our toil / and our distress //	25	3_
[8] *And YHWH brought us forth / from Egypt / with a mighty hand /*	24	3
and an outstretched arm /	11	1
[a]*And with great / terror*[a] *//*	10	2
and with signs / and with portents //	13	2_
[9] *And he brought*\\[a] *us to this place //*	14	1
and he gave to us\\[b] *this land /*	16	1
a land / flowing with milk / and honey //	13	3_
[10] *And now / behold I have brought*\\[a] *the firstfruits /*	18	2
fruit of the ground / that you have given to me / O YHWH"[b] *//*	22	3_
And you shall put it down / before\\[c] *YHWH your God /*	17	3
and you shall bow down / before / YHWH your God //	19	3_
[11] *And you shall celebrate all the bounty /*	10	1
that YHWH your God / has given to you /	15	2
[a]*And to your house*[a] *// you / and the Levite /*	15	3
and the sojourner / who is in your midst // ס	10	2_

Notes

1.a. Reading *paštā'* followed by *zāqēp qāṭôn* as conj.

2.a. Omitting כל, "all," with some Heb. MSS, SP, and LXX.

2.b-b. Omitted in most LXX witnesses. Prosodic analysis supports MT.

2.c. Reading *paštā'* followed by *zāqēp qāṭôn* as conj.

3.a. For MT אלהיך, "your God," reading אלהי, "my God," with LXX τῷ θεῷ μου, "to my God"; I take the כ as dittography.

3.b. Adding אלהי, "my God," to achieve balance in terms of mora count and word count within the larger context of 26:1–19 and 11:26–26:19 as a whole (see *Excursus:* "Deuteronomy as a Numerical Composition"). Syr. adds *'lhk* (= אלהיך, "your God").

4.a. Reading מידיך, "from your hands," for MT מידך, "from your hand," with a few Heb. MSS and LXX^{MS}.

5.a-a. LXX^{B} reads Συριαν ἀπέβαλεν, "he left Syria"; LXX^{MNmin} read Συριαν κατέλειπεν, "he left Syria"; a few Heb. MSS and Cairo Geniza fragments read ארמי אובד, "a wandering Aramean." The familiar translation "a wandering Aramean" (MOFFATT, JB, NRSV, NIV, and New Living Translation [(Wheaton, IL: Tyndale House, 1996) 215]) is retained because of its own poetic quality.

5.b. With a few Heb. MSS, SP^{W}, LXX^{L}, Syr., *Tg. Ps.-J.*, and Vg. adding *waw*-conj., which I read as emphatic.

5.c-c. Omitted in Syr. Prosodic analysis favors MT.

8.a-a. SP reads ובמראה גדול, "and with great visions," for MT ובמרא גדל, "and with great terror"; LXX reads pl.

9.a. Reading *ṭip̄ḥā'* as conj. because of misplaced *'atnāḥ*.

9.b. Reading *paštā'* followed by *zāqēp̄ qāṭôn* as conj.

10.a. Reading *paštā'* followed by *zāqēp̄ qāṭôn* as conj.

10.b. LXX adds γῆν ῥέουσαν γάλα καὶ μέλι, "a land flowing with milk and honey." Prosodic analysis supports MT.

10.c. Reading *paštā'* followed by *zāqēp̄ qāṭôn* as conj.

11.a-a. LXX^{min} (and OL) read σὺ καὶ ἡ οἰκία σου, "you and your household"; LXX^{AO} read καὶ τῇ οἰκίᾳ σου καί, "and to your household"; Caïro Geniza fragments read ולביתיך, "and to your houses," for MT ולביתך, "and to your house."

Form/Structure/Setting

Two liturgical confessions are presented from Moses' perspective prior to the eisodus; but both presuppose possession of the land and the offering to God of the fruit of that land. The language of the first confession is archaic, and is surely premonarchic in origin. It "preserves a ceremony used in the days of the tabernacle before the erection of the temple by Solomon" (G. E. Wright, *IB* 2:483).

The outer limits of 26:1–11 are marked by the *pĕtûḥā'* layout marker after 25:19 and the *sĕtûmā'* layout marker after 26:11. Within 26:1–11, the only discernible marker to indicate structure is the use of first-person direct speech in vv 3b and 5–10a. The declarations here and in vv 13b–15 are the only addresses to God with prescribed wording, which ordinary folk are to recite in a formal liturgical setting, to be found within the Torah (see also 21:7–9 for the closest parallel situation). Each of these two liturgical prayers is to be recited "before YHWH your God" (vv 5, 13); and each refers to the land as a gift from God in fulfillment of his promises to the fathers, a land described as "flowing with milk and honey" (vv 9, 15).

On the basis of prosodic analysis, vv 1–11 may be divided into five subunits:

A	You shall bring the firstfruits to the central sanctuary	26:1–2
B	Presentation of firstfruits to the priest with declaration	26:3–4a
X	Presentation at the altar with recitation of *Magnalia Dei*	26:4b–9
B′	Presentation of firstfruits to YHWH by the worshiper	26:10a
A′	You shall put it down before YHWH and rejoice	26:10b–11

In the center of this structure (vv 4b–9), we find the recitation of what G. von Rad designated the "small historical credo," or what G. E. Wright called the *Magnalia Dei* ("the mighty acts of God"). The outer frame moves from the instructions to bring the firstfruits to the central sanctuary (vv 1–2) to instructions regarding "family worship" at the central sanctuary, which includes the household of the worshiper "and the Levite and the sojourner who is in your midst" (v 11). The inner frame moves from the individual worshiper's presentation of "the basket" containing the firstfruits, which is received from his hand by the priest in charge at that time (vv 3–4a), to the presentation of the firstfruits themselves to YHWH (v 10a). Both of these presentations are followed by specific prayers that the worshiper recites within that liturgical setting.

The law in 25:17–19 (on remembering Amalekite aggression) was used to shape the narrative of Exod 17, shortly before the Israelites arrived at Mount

Sinai. The time span in the narrative from the completion of the building of the tabernacle in Exod 40:33, with its menorah, to the departure from Mount Sinai in Num 10:11 was exactly one month. The law of the firstfruits ceremony in Deut 26:1–11 is reflected in the stories of Num 13–14 at the beginning of the forty years on the edge of the promised land, where once again we meet the Amalekites. In the so-called unholy war, when the Israelites attempted to enter the promised land against the advice of Moses, following the episode with the twelve spies (Num 13) who brought back with them some of the firstfruits of the promised land (Num 13:23–24), "the Amalekites and the Canaanites who lived in that hill country came down and defeated them, pursuing them as far as Hormah" (Num 14:45 NRSV; cf. 14:25). "Now it was the season of the first ripe grapes" (Num 13:20 NRSV) when the spies entered the land; "and they came to the Wadi Eshcol, and cut down from there a branch with a single cluster of grapes, and they carried it on a pole between two of them. They also brought some pomegranates and figs" (Num 13:23 NRSV). Carmichael notes that, "As in Exod 16:3 (related to the law on weights and measures) and Exod 17:3 (related to the law on Amalek), so the Israelites had complained that God's aim was to destroy them (Num 14:3). Their failure to proceed did invoke God's wrath: the complainers were to be denied entry to the land in the future. Paying no attention to this pronouncement, they decided to invade but were defeated by the Amalekites and the Canaanites" (*LNB*, 306).

The law in Deut 26:1–2 states explicitly, "when you come into the land that YHWH your God is giving you, . . . you shall take from the first of [all] the fruit of the ground . . . and you shall put it in a basket, and you shall go to the place that YHWH your God chooses to make his name dwell there." There they were to declare, "I have entered the land that YHWH swore to our fathers to give to us; and the priest shall receive the basket from your hand" (vv 3–4). When the twelve spies returned with their firstfruits, they presented them to Moses and Aaron, the first Israelite priest, and to all the congregation of Israel. Moreover, as Carmichael puts it (*LNB*, 306), "There was no altar there but, perhaps significantly . . . the incident happened at a place whose name means 'sanctuary,' Kadesh."

The law in Deut 26:5–9 then directs the Israelites to make another declaration about YHWH's activity in their behalf from the time of their ancestor Jacob to the present. Carmichael presents impressive arguments to relate this passage to a subsequent attack at Kadesh forty years later on the part of the Edomites (Num 20). Driver also discusses common features of these two incidents at Kadesh in Num 13–14 and 20 ([1896] 31–33). Moreover, as Carmichael observes, "the Edomites and the Amalekites are related (Gen 36:12). Their attacks upon the Israelites are similar to those conflicts between brothers that have been a dominant element in the immediately preceding laws" (*LNB*, 307). In Num 20:3–5 we find the same complaints on the part of the people that were observed earlier in Num 14:3. Indeed, they make specific reference to the previous occasion at Kadesh "when our kindred died before the LORD" (Num 20:3 NRSV; cf. Num 14:36–37). Once again in the wilderness they face the same plight: "It is no place for grain, or figs, or vines, or pomegranates; and there is no water to drink" (Num 20:5 NRSV). Moreover, as was the case in Exod 17 in the incident with the Amalekites, water was provided to them from a rock (Num 20:11).

The structure and content of the speech of "your brother Israel" to the king of Edom in Num 20:14–17, which is patterned after that of the declaration in Deut 26:5–10, may be outlined as follows:

A	You know our adversity, for our ancestors went to Egypt	Num 20:14
B	The Egyptians oppressed us and our ancestors	Num 20:15
X	We cried to YHWH and he heard our voice	Num 20:16a
B′	He sent an angel and brought us out of Egypt to Kadesh	Num 20:16b
A′	Now let us pass through your land	Num 20:17

The focus of attention in this structure is on the exodus from Egypt, as the people cried out to YHWH in their distress and he heard them (v 16a). The inner frame moves from the oppression in Egypt (v 15), to the original "Passover" when YHWH brought them out of Egypt (v 16b). The outer frame moves from a presentation of their past plight, which took the ancestors to Egypt (v 14), to the present request for permission to pass through the land of Edom en route "home" to the promised land (v 17).

The structure of the above speech to the king of Edom is virtually identical to that of the worshiping Israelite in the liturgy of firstfruits at the central sanctuary in Deut 26:5–9, which may be outlined as follows:

A	A wandering Aramean was my father, who went down to Egypt	Deut 26:5
B	The Egyptians oppressed us	Deut 26:6
X	We cried to YHWH and he heard our voice	Deut 26:7
B′	YHWH brought us forth from Egypt with a mighty hand	Deut 26:8
A′	And he brought us to this place	Deut 26:9

The only real difference in the two outlines is the second half of the outer frame. In the first instance (Num 20:17), the desire is to pass through the one remaining territorial obstacle (Edom) that separates the people of Israel from the place that YHWH has chosen to establish his name (Deut 26:9).

Buber calls attention to a sevenfold repetition of the verb נתן, "to give," in the instruction and prayer presented here in 26:1–11 (*On the Bible,* 125), which may be outlined as follows:

A	When you enter the land YHWH *is giving* (נתן) to you	26:1
B	Bring from the land YHWH *is giving* (נתן) to you	26:2
C	I have entered the land YHWH swore *to give* (לתת) to us	26:3
X	The Egyptians imposed (*"gave,"* ויתנו) on us hard servitude	26:6
C′	YHWH brought us to this place and *gave* (ויתן) us this land	26:9
B′	I have brought the firstfruits you *have given* (נתתה) to me	26:10
A′	You shall celebrate the bounty YHWH *has given* (נתן) to you	26:11

"In the first three and last three cases it is used of God's gift to Israel; between the two groups of three, however, there is a strange 'giving,' . . . it is the Egyptians, who 'gave us hard bondage' (Deut. 26:6)" (Buber, *On the Bible,* 125). The outer frame in this concentric structure moves from a statement about the future when YHWH gives Israel its land (v 1) to the injunction to celebrate that gift in public worship (v 11). The second frame moves from a command to bring the firstfruits of the land (v 2) to the response of the individual landowner that he has brought the firstfruits to YHWH (v 10). The innermost frame (vv 3, 9), together with the center (v 6), connects the present act of worship with YHWH's mighty acts in times past when he delivered Israel from the "hard servitude" that Egypt had *given* them, and brought them to the promised land.

Buber also calls attention to the "twice seven times" use of the name of God in this short passage, which displays carefully structured patterning as well. For him, "this working with numbers on the part of the author or the editor has a didactic purpose" (p. 128). The structure may be outlined in a menorah pattern:

A	יהוה אלהיך . . . יהוה אלהיך . . . יהוה אלהיך	26:1–2
B	ליהוה אלהיך	26:3a
C	יהוה	26:3b
X	יהוה אלהיך . . . יהוה אלהיך	26:4–5
C′	יהוה אלהי אבתינו	26:7a
B′	יהוה . . . יהוה . . . יהוה	26:7b–10a
A′	יהוה אלהיך . . . יהוה אלהיך . . . יהוה אלהיך	26:10b–11

The structural frame (A, X, A′) consists of the three clusters of the eight occurrences of the words "YHWH your God"—three in each half of the outer frame (vv 1–2, 10–11), and two in the center (vv 4–5). The innermost frame sets the first occurrence of "YHWH" alone (v 3) over against the phrase "YHWH God of our fathers" (v 7). The second frame sets a ninth occurrence of the name "YHWH your God," to which the preposition "to" is attached (v 3), over against a threefold repetition of the name "YHWH" alone (vv 7–10). The three-plus-one patterning is also evident here in two different ways: the single word יהוה in v 3 is set over against three words יהוה אלהי אבתינו in v 7, and the expression ליהוה אלהיך in v 3 is set over against a group of three occurrences of יהוה in vv 7–10.

Buber observes that a mishnaic report (*m. Bik.* 3) of how the offering of firstfruits was celebrated reads as though the intention was

> to preserve something lost and past for the memory of future generations. We hear how the people from the surrounding country come to Jerusalem with first fruits, those living close at hand with fresh fruits, those far away with dried. In the early morning the procession enters the city headed by pipers, then the sacrificial bull with gilded horns, and behind it the men, bearing baskets filled with fruits and garlanded with grapes, each according to his wealth, golden baskets, silver baskets, and baskets woven from stripped willow-twigs. The artisans of Jersualem come out to meet them, greeting those from each place in turn: "Brothers, men from the place of such-and-such a name, may you come in peace!" But when they stood by the temple hill the king himself took his basket on his shoulders and entered in with them. In the forecourt the Levites sang the verse from the Psalms: "I will exalt Thee, YHVH, for Thou hast drawn me up." The verb described the lifting of the bucket from the well. . . . the quotation comes to mean: "Israel gives thanks to God for raising it from the well of Egypt into the daylight and freedom of its own land." (*On the Bible*, 129–30)

The evidence assembled by Labuschagne on the use of the divine-name numbers in 26:1–11 may be summarized as follows:

Words:	before *ʾatnāḥ*		after *ʾatnāḥ*		
26:1–2	26	+	13	=	39
26:1–4	37	+	34 (= 2 × 17)	=	71
26:5–11	56	+	46	=	102 (= 6 × 17)
26:1–11	93	+	79	=	172

There are 26 words before *ʾatnāḥ* in vv 1–2, 34 (= 2 × 17) words after *ʾatnāḥ* in vv 1–4, and a total of 102 (= 6 × 17) words in vv 5–11. The total of 172 words in 26:1–11 is explained by Labuschagne as the numerical value of the key phrase את־ראשית פרי האדמה, "the firstfruits of the ground," in v 10: (א = 1) + (ת = 22) + (ר = 20) + (א = 1) + (ש = 21) + (י = 10) + (ת = 22) + (פ = 17) + (ר = 20) + (י = 10) + (ה = 5) + (א = 1) + (ד = 4) + (מ = 13) + (ה = 5) = 172.

Comment

1 Buber observes that the opening instruction of this section, "when you come into the land [כי־תבוא אל־הארץ] that YHWH your God is giving you as an inheritance," appears only here and in 17:14, the law of the king (*On the Bible,* 122–23). In 17:14 the people of Israel as a whole are addressed as "you," but here the pronoun refers to the individual landowner as a member of that community, when he appears before YHWH at the central sanctuary with his offering from the firstfruits of the land.

2 The offering of "the first of [all] the fruit of the ground" acknowledges that God is the source and true owner of the land's produce. On the meaning of the term ראשית, "first," see the *Comment* on 18:4, where I interpret the term as the "first processed," and not the first ripe or first harvested crops in their natural state (with J. Milgrom, "First Fruits, OT," *IDBSup,* 336–37). The firstfruits of the new harvest were to be placed "in a basket" (בטנא) and brought "to the place that YHWH your God chooses to make his name dwell there" (i.e., the central sanctuary).

3–4 The offering was to be presented "to the priest who is there in those days" as an act of public worship, within the context of the annual pilgrimage festivals. The first words that the landowner was to speak to the priest show that the dual reference to "you" (pl. and sg.) that Buber observed in v 1 is not accidental: "I declare today to YHWH my God that I have entered the land." As Buber put it, "Here the people and the individual are merged into one. . . . The speaker identifies himself with Israel and speaks in its name" (*On the Bible,* 123). Cf. 5:2–3, where Moses says: "The Lord our God has made a covenant with us on Horeb. The Lord made not this covenant with our fathers, but with us, even us, who are all of us here alive this day" (translation of Buber, p. 124).

The firstfruits were to be presented at the Feast of Weeks and at the Feast of Booths, the two festivals that followed the harvests and the processing of their products. On the connection between the Feast of Weeks and the offering of the firstfruits, see Num 28:26. Unlike Passover and the Feast of Unleavened Bread, the offering of firstfruits was a new religious institution in ancient Israel, for before taking possession of the land, they were not an agricultural people. The individual worshiper was instructed to make a public declaration—"and the priest shall receive the basket from your hand." According to Philo, the word translated "basket" (טנא) refers to the entire ceremony (see Tigay [1996] 239). On the presentation of these firstfruits, see also 18:4–5, which as noted above is located precisely in the center of the central core of Deuteronomy within what I have called the law of the Levites (18:1–8).

5 The liturgical declaration of the individual worshiper at the central sanctuary is in the form of a prayer addressed in the first person to God, which is somewhat analogous to the use of the Lord's Prayer in Christian worship through the ages. The meaning of the Hebrew phrase ארמי אבד is not certain. The translation of אבד as "ready to perish" in KJV still has its advocates. Others suggest "straying" or "fugitive." The translation "wandering Aramean" retains the alliterative quality of the original Hebrew expression and can be understood in poetic fashion to include all of the above options. Buber interprets the word "gone astray" as pastoral language (*On the Bible*, 127), "used when a sheep has lost the flock to which it belongs (Jer. 50:6; Ezek. 34:4, 16; Psalm 119:176)." He called attention to "the same words and with the same meaning, though in quite a different tone of voice," when Abraham (whom Buber describes as a "lost Aramean") told the king of the Philistines about his life: "And it came to pass, when God caused me *to go astray* [התעו אתי] from my father's house" (Gen 20:13). "This clause is probably very ancient, for it is unlikely that Israelite tradition would have chosen to describe Israel's ancestors as 'Arameans' once the Arameans of Damascus became aggressive toward Israel in the ninth century B.C.E." (Tigay [1996] 240). (On the "Proto-Aramean" origins of the patriarchs, see J. C. L. Gibson, "Light from Mari on the Patriarchs," *JSS* 7 [1962] 44–62, esp. 51–53; idem, *JNES* 20 [1961] 217–38, esp. 229–34.) The reference here is to the ancestor Jacob, who went down into Egypt as an old man (Gen 47:9), with perhaps an allusion to Abraham as well, as Buber has observed. And "he sojourned there"—that is, he lived as a resident alien, which stands in sharp contrast with the status of the worshiper who is making his declaration at the central sanctuary in the land of Israel. On the meaning of the phrase "few in number," see the list of the seventy people in Jacob's family "who came into Egypt" in Gen 46:8–27. From that small beginning, Israel "became a great nation, mighty and populous" in the land of Egypt.

6–9 The second part of the confession spells out what happened, as "the Egyptians . . . imposed upon us hard servitude" so that the people "cried out to YHWH," who "heard our voice and . . . brought us forth from Egypt" in the great exodus with its awesome displays of God's power to bring them to the promised land, "a land flowing with milk and honey." Buber notes that no peasant farmer would describe the land of his desire in this way. When the peasant praises his land, he says: "A land of wheat and barley and vines and fig trees and pomegranates" (8:8). For Buber, "The saying refers to representative products that the land offers to the newcomer without the need of any effort on his part: milk, into which the energy of the rich pastures, as it were of one tremendous oasis, is converted and honey for the refreshment of passers-by" (*On the Bible*, 125–26).

10–11 In the eyes of some translators and interpreters, past and present, the statement "you shall put it down before YHWH" is not consistent with v 4, where the offering has already been placed "before the altar of YHWH." Rather than resort to some sort of redactional interpretation that posits conflation of alternative versions, it is best to note the concentric nature of the literary structure that alternates between description of worship and liturgical declaration. Both references are to the same act, which functions as a literary inclusion around the declaration in vv 5–9. The translation "you shall celebrate all the bounty" refers to the pilgrimage festival itself, which includes a celebratory meal at the sanctuary, much like what takes place today in the annual pilgrimage to Mecca in Islam. It should be noted, however, that the firstfruits were deposited in the central sanctuary for the priests (18:4–5). It was the annual tithe that was consumed by the worshiper and his extended family in the pilgrimage festivities at the central sanctuary. The translation "sojourner" for גר (normally part of the familiar triad: "alien," orphan, and widow) is an attempt to call the reader's attention to the inclusion it forms with ויגר, "he sojourned," in v 5, for both words come from the same verbal stem.

The prosodic analysis suggests that the *'atnāḥ* in v 11 does not represent the major break in that verse from a rhythmic point of view, and that the word translated "and to your house(hold)" is defined by what follows. In short, the Levite and the resident alien in our midst are part of our household so far as God is concerned.

Explanation

Individual worshipers in ancient Israel were instructed to present a basket of firstfruits of the harvest to God every year. The firstfruits in question are not to be equated with the so-called wave offering, when one "first put the sickle to the standing grain" (16:9) in early spring, which took place on the day after the Sabbath following the Festival of Unleavened Bread and Passover (Lev 23:10). That presentation of the firstfruits of the new barley crop was ceremonial in nature, in anticipation of the barley and wheat harvests to be completed in the next seven weeks. It marked the beginning of the countdown of forty-nine days (seven weeks) to the Feast of Weeks at which time the liturgy of 26:1–11 was presented in the ceremony of the presentation of firstfruits at the central sanctuary.

The basket of firstfruits was a token payment of the tithe, which was presented when the harvest was completed. The firstfruits of summer and fall produce were presented in like manner at the Festival of Booths (Sukkoth) in the fall. The presentation of firstfruits was a thanksgiving offering that the worshiper brought to the central sanctuary to "celebrate all the bounty that YHWH your God has given to you and to your house" (v 11).

The confession of faith that every worshiper recited before the priest at the altar explains the meaning of the ceremony. Before the basket was placed in front of the altar, the one offering sacrifice began his presentation with an acknowledgment that he has "entered the land that YHWH swore to our fathers to give to us" (v 3). The basket was then taken by the priest, who placed it before the altar (v 4), as the worshiper continued his confession of faith, recalling the bitter experience of slavery in Egypt from which God delivered them "with a mighty hand and an outstretched arm and with great terror and with signs and with portents" to bring them "to this place . . . a land flowing with milk and honey" (vv 8–9). The worshiper then declared that he had brought the firstfruits to YHWH and bowed down in worship there at the altar (v 10). When the service was completed, the offerer was charged to "celebrate all the bounty that YHWH your God has given to you" in a feast, which included the worshiper's entire household, along with "the Levite and the sojourner" (v 11). It is good that we should be cheerful in the presentation of our gifts and dues to God for his provision, and that we should enjoy the use of them in fellowship with our family, those committed to God's work, and those in our midst who are in special need.

2. *Declaration of the Triennial Tithe (26:12–15)*

Bibliography

Airoldi, N. "La Cosidetta 'Decima' Israelitica Antica." *Bib* 55 (1974) 179–210. **Baumgarten, J. M.** "On the Non-Literal Use of *maʿăśēr/dekatē*." *JBL* 103 (1984) 245–61. **Bayliss, M.** "The Cult of Dead Kin in Assyria and Babylonia." *Iraq* 35 (1973) 115–25. **Cazelles, H.** "Sur le rituel du Deutéronome (Deut 26,14)." *RB* 55 (1948) 54–71. **Fohrer, G.** "Twofold Aspects of Hebrew Words." In *FS D. Winton Thomas.* 1968. 95–103, esp. 99. **Galling, K.** "Der Beichtspiegel: Ein gattungsgeschichtliches Studium." *ZAW* 47 (1929) 125–30. **Gray, J.** *The Legacy of Canaan.* 1965. 65, 253. ———. "Ugarit." In *Archaeology and Old Testament Study.* Ed. D. Winton Thomas. Oxford: Clarendon, 1967. 149–50. **Grieshammer, R.** "Zum 'Sitz im Leben' des negativen Sündenbekenntnisses." In *XVIII. Deutscher Orientalistentag vom 1.–5. Oktober 1972 in Lübeck. Vorträge.* Ed. W. Voigt. ZDMG Sup II. Wiesbaden: Steiner, 1974. 19–25. **Hoffner, H. A.** "Second Millennium Antecedents to the Hebrew *ʾôḇ*." *JBL* 86 (1967) 385–401. **Kutsch, E.** "'Trauerbräuche' und 'Selbstminderungsriten' im alten Testament." In K. Lüthi, E. Kutsch, and W. Dantine. *Drei Wiener Antrittsreden.* ThSt 78. Zurich: EVZ, 1965. 25–42. **Lewis, T. J.** *Cults of the Dead.* 1989. 97, 102–3. **Rabban, N.** "*Lipney YHWH.*" *Tarbiz* 23 (1952) 1–8 (Heb.). **Sheriffs, D. C. T.** "The Phrases *ina IGI DN* and *lipĕnēy Yhwh* in Treaty and Covenant Contexts." *JNSL* 7 (1979) 55–68. **Sukenik, E. L.** "Arrangements for the Cult of the Dead in Ugarit and Samaria." In *Memorial Lagrange.* Paris: Gabalda, 1940. 59–65. **Wildberger, H.** *Jahwes Eigentumsvolk.* ATANT 37. Zürich: Theologischer Verlag, 1960. 18–19, 92–93 **Wilson, I.** *Out of the Midst of the Fire: Divine Presence in Deuteronomy.* SBLDS 151. Atlanta: Scholars Press, 1995. 181–87. **Yahuda, A. S.** *The Language of the Pentateuch in Its Relation to Egyptian.* London: Oxford UP, 1933. 271–73. **Zakovitch, Y.** "Some Remnants of Ancient Laws in the Deuteronomic Code." *ILR* 9 (1974) 346–51.

Translation and Prosodic Analysis

Declaration of the Triennial Tithe at Local Sanctuaries [(5:5):(6:4):(4:6):(5:5)]

12 *When you finish / tithing*[a] */ all the tithe of your produce /*	18	3
in the third year / the year of the tithe //	18	2_
[b]*You shall give*[b] *it to the Levite /*	11	1
<and>[c] *to the alien / <and>*[c] *to the orphan and to the widow /*	18	2
that they may eat in your towns / and they may be satisfied //	18	2_
13 *And you shall say / before YHWH your God /*	17	2
"I have purged the sacred portion out of the[a] *house /*	12	1

And also I have given it to the Levite / 11 1
and[b] to the alien / to[c] the orphan and[d] to the widow / 17 2_
According to all your commandment[e] / that you commanded me // 16 2
I have not passed over any of your commandments[f] / 13 1
indeed I have not forgotten // 10 1_
14*<And>[a] I have not eaten any of it / as my own wealth[b] /* 17 2
and[c] I have not purged any of it / while unclean / 16 2_
And[d] I have not given any of it\[e] to the dead // 15 1
I have hearkened / to the voice\[f] of YHWH my God / 16 2
I have done / [g]according to all / that[g] you commanded me // 18 3_
15[a]*Look down[a] from your holy habitation / from the heavens /* 18 2
and bless your people / Israel / and\[b] the ground / 19 3_
Which you have given\[c] to us // 10 1
just as you swore\[d] to our fathers / 15 1
a land / flowing (with) milk / and honey // ס 14 3_

Notes

12.a. Prosodic analysis supports MT לְעַשֵּׂר, "tithing," as the irregular inf. constr. rather than the emendation to לְעַשֵּׂר, "to tithe," suggested by *BHS.*

12.b-b. LXX reads the clause τὸ δεύτερον ἐπιδέκατον δώσεις, "the second tithe you shall give" (= שנת המעשר נתתה).

12.c. Adding *waw*-conj. with some Heb. MSS, Cairo Geniza fragments, LXX, Syr., and Vg.

13.a. LXX reads ἐκ τῆς οἰκίας μου, "out of my house." The same meaning is conveyed without emending MT הַבַּיִת, "the house," to בֵּתִי, "my house," which would add one mora to the length of the line.

13.b. Many Heb. MSS, SP, a codex of LXX, and *Tg. Ps.-J.* omit *waw*-conj.

13.c. Some Heb. MSS, LXX, Syr., and Vg. add *waw*-conj.

13.d. One LXX codex omits *waw*-conj.

13.e. One Heb. MS, SP, and Syr. read מִצוֹתֶיךָ, "your commandments." Prosodic analysis slightly supports MT מצותך, "your commandment," with one less mora.

13.f. Cairo Geniza fragments and LXX read מצותך, "your commandment." Prosodic analysis supports MT.

14.a. Adding *waw*-conj. with a few Heb. MSS, LXX, and Syr. to achieve closer balance in mora count.

14.b. Interpreting באני with Craigie and others as meaning "strength" or "wealth" (see *Comment* below).

14.c. All but one of the LXX codices omit *waw*-conj.

14.d. LXX except for the Lucianic recension omits *waw*-conj.

14.e. Reading *ṭiphā'* as conj. because of misplaced *'atnāḥ.*

14.f. Reading *pašṭā'* followed by *zāqēp qāṭôn* here as conj.

14.g-g. LXX reads καθά, "just as" (= כאשר), for MT ככל אשר, "according to all that." Prosodic analysis supports MT.

15.a-a. SP reads השקף for MT השקיפה, "look down," with no change in meaning. Prosodic analysis supports MT.

15.b. Reading *pašṭā'* followed by *zāqēp qāṭôn* here as conj.

15.c. Reading *ṭiphā'* as conj. because of misplaced *'atnāḥ.*

15.d. Reading *pašṭā'* followed by *zāqēp qāṭôn* as conj.

Form/Structure/Setting

The triennial cycle of Torah readings in ancient Israel is related to the tradition of a special tithe in Deuteronomy, which was presented at the end of every third year (see 14:28–29 and *Excursus:* "The Triennial Cycle of Torah Readings in Palestinian Judaism"). Since tithes were not presented in the seventh year of a sabbatical cycle, four years elapsed between the second "poor-tithe" and the first "poor-tithe" of the next cycle. According to the Mishnah the declaration of the "poor-tithe" was abolished in late Second Temple times (135–104 B.C.E.) by the high priest Yohanan Hyrcanus (Tigay [1996] 242).

The boundaries of the literary unit in 26:12–15 are marked by *sĕtûmā'* layout markers at the beginning and end. The shift to first-person direct speech in v 13 serves to set the actual declaration itself off as a separate literary unit, which may be outlined in a menorah pattern:

A	I have purged the sacred portion from my household	26:13ab
B	According to all your commandment, which you commanded me	26:13c
C	I have not forgotten	26:13d
X	I have not purged it while unclean	26:14a
C′	I have obeyed the voice of YHWH my God	26:14b
B′	According to all that you commanded me	26:14c
A′	Look down from the heavens and bless your people Israel	26:15

In the outer frame of this structure the worshiper declares that he has "purged" (בערתי) the sacred portion from his household as commanded (v 13), and that it is now YHWH's turn to come through with his promised blessing (v 15). The center reinforces the declaration as the worshiper swears he has avoided any ritual impurity that might defile his offering (v 14a). The inner frame states the case even more emphatically as the worshiper insists that he has not forgotten anything (v 13d), and that he has been obedient to the voice of YHWH his God (v 14b).

The declaration of the triennial tithe is in three parts: a positive statement in which the worshiper declares his fulfillment of the law relating to the tithe in the third year (v 13), a negative statement that affirms that the task has been carried out properly (v 14), and a prayer for God's continued blessing on both the people of Israel and the ground that brings forth the harvest (v 15).

This law on the triennial tithe (26:12–15) shapes further details in the narrative (Num 20) of Edom's refusal to grant Israel passage through their land (cf. Carmichael, *LNB,* 309–11). The references to "the sacred portion" (הקדש) in v 13b and "your holy habitation" (מעון קדשך) in v 15a are reflected in the statement in Num 20:1 that the people stayed "in Kadesh" (בקדש).

Comment

12 According to the law of the tithe in 14:22–27, "the tithe of your produce" was presented annually at the central sanctuary, where it was consumed by the worshiper and his household during the three pilgrimage festivals. At the end of every three years, the tithe was presented in the local towns to provide for needs of the "Levite," the "alien," the "orphan," and the "widow" (see 14:28–29). The phrase "in the third year, the year of the tithe," refers to the three-year cycle, which was repeated and then followed by the sabbatical year, when no tithe was given because no crops were planted.

13 The phrase "before YHWH" refers to God's presence, as experienced in the context of formal worship. When such worship is at the central sanctuary during one of the three annual pilgrimage festivals, the phrase "the place where YHWH chooses to establish his name" is included in the immediate context, which is not the case here. In this instance the worshiper addressed God at a local assembly, where the triennial tithe was deposited.

14 The translation "I have not eaten . . . as my own wealth [באני]" is uncertain. The word באני is sometimes rendered "while in mourning." The reading here is based on that of Craigie, "in my own wealth" ([1976] 323), using the arguments of Fohrer (*FS D. Winton Thomas,* 98). Though Galling has described the following three negative statements as a confession of innocence by which the individual declares his fitness to participate in formal worship (*ZAW* 47 [1929] 125–30), Mayes has correctly shown that ritual purity is not the primary focus in this instance ([1981] 336). The statement "I have not purged any of it while unclean" is necessary because of Num 19:22. The statement "I have not given any of it to the dead" refers to the common practice in antiquity of providing food and drink for the dead in Sheol. "In some graves excavated at Samaria, the capital of the northern kingdom, holes were found in the floors, similar to holes found in tombs at Ugarit, which served as receptacles for food and drink offerings to the dead. The Torah does not forbid this practice, but because contact with the dead is ritually defiling, it prohibits the use of the tithe for it" (Tigay [1996] 244; Lewis, *Cults of the Dead,* 97, 102–3). Cazelles proposed an interesting reading of the text (*RB* 55 [1948] 54–71), in which he interpreted the words באני and בטמא as direct objects of the verbs in the sense of "(the bread) of mourning" and "the unclean thing," referring to a cultic meal on behalf of the god Baal, who is "the dead" (למת) here. Though his interpretation fits the context well, it remains uncertain, as Mayes has noted ([1981] 336–37).

15 According to Deuteronomy, God's "holy habitation" (מעון קדשך) is in "the heavens" and not in some building made by human beings. "The words 'from heaven' seem to be an explanatory appendage intended to prevent misconstruing the expression 'holy habitation' as referring to the sanctuary" (Weinfeld, *DDS,* 198). As Tigay notes, the prayer that God would "bless your people Israel" "is typical of prescribed prayers in Judaism: the individual does not pray on his own behalf but on behalf of the entire Jewish people or the whole human race" ([1996] 244).

Explanation

The law of the triennial tithe appears in 14:28–29, which stipulates that every three years the tithe was to be used locally "in your towns" (14:28; 26:12). The principle behind the law of the triennial "poor-tithe" remains applicable: we are commanded to give of our means to assist the poor. It would be well if worshipers today faced a public moment of accountability in such matters, as did the people of ancient Israel.

B. Mutual Commitments between God and Israel in Covenant Renewal (26:16–19)

Bibliography

Buis, P. "La nouvelle alliance." *VT* 18 (1968) 1–15. **Cody, A.** "When Is the Chosen People Called a *Gôy?*" *VT* 14 (1964) 1–6. **Coppens, J.** "La doctrine biblique sur l'amour de Dieu et du prochain." *ETL* 40 (1964) 252–99. **Eichrodt, W.** "Darf Man heute noch von einem Gottesbund mit Israel reden?" *TZ* 30 (1974) 193–206. **Falk, Z. W.** *Hebrew Law in Biblical Times.* Jerusalem: Wahrmann Books, 1964. 134–53. **Levanon, M.** " *he'marta, he'emirkha.*" *Sinai* 51 (1962) 238–40 (Heb.). **Levin, C.** *Die Verheissung des neuen Bundes.* FRLANT 137. Göttingen: Vandenhoeck & Ruprecht, 1985. **Licht, J.** "The Biblical Claim of Establishment." *Shnaton* 4 (1980) 107–8 (Heb.). **Lohfink, N.** "Dt 26,17–19 und die 'Bundesformel.'" *ZKT* 91 (1969) 517–53 (repr. in *Studium zum Deuteronomium I.* 1990. 211–61). **McCarthy, D. J.** *Treaty and Covenant.* 2nd ed. 1981. 182–85. **Mercati, G.** "Una Singolare Versione di Dt 26,17–18 e l'Originale di Essa." *Bib* 24 (1943) 201–4. **Muffs, Y.** *Love and Joy.* New York: Jewish Theological Seminary, 1992. 51. **Perlitt, L.** *Bundestheologie im Alten Testament.* 1970. 106–7. **Schmid, H. H.** "Ich will euer Gott sein, und ihr sollt mein Volk sein: Die sogenannte Bundesformel und die Frage nach der Mitte des Alten Testaments." In *FS G. Bornkamm.* 1980. 1–25. **Vriezen, T. C.** "Das Hiphil von *'amar* in Dt 26,17–18." *JEOL* 17 (1964) 207–10. **Wiener, H. M.** "Zur Deuteronomiumfrage." *MGWJ* 72 (1928) 24–48. **Wildberger, H.** *Jahwes Eigentumsvolk.* ATANT 37. Zurich: Theologischer Verlag, 1960. 18–19, 92–93. **Wolff, H. W.** "Jahwe als Bundesmittler." *VT* 6 (1956) 316–20.

Translation and Prosodic Analysis

Mutual Commitments between God and Israel in Covenant Renewal [(8:7):7:8]

16 *THIS DAY / YHWH your God commands you to do /* 22 2
these statutes / and the judgments // 18 2
And you shall be careful to do / them / with all your heart / 22 3
and with all your soul // 7 1_
17a *YHWH you have declared / TODAY //* 11 2
to be your God / and to walk in his ways / 21 2
And to keep his statutes and his commands / 14 1
[b]*and his judgments*[b] */ and to hearken to his voice //* 17 2_
18a *And YHWH / has declared you TODAY /* 13 2
to be[b] *his / treasured people /* 11 2
As he has spoken [דבר] [c]*to you*[c] *//* 7 1
so keep \[d] *all his commandments //* 10 1
19 [a]*so that he will set you high /* 9 1_
Above all the nations / that he has made / for praise / 17 3
and[b] *for fame and for honor //* 10 1
And for you to be |[c] *a holy people /* 11 2
to YHWH your God / just as he has spoken [דבר] *//* ס 16 2_

Notes

17.a. In *BHS* Hemple argues that the text of vv 17–19 has been disordered and suggests rearrangement. Prosodic analysis supports the text as received in MT.

17.b-b. The term ומשפטיו, "and his judgments," is omitted in one Heb. MS, SP, and LXX. The prosodic analysis here supports MT.

18.a. See *Note* 17.a.

18.b. Some LXX texts read γενέσθαι σε, "that you should be" (= לִהְיוֹתְךָ), which appears to be an interpretive gloss. Prodosic analysis supports MT.

18.c. The term לְךָ, "to you," is omitted in one Heb. MS and some LXX witnesses. *Tg. Ps.-J.* reads pl. suff. The prosodic analysis supports MT.

18.d. Reading *ṭip̱ḥāʾ* as conj. because of the misplaced *sillûq*.

19.a. See *Note* 17.a.

19.b. The conjunction is omitted in some Heb. MSS, SP, and LXX^{MS}, which is possible in terms of the prosodic analysis presented here.

19.c. Reading *metheg* plus *dargā* on וְלִהְיֹתְךָ, "and for you to be," as disj. Letteris has two *methegs* on this word.

Form/Structure/Setting

G. E. Wright says vv 7–18 "are couched in formal, legal phraseology so that the people can have no doubt of the binding nature of the pact which they have entered" (*IB* 2:488). The power of these concluding injunctions in the laws of Deuteronomy is apparent to anyone who takes the time and effort to read the words out loud.

The text here is divided into two parts that present mutual commitments made between the people of Israel (vv 16–17) and YHWH their God (vv 18–19). The beginning of each section is marked by temporal terms ("this day" and "today") that suggest that we are dealing with ritual activity that is repeated (i.e., brought into the cultic present). The first section is framed by repetition of the words "statutes" and "judgments" (vv 16 and 17), whereas the second is framed by the parallel expressions "his treasured people" (v 18) and "a holy people to YHWH your God" (v 19).

The carefully constructed two-part unit of thought in vv 16–19 functions as the center of a concentric structure that connects the two halves of the inner frame of Deuteronomy:

Deut 26:16–19 as the Connecting Link for the Inner Frame

A	Blessing and curse in a covenant renewal under Moses	11:26–28
B	Blessing and curse in a covenant renewal at Shechem	11:29–32
X	Mutual commitments made between YHWH and Israel	26:16–19
B′	Blessing and curse in a covenant renewal at Shechem	27:1–26
A′	Blessing and curse in a covenant renewal under Moses	28:1–69 (Eng. 29:1)

The final two paragraphs in Deut 11 both deal with the matter of blessings and curses in the context of covenant renewal, with an important distinction. In 11:26–28 the focus is in the present with Moses on the plains of Moab; but in 11:29–32 the focus shifts to a time in the future, "when YHWH your God brings you into the land that you are about to enter to possess it, then you shall put the blessing on Mount Gerizim and the curse on Mount Ebal" (11:29).

In the second half of the inner frame, the situation is reversed. Deut 27 concerns the future: "in the day when you cross over the Jordan into the land that YHWH your God is giving to you, and you shall set up for yourselves great stones and . . . plaster them with plaster" (27:2). The words of the Torah are to be written on these stones, and the people are commanded to set them up on Mount Ebal (27:4). At that time, the tribes shall be assembled "to bless the people on Mount Gerizim" and "for the curse on Mount Ebal" (27:12–13). In Deut 28 the focus shifts back to the present with Moses calling the people of Israel to decision by announcing the blessings that accompany obedience and the curses that fall on disobedience to YHWH's commandments.

The center in the above structure becomes the final paragraph in Deut 26, which functions as the conclusion to the exposition of the statutes and ordinances in Deut 12–26, and the connecting link between Deut 11 and 27. At the same time, it is also a connecting link within another concentric structure that links the central core (Deut 12–26) and the section on the covenant ceremony in Deut 27–30:

Deut 26:16–19 as the Connecting Link with the Central Core

A	Ceremony of the firstfruits—first year in the land	26:1–11
B	Tithe declaration—every three years in the land	26:12–15
X	Mutual commitments between God and Israel	26:16–19
B′	Future covenant renewal at Shechem (every seven years)	27:1–26
A′	Present covenant renewal in Moab under Moses	28:1–69 (Eng. 29:1)

On either side of the summary statement about the mutual commitments between God and Israel we find two separate descriptions of liturgical activity. The outer pair in this structure focuses on the present (or the immediate future, under Joshua), with a renewal of the covenant under Moses in the plains of Moab (Deut 28:1–69) set over against the firstfruits ceremony that the people are commanded to observe in the promised land, "When you have come into the land that YHWH your God is giving you as an inheritance and you possess it" (26:1). The first half of the inner pair in this structural unit focuses on the payment of "the tithe of your produce in the third year (the year of the tithe), you shall give it to the Levites, to the alien, to the orphan, and to the widow, that they may eat in your towns and they may be satisfied" (26:12). The other half is concerned with the regular renewal of the covenant to be carried out at Shechem, in which the twelve tribes take their stand on Mount Gerizim and Mount Ebal to proclaim the blessings and curses—in times to come.

The evidence assembled by Labuschagne on the use of the divine-name numbers in 26:16–19 within its larger literary context may be summarized as follows:

Words:	before *ʾatnāḥ*		after *ʾatnāḥ*		
26:12–15	56	+	28	=	84
26:16–18	35	+	21	=	46 (= 2 × 23)
26:19	10	+	7	=	17
26:12–18	81	+	49 (= 7 × 7)	=	130 (= 5 × 26)

The final verse in Deuteronomy's central core (Deut 12–26), which has 17 (the alternate divine-name number) words, is carefully integrated into its immediate literary context with a total of 130 (= 5 × 26) words in 26:12–18. Within this section, there are a total of 46 (= 2 × 23, the number for כבוד, "glory") words in vv 16–18 and 17 words in v 19—signifying that the ancient scribes ("counters") have labored to the "glory of YHWH."

Comment

16–17 These two verses, which summarize the commitment made by the people of Israel in their covenant with YHWH, are framed by repetition of the words "statutes" (חקים) and "judgments" (משפטים, vv 16 and 17), which appear also in 12:1 to form an envelope around the laws of the central core (Deut 12–26); and by repetition of the verbal root צוה, "to command": "God is commanding you" (מצוך, v 16) and "his commands" (מצותיו, v 17). The command "to do them with all your heart and with all your soul" brings to mind the Great Commandment in 6:5–6 and 10:12–13, 20–22, to love God with "all your heart and with all your being" and to "walk in all his ways"—that is, "to fear YHWH," which is the beginning of spiritual wisdom. "Today" (היום) means both the original day on which Moses spoke these words and each subsequent day when the ceremony of covenant renewal was held. The verb האמרת, "you have declared," is the hiphil from אמר, "to say," which appears only here and in v 18 below. S. Wagner translates it with the meaning "proclaim" (*TDOT* 1:328–29). As Mayes put it, "Whatever translation is adopted, each declaration refers to the obligations undertaken by both parties to the covenant, and the reference is to a solemn legal act whereby the covenant is agreed" ([1981] 339).

18–19 These two verses are framed by reference to the special relationship between YHWH and his people: the people of Israel are "his treasured people" (v 18). Consequently they are called to "be a holy people to YHWH" (v 19). The parallel text in Exod 19:6 has "a holy nation." In Deuteronomy, however, the term for "nations" (גוי) is reserved for non-Israelite peoples, as Mayes observes ([1981] 339). The phrase "just as he has spoken" is repeated to form a frame around the concluding summation, in which the people are urged once again to keep all of YHWH's commands (v 18), "so that he will set you high above all the nations" (v 19) to be an object of praise and honor to YHWH among those peoples.

The hiphil of אמר, which appears nowhere else in the Hebrew Bible, is to be taken in an intensive and not a causative sense. Israel does not cause God to say anything, nor does God cause Israel to say or do anything. The commitments made between God and Israel in covenant renewal are mutual. The translation "YHWH has declared you" is intended to suggest that the covenant relationship is seen as a marriage, as argued by M. A. Friedman ("Israel's Response to Hosea 2:17b: 'You Are My Husband,'" *JBL* 99 [1980] 20 n. 14). Z. W. Falk suggests that the mutual commitments of vv 16–17 reflect a marriage ceremony between YHWH and his bride, Israel. He points out that in subsequent rabbinic literature מאמר "had the meaning of the marriage formula used by the levir and of the oral declaration of divorce" (*Hebrew Law in Biblical Times* [1964] 135).

Explanation

The brief exhortation in 26:16–19 functions as the conclusion to the exposition of the law in Deut 5–26, which was used in a covenant renewal ceremony in ancient Israel. It summarizes what has happened in that ceremony, where the words "this day" and "today" (vv 16, 17, 18) refer to both the original day on which Moses spoke and each subsequent time thereafter when the ceremony was held. S. J. DeVries has made a detailed study of the use of the word "today" (and its equivalents, which appear 49 times in Deuteronomy), in which he concludes: "his revelation is now. He is very alive and present. Israel must respond one way or another, because the voice of God is near. The word they must obey is not far off in the heavens or belonging to remote antiquity. Therefore do not defer your choice to still another 'today'!" ("The Development of the Deuteronomic Promulgation Formula," *Bib* 55 [1974] 316; see Maxwell [1987] 288–89; for an expanded discussion of this matter, see S. J. De Vries, *Yesterday, Today and Tomorrow* [Grand Rapids, Eerdmans, 1975).

The recitation of the laws that God revealed to Moses is now complete, and attention shifts to the covenant relationship between God and his chosen people. The people solemnly declare that YHWH is their God and that they will obey him (v 17); and God, on his part, affirms that he will set them "high above all the nations . . . for praise and for fame and for honor" and that Israel shall be a holy people (vv 18–19). "These concluding verses . . . lead by implication to the substance of chs. 5–11, in which the intimate, personal relationship with God is emphasized, one which is the substance of the covenant agreement. Obedience now assumes a new aspect; it is not so much a legal duty as a response to a personal relationship with the community's Lord and Savior" (Wright, *IB* 2:488).

Though Israel, as the people of God, were commanded to observe the laws as delineated in Deut 12–26, the matter of greatest importance is their attitude. That they were chosen as YHWH's "treasured people" is not a basis for pride. The privilege carries a heavy responsibility. If their obedience to God's laws comes from the heart, then God will exalt them in such a manner that they become a source of praise and honor among the nations.

How very different the situation often became through the ages. We tend to set our focus on external matters, in the mere keeping of those many commandments. When we do so, we lose sight of what it means to be God's "treasured people" whom he sets "high above all the nations that he has made—for praise, and for fame, and for honor" (v 19). The object of that praise is not the people of Israel; it is God himself. The name we are to lift up is not ours, but his. It is not our honor that is spoken of here, but his. To be a holy people is to be a people set apart for God, and for that special task among the nations to which he has called us. The keeping of God's commandments is not the means of our own vindication or justification before God. God chose Israel to be a special people on the basis of his own lovingkindness—it is a matter of God's grace, and God's grace alone. It is our heartfelt response to God's love and commitment to us as his "treasured possession" that he desires of us by means of obedience to his commands. That is what will bring forth his praise and honor among the nations.

C. Writing the Torah on Stones and Covenant Renewal at Shechem (27:1–26)

Bibliography

Bowman, J. "The Samaritans and the Book of Deuteronomy." *GOST* 17 (1957–58) 9–18. **Bülow, S.** "Der Berg des Fluches (Ebal)." *ZDPV* 73 (1957) 100–107, esp. 104 n. 14. **Eisenbeis, W.** *Die Wurzel* שלם *im Alten Testament.* BZAW 113. Berlin: de Gruyter, 1969. 234–39. **Eissfeldt, O.** "Deuteronomium und Hexateuch." *Mitteilungen des Institus für Orientforschung* 12 (1966) 17–39 (repr. in *KlSchr* 4:238–58). ———. "Gilgal or Shechem?" In *FS G. H. Davies.* 1970. Repr. 1983. 90–101. **Fabry, H.-J.** "Noch ein Dekalog! Die Thora des lebendigen Gottes in ihrer Wirkungsgeschichte: Ein Versuch zu Deuteronomium 27." In *Im Gesprach mit dem dreinen Gott: Elemente einer trinitarischen Theologie. FS W. Breuning.* Dusseldorf: Patmos, 1985. 75–96. **Jaroš, K.** *Sichem: Eine archäologische und religionsgeschichtliche Studie mit besonderer Berücksichtigung von Jos 24.* OBO 11. Fribourg: Universitaires, 1976. **Langlamet, F.** *Gilgal et les récits de la traversée du Jourdain (Jos III-IV).* CahRB 11. Paris: Gabalda, 1969. 67–68, 83. **Lewy, I.** "The Puzzle of Deuteronomy 27: Blessings Announced, but Curses Noted." *VT* 12 (1962) 207–11. **L'Hour, J.** "L'alliance de Sichem." *RB* 69 (1962) 5–36, 161–84. **Mölle, H.** *Der sogenannte Landtag zu Sichem.* FB 42. Würzburg: Echter, 1980. **Nielsen, E.** *Shechem: A Traditio-Historical Investigation.* 2nd ed. Copenhagen: Gad, 1959. **Schmitt, G.** *Der Landtag von Sichem.* AzT 1.15. Stuttgart: Calwer, 1964. **Schulz, H.** "Die Fluchreihe Dtn 27." In *Das Todesrecht im Alten Testament.* BZAW 114. Berlin: Töpelmann, 1969. 61–71. **Seebass, H.** "Erwägungen zum altisraelitischen System der zwölf Stämme." *ZAW* 90 (1978) 196–220, esp. 213–15. **Soggin, J. A.** "Zwei umstrittene Stellen aus dem Überlieferungskreis um Schekem." *ZAW* 73 (1961) 78–87. **Tsumura, D. T.** "Hab 2,2 in the Light of Akkadian Legal Practice." *ZAW* 94 (1982) 294–95. **Ulrich, E.** "4QJoshua[a] and Joshua's First Altar in the Promised Land." In *New Qumran Texts and Studies.* Ed. G. J. Brooke. Leiden: Brill, 1994.89–104. **Wächter, L.** "Das Baumheiligtum bei Sichem." *FolOr* 17 (1976) 71–86. ———. "Die Bedeutung Sichems bei der Landnahme der Israeliten." *Wissenschaftlich Zeitschrift der . . . Rostock* 17 (1968) 411–19. **Weinfeld, M.** "Traces of Assyrian Treaty Formulae in Deuteronomy." *Bib* 41 (1960) 417–27. **Wright, G. E.** *Shechem: The Biography of a Biblical City.* New York: McGraw-Hill, 1965. **Wright, G. R. H.** "Shechem and League Shrines." *VT* 21 (1971) 572–603.

1. Shechem Ceremony Dramatizing Israel's Covenant Responsibilities (27:1–10)

Bibliography

Anbar, M. "The Story about the Building of an Altar on Mount Ebal: The History of Its Composition and the Question of the Centralization of the Cult." In *Das Deuteronomium.* Ed. N. Lohfink. 1985. 304–9. **Bowman, J.** "The Exegesis of the Pentateuch among the Samaritans and among the Rabbis." *OTS* 8 (1950) 220–62, esp. 228. **Brichto, H. C.** *Problem of "Curse."* 1963. 184–86. **Cazelles, H.** "Les structures successives de la '*berît*' dans l'Ancien

Testament." In *FS R. Martin-Achard.* 1984. 2–7, 33–46, esp. 38. **Coogan, M. D.** "Of Cults and Cultures: Reflections on the Interpretation of Archaeological Information." *PEQ* 119 (1987) 1–8. **Dexinger, F.** "Das Garizimgebot im Dekalog der Samaritaner." In *FS W. Kornfeld.* 1977. 111–33, esp. 127–28. **Falk, Z. W.** "Sociological Notes on Deuteronomy." *DiIs* 3 (1972) 37–43, esp. 43. **Gill, D.** " *Thysia* and *šělāmîm*: Questions to R. Schmid's *Das Bundesopfer in Israel.*" *Bib* 47 (1966) 255–62. **Jacob ben Aaron.** "Mount Gerizim the One True Sanctuary." *BSac* 64 (1907) 489–518, esp. 508. **Janowski, B.** "Erwägungen zur Vorgeschichte des israelitischen *šělāmîm*-Opfers." *UF* 12 (1980) 231–59. **Kempinski, A.** "Joshua's Altar—An Iron Age I Watchtower." *BARev* 12.1 (1986) 42–53. **Lemaire, A.** "L'inscription de Balaam trouvée à Deir ʿAlla: Épigraphie." In *Proceedings of the International Congress on Biblical Archaeology, April 1984.* Jerusalem: Israel Exploration Society, 1985. 313–25, esp. 322 **Levine, B. A.** *In the Presence of the Lord.* SJLA 5. Leiden: Brill, 1974. 3–52, 118–22. **Licht, J.** "The Biblical Claim of Establishment." *Shnaton* 4 (1981) 98–128 (Heb.; Eng. summary, vii). **Lods, A.** "Review of Löhr, *Deuteronomium;* Wiener, *Altars;* Siebens, *Origine.*" *RHR* 50 (1929) 229–37, esp. 232–34. **MacDonald, J.** "Samaritans." *EncJud* 14:726–58. **Machlin, M.** *Joshua's Altar: The Dig at Mount Ebal.* New York: Morrow, 1991. **Merendino, R. P.** "Dt 27,1–8: Eine literarkritische und überlieferungsgeschichtliche Untersuchung." *BZ* 24 (1980) 194–207. **Milgrom, J.** "Sacrifices and Offerings." *IDBSup.* 769. **Muhly, J.** "How Iron Technology Changed the Ancient World." *BARev* 8.6 (1982) 46. **Nelson, R. D.** "Josiah in the Book of Joshua." *JBL* 100 (1981) 531–40, esp. 533. **Nielsen, E.** "Historical Perspectives and Geographical Horizons: On the Question of North-Israelite Elements in Deuteronomy." In *Law, History, and Tradition.* Copenhagen: Gad, 1983. 82–92. ———. *Shechem: A Traditio-Historical Investigation.* Copenhagen: Gad, 1955. 59–61. **Rothstein, W.** *Die Juden und Samaritaner.* BWAT 3. Leipzig: Hinrichs, 1908. **Shanks, H.** "Two Israelite Cult Sites Now Questioned." *BARev* 14.1 (1988) 48–52. **Vaux, R. de.** *Studies in Old Testament Sacrifice.* 1964. 32–33. **Walkenhorst, K. H.** *Der Sinai im liturgischen Verständis der deuteronomistischen und priesterlichen Tradition.* BBB 33. Bonn: Hanstein, 1969. **Weinfeld, M.** "The Emergence of the Deuteronomic Movement: The Historical Antecedents." In *Das Deuteronomium.* Ed. N. Lohfink. 1985. 83. **Wiener, H. M.** *The Altars of the Old Testament.* Beigabe zur *OLZ.* Leipzig: Hinrichs, 1927. **Wright, G. E.** *Shechem: The Biography of a Biblical City.* New York: McGraw-Hill, 1965. 9. **Zertal, A.** "A Cultic Center with a Burnt-Offering Altar from Early Iron Age I Period at Mount Ebal." In *Wünschet Jerusalem Frieden.* Ed. M. Augustin et al. Frankfurt: Peter Lang, 1988. 137–54. ———. "Has Joshua's Altar Been Found on Mount Ebal?" *BARev* 11.1 (1985) 26–43. ———. "How Can Kempinski Be So Wrong?" *BARev* 12.1 (1986) 43–53. ———. "Mount Ebal—1983/84." In *Excavations and Surveys in Israel 1984, Vol. 3.* Jerusalem: Israel Department of Antiquities and Museums, 1985. 82–86.

Translation and Prosodic Analysis

Moses and the Elders Command the People to Keep the Commandment [4:5]

1 *Now Moses / and the elders of Israel commanded /* [15 2
[a]*the people*[a] */ saying //* 9 2
"Keep[b] */ all the commandment /* [10 2
that I / command you / TODAY // <u>16</u> 3_

Write the Torah on Plastered Stones on Mount Ebal [(6:5):(5:6):(4:5)]

2 And it shall be / in the day / when you cross over the Jordan / [19 3
into the land / that YHWH *your God / is giving to you //* 23 3_

And you shall set up for yourselves / great stones / 19 2
and you shall plaster them / with plaster // 11 2
3 *and you shall write upon them /* <u>10</u> 1_
All the words / of this Torah / when you[a] *cross over //* 17 3
in order / that you[a] *may come into the land /* 17 2_
That YHWH your God / is giving to you / 16 2
a land flowing with milk\[b] *and honey /* 13 1
just as YHWH God of your fathers / spoke / to you // <u>20</u> 3_
4 *And it will be / when* you cross over the Jordan / 14 2
you shall set up / these stones / 19 2_
That I / command you / TODAY\[a] on [b]Mount Ebal[b] // 22 3
and you shall plaster them / with plaster // <u>10</u> 2_

Erect the Altar of YHWH on Mount Ebal and Offer Sacrifices [(5:4):(4:5)]

5 *And you shall build there / an altar / to YHWH / your God //* 24 4
an altar of stones / 8 1
You shall not wield upon them[a] */ an iron tool //* 12 2
6 *of unhewn stones / you shall build it /* <u>12</u> 2_
It is the altar\[a] *of YHWH your God //* 12 1
and you shall offer upon it\[b] *burnt offerings /* 14 1
to YHWH / your God // 10 2_
7 *And you shall sacrifice peace offerings*[a] */ and eat there //* 17 2
and you shall rejoice / before / YHWH your God // <u>18</u> 3_

Write the Torah on Plastered Stones "Very Plainly" [4]

8 *And you shall write upon the stones / all the words /* 18 2
of this Torah / very plainly[a] *//* ס 16 2_

Moses' Pronouncement and Summation [7:(7:4)]

9 *And Moses spoke / together with the Levitical*[a] *priests /* 20 2
to all Israel / saying // 11 2
"Keep silence / and hear / O Israel / 11 3_
THIS DAY / *you have become the people*[b] */ of YHWH / your God //* 23 4
10 *and you shall hearken / to the voice / of YHWH your God //* 18 3_
And you shall observe [a]*his commandments*[a] \[b] *and his statutes /* 17 1
that / I command you / TODAY" // ס <u>15</u> 3_

Notes

1.a-a. Some LXX witnesses omit את־העם, "the people." Prosodic analysis supports MT.

1.b. Some Heb. MSS read שמור, add the missing vowel, for MT שמר, "keep"; SP, Syr., Tg., and Vg. read שמרו, "they kept." The more difficult reading of MT is retained, with inf. functioning as impv.

3.a. Some LXX witnesses and *Tg. Ps.-J.* read 2 pl. forms.

3.b. Reading *paštā'* followed by *zāqēp qāṭôn* as conj.

4.a. The *'atnāḥ* is misplaced in this verse, and should be placed after האלה, "these." The *ṭipḥā'* under היום, "today," is read as conj.

4.b-b. SP reads Mount Gerizim.

5.a. A number of Heb. MSS read ־הן (3 fem. pl.) to agree with אבנים, "stones."
6.a. Reading *ṭipḥā'* as conj. because of misplaced *'atnāḥ*.
6.b. Reading *paštā'* followed by *zāqēp parvum* as conj.
7.a. Some LXX witnesses add κυρίῳ (τῷ θεῷ σου), "to the Lord (your God)." Prosodic analysis supports MT.
8.a. A number of Heb. MSS read בָּאֵר, "to make clear." See *Comment* on 1:5.
9.a. Some Heb. MSS, Syr., and some LXX witnesses add *waw*-conj., reading "the priests *and* the Levites." The more difficult reading of MT is followed here.
9.b. SP and some LXX witnesses add קדש, "holy"; cf. 28:9.
10.a-a. Reading מצותיו, "his commandments," with Q and Cairo Geniza fragments.
10.b. Reading *paštā'* followed by *zāqēp qāṭôn* as conj.

Form/Structure/Setting

The structure of Deut 27 has puzzled scholars through the centuries. Its content interrupts the natural connection between Deut 26 and 28, centered in events on the plains of Moab under Moses. Here the focus shifts to Shechem, which is somewhat distant from where the people of Israel crossed the Jordan River near Jericho and further than the people could journey in a single day, contrary to what a superficial reading of 27:2 might suggest.

Important examples of covenant documents and ceremonies have emerged in the large number of international treaties preserved in texts from all over the ancient Near Eastern world. Although these treaties are known primarily from Hittite sources, there is no reason to believe that the Hittites originated the treaty form. Such treaties are intrinsically cross-cultural in nature and certainly influenced the structure and nature of the Sinai covenant and its renewal, especially as reflected in the covenant ceremony presented in Deut 27–30.

In terms of the prosodic analysis of the Hebrew text, 27:1–10 is in five parts: vv 1, 2–4, 5–7, 8, and 9–10. The *Numeruswechsel* before the temporal marker "today" separates the opening verse from what follows and establishes the boundaries of 27:2–4, which are also marked by repetition of the words "cross over the Jordan" followed by "you shall plaster them with plaster." The *sĕtûmā'* layout marker after v 8 breaks vv 8–10 into two parts.

Before examining further the structural detail from a prosodic point of view, it is useful to review the overall structure of Deut 27, which may be outlined as follows:

A	Keep all the commandment that I command you today	27:1
B	Write the Torah on stones and build an altar on Mount Ebal	27:2–8
X	Summary appeal for obedience	27:9–10
B′	Proclamation of blessings and curses by the twelve tribes	27:11–13
A′	Twelve curses recited from Mount Ebal on hidden sins	27:14–26

The outer frame in this structure moves from a summary command to keep all the commandment (v 1) to twelve curses that are to be recited from Mount Ebal concerning hidden sins (vv 14–26), with a second summary appeal for obedience to God's commandments in the center (vv 9–10). The inner frame moves from the command to write the words of the Torah on plastered stones and to build a stone altar on Mount Ebal (vv 2–8) to the proclamation of blessings and curses by the twelve tribes there at Shechem (vv 11–13).

The stones of 27:5–6 are the unhewn stones from which the altar is built, whereas the stones of v 8 are the great plastered stones of vv 2–4, on which the Torah is inscribed for all to see. This becomes clear in light of the five-part concentric structure of vv 1–10, which may be outlined as follows:

A	Moses' summary commandment	27:1
B	Write the Torah on plastered stones on Mount Ebal	27:2–4
X	Erect an altar of unhewn stones there and offer sacrifices	27:5–7
B′	Write the Torah on plastered stones—very plainly	27:8
A′	Moses' pronouncement and summary commandment	27:9–10

The boundary between vv 8 and 9 is marked by the *sĕtûmāʾ* layout marker, which suggests that vv 9–10 are set off from what precedes and that they play a role in larger structures within Deuteronomy. For the section as a whole, the phrase "all the commandment" (v 1) forms an inclusion with "all the words of this Torah" in v 8, and with the words "his commandments and his statutes" in v 10. It is the whole of Deuteronomy that is to be made "very plain" for all the people assembled there by displaying the Torah on great plastered stones for all to see. "Rabbinic exegesis took the requirement of making the Teaching clear to mean that it was to be written on the stones in seventy languages so that all nations might avail themselves of it" (Tigay [1996] 250, citing *m. Sot.* 7:5; *t. Sot.* 8:6; *Tg. Ps.-J.* and Tg. Yerushalmi).

The word אבנים, "stones," appears as a framing device around vv 2–8, and in the structural center of that subunit, which may be outlined as follows:

A	Set up stones and write on them the words of this Torah	27:2–3
B	Set up these plastered stones on Mount Ebal	27:4
X	Build there an altar of unhewn stones to YHWH	27:5–6a
B′	Offer sacrifices, eat there, and rejoice before YHWH	27:6b–7
A′	Write upon the stones the words of this Torah	27:8

The stones of vv 5–6 are the unhewn stones from which the altar is built, whereas the stones of vv 2–4 and 8 are the great plastered stones, on which the Torah is inscribed for all to see.

It is interesting to note that, in spite of its brevity, this summary appeal for obedience may be outlined in similar fashion:

A	Moses and Levitical priests speak to the people:	27:9a
B	Keep silence and hear, O Israel!	27:9b
X	This day you have become the people of God.	27:9c
B′	Hear the voice of YHWH!	27:10a
A′	You shall do as I have commanded you.	27:10b–c

At the center of this structure, which is also the structural center of chap. 27 itself, we have the simple affirmation: "This day you have become the people of YHWH your God" (v 9d). The verb "to hear" appears in the imperative form on either side urging the people of Israel to listen to the voice of YHWH. The larger frame indicates that Moses (along with the Levitical priests) told the people to do what YHWH has commanded them to do (cf. the discussion of 1:1–6a).

The evidence gathered by Labuschagne on the use of the divine-name numbers in 27:1–11 may be summarized as follows:

Words:	before *'atnāḥ*		after *'atnāḥ*		
27:1–4	43 (= 17 + 26)	+	39	=	82
27:5–8	26	+	15	=	41
27:9	8	+	9	=	17
27:10	4	+	9	=	13
27:1–10	81	+	72	=	153 (= 9 × 17)

There are a total of 153 (= 9 × 17) words in this section, which is also the sum of the numbers one through seventeen. There are 43 (= 17 + 26) words before *'atnāḥ* in vv 1–4 and 26 words before *'atnāḥ* in vv 5–8. The 17 words of v 9 are augmented by 13 words in v 10, so as to reach the grand total of 153 (= 9 × 17) words in the passage as a whole. On the use of the numbers 17 and 26 as divine-name numbers, see *Excursus:* "Deuteronomy as a Numerical Composition."

Comment

1 "Moses and the elders of Israel"—this is the only place in which Moses is joined by the elders in commanding the people to observe "the commandment" (cf. also v 9, where Moses is joined by the Levitical priests). Craigie says the wording here is appropriate because Moses would not be present at the ceremony of covenant renewal on Mount Ebal: "Therefore a particular responsibility would fall on the elders of the people to ensure that the injunction was carried out" ([1976] 327). The phrase "all the commandment" refers to all the laws of Deuteronomy, which is equivalent to "all the words of this Torah" in vv 3 and 8. The phrase "that I command you" appears to be in some tension with the opening words of the verse, in which "Moses and the elders of Israel" are speaking.

2–3 The phrase "in the day when you cross over the Jordan" cannot be meant literally, since Mount Ebal is thirty miles from Jericho and four thousand feet higher. Nonetheless, as Mayes puts it, "this definite statement cannot be taken vaguely . . . [but rather] points to an action to be undertaken as soon as the Jordan has been crossed" ([1981] 340). With a number of other scholars, Mayes argues for "an intentional conflation of traditions, those of Shechem where Israel's covenant tradition was particularly preserved, and those of Gilgal . . . where memories of Israel's first entry into the land were preserved" ([1981] 341). Zertal suggests that the historical crossing of the Jordan was actually farther north near the village of Adam where the Jabbok enters the Jordan—opposite the Wadi Faria. This is where Abraham entered Canaan in an earlier era, when he "traveled through the land as far as the site of the great tree of Moreh at Shechem. . . . So he built an altar there to the LORD" (Gen 12:6–7 NIV). If so, Gilgal is to be located in the vicinity of Mount Ebal, and the injunction here to set up the great plastered stones and the altar of unhewn stones on that very day is to be taken literally. The covenant ceremony was to take place at the Israelites' first camp in the promised land near Shechem. While they were encamped there, a number of momentous events occurred: Joshua circumcised all the males who had been born in their wilderness sojourn, the people celebrated the first Passover in the land, the manna ceased, the people ate the produce of the land, and the Israelites launched their military campaign for the land from there. That "conquest" was subsequently celebrated annually as YHWH's "Holy War," with Jericho and Ai as the primary focus in the repeated celebration of the ritual conquest in the spring festival of Passover.

Tigay suggests that the writing on "plaster" was done by engraving the text "through the plaster into the stone" such that "the white plaster would highlight the dark color of the letters" ([1996] 248). On the phrase "a land flowing with milk and honey," see the *Comment* on 6:3 and literature cited in the bibliography there.

4 The summit of Mount Ebal allows a person to see most of the marvelous vision of the promised land that Moses saw from Mount Nebo (cf. 34:1–3). The ancient city of Shechem is located in the valley, some 1,200 feet below the summit of Mount Ebal and its sister Mount Gerizim, and was an important site in Israel's traditions (see Gen 33:19, 20; Josh 24). Excavations by Adam Zertal have revealed a structure from the early Iron Age on Mount Ebal that a number of scholars believe to be Joshua's altar (see picture of artist's sketch in the front of WBC 6A, and Machlin, *Joshua's Altar,* 112). Though Coogan's conclusion that "it is misleading and ultimately unhelpful for the larger historical task of a biblical archaeologist . . . to presume that [it was] Israelite" (*PEQ* 119 [1987] 1–8), the fact remains that the site fits all four of his own criteria for a cultic site from archeological remains as well as the general picture in terms of the biblical account. Some scholars have suggested that the reading of "Gerizim" for "Ebal" in SP is original and that the subsequent change in MT is to be explained as anti-Samaritan polemic (cf. Bülow, *ZDPV* 73 [1958] 104 n. 14; Mayes [1981] 341). It is more likely that the Samaritan tradition of celebrating Passover on the mountain associated with the blessing emerged in a later period when the covenant renewal at the original central sanctuary in Shechem was no longer observed there. By then, the celebration of Passover as a pilgrimage festival was already held on an annual basis at the battle camp of Gilgal located near Jericho. The second half of v 4, "and you shall plaster them with plaster," repeats the command given in v 2 to form a frame around the vv 2–4 as a literary subunit.

5–7 According to the prescription of Exod 20:25, "an altar of stones" was constructed of uncut stones. Such an altar was found in the excavations at Arad and earlier in various Canaanite sites. The reason for prohibiting the use of "an iron tool" in connection with religious ceremonies is not known. In the "burnt offerings" and the "peace offerings" offered in the covenant on Mount Sinai (Exod 24:5), most of the flesh was eaten by the worshiper and thus the offering was appropriate for a festival. Levine argues that what is called a "peace offering" here was "an ancient sacrifice, probably introduced into the Israelite cult before the beginnings of the monarchy" (*In the Presence of the Lord,* 45). It later became an element of regular public worship, particularly within the context of the Festival of Weeks (Lev 23:15–21).

8 The "stones" here refers to the plastered stones of vv 2–4, not the unhewn stones of the altar (in vv 5–7). The phrase translated "very plainly" (באר היטב) includes a form of the verb that appears elsewhere in the Hebrew Bible only in Deut 1:5 and Hab 2:2, with the sense of making a written statement plain or distinct. In postbiblical Hebrew the term בֵּיאוּר denotes an exposition, or commentary. Tsumura has argued for parallels in Akkadian *burru,* the D stem of *bâru,* meaning "to establish the true legal situation (ownership, liability, etc.) by a legal procedure involving ordeal, oath, or testimony" (*ZAW* 94 [1982] 294–95).

9–10 On the phrase "Moses . . . with the Levitical priests," see v 1 above. It is interesting to note that the shift from third-person address (v 9) to first-person singular, "that I command you," parallels the usage in v 1 to form an envelope around vv 1–10 as a literary unit. The unusual grouping of leadership titles with and without Moses in vv 1, 9, 11, and 14 serve as rhetorical markers for the beginning of the four major sections of the chapter: vv 1–8, 9–10, 11–13, and 14–26. The terminology "you shall observe his commandments and his statutes" (v 10) connects with that of 26:16–19, as Mayes ([1979] 343) observes. The phrase כל־ישׂראל, "all Israel" (v 9), also functions as an envelope around Deuteronomy as a whole (in 1:1 and 34:12).

Explanation

Deuteronomy constitutes the essence of the culture of ancient Israel. As such, its content needed to be communicated to each member of that national entity. To that end the book became part of the public observance of covenant renewal at Shechem. Like the Code of Hammurabi in Mesopotamia, the "Code of Moses," as recorded in the Hebrew text of Deuteronomy, was inscribed on great stone stela for all to see when they assembled to offer sacrifices on Mount Ebal and to remember YHWH's Holy War in the days of Moses and his successor Joshua.

Much effort was spent in ancient Israel to put the content of Deuteronomy in the hearts and minds of the common people by means of musical recitation and dramatic performance within the context of public festivals. The text was on public display for all to see, on great plastered stela alongside the altar that was the focus of sacrificial offerings in Mount Ebal. That same text was sung by the Levitical priests and committed to memory by the worshipers as well.

The Christian church can learn much from the example of ancient Israel in this regard. It is not enough merely to hand out copies of the Bible to our children as they move from the third to the fourth grade. We must find ways to get the content of that book into the hearts and minds of all our people by various means, which include the prominent display of the text itself in public worship.

One of the curious features of modern worship within the evangelical churches today is the absence of public recitation of the Scriptures as an end in itself. Much time is given to singing songs of praise, many of which are simply biblical texts put to music. But very little time is given to "hearing" the Bible recited, other than perhaps the text on which the pastor's sermon of the morning is based. We need to find ways to expose our people to the whole of the Bible in public worship in the manner that ancient Israel experienced Deuteronomy on Mount Ebal.

The reason that the text of Deuteronomy was written on great stone stela for all to see was that the people might learn to "keep all the commandment that I command you today" (27:1). The text of "all the words of this Torah" was to be written "very plainly" (v 8) so that everyone would know what God requires of them. We need to find ways today to accomplish the same end more effectively. If we love God, we will keep his commandments "with all our heart and with all our being." We are indeed a "treasured" and a "holy people"; but if we are to be truly set on high "above all the nations . . . for praise, and for fame, and for honor . . . to YHWH [our] God" (26:18–19), we need to see that God's law is written in our minds and on our hearts for everyone to see (cf. Jer 31:31–33).

2. *Positioning of the Tribes at Shechem and a Litany of Curses (27:11–26)*

Bibliography

Alt, A. *Essays on Old Testament History and Religion.* 1966. 114–15, 147–48, 155–57, 161–68. **Bellefontaine, E.** "The Curses of Deuteronomy 27: Their Relationship to the Prohibitives." In SBTS 3:256–68. ———. "A Study of Ancient Israelite Laws and Their Function as Covenant Stipulations." Diss., Notre Dame, 1973. **Brichto, H. C.** *Problem of "Curse."* 1963. 77–96, 132–35. **Broyde, M. J.,** and **Weiner, S. S.** "A Mathematical Analysis of the Division of the Tribes and the Role of the Levites on Grizim and Aval in Deuteronomy 27." *Tradition* 27 (1992) 48–57. **Buis, P.** "Deutéronome XXVII 15–26: Malédictions ou exigences de l'alliance?" *VT* 17 (1967) 478–79. **Cardascia, G.** "Egalité et inégalité des sexes en matière d'atteinte aux moeurs dans le Proche-Orient ancien." *WO* 11 (1980) 7–16, esp. 12. **Daube, D.** "The Culture of Deuteronomy." *Orita* 3 (1969) 27–52, esp. 38–39. ———. "Some Forms of Old Testament Legislation." In *Oxford Society of Historical Theology: Abstracts of Proceedings for the Academic Year 1944–45.* 36–46, esp. 39. **Fensham, F. C.** "Aspects of Family Law in the Covenant Code in Light of Ancient Near Eastern Parallels." *DiIs* 1 (1969) 5–19, esp. 15–16. **Garbini, G.** "Il Sangue dell'innocente." In *Atti della Settimana Sangue e Antropologia nela letteratura cristiana.* Ed. F. Vattioni. 3 vols. Rome: Pia Unione Preziosissimo Sangue, 1983. 1:513–24. **Good, E. M.** "Capital Punishment and Its Alternatives in Ancient Near Eastern Law." *SLR* 19 (1967) 947–77, esp. 959–60. **Hoffner, H. A.** "Incest, Sodomy and Bestiality in the Ancient Near East." In *FS C. H. Gordon.* 1973. 81–90. ———. "Some Contributions of Hittitology to Old Testament Study." *TynBul* 20 (1969) 27–55, esp. 41–42. **Klopfenstein, M. A.** *Scham und Schande nach dem Alten Testament.* ATANT 62. Zurich: Theologischer Verlag, 1972. 190–93. **Lewy, I.** "The Puzzle of Deuteronomy 27: Blessings Announced, but Curses Noted." *VT* 12 (1962) 207–11. **Mitchell, T. C.** "The Meaning of the Noun ḤTN in the Old Testament." *VT* 19 (1969) 93–112, esp. 112. **Nielsen, E.** *Shechem: A Traditio-Historical Investigation.* Copenhagen: Gad, 1955. 39–85, 315–57. **Phillips, A.** "Uncovering the Father's Skirt." *VT* 30 (1980) 38–43. **Schottroff, W.** *Der altisraelitische Fluchspruch.* WMANT 30. Neukirchen-Vluyn: Neukirchener Verlag, 1969. **Schulz, H.** *Das Todesrecht im Alten Testament.* BZAW 114. Berlin: Töpelmann, 1969. 61–71 **Seebass, H.** "Garizim und Ebal als Symbol von Segen und Fluch." *Bib* 63 (1982) 22–31. **Smith, W. R.** *Kinship and Marriage.* 1903. 191–98. **Sole, F. M.** "La Proprietà fondiaria in Israele." *PalCl* 43 (1964) 673–76. **Steinmetzer, F. X.** *Die babylonischen Kudurru (Grenzsteine) als Urkundenform.* SGKA XI 4/5. Paderborn, Schoningh, 1922. ———. "Über den Grundbesitz in Babylonien zur Kassitenzeit nach den sogenannten Grenzsteinen dargestellt." *Der Alte Orient* 19 (1919). **Tigay, J.** *You Shall Have No Other Gods.* HSS 31. Atlanta: Scholars Press, 1986. 91–96. **Wallis, G.** "Der Vollbürgereid in Dt 27,15–26." *HUCA*

45 (1974) 47–63. **Weinfeld, M.** *DDS.* 147. ———. *Deuteronomy 1–11.* 1991. 253–54. ———. "The Origin of the Apodictic Law: An Overlooked Source." *VT* 23 (1973) 63–75, esp. 63–65. ———. "Social and Cultic Institutions in the Priestly Source against Their Ancient Near Eastern Background." In *Proceedings of the Eighth World Congress of Jewish Studies Panel Sessions: Bible Studies and Hebrew Language.* Jerusalem: World Union of Jewish Studies, 1983. 95–129, esp. 105–6. ———. "Zion as a Religious Capital." In *The Poet and the Historian.* Ed. R. E. Friedman. Chico, CA: Scholars Press, 1983. 81–85. **Wilson, C. W.** "Ebal and Gerizim, 1866." *PEQ* (April 1873) 66–70.

Translation and Prosodic Analysis

Positioning on Mounts Gerizim and Ebal and the First Curse [(6:3):(4:4):(4:4)] [3:6]

11 *And Moses commanded / the people / IN THAT DAY / saying //*	21	4
12 *these / shall stand /*	7	2_
To bless the people\[a] on [b]Mount Gerizim[b] /	17	1
when you cross / the Jordan //	9	2_
Simeon / and[c] Levi and[c] Judah / and[c] Issachar /	20	3
and[c] Joseph and Benjamin //	12	1
13 and these / shall stand |[a] for the curse / on Mount Ebal //	21	4_
Reuben / Gad and Asher /	12	2
[and][b] Zebulun / Dan[c] and Naphtali //	14	2_
14 And the Levites shall respond / and they shall say /	15	2
to every man in Israel / with a loud voice // ס	13	2_

15 Cursed is the man / who makes a graven or molten image /	21	2
an abomination to YHWH /	7	1_
A work / by hands of a craftsman /	11	2
and he sets it up in secret //	7	1
And all the people shall respond /	10	1
and they shall say / Amen // ס	10	2_

Four Curses on Social Sins from Mount Ebal {[5] [5] [5] [6]}

16 Cursed is the one / who dishonors[a] his father / or his mother //	15	3
and all the people shall say[b] / Amen // ס	15	2_

17 Cursed is the one / who moves back / his neighbor's landmark //	16	3
and all the people shall say / Amen // ס	15	2_

18 Cursed is the one / who misleads a blind man / in the way //	13	3
and all the people shall say / Amen // ס	13	2_

19 Cursed is the one / who perverts[a] / justice for alien [b]orphan /	14	3
and widow //	6	1
and all the people shall say / Amen // ס	13	2_

Four Curses on Sexual Sins from Mount Ebal {[5] [5] [5] [5]}

20 Cursed is the one / who lies \\[a] with his father's wife /	16	2
because he has removed \\[b] his father's garment //	11	1
and all the people shall say / Amen // ס	15	2_
21 Cursed is the one / who lies / with any beast //	15	3
and all the people shall say / Amen // ס	15	2_
22 Cursed is the one / who lies \\[a] with [b]his sister /	14	2
the daughter of his father \\[c] or daughter of his mother[b] //	11	1
and all the people shall say / Amen // ס	13	2_
23 Cursed is the one / who lies / with his mother-in-law //	14	3
and all the people shall say / Amen // ס	13	2_

Two Curses on Social Sins from Mount Ebal {[5] [5]}

24 Cursed is the one / who strikes down his neighbor / in secret //	17	3
and all the people shall say / Amen // ס	15	2_
25 Cursed is the one / who takes a bribe /	12	2
so as to strike down a life \\[a] (taking) [b]innocent blood[b] //	12	1
and all the people shall say / Amen // ס	13	2_

Final Curse on Those Who Do Not Keep the Words of This Torah [6]

26 Cursed is he / who does not uphold /	12	2
<all>[a] the words of this Torah /	13	1
[b]To do them[b] //	8	1
and all the people shall say / Amen // פ	15	2_

Notes

12.a. Reading *paštā'* followed by *zāqēp parvum* as conj.

12.b-b. Reading גרזים, "Gerizim," with MT, against B and SP, which read גריזים, in order to achieve closer balance in terms of mora count. The term is counted five morae.

12.c. Reading the *waw*-conj. with MT on the basis of prosodic analysis in all four instances against some Heb. MSS, LXX, and Vg.

13.a. Reading disj. accent here for *metheg* plus *mêrĕkā.*

13.b. Deleting *waw*-conj. with some Heb. MSS and SP.

13.c. Reading with MT; Syr. adds *waw*-conj.

16.a. Reading מַקְלֶה, "he dishonors," with MT; two Heb. MSS read מְקַלֵּל.

16.b. Here and in the repetition of this refrain in vv 17–26, I read sg. with MT; SP reads pl.

19.a. Some Heb. MSS and B read מַטֵּה rather than מַטֶּה, "he perverts," with no change in meaning.

19.b. LXX and Syr. add *waw*-conj. Prosodic analysis supports MT.

20.a. Reading *paštā'* followed by *mûnāḥ* as conj.

20.b. Reading *ṭipḥā'* as conj. because of misplaced *'atnāḥ.*

22.a. Reading *paštā'* followed by *zāqēp parvum* as conj.

22.b-b. Some LXX witnesses read אחות אביו ואמו, "sisters of his father and his mother." Prosodic analysis supports MT.

22.c. Reading *ṭipḥāʾ* as conj. because of misplaced *ʾatnāḥ*.
25.a. Reading *ṭipḥāʾ* as conj. because of misplaced *ʾatnāḥ*.
25.b-b. B reads דם נקי(א), with the same meaning as MT דם נקי, "innocent blood." Cf. 19:10 and Jonah 1:14.
26.a. Adding כל, "all," with a few Heb. MSS, SP, and most LXX witnesses. Restoring the word completes the pattern in the use of the divine-name numbers throughout 27:11–26 (see discussion under *Form/Structure/Setting*).
26.b-b. SP reads לַעֲשׂוֹתָם, "to do them," for MT לעשות אותם, "to do them." Prosodic analysis supports MT.

Form/Structure/Setting

There are significant problems in the interpretation of this section. There are two ways to interpret 27:11–13. Either the preposition על (v 12) is to be read as equivalent to אל־מול, "in front of" (Josh 8:33), or we are dealing with more than one ceremony. A further complexity is introduced by the fact that v 12 refers to six tribes standing there "to bless the people on Mount Gerizim," but there are no blessings given in the text until we get to Deut 28. The best way to explain this situation is in terms of the function of 27:11–26 within the larger literary structure of Deut 27–28 as a whole, which may be outlined as follows:

A	Shechem ceremony—Torah inscribed on stones and sacrifices on Ebal	27:1–10
B	Positioning of the tribes at Shechem—litany of twelve curses	27:11–26
X	Six ritual blessings in Moab under Moses	28:1–14
B′	Six ritual curses that echo the old Shechem ceremony	28:15–19
A′	Moab ceremony—commentary and expansion of covenant curses	28:20–69

From this structure it is clear that we are dealing with more than one covenant ceremony in the text of Deut 27–28—that of covenant renewal under Moses on the plains of Moab and the anticipated covenant renewal under Joshua in the promised land. Joshua's renewal of the covenant of Shechem became an ongoing part of worship experience in the life of ancient Israel.

The outer frame in the above structure moves from a description of the anticipated setting for covenant renewal in the promised land at Shechem under Joshua (27:1–10), to a detailed commentary and expansion of the covenant curses as enunciated by Moses on the plains of Moab (28:20–69). The inner frame moves from a description of the positioning of the twelve tribes on Mount Gerizim and Mount Ebal for the blessing and curse, which includes a litany of twelve curses to be recited in that context (27:11–19), to six ritual curses of the original ceremony of covenant renewal in Moab (28:15–19). These six ritual curses are preceded by the account of the corresponding six ritual blessings in the center of the structure (28:1–14).

The continued observance of Passover by the Samaritan community on Mount Gerizim (see *Explanation* of 16:1–8) reveals that there is a place for both events depicted in Deut 27 and Josh 8:30–35 within the context of festival observance and covenant renewal at Shechem. In particular, the last day of the annual Samaritan observance begins early in the morning when all the males make their way to the top of Mount Gerizim to recite long doxologies, prayers, and songs to God, interspersed with biblical readings. The antiphonal recitation of blessings and curses on the part of tribal representatives on the two mountains of Deut 27 makes perfect sense along with the corporate experience of the assembly of the entire community facing the two mountains (Josh 8:33).

In terms of prosodic structure, 27:11–26 is in two major sections, the first of which is divided further in two parts (vv 11–14 and 15).

27:11–15	Positioning of the twelve tribes
27:16–26	Twelve curses recited from Mount Ebal by the Levites

The boundaries of the first prosodic unit (27:11–15) are marked by *sĕtûmāʾ* layout markers and the *Numeruswechsel* (change from second sg. to second pl.) in v 12. It should be noted, however, that there is another *sĕtûmāʾ* layout marker at the end of v 14 and after each of following verses that delineate the individual curses. Consequently the structure is determined primarily on the basis of content, which may be outlined as follows:

Proclamation of Blessings and Curses by the Twelve Tribes		*27:11–14*
A	These shall stand on Mount Gerizim to bless the people	vv 11–12a
B	Simeon, Levi, Judah, Issachar, Joseph, and Benjamin	v 12b
X	These shall stand for the curse on Mount Ebal	v 13a
B′	Reuben, Gad, Asher, Zebulun, Dan, and Naphtali	v 13b
A′	And the Levites shall respond with a loud voice	v 14

Twelve Curses Pronounced by the Levites on Clandestine Sins		*27:15–26*
A	First curse: on relations with God (making images of God)	v 15
B	Four curses on social sins	vv 16–19
X	Four curses on sexual sins (incest and bestiality)	vv 20–23
B′	Two curses on social sins	vv 24–25
A′	Summary curse: on relations with God (keeping the Torah)	v 26

The boundary after 27:14 is marked by the *sĕtûmāʾ* layout marker and by singling out of the Levites as the ones to pronounce the twelve curses that follow in 27:15–26.

The list of sins delineated here is similar to other such representative lists that appear elsewhere in the Torah, the Prophets, and the Psalms (cf. Ezek 18; Ps 15). Where relations with God are included in these lists, that matter is always placed first. A number of scholars have argued in favor of an original series of ten curses. The conclusion reached by Mayes is apropos: "in its allusions to various laws, it may function in a representative way . . . to bring to mind the whole field of law and morality which must characterize the life of the people of Yahweh" ([1981] 345–46).

It should be noted that the curses of 27:15–26 are not the ceremony described in vv 11–14, as Lewy (*VT* 12 [1962] 207–11) and others have noted. They appear here as part of larger concentric structural patterns. In particular, the twelve curses recited from Mount Ebal by the Levites are set over against the mutual commitments between God and the people of Israel in 26:16–19. They spell out what will happen if, by choosing not to observe the Torah, Israel fails to be the "holy people" YHWH desires.

The conclusion Craigie reached about the omission of the blessings is indeed credible: when the text of the blessings in 28:3–6 is compared to the curses of

28:16–19, "it is not unlikely . . . that the twelve blessings, which are not mentioned here, would have been the exact reverse of the twelve curses that are stated" ([1976] 331).

The evidence assembled by Labuschagne on the use of the divine-name numbers in 27:11–26, modified by the addition of the word כל, "all," in the first half of v 26, may be summarized as follows:

Words:	before *ʾatnāḥ*		after *ʾatnāḥ*		
27:11	7	+	0	=	7
27:12–15	39	+	17	=	56
27:16–19	18	+	16	=	34 (= 2 × 17)
27:20–23	27	+	16	=	43 (= 17 + 26)
27:24–26	22	+	12	=	34 (= 2 × 17)
27:12	11	+	6	=	17
27:12–13	17	+	12	=	29
27:12–14	26	+	12	=	38
27:15–16	17	+	9	=	26
27:15–17	21	+	13	=	34 (= 2 × 17)

Following the introductory seven words of v 11, each subunit makes use of either or both of the divine-name numbers 17 and 26. There are 17 words in v 12, which concerns the blessing proclaimed from Mount Gerizim. In the whole of vv 12–14, on the positioning of the twelve tribes on Mounts Gerizim and Ebal for the blessings and curses, there are 26 words before *ʾatnāḥ*. In vv 12–15, which includes the first curse (v 15), there are 17 words after *ʾatnāḥ*. In vv 15–16, which present the first two curses, there are 17 words before *ʾatnāḥ* and a total of 26 words. In vv 15–17, which include the first three curses, there are a total of 34 (= 2 × 17) words; and in vv 16–19 on the four social sins proclaimed from Mount Ebal, there are a total of 34 (= 2 × 17) words. In vv 20–23 on the four sexual sins proclaimed from Mount Ebal, there are a total of 43 (= 17 + 26) words. And in vv 24–26 on the final three curses spoken from Mount Ebal, there are a total of 34 (= 2 × 17) words. The divine-name numbers appear to be the primary numerical pattern on which the text itself is built, expanding one subunit on another to build a structure in which God's name is carefully woven into the fabric of the Hebrew text.

Comment

12–13 On the association of "Mount Gerizim" and "Mount Ebal" with the covenant blessings and curses, see the *Comment* on 11:29 and Plate 4. Tigay notes that the Levites' "pronouncements would be most audible if [the people] stood on the slopes of the mountains," since the text actually states "'on,' not 'atop,' the mountains" ([1996] 252).

15 The first curse in the Dodecalog (vv 15–26) concerns the breaking of the first two of the Ten Commandments, by making a "graven or molten image." The term "cursed" (ארור) was defined by Brichto as "destined for misfortune" (*Problem of "Curse,"* 77). It is the opposite of ברוך, "to be blessed." A פסל, "graven image," may be rendered as "idol," since this noun is used only for images of gods in wood, metal, or stone. "Amen" is rendered in the LXX as "Let it be so." Tigay calls attention to the fact that its meaning is spelled out by Jeremiah, who expressed assent to what Hananiah had just said by responding "Amen! May YHWH do so!" (Jer 28:6). He also calls attention to Num 5:22, where the suspected adulteress is commanded to drink a certain potion that will harm her if she is guilty, and she must respond "Amen, amen!" ([1996] 255). The Talmud explains that, "Answering 'amen' after an oath is equivalent to pronouncing the oath with one's own mouth" (*b. Shebu.* 29b, cited by Tigay).

16 The term "dishonors" means to insult, or to treat with disrespect, which is the reverse of the verb to "honor" in the fifth commandment (see also 21:18–21).

17 To "remove a neighbor's landmark" was considered a sin against God because property was owned by God, who assigned it to the original tribes in the days of Joshua (see also 19:14). If the reference is to something like the Mesopotamian *kudurru*-stone, as suggested by Craigie, the crime in question would be the "total appropriation of another person's property" ([1976] 332; see also A. L. Oppenheim, *Ancient Mesopotamia* [Chicago: Univ. of Chicago Press, 1964] 123, 149).

18 The curse of "one who misleads a blind man" is interpreted broadly in Jewish tradition (cf. Lev 19:14). As Tigay put it, "Halakhic exegesis took the prohibition to include misleading uninformed people with incorrect information or bad advice, or abetting sinners and criminals, who are blinded by their desires" ([1996] 255; cf. Josephus *Ant.* 4.8.31 §276, cited by Tigay [1996] 395 n. 55).

19 The "alien, orphan, and widow" were vulnerable because they often lacked the power to defend themselves in legal proceedings (cf. 10:18). The subject of perverting justice to the vulnerable in society is taken up in the laws of 24:6–25:16, and particularly in 24:17–22.

20–23 On the meaning of the phrase "he has removed his father's garment," see also the *Comment* on 23:1 (Eng. 22:30), the law prohibiting marriage to one's father's wife. The statement seems to be a euphemistic description of the invasion of the privacy of the sexual relationship between the father and (step)mother by the father's son. Tigay says the absence of adultery here has to do with the very nature of the crimes listed. "A man would arouse suspicion if seen in the company or home of another man's wife, but not if seen in the company of his stepmother, sister, mother-in-law, and cattle" ([1996] 256). The defining of "sister" as "daughter of his father or daughter of his mother" excludes marriage with a half sister, which was clearly permitted in the stories of Abraham and Sarah (Gen 20:12), and Tamar and Amnon (2 Sam 13:13).

It is interesting to note that the list of sexual sins here does not include sexual relations between persons of the same sex, as is also the case in the list of twelve sexual prohibitions in Lev 18:6–18. The prohibition of homosexual acts comes rather far down the list of sexual evils in ancient Israel. In Lev 18:22 and 20:13 sexual union of males is prohibited; but nothing is said in the laws of the Torah in the matter of same-sex relations with females. Moreover, there is nothing in the laws of Deuteronomy on the subject of homosexuality at all. On the matter of transvestism, see Deut 22:5 and the *Comment* there.

24–25 Though the word מכה, "strikes down," is often translated "slays," a different verb is normally used to convey the meaning "to kill," as in Exod 21:12. Nonetheless, the crime in question here remains that of slaying one's "neighbor in secret." The perpetrator of such a deed may escape trial and punishment on the part of legal authorities, but he or she cannot escape the curse of God. Biblical laws about "the one who takes a bribe" normally refer to judges, so Tigay concludes that the reference here is to corrupt application of the death penalty ([1996] 257; cf. Exod 23:7–8; Deut 16:22; Ezek 22:12).

26 The twelfth and final curse refers to all other commands in "this Torah."

Explanation

The concentric structure of the curses here suggests that the sins of incest and bestiality are of primary concern and that they are in some way connected with the sins regarding human relations with God in the first and last of the curses (27:14–15 and 26). That homosexual acts are not included in the list of four curses on sexual sins from Mount Ebal here or in the parallel list of twelve prohibitions of sexual relations in Lev 18:7–18 should not be construed as evidence condoning or condemning such relationships. Same-sex relations between males are condemned in Lev 18:22 and 20:13. In the latter instance the prohibition appears in conjunction with the prohibition of sexual union with animals by either sex (Lev 20:15–16), a prohibition listed here in Deut 27:21.

The sins against God here focus on the issue of idolatry (making images of God) and the keeping of the Torah. Though these matters are of primary importance throughout Deuteronomy, it is not immediately clear what connection, if any, exists between them and the four curses on the sexual sins of incest and bestiality in 27:20–23.

In his letter to the church at Corinth the apostle Paul saw a connection with glorifying God in our bodies. "The body is not meant for immorality, but for the Lord, and the Lord for the body. . . . Every other sin which a man commits is outside the body; but the immoral man sins against his own body. Do you not know that your body is a temple of the Holy Spirit within you, which you have from God? You are not your own; you were bought with a price. So glorify God in your body" (1 Cor 6:13–20). It makes no difference whether such sins are actually found out. Their effect is real and permanent—in our own bodies, in the life of the objects of our sexual actions, and in our relationship with God. Paul expounds the meaning of this curse in his letter to the Galatians (3:10–14), concluding that we cannot claim justification before God on the basis of "works of the law." Since the all-embracing nature of this law turns our eyes to Christ, Paul then shifts his attention to the fact that "Christ redeemed us from the curse of the law, having become a curse for us—for it is written, 'Cursed be every one who hangs on a tree'" (Gal 3:13; see Deut 21:23 and *Comment* there).

D. *If You Keep Covenant (28:1–69 [Eng. 28:1–29:1])*

Bibliography

Blank, S. H. "The Curse, the Blasphemy, the Spell, and the Oath." *HUCA* 23 (1950/51) 73–95. **Borger, R.** "Zu den Assarhaddon-Verträgen aus Nimrud." *ZA* 54 (1961) 191–92. **Brichto, H. C.** *Problem of "Curse."* 1963. 186. **Buis, P.** "Comment au septième siècle envisageait-on l'avenir de l'alliance: Étude de Lv. 26,3–45." In *Questions disputées d'Ancien Testament.* Ed. C. Brekelmans. 1974. 131–40. **Chołewinski, A.** *Heiligkeitsgesetz und Deuteronomium.* AnBib 66. Rome: Pontifical Biblical Institute, 1976. **Fensham, F. C.** "Common Trends in Curses of the Near Eastern Treaties and Kudurru-Inscriptions Compared with Maledictions of Amos and Isaiah." *ZAW* 75 (1963) 155–75. ———. "Maledictions and Benedictions in Ancient Near Eastern Vassal-Treaties and the Old Testament." *ZAW* 74 (1962) 1–9. **Frankena, R.** "The Vassal-Treaties of Esarhaddon and the Dating of Deuteronomy." *OTS* 14 (1965) 122–54. **Gevirtz, S.** "West-Semitic Curses and the Problem of the Origins of Hebrew Law." *VT* 11 (1961) 137–58. **Hillers, D. R.** *Treaty-Curses and the Old Testament Prophets.* BibOr 16. Rome: Pontifical Biblical Institute, 1964. **Horst, F.** "Der Eid im Alten Testament." *EvT* 17 (1961) 292–314. **Jeremias, J.** *Kultprophetie und Gerichtsverkündigung in der späten Königszeit.* WMANT 35. Neukirchen-Vluyn: Neukirchener Verlag, 1970. 164–75. **Lohfink, N.** "Die Abänderung der Theologie des priesterlichen Geschichtswerks im Segen des Heiligkeitsgesetzes: Zu Lev. 26,9.11–13." In *FS K. Elliger.* 1973. 129–36. **Mendenhall, G. E.** "Covenant Forms in Israelite Tradition." *BA* 17 (1954) 50–76. ———. "The Suzerainty Treaty Structure: Thirty Years Later." In *Religion and Law.* Ed. E. B. Firmage et al. 1990. 85–100. ———, and **Herion, G. A.** "Covenant." *ABD* 1:1179–1202. **Moran, W. L.** "The Ancient Near Eastern Background of the Love of God in Deuteronomy." *CBQ* 25 (1963) 77–87. **Mørstad, E.** *Wenn du der Stimme des Herrn, deines Gottes, gehorchen wirst: Die primären Einführungen zu Dt 28,3–6 und 16–19.* Oslo: Forlaget Land og Kirke, 1960. **Noth, M.** "For All Who Rely on Works of the Law Are under a Curse." In *The Laws in the Pentateuch.* 1966. 118–31. **Pedersen, J.** *Der Eid bei den Semiten.* Strassburg: Trubner, 1914. **Plöger, J. G.** *Literarkritische, formgeschichtliche und stilkritische Untersuchungen.* 1966. 130–217. **Schächter, E. A.** "Bundesformular und prophetischer Urteilsspruch: Bemerkungen zu D. R. Hillers, *Treaty Curses and the Old Testament Prophets.*" *Bib* 48 (1967) 128–31. **Scharbert, J.** "'Fluchen' und 'Segnen' im Alten Testament." *Bib* 39 (1958) 1–26. **Schottroff, W.** *Der altisraelitisch Fluchspruch.* WMANT 30. Neukirchen-Vluyn: Neukirchener Verlag, 1969. 225–27. **Seitz, G.** *Redaktionsgeschichtliche Studien zum Deuteronomium.* BWANT 93. Stuttgart: Kohlhammer, 1971. 254–302. **Seybold, K.** *Das Gebet der Kranken im Alten Testament.* BWANT 99. Stuttgart: Kohlhammer, 1973. 17–29, 39–55, 169. **Sumner, W. A.** "A Study of Deuteronomy 28, with Special Reference to the Parallels with Jeremiah." Diss., Oxford, 1967/68. **Thompson, J. A.** *The Ancient Near Eastern Treaties and the Old Testament.* London: Tyndale, 1964. 17. **Urbach, W. J.** "Blessings and Curses." *ABD* 1:755–61. **Wächter, L.** *Der Tod im Alten Testament.* Stuttgart: Calwer, 1967. 129–57. **Weinfeld, M.** "Traces of Assyrian Treaty Formulae in Deuteronomy." *Bib* 46 (1965) 417–27. **Welch, A. C.** *Deuteronomy: The Framework of the Code.* 1932. 75–96. **Wolfers, D.** "Is Job after All Jewish?" *DD* 14 (1985) 39–44.

Introduction

The final verse (28:69) functions as a bridge connecting the "Covenant Blessings and Curses" under Moses and Joshua in Deut 28 with Deut 29, which makes clear that the terms of this ancient covenant apply to all future generations of the people of God as well.

Because of the nature of the content of these curses, the custom emerged within Judaism of chanting them in a whisper during the Torah reading. A Jewish tomb inscription of the third century C.E. invokes "all the curses written in Deuteronomy" on the person who violates it (*Corpus inscriptionum judaicarum* [Rome: Pontificio Istituto di Archeologia Cristiana, 1952] 2:24, no. 760; Tigay [1996] 261, 396 n. 22).

The boundaries of Deut 28 are marked by *pĕtûḥāʾ* layout markers in *BHS*, which indicates that in L the extra space left after 27:26 and 28:69 are similar: the second half of the previous line was left blank and the text is written flush right with no indentation. For the *sĕtûmāʾ* layout markers after vv 14 and 68, extra space was left in the middle of the line. It appears that the two *sĕtûmāʾ* layout markers are calling attention to the fact that vv 1–14 and v 69 are part of other structures that extend beyond Deut 28. The only further rhetorical markers for internal structure in this lengthy chapter are the *Numeruswechsel* in vv 62 (twice), 63 (twice), and 68. Nonetheless, the chapter is one of the most tightly structured of the entire book, consisting of five parts, four of which are divided further into five parts, and one of these (vv 58–68) divided still further into five parts, as the following outline indicates:

A	Blessings for obedience and curses for disobedience	28:1–19
a	Six covenant blessings (in three pairs)	vv 1–6
b	Promises expanding on the blessings	vv 7–10
x	Threefold blessing: progeny, livestock, and produce	v 11
b′	Promises expanding on the blessings	vv 12–14
a′	Six covenant curses (in three pairs)	vv 15–19
B	Expansion of curses: pestilence, famine, and disease	28:20–32
a	General theme: curse, confusion, and cumbrance	v 20
b	Seven afflictions from pestilence	vv 21–22
x	Destruction by famine and the sword	vv 23–26
b′	Seven more afflictions ("boils of Egypt")	vv 27–29
a′	Violent loss of family, home, and property	vv 30–31
X	Expansion of curses: oppression, exile, and slavery	28:32–44
a	Oppression that produces insanity	vv 32–34
b	Afflictions from disease ("boils" [like Job])	v 35
x	Exile from the land of Israel	vv 36–37
b′	Afflictions of pestilence and war	vv 38–42
a′	Impoverishment and debt	vv 43–44
B′	Expansion of curses: utter privation in siege warfare	28:45–68
a	These curses will pursue you until you are destroyed	v 45
b	Israel's utter privation "in want of all things"	vv 46–48
x	Military siege and the undoing of God's blessings	vv 49–52
b′	A gruesome climax: cannibalism	vv 53–57
a′	The complete reversal of Israel's history	vv 58–68

a You will experience the diseases of Egypt 28:58–61
b Your numbers will be decimated v 62
x YHWH takes delight in destroying you v 63
b′ YHWH will scatter you among the nations v 64–65
a′ YHWH will make you "return to Egypt" vv 66–68

A′Summation: "These are the words of the covenant" 28:69

Detailed discussion of each of these passages is presented below, including the prosodic analysis on which this outline is based.

Most of the covenant or international treaty texts recovered from the ancient Near East include a section on blessings and curses, which describe in detail the consequences of obedience and disobedience on the part of the vassal. Because the witnesses mentioned in these texts were deities or deified elements of the natural world, the blessings and curses were appropriately those experiences that are beyond normal human ability to predict, much less to control. The most important of these concern health, productivity of fields and flocks and wives, and the ravages of war.

It should be noted that treaty texts from the Late Bronze Age (before 1200 B.C.E.) included not only punitive threats (curses) to be carried out by the divine witnesses to the covenant agreement but also positive rewards (blessings) of similar origin. Later in the Iron Age (after 1200 B.C.E.), particularly in the period of the Assyrian Empire (ca. 750–620 B.C.E.), only the curses were included. In Deut 28 both blessings and curses appear in the first section (28:1–19), but the great bulk of the material (28:20–68) is an expansion of the curses. Moreover, as Mendenhall and others have noted [*ABD* 1:1183], all of the various elements of ancient Near Eastern suzerainty treaties are present in Deuteronomy, which thus represents an early form of covenant tradition. At the same time, it is also true that the development of the treaty analogy in Deuteronomy appears to be a creative response to and polemic against the crisis of Assyrian domination in Israel, as Lohfink has argued (*IDBSup*, 229–32).

The longest chapter in the book, Deut 28 is discussed in most commentaries as two literary units: the blessings (vv 1–14) and the curses (15–68). The prosodic analysis presented here, however, suggests that the chapter is made up of five subsections: vv 1–19, 20–32, 33–44, 45–68, and 69, the first of which presents both blessings and curses in summary form, with the focus of attention on the blessings. This is contrary to parallels in other ancient Near Eastern international treaty texts, where the usual order presents curses before blessings. After the summary statement of six covenant curses in vv 15–19, which are almost identical in form to the six covenant blessings of vv 1–6, the curses are expanded in three cycles, and a fourth cycle contained within the third cycle in vv 58–61, as a "wheel within a wheel."

1. Blessings for Obedience and Curses for Disobedience (28:1–19)

Bibliography

Aejmelaeus, A. "Function and Interpretation of כי in Biblical Hebrew." *JBL* 105 (1986) 193–209, esp. 208. **Aull, J. S.** "Obey My Voice: A Form-Critical Study of Selected Prose Speeches from the Book of Deuteronomy." Diss., Duke Univ., 1971. **Dahood, M.** "Hebrew-Ugaritic Lexicography II." *Bib* 45 (1964) 393–412. ———. "A Note on *tôb* "Rain." *Bib* 54 (1973) 404. **Diringer, D.,** and **Brock, S. P.** "Words and Meanings in Early Hebrew Inscriptions." In *FS D. Winton Thomas.* 1968. 41–42. **Evans, G.** "'Coming' and 'Going' at the City Gate: A Discussion of Prof. Speiser's Paper." *BASOR* 150 (1958) 28–35. **Galling, K.** "Die Ausrufung des Namens als Rechtsakt in Israel." *TLZ* 81 (1956) 65–70. **Gammie, J. G.** "The Theology of Retribution in the Book of Deuteronomy." *CBQ* 32 (1970) 1–12, esp. 8. **Gaster, T. H.** *Thespis: Ritual, Myth, and Drama in the Ancient Near East.* 2nd ed. Garden City, NY: Doubleday, 1961. 305, 321. **Giesen, G.** *Die Wurzel* שׁבע. 1981. 304–5. **Gray, J.** *Legacy of Canaan.* 2nd ed. 1965. 298. **Izre'el, S.** "*'Et* = 'to, toward' in Biblical Hebrew." *Shnaton* 3 (1978/79) 205–12 (Heb.). **Kraus, H. J.** *Worship in Israel.* Tr. G. Buswell. Richmond: John Knox, 1966. 85–87. **Scharbert, J.** "Die Geschichte der *bārûk*-Formel." *BZ* 17 (1973) 1–28, esp. 14–15. **Speiser, E. A.** "'Coming' and 'Going' at the City Gate." *BASOR* 144 (1956) 20–23. **Tawil, H.** "A Curse Concerning Crop-Consuming Insects in the Sefire Treaty and in Akkadian: A New Interpretation." *BASOR* 225 (1977) 61. **Troadec, H.** "Faut-il désirer la richesse? (Deutéronome 28,1–14)." *BVC* 37 (1961) 46–52. **Weippert, H.** "Speicher." *BRL.* 308–9.

Translation and Prosodic Analysis

Six Covenant Blessings [4:(5:5):6] [4:(3:3):4)]

1 *And it shall be / if you*[a] *surely hearken /*	13	2
to the voice / of YHWH your God /	12	2_
To be careful [b]*to do / all his commandments /*	14	2
that / I command you / TODAY //	15	3_
Then YHWH your God / will make you / most high /	18	3
above / all the nations[c] *of the earth //*	11	2_
2 *And all these blessings / will come upon you /*	23	2
and they will overtake you //	7	1
when you hearken / to the voice / of YHWH your God //	16	3_
3 *Blessed are you / in the city //*	11	2
and blessed are you / in the (open) field //	13	2_
4 *And blessed is the fruit of your womb /*	10	1
and the fruit of your ground /	10	1
[a]*and the fruit of your beasts*[a] *//*	9	1_
The increase of your cattle\\[b] *and the young of your flock //*	16	1
5 *blessed is your basket / and your kneading trough //*	13	2_

6 *Blessed are you / in your coming in //*	12	2
and blessed are you / in your going out //	14	2_

Promises Expanding on the Blessings [(7:5):(4:4):(5:7)]

7 *May YHWH grant in regard to your enemies /*	13	1
the ones rising[a] *against you /*	10	1
that they be struck down / before you //	11	2
In one[b] *road*[c] *they shall go out against you /*	15	1
and in seven roads / they shall flee before you //	22	2_
8 *May YHWH command*[a] *that the blessing / be with you /*	16	2
in your granaries[b] */ and in every / enterprise of your hand*[c] *//*	19	3_
And he will bless you / in the land /	12	2
that YHWH your God / is giving to you //	17	2
9 *YHWH will establish you *[a] *for himself / to be a holy people /*	17	2
just as / he swore to <your fathers>[b] *//*	12	2_
When you keep / the commandments / of YHWH your God /	18	3
and you walk / in his ways //	10	2_
10 *Then all the peoples of the earth / shall see /*	14	2
that / the name of YHWH / is proclaimed over you //	16	3
and they shall be afraid / of you //	10	2_

The Threefold Blessing: Progeny, Livestock, and Produce [5:5]

11 *And YHWH will make you abound / in prosperity*[a] */*	13	2
in the fruit of your womb /	6	1
and in the fruit of your[b] *cattle /*	9	1
and in the fruit of your ground //	10	1_
Upon / the ground / that YHWH swore /	15	3
to your fathers / to give to you //	12	2_

Promises Expanding the Blessings [(6:7):(7:6):(5:5)]

12 *May YHWH open / to you / his good treasury / the heavens /*	23	4
by giving rain [a]*on your land*[a] */ in its time /*	13	2_
And[b] *by blessing / all / the work of your hand*[c] *//*	18	3
and you shall lend / to many nations /	11	2
but as for you / you shall not borrow //	8	2_
13 *And YHWH will make you / to be the head / and not the tail /*	20	3
and you shall be / only above /	11	2
and you shall not be / beneath //	9	2_
When you hearken / to the commands / of YHWH your God /	16	3
that I command you / TODAY / to keep and to do (them) //	23	3_
14 *And you shall not turn aside /* [a]*from all the words /*	15	2
that I / [b]*command <you>*[b] */ TODAY*[a] */*	15	3_
To the right or to the left //	8	1
to walk / after / other gods / to serve them // ס	22	4_

Six Covenant Curses [(5:4):(3:3):(4:5)]

15 *And it shall be / if you will not hearken / to the voice /*	13	3
of YHWH your God / [a]*to keep and* [b]*to do*[b] */*	16	2
[c]*All his commands*[c] *and* [d]*his statutes*[d] */*	13	1
that / I command you / TODAY[a] *//*	16	3_
Then all these curses / shall come upon you /	23	2
and they shall overtake you //	7	1
16 *Cursed are you* \\[a] *in the city //*	11	1
and cursed are you / in the field //	12	2_
17 *Cursed is your basket / and your kneading trough //*	13	2
18 *cursed is the fruit of your womb /*	11	1
and the fruit of the ground[a] *//*	11	1_
The increase of your cattle /	8	1
and the offspring of your flock //	10	1
19 *Cursed are you* \\[a] *in your coming in //*	12	1
and cursed are you / in your going out //	13	2_

Notes

1.a. LXX has 2 pl. verbal form.

1.b. Some Heb. MSS, SP, LXX, and *Tg. Ps.-J.* add *waw*-conj.

1.c. A few Heb. MSS and SP read גוי, "nation," for MT גויי, "nations of (the earth)."

4.a-a. Omitted in LXX by homoeoteleuton. Prosodic analysis supports MT.

4.b. Reading *ṭipḥā'* as conj. because of misplaced *sillûq*.

7.a. Some SP MSS read הקאמים for MT הקמים, "the ones rising." The roots קאם and קום appear to be interchangeable (see BDB, 866).

7.b. Some SP MSS read אחת, "one," for MT אחד, "one."

7.c. Reading *pašṭā'* followed by *zāqēp qāṭôn* as conj.

8.a. SP reads יצוה for MT יצו, "he will command," with no change in meaning.

8.b. SP reads באסימך, "in your barn," for MT באסמיך, "in your barns."

8.c. Many Heb. MSS, SP, Tg., and Vg. read pl. ידיך, "your hands," for MT ידך, "your hand." *Tg. Ps.-J.* reads ידיכם, "your [pl.] hands."

9.a. Reading *pašṭā'* followed by *mêrĕkā* as conj.

9.b. Emending with LXX τοῖς πατράσιν σου, "to your fathers," for MT לָךְ, "to you." Mayes ([1981] 353) says the verb שׁבע, "to swear," in Deuteronomy with YHWH as subject is used elsewhere only with reference to the promise to the fathers (e.g., 1:8; 4:31; 6:10; 7:12; etc.; though cf. 2:14).

11.a. SP reads לטוב, "for good [masc.]," for MT לטובה, "for good [fem.]," which is possible in terms of the prosodic analysis.

11.b. SP omits pronominal suff.

12.a-a. SP inserts את before ארצך, "your land."

12.b. One Heb. MS and some SP MSS omit *waw*-conj.

12.c. Cairo Geniza text, LXX, SP, Syr., and Vg. read pl. ידיך, "your hands" for MT ידך, "your hand."

14.a-a. Omitted in LXX (Vg. reads *ab eis*, "from them"). Prosodic analysis supports MT.

14.b-b. Reading מצוך for MT מצוה אתכם, "(that I) command you [sg.]," with one Heb. MS, SP, LXX, and Syr. (cf. 4:40; 6:2, 6, and numerous other occurrences, including 28:13). There is no change in meaning. The *sĕtûmā'* layout marker makes a significant boundary here, which may have attracted the use of the *Numeruswechsel* within the Masoretic tradition (cf. 28:62, 63, 68). The elimination of one word here brings the total word count for 28:11–14 to 78 (= 3 × 26) and the word count before *'atnāḥ* to 119 (= 7 × 17). It also brings the total word count before *'atnāḥ* in 28:1–69 to 595 (= 35 × 17). See discussion under *Form/Structure/Setting.*

15.a-a. Omitted in LXX minuscules. Prosodic analysis supports MT.

15.b-b. Omitted in SP and LXX[B]; some Heb. MSS add *waw*-conj. Prosodic analysis supports MT.

15.c-c. Omitted in SP and LXX minuscules. Prosodic analysis supports MT.

15.d-d. Omitted in some Heb. MSS, some LXX witnesses, and Syr. Prosodic analysis supports MT.
16.a. Reading *ṭipḥā'* as conj. because of misplaced *'atnāḥ*.
18.a. One Heb. MS adds ופרי בהמתך, "and fruit of your livestock." Prosodic analysis supports the shorter MT.
19.a. Reading *ṭipḥā'* as conj. because of misplaced *'atnāḥ*.

Form/Structure/Setting

From a prosodic point of view, Deut 28:1–19 is in five parts (vv 1–6, 7–10, 11, 12–14, and 15–19), which are carefully structured in terms of content in a concentric pattern:

A Six blessings (in three pairs) — 28:1–6
B Promises expanding on the blessings — 28:7–10
X Threefold blessing (fruit of womb, cattle, ground) — 28:11
B′ Promises expanding on the blessings — 28:12–14
A′ Six curses (in three pairs) — 28:15–19

The six blessings (28:1–6) and six curses (28:15–19) are arranged in three pairs using virtually identical language:

1. Blessed/cursed are you in the city — 28:3a, 16a
2. Blessed/cursed are you in the field — 28:3b, 16b

3. Blessed/cursed is the fruit of you womb, . . . ground, and . . . beasts — 28:4, 18
4. Blessed/cursed is your basket and your kneading trough — 28:5, 17

5. Blessed/cursed are you in your coming in — 28:6a, 19a
6. Blessed/cursed are you in your going forth — 28:6b, 19b

The inner frame in the above concentric structure (28:7–10 and 12–14) consists of promises that elaborate on the concise blessings of vv 3–6. These sections highlight that God is the source of the blessings. Israel will be successful because God will honor what he promised in 26:18–19. The expansion of the covenant blessings in 28:7–10 may be outlined as follows:

A YHWH will destroy your enemies before you — 28:7
B YHWH will ordain blessings for you — 28:8a
X And he will bless you in the land that YHWH is giving you — 28:8b
B′ YHWH will establish you as his holy people — 28:9
A′ All the peoples of the earth shall see and fear — 28:10

The outer frame moves from YHWH's promise to destroy Israel's enemies (v 7) to the great fear that will spread among all the peoples of the earth who see what God is doing in behalf of Israel (v 10). In the inner frame YHWH declares that he will surely bring his blessings on Israel (v 8a), for he will establish them as his holy people (v 9). The center summarizes the matter: God will bless his people in the land that he is giving them (v 8b). The nature of that blessing is spelled out again in v 11, in a circular sentence:

A	YHWH will make you abound in prosperity	והותרך יהוה לטובה
B	in the fruit of your womb	בפרי בטנך
X	in the fruit of your cattle	ובפרי בהמתך
B′	in the fruit of your ground	ובפרי אדמתך
A′	upon the ground	על האדמה
	that YHWH swore to your fathers to give you	אשר נשבע יהוה לאבתיך לתת לך

YHWH will cause his people to abound in prosperity in the promised land: in progeny, in livestock, and in agricultural produce.

The second expansion of the blessings in terms of promises on the part of YHWH in 28:12–14 may be outlined in similar fashion:

A	YHWH will open for you his rich storehouse	28:12a
B	You will be a creditor to many nations, but debtor to none	28:12b
X	YHWH will make you the head, not the tail	28:13a
B′	If you keep the commandments of YHWH that I command you today	28:13b
A′	Do not turn to the worship of other gods	28:14

YHWH will open "his good treasury" to bless his people in all they do (v 12a), so do not turn "to the right or to the left, to walk after other gods to serve them" (v 14). If Israel keeps YHWH's commandments (v 13b), they will be blessed above all nations (v 12b). Israel will lend to many nations, but borrow from none, for Israel will be exalted high above all peoples (v 13a).

There are other ways to show the concentric structure of this passage in matters of detail. Tigay presents the relationship between the blessings in vv 3–6 and the promises of vv 7–13 as follows ([1996] 490):

A	economic success	28:3a
B	fertility of soil	28:3b
C	fertility of humans and animals	28:4
D	abundant food	28:5
E	military success	28:6
E′	military success	28:7
D′	abundant food	28:8
C′	fertility of humans and animals	28:11
B′	fertility of soil	28:12a
A′	economic success	28:12b–13

This particular analysis, which is based on repetition of ideas as well as on specific vocabulary items, was apparently first observed by Rofé (Tigay [1996] 542 n. 6).

The evidence Labuschagne has gathered on the use of the divine-name numbers in 28:1–19, with a minor correction in v 14, may be summarized as follows:

Words:	before *ʾatnāḥ*		after *ʾatnāḥ*		
28:1–6	38 (= ברכה)	+	23	=	61
26:3–6	16	+	10	=	26
28:7–10	34 (= 2 × 17)	+	25	=	59
28:7–8	17	+	15	=	32
28:9–10	17	+	10	=	27

28:11–14	47 (= ארור)	+	31	= 78 (= 3 × 26)
28:11	9	+	8	= 17
28:12	17	+	6	= 23
28:13	11	+	12	= 23
28:11–12	26	+	14	= 40
28:12–14	39	+	23	= 62
28:13–14	21	+	17	= 38 (= ברכה)
28:15–19	31	+	16	= 47 (= ארור)
28:1–14	119 (= 7 × 17)	+	79	= 198
28:15–69	476 (= 4 × 7 × 17)	+	318	= 794

The divine-name numbers are woven into the text of 28:1–14 in numerous ways, along with both 23 and 32, the two numerical values of כבוד, "glory." A close look at the prosodic analysis presented here in relation to the data assembled by Labuschagne reveals that each of the prosodic units, and the subdivisions within these units as well, is structured in terms of these sacred numbers. Moreover, 28:1–14 as a whole has 119 (= 7 × 17) words before *ʾatnāḥ*; and 28:15–69 as a whole has 476 (= 4 × 7 × 17) words before *ʾatnāḥ*. It may also be significant that there are 38 words before *ʾatnāḥ* at the beginning (vv 1–6) and 38 words in vv 13–14 near the end of this unit; for this is the numerical value of the word ברכה, "blessing," which is the subject of the passage. There are 47 words in vv 15–19, which is the numerical value of the key word ארור, "cursed," which appears six times in vv 16–19. Symbolically the word "curse" appears a seventh time in the total number of 47 words in this passage.

Comment

1–2 The opening words, "if you surely hearken to the voice of YHWH your God," form an inclusion with the concluding words of v 2 that separates vv 1–2 from the sixfold covenant blessing of vv 3–6.

3–4 The word ברוך, "blessed," which carries the connotation of being "prosperous," is repeated six times in vv 3–6 within the space of twenty-six words. The phrases "in the city" and "in the field" function as a merism to indicate totality of place (see J. Krašovec, *Der Merismus im Biblisch-Hebraischen und Nordwestsemitischen*, BibOr 33 [Rome: Pontifical Biblical Institute, 1977]). Wherever you are, you will prosper. The word פרי, "fruit," is used in a broader sense in Hebrew than is normally the case in English. See 28:53 below, where it is used in the expression "fruit of your own womb" in reference to human beings who are consumed in the horrors of starvation in times of military siege. The word appears three times here: of human beings, of agricultural produce, and of livestock.

5 The "kneading trough" was a wide shallow bowl employed for the preparation of dough with which to make bread. The blessing here refers to provision of daily food for the family.

6 The phrases "your coming in" and "your going out" are often used of military activity, which is clearly the case in the parallel passage in 28:7. See the discussion below in 31:2, where Moses' inability "to go out and to come in" refers to his concern for the military leadership that he is turning over to Joshua (cf. Num 27:17, 21 and 1 Sam 18:13, 16; 29:6).

7 Security is assured by God against external threats from enemies. The phrase "seven roads" is used figuratively to express the idea of a large number, with the notion of completeness and fullness. Thus the translation in JPS *Tanakh* renders it "by many roads."

8 On the meaning of the phrase "every enterprise of your hand," see the *Comment* on 12:7. The phrase has a double meaning: "labor" itself, in the sense of "that to which one sets one's hand," and the products of one's labor (cf. 26:11).

9 On the peculiar calling of the people of Israel "to be a holy people," see also Exod 19:6, where the concept of Israel as "a holy nation" is linked with that of their being "a kingdom of priests." Without the proposed textual emendation from LXX (adding "your fathers"), this would be the only use of the phrase "just as he swore" with reference to the Sinai covenant in Deuteronomy.

10–11 "They shall be afraid of you," because "the name of YHWH is proclaimed over you." Tigay has noted that the same concept on a human level appears in an appeal from a Canaanite vassal to Pharaoh in Amarna Tablet 287 ([1996] 260): "Behold, the king has set his name in the land of Jerusalem for ever; so he cannot abandon the lands of Jerusalem!" (*ANET*, 488). To proclaim the name over something was a legal act by which ownership was claimed and established in ancient Israel (Galling, *TLZ* 76 [1956] 65–70). On the threefold blessing of v 11, cf. v 4.

12 Craigie says, "The language of the verse is poetic and the imagery . . . is reminiscent of Ps. 104:3, 13, where God is described as watering the mountains from his lofty abode" ([1976] 337). Israel shall enjoy such an excess of prosperity that they "shall lend to many nations" and "shall not borrow." On God's provision of the rain, see 11:11–17.

13–14 The idea that God will make Israel "to be the head and not the tail" expresses in new language what was said in the previous verse.

15–19 On the phrase "all his commands and his statutes" see also v 45 (and cf. v 1). The curses begin with the conditional clause, "if you will not hearken to the voice of YHWH your God," similar to some ancient treaties.

Explanation

The threefold blessing of progeny, livestock, and produce of v 11 is expanded in vv 1–19 in parallel units that epitomize the essence of Deuteronomic theology, which may be summarized as follows: "obey the commands of YHWH and be blessed; disobey them and be cursed." That this is an oversimplification of reality is demonstrated by the question posed by the prophet Habakkuk—"why do you look on the treacherous, and are silent when the wicked swallow those more righteous than they?" (Hab 1:13 NRSV)—and by the book of Job. Job is actually singled out for suffering because he "was blameless and upright, one who feared God and turned away from evil" (Job 1:1, 8), not because of any sin on his part. Some scholars have even suggested that the book of Job was written expressly to challenge the simplistic interpretation of Deuteronomic theology.

One's circumstances in life are not necessarily a result of one's character. Hundreds of thousands of innocent children died in the Nazi holocaust, not because of sin on their part but because of an enormous evil force that surged across the length and breadth of Europe at that time. There are countless examples of disasters in all ages in which innocent people suffer and die. When Jesus' disciples saw a man blind from birth, they asked Jesus, "Rabbi, who sinned, this man or his parents, that he was born blind?" (John 9:2). Jesus responded, "Neither this man nor his parents sinned" (John 9:3 NRSV). As so many in various twelve-step recovery programs remind themselves again and again in their attempts to break free from the sense of guilt that tends to paralyze them, life is not fair. None of us is totally free from the effects of the evil one, however righteous we may be.

As Maxwell noted ([1987] 303–4), a close reading of the Former Prophets shows that even the so-called Deuteronomistic History does not follow the simplistic reading of Deuteronomic theology proposed by a surface reading of Deut 28:1–19. In 2 Sam 11:25 we read that "the sword devours now one and now another," so that the innocent are taken along with the guilty. The untimely deaths of the priests of Nob at the hands of King Saul (1 Sam 22:18–19) and the deaths of the seventy brothers of Abimelech (Judg 9:1–6) had nothing to do with retributive justice. On the other side, the long succession of kings in ancient Israel and Judah who ruled in luxury in spite of the fact that they refused to obey the words of YHWH's Torah bears witness to the other side of the coin. Evil is not always punished in this life.

The most striking example of innocent suffering in the literature of the Latter Prophets is that of the "suffering servant" of Isaiah 53. In spite of his obedience to God's commandments, the servant suffers as did the prophet Jeremiah before him, and others in the long line of men and women who faithfully proclaimed the word of God in difficult circumstances.

A close reading of Deuteronomy itself shows the folly in a simplistic interpretation of blessings and curses in terms of moral behavior alone. Israel's wealth is presented as a gift of God, not something earned (8:18). God did not give the blessing of the land to Israel because they were more righteous than other nations (9:4–6). In the episode of the golden calf, the people were spared because Moses interceded for them, not because of righteousness on their part (9:25–29).

2. *Expanded Description of Future Disaster (28:20–69 [Eng. 29:1])*

a–b. *First and Second Expansions of the Covenant Curses (28:20–44)*

Bibliography

Aharoni, I. "Animals Mentioned in the Bible." *Osiris* 5 (1938) 478. **Alexander, R. D.** "Cricket." In *EncBrit.* 1966. 6:753. **Ben-Hayyim, Z.** "Observations on the Hebrew and Aramaic Lexicon from the Samaritan Tradition." In *FS W. Baumgartner.* 1967. 12–24, esp. 16–17, 19. **Branden, A. van den.** "'Reseph' nella Bibbia." *BeO* 13 (1971) 211–25, esp. 213. **Carmichael, C. M.** "Uncovering a Major Source of Mosaic Law: The Evidence of Deut 21:15–22:5." *JBL* 101 (1982) 505–20, esp. 514 n. 19. **Cathcarth, K. J.** "Micah 5,4–5 and Semitic Incantations." *Bib* 59 (1978) 38–48, esp. 46–47. **Cazelles, H.** "Jérémie et le Deutéronome." *RSR* 38 (1951/52) 5–36, esp. 12. **Dion, P. E.** "Un nouvel éclairage sur le context culturel des malheurs de Job." *VT* 34 (1984) 213–15. ———. "Quelques aspects de l'interaction entre religion et politique dans le Deutéronome." *ScEs* 30 (1978) 39–55, esp. 48–50. **Driver, G. R.** "The Plague of the Philistines." *JRAS* (1950) 51. **Fensham, F. C.** "Ordeal by Battle in the Ancient Near East and in the Old Testament." In *FS E. Volterra.* 1971. 1969. 127–35, esp. 133–34. **Frankena, R.** "The Vassal-Treaties of Esarhaddon and the Dating of Deuteronomy." *OTS* 14 (1965) 122–54. **Greenfield, J. C.** "Some Phoenician Words." *Sem* 38 (1990) 156. **Gruber, M.** *Aspects of Nonverbal Communication in the Ancient Near East.* Studia Pohl 12.I–II. Rome: Biblical Institute Press, 1980. 1:386–400. **Hillers, D.** *Treaty-Curses and the Old Testament Prophets.* BibOr 16. Rome: Pontifical Biblical Institute, 1964. 30–42. **Hort, G.** "The Plagues of Egypt." *ZAW* 69 (1957) 101–2. **Kim, Y.** "The Vocabulary of Oppression in the Old Testament: *ʿsq, ynh, lhs,* and Congeners." Ph.D. diss., Drew Univ., 1981. **Linsenmaier, W.** *Insects of the World.* New York: McGraw-Hill, 1972. 78–79. **Lohfink, N.** "'I Am Yahweh, Your Physician' (Exodus 15:26): God, Society and Human Health in a Postexilic Revision of the Pentateuch (Exod. 15:25b, 26)." In *Theology of the Pentateuch.* 1994. 35–95. **Macalister, A.** "Medicine." *Dictionary of the Bible.* Ed. J. Hastings. 5 vols. New York: Scribner, 1902–4. 3:323–25, 329. **MacIntosh, A. A.** "A Consideration of Hebrew *gʿr.*" *VT* 19 (1969) 471–79, esp. 477, 479. **Malusa, L.** "L'interpretazione Geronimiana de '*ḥrb*' in tre passi biblici." *BeO* 19 (1977) 259–61. **McCarthy, C.** *The Tiqqune Sopherim and Other Theological Corrections in the Masoretic Text of the Old Testament.* OBO 36. Fribourg; Göttingen: Vandenhoeck & Ruprecht, 1981. 197–204, 211–14. **McCarthy, D. J.** *Treaty and Covenant.* AnBib 21. Rome: Pontifical Biblical Institute, 1963. 121–22, 124. **Montet, P.** *Egypt and the Bible.* Tr. L. R. Keylock. Philadelphia: Fortress, 1968. 98. **Neustätter, O.** "Where Did the Identification of the Philistine Plague as Bubonic Plague Originate?" *Bulletin of the History of Medicine* 11 (1942) 36–47. **Nielsen, B. E.** "תיקוני סופרים." M.Div. Thesis, Union Theological Seminary, 1977. 1–32, 111–24. **Oded, B.** *Mass Deportations and Deportees in the Neo-Assyrian Empire.* Wiesbaden: Reichert, 1979. **Palmoni, Y.** "Locust" *IDB* 3:144–48. **Plöger, J. G.** *Literarkritische, formgeschichtliche und stilkritische Untersuchungen.* 1967. 189–90. **Pons, J.** *L'Oppression dans l'Ancien Testament.* Paris: Letouzey, 1981. **Preuss, J.** *Biblical and Talmudic Medicine.* Tr. F. Rosner. New York: Sanhedrin Press, 1978. 154–57, 164–66, 339–43. **Reif, S. C.** "A Note on *gʿr.*" *VT* 21 (1971) 241–44. **Saggs, H. W. F.** *The Greatness That Was Babylon.* London: Sidgwick & Jackson, 1962. 97. **Sasson, J. M.** *The Military Establishments at Mari.* Studia Pohl 3. Rome: Pontifical Biblical Institute, 1969. 47–49. **Steiner, F.** *Taboo.* 2nd ed. London: Cohen & West, 1967. 68–93, 149–53. **Watson, W. G. E.** "Reclustering Hebrew *lʾlyd-.*" *Bib* 58 (1977) 213–15. **Weidner, E. F.** "Der Staatsvertrag Assurniraris V mit Mati'ilu von Bit-Agusi." *AfO* 8 (1932–33) 17–26. **Weil, H. M.** "Gage et cautionnement dans la Bible." *AHDO* 2 (1938) 171–241, esp. 178. **Weinfeld, M.** *DDS.* 116–29. ———. "Traces of Assyrian Treaty Formulae in Deuteronomy." *Bib* 46 (1965) 417–27, esp. 418 n. 3, 420–23. **Westbrook, R.** *Studies in Biblical and Cuneiform Law.* Paris: Gabalda, 1988. 15–35. **Wilkinson, J.** *The Bible and Healing: A Medical and Theological Commentary.* Grand Rapids: Eerdmans, 1998. **Wilson, J. V. K.** "Medicine in the Land and Times of the Old Testament." In *Studies in the Period of David and Solomon and Other Essays.* Ed T. Ishida. Winona Lake, IN: Eisenbrauns, 1982. 337–65. **Winckler, A. J.** "Pests and Diseases." *EncBrit.* 1966. 10:691. **Wiseman, D. J.** "'Is It Peace?'—Covenant and Diplomacy." *VT* 32 (1982) 311–26, esp. 321. ———. *The Vassal-Treaties of Esarhaddon (= Iraq 20).* London: British School of Archaeology, 1958. 88.

Translation and Prosodic Analysis

First Expansion: Pestilence, Famine, and Disease [(5:4):(4:4):(4:5)]

General Theme: Curse, Confusion, and Cumbrance [(5:4)]

[20] *YHWH will send\[a] upon you / curse[b] <and>[c] confusion /* 22 2
and cumbrance / in all the undertakings of your hand[d] / 14 2
[e]that you will do[e] // 5 1_
Until [f]you are destroyed and you perish[f]\[g] quickly / 16 1
because of / your evil doing / in forsaking me // 22 3_

Seven Afflictions from Pestilence [(4:4):(4:5)]

[21] *YHWH will make\[a] the pestilence cling / to you //* 13 2
until / he has put an end to you / 10 2
From upon / the ground / 10 2
that you are coming there / to possess // 14 2_
[22] *YHWH [a]will strike you[a] / with consumption and with fever /* 17 2
and with inflammation / and with fiery heat / 12 2_
And with drought[b] / 5 1
and with scorching / and with mildew // 17 2
[c]and they will pursue you / until you perish[c] // 13 2_

Destruction by Famine and the Sword [6:7:7:6]

[23] *And your heavens[a] /* 10 1
that are over your head\[b] will become brass // 12 1
and the land that is beneath you\[c] iron // 14 1
[24] *And YHWH will make / the rain of your land /* 12 2
powder and dust // 9 1_
From the heavens / it will come down upon you / 15 2
until\[a] you are destroyed[b] // 5 1
[25] *And YHWH / will cause you /[a] to be defeated /* 9 3
before your enemies / 9 1_
By one[b] road / you will go forth against him / 14 2
indeed by seven roads / 11 1
you will flee before him // 9 1
And you will become [c]an object of trembling[c] / 11 1
to all / the kingdoms of the land // 12 2_
[26] *And your corpses will be / food /* 17 2
[a]for every bird[a] of the heavens / 9 1
And for the beasts of the land // 11 1
and there will be none / to frighten them off // 7 2_

Seven More Afflictions ("Boils of Egypt") [(6:4):(4:6)]

[27] *And YHWH will strike you /* 7 1
with boils of Egypt\[a] and with piles[b] / 13 1

and with scurvy / and with itch[c] *//* 13 2
of which you are not able / to be healed // 13 2_
28 *And YHWH will strike you /* 7 1
with madness\[a] *and*[b] *with blindness //* 14 1
and[b] *with confusion / of heart //* 10 2_
29 *And you will / grope about at noonday /* 15 2
just as the blind man gropes about / in the dark / 19 2_
And you will not prosper / in your ways[a] *//* 14 2
and you will be / only[b] *maltreated and robbed / all the days /* 22 3
and there will not be[c] *a savior //* 8 1_

Violent Loss of Family, Home, and Property [7:(4:7)]

30 *A woman you will betroth /* 8 1
but another man / will rape[a] *her /* 12 2
A home you will build / 4 1
but you will not dwell in it // 9 1
A vineyard you will plant / 4 1
but you will not put it to use // 9 1_
31 *Your ox / will be slaughtered before your eyes /* 15 2
and you will not eat / any of it / 10 2_
Your ass / will be stolen from before you / 16 2
and it will not be returned / to you // 9 2_
Your sheep\[a] *will be given to your enemies /* 16 1
and there will not be for you / a savior // 10 2_

Second Expansion: Oppression, Exile, and Slavery

Oppression That Produces Insanity [(7:4):7]

32 *Your sons and your daughters / will be given to another people /* 23 2
and your eyes will look on / 10 1
And they will be spent with tears for them / [a]*all the day*[a] *//* 13 2
and there will be no power (to help) / in your hand<s>[b] *//* 11 2_
33[a] *The fruit of your ground / and of all your toil /* 15 2
a people will devour / that you have not known // 19 2_
And you will be / 6 1
only / maltreated and crushed / all the days // 16 3_
34 *And you will be*\[a] *driven mad //* 10 1
by the sight of your eyes / that you will see // 13 2_

Afflictions of Disease ("Boils [like Job]") [4:4]

35 *YHWH will strike you / with evil boils /* 11 2
on the knees / and on the legs / 12 2
Of which you will not be able / to be healed // 14 2
from the sole of your foot / to the crown of your head // 11 2_

Exile from the Land of Israel [5:5:5]

[36] *And YHWH will bring*[a] */ you / and your*[b] *king /*	18	3
that you will set up over you / to a nation /	15	2_
That you have not known \\[c] *you and your fathers //*	17	1
and you[d] *will serve there / other gods / of wood and stone //*	24	3
[37] *and you will become a horror*[a] */*	10	1_
[b]*A proverb* \\[c] *and a byword //*	11	1
among all / the peoples /	8	2
to which YHWH will lead you / there //	13	2_

Afflictions of Pestilence and War [(4:5):(3:3):(5:4)]

[38] *Much seed* \\[a] *you will carry to the field //*	11	1
and little will you gather in /	8	1
for the locust swarm / will consume it //	11	2_
[39] *Vineyards you will plant* \\[a] *and you will till them //*	14	1
but wine you will not drink /	8	1
And you will not gather in fruit /	7	1
for the worm / will devour it //	14	2_
[40] *Olive trees / you will have / throughout all your territory //*	16	3
but oil \\[a] *you will not have to anoint yourself /*	9	1
for your olives / [b]*will drop off*[b] *//*	8	2_
[41] *Sons and daughters / you will bear //*	14	2
but they will not be yours /	8	1
for they will go / into captivity //	11	2_
[42] *All your trees / and the fruit of your ground //*	15	2
the buzzing cricket / [a]*will possess*[a] *//*	9	2_

Impoverishment and Debt [6:6]

[43] *The alien / who is in your midst / will rise above you /*	17	3
higher and higher // but you will go down /	16	2
lower and lower //	7	1_
[44] *He will lend to you / and you / will not lend to him //*	16	3
he will be the head / and you / will be the tail //	18	3_

Notes

20.a. Reading *lĕgarmēh* as conj.

20.b. SP reads המרה, "the bitterness," for MT המארה, "the calamity."

20.c. A number of Heb. MSS, Cairo Geniza texts, SP, LXX, α′, and Vg. add *waw*-conj. Prosodic analysis supports the emendation.

20.d. Some Heb. MSS and SP read ידיך, "your hands," for MT ידך, "your hand."

20.e-e. LXX[B] omits this phrase. Prosodic analysis supports MT.

20.f-f. SP reads השמיד(ו)ך ועד (ה)אב(י)ד(ו)ך, "they destroy you and until they cause you to perish," for MT השמדך ועד־אבדך, "you are destroyed and until you perish." Prosodic analysis supports MT.

20.g. Reading *paštā'* followed by *zāqēp̄ qāṭôn* as conj.

21.a. Reading *ṭip̄ḥā'* on בך as conj. because of misplaced *'atnāḥ*.

22.a-a. Reading MT יַכְּכָה as equivalent to יַכֶּכָּה (cf. SP יכך), "he will strike you" (see also 28:27, 28, 35).

22.b. Omitted in LXX[B]. Reading חֹרֶב, "dryness" or "heat," with Vg., which reads *et aestu,* "and heat." MT reads חֶרֶב, "sword."

22.c-c. SP and Syr. read ירדפוך עד אב(י)ד(ו)ך, "they will pursue you until they cause you to perish," for MT ורדפוך עד אבדך, which is possible from a prosodic perspective.

23.a. Syr., Tg., and Vg. read השמים, "the heavens," for MT שמיך, "your heavens." MT is retained as *lectio difficilior.*

23.b. Reading *tip̄ḥā'* as conj. because of misplaced *'atnāḥ.*

23.c. Reading *tip̄ḥā'* as conj. because of misplaced *sillûq.*

24.a. Reading *tip̄ḥā'* as conj. because of misplaced *sillûq.*

24.b. LXX[B] adds ἐν τάχει, "quickly" (= מהר). Prosodic analysis supports MT.

25.a. Reading the unusual sequence of accents *mêrĕkā* with *pāsēq* as disj.

25.b. Some SP MSS read אחת, "one," for MT אחד, "one" (see 28:7).

25.c-c. One Heb. MS and SP read לזועה, "an object of trembling," by transposition, for MT לזעוה, "an object of trembling." See Isa 28:19.

26.a-a. Some Heb. MSS, SP, LXX, and Syr. read לעוף, "for birds," for MT לכל־עוף, "for every bird."

27.a. Reading *pašṭā'* followed by *zāqēp̄ qāṭôn* as conj.

27.b. Reading ובעפלים, "piles" or "hemorrhoids," with K, which was apparently considered too vulgar for public reading. The Q ובטחרים, "swellings," or "tumors," appears in some Heb. MSS, DSS, Syr., and Tg.

27.c. Some SP witnesses read ובהרם, "and with destruction," for MT ובחרס, "and with itch."

28.a. Reading *tip̄ḥā'* as conj. because of misplaced *'atnāḥ.*

28.b. Some LXX witnesses omit *waw*-conj. Prosodic analysis supports MT.

29.a. Some Heb. MSS, SP, and Syr. read sg. דרכך, "your way," for MT pl. דרכיך, "your ways." Prosodic analysis supports MT.

29.b. SP reads רק, "only," for MT אך, "only" or "surely."

29.c. Some of the more important LXX witnesses add σοι, "for you" (= לך) (cf. v 31 below). Adding a word here disturbs the numerical composition, which totals 51 (= 3 × 17) words in vv 29–31. It appears that the phrase "and there will not be a savior" is to be taken as a coda from a musical point of view.

30.a. Reading with K ישגלנה, "he shall rape her," a verb never used of legitimate sexual relations. Since this word was considered too vulgar for public reading, Q and other textual traditions used the words ישכב עמה, "lie with her," instead (cf. *Note* 27.b).

31.a. Reading *pašṭā'* followed by *zāqēp̄ qāṭôn* as conj.

32.a-a. Omitted in some Heb. MSS and LXX. Prosodic analysis supports MT.

32.b. Reading pl. ידיך, "your hands," with a number of Heb. MSS, Cairo Geniza fragments, and Syr. MT reads ידך, "your hand"; *Tg. Ps.-J.* reads ידיכם, "your [pl.] hands."

33.a. Some SP witnesses add *waw*-conj. Prosodic analysis supports MT.

34.a. Reading *tip̄ḥā'* as conj. because of misplaced *'atnāḥ.*

36.a. Some SP witnesses read יוליך for MT יולך, "he will bring," with no change in meaning.

36.b. *Tg. Ps.-J.* reads 2 pl.

36.c. Reading *tip̄ḥā'* as conj. because of misplaced *'atnāḥ.*

36.d. Lucianic tradition of LXX, OL, and *Tg. Ps.-J.* read 2 pl.

37.a. SP reads לשם for MT לשמה, "become a horror," with no change in meaning.

37.b. SP and LXX add *waw*-conj.

37.c. Reading *tip̄ḥā'* as conj. because of misplaced *'atnāḥ.*

38.a. Reading *tip̄ḥā'* as conj. because of misplaced *'atnāḥ.*

39.a. Reading *tip̄ḥā'* as conj. because of misplaced *'atnāḥ.*

40.a. Reading *pašṭā'* followed by *zāqēp̄ qāṭôn* as conj.

40.b-b. Some SP witnesses, Syr., Tg., and Vg. read יש(ע)לו, "they will drop off," for MT ישל, "it will drop off."

42.a-a. Reading יוריש, "it shall possess," with SP for MT יירש, "it will be dispossessed (by the locust)."

Form/Structure/Setting

Since about 1960, scholars have looked to international treaty texts from the ancient Near East as a model to explain the form of Deuteronomy. At first, interest focused on parallels with Hittite vassal treaty texts of the Late Bronze Age (pre-1200 B.C.E.); but other parallels were noted with later Assyrian treaty texts from the Iron Age (post-1200 B.C.E.). In keeping with the structure of what have come to be called "Iron Age Loyalty Oaths," Deut 28:20–68 is an expanded definition of the acts of commission and omission that subject a vassal to the covenant curses. The Iron Age treaties give the impression that a promise to obey has simply been imposed by superior military force and is reinforced by means of the elaboration of curses. Weinfeld has appropriately called these treaties "loyalty oaths" (*JAOS* 90 [1970] 184–203; idem, *UF* 8 [1976] 392–93).

Like the Assyrian loyalty oaths, Deut 28:20–44 is an expanded description of disasters, including natural calamities, diseases, and the ravages of war, that may be outlined as follows:

A	Agricultural disaster (drought and hardened soil)	28:20–24
B	Human afflictions (defeat → boils → madness → oppression)	28:25–29
X	Undoing of the blessings (in 28:4, 8, 11)	28:30–31
B′	Human afflictions (oppression → madness → boils → defeat)	28:32–37
A′	Agricultural disaster (crop-destroying pests)	28:38–44

In this reading the outer frame consists of parallel groups of curses that focus on agricultural disaster in terms of drought (vv 20–24) and pestilence (vv 38–44). The inner frame focuses on human afflictions (vv 25–29 and 32–37). In the center (vv 30–31) we find the reversal of the covenant blessings of prosperity in progeny, livestock, and agricultural produce. The elaboration here is far more expansive than that which accompanies the blessings in 28:7–14. Though this section is complex from a prosodic point of view, with ten rhythmic units, it contains an elaborate concentric structural design embracing the whole, which may be outlined as follows:

A	Triad of afflictions: curse, confusion, and cumbrance	28:20–22
B	Agricultural disaster (drought and hardened soil)	28:23–24
C	War: defeat leading to Israel becoming an object lesson	28:25–26
D	Boils of Egypt (sent from YHWH)	28:27
E	Madness and blindness	28:28–29a
F	Oppressed and robbed all the days	28:29b
X	Undoing of the blessings (in 28:4, 8, 11)	28:30–31
F′	Oppressed and crushed all the days	28:32–33
E′	Madness from what one sees	28:34
D′	Boils (sent from YHWH)	28:35
C′	War: exile leading to Israel becoming an object lesson	28:36–37
B′	Agricultural disaster (crop-destroying pests)	28:38–42
A′	Economic collapse—impoverishment and debt	28:43–44

The center of this structure (vv 30–31) contains a list of calamities that essentially undo the blessings of vv 4, 8, and 11. Everything the people of Israel have will be taken by those who conquer them: their fiancées will be raped, their homes and vineyards taken, their oxen slaughtered, their asses and sheep stolen, their children enslaved, and their produce consumed.

Since there are no markers in MT to indicate either the boundaries of vv 20–44 or the subunits within it, the structure must be determined on the basis of content, prosodic analysis, and the use of divine-name numbers. The list of curses that emerges from this study is arranged in ten prosodic units, perhaps to reflect the "ten plagues" of Exod 7–11. These units may be outlined in two five-part structural units (vv 20–32 and 33–44):

A	General theme: curse, confusion, and cumbrance	28:20
B	Seven afflictions from pestilence	28:21–22
X	Destruction by famine and war	28:23–26
B′	Seven more afflictions (including "boils of Egypt")	28:27–29
A′	Undoing of the blessings	28:30–31

A	Oppression that produces insanity	28:32–34
B	YHWH will strike you with boils (like Job)	28:35
X	Exile from the land	28:36–37
B′	Undoing of the blessings	28:38–42
A′	Impoverishment and debt	28:43–44

These individual prosodic units are carefully arranged in parallel structures. In this reading the focus of attention is on destruction by famine and war and the exile of the people of Israel from their land. Three categories of punishment are presented here: disease (vv 21–22), drought with subsequent famine (vv 23–24), and war (vv 25–26). Compare the familiar "pestilence, sword, and famine" in other texts (Jer 21:7; 32:24; 38:2; 43:11; Ezek 5:12; 7:15).

In the outer frame of the first five-part structure, the opening verse (v 20) is set over against a summation of the undoing of the blessings (vv 29b–32) given earlier in vv 3–13. Inside this frame we find the familiar triad of pestilence, famine, and sword, in which the climax is reached in v 26 with its portrayal of ignoble death in warfare where the corpses remain unburied. The inner frame around the unit I have titled "Destruction by famine and war" presents parallel structures on the subject of pestilence, each of which presents a list of seven afflictions.

As the first five-part structure highlights in its center (v 26) the ravages of war, so the second has its focus on the exile from the land of Israel that is the result of that military debacle (vv 36–37). The word שחין, "boils," appears in v 27 ("boils of Egypt") and again in v 35, where it is set over against another summation of the undoing of the earlier blessings (vv 38–42). The description of these "evil boils" in v 35 is virtually identical to Job's affliction as presented in Job 2:7.

The general theme of the curses to follow is announced in v 20 in poetic fashion with alliteration in Hebrew: YHWH will send מארה, מהומה, and מגערת, "curse, confusion, and cumbrance." The inner frame (vv 21–22 and 27–29) follows with two parallel presentations of seven afflictions:

A	YHWH will make pestilence cling to you until you are destroyed	28:21
B	Consumption, fever, and inflammation (בשחפת בקדחת ובדלקת)	28:22a
X	Fiery heat (ובחרחר)	28:22a
B′	Drought, scorching, and mildew (ובחרב ובשדפון ובירקון)	28:22a
A′	These will pursue you until you perish	28:22b

A	YHWH will strike you with boils of Egypt and with hemmorrhoids	28:27a
B	And with scurvy and with itch of which you cannot be healed	28:27a

X	YHWH will strike you with madness, blindness, confusion of heart	28:28a
B′	You shall grope about like a blind man—you shall not prosper	28:29a
A′	You will be mistreated and robbed—without anyone to help	28:29b

In the first series, the seven deadly forms of pestilence become reified; for "they will pursue you until you perish" (v 22b). The second series is introduced with the "boils" (שחין) of Egypt, and the structure focuses on the psychological torment that produces insanity (v 28a).

The central section, which describes the destruction by famine and war, is framed by repetition of the words שמים, "heavens," and ארץ, "earth," in vv 23 and 26, which appear in reverse order in v 24 as well. The structure of the subunit as a whole may be outlined as follows:

A	The skies shall be as brass and the earth as iron	28:23–24
B	YHWH will cause you to be defeated before your enemies	28:25a
X	You shall go out against them one way and flee seven ways	28:25b
B′	You shall become an object of trembling to all kingdoms	28:25c
A′	Your corpses—food for birds of the heavens and beasts of the earth	28:26

The structure highlights the totality of the destruction, which moves from the heavens to the earth—from drought to military defeat—leaving nothing but corpses to be consumed by birds of the heavens and beasts of the earth.

The expansion of the curses in vv 20–32 concludes with a portrayal of the reversal of the threefold blessing of vv 4 and 11:

A	Loss of wife and home	28:30a
B	A vineyard you shall plant and you shall not use it	28:30b
X	Your ox eaten by others and your ass stolen	28:31a
B′	Your sheep shall be given to your enemies	28:31b
A′	Loss of sons and daughters—helpless, you will see it all	28:32

The concluding note on the bitter sorrow for the great loss of family, home, and property, with "no power (to help) in your hand," sets the stage for the further expansion of the curses in 28:33–44.

The powerlessness to do anything at all produces insanity (vv 33–34); for "YHWH shall strike you with evil boils . . . from the sole of your foot to the crown of your head" (v 35). The picture is that of the suffering of Job at the hands of Satan. In this instance it leads to exile from the promised land "to a nation that you have not known . . . and you will serve there other gods of wood and stone" (v 36).

Another portrayal of the reversal of the threefold blessing of vv 4 and 11 follows in vv 38–42, which may be outlined as follows:

A	The locust (הארבה) shall consume your crops	28:38
B	Your vineyards shall be consumed by the worm (התלעת)	28:39
X	Your olive trees will produce no fruit for oil	28:40
B′	Your sons and daughters shall go into captivity	28:41
A′	All your crops will be consumed by the grasshopper (הצלצל)	28:42

The oil of the olive tree is a symbol for joy and comfort lost, for the olives will drop to the ground prematurely—there will be no oil of gladness (v 40). The vineyards will produce no wine because of the worm, which bred in the stale manna of the wilderness (see Exod 16:20). The outer frame moves from the reference to a plague of locusts (v 38) to that of grasshoppers (v 42), the proverbial source of agricultural disaster.

The expansion of the curses in vv 20–44 concludes with a brief note on the reversal of fortune as the alien, who in times past was a symbol of poverty in the midst of the people of Israel, is now the one to whom the people turn for subsistence: "he will be the head and you will be the tail" (v 44). It should be noted that this is a reversal of the final blessing in the original expansion of the covenant blessings in vv 12–13.

The prosodic analysis suggests that v 20 belongs with the seven afflictions from pestilence in vv 21–22 as a literary unit that scans (4:4):(6:6):(4:4) in accentual stress units. With other minor adjustments in vv 26 and 35, the resultant nine-part structure is essentially the "chiasm" observed by Tigay ([1996] 491):

A	Seven afflictions from pestilence	28:20–22
B	Drought and famine	28:23–25
C	The "sword"—ignoble death in warfare	28:26
D	Seven more afflictions (including boils)	28:27–29
X	Undoing of the blessings	28:30–32
D′	Oppression and boils sickness (cf. Job)	28:33–35
C′	Exile from the land	28:36–37
B′	Undoing of the blessing	28:38–42
A′	Impoverishment and debt	28:43–44

Tigay noted that the curses delineated here include virtually all of those mentioned in vv 16–19 and also appear to be an elaboration, in reverse order, of the blessings and promises of vv 1–15 ([1996] 542 n. 9). A similar chiastic structure was found by Thompson for vv 25–37, with vv 30–32 as the focal point ([1974] 273).

The evidence assembled by Labuschagne on the use of the divine-name numbers in vv 20–44 may be summarized as follows:

Words:	before *ʾatnāḥ*		after *ʾatnāḥ*		
28:20–22	28	+	23	=	51 (= 3 × 17)
28:23–26	34 (= 2 × 17)	+	17	=	51 (= 3 × 17)
28:27–28	11	+	6	=	17
28:29–31	33	+	18	=	51 (= 3 × 17)
28:32–35	34 (= 2 × 17)	+	17	=	51 (= 3 × 17)
28:36–39	26	+	25	=	51 (= 3 × 17)
28:40–42	12	+	14	=	26
28:43–44	12	+	10	=	22
28:20–44	190	+	130 (= 5 × 26)	=	320
28:1–44	340 (= 20 × 17)	+	226	=	565
28:23–24	13	+	10	=	23

28:47–48	22	+	10	=	32
28:33–44	73	+	63	=	136 (= 8 × 17)
28:38–44	31	+	37	=	68 (= 4 × 17)
28:20–31	106	+	64	=	170 (= 10 × 17)
28:23–31	78 (= 3 × 26)	+	41	=	119 (= 7 × 17)
28:27–31	44	+	24	=	68 (= 4 × 17)
28:30–31	22	+	10	=	32

Once again, we find the divine-name numbers 17 and 26, along with the two numerical values for כבוד, "glory" (23 and 32) woven into the Hebrew text of vv 20–44 in a variety of ways. The most striking observation is that there are a total of 51 (= 3 × 17) words in five of the first six subunits in vv 20–39. Moreover, a major break is found at the end of v 31 with the words ואין לך מושיע, "and there will not be for you a savior," which marks the boundary between the two expanded descriptions of future disaster in the prosodic analysis presented in this commentary (vv 20–31 and 32–44).

Comment

20 The three afflictions are alliterated in Hebrew: מארה, מהומה, and מגערת, which Tigay reproduces in English translation as "Curse, Confusion, and Cumbrance" ([1996] 261). The noun מארה, "calamity," comes from the root ארר, which means "to curse," and is the opposite of ברכה, "blessing," in v 8. The term מהומה, "confusion," refers to the turmoil and panic inspired by God in the traditions of Holy War in ancient Israel, often translated "panic" or "discomfit" in the KJV (Josh 10:10; Judg 4:15; 1 Sam 5:11; 7:10, etc.). What we have here is a reversal of YHWH's Holy War. The term מגערת, "cumbrance," which appears only here in the Hebrew Bible, comes from the root גער, "rebuke" or "restrain," which refers to God "restraining" the rain in vv 23–24 with the resultant crop failures (cf. vv 38–42). According to Craigie ([1976] 342), מגערת "denotes the physical expression of God's anger" (based on MacIntosh, *VT* 19 [1969] 471–79; and Reif, *VT* 21 [1971] 241–44). As Mayes put it, "With God as subject it may also denote the effective working out of his anger, and so come close to the sense of 'curse'" ([1981] 354).

21 The "pestilence" is a severe epidemic of some sort that produces the seven afflictions of the next verse (v 22).

22 Of the seven afflictions listed, some are uncertain because of our limited knowledge of ancient medical terminology: שחפת, "consumption," is probably tuberculosis; קדחת, "fever," may have been malaria; דלקת, "inflammation," is some kind of "burning" disease; חרחר, "fiery heat," may apply to "burning up" of vegetation in the drought; חרב, "drought," is the "heat" of both the sun and of fever; שדפון, "scorching," and ירקון, "mildew," normally refer to crop afflictions but may also be interpreted as human illness such as jaundice and emaciation. For useful discussions of disease in the Bible, see R. K. Harrison (*IDB* 1:847–54) and M. Sussman (*ABD* 6:6–15).

23–24 The likeness of the "heavens" to "brass" (נחשת) and the "land" to "iron" (ברזל) refers to hot sun and dry ground. The dryness of the cursed soil here stands in sharp contrast to the moist soil of the blessed land in v 12. Wiseman (*Vassal-Treaties,* 88) called attention to a significant parallel to this particular curse in the Esarhaddon treaty, which Thompson ([1974] 273) quotes as follows (ll. 530–33):

> Just as rain does not fall from a brazen heaven
> So may rain and dew not come upon your fields
> And your meadows; may it rain burning coals instead of dew on your land.

The terms "powder and dust" refer to the duststorms stirred up by the parched soil.

25–26 The phrase "seven roads" is used figuratively to express the idea of a large number (cf. v 7 above). The term rendered "object of trembling" (זעוה) derives from the Hebrew root זוע, "to tremble, quake." On the image of Israel as an object of trembling, see Jer 15:4; 24:9; 29:18; 34:17. The phrase "your corpses will be food" refers to the unburied bodies of Israel's fallen warriors (cf. Jer 7:33; 34:20). The phrase "to frighten them off" refers to protecting the corpses from being consumed by birds of prey. See 2 Sam 21:10.

27 The identifications of the four diseases mentioned here are not certain. The familiar translation "boils of Egypt" is retained here for Hebrew שחין, even though the term probably refers to some kind of dermatitis characteristic of Egypt; Tigay equates it with the sixth of the ten plagues in Egypt (Exod 9:8–12), perhaps skin anthrax ([1996] 263; see also Hort, *ZAW* 69 [1957] 101–2). Mayes suggests possible candidates for the "boils of Egypt" in such diverse ailments as elephantiasis, the "Baghdad Button," or the "Jericho Rose" ([1981] 354). More recently, Wilkinson identified the boils mentioned here as cutaneous anthrax (*Bible and Healing,* 48). According to rabbinic tradition, both K עפלים and Q טחרים mean "hemorrhoids"; but the former "was considered vulgar (like English 'piles') and was therefore replaced with the more polite *teḥorim* when the Torah was read in the synagogue" (Tigay [1996] 264; cf. v 30 below). On the identification of this disease see Neustätter, *Bulletin of the History of Medicine* 11 (1942) 36–47. The old Douay version put it rather well when it paraphrased the Hebrew text "the part of thy body, by which the dung is cast out." The afflictions of גרב, "scurvy," and חרס, "itch," are also serious skin afflictions, according to cognates in other Semitic languages. Weinfeld has identified גרב with a form of leprosy (*Bib* 41 [1960] 418 n. 3; cf. Craigie [1976] 344 n. 23).

28–29 The term שגעון, "madness," is used in 2 Kgs 9:20 to describe the manner in which Jehu drove his chariot in Jezreel. In the present context it probably means ranting and raving. The עורון, "blindness," here probably refers to psychological incapacitation, along with תמהסן לבב, "confusion of heart," which means consternation or bewilderment. The people, as if they were blind, will "grope about at noonday" as one does "in the dark." The interpretation of v 28 in terms of syphilis is debatable, as Craigie has shown ([1976] 344 n. 24).

30–32 The statement that "your eyes . . . will be spent with tears for them" presents the picture of "cried-out eyes," somewhat like the English idiom "to cry one's eyes out for them." The specific meaning of the Hebrew idiom אין לאל ידך, translated here as "there will be no power (to help) in your hand," is problematic. The key phrase here is אל יד, "god of the hand" or "the god who is at one's side" (C. Brockelmann, "אל ידי," *ZAW* 26 [1906] 29–32). The full meaning of the idiom would then be "the god of PN's hand has the power to. . . ." Such a reading, however, presupposes "a survival from a pre-monotheistic stage of Hebrew," as Tigay has noted ([1996] 396 n. 54).

33–34 The reference to "all your toil" is to the products of hard physical labor. The people of Israel will be left with nothing.

35 The שחין רע, "evil boils," cover the body "from the sole of your foot to the crown of your head"; Job suffered the same affliction (cf. v 27 above and Job 2:7).

36–37 The people of Israel will be sent into exile "to a nation that you have not known." The wording here, "your king that you will set up over you," is similar to that of 17:14–20. The institution of kingship is presented as a necessary evil (cf. also 1 Sam 12:13). Hope in the leadership of a king is futile if the people are not faithful to their covenant agreement with YHWH: "you will become a horror [שמה]," a source of consternation. The terms משל, "proverb," and שנינה, "byword," indicate that Israel will become an object lesson to others, an object of "sharp" or "cutting" remarks (so Driver [1895] 312).

38–40 The curses here elaborate the summary statement of v 18 and are the converse of the blessings in vv 11–13. An attack of locusts was the eighth of the ten plagues in Egypt. The "worm" (תלעת) will consume their "vineyards." "And oil you will not have to anoint yourself" because the olive trees will fail.

41–42 With so few people left to work the land, it will be overrun with destructive insects. That צלצל, "buzzing cricket," here forms an inclusion with ארבה, "locust swarm," of v 38 suggests that we have here another destructive insect, which "will possess (the land)." If so, the so-called mole cricket (Gryllotalpa) is a good candidate for צלצל (Aharoni, *Osiris* 5 [1938] 478; see Tigay [1996] 397 n. 69).

Explanation

One of the more important lessons of the long list of curses in Deut 28 is also a primary lesson in the story of the prophet Jonah: the simple fact that "there is no running from God but by running to him, no fleeing from his justice but by fleeing to his mercy" (M. Henry, *Exposition of the Old and New Testament* [1828] 681). Jonah was convinced that he was free to disobey God by fleeing to Tarshish. A close reading of that text, however, reveals that Jonah was not in fact free to disobey God. Nor are we. The only person in the story of Jonah who is actually free is God, who is even free to change his own mind (Jonah 3:10 NRSV: "God *changed his mind* about the calamity that he had said he would bring upon them; and he did not do it"), and to give the very words he entrusts to his prophet a meaning other than what the prophet himself understands.

According to the text of Deut 28, the curse of God follows a person wherever one may choose to go, for there is no escape from the relentless "hound of heaven." Jonah's flight from God's presence took him to "the roots of the mountains" in the nether world; but even in the Pit there was no way to escape from God (Jonah 2:5–6). As the summary curses here in Deut 28:16–19 put it, "Cursed are you in the city; and cursed are you in the field. . . . Cursed are you in your coming in; and cursed are you in your going out" (cf. Prov 3:33). The book of Job speaks to the same issue: "They will flee from an iron weapon; a bronze arrow will strike them through" (Job 20:24 NRSV). The imagery is similar to that of the prophet Amos, when he described the "day of the LORD": it is "as if someone fled from a lion, and was met by a bear; or went into the house and rested a hand against the wall, and was bitten by a snake" (Amos 5:19 NRSV).

Whatever the sinner does is under the curse—"in all the undertakings of your hand that you shall do," (v 20) there is constant vexation of disappointment, for God's curse in vv 15–19 is the opposite of his blessing in vv 1–14. The enumeration of those curses in the expansions that follow (vv 20–44, 45–68) in ever more focused detail of horror is intended to evoke a deep and lasting impression on the hearer. The judgments of God in vv 20–44 focus primarily on sufferings from pestilence (vv 21–22), famine, and war (vv 23–26), leading to the loss of everything, including the very promised land itself in the bitterness of exile (vv 36–37).

Those who are subject to the covenant curses will be plundered of all their enjoyments, including their homes and their families (vv 30–32). Their sons and daughters will be carried into captivity (v 41). Those who remain shall be insulted and tyrannized by strangers (vv 43–44). Such was the case with the Northern Kingdom, which fell to the might of the Assyrian Empire in the eighth century B.C.E. (2 Kgs 17:24), and to the Southern Kingdom of Judah that fell to King Nebuchadnezzar of Babylon at the beginning of the sixth century B.C.E. (2 Kgs 24–25).

When the text of Deut 28:15–68 is read with knowledge of the subsequent history of ancient Israel, the curses assume the nature of prophetic speech in describing what Craigie called "an aweful inevitability" ([1976] 341). It is not hard to understand the response of King Josiah to these very words: "And when the king heard the words of the book of the law, he rent his clothes" in dismay (2 Kgs 22:11). Moreover, when we realize that we as God's people today have the same sinful nature as they, then the inevitability of the curse weighs heavily upon us too. "It is at this point that the gospel message of the New Testament casts light into the darkness evoked by the curse" (Craigie [1976] 341). He then cites the words of William Blake, in his poem "The Everlasting Gospel," which merit repetition:

> Jesus was sitting in Moses' chair.
> They brought the trembling woman there.
> Moses commands she be stoned to death.
> What was the sound of Jesus' breath?
> He laid his hand on Moses' law.
> The ancient heavens in silent awe,
> Writ with curses from pole to pole.
> All away began to roll.

"The inevitability of the curse can be removed only by Jesus, and that is possible only because 'he redeemed us from the curse of the law, having become a curse for us' (Gal. 3:13)" (Craigie [1976] 341).

c. Third Expansion: Utter Privation in Siege Warfare (28:45–57)

Bibliography

Baker, J. A. "Deuteronomy and World Problems." *JSOT* 29 (1984) 3–17, esp. 87. **Cutler, B.**, and **MacDonald, J.** "Identification of the *Naʿar* in the Ugaraitic Texts." *UF* 8 (1976) 27–35. **Fensham, F. C.** "Ordeal by Battle in the Ancient Near East and the Old Testament." In *FS E. Volterra.* 1971. 127–35, esp. 133–35. **Gray, J.** *Legacy of Canaan.* 2nd ed. 1965. 185. **Gruber, M. I.** "The Many Faces of Hebrew נשׂא פנים 'lift up the face.'" *ZAW* 95 (1983) 252–60, esp. 253–54. **Jenni, E.** "Faktitiv und Kausativ von *ʾbd* 'zugrunde gehen.'" In *FS W. Baumgartner.* 1967. 143–57. **Johnson, A. R.** "Aspects of the Use of the Term פָּנִים in the Old Testament." In *Festschrift Otto Eissfeldt zum 60. Geburtstag.* Ed. J. Fuck. Halle: Niemeyer, 1947. 155–59, esp. 157. **MacDonald, J.** "The Status and Role of the *NAʿAR* in Israelite Society." *JNES* 35 (1976) 147–70. **Muffs, Y.** "Joy and Love as Metaphorical Expressions of Willingness and Spontaneity in Cuneiform, Ancient Hebrew, and Related Literatures: Divine Investitures in the Midrash in the Light of Neo-Babylonian." In *Christianity, Judaism, and Other Greco-Roman Cults: FS Morton Smith at Sixty, Part Three.* Ed. J. Neusner. 4 vols. SJLA 12. Leiden: Brill, 1975. 1–36, esp. 5ff. ———. *Love and Joy.* New York: Jewish Theological Seminary, 1992. 103–5, 121–25. ———. *Studies in the Aramaic Legal Papyri from Elephantine* [on Deut 28:47, *twb lēbāb*]. Studia et Documenta ad Iura Orientis Antiqui Pertinentia 8. Leiden: Brill, 1969. Esp. 27–62. **Oppenheim, A. L.** "Siege Documents from Nippur." *Iraq* 17 (1955) 77–78. **Weinfeld, M.** *DDS.* 126–29. **Welch, A. C.** *Deuteronomy: The Framework to the Code.* 1932. 126–40.

Translation and Prosodic Analysis

These Curses Will Pursue You Until You Are Destroyed [6:6]

45 *And all these curses / will come upon you //*	24	2
and they will pursue you / and they will overtake you /	16	2
until / you are destroyed[a] *//*	7	2_
Because you did not hearken / to the voice / of YHWH your God /	20	3
to keep / his commandments and his statutes /	14	2
that he commanded you //	5	1_

Israel's Utter Privation—"in want of all things" [(5:6):(6:5)]

46 *And they will be with you / as a sign / and as a wonder //*	18	3
and with your descendants / forever //	11	2_
47 *Because / you did not serve / YHWH your God /*	19	3
with joy \[a] *and with goodness of heart //*	13	1
from the abundance / of everything //	6	2_
48 *And you will serve*[a] [b]*your enemies*[b] */*	13	1
the ones whom YHWH will send / against you /	13	2
In hunger [c]*and in thirst /*	12	1
and in nakedness[c] */ and in want of everything //*	15	2_

And he will put / a yoke of iron / upon your neck / 15 3
until he has destroyed / you // 10 2_

Military Siege and the Undoing of God's Blessing [(5:7):(6:6):(7:5)]

49 *YHWH will raise up against you a nation / from afar /* 19 2
from the end of the earth / 8 1
that will swoop[a] */ like the eagle //* 9 2_
A nation / whose language\[b] *you do not understand //* 13 2
50 *a nation*\[a] *of fierce countenance //* 7 1
Who will show no regard / to the old / 16 2
and the young / will receive no compassion / 9 2_
51 *And it will devour / the fruit of your livestock* |[a] 11 2
and the fruit of your ground / until [b]*you are destroyed*[b] / 17 2
who will not leave behind / for you / 10 2_
Grain / [c]*new wine and oil /* 12 2
the calving of your herds / and the lambing of your flock // 17 2
until it annihilates / you // 11 2_
52 *And it will besiege you / in all*[a] *your towns /* 14 2
until your walls come down / 10 1
The high and the fortified ones / 12 1
in which you / are trusting / throughout all your land // 19 3_
And it will besiege you\[b] *in all*[c] *your towns /* 14 1
[d]*in all your land*[d] / 5 1
that [e]*YHWH your God*[e] */ has given / to you //* 16 3_

A Gruesome Climax: Cannibalism [(5:4):(5:4):(5:5):(4:5):(4:5)]

53 *And you will eat the fruit of your own womb /* 11 1
the flesh of your sons / and your daughters / 13 2
that [a]*YHWH your God*[a] */ has given to you //* 18 2_
In the siege / and in the straits / 12 2
with which your enemy[b] */ besieges*[c] *you //* 13 2_
54 *The man / the tenderest among you / and dainty / exceedingly //* 18 4
his eye will be evil |[a] 7 1_
Against his brother / 5 1
and against the woman of his bosom / 10 1
and against the rest of his children / that he has spared // 15 2_
55 *From giving*\[a] *to one of them /* 9 1
some of the flesh of his children / that he is eating / 13 2
because he has nothing left to him / of anything // 11 2_
In the siege / and in the straits / 12 2
with which [b]*your enemy / besieges you*[b] */ in all your towns //* 23 3_
56 *The tenderest woman* [a]*among you*[a] */ indeed the daintiest*[b] *one /* 15 2
who would not try to set[c] *the sole of her foot / on the land /* 21 2_
In spite of her daintiness\[d] *and her tenderness //* 12 1
her eye will be evil / against the man of her bosom / 14 2
and[e] *against her son / and against her daughter //* 11 2_

57 *And her afterbirth / that goes out*[a]\[b] *from between her legs /* 20 2
and her children[c] */ that she bears /* 14 2_
Indeed she will eat them out of lack of everything\[d] *in secret //* 17 1
in the siege\[e] *and in the straits /* 12 1
to which [f]*your enemy / reduces you*[f] */ in <all>*[g] *your towns //* 22 3_

Notes

45.a. SP, OL, and Syr. read השמיד(ו)ך, "they will destroy you," for MT השמדך, "(until) you are destroyed" (cf. vv 20 and 24).

47.a. Reading *ṭip̄ḥā'* as conj. because of misplaced *'atnāḥ*.

48.a. Some LXX witnesses add ἐκει, "there" (= שם). Prosodic analysis supports MT.

48.b-b. Vg. reads *inimico tuo*, "your enemy" (= איבך) for MT איביך, "your enemies"; *Tg. Ps.-J.* reads איביכם, "your [pl.] enemies."

48.c-c. Omitted in LXX^{B}. Prosodic analysis supports MT.

49.a. SP reads יראה, "it will see," for MT ידאה, "it will swoop."

49.b. Reading *ṭip̄ḥā'* as conj. because of misplaced *sillûq*.

50.a. Reading conj. accent *mahpāk*, which is the same sign as *yĕtîb*.

51.a. Reading the sequence of *'azlā* followed by *mêrĕkā* as disj.

51.b-b. Some Heb. MSS, SP, and Syr. read השמידך, "it will cause you to be destroyed," for MT השמדך, "you are destroyed." OL presupposes השמידוך, "they will destroy you" (cf. v 45 above).

51.c. A few Heb. MSS, OL, and Syr. add *waw*-conj. Prosodic analysis supports MT.

52.a. LXX^{B} omits כל, "all."

52.b. Reading *paštā'* followed by *zāqēp̄ qāṭôn* as conj.

52.c. LXX^{B} omits כל, "all."

52.d-d. Omitted in LXX^{-L}. Prosodic analysis supports MT.

52.e-e. Omitted in LXX^{B}. Prosodic analysis supports MT.

53.a-a. Omitted in SP, LXX^{B}; one Heb. MS omits אלהיך, "your God."

53.b. A number of Heb. MSS, Cairo Geniza fragments, and SP read איביך, "your enemies," for MT איבך, "your enemy."

53.c. SP and *Tg. Ps.-J.* read pl. for MT sg. יציק, "he besieges."

54.a. Reading the sequence of *'azlā* followed by *mahpāk* as disj.

55.a. Reading *lĕgarmēh* as conj.

55.b-b. SP, LXX, OL, and Vg. read pl. forms יציקו לך איביך, "your enemies will reduce you."

56.a-a. Omitted in Vg.; LXX and *Tg. Ps.-J.* read 2 pl.

56.b. LXX adds σφόδρα, "exceedingly" (= מאד from v 54).

56.c. SP reads הציגה for MT הצג, "to set her foot," with no change in meaning.

56.d. Reading *ṭip̄ḥā'* as conj. because of misplaced *'atnāḥ*.

56.e. SP, LXX, and Vg. omit *waw*-conj.

57.a. Reading הי(ו)צאת, "it comes (forth)," with a number of Heb. MSS and SP for MT היוצת, with no change in meaing.

57.b. Reading *lĕgarmēh* as conj.

57.c. LXX reads καὶ τὸ τέκνον αὐτῆς, "and her (young) child," for MT ובניה, "and her (newborn) children."

57.d. Reading *ṭip̄ḥā'* as conj. because of misplaced *'atnāḥ*.

57.e. Reading *paštā'* followed by *zāqēp̄ qāṭôn* as conj.

57.f-f. SP reads יציקו לך איביך, "your enemies reduce you."

57.g. Reading בכל־שעריך, "in all your towns," with most LXX (= ἐν πάσαις ταῖς πόλεσίν σου), as in v 55. Adding the word "all" (כל) here brings the total word count in 28:45–57 to 221 (= 13 × 17).

Form/Structure/Setting

The ravages of war and exile from the land of Israel, which were in focus at the center of the two five-part concentric structures in the first and second expanded description of future disaster (vv 20–44), are developed further in vv 45–57, which deals primarily with military defeat and its consequences. The section opens with an introductory verse (v 45) stating the theme that is reiterated in detail: servitude, starvation, and abject poverty (vv 47–48). It then describes a natural sequence of dire consequences: invasion on the part of a distant nation who will show no mercy (vv 49–50), pillage of livestock and crops (v 51), siege (v 52), and starvation leading to cannibalism, which is described at length in horrible detail (vv 53–57).

The opening verse (28:45) functions as a connecting link. It looks back to 28:15, which marked the beginning of the six curses in the covenant ceremony at Shechem, for the two verses are virtually identical, though in reverse order, as Tigay points out ([1996] 268):

A	If you will not hear the voice of YHWH your God . . .	28:15a
B	All these curses will overtake you	28:15b
X	The curses of 28:16–19 and 20–44	28:16–44
B′	All these curses will . . . overtake you	28:45a
A′	Because you have not heard the voice of YHWH your God	28:45b

It also looks back to 28:20, as Craigie has noted ([1976] 347), such that we may outline the three verses in a similar manner:

A	If you will not hear the voice of YHWH your God . . .	28:15a
B	All these curses will overtake you	28:15b
X	YHWH will send upon you curse, confusion, and cumbrance	28:20
B′	All these curses will . . . overtake you	28:45a
A′	Because you have not heard the voice of YHWH your God	28:45b

At the same time, the verse introduces the disasters of 28:46–57.

From a prosodic point of view, the remainder of this section is in three parts: 28:46–48, 49–52, and 53–57. Israel's coming punishment is presented as a just reversal of their former prosperity: "Because you did not serve YHWH your God . . . from the abundance of everything" (28:47). For that reason they now face utter privation "in want of everything" (28:48).

The course of the coming military conquest in 28:49–52 is presented in concentric fashion:

A	YHWH will raise up against you a nation from afar	28:49
B	Who will show no mercy to the old or the young	28:50
X	That nation will undo the blessing of 28:3–13	28:51a-b
B′	Until it annihilates you	28:51c
A′	That nation will besiege you in all your towns	28:52

The central verse (28:51) includes most of the familiar phrases of Israel's blessing from 28:4 and 11, and the undoing of that blessing in 28:30–32 and 38–42. The first half of the outer frame in this structure has the word "nation" functioning as an envelope in 28:49–50a, whereas the second half has the statement "it will besiege you in all your towns" functioning in the same manner in 28:52. The two sentences may be outlined as follows:

A	"YHWH will raise up against you *a nation*"	ישא יהוה עליך גוי	28:49a
B	"from afar, from the end of the earth,"	מרחוק מקצה הארץ	
X	"that will swoop like the eagle,"	כאשר ידאה הנשר	
B′	"a nation whose language you do not understand,"	גוי אשר לא־תשמע לשנו	28:49b
A′	"*a nation* of fierce countenance"	גוי עז פנים	28:50a

A	*"And it will besiege you in all your towns"*	וחצר לך בכל־שעריך	28:52a
B	"until your walls come down,"	עד רדת חמתיך	
X	"the high and the fortified ones"	הגבהות והבצרות	
B′	"in which you are trusting throughout all your land"	אשר אתה בטח בהן בכל־ארצך	
A′	*"and it will besiege you in all your towns"*	והצר לך בכל־שעריך	28:52b

In this reading, the nation whom God has appointed to undo Israel's covenant blessings is described in the regal image of an eagle swooping down on its prey to destroy "impregnable" fortresses in his path.

The final gruesome scene of the inhabitants of Israel reduced to cannibalism may also be outlined in a five-part concentric structural pattern:

A	You shall eat your children *"in the siege and in the straits"*	28:53
B	The man—"his eye will be evil against his brother"	28:54
X	He will not share *"in the the siege and in the straits"*	28:55
B′	The woman—"her eye will be evil against the man of her bosom"	28:56
A′	She will eat them in secret *"in the the siege and in the straits"*	28:57

The curse here is made more painful by repetition of the words "fruit of your own womb" (28:53), which also appear as part of the covenant blessing in 28:4. The famine in the land will cause such utter desperation that even the most natural human instincts of compassion will be destroyed: husbands and wives will turn against each other and their own children, refusing to share their meager portion of human flesh.

Identical words appear at the beginning, in the middle, and at the end of the above concentric structure: במצור ובמציק אשר יציק לך איבך, "in the the siege and in the straits with which your enemy besieges you." These words constitute the motivating cause for the horrible scenes delineated on the part of husbands (vv 54–55a) and their wives (vv 56–57a), who eat the flesh of their own children in order to survive. For parallel references to cannibalism in ancient Near Eastern texts, see Weinfeld, *DDS,* 126–29.

The gruesome climax of the curses in 28:53–57 are used to shape the telling of the narrative in 2 Kgs 6:24–31 on the siege and fall of Samaria to Ben-hadad, king of Syria. The use of the curses here on the part of the prophet Jeremiah are evident in Jer 4:13; 5:15, 17; 19:9; 28:14; 48:40; and 49:22. See also Lam 2:20; 4:10.

The evidence assembled by Labuschagne on the use of the divine-name numbers in 28:45–57, modified by the addition of the word כל, "all," in the second half of v 57, may be summarized as follows:

Words:	before *ʾatnāḥ*		after *ʾatnāḥ*		
28:45	9	+	11	=	20
28:46–48	26	+	13	=	39

28:49–50	13		+	13	=	26	
28:51–52	33		+	14	=	47	(= ארור)
28:53–57	52	(= 2 × 26)	+	37	=	89	
28:45–57	133		+	88	=	221	(= 13 × 17)
28:47–48	22		+	10	=	32	
28:52–53	26		+	17	=	43	(= 17 + 26)
28:52	15		+	11	=	26	
28:53	11		+	6	=	17	
28:54–55	16		+	17	=	33	

Once again, the use of the divine-name numbers here corroborates the structure determined independently on the prosodic analysis presented in this commentary with each of the subunits, except for vv 45 and 51–53, having the divine-name number 26 woven into the fabric of the Hebrew text. Moreover, the total number of words in 28:45–57 as a whole comes to 221 (= 13 × 17). Both divine-name numbers appear in the totals for vv 52 and 53 and various combinations of the verses throughout the unit. The numerical value of Hebrew ארור, "cursed," appears as the total word count for vv 51–52 (cf. 28:15–19).

Comment

45 "All these curses" are reified in the sense that "they will pursue you and they will overtake you." Nonetheless, they remain under God's absolute control (see *Comment* on 28:2 and 28:20).

46 "They will be with you as a sign and as a wonder." Since the terms אותות, "signs," and מופתים, "wonders," are used for the ten plagues in Egypt (see 4:34; 6:22; 34:11), we have here another grand reversal with Israel treated as Egypt was in times past. In Num 17:3 and 25, the term אות has the meaning "warning" or "lesson," which is probably the intent here as well.

47–48 The verb (לא)־עבדת, "you did (not) serve," is in the perfect tense. Craigie observes, "Within the address on the curse, the speaker is so carried away by his theme that it now seems that the curse is inevitable, and the words are almost as if the curse had already been put into effect" ([1976] 348). Because the people did not serve YHWH "with joy and with goodness of heart" over the "abundance of everything," they "will serve their enemies . . . in hunger and in thirst and in nakedness and in want of everything." Muffs finds significant linguistic parallels in Akkadian literature to the phrase בשמחה ובטוב לבב, "with joy and goodness of heart," in which the words are used metaphorically to mean "willingly" and "with spontaneity" (*Love and Joy*, 121–24). To receive the blessing of God and to experience no joy in it and to offer no thanks for it was to invite the curse of God. The total privation conveyed in the phrase "in want of everything" (בחסר כל; cf. v 57) comes as the result of military conquest. The "yoke of iron" is a common metaphor to express submission to foreign rule (cf. Jer 27:8–12; 28:2–4, 11–14). In short, "The curse of God reverses the history of salvation: God had brought his people out of Egypt, where they served an enemy; but because in the course of time they rejected God's love, they would be assigned once again to serve an enemy, forfeiting all the privileges of the covenant" (Craigie [1976] 348).

49–50 Mayes argues that the existence of a common tradition in the language of treaty curses, not direct literary dependence, explains the contacts between these two verses and Isa 5:26–29; Jer 5:15–19; 6:22–24; Hab 1:5–11 ([1981] 356). The nation "will swoop like the eagle" in the sense that its appearance will be sudden and without warning (cf. Hos 8:1; Jer 48:40). The phrase עז פנים, "fierce countenance," refers to the ruthless character of the enemy as spelled out in what follows: they "will show no regard to the old, and the young will receive no compassion" (cf. Isa 13:18; 47:6; Lam 4:16; 5:12–13). On the word עז as meaning "angry," see Muff's discussion ("Hebrew *ʿoz* = Akkadian *ezzu*, 'anger,'" in *Love and Joy*, 103–5). Craigie calls attention to the play on words here ([1976] 349): "a nation fierce of face who do not lift up faces" (i.e., "show no compassion").

52 Though the term והצר, which appears twice in this verse, comes from the root צרר, "to bind, be restricted," rather than צור, "to besiege," it means essentially the same thing in this context, as Tigay notes: "it will besiege you" ([1996] 397 n. 84; cf. Jer 4:31; 49:24).

53–57 Israel is here presented in sharp moral contrast to the fierce enemy of the previous verses. The siege and famine that result will be so intense that the people will eventually resort to cannibalism, even eating their own children; and husbands and wives will be unwilling to share their meager portion of human flesh with each other. On cannibalism in ancient Israel see 2 Kgs 6:28–29; Isa 9:19; Lam 2:20; 4:10. It also occurred during the final siege of Jerusalem in the days of the Second Temple as reported by Josephus (*J.W.* 6.3.4 §§201–13). The phrase translated "the fruit of your own womb" appears also in the blessing of v 4. In the phrase במצור ובמצוק, translated here as "in the siege and in the straits," a double meaning appears to be intended for the first word. Normally the word מצור means "siege," as the RSV has rendered it. The meaning "distress," which appears in the JPS *Tanakh* translation, is reading מֵצַר, "straits, distress," for MT מָצוֹר. Tigay says the reading מָצוֹר was selected to rhyme with מָצוֹק such that the text intends "both meanings as a double-entendre" ([1996] 270). "The man, the tenderest among you and dainty exceedingly," will eat the most disgusting food, which he will jealously guard from even "the woman [wife] of his bosom," toward whom one would expect the warmest feelings (v 54). "His eye will be evil" means that he will "eye grudgingly." The gender of the same words is reversed in v 56 so as to read "the most refined and gentle woman," where the horror is carried even further as she secretly consumes "her afterbirth that goes out from between her legs," and the newborn infant as well, to avoid sharing them with her husband and older children. The phrase "who remain" (אשר יותיר), in the sense of surviving the invasion and famine (with RSV), can be rendered, as it is here, "that he has spared" (v 54)—those whom the fastidious man has not slaughtered and eaten (with *Tanakh*).

Explanation

The portrayal of destruction that follows is more dreadful, with Israel experiencing utter privation in siege warfare (vv 45–57), culminating in the complete reversal of Israel's history (vv 58–68), in which YHWH causes them to return to Egypt (vv 66–68). If the people of Israel refuse to "hearken to the voice of YHWH your God to keep his commandments and his statutes," then "all these curses will come upon you and they will pursue you and they will overtake you until you are destroyed" (v 45). The severity of the destruction shall stand "as a sign and as a wonder" to future generations (v 46). If they would not serve God "with joy and with goodness of heart" (v 47), they shall be compelled to "serve [their] enemies . . . in want of everything" (v 48). The coming military siege will result in the total undoing of God's blessing of times past at the hands of "a nation from afar, from the end of the earth, that will swoop down like the eagle . . . until it annihilates you" (vv 49–51).

The climactic portrayal of utter depravation is the most gruesome scene in the Bible, as the severity of the ensuing famine reduces the populace to starvation and the inhuman behavior of cannibalism in which they kill and eat their own children (v 53). It is interesting to note that Jesus, in his farewell address to his disciples, spoke in somewhat similar fashion of a "desolating sacrilege" in the city of Jerusalem, as foretold by the prophet Daniel, in which there would be "great suffering, such as has not been from the beginning of the world until now, no, and never will be" (Matt 24:15–21 NRSV).

d. The Complete Reversal of Israel's History (28:58–68)

Bibliography

Brueggemann, W. "Weariness, Exile and Chaos (A Motif in Royal Theology)." *CBQ* 34 (1972) 19–38, esp. 30 (on Deut 28:65). **Clements, R. E.** *God's Chosen People: A Theological Interpretation of the Book of Deuteronomy.* London: SCM Press, 1968. 57. **Dahood, M.** "Hebrew-Ugaritic Lexicography VI." *Bib* 49 (1968) 355–69, esp. 365. ———. "Ugaritic Studies and the Bible." *Greg* 43 (1962) 55–79, esp. 64. **Daniélou, J.** "Das Leben, das am Holze hängt: Dt 28,66 in des altchristlichen Katechese." In *FS J. R. Geiselmann.* 1960. 22–34. ———. "La vie suspendue au bois: Dt 28,66 dans la catéchèse archaïque." In *Eglise et Tradition.* Ed. J. Betz et al. Le Puy: Mappus, 1963. 35–45. **Duffy, C.** *Siege Warfare.* 2 vols. London: Routledge and Kegan Paul, 1979. 1:253. **Gruber, M. I.** "Hebrew *da'ăbôn nepeš* 'Dryness of Throat': From Symptom to Literary Convention." *VT* 37 (1987) 365–69. **Hausmann, J.** *Israels Rest: Studien zum Selbstverständnis der nachexilischen Gemeinde.* BWANT 124. Stuttgart: Kohlhammer, 1987. 120–22. **Held, M.** "The Terms for Deportation in the Old Babylonian Royal Inscriptions with Special Reference to Yahᵉdunlim." In *Near Eastern Studies in Memory of M. M. Bravmann.* Ed. E. Greenstein. *JANESCU* 11 (1979) 53–67. **Lipiński, E.** "Sale, Transfer and Delivery in Ancient Semitic Terminology." In *Gesellschaft und Kultur im alten Vorderasien.* Ed. H. Klengel. SGKAO 15. Berlin: Akademie-Verlag, 1982. 173–85. **Lohfink, N.** "'I Am Yahweh, Your Physician' (Exodus 15:26): God, Society and Human Health in a Postexilic Revision of the Pentateuch (Exod. 15:25b, 26)." In *Theology of the Pentateuch.* 1994. 35–95. **Muffs, Y.** "The Lesson of the Almond Tree." *Proceedings of the Rabbinical Assembly* 56 (1995) 32–34. **Oded, B.** "Mass Deportations in the Neo-Assyrian Empire—Facts and Figures." *EI* 14 (1978) 62–68 (Heb.; Eng. summary, 124). **Salisbury, H. E.** *The 900 Days: The Siege of Leningrad.* New York: Harper & Row, 1969. 376–77, 492, 507.

Schley, D. G. "'YHWH Will Cause You to Return to Egypt in Ships' (Deuteronomy XXVIII 68)." *VT* 35 (1985) 369–72. **Stoebe, H. J.** "Anmerkungen zu Wurzel *pl'im* Alten Testament." *TZ* 28 (1972) 13–23. **Widengren, G.** "Yahweh's Gathering of the Dispersed." In *FS G. W. Ahlström.* 1984. 227–45. **Wildberger, H.** "'Glauben': Erwägungen zu *h'mjn.*" In *FS W. Baumgartner.* 1967. 372–86, esp. 379. **Zeitlin, S.** "Some Reflections on the Text of the Pentateuch." *JQR* 51 (1960/61) 321–31.

Translation and Prosodic Analysis

You Will Experience the "Plagues" of Egypt [(6:6:8):(8:8)]

58 *If you are not careful / to do / all the words / of this Torah /* 23 4
written / in this scroll // 12 2_
To fear / the name / this honored and awesome / One / 20 4
namely / YHWH your God // 11 2_
59 *Then YHWH*[a] *will inflict / on you blows*[b] */* 14 2
and / blows on your descendants // 9 2_
Blows that are great / and lasting / 15 2
and afflictions[c] *that are evil / and lasting //* 17 2_
60 *And he will return upon you / every disease*[a] *of Egypt /* 16 2
from which you were in dread / of them // 9 2
and they[b] *will cling / to you //* 8 2
61 *indeed every sickness / and every blow /* 10 2_
That / is not written / in the scroll / of this[a] *Torah //* 19 4
YHWH will bring / against you / until / you are destroyed[b] *//* 16 4_

Your Numbers Will Be Decimated [8]

62 And you will be left / a scant few / after having been / 18 3
as the stars of the heavens / for multitude // 15 2
because *you*[a] *did not heed / the voice / of YHWH your*[b] *God //* 19 3_

YHWH Takes Delight in Destroying You [6:6]

63 *And it shall be / just as YHWH took delight /* in you / 17 3
by doing good for you / and by multiplying you / 15 2
so YHWH will take delight \[a] in you / 13 1_
By causing you to perish / and by destroying you // 15 2
and you will be plucked[b] / from off the ground / 14 2
that *you are entering / to possess it //* 14 2_

YHWH Will Scatter You among the Nations [(4:4):(4:4)]

64 *And YHWH will scatter you / among all the peoples /* 16 2
from one end of the land / to the other end of the land // 18 2_
And you will serve there other gods / 17 1
that you have not known / you or your fathers / 18 2
of wood and stone // 7 1_

[65] *And among these nations / you will find no ease /* 17 2
and there will be no rest / for the sole of your foot // 15 2
And YHWH will give you there / an anguished heart / 16 2
and[a] *cried-out eyes / and a dry*[b] *throat //* 16 2

YHWH Will Make You Return to Egypt [(7:4):(2:2):(7:4)]

[66] *And your life will / hang in doubt / before you //* 18 3
and you will be in dread / night and day / 14 2
and you will have no assurance / of your life // 12 2
[67] *In the morning you will say / If only it were evening /* 14 2
and in the evening you will say / If only it were morning // 17 2
From the dread of your heart / that you will dread / 14 2
and from the sight of your eyes / that you will see // 15 2
[68] *And YHWH will return you / to Egypt*[a] */ in mourning*[b] */* 18 3
by the way / that I told you[c] */* 13 2
never again will you[c] */ see it //* 13 2
And you[d] will sell yourselves there |[e] to *your*[f] *enemies /* 14 2
as male and female slaves / but there will be no buyer // ס 18 2

Notes

59.a. Some Heb. MSS and SP add אלהיך, "your God." Prosodic analysis supports the shorter text of MT.

59.b. A few Heb. MSS, Syr., and Vg. read מכ(ו)תיך for MT מכתך, "blow(s) upon you," with no change in meaning.

59.c. A few Heb. MSS read וחלאים (from חלא, "to be sick") for MT וחלים, "and afflictions"; two Heb. MSS and Cairo Geniza fragments read וחליים.

60.a. Reading מדוי, "disease of" (constr. form), with some Heb. MSS, Cairo Geniza fragments, SP, Syr., Tg., and Vg., for MT מדוה, "disease of."

60.b. SP reads 3 sg. ודבק, "it will cling," for MT ודבקו, "they will cling."

61.a. Reading masc. sg. הזה, "this," to agree with ספר, "scroll," with some Heb. MSS, SP, LXX, OL, Syr., and Tg. for MT הזאת (fem. sg.) to agree with תורה, "Torah, instruction" (cf. 29:20; 30:10; 31:26).

61.b. One Heb. MS, SP, Syr., and Vg. read השמידך, "he exterminates you," for MT השמדך, "you are destroyed."

62.a. SP, LXX, OL, and *Tg. Ps.-J.* read 2 pl.

62.b. See previous note; some LXX witnesses read 1 pl. here.

63.a. Reading *paštā'* followed by *zāqēp qāṭôn* as conj.

63.b. LXX[B] adds ἐν τάχει, "quickly" (= מהר), which is possible in terms of mora count. The emendation would disturb the carefully worked out numerical composition of 28:58–68, which has 78 (= 3 × 26) words after *'atnāḥ*. The passage is closely connected to 28:69, for the total of words in 28:58–69 is 208 (= 8 × 26). Adding a word here would destroy both of these features.

65.a. SP omits *waw*-conj.

65.b. SP reads ודיבון, "Dibon" (?), with one MS reading ומדיבון, "and from Dibon" (?), for MT ודאבון, "dryness (of throat)."

68.a. Sebire and SP read מצרימה, "to(ward) Egypt," for MT מצרים, "Egypt"; a few MSS have צ maj.

68.b. Reading MT בָּאֳנִיּוֹת, "in ships," as בַּאֲנִיּוֹת, an abstract pl. of בַּאֲנִיָּה, "in mourning" or "in a lamentful condition," with J. Z. Meklenburg (*Ha-Ketav ve-ha-Kabbalah* [Leipzig, 1839], cited by Tigay [1996] 397 n. 104) and others. One SP MS reads באוניות.

68.c. SP and *Tg. Ps.-J.* read 2 pl.

68.d. Vg. reads *venderis*, "you [sg.] will sell yourself" (= התמכרתָּ); a few MSS read כ maj.

68.e. Reading the sequence of *paštā'* followed by *dargā* as disj.

68.f. SP, LXX, Syr., and Tg. read 2 pl. לאיביכם, "to your [pl.] enemies," for MT לאיביך, "to your [sg.] enemies."

Form/Structure/Setting

The content of 28:58–68 forms the conclusion to the long and complex list of covenant curses in Deut 28; taken as a whole, the content may be outlined as follows:

A Blessings for obedience and curses for disobedience 28:1–19
B Expansion of curses: pestilence, famine, and disease 28:20–32
X Expansion of curses: oppression, exile, and slavery 28:33–44
B′ Expansion of curses: utter privation in siege warfare 28:45–57
A′ The complete reversal of Israel's history 28:58–68

The outer frame in this structure moves from the summary statement of the covenant blessings and curses (vv 1–19), to the complete reversal of Israel's history for violating the terms of the covenant (vv 58–68), followed by a brief summation of the whole matter in v 69. Within that frame we find a three-part expansion of the covenant curses with a description of oppression, exile, and a return to slavery in the middle (vv 33–44).

The structure of 28:45–68 may be outlined in a similar five-part concentric structure, a "wheel within a wheel":

A These curses will pursue you *until you are destroyed* 28:45
B Israel's utter privation— *in lack of everything* 28:46–48
X Military siege and the undoing of God's blessings 28:49–52
B′ Israel reduced to cannibalism— *in lack of everything* 28:53–57
A′ Complete reversal of Israel's history *until you are destroyed* 28:58–68

The disasters presented in 28:58–68 not only undo the blessings promised in 28:1–15 but also completely reverse Israel's history—sending them back to "slavery" in Egypt! The outer frame includes repetition of the words עד השמדך, "until you are destroyed" (vv 45, 61). The inner frame in this structure is made up of parallel accounts of utter privation, both of which contain the words בחסר כל, "in want of everything" (vv 48, 57). In the center we find an account of a military siege to be waged against Israel that results in the undoing of the covenant blessings (vv 49–52).

The structure of 28:58–68 may be described as another "wheel within a wheel." From a prosodic point of view this section is in five parts: vv 58–61, 62, 63, 64–65, and 66–68. The boundaries of the first three of these units are marked by the *Numeruswechsel* at the beginning and end of vv 62 and 63. The boundary at the end of v 68 is marked with both the *Numeruswechsel* and the *sĕtûmāʾ* layout marker. It is only the boundary between vv 65 and 66 that must be determined on the basis of content and internal prosodic structure. The content of the whole may be outlined in a five-part concentric structure:

A YHWH will bring back upon you the *"plagues" of Egypt* 28:58–61
B You will be decimated in numbers 28:62
X YHWH takes delight in destroying you 28:63
B′ YHWH will scatter you among the nations 28:64–65
A′ YHWH will make you *return to Egypt* 28:66–68

What is most disturbing about this climactic structure, within the lengthy presentation of the covenant curses of Deut 28, is its center. Here YHWH himself declares that he takes delight in destroying Israel (v 63). In this reading the first and last prosodic units (vv 58–61 and 66–68) form an inclusion that focuses attention on Egypt in different ways. In the former instance, YHWH is bringing back upon the people of Israel the diseases of Egypt (v 60), one of which is מכה, translated as "blow" here (it may also be translated "plagues"; see also v 59, where this word appears three times). This unit (vv 58–61) is set over against vv 66–68, in which YHWH declares that he will make the people "return to Egypt in mourning" (see *Comment*). What we have here is a grand reversal of the epic story of Israel's exodus from Egypt. Israel made their original descent into Egypt because of famine. Once again they will experience famine and poverty so severe that in order to obtain sustenance they will seek to become slaves in Egypt, only to suffer refusal; for "there will be no buyer" (v 68).

In the first half of the inner frame (v 62), we learn that their numbers will be reduced to what they were before the "blessing in Egypt" (Exod 1:1–7), which set the stage for the birth of Moses and the exodus from Egypt. The means to that end are presented in the parallel prosodic unit (vv 64–65): "YHWH will scatter you among all the peoples from one end of the land to the other." In that setting there will be no rest for the weary.

The evidence from Labuschagne's analysis on the use of the divine-name numbers in 28:58–69 may be summarized as follows:

Words:	before *ʾatnāḥ*			after *ʾatnāḥ*				
28:58–61	39		+	22		=	61	
28:62	9		+	6		=	15	
28:63	17		+	8		=	25	
28:64–65	18		+	21		=	39	
28:66–68	27		+	21		=	48	
28:58–68	110	(= 2 × 55)	+	78	(= 3 × 26)	=	188	
28:58–69	124		+	84		=	208	(= 8 × 26)
28:1–69	595	(= 35 × 17)	+	397		=	992	
28:58–59	19		+	15		=	34	(= 2 × 17)
28:58–60	28		+	17		=	45	
28:62–63	26		+	14		=	40	
28:63–64	26		+	19		=	45	
28:66–69	41		+	27		=	68	(= 4 × 17)
28:68–69	26		+	13		=	39	

Although the divine-name numbers 17 and 26 are not a dominant feature within the five rhythmic subunits, as determined by the prosodic analysis, the evidence does suggest that the scribes of ancient Israel labored carefully to integrate this passage into the larger pattern of their numerical composition. The divine-name number 17 appears in v 63, which occupies the central position in the concentric structure of the five major subunits in 28:58–68. In this verse, which declares that YHWH takes delight in destroying Israel, there are 17 words before *ʾatnāḥ*. Moreover, there are a total of 78 (= 3 × 26) words after *ʾatnāḥ* in 28:58–68 taken as a whole. The total number of words before *ʾatnāḥ* is 110 (= 2 × 55). Labuschagne has much to say about what he calls the "minor tetraktys," in which the number 55 is the triangular number of 10 (the triangular number of 10 is the sum of the numbers 1 through 10), the decade, which is the triangular number of 4 (1 + 2 + 3 + 4 = 10). The compositional model 55 = 23 + 32 is used frequently throughout the Hebrew Bible. Labuschagne explains the significance of the numbers 23 and 32 in terms of the numerical value of the word כבוד, "glory." כבוד = 23 or 32 depending on whether כ = 11 or 20; without the *waw* כבד = 17 or 26 (i.e., the divine-name number). See *Excursus:* "Deuteronomy as a Numerical Composition."

It is the integration of 28:58–68 into its larger literary context where the use of the divine-name numbers is most impressive, for there are exactly 208 (= 8 × 26) words in 28:58–69, and 595 (= 35 × 17) words before *ʾatnāḥ* in 28:1–69. In short, God's name is carefully woven into the fabric of the Hebrew text throughout the long list of covenant curses in Deut 28.

Comment

58 At this point in the long list of curses, which is presented with a sense of inevitability, Moses reminds the reader/hearer once again that the matter is conditional. That v 58 does not begin with והיה, "and it will come to pass" (as in v 15), indicates that this verse can be read as the conclusion to vv 46–57. All these things will come to pass "if you are not careful to do all the words of this Torah." At the same time, the primary function of the verse is that of the protasis of a conditional sentence that continues in v 59.

The reference to "all the words of this Torah written in this scroll," which functions as a frame around vv 58–61, anticipates 31:9, where the Torah is first written down by Moses and entrusted to the Levites. The repeated words in v 61 appear in reverse order: "written in the scroll of this Torah." Attention is already focused here on future generations who will receive the teachings (Torah) of Moses in written form. On the meaning of the injunction to "fear" God, see the *Comment* on 10:12 and on 6:2. The use of "the name" (השם) without a pronominal suffix to refer to God himself is unusual in the Pentateuch, appearing only here and in Lev 24:11. This usage is common in subsequent Jewish practice to the present day. One wonders if this reference to the ineffable Name is also an attempt to call attention to the hidden ways in which this name is woven into the fabric of the Hebrew text in terms of its numerical composition.

59–60 The term מכות, "blows," which appears three times in v 59 and again in v 61, is often translated as "plagues." These plagues will be "extraordinary ones" in the sense that they will be "great [i.e., 'severe'] and lasting." God will afflict Israel with "every disease of Egypt" from which he had earlier promised to protect them (7:15). See also v 27 above and the *Comment* there on the so-called boils of Egypt.

61 The reference to what "is not written in the scroll of this Torah" has parallels in statements appended to extant Near Eastern treaty documents outside the Bible. Tigay says the expression "a plague that is not written in the Torah" is still used today in modern Hebrew to refer to a severe and unusual affliction ([1996] 272).

62 The population of Israel will once again become what it was before the multiplication in Egypt (Exod 1:7). The two phrases מתי מעט, "a scant few" and ככוכבי השמים, "as the stars of the heavens for multitude," appear earlier 1:9; 10:22; and 26:5 in reference to YHWH's blessing in multiplying his people in times past. The process is reversed here.

63 Y. Muffs says the term שׂשׂ, translated here as "took delight," carries a volitional sense: "was determined to . . . will be determined to" (*Love and Joy* [New York: Jewish Theological Seminary, 1992] 121–93; see also Tigay [1996] 272). The wording "to cause you to perish" implies a strong contrast to 26:5, where the same verbal root appears (אבד, "to perish"). God took a single "perishing" (אבד) Aramean and made from him a people of vast numbers, so long as they were obedient. If they proved to be disobedient, he would diminish those numbers again by making his people "perish" (להאביד). The verb נסח, which appears in the statement "you shall be plucked from off the ground," has cognates outside the Bible with the same sense of "deportation" (Tigay [1996] 397 n. 100; Held, *JANESCU* 11 [1979] 53–67).

64–65 On serving "other gods that you have not known . . . of wood and stone," see the *Comment* on 4:28. In exile the people of Israel "shall find no ease and there shall be no rest." On the image of "cried-out eyes" see the *Comment* on 28:32. The translation of ודאבון נפש as "a dry throat" is taken from Tigay ([1996] 273, 397 n. 101), who cites Gruber (*VT* 37 [1987] 365–69; cf. Pss 69:4 [Eng. 3]; Jer 2:25).

66–67 Their "life will hang in doubt" as the refugees face horror "night and day," finding each so unbearable that they long for the other—in the morning they long for evening; and in the evening they long for morning.

68 The Hebrew והשׁיבך, which is translated here as "shall make you return (to Egypt)," forms an inclusion with the "diseases of Egypt" in v 60. The reading they are to be returned "in mourning" (אניות) is that of Meklenburg as cited by Tigay ([1996] 273). Craigie suggests the possibility of translating אניות here as "in ease, casually," on the basis of Ugaritic evidence, following J. Gray, who offered a similar rendering in Judg 5:17 (*Joshua, Judges and Ruth,* NCBC [London: Nelson, 1967] 287–88). Such a reading offers "a further contrast between the blessing and the curse. God had brought his people out of Egypt, and together they had fought every inch of the way. Forgetting that great redemption, the people under the curse would be permitted to return casually to Egypt, the land of their bondage" (Craigie [1976] 353). The statement that they are to return to Egypt "by the way that I told you never again will you see it" is connected in some way with similar words in the so-called Law of the King in 17:14–20 (see *Comment* on 17:16). The people of Israel will attempt to sell themselves as slaves in Egypt; but "there will be no buyer."

Explanation

The undoing of the blessings in 28:58–68 is essentially a final reversal of Israel's history. The curses reverse the blessings of God and constitute a final and awesome warning for future generations. In Egypt of times past, God afflicted the Egyptians with severe diseases in order to bring the people of Israel to their blessing. In the curse of God, the diseases of Egypt will be inflicted on Israel, not on their enemies; and for good measure, God will add disease and affliction that even the Egyptians never knew (vv 60–61). In the blessing of God, Israel's ancestors went down into Egypt few in number and multiplied there according to God's ancient promises. In the curse of God, they will become few in number once again, their numbers growing smaller and smaller until finally they are destroyed altogether (v 63). In the blessing of God, the people of Israel looked forward to the gift of the promised land, a gift that was partially fulfilled for the two and a half tribes who had already gained possession of their land. In the curse of God, the people would be forcibly removed from the promised land and scattered abroad among the nations, where they will find no rest (vv 64–65).

The fullness of God's blessing lay in serving and loving YHWH alone (6:4–5). The emptiness of living under God's curse will be experienced in serving lifeless gods of wood and stone (28:64b). In the blessing of God, distant nations will fear Israel, who is confident in God. In the curse of God, the people of Israel will be constantly suspended in fear (vv 65–67). The blessing of God meant a long life in the promised land. But under the curse of God the people would not know from one moment to the next if they would even be allowed to remain alive (vv 66–67). In the blessing of God, the people of Israel were brought out of Egypt and freed from slavery. In the curse of God, they will return once again to Egypt, where they will offer themselves for sale as slaves; but the Egyptians will consider them of no value (v 68). Having rejected the honor of serving God, they will no longer be fit even to be slaves in Egypt.

The great reversal of Israel's history described in 28:58–68 is YHWH's own doing. It is YHWH himself who "will take delight in you by causing you to perish, and by destroying you" (v 63). The same conclusion was reached in Lam 2:1–17 and 4:11–12, which function as a framework around a marvelous portrayal of the other side of the coin, namely that YHWH will not reject his people forever. Though this conclusion is not reached in Deut 28 itself, it is the central message in Lamentations, the content of which is shaped in large measure by the covenant curses of Deuteronomy. Lamentations may be outlined as follows:

A	The desolation of Zion (Jerusalem)	Lam 1
B	YHWH has done what he purposed	Lam 2
X	YHWH will not reject his people forever	Lam 3
B′	Zion's children are ravaged by YHWH's own wrath	Lam 4
A′	The desolation of Zion (Jerusalem)	Lam 5

Much of the content of desolation of Zion in the outer frame of this structure reflects in detail the horrible curses of Deut 28, including the section on cannibalism (vv 53–57; cf. Lam 4:10) and the great reversal of Israel's history in Deut 28:58–68.

A simple lesson emerges from careful reflection on the whole of this lengthy account of the covenant curses in Deut 28: to stand in awe before God and to turn from our sin. When King Josiah heard the words of this Torah read in Jerusalem, "he tore his clothes" and declared: "great is the wrath of the LORD that is kindled against us, because our ancestors did not obey the words of this book, to do according to all that is written concerning us" (2 Kgs 22:11–13 NRSV). In sharp contrast, King Jehoiakim took the scroll of the prophet Jeremiah and cut it up with a penknife and burned it piece by piece (Jer 36:23) rather than heed its message. We do well to emulate the example of Josiah rather than Jehoiakim; for destroying or ignoring the text of these covenant curses accomplishes nothing. The message stands true now, as then, that God has determined that indeed "the wages of sin is death" (Rom 6:23), whether we choose to hear and obey, or harden our hearts and go our own way. At the same time, God's mercy remains extended to all, for "the free gift of God is eternal life in Christ Jesus our Lord" (Rom 6:23).

e. Summation: "These Are the Words of the Covenant" (28:69 [Eng. 29:1])

Bibliography

Baltzer, K. *Covenant Formulary.* 1971 (Ger. original, 1960). 34–38. **Cazelles, H.** "Les structures successives de la 'berît' dans l'Ancien Testament." In *FS R. Martin-Achard.* 1984. 2–7, 33–46, esp. 40. **Chołewinski, A.** "Zur theologischen Deutung des Boabbundes." *Bib* 66 (1985) 96–111. **Lohfink, N.** "Der Bundesschluss im Land Moab: Redaktionsgeschichtliches zu Dtn. 28:69–32:47." In *Studien zum Deuteronomium I.* 1990. 53–82. ———. *The Covenant Never Revoked: Biblical Reflections on Christian-Jewish Dialogue.* Tr. J. J. Scullion. New York: Paulist Press, 1991. **Radjawane, A. N.** "Israel zwischen Wüste und Land: Studie zur Theologie von Deuteronomium 1–3." Diss., Mainz, 1972. 209–10.

Translation and Prosodic Analysis

Summary: "These Are the Words of the Covenant" [4:4]

28:69(29:1) *These[a] are the words of the covenant /*	10	1
that YHWH commanded Moses / to make /	15	2
with the children of Israel /	9	1
In the land of Moab // in addition to the covenant /	14	2
that he made with them / at Horeb // פ	13	2

Notes

1.a. SP and LXX add *waw*-conj., which is possible from a prosodic point of view. MT is followed here because it is easier to explain the addition of the conj. than its omission. Adding it strengthens the tie with what precedes, and the verse already appears in MT as the concluding verse of Deut 28 rather than the first verse of Deut 29.

Form/Structure/Setting

Scholars have long noted a series of titles in Deuteronomy, and these have been explained in various ways. Thus 4:45 is sometimes taken to be the introduction to the original scroll of Deuteronomy, prior to its insertion within the so-called Deuteronom(ist)ic History (Joshua through 2 Kings). The conclusion to that scroll is presumed to be the covenant blessings and curses of Deut 28, and thus 4:45 and 28:69 are sometimes explained as an envelope around 4:44–11:32 // 27:1–28:69, which constitutes the major part of the inner frame of Deuteronomy (chaps. 4–11 and 27–30).

It is better to see this verse as the structural center of Deut 26–30 (weekly readings 7 and 8 taken together) as outlined in detail above in the introduction to the seventh weekly portion (26:1–29:8). That outline may be summarized as follows:

A	Public worship at the festivals in the promised land	Deut 26
B	The covenant blessings and curses	Deut 27–28
X	Summation: "These are the words of the covenant"	Deut 28:69
B′	The covenant is for future generations too	Deut 29
A′	The terms of the covenant are doable	Deut 30

Deut 28:69 thus functions both as the conclusion to the basic covenant renewal ceremony in 26:16–28:69 (as Craigie and others have argued) and the beginning of the covenant in the land of Moab, which Lohfink and others have identified with 28:69–32:47.

It is useful to place 28:69 within the context of the seventh weekly portion of Torah readings from Deuteronomy in terms of the specific prosodic subunits as determined in the prosodic analysis presented here. The content of the seventh reading may be outlined in a menorah pattern:

A	Preview: two liturgies for worship in the promised land	26:1–15
B	Transition: mutual commitments in covenant renewal	26:16–19
C	Covenant renewal at Shechem—a litany of curses	27:1–26
X	Blessings and curses of the covenant in Moab	28:1–57
C′	Final curse—a complete reversal of Israel's history	28:58–68
B′	Transition: "These are the words of the covenant"	28:69
A′	Review: the *Magnalia Dei* as the basis of the covenant	29:1–8

The ceremonies of public worship at the central sanctuary in ancient Israel in the first half of the outermost frame in this structure include a liturgy for the annual presentation of firstfruits at the central sanctuary (26:1–11) and a liturgy for the triennial tithe (26:12–15), which was stored in local towns. This preview of future worship in the promised land is set over against a brief review of the "mighty acts of God" *(Magnalia Dei)* in times past, which acts constitute the basis of the covenant relationship between YHWH and his people Israel (29:1–8). The second frame is made up of two brief transitional passages: mutual commitments made between the people and YHWH (26:16–19) and the summary statement, "These are the words of the covenant" (28:69). The inner frame opens with the account of the Shechem ceremony of covenant renewal that dramatizes Israel's covenant responsibilities (27:1–10) and the litany of ten covenant curses pronounced by the twelve tribes from Mount Ebal and Mount Gerizim (27:11–26). It concludes with the final curse, which is the complete reversal of Israel's history (28:58–68). In the center we find the long section on the blessings for obedience and curses for disobedience to the covenant stipulations (28:1–57).

The summary command in 28:69 and the similar such summary command in 29:8 function as a frame around a brief summary of YHWH's Holy War (see *Excursus:* "Holy War as Celebrated Event in Ancient Israel") from the perspective of Moses, which may be outlined as follows:

A	Summary: "These are the words of the covenant"	28:69
B	The exodus from Egypt remembered	29:1–3
X	God's provision for forty years in the wilderness	29:4–5
B′	The conquest of the two Amorite kings in Transjordan	29:6–7
A′	Summary: "You shall keep the words of this covenant"	29:8

In short, 28:69 is a pivotal text, which ties together a number of different structures within Deuteronomy. From a prosodic perspective, it is primarily a part of what follows in 29:1–8, as shown in the next section of this commentary.

From antiquity there has been difference of opinion in regard to how this verse functions within its larger context. In the MT the verse concludes chap. 28 and thus belongs with the blessings and curses. In the LXX tradition and other translations, including English Bibles, the verse is considered to be the first verse of chap. 29. The reason for this ambiguity is simply that the verse belongs to both sections. Besides its function as a bridge connecting Deut 28 and 29, this verse is also connected with more distant texts—in particular, with Deut 1:1, which begins: "These are the words that Moses spoke." The text goes on to spell out that Moses spoke what YHWH commanded him to say (1:3). Moreover, he began to expound what these words meant in the form of "this Torah" (1:5). The text echoes Moses' words in 5:2: "YHWH our God has cut with us a covenant in Horeb." Here in 28:69 we find: "These are the words of the covenant that YHWH commanded Moses to make with the children of Israel."

Deut 28:69 also forms an inclusion with 28:58 and its reference to "all the words of this Torah written in this scroll." Its place within that context may be outlined in another menorah pattern:

A	If you are not careful to do *all the words of this Torah*	28:58
B	You will experience the plagues of Egypt	28:59–61
C	Your numbers will be decimated	28:62
X	YHWH will take delight in destroying you	28:63
C′	YHWH will scatter you among the nations	28:64–65
B′	YHWH will make you return to Egypt	28:66–68
A′	These are *the words of the covenant*	28:69

It appears that 28:69 is an important part of the editorial structuring of Deuteronomy as a whole. Lohfink argues that the verse is to be taken as the first verse of a new unit and traces elements of the treaty pattern in the section that follows (*BZ* 6 [1962] 32–56). This conclusion stands, but so does the close structural connection to what precedes it as well.

Comment

69 The reference to "the covenant that he made with them at Horeb" as well as the covenant "in the land of Moab" makes clear that there is direct continuity between these two covenant ceremonies. In Moab "the covenant that he made with them at Horeb" was renewed—as it was again later at Shechem. At the same time, both covenants are new in the sense that each reflects the continuing living relationship established between YHWH and his people. It should be noted that this verse is closely connected with 29:9, as is shown in the following section, where the word ברית, "covenant," also appears. That word appears five times in Deut 29 (vv 9, 12, 14, 21, 25), while it is used only once in all the laws in the central core (in 17:2). The verse functions as an introduction to what follows; but at the same time it is dependent on the preceding chapters, as an essential connecting link within the macrostructure of Deuteronomy and the Book of the Covenant in Exodus. The law of Moses in Moab is covenant law, and is thereby placed on the same footing as the covenant law given at Sinai.

Explanation

The prophet Jeremiah later spoke of "a new covenant" that YHWH "will make with the house of Israel after those days" (Jer 31:31–34). Later still, Jesus at the Last Supper declared: "This cup . . . is the new covenant in my blood" (Luke 22:20; 1 Cor 11:25), which will be poured out for the forgiveness of sins (Matt 2:28). Like the old covenant at Sinai, this new one is sealed with a fellowship meal and blood sacrifice. Like Moses on Mount Sinai, Jesus, on another mountain, gave a new covenant law (Matt 5–7). The teaching of Jesus, his example, and his life constitute the commandments of the new covenant (John 15:12; 13:14–15, 34). For Christians, the promise of the Mosaic covenant at Horeb and Moab (and Shechem) continues. It is part of God's unfolding redemptive plan; and, as such, the covenant remains essentially one. As Lohfink once put it in the title of a provocative study, "the covenant was never revoked" *(The Covenant Never Revoked)*.

E. Remembering the Past: The Magnalia Dei *(29:1–8 [Eng. 2–9])*

Bibliography

Baltzer, K. *Covenant Formulary.* 1971 (Ger. original, 1960). 34–35. **Begg, C. T.** "'Bread, Wine and Strong Drink' in Deut 29:5a." *Bijdragen* 41 (1980) 266–75. **Blenkinsopp, J.** "Are There Traces of the Gibeonite Covenant in Deuteronomy?" *CBQ* 28 (1966) 207–19, esp. 209. **Brichto, H. C.** *Problem of "Curse."* 1963. 28–31. **Briggs, C. A.** "A Study of the Use of לֵב and לֵבָב in the Old Testament." In *FS A. Kohut.* 1897. 94–105, esp. 95. **Cazelles, H.** "Les structures successives de la 'berît' dans l'Ancien Testament." In *FS R. Martin-Achard.* 1984. 2–7, 33–46, esp. 40. **Chołewinski, A.** "Zur theologischen Deutung des Moabbundes." *Bib* 66 (1985) 96–111. **Davies, G. I.** "The Wilderness Itineraries and the Composition of the Pentateuch." *VT* 33 (1983) 1–13, esp. 12. **Greenberg, M.** "Mankind, Israel and the Nations in the Hebraic Heritage." In *No Man Is Alien: Essays on the Unity of Mankind.* Ed. J. R. Nelson. Leiden: Brill, 1971. 15–40, esp. 28. **Greenfield, J. C.** "An Ancient Treaty Ritual and Its Targumic Echo." In *Salvación en la Palabra . . . Homenaje al Profesor Alejandro Diez Macho.* Madrid: Ediciones Cristiandad, 1986. 391–97. **Halbe, J.** "Gibeon und Israel." *VT* 25 (1975)

613–41. **Halpern, B.** "Gibeon: Israelite Diplomacy in the Conquest Era." *CBQ* 37 (1975) 303–16. **Kearney, P. J.** "The Role of the Gibeonites in the Deuteronomic History." *CBQ* 35 (1973) 1–19. **Koch, D.-A.** *Schrift als Zeuge des Evangeliums.* BHT 69. Tübingen: Mohr, 1986. 170–71. **Kutsch, E.** *Verheissung und Gesetz: Untersuchungen zum sogenannten "Bund" im Alten Testament.* BZAW 131. Berlin: de Gruyter, 1973. 140–41. **Lohfink, N.** "Der Bundesschluß im Land Moab: Redaktionsgeschichtliches zu Dt 28,69–32,47." In *Studium zum Deuteronomium I.* 1990. 53–82. **Mayes, A. D. H.** "Deuteronomy 29, Joshua 9 and the Place of the Gibeonites in Israel." In *Das Deuteronomium.* Ed. N. Lohfink. 1985. 321–25.

Translation and Prosodic Analysis

YHWH's Mighty Acts in Egypt [8]

1(2) *And Moses summoned / all Israel /*	14	2
and he said to them // "You yourselves have seen /	14	2
all that YHWH did before your eyes /	18	1
In the land of Egypt / to Pharaoh and to all his servants /	19	2
and to all his land //	7	1_

Israel's Lack of Understanding [7:7]

2(3) The great / feats / that *your*[a] *eyes / have seen //*	21	4
[b]*these / great / signs and the marvels //*	21	3_
3(4) *Indeed*[a] *YHWH has not given /* you a mind / to understand /	18	3
nor eyes to see / nor ears to hear // to / THIS DAY //	22	4_

YHWH's Provisions for Forty Years in the Wilderness [7:7]

4(5) "'I[a] led you / forty years / in the wilderness //	21	3
[b]Your garments[b] did not wear out / from upon you /	18	2
[c]and *your sandal(s) did not wear out / from upon your feet*[c] //	19	2_
5(6) *Bread* \[a] you did not eat /	7	1
and wine or other intoxicant / you did not drink //	14	2
so \[b] you may know / [c]that / I am YHWH / your God'[c] //	22	4_

The Conquest and Settlement of Transjordan [7:7]

6(7) "And you came / to this place //	15	2
and Sihon king of Heshbon came out /	14	1
And Og king of Bashan |[a] to meet us[b] / for battle /	23	3
and we struck them //	4	1_
7(8) And we took / their land / and we[a] gave it as an inheritance[b] /	17	3
to the Reubenites / and to the Gadites //	14	2
and to the half / tribe of Manasseh //	13	2_

Summary Command to Keep the Terms of the Covenant [8]

8(9) "And you shall keep / <all>[a] the words / of this covenant /	17	3
and you shall do / them //	9	2
so that you will be successful / with / all that you do // פ	17	3_

Notes

2.a. LXX[L], Syr., and *Tg. Ps.-J.* read 2 pl.
2.b. Some Heb. MSS, one LXX MS, and OL add *waw*-conj. Prosodic analysis supports MT.
3.a. Reading *waw emphaticum.*
4.a. LXX, Syr., and Vg. read 3 masc. sg.
4.b-b. Some Heb. MSS and SP read שמל(ו)תיכם for MT שלמתיכם. Both terms are used for an outer garment.
4.c-c. SP, LXX, Syr., *Tg. Ps.-J.*, and Vg. read ונעליכם לא בלו מעל רגליכם, "and your [pl.] sandals did not wear out from upon your [pl.] feet." MT, which reads 2 sg. forms, is retained as *lectio difficilior.*
5.a. Reading *yĕtîb* as conj.
5.b. Reading *pašṭāʾ* followed by *zāqēp qāṭôn* as conj.
5.c-c. LXX[B] reads ὅτι οὗτός (ἐστιν) κύριος ὁ θεὸς ὑμῶν, "that this is the Lord your God."
6.a. Reading the sequence of *ʿazlā* followed by *dargā* as disj. Note in particular the *metheg* under the מלך, "king."
6.b. Some of the more important LXX witnesses read 2 pl.
7.a. LXX reads 1 sg.
7.b. The term לנחלה, "as an inheritance," is omitted in one Heb. MS; SP, Syr., and *Tg. Ps.-J.* omit the *waw*-conj. Prosodic analysis supports MT.
8.a. With LXX adding πάντας (= כל, "all"). The addition of this one word to the Hebrew text brings the total of words in 27:1–29:8 to 1,428 (= 7 × 12 × 17). See discussion at the end of *Form/Structure/Setting.*

Form/Structure/Setting

The seventh of the eleven weekly portions of the Torah readings from Deuteronomy (26:1–29:8) comprises eight verses of chap. 29 that function as a fitting conclusion to the section as a whole. The content of these verses may be described with the phrase G. Ernest Wright used so often, the *Magnalia Dei* ("mighty acts of God"), which may be outlined as follows:

A	Preview: two liturgies for worship in the promised land	26:1–15
B	Transition: mutual commitments in covenant renewal	26:16–19
X	Covenant renewal in Moab and Shechem: blessings and curses	27:1–28:68
B′	Transition: "These are the words of the covenant"	28:69
A′	Review: the basis of the covenant in the mighty acts of God	29:1–8

The section begins with the words, "when you come into the land that YHWH your God is giving you" (26:1); and it ends with the injunction, "you shall keep the words of this covenant . . . so that you will be successful with all that you do" (29:8). The outer frame in this structure moves from a pair of litanies that anticipate future worship in the promised land (26:1–15) to a brief review of God's redemptive activity in Israel's behalf, from the exodus from Egypt to the conquest and settlement of Transjordan (29:1–8). The inner frame is made up of two brief transitional passages (26:16–19 and 28:69), which function as a frame around the central concern of the whole: the matter of covenant renewal in the days of Moses in Moab, and in the promised land at Shechem in time to come.

Deut 26:1–11 includes a liturgical confession that every male Israelite used each year as he presented the firstfruits of his labors to YHWH at the central sanctuary in behalf of his household. This was followed by another brief confession to be used every three years when the special triennial tithe was presented symbolically in a basket at the central sanctuary (26:12–15), though the tithe itself was stored for use in local towns throughout the land. Then the focus shifts to the matter of the covenant renewal itself (27:1–29:8), which was celebrated in a special way in the sabbatical year, beginning with the observance of Passover and the Feast of Unleavened Bread at Shechem "in the day when you cross over the Jordan into the land that YHWH your God is giving you" (27:2), in which "all the words of this Torah" were to be written on large plastered stones for the people to see and read. The season of covenant renewal "every seventh year, at the set time, the year of release, at the Festival of Booths" (31:10), climaxed with a memorable recitation of Deuteronomy to musical accompaniment.

The boundaries of the five prosodic subunits in 29:1–8 are marked with the *Numeruswechsel* (changing between second singular and plural forms) in each of the first five verses and the *pĕtûḥā᾽* marker after v 8. Moreover, the fourth unit (vv 6–7) displays an extension of the *Numeruswechsel* with a change from second-person plural to first-person plural forms in vv 6 and 7, which separates v 8 from what precedes. The *Numeruswechsel* in the middle of the third unit (vv 4 and 5) marks the center of 28:69–29:8, taken as a whole. The change in speaker in vv 4–5, as Moses here quotes YHWH directly, should also be noted.

The five-part concentric structure of 28:69–29:8 may be outlined as follows:

A	Summary: "These are the words of the covenant"	28:69
B	Moses speaks: the exodus from Egypt remembered	29:1–3
X	YHWH speaks: "I led you forty years in the wilderness"	29:4–5
B′	Moses speaks: conquest of the Amorite kings in Transjordan	29:6–7
A′	Summary: "You shall keep the words of this covenant"	29:8

The text of 29:1–8 can be analyzed further into three prosodic subunits that highlight the specific message in matters of detail:

A	*You have seen* what YHWH did before *your eyes*	29:1a
B	In the land of Egypt to Pharaoh and all his servants	29:1b
X	Great feats that *your eyes have seen*	29:2a
B′	These great signs and marvels	29:2b
A′	YHWH has not given *eyes to see* nor ears to hear	29:3

From a structural point of view, the key words in vv 1–3 are the noun עינים, "eyes," and the verb ראה, "to see," each of which appears three times in three verses. The outer frame presents a contrast: you have seen what YHWH has done before your eyes (v 1a); but, even so, YHWH has not given you "eyes to see" in the sense of understanding (v 3). In the land of Egypt, YHWH has done great signs and marvels "that your eyes have seen" (vv 1b–2).

At this point, the narrative shifts to first person, with Moses quoting the words of YHWH himself:

A	I have led you forty years in the wilderness	29:4a
B	Your garment and sandals did not wear out from upon you	29:4b
B′	It was not bread you ate nor wine and liquor that you drank	29:5a
A′	So you may know that I am YHWH your God	29:5b

The point is that it was not natural food that God provided in the wilderness. The people survived on manna, quail, and water provided directly by God, for "not by bread alone do humans live" (8:3). The outer frame in this structure is in the first person singular (vv 4a and 5b), and the inner frame (vv 4b and 5a) is in the second person.

The narrative continues with Moses describing the conquest and settlement of the two Amorite kingdoms in Transjordan:

A	And you came to this place	29:6a
B	And Sihon and Og came to meet us for battle and we struck them	29:6b
B′	And we gave their land to Reuben, Gad, and Manasseh (east)	29:7
A′	You shall keep the words of this covenant to be successful	29:8

The first phase of YHWH's Holy War within the promised land was the defeat of the two Amorite kings, Sihon and Og, and the settlement of the tribes of Reuben, Gad, and half of the tribe of Manasseh in their place. The outer frame in this structure is in the second person (vv 6a and 8), whereas the inner frame (vv 6b and 7) is in the first person plural.

The recital of the *Magnalia Dei* in 29:1–8 functions in two different ways. Within the context of the seventh of the eleven weekly readings of the Torah in the lectionary cycle (26:1–29:8), it is a fitting conclusion to YHWH's Holy War as celebrated event in the life of ancient Israel. By "Holy War" I mean the events of the exodus-eisodus, the mighty acts of God in delivering Israel from bondage in Egypt under Moses and the possession of the promised land that took place in two phases: Transjordan under Moses, and Cisjordan under Joshua. The two great covenant renewal ceremonies—on the plains of Moab with Moses and on Mount Ebal with Joshua—are the focus of interest in this larger structural entity.

Deut 29:1–8 also introduces what follows in 29:9–32:52 (the eighth and ninth of the weekly readings in the lectionary cycle), where the focus shifts to the matter of covenant renewal in future generations, extending even beyond the actual breaking of the covenant and the experience of the covenant curses as spelled out in Deut 28. The relation between 29:1–8 and what follows may be outlined in a menorah pattern:

A	Brief recitation of the mighty acts of God in times past	29:1–8
B	An appeal for covenant faithfulness in generations to come	29:9–28
C	Restoration remains possible / Torah and song as a witness	30:1–31:30
X	Recital of YHWH's saving deeds in days of old	32:1–14
C′	Israel's future rebellion and restoration	32:15–45
B′	Summary command to observe all the words of the Torah	32:46–47
A′	God instructs Moses to ascend Mount Nebo to "see" the land	32:48–52

The framework in this structure (A, X, A′) moves from the recital of YHWH's mighty acts in the days of Moses (29:1–8 and 32:1–14), to the final scene in the life of Moses (32:48–52) in which YHWH allows him to see the whole of the promised land—the culmination of that epic journey. The outermost of the frames (B, B′) within this framework focuses on the fact that the covenant made in the days of Moses is binding for all time; even after the people experience the covenant curses for violating its terms (29:9–28), the command to observe all the words of the Torah still stands (32:46–47). The innermost frame (C, C′) focuses on the restoration of Israel when they heed the words of this Torah and the Song of Moses, which was preserved in their midst as a witness (30:1–31:30 and 32:15–45).

The data assembled by Labuschagne on the use of the divine-name numbers, with three minor textual corrections (27:26; 28:14; 29:8), may be summarized as follows:

Words:	before *ʾatnāḥ*		after *ʾatnāḥ*		
28:69–29:2	26	+	25	=	51 (= 3 × 17)
29:1–5	34 (= 2 × 17)	+	37	=	71
29:4–7	23	+	28	=	51 (= 3 × 17)
29:4–8	30	+	34 (= 2 × 17)	=	64 (= "Israel")
27:1–10	81	+	72	=	153 (= 9 × 17)
27:11–26	113	+	61	=	174
28:1–14	119 (= 7 × 17)	+	79	=	198
28:15–69	476 (= 4 × 7 × 17)	+	318	=	794
29:1–8	53	+	56	=	109
27:1–29:8	841	+	587	=	1,428 (= 7 × 12 × 17)

Once again the divine-name numbers 17 and 26 are woven into the fabric of the text in different ways. The total number of words in vv 4–8, which is essentially a review of Israel's past (i.e., the forty years in the wilderness and the conquest and settlement of Transjordan), is 64—the numerical value of the word "Israel." There are 23 (= כבוד, "glory") before *ʾatnāḥ* in these same five verses. The two divine-name numbers 17 and 26 are used to tie 29:1–2 together with 28:69. The most intriguing figure, however, is the total number of words in 27:1–29:8 (on the covenant renewal ceremony in Moab and Shechem): 1,428 (7 × 12 × 17). The number 7 signifies "worship" (the Sabbath is the seventh day), the number 12 stands for Israel (12 tribes), and the number 17 is associated with both the divine name YHWH and כבד, "glory." Once again, the scribes of ancient Israel have labored to the glory of YHWH in the numerical composition of the biblical text.

Comment

1–2 The opening statement that Moses "summoned" (ויקרא אל) indicates that he is continuing the proclamation of the covenant ceremony that includes the blessings and curses of 28:1–68. Moses reminds the people what God did in their behalf "in the land of Egypt to Pharaoh and to all his servants." "The great feats . . . these signs and marvels" refer to the ten plagues that led to the crossing of the sea in the exodus from Egypt.

3 In spite of the mighty acts of God in delivering the people of Israel from slavery in Egypt, they still were not able to grasp what this meant. At first glance their obtuseness appears to be the responsibility of God himself, for the text says: "YHWH has not given you a mind to understand, nor eyes to see, nor ears to hear." The Hebrew לב, "mind," is literally "heart" (see *Comment* on 6:5). As Tigay has observed, "Moses' statement that God had not given Israel the capacity to understand its experiences has puzzled commentators. If it means that the perception necessary to understand the religious meaning of historical experiences . . . comes only from God, how could God have held the rebellious Exodus generation responsible for its faithlessness? . . . However, a similar thought is expressed in 30:6, where Moses promises that after Israel repents in exile, God will open up the people's hearts and enable them to love Him. This seems to imply that God does give the heart the capacity for faith, but that He does so for those who seek it. . . . as the Talmud says, 'When a person seeks to purify himself, he receives help in doing so'" ([1996] 275–76, citing *b. Shab.* 104a and parallels).

4–5 Moses here quotes God, who reminds the people of his care for them for "forty years in the wilderness." On their supernatural food and the miraculous preservation of their clothing, see *Comment* on 8:1–6. The emphatic position of לחם, "bread," and ויין ושכר, "and wine or other intoxicant," here indicates that it was supernatural food and water that sustained them up to this point in time. The word תדעו, "know," is used here in the sense of legal recognition, as found also in ancient treaty texts, where it refers to the overlord's recognition of his vassal and vice versa.

6–7 The phrase "this place" refers to the land of the two Amorite kings, "Sihon king of Heshbon" and "Og king of Bashan." Their defeat by Israel under Moses' leadership marks the end of the first phase of YHWH's Holy War in Transjordan, which will continue under Joshua in Cisjordan. It is possible that we have here an extension of the more familiar *Numeruswechsel,* which normally involves the change between singular and plural forms. Here we move from second plural (vv 5–6) to first plural forms (vv 6–7), perhaps to mark the boundaries of subunits in the larger literary structure (cf. also the "we" passages in 1:19; 2:1; 3:1; 29:14–15, 18, 28; 30:12–13).

8 The summary command "you shall keep the words of this covenant" forms an inclusion with "the words of the covenant" in 28:69.

Explanation

An important lesson to be learned from 29:1–3 concerns spiritual blindness. In spite of great "signs and marvels" witnessed by the people of Israel, in which their clothing did not wear out and they ate extraordinary food supplied by God himself, the people were without understanding. They lived in full view of God's marvelous handiwork, and yet they did not have "a mind to understand, nor eyes to see, nor ears to hear" (v 3). Jesus spoke of this phenomenon by quoting the words of the prophet Isaiah in Matt 13:13–15 to the effect that God himself must in some way be responsible for spiritual blindness. The text here, however, suggests that the reason is simply that God has not yet given them eyes to see and ears to hear. John Calvin once said, "Men are ever blind in the brightness of light, until they have been enlightened by God" (citation from G. E. Wright, *IB* 2:503).

As Paul put it in another quotation from Isaiah, "All day long I have held out my hands to a disobedient and contrary people" (Rom 10:21). They cannot see because their eyes are blinded through disobedience to what God has already revealed to them (cf. Rom 11:1–10).

Reading 8: Appeal for Covenant Loyalty (29:9–30:20 [Eng. 29:10–30:20])

The eighth of the eleven weekly portions in the lectionary cycle of Torah readings from Deuteronomy (29:9–30:20) is known as נִצָּבִים, "taking one's stand," which is descriptive of its content, as individuals are invited to take their stand as obedient members of the covenant community. The covenant is intended not only for those who are "here with us standing today before YHWH our God"; it is also with those who are "not here with us today" (29:14)—that is, for all future generations of God's people. The entire weekly portion in 29:9–30:20 may be outlined in a menorah pattern:

A	The covenant is binding on future generations too	29:9–14
B	Warning to those with reservations about keeping the covenant	29:15–20
C	The exile from the land of Israel foretold	29:21–27
X	Secret and revealed things: Do all the words of this Torah!	29:28
C′	The possibility of restoration after exile	30:1–10
B′	God's commandments are doable	30:11–14
A′	The choice before you is between life and death—choose life	30:15–20

The framework (A, X, A′) in this structure moves from a statement of the situation that the covenant is binding on future generations (29:9–14) to urging each individual to choose life rather than death (30:11–20)—by deciding to "do all the words of this Torah" (29:28). The first frame (B, B′) moves from a warning to those with reservations about keeping the covenant (29:15–20) to an assurance that God's commandments are indeed doable (30:11–14). The innermost frame moves from a prediction of exile from the land of Israel (29:21–27) to a presentation of the possibility of restoration after exile (30:1–10).

Each of the two chapters (Deut 29 and 30) may be outlined in a five-part concentric structure:

A	Summary command to keep the terms of the covenant	29:1–8
B	The covenant is binding on future generations too	29:9–14
X	Warning to those with reservations on keeping the covenant	29:15–20
B′	Exile from the land is foretold for breaking the covenant	29:21–27
A′	Secret and revealed things: Do all the words of this Torah!	29:28

In this reading, the message of Deut 29 presents the warning of what will happen to those who do not keep the covenant in times to come: "YHWH uprooted them from their soil in anger and in fury and in great rage; and he cast them into another land" (29:27).

A	The possibility of returning to YHWH is there	30:1–5
B	When you return, YHWH will return the covenant blessings	30:6–10
X	God's commandments are doable	30:11–14
B′	I have set before you the choice between life and death	30:15–18
A′	So choose life by obeying YHWH's commandments	30:19–20

The message is clear: even in exile, the possibility of returning to YHWH is there (vv 1–5), so make the choice to live in obedience to YHWH's commandments (vv 19–20). When the people choose to return to YHWH, he will once again restore the covenant blessings (vv 6–10). The choice between life and death is before God's people (vv 15–18), for his commandments are doable (vv 11–14).

A. The Covenant Is Binding on Future Generations Too (29:9–14 [Eng. 10–15])

Bibliography

Begg, C. T. "The Reading *šbṭy(km)* in Deut 29,9 and 2 Sam 7,7." *ETL* 58 (1982) 87–105. **Blenkinsopp, J.** *Gibeon and Israel: The Role of Gibeon and the Gibeonites in the Political and Religious History of Early Israel.* SOTSMS 2. Cambridge: Cambridge UP, 1972. **Brenner, A.** "Concerning *maṭṭeh* and *šebeṭ* and Their Semantic Classification." *Leš* 44 (1980) 100–108 (Heb.). **Brichto, H. C.** *Problem of "Curse."* 1963. 28–31. **Cazelles, H.** "La rupture de la *berît* selon les Prophètes." In *FS Y. Yadin.* 1982. 133–44, esp. 136. ———. "Les structures successives de la 'berît' dans l'Ancien Testament." In *FS R. Martin-Achard.* 1984. 40. **Falk, Z. W.** "Ruler and Judge." *Leš* 30 (1965–66) 243–47 (Heb.). **Friedrich, J.** "Der hethitische Soldateneid." *ZA* 35 (1924) 161–91, esp. 170–72. **Gevirtz, S.** "On Hebrew *šebeṭ* = 'Judge.'" In *FS C. H. Gordon.* 1980. 61–66. **Giesen, G.** *Die Wurzel* שׁבע. 1981. 303–4. **Guillén Torralba, J.** "La Formula *kol 'îš yiśra'ēl.*" *EstBib* 34 (1975) 5–21. **Hasel, G. F.** "The Meaning of the Animal Rite in Genesis 15." *JSOT* 19 (1981) 61–78. **Henninger, J.** "Was bedeutet die rituelle Teilung eines Tieres in zwei Hälften?" In *Arabica Sacra: Aufsätze zur Religionsgeschichte Arabiens und seiner Randgebiete.* OBO 40. Freiburg: Universitäts Verlag; Göttingen: Vandenhoeck & Ruprecht, 1981. 275–85. **Laubscher, F. D. T.** "Notes on the Literary Structure of 1QS 2:11–18 and Its Biblical Parallel in Deut. 29." *JNSL* 8 (1980) 49–55. **Levin, C.** *Der Sturz der Königin Atalja: Ein Kapitel zur Geschichte Judas im 9. Jahrhundert v. Christ.* SBS 105. Stuttgart: Katholisches Bibelwerk, 1982. 59–77. **Loewenstamm, S. E.** *Comparative Studies in Biblical and Ancient Oriental Literatures.* Kevelaer: Butzon and Bercker; Neukirchen-Vluyn: Neukirchener Verlag, 1980. 270–72. **Milgrom, J.** "Excursus 34: The 'Ger.'" In *Numbers.* 1990. 398–402. **Reid, P. V.** "*šbṭy* in 2 Samuel 7:7." *CBQ* 37 (1975) 17–20. **Reviv, H.** "The Pattern of the Pan-Tribal Assembly in the Old Testament." *JNSL* 8 (1980) 85–94. **Robert, P. de.** "Juges ou tribus en 2 Samuel vii 7." *VT* 21 (1971) 116–18. **Rösel, H.** "Die 'Richter Israels': Rückblick und neuer Ansatz." *BZ* 25 (1981) 180–203. **Ruprecht, E.** "Exodus 24,9–11 als Beispiel lebendiger Erzähltradition aus der Zeit des babylonischen Exils." In *FS C. Westermann.* 1980. 138–73, esp. 143 ("elders"). **Sheriffs, D. C. T.** "The Phrases *ins IGI DN* and *lipeney Yhwh* in Treaty and Covenant Contexts." *JNSL* 7 (1979) 55–68. **Thiel, W.** "Altorientalische und israelitisch-jüdische Religion." *JLH* 28 (1984) 166–91, esp. 168, 178. **Trever, J. C.** "Gall" and "Wormwood." *IDB.* 2:350 and 4:878–79. **Vos, C. J.** "Woman in Old Testament Worship." Diss., Amsterdam, 1968.

Translation and Prosodic Analysis

The Covenant Is Binding on Future Generations Too [9:7] [(4:5):(5:4)] [7:9]

9(10) You are stationed TODAY / all of you /	13	2
before the presence of / YHWH your God //	12	2
[a]Your heads your judges[a] / your elders / and your officials /	22	3
every / man of Israel //	9	2_
10(11) Your little ones [a]your wives / and *your resident alien* /	12	2
who / are in the midst of your camp[b] //	9	2
from your woodchopper / to[c] */ your water hauler* //	21	3_
11(12) *That* [a]*you may enter*[a] */ into the covenant / of YHWH your God /*	18	3
and into his oath of fealty //	9	1_
That / YHWH your God /	11	2
is cutting with you / TODAY //	11	2
12(13) *in order that he may establish you TODAY* /[a]	15	1_
For him as a people / with him being for you / as a God /	19	3
just as / he promised you //	7	2_
And just as he swore /	6	1
to your fathers / to Abraham and to Isaac / and to Jacob //	24	3_
13(14) *And it is not* with you / you alone //	10	2
I / cut / this covenant / and this / oath //	29	5_
14(15) But with the one who is / here / with us /	15	3
standing TODAY / before / YHWH our[a] God //	20	3
and with the one who is not / here / with us[b] TODAY //	20	3_

Notes

9.a-a. Emending MT שבטיכם, "your tribes," to read שפטיכם, "your judges," with LXX, which reads οἱ ἀρχίφυλοι ὑμῶν καὶ ἡ γερουσία ὑμῶν καὶ οἱ κριταὶ ὑμῶν καὶ οἱ γραμματοεισαγωγεῖς ὑμῶν, "your heads and your elders and your judges and your officials" (= ראשיכם וזקניכם ושפטיכם ושטריכם), where the order of the second and third items in the list are reversed from that of MT. These four terms for leaders in ancient Israelite society appear together in Josh 23:2 and 24:1, but in different order from either LXX or MT as emended here, namely: elders, heads, judges, and officials. Syr. and *Tg. Ps.-J.* read ראשי שבטיכם, "heads of your tribes."

10.a. DSS, SP, LXX, Syr., *Tg. Ps.-J.*, and Vg. add *waw*-conj. Prosodic analysis supports MT.

10.b. Reading מחנך, "your [sg.] camp," with some Heb. MSS, SP, and Syr.; LXX reads τῆς παρεμβολῆς ὑμων, "your [pl.] camp" (= מחנכם); *Tg. Ps.-J.* reads מחניכם.

10.c. One Heb. MS, SP, some major LXX witnesses, Syr., and Vg. add *waw*-conj.

11.a-a. Syr. reads 2 pl. in place of 2 sg. in MT; some SP MSS and Tg. read להעבירך, "to cause you [sg.] to cross"; *Tg. Ps.-J.* reads להעבירכם, "to cause you [pl.] to cross."

12.a. The anomalous *pāsēq* in *BHS* suggests that the disj. break belongs here instead of with the *gereš* on the following word. The *pāsēq* is missing in the Letteris edition of the Hebrew text.

14.a. LXX reads 2 pl.

14.b. DSS, some LXX witnesses, and OL read 2 pl.

Form/Structure/Setting

It is possible to read Deut 29 within a more elaborate concentric structure with 29:9–14 in the center:

A	Introduction: These are the words of the covenant	28:69
B	The exodus from the land of Egypt recalled	29:1–2
C	Moses reminds them of God's provision in times past	29:3–8
X	The covenant is binding on future generations too	29:9–14
C′	Moses warns those with reservations about the covenant	29:15–20
B′	The exile from the land of Israel foretold	29:21–27
A′	Conclusion: Observe the words of the Torah	29:28

In this reading the central message remains much the same as that of Deut 27–28, with Moses reminding the people of past blessings and warning them of future curses for breaking the covenant with YHWH (vv 3–20). The focus of attention in the center of this structure, however, is that the covenant applies to future generations as well (29:9–14). The outer frame picks up the image of "the land of Egypt" (ארץ מצרים) as a key concept in vv 1 and 24, in both instances calling attention to God's redemptive power in times past.

The boundaries of the three prosodic units here are marked with the *Numeruswechsel* in vv 10 and 13. The section as a whole begins with reference to all of the people who are standing before YHWH in the covenant ceremony there on the plains of Moab (v 9) and closes with a statement that this covenant also applies to "those who are not here with us today" (v 14). This inclusion becomes the outer frame in a concentric structural design that Tigay (following Mayes) has outlined as follows ([1996] 277):

A	You [present generation] stand today before YHWH your God	29:9–10
B	to enter the covenant . . . with its sanctions	29:11
X	that YHWH may establish you as his people and be your God	29:12
B′	I am concluding this covenant . . . with its sanctions	29:13
A′	those standing here today and [future generations]	29:14

This structure has the covenant formula as its focal point in v 12 and focuses attention on repetition of the words "covenant" and "oath" in vv 11 and 13.

Another way of looking at the concentric structural design is to add another structural frame to form a menorah pattern:

A	Present: you are all standing here today before YHWH	29:9–10
B	Stipulations: "the covenant of YHWH . . . and his oath"	29:11a
C	Present: YHWH is making this covenant with you today	29:11b
X	Formula: to establish you as his people and he as your God	29:12a
C′	Past: the covenant was promised to Abraham, Isaac, and Jacob	29:12b
B′	Stipulations: "this covenant and this oath"	29:13
A′	Future: this covenant is also with those not here today	29:14

The inner frame in this structure (vv 11, 12b) focuses on the fact that this covenant, which the people are about to make with YHWH, is the same covenant that was promised to the ancestors Abraham, Isaac, and Jacob in Genesis. The center of this structure presents the unique relationship that this covenant establishes between God and Israel: they are to become his people and he will henceforth be their God.

The evidence gathered by Labuschagne on the numerical composition of 29:9–20 may be summarized as follows:

Words:	before *ʾatnāḥ*		after *ʾatnāḥ*		
29:9–13	34 (= 2 × 17)	+	32	=	66
29:9–16	58 (= 26 + 32)	+	51 (= 3 × 17)	=	109
29:14	11	+	6	=	17
29:15–16	13	+	13	=	26
29:15–18	52 (= 2 × 26)	+	25	=	77
29:15–20	78 (= 3 × 26)	+	38	=	116
29:17	23	+	7	=	30
29:17–18	39	+	12	=	51 (= 3 × 17)
29:19	20	+	6	=	26
29:19–20	26	+	13	=	39
29:9–14	45	+	38	=	83
29:9–30:20	357 (= 21 × 17)	+	306 (= 18 × 17)	=	663 (39 × 17)

The divine-name numbers 17 and 26 have been woven into the fabric of this text in a variety of ways, along with the numbers 23 and 32 (= כבוד, "glory; see *Excursus:* "Deuteronomy as a Numerical Composition"). Though these numbers are not present for 29:9–14 as such, it is interesting to note the larger context of Reading 8 (29:9–30:20) as a whole. In this instance all three numbers are exact multiples of the divine-name number 17, with 663 (= 39 × 17) total words, which is 357 (= 21 × 17) words before *ʾatnāḥ* plus 306 (= 18 × 17) words after *ʾatnāḥ*. And 29:9–14 is an integral part of this structure. The labor on the part of ancient scribes to achieve this phenomenon was done to the glory of YHWH.

Comment

9–10 The Hebrew נצבים, translated here as "stationed," means to present oneself in the formal sense of "taking one's stand." Craigie suggests that the word "implies some kind of formal arrangement (almost a 'parade')" ([1976] 356 n. 4). The word היום, "today," appears five times in vv 9–14 referring to the cultic present, in the sense of that time in which the covenant was formally renewed in ancient Israel. "Your heads, your judges, your elders, and your officials" (see *Comment* on 1:13–15)—the textual corruption in MT (see *Notes*) may have been influenced by 31:28, which reads זקני שבטיכם ושטריכם, "elders of your tribes and your officers." The phrase כל איש ישראל, "every man of Israel," can also be translated "every person in Israel" (cf. Vg. *omnis populus Israel,* "all the people of Israel"), as the NRSV renders the same phrase in 1 Chr 16:3. It is not just the leaders and other adult males who are included. The covenant ceremony is for every single person in ancient Israel, including "your little ones, your wives, and your resident alien." These resident aliens, or strangers (see *Comment* on 1:16–18), are divided into subcategories "from your woodchopper to your water hauler," the tasks that Joshua later assigned to the Gibeonites (Josh 9:21–27). In Ugaritic texts these roles appear as tasks for women (Craigie [1976] 357 n. 7; *ANET,* 144, iii, 112–15). Tigay says the list may be expanded from other ancient Near Eastern texts to include such menial laborers as washermen, gardeners, and straw collectors ([1996] 278).

11–12 The word לעברך, translated here as "that you may enter," means literally "for your crossing over (into the covenant)." The sense is aptly rendered in JPS *Tanakh* "to enter into the covenant . . . with its sanctions." According to Tigay ([1996] 278), the combination of ברית ואלה, rendered here as "covenant . . . oath of fealty," is a hendiadys that means "a covenant guarded by curses" (detailed in 28:15–68). The purpose of the covenant is to establish a lasting relationship in which the people of Israel become God's people and he in turn becomes their God. This is what God promised "to Abraham" and his descendants in Gen 17:7–8.

13–14 The reference to those who are "not here with us today" is to future generations on whom the covenant stipulations are also binding, as well as to those who may be detained at home, for whatever reasons, or away on business and thus unable to make the pilgrimage to the central sanctuary for the service of covenant renewal. For parallels in other ancient Near Eastern treaty texts, which also stipulate that they are binding on the descendants of the parties involved, see the Vassal Treaties of Esarhaddon (*ANET,* 534 and 539) and Sefire IA (*ANET,* 659).

Explanation

When Peter addressed the first Christian converts on Pentecost, the words he used echo those of Deut 29:9–14: "for the promise is for you, for your children and for all who are far away, everyone whom the Lord our God calls to him" (Acts 2:39 NRSV). In the words of the covenant made on the plains of Moab in the days of Moses, "it is not with you, you alone, I cut this covenant . . . but with the one who is here with us . . . and with the one who is not here with us today" (Deut 29:13–14). The covenant is binding on future generations, as well as on those assembled in Moab or at Shechem.

The political leaders and officials among the men are mentioned first (v 1), but it is not only the men who are included. The wives and children must also enter the covenant (v 10). In this regard it is interesting to note that little children are considered capable of entering the covenant along with their parents. As Jesus put it on another occasion, "Let the little children come to me; do not stop them; for it is to such as these that the kingdom of God belongs" (Mark 10:14 NRSV). It should also be noted that it is not only the Israelites who are included in the covenant community, but the aliens in their midst as well, no matter how menial their social position ("from your woodchopper to your water hauler")—so long as they had renounced false gods. We sometimes forget how inclusive the covenant community of ancient Israel was from its very beginning.

Some take the reference to those who are "not here with us today" (v 14) to mean those who remained at home, for whatever reason. Every Israelite shares in the common blessings and responsibilities. Those who are unable to go up to the house of YHWH for the public renewal of the covenant are present in spirit and bound to the commitments made in their behalf as members of the covenant community. At the same time, it is clear that the reference to those who are not here today refers to generations to come as well, as one of the Targums renders it: "All the generations that have been from the first days of the world, and all that shall arise to the end of the whole world, stand with us here this day" (taken from M. Henry, *Exposition of the Old and New Testament* [1828] 687).

B. Those with Reservations about Keeping the Covenant Are Warned (29:15–20 [Eng. 16–21])

Bibliography

Becker, J. P. "Wurzel und Wurzelspross." *BZ* 20 (1976) 22–44. **Berg, W.** "Die Eifersucht Gottes—Ein problematischer Zug des alttestamentlichen Gottesbildes?" *BZ* 23 (1979) 197–211, esp. 206. **Brichto, H. C.** *Problem of "Curse."* 1963. 28–31. **Daube, D.** "The Extension of a Simile." In *FS E. I. J. Rosenthal.* 1982. 57–59. **Farbridge, M. H.** *Studies in Biblical and Semitic Symbolism.* 1923. Repr. New York: Ktav, 1970. 48–49. **Ginsberg, H. L.** "'Roots Below and Fruits Above' and Related Matters." In *FS G. R. Driver.* 1963. 72–76, esp. 75. **Goshen-Gottstein, M.** "*ʿl hbrkh.*" *Lěš* 32 (1967–68) 52–62 (Heb.). **Haran, M.** "Book-Scrolls in Israel in Pre-Exilic Times." In *FS Y. Yadin.* 1983. 161–73, esp. 166. **Koch, D.-A.** *Die Schrift als Zeuge des Evangeliums.* BHT 69. Tübingen: Mohr, 1986. 164–65. **McKane, W.** "Poison, Trial by Ordeal and the Cup of Wrath." *VT* 30 (1980) 474–92, esp. 478–84. **Paschen, W.** *Rein und Unrein: Untersuchung zur biblischen Wortgeschichte.* Munich: Kosel, 1970. 66–67, 120. **Paul, S.** "Euphemism and Dysphemism." *EncJud* 6:959–61. **Pope, M.** "Bible, Euphemism and Dysphemism in the." *ABD* 1:720–25. **Preuss, H. D.** "*gillûlim.*" *TDOT* 3:1–5. **Spencer, A. B.** "שרירות as Self-Reliance." *JBL* 100 (1981) 247–48.

Translation and Prosodic Analysis

Warning to Those with Reservations about Keeping the Covenant
[(5:7):(4:5):(7:7):(5:4):(7:5)]

15(16)For you indeed know / how we dwelt \[a] in the land of Egypt // 23 2
and how we passed over / in the midst of the nations / 18 2
that you passed over // 5 1
16(17)You saw / their detestable things / indeed / their idol-turds // 20 4
of wood and stone / of silver and gold / that they have // 19 3
17(18)Beware lest there is among you / a man or a woman / 13 2
or a family or a tribe / whose heart is turning away TODAY[a] / 23 2
From / YHWH our[b] God / to go to serve / 21 3
the gods / of these nations // 15 2
Beware lest there is among you / a stock / 10 2
sprouting poison / and bitterness // 11 2

18(19)and it shall be / when he hears the words of this / oath /	22	3_
And he fancies himself blessed saying /	16	1
"May I be safe / though / my own willful heart \[a] I follow //	21	3
to the / utter ruin of moist[b] / and dry alike" //	19	3_
19(20)YHWH will not agree / [a]to pardon him[a] /	14	2
but rather \[b] YHWH's anger and his jealousy / will smoke[c] /	12	2
against that man /	7	1
till every curse / written / in this scroll / settles[d] on him //	27	4_
YHWH [e]will blot out[e] / his name / from under \[f] the heavens //	18	3
20(21)and YHWH will single him out /	9	1
for misfortune / from all / the tribes of Israel //	16	3_
According to all / the curses of the covenant /	11	2
(that are) written[a] / in this[b] / scroll of the Torah //	17	3_

Notes

15.a. Reading *tiphā'* as conj. because of misplaced *'atnāḥ*.

17.a. Omitted in LXX except for the Lucianic tradition; Origen inserts with asterisk. Prosodic analysis supports MT.

17.b. LXX reads 2 pl.

18.a. Reading *tiphā'* as conj. because of misplaced *'atnāḥ*.

18.b. Some SP witnesses read הרוחה, "respite, relief," and others הרואה (meaning uncertain) for MT הרוה, "watered."

19.a-a. SP, Syr., and Tg. read לסלח for MT סלח, "(to) pardon (him)."

19.b. Reading the *tĕlîsā gĕdôlā* as conj.

19.c. SP reads יחר, "it will burn," for MT יעשן, "it will smoke."

19.d SP reads ורבצו, "they lie down," for MT ורבצה, "he lies down"; 4QDeut[c] reads דבקה, "it clings (to him)," which appears to be reflected in LXX and Tg. Onqelos. Tigay suggests that this reading is "an attempt at softening the animal imagery" ([1996] 280).

19.e-e. Reading יִמְחֶה for MT וּמָחָה, "he will blot out," to improve balance in mora count.

19.f. Reading *tiphā'* as conj. because of misplaced *sillûq*.

20.a. SP and Syr. read הכתובים, "the things written," for MT הכתובה, "(that are) written."

20.b Syr. and Vg. read fem., perhaps הזאת, "this." Prosodic analysis supports MT.

Form/Structure/Setting

In 29:15–20 Moses warns the people of Israel about the consequences of idolatry. They will not get away with it (vv 17–18), for YHWH will single them out for misfortune (vv 19–20). They will bring down the covenant curses on themselves, which will result in exile from the land of Israel (vv 21–27). Nonetheless, YHWH will continue to extend mercy and will extend further opportunities to renew the covenant (30:1–5); and when they choose to return to YHWH, he will return his covenant blessings to them (30:6–10). The choice before God's people, then and now, is between life and death; and they are urged to choose life (30:11–20).

The boundaries of the prosodic subunits in this section are not marked in L. Internal structure is indicated by the use of the expression פן־יש ("beware lest" or "perchance there is") at the beginning of the second and third prosodic subunits, and the imperfect form of the verb with YHWH as the subject at the beginning of the fourth and fifth such units (vv 19 and 20).

Within the structure of Deut 29 as a whole, vv 15–20 constitute the center of a concentric structure of its own (see introduction to 29:9–30:20 above). The content of 29:15–20 may be outlined as follows:

A	You know about the detestable idols of other nations	29:15–16
B	There may be among you those who turn to other gods	29:17a
X	They may think they will get away with it	29:17b–18
B′	They will bring down the curses on themselves	29:19a
A′	YHWH will single them out for misfortune	29:19b–20

The center of this structure contains a difficult clause that has produced a host of interpretations (see *Comment* on the phrase "to the utter ruin of moist and dry alike" in v 18). The point is that those who think they can follow their own willful heart in matters of covenant loyalty are in for bitter disappointment. When they turn to other gods in times to come (v 17a), they will bring down upon themselves the covenant curses (v 19a). The people are warned that they have been exposed to other nations and their idolatry that may lead some to the worship of idols (vv 15–16). The consequences of such action are horrendous, for YHWH himself "will single them out for misfortune, and they will surely experience all the curses of the covenant written in this book of the Torah" (v 20).

For the data on the numerical composition of 29:15–20 see the discussion at the end of the section on *Form/Structure/Setting* under 29:9–14.

Comment

15–16 The people are reminded of their experience "in the land of Egypt" and "in the midst of the nations" through which they passed in Transjordan. The concern here is not to illustrate the power of YHWH in delivering Israel from slavery in Egypt, but to draw attention to the idolatrous practices of the nations that the covenant people must be careful to avoid. In their journeys from Egypt to the edge of the promised land, they "saw their detestable things" (שקוציהם), that is, "their idol-turds of wood and stone, of silver and gold." Pope (*ABD* 1:725) says that גלליהם, translated "idol-turds" here, is a dysphemism from the root גלל, "to roll," which makes allusion to excrement (cf. the noun גָּלָל, "dung," in 1 Kgs 14:10; Zeph 1:17). He suggests the English translation "turds," a word that entered the English language a thousand years ago from Latin *tordere,* "to roll."

17–18 The list of those who may be turning away from YHWH to worship other gods begins with reference to "a man or a woman" in keeping with the fact that every single person is invited to enter the covenant individually in v 9. The reference to "gods of these nations" is to the idols of v 16, for Deuteronomy does not recognize the existence of other gods as such, but simply these images that are made by human beings (cf. 4:28).

Tigay identifies the word לענה with wormwood and suggests that "these two plants serve as a metaphor for punishment" ([1996] 279). On the translation of בשררות לבי, "my own willful heart," cf. Jer 3:17; 7:24; 9:13; 11:8; 13:10; 16:12; 18:12; 23:17; Ps 81:13 (Eng. 12). The phrase "to the utter ruin of moist and dry alike" is obscure and probably represents a lost idiom, as Tigay suggests ([1996] 280). Craigie thinks that it may be an ancient proverb that means essentially that "no one would escape judgment" ([1976] 359 n. 14). The reading taken here is that of the majority of commentators, who see a merism meaning essentially "everything." The person's delusion will bring about a calamity that will bring everything to ruin.

19 According to Weinfeld the four motifs of this verse are all found in treaties and other legal documents of the ancient Near East: divine wrath; the curse that settles upon and pursues the malefactor; the oath-imprecation inscribed in a written document; and the obliteration of the malefactor's name and memory (*DDS,* 107–9).

20 The term והבדילו, translated here "to single him out," is normally used in a positive sense in Deuteronomy (cf. 4:41; 10:8). Here the person is singled out "for misfortune."

Explanation

The covenant community must be on guard against any member who, having taken the vows to YHWH, then decides that it is safe to do as he or she pleases (vv 18–19). The promises of God are conditioned on sincere and continued obedience, and the danger is that defection on the part of one person will infect the whole community. The whole community hence stands responsible for the individuals in their midst who make light of the obligations of the covenant. At the same time, these very individuals, with their reservations about keeping the covenant, stand responsible under the law for their own behavior. If an individual member of the community chooses the path of willful rebellion, "YHWH will single him out for misfortune from all the tribes of Israel according to all the curses of the covenant (that are) written in this scroll of the Torah" (v 20). The teaching of individual responsibility inherent in this text is developed further in Jeremiah, and even more so in Ezekiel.

The sin of idolatry begins in the human heart (v 17). Those who begin to turn from God by neglecting their duty to him are easily drawn into the service of other gods. Such folk are dangerous, for they soon corrupt others, drawing them into idolatry as well. The writer of the letter to the Hebrews refers to the same thing when he cautions us to take heed of those who would seduce us in the Christian walk, causing "trouble, and through it many become defiled" (Heb 12:15 NRSV). As Paul put it on another occasion, "a little yeast leavens the whole batch of dough" (1 Cor 5:6 NRSV).

When the idolater "hears the words of this oath," so that he cannot plead ignorance of the danger, he still "fancies himself blessed" in the willfulness of his own heart and thinks himself safe from the wrath of God (v 18). The text declares that "YHWH will not agree to pardon him, but rather YHWH's anger and his jealousy will smoke against that man till every curse written in this scroll settles on him; YHWH will blot out his name from under the heavens" (v 19). This is not mere rhetoric to frighten children, but a real declaration of the wrath of God against human presumption.

C. Exile from the Land Foretold for Breaking the Covenant (29:21–27 [Eng. 22–28])

Bibliography

Albrektson, B. *History and the Gods.* ConBOT 1. Lund: Gleerup, 1967. 39, 105–6. **Cazelles, H.** "La rupture de la *berît* selon les Prophètes." *JJS* 33 (1982) 133–44, esp. 137. **Daube, D.** "The Culture of Deuteronomy." *Orita* 3 (1969) 51. **Deatrick, E. P.** "Salt, Soil, Savior." *BA* 25 (1962) 45. **Fensham, F. C.** "Salt as Curse in the Old Testament and the Ancient Near East." *BA* 25 (1962) 48–50. **Frankena, R.** "The Vassal-Treaties of Esarhaddon and the Dating of Deuteronomy." *OTS* 14 (1965) 122–54. **Gevirtz, S.** "Jericho and Shechem: A Religio-Literary Aspect of City Destruction." *VT* 13 (1963) 52–62. **Greenfield, J. C.** "A Hapax Legomenon: *mimšak ḥarul.*" In *Studies in Judaica, Karaitica, and Islamica Presented to Leon Nemoy.* Ed. S. R. Brunswick. Ramat Gan: Bar Ilan UP, 1982. 79–82. **Levenson, J. D.** "Who Inserted the Book of the Torah?" *HTR* 68 (1975) 208. **Long, B. O.** "Two Question and Answer Schemata in the Prophets." *JBL* 90 (1971) 129–39. **Mayes, A. D. H.** "Deuteronomy 4 and the Literary Criticism of Deuteronomy." *JBL* 100 (1981) 50–51. **McCarthy, D. J.** "*bĕrît* in Old Testament History and Theology." *Bib* 53 (1972) 110–21, esp. 120. **Ridley, R. T.** "To Be Taken with a Pinch of Salt: The Destruction of Carthage." *CP* 81 (1986) 140–46. **Skweres, D. E.** "Das Motiv der Strafgrunderfahrung in biblischen und neuassyrischen Texten." *BZ* 14 (1970) 181–97. **Streck, M.** *Assurbanipal und die letzten assyrischen Könige bis zum Untergange Niniveh*s. Part 3. *Texte.* Vorderasiastische Biliothek 7.2. Leipzig, Hinrichs, 1916. **Vargyas, P.** "Le cylindre Rassam et la Bible: Les parallèles du Dtn 29,23–26." *Oikumene* 3 (1982) 157–62. ———. "Deuteronomium 29,23–26 e la forma assira del Patto." *Evkönyv* (1977) 411–18. **Weinfeld, M.** *DDS.* 63 n. 5, and 109. **Zenger, E.** "Funktion und Sinn der ältesten Herausführungsformel." *ZDMG* Sup 1 (1969) 334–42, esp. 335.

Translation and Prosodic Analysis

Exile from the Land Foretold for Breaking the Covenant
[(7:6):(8:5:5):(5:5:8):(6:7)]

21(22) And later generations / will say / 13 2
your children / who appear \[a] after you / and the foreigner / 24 3
who comes / from a distant land // 15 2
And they[b] see / the blows (dealt) / to that land / 17 3
and the diseases / that YHWH has inflicted[c] / on it // 20 3
22(23) With brimstone and salt / burnt is all her land / 16 2
it is not sown[a] / and it produces nothing / 12 2
And there does not grow on it / any grass // 12 1
it is like the overthrowing / of Sodom and Gomorrah / 14 2
of Admah and Zeboiim[b] / 14 1
Which / YHWH overthrew / in his anger \[c] and in his wrath // 20 3
23(24) and all the nations / will say / 12 2
"For what reason has YHWH done / thus \[a] to this land? // 20 2
[b]Why the burning / of this / great anger?" // 14 3
24(25) And they will say / "Because / they forsook / 14 3
the covenant of YHWH / God of their fathers // 17 2

That / he cut with them / when he delivered them /	19	3
from the land of Egypt // 25(26) and they went /	14	2_
And they served / other gods / [a]and they worshiped[a] / them //	24	4
gods[b] / whom they had not known /	14	2
and whom he had not allotted / to them" //	9	2_
26(27) And the anger of YHWH was kindled / at that land //	15	2
to bring upon it / every curse / written / in this scroll //	30	4_
27(28) And YHWH uprooted them /	9	1
from their soil / in anger and in fury / and in great rage //	26	3
and he cast[a] them / into another land / as at THIS DAY //	17	3_

Notes

21.a. Reading *paštā'* followed by *zāqēp qāṭôn* as conj.
21.b. SP reads sg. וראה, "he will see," for MT וראו, "they will see."
21.c. One Heb. MS and some SP Mss read חלא, "he defiled," for MT חלה, "he afflicted."
22.a. SP reads חִזְרִיעַ, "it produced seed," for MT תִזָּרַע, "it is sown."
22.b. Reading the K וצב(ו)ים, "and Zeboiim," with some Heb. MSS, DSS, and some SP MSS; SP and Tg. read וצב(ו)אים, with no change in meaning.
22.c. Reading *ṭipḥā'* as conj. because of misplaced *sillûq*.
23.a. Reading *ṭipḥā'* as conj. because of misplaced *'atnāḥ*.
23.b. Some Heb. MSS, SP, and Syr. add *waw*-conj. reading ומה, "and why," for MT מה, "why." Prosodic analysis supports MT.
25.a-a. Omitted in some LXX witnesses. Prosodic analysis supports MT.
25.b. Omitted in LXX except for Lucianic recension (Origen has it with asterisk). Prosodic analysis supports MT.
27.a. A number of Heb. MSS and B read ל maj (written larger) in וישלכם.

Form/Structure/Setting

The loss of the land depicted here (29:21–27) constitutes the reversal of YHWH's Holy War, which is essentially the epic journey of the people of Israel from slavery in Egypt (the exodus) to the entry into the promised land (the eisodus). The complete reversal of Israel's history in 28:58–68 marks the climax of the covenant curses of Deut 28. Moreover, the subject of exile from the land of Israel is in the structural center of that lengthy chapter (vv 36–37), and is further expanded in its final section (vv 64–68). That same subject of exile from the land of Israel is explored further here in graphic detail.

The prosodic analysis indicates that the internal structure of 29:21–27 is marked by the introduction of direct speech on the part of the nations in vv 24–25, and the shift back to narrative discourse with YHWH as subject in v 26. The content of the section as a whole may be outlined in a five-part concentric structure:

A	Later generations will see the devastation of the land	29:21–22
B	They will ask: "Why the burning of this great anger?"	29:23
X	Answer: YHWH did it because Israel broke the covenant	29:24–25
B′	The exile and destruction are the covenant curses	29:26
A′	It was YHWH who uprooted them and cast them into exile	29:27

In times to come, the people of Israel will violate the terms of the covenant and bring upon themselves the curses in the form of devastation and exile from their land. Members of the community of faith, and foreigners as well, will ask: "For what reason has YHWH done thus to this land? Why the burning of this great anger?" They will answer their own question, for the reason is obvious: YHWH has done this because Israel broke their covenant agreement. The same message is conveyed in a concentric reading of vv 24–27:

A	They forsook the covenant of YHWH God of their fathers	29:24
B	And they went and served other gods and worshiped them	29:25
X	And the anger of YHWH was kindled to bring the curses	29:26
B′	So YHWH uprooted them from their land	29:27a
A′	And he cast them into another land	29:27b

Because they forsook his covenant with them and turned to the worship of other gods, YHWH uprooted them from their land and cast them into exile.

The key word in 29:21–27 is ארץ, "land," which appears seven times in a carefully structured menorah pattern:

A	Foreigners will come from a distant land	והנכרי אשר יבא מארץ רחוקה	v 21a
B	They will see the destruction of that land	וראו את־מכות הארץ ההוא	v 21b
C	Brimstone and salt, burnt is all her land	גפרית ומלח שרפה כל־ארצה	v 22
X	Why has YHWH done thus to this land?	על־מה עשה יהוה ככה לארץ	v 23
C′	He delivered them from the land of Egypt	בהוציאו אתם מארץ מצרים	v 24
B′	YHWH's anger was kindled in that land	ויחר־אף יהוה בארץ ההוא	v 26
A′	And he cast them into another land	וישלכם אל־ארץ אחרת	v 27

When foreigners come to the land and see its devastation (v 21–22), they will ask the central question: Why has YHWH destroyed this land? (v 23). He delivered this people from the land of Egypt in the distant past (v 24); but now in his anger he has cast them into another land (vv 26–27). The pattern here is that of the menorah (candelabrum), with three related uses of the word ארץ, "land," on either side of the central column, which contains the great question: Why has all this happened?

Along with others before him, Tigay presents a useful parallel situation in the inscriptions of King Ashurbanipal of Assyria (668–627 B.C.E.). The situation concerns his response to the king of the Arabs who violated his treaty obligations in revolt against Assyria. The Ashurbanipal text deals with "how the gods afflicted Arabia with all the curses written in the treaty, so that whenever the inhabitants of Arabia ask each other: 'On account of what have these calamities befallen Arabia? [They themselves answered:] Because we did not keep the solemn oaths [sworn in the name of the god] Ashur, because we violated the pact of good relations with Ashurbanipal'" ([1996] 281; *ANET,* 297, 300; cf. the discussions of Frankena [*OTS* 14 (1965) 122–54] and Weinfeld [*DDS*, 109–16] on the Esarhaddon inscriptions).

The evidence assembled by Labuschagne on the numerical composition of 29:21–28 may be summarized as follows:

Words:	before *'atnāḥ*		after *'atnāḥ*			
29:21	12	+	11	=	23	
29:21–22	26	+	21	=	47	
29:21–24	45	+	33	=	78	(= 3 × 26)
29:23–28	41	+	44	=	85	(= 5 × 17)
29:25–26	11	+	15	=	26	
29:27–28	11	+	17	=	28	

Once again, the scribes of ancient Israel have carefully woven the two divine-name numbers 17 and 26 into the fabric of the text in different ways, as well as the number 23. On the details of this system of numerical composition, see *Excursus:* "Deuteronomy as a Numerical Composition."

Comment

21 The הדור האחרון, "later generations," could refer to "the following generation," as Tigay suggests. It is more likely, however, that the author has more distant generations in mind. According to rabbinic tradition, the reference to "that land" here applies to the Northern Kingdom of Israel, whose people were exiled to Assyria in the eighth century B.C.E. (*m. Sanh.* 10:3; *t. Sanh.* 13:12; *b. Sanh.* 110b). The land is described as being afflicted by מכות, "blows" (also translated "plagues"), and תחלאיה, "diseases," sent by God in retribution for Israel's sin.

22 The association of "brimstone and salt" with the "overthrowing of Sodom and Gomorrah" in this verse suggests that the curse is something along the lines of the story in Genesis in which "brimstone [sulfur] and fire" fell out of heaven on those cities (Gen 19:24). Tigay argues, however, that the association of salt and infertility here suggests a different picture. In antiquity conquerors sometimes spread salt on the soil they conquered to make it infertile (see Judg 9:45). For parallels in the ancient Near East, see S. Gevirtz, *VT* 13 (1963) 52–62, cited by Tigay ([1996] 399 n. 57) with the comment: "the idea that Carthage was salted at the end of the Punic Wars is an invention of modern historians who mistakenly transferred the idea from Judg. 9:45" (see Ridley, *CP* 81 [1986] 140–46). The translation "burnt [שרפה] is all her land" probably refers to the withering effect salt and sulfur have on plants (Deatrick, *BA* 25 [1962] 45).

On the destruction of Sodom and Gomorrah, see Gen 19. These two cities, along with the cities of Admah and Zeboiim, which appear with them in Gen 10:9; 14:2–8, were destroyed in the time of Abraham. Though the destruction of Admah and Zeboiim is referred to in Hos 11:8; 13:19, there is no narrative account of their overthrow recorded in the Bible. Further references to the destruction of Sodom and Gomorrah are found in Amos 4:11; Isa 1:9; 13:19; and Jer 49:18; 50:40.

23 The destruction will be such that "all the nations" (i.e., the whole world) will hear of it. From far and wide, foreigners will join with future Israelites and those who pass by to inquire why this has happened. As the wording of their question indicates, it will be obvious to all that the destruction of Israel is an act of God's judgment.

24–25 The question of why God has done this to the land appears to be answered by the very persons who asked it, as they acknowledge that Israel "forsook the covenant of YHWH, God of their fathers." They offended God, the God who "delivered them from the land of Egypt" and "served other gods" whom God "had not allotted to them" (see 4:19 and *Comment* on 32:8–9).

26–27 The reference to what is "written in this scroll" indicates that the response on the part of the nations to their own question ends with v 25. The verb translated "uprooted them," ויתשם, does not occur elsewhere in the Pentateuch, as Mayes notes ([1981] 366–67), but does appear in Jeremiah (1:10; 12:14–15; 18:7). "In anger and in fury" YHWH "cast them into another land." On the synonymous use of these two verbs for "anger," see Jer 21:5; 32:37; and for "another land," see Jer 22:26. The *lamed* in וישלכם, translated "he cast them," is written as a majuscule (a large letter) in Torah scrolls. Tigay notes that "majuscules are sometimes used to highlight the first or middle letter of a book" ([1996] 282). This observation suggests that they have something to do with the numerical composition of the text (see *Excursus:* "Deuteronomy as a Numerical Composition"). Further support for this conclusion is found in the majuscule in 32:6, where an interrogative *he* is treated as a separate word by means of a *maqqeph*.

Explanation

The word ארץ, "land," appears seven times in vv 21–27 in a carefully structured concentric pattern, as shown above in *Form/Structure/Setting*. When human beings cast God out, a blight comes upon the created order itself—"with brimstone and salt burnt is all her land; it is not sown, and it produces nothing" (v 22). The Oklahoma "dust bowl" from which the Joad family fled in Steinbeck's novel *The Grapes of Wrath* portrays in vivid imagery a modern example of the land that is "burnt" and "it is not sown, and it produces nothing." Though the cause of the disaster in this instance was in large part beyond human control in the form of a great drought, human error contributed to the misery as marginal grazing land was plowed up and blown away in devastating dust storms.

The effects of sin are felt in the productivity of the earth itself. In recent decades we have been reminded again and again of other results of "sinning against the land." In Bangladesh the wanton consumption of trees for fuel has produced ecological disaster of enormous proportions, with ensuing floods devastating the land year by year. As self-centered exploiters turn their back on the stipulations of God's covenant and cut down the rain forests of the Amazon valley with no thought except personal gain, the ensuing erosion washes away millions of acres of fertile soil. And other powerful forces of ecological disaster are released, which we only partially understand, with potential to harm human life throughout the entire world. The destruction of tropical rain forests in Borneo and other distant lands appears to be intricately linked to the arrival of the El Niño weather phenomenon—which in turn is linked with devastating floods, drought, hurricanes, and other so-called natural disasters. The price we pay for breaking God's covenant is exile from the land. This is as true today as it was in ancient Israel.

D. Secret and Revealed Things: "Do All the Words of This Torah!" (29:28 [Eng. 29])

Bibliography

Balentine, S. E. "A Description of the Semantic Field of Hebrew Words for 'Hide.'" *VT* 30 (1980) 137–53. **Butin, R.** *The Ten Nequdoth of the Torah.* 1906. Repr. New York: Ktav, 1969. **Grimme, H.** "Zur Annahme eines salomonischen Gesetzes." *OLZ* 11 (1908) 188–93. ———. "Zur Auffindung des salomonischen Gesetzbuches unter Josia." *OLZ* 10 (1907) 610–15. **Haag, H.** "'Offenbaren' in der hebräischen Bibel." In *Das Buch des Bundes: Aufsätze zur Bibel und ihrer Welt.* Düsseldorf: Patmos, 1980. 73–78, esp. 75. **Haupt, P.** "Salomons Deuteronomium." *OLZ* 11 (1908) 119–25. **Jervell, J.** "Die offenbarte und die verborgene Tora: Zur Vorstellung über die neue Tora im Rabbinismus." *ST* 25 (1971) 90–108. **Perlitt, L.** "Die Verborgenheit Gottes." In *FS G. von Rad.* 1971. 367–82, esp. 379. **Tov, E.** *Textual Criticism of the Hebrew Bible.* Minneapolis: Fortress, 1992. 55–57, 213. **Urbach, E. E.** *The Sages.* Cambridge: Harvard UP, 1987. 539. **Zeitlin, S.** "Some Reflections on the Text of the Pentateuch." *JQR* 51 (1960–61) 321–31.

Translation and Prosodic Analysis

Secret and Revealed Things: "Do All the Words of This Torah!" [4:4]

28(29) The secret things / belong to YHWH \[a] our[b] God //	[17	2
and the revealed things /	5	1
[c]to us and to our children[c] /	13	1
forever / to do / all the words [דברי] / of this Torah // ס	<u>22</u>	4_

Notes

28.a. Reading *ṭip̄ḥā'* as conj. because of misplaced *'atnāḥ*.

28.b. Some LXX witnesses read 2 pl. אלהיכם, "your [pl.] God."

28.c-c. This is one of the ten locations of the *Nequdoth* (extraordinary points) in the Torah (see *Comment* below).

Form/Structure/Setting

One of the characteristic features of narrative structure in the Hebrew Bible is what I have described elsewhere as the "riddle at the middle" (see D. L. Christensen, "Janus Parallelism in Gen. 6:3," *HS* 27 [1986] 20–24). The center of concentric structures is often relatively short and enigmatic. This is particularly true in regard to 29:28. The work of C. Labuschagne suggests that one aspect of the mystery presented here in summary form has to do with hidden or coded information contained in the text ("Divine Speech in Deuteronomy," in SBTS 3:375–93; idem, *Deuteronomium* [1987–97]). In this instance, the text itself speaks of "secret things" and "revealed things." Moreover, the verse contains the tenth and final instance of the phenomenon of the *Nequdoth*, where each of ten successive consonants in the Hebrew text has a special mark over it in L. For more on this see the *Comment*.

The structure of 29:9–30:20, the eighth of the eleven weekly portions of Torah readings in Deuteronomy, is outlined at the beginning of this section in a menorah pattern:

A	The covenant is binding on future generations too	29:9–14
B	Warning to those with reservations about keeping the covenant	29:15–20
C	The exile from the land of Israel foretold	29:21–27
X	Secret and revealed things: Do all the words of this Torah!	29:28
C′	The possibility of returning to YHWH is there	30:1–5
B′	When you return, YHWH will return the covenant blessings	30:6–10
A′	The choice before you is between life and death—choose life	30:11–20

Within this structure, 29:28 occupies the center, and the ten *Nequdoth* are in the center of this center.

Deut 29:28 is connected with more distant texts as well in other structures, one of which ties together chaps. 28 and 29 of Deuteronomy as follows:

A	Introduction: These are the words of the covenant	28:69
B	The exodus from the land of Egypt recalled	29:1–3
C	Moses reminds them of God's provision in times past	29:4–8
X	The covenant is binding on future generations too	29:9–14
C′	Moses warns those with reservations about the covenant	29:15–20
B′	Exile from the land of Israel foretold	29:21–27
A′	Conclusion: Observe all the words of the Torah	29:28

In this reading the focus of attention is on the fact that the words of the covenant are binding on future generations too—they belong "to us and to our children forever, to do all the words of this Torah" (29:28).

In a similar manner, 29:28 also functions as the center of a structure that ties together chaps. 29 and 30, as shown in the following outline:

A	Introduction: These are the words of the covenant	28:69
B	Moses reminds them of God's provision in times past	29:1–8
C	The covenant is binding on future generations too	29:9–14
D	Moses warns those with reservations about the covenant	29:15–20
E	Exile from the land of Israel foretold	29:21–27
X	Secret and revealed thing: Do all the words of this Torah!	29:28
E′	The possibility of restoration is there	30:1–5
D′	When you seek to purify yourselves you will receive help	30:6–10
C′	This instruction is not beyond your reach	30:11
B′	God's requirements are known, understandable, and doable	30:12–14
A′	Conclusion: Choose life and blessing, not death and cursing	30:15–20

The outer frame in this particular structure places the pivotal verse 28:69, which also functions as the summation of 26:19–28:68, over against 30:15–20, with its moving call to decision: "I set before you today life and good or death and evil. . . . I set before you the blessing and the curse, so choose life that you . . . may live" (30:15, 19).

Comment

28 "The secret things" (הנסתרת) and "the revealed things" (הנגלת) have been explained in many different ways in Jewish tradition (see Tigay [1996] 283). Mayes explains the verse as "a wisdom maxim, which affirms the limits of any human wisdom apart from the law which God has revealed" ([1981] 368). Another reading is to note that both the "secret things" and the "revealed things" "belong to YHWH our God." It is all his; and it is entrusted "to us and to our children forever—to do all the words of this Torah." We can only teach what is revealed to us from this treasury of information. As God reveals more and more of the meaning of "these words" (אלה הדברים, the opening words, and the title of the book of Deuteronomy) to us as we ponder the details of his mysterious and marvelous revelation, we as scholars have the responsibility to communicate what we find "to our children," for the "revealed things" are then no longer "hidden things." The reading proposed here associates the verse with 30:15–20, with its injunction to choose life and blessing rather than death and cursing, as a literary framework around 30:1–14.

Prosodic analysis reveals a pivot pattern, in which the words לנו ולבנינו, "to us and to our children," belong to both halves of this verse. These words are unique in Deuteronomy in the sense that each of the ten consonants in the Hebrew text has a special mark over it—what the scholars have called the *Nequdoth* (נקודות). This is the tenth and final such instance of the phenomenon within the Pentateuch (see Butin, *Ten Nequdoth*). The meaning of the extraordinary points is explained in various ways.

It should be noted that the *Nequdoth* in 29:28 of L are written over ten successive letters that make up the two words לנו ולבנינו, "to us and to our children." The Aleppo Codex, however, has twelve dots, starting with the ה of the previous word and ending with the ע on the word עד. Tigay notes: "Rabbinic interpretation takes the dots as calling attention to midrashic explanations that limit the application of the words: it was not *until* (*'ad*, whose first letter is flagged by a dot) Israel entered the promised land that God held them collectively accountable ('us and our children') for concealed sins or, in another view, for overt ones" ([1996] 283). A simpler explanation is to note that the dots are themselves a form of commentary, or homiletical notes to such commentary, on the Hebrew text. The twelve dots of the Aleppo Codex may refer to the twelve tribes, that is, Israel—which the scribe understood to be the meaning of the words "to us and our children." The secret things belong to God; but God's revelation in "the words of this Torah" belongs to Israel. The ten dots of L, on the other hand, may refer to the Ten Words (Ten Commandments), which are expanded into what eventually became the book of Deuteronomy as we now have it.

The scribe who added the *Nequdoth* in L may have been aware that the numerical value of the two words under these dots is 32 + 64 (= 2 × 32) = 96 (= 3 × 32). In terms of the usual association of the number 32 with כבוד, "glory" (= 32), in the numerical composition of Deuteronomy, this number is used to call attention to the glory of YHWH. The ten curious dots over ten successive letters in the Hebrew text stand for the "Ten Words," which are entrusted to Israel. And those words are "to us and to our children," that is, for all Israel. In short, the book of Deuteronomy has the title אלה הדברים, "these are the words," which are in essence an expansion of the original "Ten Words" (the Ten Commandments). The secret things belong to God, but the revealed things belong to us and to our children forever—namely, "to do all the words of this Torah." The *Nequdoth* in this instance may then be a form of homiletical notes for the informed rabbi to teach the central message of Deuteronomy.

Explanation

Tigay ([1996] 283) presents a brief but useful description of various interpretations of the words of this verse within Judaism, past and present, from which he selects the meaning expressed in *Tg. Ps.-Jonathan* as the one he prefers: "concealed acts (that is, concealed sins) are known to God, and He will punish them, but overt ones are our responsibility to punish ('to apply all the provisions of this Teaching')." This is true, as is the second of his possible interpretations: "although it is true that only overt sins can be punished by human authorities, God will detect and punish concealed ones." The same holds for the reading of Maimonides, who according to Tigay argues that "'concealed things' refers to the reasons for the commandments, which are known to God, whereas 'overt acts'—the physical performance of the commandments—are assigned to Israel. People may not exempt themselves from performing commandments even if they know their reasons and think that that makes their performance superfluous."

The plain reading of the text of 29:28, however, suggests that although God has revealed many things to us, it has also pleased him to conceal much from us. For as Thomas Scott put it long ago, "who can penetrate into the secrets of his wisdom; or discover his decrees and counsels, the reasons of his conduct, and the mysteries of his nature, further than he reveals them?" (*Holy Bible* [1823] 1:562–63). Anyone who ponders the words of Deuteronomy faces questions and may even raise objections against God's dealings with his people, for the awful curses seem to be needlessly severe.

In 29:28 we are cautioned in such inquiry by an important distinction between the "secret things" and the "revealed things." We must leave some things alone, as belonging to God, and put our primary attention to the task of doing "all the words of this Torah," which are revealed "to us and to our children" in plain language. God has revealed the things that are beneficial to us; and our attention should focus on these discoveries, and end with them. As Scott observes (p. 563),

> Almost all the heresies and controversies, which have corrupted the purity, or disturbed the peace of the church in every age, have originated from disregard to this distinction; from vain attempts, by human reasonings and authority, to fill up supposed chasms in revelation, and to make it more apparently consistent and systematical, than it has pleased God to make it; from deducing disputable consequences from revelation; or from tracing back its sacred mysteries to some *unrevealed* antecedent causes.

Silence is an appropriate response in the face of ultimate mystery. As the prophet Isaiah put it, "For my thoughts are not your thoughts, nor are your ways my ways, says the LORD. For as the heavens are higher than the earth, so are my ways higher than your ways and my thoughts than your thoughts" (Isa 55:8–9 NRSV).

There is danger on the other side as well, in the disposition to speak too much of matters that are revealed—arguing that it would have been better had such not been written. Some writers today advise the omission of many parts of revealed truth, particularly in the letters of Paul. The text here declares that all the revealed things belong to us.

The Scriptures reveal plainly all that is needed for us to know God and to love and to serve him; to know our state as sinners, and to know the way of acceptance in Jesus Christ; to understand our duty as redeemed sinners, with respect to our talents and opportunities for service to others; and to know the nature of the spiritual enemies and dangers to which we are exposed. All this belongs to the "revealed things" that are the substance of useful knowledge and, when put into practice, are the substance of heavenly wisdom. But all those things that we are tempted to add to revealed truth, or substitute in its place, serve only to bewilder and confuse the benighted traveler. Such speculations may amuse and distract the curious; but they often mislead as well, leading the unwary to the pit of destruction. The prophet Isaiah warned against those who consult other gods "for teaching and for instruction": "Surely, those who speak like this will have no dawn!" (Isa 8:20 NRSV).

E. Possibility of Restoration: When You Return, God Will Return (30:1–10)

Bibliography for 30:1–20

Baker, D.W. "The Uniqueness of the Mosaic Covenant." *South African Judaica* 1 (1984) 1–11. **Barth, C.** "Notes on 'Return' in the Old Testament." *Ecumenical Review* 19 (1967) 310–12. **Braulik, G.** "Gesetz als Evangelium: Rechtfertigung und Begnadigung nach der deuteronomischen Tora." *ZTK* 79 (1982) 127–60, esp. 155–60. **Brueggemann, W.** "The Kerygma of the Deuteronomistic Historian: Gospel for Exiles." *Int* 22 (1968) 387–402, esp. 393–94. **Buis, P.** "Comment au septième siècle envisageait-on l'avenir de l'Alliance? Étude de Lv. 26,3–45." In *Questions disputées d'Ancien Testament.* Ed. C. Brekelmans. 1974. 131–40, esp. 139. ———. "La Nouvelle Alliance." *VT* 18 (1968) 1–15. **Gamper, A.** "Die heilsgeschichtliche Bedeutung des salominischen Tempelweihgebetes." *ZKT* 85 (1963) 55–61, esp. 60–61. **Gressmann, H.** "Josia und das Deuteronomium." *ZAW* 42 (1924) 313–46, esp. 335. **Holladay, W. L.** *The Root ŠÛBH* in the Old Testament with Particular Reference to Its Usages in Covenantal Contexts. Leiden: Brill, 1958. **Köckert, M.** "Das nahe Wort: Zum Gesetzesverständnis im Alten Testament." *TP* 60 (1985) 496–519. **Levenson, J. D.** "The Paronomasia of Solomon's Seventh Petition." *HAR* 6 (1982) 135–38. **Lohfink, N.** "Der Bundesschluß im Land Moab: Redaktionsgeschichtliches zu Dt 28,69–32,47." In *Studien zum Deuteronomium I.* Ed. N. Lohfink. 1990. 53–82, esp. 63–64. ———. *Höre Israel: Auslegung von Texten aus dem Buch Deuteronomium.* Dusseldorf: Patmos-Verlag, 1965. 119–20. **Schenker, A.** "Unwiderrufliche Umkehr und neuer Bund: Vergleich zwischen der Wiederherstellung Israels in Dt 4,25–31: 30,1–14 und dem neuen Bund in Jer 31,31–34." *FZPhTh* 27 (1980) 93–106.

Bibliography for 30:1–10

Aho, G. "The Eighth Sunday after Pentecost." *CTQ* 47 (1983) 48–49. **Brichto, H. C.** *Problem of "Curse."* 1963. 32, 187. **Chołewinski, A.** "Zur theologischen Deutung des Moabbundes." *Bib* 66 (1985) 96–111, esp. 108–9. **Fishbane, M.** "The Biblical *'ôt.*" *Shnaton* 1 (1975) 213–34 (Heb.; Eng. summary, x–xi). **Fitzmyer, J.** "The Aramaic Suzerainty Treaty from Sefire in the Museum of Beirut." *CBQ* 20 (1958) 444–46. **Greenfield, J. C.** "Stylistic Aspects of the Sefire Treaty Inscription." *AcOr* 29 (1965) 4. **Le Déaut, R.** "Le thème de la circoncision du coeur (Dt. xxx 6; Jér. iv 4) dans les versions anciennes (LXX et Targums) et à Qumrân." In *Congress Volume, Vienna 1980.* Ed. J. Emerton. VTSup 32. Leiden: Brill, 1981. 178–205. **Melamed, E. Z.** *Biblical Studies in Texts, Translations, and Commentators.* Jerusalem: Magnes, 1984. 131–36 (Heb.). **Mendecki, N.** "Dtn 30,3–4—Nachexilisch?" *BZ* 29 (1985) 267–71. **Schröter, U.** "Jeremias Botschaft für das Nordreich, zu N. Lohfinks Überlegungen zum Grundbestand von Jeremiah xxx-xxxi." *VT* 35 (1985) 312–29. **Sheppard, G. T.** "Wisdom and Torah: The Interpretation of Deuteronomy Underlying Sirach 24,24." In *FS W. S. LaSor.* 1978. 166–76, esp. 170–73. **Sklba, R. J.** "The Call to New Beginnings: A Biblical Theology of Conversion." *BTB* 11 (1981) 67–73. **Thompson, J. A.** "Israel's 'Haters.'" *VT* 29 (1979) 200–205. **Vanoni, G.** "Der Geist und der Buchstabe: Überlegungen zum Verhältnis der Testamente und Beobachtungen zu Dtn 30,1–10." *BN* 14 (1981) 65–98. **Weinfeld, M.** "Jeremiah and the Spiritual Metamorphosis of Israel." *ZAW* 88 (1976) 17–56. **Widengren, G.** "The Gathering of the Dispersed." *SEÅ* 41–42 (1976–77) 224–34. **Wolff, H. W.** "The Kerygma of the Deuteronomic Historical Work." Tr. F. C. Prussner. In W. Brueggemann and H. W. Wolff, *The Vitality of Old Testament Traditions.* 2nd ed. Atlanta: John Knox, 1982. 83–100.

Translation and Prosodic Analysis

The Possibility of Returning to YHWH Is There [(6:6):(5:4):(4:5):(6:6)]

1 And it shall be when *all these words / come upon you /*	30	2
the blessing / and the curse /	13	2
that I have set / before you //	12	2_
And you take them / to[a] *heart / among all the nations /*	21	3
where YHWH [b]*your God*[b] */* [c]*has banished you*[c] */ there //*	21	3_
2 *And you return / to YHWH your God /*	14	2
and you hearken to his voice /	10	1
according to all[a] *that I command you / TODAY //*	18	2_
[b]*You* |[c] *and your children*[b] */*	10	2
with all your heart / and with all your soul //	14	2_
3 *Then YHWH your God will restore*[a] */ your fortunes*[b] */*	18	2
and he will show compassion on you // and he will return /	11	2_
And he will gather you / from all the peoples /	11	2
where [c]*YHWH your God*[c] */ has scattered you / there //*	20	3_
4 *If you be banished away*\[a] *to the ends of the heavens //*	16	1
from there / YHWH your God / will gather you /	17	3
and from there / he will take you[b] *//*	10	2_
5 *And YHWH*[a] *your God*[b] */ will bring you /*	15	2
to the land / your fathers possessed\[c] *for you to possess //*	24	2
And he will make you more [d]*prosperous and*[d] *numerous /*	11	1
than your fathers //	7	1_

When You Return, God Will Return the Covenant Blessings to You
[(7:5):(6:4):(4:6):(5:7)]

[6]*And YHWH your God will circumcise / your heart /* 18 2
and the heart of your descendants // 7 1
To love / YHWH your God / 15 2
with all your heart and with all your soul / 14 1
in order that you may live // 7 1_
[7]*And YHWH your God / will put / all these*\[a] *curses //* 27 3
on your enemies[b] *and on your foes / who persecuted you //* 23 2_
[8]*And you yourself will return /* 8 1
and you will hearken\[a] *to the voice of YHWH*[b] *//* 11 1
And you will do\[c] *all his commandments /* 13 1
that / I command you / TODAY // 15 3_
[9]*And YHWH your God |*[a] *will grant you abundance /* 17 2
in all / the work of your hand<s>[b] */* 12 2_
In the fruit of your womb / and in the fruit [c]*of your cattle /* 15 2
and in the fruit of your ground[c] */ for good //* 15 2
For / YHWH will return / to delighting in you / for good / 20 4
just as he delighted / in your fathers // 11 2_
[10]*When you hearken / to the voice / of YHWH your God /* 15 3
by keeping his commandments / and his statutes / 14 2_
The ones written / in this[a] */ book of the Torah //* 14 3
when you return / to YHWH your God / 15 2
with all your heart / and with all your soul // פ 14 2_

Notes

1.a. Some SP MSS read על for MT אל, "to(ward)," with no change in meaning.
1.b-b. Omitted in LXX[B], OL, and *Tg. Ps.-J.*
1.c-c. SP reads ידיחך, "he will banish you," for MT הדיחך, "he banished you."
2.a. Reading *tĕbîr* under ככל as conj.
2.b-b. Omitted in LXX[L] (Origen adds with asterisk).
2.c. Reading *mûnāḥ* under אתה as disj.
3.a. LXX reads καὶ ἰάσεται (-ηται) "and he will heal (your iniquities)"; LXX[L] reads καὶ ἐξελάσεται. The use of the root שוב in this verse is idiomatic: ושב את שבותך, "to return your captivity," means to undo it—"to restore your fortunes."
3.b. SP reads שובתך for MT שבותך, "your fortunes," by metathesis; the SP was probably understood to have the same meaning.
3.c-c. Omitted in Vg.; LXX[B] and some other witnesses omit אלהיך, "your God." Prosodic analysis supports MT.
4.a. Reading *ṭip̄ḥā'* as conj. because of misplaced *'atnāḥ*.
4.b. LXX[B] and some other MSS add κύριος ὁ θεός σου, "the Lord your God." Prosodic analysis supports MT.
5.a. Omitted in LXX[B]. Prosodic analysis supports MT.
5.b. LXX (except for LXX[B]) add ἐκεῖθεν, "(from) thence." Prosodic analysis support MT.
5.c. Reading *ṭip̄ḥā'* as conj. because of misplaced *'atnāḥ*.
5.d-d. SP omits והיטבך, "and make you prosperous." Prosodic analysis supports MT.
7.a. Reading *ṭip̄ḥā'* as conj. because of misplaced *'atnāḥ*.
7.b. Two Heb. MSS and Cairo Geniza fragments read איבך, "your enemy," for MT איביך, "your enemies." Prosodic analysis tends to support MT.
8.a. Reading *ṭip̄ḥā'* as conj. because of misplaced *'atnāḥ*.

8.b. A few Heb. MSS, SP, LXX, Syr., and Vg. add אלהיך, "your God." Adding a word here, however, disturbs the pattern in the numerical composition of the text.

8.c. Reading *paštā'* followed by *zāqēp qāṭôn* as conj.

9.a. Reading *tĕlîšā qĕṭannā* after והותירך, "he will grant you abundance," as disj.

9.b. Reading ידיך, "your [sg.] hands," for MT ידך, "your [sg.] hand," with a number of Heb. MSS, Cairo Geniza fragments, SP, LXX, Syr., and Vg. *Tg. Ps.-J.* reads ידיכם, "your [pl.] hands."

9.c-c. SP reads אדמתך ובפרי בהמתך, "of your ground and in the fruit of your cattle," for the phrase in MT בהמתך ובפרי אדמתך, "of your cattle and in the fruit of your ground."

10.a. Cairo Geniza fragments read fem.

Form/Structure/Setting

The phrase "YHWH your God" appears twelve times—at least once in each verse except v 8. Tigay calls attention to the fact that the key word שוב, "to return," appears in seven clauses in a carefully constructed chiastic pattern ([1996] 283–84). The message is clear: if Israel chooses to "return" to YHWH their God, YHWH will "return" to them in more ways than one.

The content of Deut 30 as a whole may be outlined in a five-part concentric structural design:

A	The possibility of restoration is there, so return to YHWH	30:1–5
B	When you return, YHWH will return the blessing	30:6–10
X	This Torah is not beyond your reach—it is doable	30:11–14
B′	I have set before you a choice: life or death	30:15–18
A′	Choose life through obedience to YHWH	30:19–20

Even after exile from the promised land, the possibility of restoration is still there (vv 1–5), through obedience to the commandments in the Torah, which are doable (vv 11–14). If the people return to YHWH, he will return the blessing (vv 6–10). The way to renewed life in the land is thus a matter of choice (vv 15–18), through obedience to YHWH (vv 19–20).

Within the larger concentric structural design of Reading 8 (29:9–30:20) as a whole, the content moves from a warning of exile to come for violation of the covenant (29:15–27), which is set over against God's promise that even if Israel suffers exile, he will return the blessing to them when they choose to return to him (30:1–10). The key term here is the Hebrew root שוב, "turn" or "return," which appears in carefully structured patterns in the Hebrew text. Unfortunately, it is not possible to translate each of these occurrences of that Hebrew root with the same English words, so the patterns do not survive translation. The Hebrew root expresses both Israel's return to God and God's return of Israel's blessing. In grammatical terms, the verb "return" may be used either intransitively or transitively. The sense of the text in 30:6–10 may be summarized in the circular sentence: "When you return, God will return you!"

The Hebrew verb שוב also appears in idiomatic expressions, such as "taking to heart" (v 1) and "return your captivity" in the sense of restoring your fortune (v 3). Moreover, as Tigay puts it, "Appropriately, this paragraph is part of the Torah portion read in the synagogue on the Sabbath preceding the Ten Days of Repentance (*teshuvah*, lit. "return") that extend from Rosh Hashanah to Yom Kippur" ([1996] 284).

The boundaries of 30:1–10 are marked by the *sĕtûmā'* layout marker, the

Numeruswechsel at the beginning, and the *pĕtûḥā'* layout marker at the end. No further indications of internal structure are given other than the content itself. The key word in this text is the Hebrew root שוב, "return," which appears in seven clauses within the following menorah pattern:

A Recall [והשבת] these words and return [ושבת] to YHWH 30:1–2

B YHWH will restore [ושב שבות] you and he will return [ושב] 30:3

C YHWH will bring you back to the land of your fathers 30:4–5

X Love God with all your heart and with all your soul 30:6–7

C′ You will return [תשוב] and heed the voice of YHWH 30:8

B′ YHWH will return [ישוב] to take delight in you 30:9

A′ You will heed YHWH's voice when you return [תשוב] to him 30:10

Three of the occurrences of the root שוב are in the outermost frame, which focuses on the need to return to YHWH at that point in the future when the terms of the covenant have been broken (vv 1–2). The way "to return" is to obey YHWH's voice (v 10). The next frame also contains three occurrences of the root שוב in parallel verses (vv 3 and 9), which focus on the assurance that YHWH will return to his people and that he will restore their fortunes after the captivity (v 3). The inner frame has its focus on the fact that when the people return by obeying YHWH (v 8), YHWH will bring them back to the land of their fathers (vv 4–5). And in the center we find a restatement of the "great commandment": "to love YHWH your God with all your heart and with all your soul" (vv 6–7).

Careful prosodic analysis reveals two subunits, the first of which (vv 1–5) may be outlined as follows:

A Recall ("return" your heart to) these words among the nations 30:1

B And return to YHWH your God with all your heart 30:2

X YHWH will restore your fortunes ("return your captivity") 30:3a

B′ YHWH will return and gather you from all the peoples 30:3b

A′ YHWH will restore you to the land of your fathers 30:4–5

The outer frame in this structure moves from the command to remember these words from captivity among the nations (v 1) to, if the people do so, God restoring them to the land of their fathers (vv 4–5). These two parts are in parallel rhythmic subunits, each of which scans 6:6 in syntactic accentual stress units. The inner frame reiterates the conditional statement: if you return to YHWH with all your heart (v 2), then YHWH will return to you (v 3b); and he will restore your fortunes as in times past (v 3a).

The second subunit in vv 6–10 may be outlined in similar fashion:

A Love God *with all your heart and with all your soul* 30:6–7

B You shall return [תשוב] and do all his commandments 30:8

X YHWH will bless you with his covenant blessings 30:9a

B′ YHWH will return [ישוב] to take delight in you again 30:9b

A′ When you return *with all your heart and with all your soul* 30:10

Here the "great commandment" is the focus of the outer frame: the way to show that you love God with all your heart and with all your soul (vv 6–7) is to return to him in that very manner (v 10); and, when you do so, God will bless you once again with his covenant blessings (v 9a). The inner frame picks up two more usages of the root שׁוב in parallel statements: you shall return to YHWH by keeping his commandments (v 8); and when you do so, YHWH will return to you (v 9b).

Another way of looking at the structure of 30:6–10 is to focus attention on the seven occurrences of the phrase "YHWH your God," which may be outlined in a menorah pattern:

A	YHWH your God will "circumcise your heart"	30:6a
B	to love YHWH your God with all your heart and soul	30:6b
C	YHWH your God will put these curses on your enemies	30:7
X	You shall obey the voice of YHWH your God	30:8
C′	YHWH your God will restore the blessings to you	30:9
B′	when you hear (obey) the voice of YHWH your God	30:10a
A′	when you return to YHWH your God with all your heart and soul	30:10b

The summary command at the center of this structure in v 8 functions like the central column of the candelabrum. On either side we find three related uses of the phrase "YHWH your God." On one side we see that YHWH will "circumcise" the hearts of his people so as to enable them to love him (v 6). YHWH will put the covenant curses on Israel's enemies (v 7), as he restores the blessings to his own people (v 9)—when they obey his voice and return to him with all their heart and with all their soul (v 10).

Craigie notes that the reference point of vv 1–10 is the whole of the blessings and curses of Deut 28 ([1976] 363). Various themes are repeated here from other parts of Deuteronomy as well, often stated in reverse terms (e.g., the curses in Deut 28).

The data from Labuschagne on the numerical composition of Deut 30 may be summarized as follows:

Words:	before *ʾatnāḥ*		after *ʾatnāḥ*		
30:1–5	43 (= 17 + 26)	+	34 (= 2 × 17)	=	77
30:6–10	45	+	43 (= 17 + 26)	=	88
30:11–14	19	+	32	=	51 (= 3 × 17)
29:28–30:3	32	+	36	=	68 (= 4 × 17)
30:1–2	23	+	16	=	39
30:1–4	34 (= 2 × 17)	+	31	=	65
30:2	11	+	6	=	17
30:2–3	17	+	15	=	32
30:2–4	22	+	21	=	43 (= 17 + 26)
30:3–4	11	+	15	=	26
30:5–6	17	+	13	=	30
30:5–7	24	+	19	=	43 (= 17 + 26)
30:6–9	33	+	34 (= 2 × 17)	=	67
30:7–8	12	+	14	=	26
30:9	13	+	10	=	23
29:9–30:20	357 (= 21 × 17)	+	306 (= 18 × 17)	=	663 (= 39 × 17)

Once again, the scribes of ancient Israel have woven the divine-name numbers 17 and 26 into the fabric of the Hebrew text in a variety of ways. In addition to these two numbers, we find 34 (= 2 × 17), 51 (=3 × 17), and 43 (= 17 + 26). The numbers 23 and 32, which are associated with the word כבוד, "glory," appear as well, for these scribes have so labored to the glory of YHWH.

Comment

1 The reference to "the blessing and the curse" looks back to the content of Deut 28. The prosodic analysis suggests that the relative clause here, like that in v 5, functions primarily as the introduction to what follows. "That which I have set before you," namely "all these words" of the covenant blessings and curses, shall be "returned to your heart" (והשבת)—that is, they shall be recalled or remembered in the sense of being brought back into one's mind. The verbal root שוב, "to return," appears seven times in vv 1–10 with a wide range of meanings. The translation here attempts to convey that verbal repetition as much as possible, with the divergent meanings spelled out in the *Comment* for each verse. The verb הדיחך, "he has banished you," is not otherwise used in this sense in Deuteronomy, though it does appear with this meaning in Jeremiah (8:3; 16:15; 24:9), as Mayes notes ([1981] 368); but his conclusion that "the exile is clearly presupposed" does not follow, if he means by this that these words could not have been written to anticipate the possibility of restoration following future apostasy and its punishment by exile. We have already seen in the discussion of the covenant curses in 28:36–37 that exile was a common motif in the treaty language of the ancient Near East.

2 The second use of the verbal root שוב is in the phrase "you shall return" (תשוב), which points to a change in behavior. Milgrom notes that the concept of returning to God in Deuteronomy is different from what it becomes in the prophets ("Repentance in the OT," *IDBSup*, 737). Here it is mentioned as something that occurs after punishment has taken place, as a means of terminating the punishment. The prophets extend this concept to call the people to repent before it is too late, so as to avert punishment altogether. On the meaning of "with all your heart and with all your soul," see the *Comment* on 6:5—the people are to love God with their whole being. The Hebrew לבב refers to what we would call the "mind." The pairing of לבב, "heart," and נפש, "soul," suggests a distinction of some sort between mental and emotional energy and activity. In terms of modern depth psychology, we would say that our love for God is to embrace the whole of our mind, both conscious and unconscious. It is to permeate our very being.

3 The third use of the root שוב is in the form of an idiom, ושב שבות, translated here as "restore your fortunes" (lit. "return a return" or "return [your] captivity"), which means "restore" in the sense of returning to their former state before being taken into captivity. The fourth use of the root שוב is in reference to YHWH, who "will return" (ישוב) and "gather you from all the peoples where [he] has scattered you." As Thompson notes, the picture of a repentant people being restored to their homeland here in vv 3–5 is "a very different picture from that which obtains in modern Israel, where there is little evidence of repentance and where great numbers of people are agnostic" ([1974] 285).

4–5 The words of v 4 are familiar to modern Jews because they are part of the "Prayer for the Welfare of the State of Israel," which urges God to continue gathering the outcasts from all corners of the Diaspora to Israel (from Tigay [1996] 284). The phrase "the ends of the heavens" is an idiom for expressing geographical limits (see *Comment* on 4:32–34). The reference to "your fathers" here is to those about to enter the promised land and their successors, up to the time of the future judgment envisioned in the covenant violation and exile of 29:21–27. The two verbs translated "make you more prosperous and numerous" occur together in 28:63.

6–7 The promise that "YHWH your God will circumcise your heart" means that God himself will remove whatever prevents the people from choosing to follow God's teachings (see *Comment* on 10:16). "The rabbis described this process as follows: 'When a person seeks to purify himself, he receives help in doing so'" (Tigay [1996] 285). See also 10:16, where Moses exhorted Israel "to circumcise the foreskin of your hearts." On what it means "to love YHWH your God," see the *Comment* on 6:5.

8–9 The fifth use of the root שוב in 30:1–10 speaks of the future when תשוב, "you yourself shall return," which is defined in the parallel line of the verse as hearkening to the voice of YHWH by obeying "all his commandments." The result of such action on Israel's part is that "YHWH will return [ישוב] to delighting in you for good"—by restoring the threefold covenant blessing of 28:4 (in progeny, livestock, and produce of the soil), to which is added a significant addition in the promise that "YHWH your God will grant you abundance in all the work of your hands." The first half of v 9 repeats 28:11 with only slight modification, as Mayes observes ([1981] 370).

10 The seventh use of the root שוב in vv 1–10 appears in the clause "when you return [תשוב] to YHWH your God with all your heart and with all your soul," which forms an inclusion with vv 2 and 6, where all these words appear except "when you return" (כי תשוב). In the latter instance (v 6), we find in the place of the key word שוב what it means "to return": "to love YHWH your God with all your heart and with all your soul" (see *Comment* on 6:5).

Explanation

Unlike most judges today, God never closes the case in his dealings with his people. The terrifying list of curses that reaches its climax in the horrors of siege warfare and exile to a foreign land are followed by an affirmation that the door remains open for the return of the prodigal son. Moreover, when the people choose to return to the covenant agreement, God will make them more prosperous and numerous than they were before, provided of course that their obedience to the covenant is sincere and wholehearted.

The repentance God wants is more than mere turning away from an evil past. God wants wholehearted commitment to covenant loyalty and obedience. In this regard, an illustration by J. Maxwell ([1987] 318) merits repetition. A cartoon appeared in the *Saturday Review of Literature* in which George Washington as a boy is standing with an axe in his hand. Lying on the ground before him is the famous cherry tree. He has already admitted that he chopped it down—after all, "he cannot tell a lie." But his father is standing there, exasperated, saying, "All right, so you admit it! You *always* admit it. The question is, when are you going to stop *doing* it."

As so many have learned the hard way—in Alcoholics Anonymous and other twelve-step programs—one must first experience the full force of the "curses" before one is ready to exercise the will to change. The people of Israel must experience the covenant curses, including exile to a foreign land, before they will begin to think right and choose to turn themselves around to go in another direction.

As Craigie puts it, "Moses, in his address, employs both the experience of the past and his notion of the potential future to force home upon the Israelites the need for obedience in the present. Before they have even entered the land, he warns of their being driven out again and scattered, and then brought back in" ([1976] 364). This great vision does eventually come to be seen as prophetic, as Craigie also notes (cf. Jer 29:14; Ezek 36:24; Matt 24:31; Mark 13:27). Cf. vv 6–10 with Jer 31:31–34 and Ezek 36:24–32. Thompson invites comparison with Ezek 36:24–36; 37:23–28; and Rom 11:25–27, where "God seems to be taking the initiative in restoring his people . . . before they repent. . . . God himself will carry out the inward renewal of Israel (*circumcise your heart*), so that Israel will love Yahweh with all their heart. . . . Repentance in itself will not suffice. Perhaps, indeed, the origin of repentance itself lies in the divine activity. Certainly, the origin of heart-love for Yahweh lies in Yahweh himself" ([1974] 285).

The power to change comes from God. There is an old saying that "God does not make us to go 'gainst our will, he just makes us willing to go!" God's commandments are his enablements. He has not commanded us to do anything that he will not empower us to do. For, indeed, "YHWH your God will circumcise your heart, and the heart of your descendants, to love YHWH your God with all your heart and with all your soul, in order that you may live" (30:6).

F. God's Commandments Are Doable (30:11–14)

Bibliography

Aho, G. "The Eighth Sunday after Pentecost." *CTQ* 47 (1983) 48–49. **Collins, J. J.** "The Place of Apocalypticism in the Religion of Israel." In *FS F. M. Cross.* 1987. 548. **Couroyer, B.** "La tablette du coeur." *RB* 90 (1983) 416–34. **Dumortier, F.** "Une loi, principe de vie, Dtn 30,10–14." *AsSeign* 46 (1974) 52–56. **Dus, J.** "Der ferne Gott und das nahe Gebot (Eine Studie zum Deuteronomium)." *CV* 7 (1964) 193–200. **Glasson, T. F.** "Gospel of Thomas, Saying 3, and Deuteronomy xxx 11–14." *ExpTim* 78 (1966–67) 151–52. **Goldberg, A. M.** "Torah aus der Unterwelt? Eine Bemerkung zu Röm 10,6–7." *BZ* 14 (1970) 127–31. **Holladay, W. L.** "A Proposal for Reflections in the Book of Jeremiah of the Seven-Year Recitation of the Law in Deuteronomy (Deut 31,10–13)." In *Das Deuteronium.* Ed. N. Lohfink. 1985. 326–28. **Jervell, J.** "Die offenbarte und die verborgene Tora: Zur Vorstellung über die neue Tora im Rabbinismus." *ST* 25 (1971) 90–108, esp. 93–95. **Koch, D.-A.** *Die Schrift als Zeuge des Evangeliums.* BHT 69. Tübingen: Mohr, 1986. 107, 153–60, 185–86, 197–98, 295–96. **Köckert, M.** "Das nahe Wort: Zum entscheidenden Wandel des Gesetzesverständnis im Alten Testament." *TP* 60 (1985) 496–519. **Kutsch, E.** "Menschliche Weisung—Gesetz Gottes: Beobachtungen zu einem aktuellen Thema." In *Gott ohne Eigenschaften?* Ed. S. Heine and E. Heintel. Vienna: Evangelischer Presseverband, 1983. 77–106, esp. 99–100. **Lemke, W.** "The Near and Distant God: A Study of Jer 23:23–24 in Its Biblical Theological Context." *JBL* 100 (1981) 541–55, esp. 545, 552. **Sheppard, G. T.** "Wisdom and Torah: The Interpretation of Deuteronomy Underlying Sirach 24,23." In *FS W. S. LaSor.* 1978. 166–76. **Suggs, M. J.** "'The Word Is Near You': Romans 10:6–10 within the Purpose of the Letter." In *Christian History and Interpretation: FS J. Knox.* Ed. W. Farmer et al. Cambridge: Cambridge UP, 1967. 289–312. **Veerkammp, T.** "Predigt zum Barmen-Jubiläum in Dresden über 5. Mose 30.11–14." *Junge Kirche* 45 (1984) 386–88. **Vicent, R.** "Derash homilético en Romanos 9–11." *Salm* 42 (1980) 751–88.

Translation and Prosodic Analysis

God's Commandments Are Doable [(6:7):(7:6)]

11 *For this commandment / that / I command you\\[a] TODAY //*	24	3
it[b] is not too hard\\[c] for you /	10	1
and it[d] is not / too far away //	10	2
12 *It[a] is / not in the heavens // that you should say /*	13	3
"Who will go up for us to the heavens[b] / and get it for us /	26	2
and cause us to hear it / that we may do it?" //	18	2
13 *And it[a] is not across / the sea //*	13	2
that you should say / "Who will cross over for us /	14	2
to the other side of the sea / and get it for us /	18	2
and impart it to us?" /	12	1
So let us do it // 14 *for the word / is very / near to you //*	25	4
in your mouth and in your heart / to do it // ס	18	2

Notes

11.a. Reading *tiphā'* as conj. because of misplaced *'atnāḥ*.
11.b. Many Heb. MSS have ו maj (written larger) in הוא.
11.c. Reading *paštā'* followed by *zāqēp qāṭôn* as conj.
11.d. Many Heb. MSS have ו maj (written larger) in הוא.
12.a. Many Heb. MSS have ו maj (written larger) in הוא.
12.b. SP reads השמים, "the heavens," for MT השמימה, "to the heavens" (cf. 4:19). Prosodic analysis supports MT.
13.a. Many Heb. MSS have ו maj (written larger) in הוא.

Form/Structure/Setting

The boundaries of 30:11–14 are marked by the *pĕtûḥā'* layout marker after v 10 and the *sĕtûmā'* layout marker after v 14, with no internal indicators of structure other than the content itself, which may be outlined as follows:

A	This is the commandment—it is not too hard for you	30:11
B	It is not in the heavens—"Who will go up for us?"	30:12ab
X	"and cause us to hear it that we may do it"	30:12c
B′	It is not beyond the sea—"Who will cross over for us?"	30:13
A′	It is near to you—in your mouth and in your heart to do it	30:14

The outer frame asserts that the commandment is not too difficult, nor is it inaccessible (v 11); it is near at hand: "in your mouth and in your heart to do it" (v 14). The inner frame is made up of two parallel statements, virtually identical in form, expanding the point that YHWH's commandment is not beyond our reach—"in the heavens" (v 12a) or "across the sea" (v 13a); and "cause us to hear it that we may do it" (v 12c).

The prosodic analysis suggests that the words וישמענו אתה ונעשׂנה, "and cause us to hear it and we will do it," are to be taken in a slightly different sense at the end of v 13 than at the end of v 12. The "stereotyped phrase" is broken up, since the word ונעשׂנה now belongs with v 14 as the first word in a circular sentence, which may be outlined as follows:

A	"So let us do it—"	ונעשׂנה	30:13d
B	"for it is near to you"	כי־קרוב אליך	30:14aα
X	"the word, exceedingly so"	הדבר מאד	30:14aβ
B′	"in your mouth and in your heart"	בפיך ובלבבך	30:14bα
A′	"to do it"	לעשׂתו	30:14bβ

The word ונעשׂנה is read here as a cohortative, "let us do it"—namely, "the word" (הדבר) of God, which is exceedingly near to you, "in your mouth and in your heart." This single sentence, which concludes the central section in Deut 30, also summarizes the content of the whole chapter.

The data assembled by Labuschagne on the numerical composition of 30:11–14 may be summarized as follows:

Words:	before *ʾatnāḥ*		after *ʾatnāḥ*		
30:11	7	+	7	=	14
30:11–12	10	+	17	=	27
30:11–13	14	+	29	=	43 (= 17 + 26)
30:11–14	19	+	32	=	51 (= 3 × 17)
29:9–30:20	357 (= 21 × 17)	+	306 (= 18 × 17)	=	663 (= 39 × 17)

Within the space of four verses, both the divine-name numbers 17 and 26 are woven into the text, as well as the number 32, which is associated with the word כבוד, "glory." The process is simply that of building one verse at a time on the base of v 11 with its seven words before and after *ʾatnāḥ*. Adding v 12 results in 17 words after *ʾatnāḥ*. Adding another verse results in a total of 43 words, which is 17 + 26. The next verse brings the total number of words after *ʾatnāḥ* in 30:11–14 to 32, which completes the hidden message, for now the total number of words is 51 (3 × 17). The scribes have extended their labor here in the numerical composition of 30:11–14 to the glory of YHWH.

Comment

11 God's commandment is doable—"it is not too hard for you," that is, unintelligible (v 11); "and it is not too far away," nor is it in some inaccessible place (vv 12–14), among the "secret things" (29:28). In subsequent tradition the Jewish group that produced the apocalyptic writings associated with Enoch significantly modified this simple statement as they sought revelation through higher angelic mediation (Collins, *FS F. M. Cross,* 548).

12 "It is not in the heavens"—the commandment is not inaccessible, it does not require some specially qualified person to make it all clear. In short, the law was specifically designed for our instruction in daily living and not to be part of the mystery of God that we could not approach and that was retained "in the heavens." There is no ground for excuse in relation to our response to God's commandment. According to Tigay, the statement that God's Torah "is not in heaven is invoked in rabbinic literature to express fundamental concepts of Judaism. In the Talmud it is used to represent the idea that the authority for *interpreting* the Torah is not in God's hands. Once God gave the Torah to Israel, He gave the authority to decide how it is to be applied entirely to legal scholars, and retained none for Himself" ([1996] 286; see E. Berkovits, *Not in Heaven: The Nature and Function of Halakha* [New York: Ktav, 1983]). Thompson ([1974] 286) calls attention to the fact that the expression "ascend to heaven" appears in the Amarna letters written by Egyptian vassals in Palestine to their overlords in Egypt in the fourteenth century B.C.E. (J. A. Knudtzon, *Die El-Amarna Tafeln* [Leipzig: Hinrichs, 1915] no. 264, ll. 14–19; cf. "A Pessimistic Dialogue between Master and Servant," *ANET,* 438, XII). The idiomatic usage in regard to the God's commandments being "near" or "far away" was known over many centuries (cf. Eph 2:13).

13–14 "And it is not across the sea," so as to require an arduous journey to acquire it. As Craigie notes, the Mesopotamian hero Gilgamesh in his quest to find eternal life had to cross the sea. In sharp contrast to this heroic journey in the Epic of Gilgamesh, Moses declared that life is to found in God's commandment, which is "very near to you." The expression "in your mouth and in your heart" indicates that the Torah is to be memorized—it is to be "known by heart." See 31:9–13, the *Comment* on 6:7, and *Excursus:* "Law, Poetry, and Music in Ancient Israel." In the culture of ancient Israel, the educational process was primarily by means of oral recitation.

Explanation

The content and demands of the covenant are not too difficult to understand and achieve. The covenant is something that can and should be acted on now—"I did not speak in secret, in a land of darkness; . . . I the LORD speak the truth, I declare what is right" (Isa 45:19). It is not a matter of erudition. As Saint Bonaventura put it long ago, "Any old woman can love God better than a doctor of theology can!"

The apostle Paul found inspiration in the text of Deut 30:11–14 to argue his case that salvation is not for the privileged few, based on some elaborate system of works. Salvation is for all who choose to believe "the word of faith." In short, "The word is near you, on your lips and in your heart" (Rom 10:6–9). Paul, and Jesus before him, understood the message of Deuteronomy, which declares that the heart of the matter is found in two commandments: to love God and to love one's neighbor as oneself. God's word is not esoteric, hidden away in heaven or beyond the sea, to be apprehended only at great cost and human effort.

Moses taught the Torah to the people by heart—in oral recitation, as a "musical" experience. This was the form in which the Torah was "published," even though a copy was written down and entrusted to the Levites for transmission to subsequent generations (31:9). The oral "publication" of the Torah continued long after the death of Moses, as the text of Josh 1:8 bears witness: "Let not this book of the Torah depart out of your mouth; but recite it day and night, so that you may observe faithfully all that is written in it" (author's translation). It should be noted, however, that we are not talking about merely knowing the Torah by rote. It was to be known internally; that is, it was to be written in one's heart. In one sense, then, the "new covenant" Jeremiah envisioned (Jer 31:31–34) was a return to the original intention of the covenant relationship between God and his people as expressed in Deuteronomy: "I will write it on their hearts; and I will be their God, and they shall be my people" (Jer 31:33 NRSV).

G. *The Choice before You Is between Life and Death—Choose Life (30:15–20)*

Bibliography

Brand, R. C. "Freedom's Just Another Word." *ExpTim* 90 (1979) 174–75. **Brichto, H. C.** *Problem of "Curse."* 1963. 187. **Carmichael, C. M.** *The Laws of Deuteronomy.* 1974. 5. **Delcor, M.** "Les attaches littéraires, l'origine et la signification de l'expression biblique 'Prendre à temoin le ciel et la terre." *VT* 16 (1966) 8–25. **Friedman, R.** "The Biblical Expression *mastîr pānîm.*" *HAR* 1 (1977) 139–47. **Giesen, G.** *Die Wurzel* שׁבע. 1981. 283–85. **Greenfield, J. C.** "Stylistic Aspects of the Sefire Treaty Inscriptions." *AcOr* 29 (1965) 7. **Henry, M. L.** "'Tod' und 'Leben,' Unheil und Heil als Funktionendes richtenden und rettenden Gottes im Alten Testament." In *FS. H. Thielicke.* 1968. 1–26. **Hurowitz, A.** *Ina Anum rum: Literary Structures in the Non-Juridical Sections of Codex Hammurabi.* Philadelphia: Samuel Noah Kramer Fund, 1994. 27–29. **Lévy-Valensi, E. A.** "Une énigme pour les peuples: Israel ou le choix de la vie." In *Studies in Judaism: Jubilee Volume Presented to David Kotlar.* Ed. A. Rabello. Tel Aviv: Am Hassefer, 1975. iii–xiii. **Merendino, R. P.** "La via della vita (Dt 30,15–20)." *Parola, Spiritu e Vita* 5 (1982) 35–51. **Orbe, A.** "El dilema entre la vida y la muerte: Exegesis prenicena de Deut. 30,15.19." *Greg* 51 (1970) 305–65, 509–36. **Seebass, H.** "Landverheißungen an die Väter." *EvT* 37 (1977) 210–29, esp. 222. **Steiger, L.** "Das Leben wählen: Predigt über 5. Mose 30,15–20." In *FS H.-J. Kraus.* 1983. 523–28. **Veijola, T.** "Zu Ableitung und Bedeutung von *Hēʿîd* I im Hebräischen: Ein Beitrag zur Bundesterminologie." *UF* 8 (1976) 343–51.

Translation and Prosodic Analysis

I Have Set before You the Choice between Life and Death [(5:4):6:(6:6):(4:5)]

15 *See, I set before you / TODAY*[a] / [17 2
life\[b] *and good // or death /* 16 2
and evil // 6 1

16 *<If you obey the commandments / of YHWH your God />*[a] 16 2
that I command you / TODAY / 15 2_
To love / YHWH your God / [b]*to walk* [c]*in his ways*[c] / 24 3
and to keep / [d]*his commandments and his statutes*[d] / 15 2
and his judgments // 7 1_
Then you will live and multiply / 12 1
and [e]*YHWH your God*[e] */ will bless you /* 15 2
in the land / to which you are coming / 15 2
to possess it // 4 1_
17 *But if your heart turns / and you will not hearken //* 15 2
and you are drawn away / 5 1
and you worship / other gods / and you serve them // 22 3_
18 *I declare* to you[a] / TODAY / that you will surely \\[b] perish // 22 3
you will not prolong your days / 12 1_
[c]Upon the ground / that [d]*you are crossing over*[d] / *the Jordan /* 22 3
[e]*to come*[e] *thither / to possess it //* 12 2_

So Choose Life by "Loving" YHWH Your God [(5:6):(6:5)]

19 *I call to witness* against you |[a] TODAY / heaven and earth / 26 3
life and death / 8 1
I set *before you*[b] / 11 1_
The blessing / and the curse // 13 2
so choose / life / that you and your offspring / may live // 23 4_
20 *By loving / YHWH your God /* 15 2
[a]*by obeying his voice / and by cleaving to him //* 17 2
for he is your life / and the length of your days / 17 2_
That you may dwell upon the ground / 12 1
that YHWH your God swore to your fathers / 14 1
to Abraham / to Isaac and to Jacob / to give to them[b] // פ 24 3_

Notes

15.a. SP omits היום, "today." Prosodic analysis supports MT.

15.b. Reading *ṭiphā'* as conj. because of misplaced *'atnāḥ*.

16.a. Adding an entire line (six words in the Hebrew text) with LXX, (καὶ) εἰσακούσῃς τὰς ἐντολὰς κυρίου τοῦ θεοῦ σου (= אם תשמע אל מצות יהוה אלהיך); cf. 11:27.

16.b. Some Heb. MSS, one SP MS, LXX[LO], Syr., *Tg. Ps.-J.*, and Vg. add *waw*-conj.

16.c-c. LXX reads ἐν πάσαις ταῖς ὁδοῖς σου (= בכל דרכיך, "in all your ways").

16.d-d. SP and some LXX witnesses read חקיו ומשפטיו, "his statutes and his commandments," for MT מצותיו וחקתיו, "his commandments and his statutes"; other LXX witnesses omit מצותיו. Prosodic analysis supports MT.

16.e-e. OL and Vg. omit יהוה אלהיך, "YHWH your God"; one LXX witness reads κύριος ὁ θεός, "the Lord God" (= יהוה אלהים). Prosodic analysis favors MT as it stands.

18.a. LXX and Vg. read 2 sg. לך, "to you."

18.b. Reading *ṭiphā'* as conj. because of misplaced *'atnāḥ*.

18.c. Omitted in one LXX MS; many Heb. MSS, LXX, Syr., *Tg. Ps.-J.*, and Vg. add *waw*-conj. Prosodic analysis supports MT.

18.d-d. SP, LXX, Syr., and *Tg. Ps.-J.* read 2 pl.

18.e-e. Omitted in LXX[L] and in the parallel passage in 4:26. Prosodic analysis supports MT.

19.a. Reading the sequence *'azlā* followed by *mûnāḥ* as disj. Note that Letteris has a *metheg* under העידתי, "I call to witness."

19.b. LXX, Syr., *Tg. Ps.-J.*, and Vg. read 2 pl.

20.a. Two Heb. MSS, Cairo Geniza fragments, one LXX MS, SP MSS, OL, Syr., and Vg. add *waw*-conj. Prosodic analysis supports MT.

20.b. SP and LXX^{L} read 2 pl.; LXX^{min} and Syr. read 2 sg.

Form/Structure/Setting

The *Numeruswechsel,* which appears twice in both v 18 and v 19, divides 30:15–20 into two subunits: vv 15–18 and 19–20. At the same time, the passage as a whole constitutes a unified structure that may be outlined as follows:

A	I have set before you the choice between life and death	30:15
B	I command you to love YHWH your God by obeying him	30:16a
X	And YHWH will bless you in the land you possess	30:16b
B′	If you turn aside to worship other gods, you will perish	30:17–18
A′	So choose life by loving YHWH, by obeying his voice	30:19–20

The outer frame in this structure concerns the choice YHWH has set before his people between life and death (v 15), in which they are urged to choose life (vv 19–20) by obeying him (v 16a). YHWH will bless them in the land if they obey (v 16b); but if they turn aside to worship other gods, they will perish (vv 17–18).

The key words in this passage are the noun חיים, "life," and the verb חיה, "to live," which appear a total of six times, in five specific contexts, arranged in a concentric structural pattern:

A	I have set before you *life* or death	נתתי לפניך היום את־החיים	30:15a
B	And you shall *live* and multiply	וחיית ורבית	30:16b
X	*Life* and death I have set before you	החיים והמות נתתי לפניך	30:19a
B′	So choose *life* that you may *live*	ובחרת בחיים למען תחיה	30:19b
A′	For he is your *life*	וכי הוא חייך	30:20b

In the center we find the specific choice that YHWH has set before his people between life and death (v 19a). The outer frame moves from a statement of the same choice (v 15a), to the identification of YHWH with life (v 20b). The inner frame contains the two occurrences of the verb חיה with the promise that "you will live" and multiply (v 16b) when you choose "to walk in his ways" (v 16a) by keeping the Torah.

When vv 15–20 are examined within the larger context of 30:11–20, the reason for the *Numeruswechsel* in v 19 becomes clearer, for it functions as a structural marker to separate v 19a from what follows as a distinct unit of thought within another five-part concentric structure:

A	This command is not too hard for you	30:11
B	The word of YHWH is "not in the heavens"—it is near	30:12–14
X	I have set before you a choice between life and death	30:15–18
B′	The heavens and the earth are summoned as witnesses	30:19a
A′	Choose life by obeying YHWH's voice	30:19b–20

In the inner frame of this structure, the reference to "in the heavens" (בשמים) in v 12 is set over against the summoning of "the heavens" (השמים) as witnesses in the covenant commitment in v 19a. The outer frame states the central issue:

YHWH's commandment is not too difficult for you to do (v 11); so choose life by choosing to obey YHWH's voice (vv 19b–20).

The choice between life and death in vv 15–18, the center of the previous structure (vv 15–18), may be outlined in the same manner:

A	I have set before you *today* life and good or death and evil	30:15
B	*If you will heed ("hear")* the commandments and love YHWH	30:16a
X	Then you shall live and multiply in the land	30:16b
B′	*If you will not hear* and you turn to worship other gods	30:17
A′	I declare to you *today* that you will surely perish	30:18

The message remains essentially the same. The outer frame presents the choice between life and death at the outset (v 15), with the promise that "you will live and multiply . . . in the land" at the center (v 16b) and the declaration that "you will surely perish" at the end (v 18). The inner frame presents the way to life or death—it depends on whether you choose to "hear" the commandments of YHWH (v 16a) or "not hear" (v 17).

The data from Labuschagne on the numerical composition of 30:15–20 may be summarized as follows:

Words:	before *ʾatnāḥ*		after *ʾatnāḥ*	
30:15–16	28	+	15	= 43
30:15–18	39	+	33	= 72
30:19–20	21	+	23	= 44
30:20	8	+	17	= 25
29:9–30:20	357 (= 21 × 17)	+	306 (= 18 × 17)	= 663 (= 39 × 17)

Once again, the scribes in ancient Israel have managed to weave both of the divine-name numbers 17 and 26 into the fabric of the Hebrew text, along with the number 23 (associated with the word כבוד, "glory"). But more impressive are the totals for Reading 8 (29:9–30:20) as a whole. The total number of words both before and after *ʾatnāḥ* are multiples of the divine-name number 17; and of course their total is also a multiple of that same number, 663 (= 39 × 17).

Comment

15 Though the words הטוב, "good," and הרע, "evil," mean essentially "prosperity" and "adversity," as in the NRSV and JPS *Tanakh,* I render them literally here so as to call the reader's attention to the nature of the dichotomy: the choice is between life and death; and life is to be chosen as the "good." The verse here forms an inclusion with 11:26–28, where the alternatives are between blessing and cursing. Thus, as Thompson notes ([1974] 287), the full list of alternatives is threefold: life, good, and blessing; or death, evil, and cursing.

16–18 The way to "life" is to choose "to love YHWH your God," which in Deuteronomy means "to fear" God by obeying him (see *Comment* on 6:5 and on 10:12–13). "To walk in his ways and to keep his commandments and his statutes and his judgments" is what it means "to love YHWH your God." To forsake God by choosing to "worship other gods and . . . serve them" is to choose the way of death—"you will surely perish."

19–20 In the treaty texts of the ancient Near East, "the heavens and the earth" are included as deities cited to witness the treaty (see in particular *PRU* IV, 17.365 and 17.338; and Craigie's discussion [1976] 139). In Deuteronomy they are not considered to be gods as such, but metaphorical "witnesses." A person chooses to love God "by obeying his voice and by cleaving to him." The reading "he is your life," rather than "that means life to you" (NRSV), is found in NIV and some earlier Jewish commentators (Ibn Ezra and Shadal). Tigay calls attention to the fact that the biblical phrase here has been adapted in the evening liturgy in Judaism as "For they [God's commandments and the words of his Torah] are our life and the length of our days" ([1996] 288).

Explanation

Life is a constant stream of opportunities demanding choices. We can choose to stand up and be counted, or we can choose to do nothing at all. But either way we still must choose. If we choose the former, it is good to remember that there are many different ways to take one's stand in life. Rosa Parks took her stand by refusing to stand and give up her seat on the bus to a white man in Montgomery, Alabama, in 1955. In so doing, a seemingly powerless individual became "the mother of the civil rights movement" in America. The Montgomery bus strike that emerged from the choice of that single person led to a demonstration of the power of collective choice, when a people takes a stand in nonviolent resistance to the sin of social injustice.

As Matthew Henry pointed out, Moses concludes his appeal for covenant loyalty in Deut 29:9–30:20 with powerful words, which are certainly reasonable. We all want life and good, and to escape death and evil. And so Moses declares that we can choose between these alternatives: "I have set before you today life and good or death and evil. . . . So choose life that you and your offspring may live, by loving YHWH your God—by obeying his voice and cleaving to him; for he is your life and the length of your days" (30:15–20). Adam and Eve ate the forbidden fruit in the Garden of Eden in hopes of gaining the knowledge of good and evil. They learned the knowledge of good by losing it; and they learned death and evil by experiencing it. Moses argues that the choice to obey God brings real advantages our way and the choice to disobey brings with it the certainty of ruin. We have the power to choose life and good instead of death and evil.

When I was first asked to write this commentary on Deuteronomy, a friend said she wanted to share something with me that she thought might be useful at some point. It was a personal experience with this text, one that she had shared with no one, not even her husband. It seems that she was struggling with great depression to the point that she finally decided to end her life by suicide. As a final attempt to find some kind of direction or meaning in her life, she opened a Bible at random and placed her finger on the text of Deut 30:19—"life and death I set before you, the blessing and the curse, so choose life." She said, "That's what I did. If it were not for the book of Deuteronomy, I wouldn't be here today." I am sure that this is not a model of how we are to make use of Scripture in seeking guidance and direction in our lives; but I am also sure that God chose to use the biblical text in that particular way on that specific occasion.

Readings 9–11: Anticipating the Eisodus into the Promised Land under Joshua (31:1–34:12)

Bibliography

Baltzer, K. *Covenant Formulary.* 1971. 68–72. **Eissfeldt, O.** "Die Umrahmung des Mose-Liedes Dt 32,1–43 und des Mose-Gesetzes Dt 1–30 in Dt 31,9–32,47." In *KlSchr* 3:322–34. **Harrington, D. J.** "Interpreting Israel's History: The Testament of Moses as a Rewriting of Deuteronomy 31–34." In *Studies on the Testament of Moses.* Ed. G. W. E. Nickelsburg. SBLSP 1973. SBLSCS 4. Cambridge, MA: SBL, 1973. 59–68. **Labuschagne, C. J.** "The Setting of the Song of Moses in Deuteronomy." In *FS C. H. W. Brekelmans.* 1997. 111–29. ———. "The Song of Moses: Its Framework and Structure." In *FS A. van Selms.* 1971. 85–98. **Lohfink, N.** "The Deuteronomistic Picture of the Transfer of Authority from Moses to Joshua." In *Theology of the Pentateuch.* 1994. 234–47 (Ger. original 1962; repr. in *Studien zum Deuteronomium I.* 1990. 83–97). **Noar, M.** "*Dĕbarim* 31–34: Reconstructed Text." In *Sepher J. Braslavi.* Ed. I. Ben-Shem. Jerusalem: Kiryat Sefer, 1971. 216–29 (Heb.). **Nordheim, E. von.** *Die Lehre der Alten II: Das Testament als Literaturgattung im Alten Testament und im alten vorderen Orient.* ALGHJ 18. Leiden: Brill, 1985. **Porter, J. R.** "The Succession of Joshua." In *FS G. H. Davies.* 1970. 102–32. **Schröter, R.** "Bar Hebraus' Scholien zu Gen. 49.50, Ex. 14.15, Dt. 32–34 und Jud. 5." *ZDMG* 24 (1870) 495–562, 517–20, 546–57. **Watts, J. W.** *Psalm and Story: Inset Hymns in Hebrew Narrative.* JSOTSup 139. Sheffield: JSOT Press, 1992.

Introduction

The concept of an "outer frame" in Deuteronomy, made up of chaps. 1–3 and 31–34, suggests a close literary connection between these two blocks of material, which is easy to demonstrate in terms of repetition of specific words and phrases from the concluding paragraphs of Deut 3 in Deut 31–34, and comparison of the overall literary structure of these two sections. Joshua is introduced in 1:38, where he is presented as Moses' assistant who is destined to bring Israel into possession of the promised land in times to come. The concluding section of the first half of the outer frame in 3:23–29, which also focuses attention on the transition in leadership from Moses to Joshua, may be outlined as follows:

A	Moses requests permission to cross over into the land	3:23–25
B	YHWH is "cross" with Moses	3:26
X	Moses is permitted to "see" the land	3:27a
B′	Moses is not permitted to cross over the Jordan	3:27b
A′	Moses is told to command Joshua to cross over	3:28

This text is aptly titled "Crossing Over" in that it focuses attention on the question of who will be granted the privilege of leading the people of Israel as they cross over into the promised land. Moses pleads with God for the privilege: אעברה, "let me cross over," in the first word of 3:25; and in the first word of the next verse, it is YHWH who is ויתעבר, "cross," with Moses (3:26). Both words come from the same Hebrew root, עבר, "to cross over." The attentive reader, however, soon discovers a third meaning of this verb, in its repetition in 3:28 and twice again in 31:3, where it is used once with YHWH as the subject and again with

Joshua as the subject. In short, the reader is invited to "cross over" from the first half of the outer frame at the end of chap. 3 to the second half, which continues in Deut 31. The vocabulary of 3:28 is repeated in 31:6–7, where Moses encourages Joshua to be strong and courageous in his new role as he brings the people across the Jordan into the land YHWH swore to give to their fathers.

The close tie between the closing paragraph of the first half of the outer frame (3:23–28) and the content of Deut 31–34 may also be shown by careful study of literary structure and content, as the following outline suggests:

The Covenant Concluded—from Moses to Joshua	*31:1–34:12*
A Commissioning of Joshua and deposition of the Torah	31:1–29
B The Song of Moses	31:30–32:47
X Moses commanded to climb Mount Nebo to "see" the land	32:48–52
B′ Testamentary blessing of Moses	33:1–29
A′ Death of Moses and succession of Joshua	34:1–12

In short, the subject of the transfer of leadership from Moses to Joshua functions as a frame around both Deut 4–30 and Deut 31–34 (the second half of the outer frame). Moreover, the presentation of the impending death of Moses at the center of this structure in 32:48–52, which is taken up again in 34:1, uses the language of 3:27, where Moses is commanded: "Go up to the top of Pisgah and . . . see with your eyes [the land of Canaan, which I am giving to the children of Israel for a possession]."

Another way of looking at the overall structure of Deut 31–34 is to divide the whole into two parts, which may be outlined as follows:

Writing and Reading of the Torah and the Song of Moses	*31:1–32:47*
A Appointment of Joshua and deposition of the Torah	31:1–27
B Moses gathered the leaders to hear the words of the song	31:28–30
X Song of Moses—future rebellion, judgment, and restoration	32:1–43
B′ Moses and Joshua spoke the words of the song to the people	32:44
A′ Moses' final exhortation to observe the Torah	32:45–47

Death of Moses and Succession of Joshua	*32:48–34:12*
A Moses commanded to ascend Mount Nebo to "see" the land	32:48–52
B The Testamentary Blessing of Moses within a hymnic frame	33:1–29
X Moses ascends Mount Nebo where he "sees" the land	34:1–4
B′ The death and burial of Moses	34:5–8
A′ Joshua takes Moses' place of leadership in Israel	34:9–12

The two centers in this reading of Deut 31–34 focus attention on the content and function of the Song of Moses as a witness to future generations in Israel (32:1–43), and the ascent of Moses to the top of Mount Nebo, where YHWH shows him the whole of the promised land that the children of Israel are about to possess under Joshua's leadership (34:1–4).

An even more instructive way of reading this section of Deuteronomy is to divide each of these halves in half, to find four "wheels of the same likeness" with a brief summary statement at the center that contains a command to observe the words of the Torah (32:46–47):

A	*Appointment of Joshua and Deposition of the Torah*	*31:1–30*
a	Moses announces his departure and his successor Joshua	31:1–8
b	Deposition of the Torah to teach Israel "to fear" YHWH	31:9–13
x	Moses and Joshua in the tent of meeting	31:14–15
b′	The Song of Moses as a witness to future generations	31:16–22
a′	Joshua succeeds Moses—Torah and song given as a witness	31:23–30
B	*The Song of Moses as a Witness for Future Generations*	*31:30–32:45*
a	Moses speaks the words of this song to all the assembly	31:30
b	Recital of YHWH's saving deeds in days of old	32:1–14
x	Israel's future rebellion and YHWH's indignation	32:15–25
b′	YHWH will restore Israel and punish his enemies	32:26–43
a′	Moses speaks all the words of this song to the people	32:44–45
X	*Summary Command to Observe All the Words of the Torah*	*32:46–47*
B′	*The Testamentary Blessing of Moses*	*32:48–34:4*
a	Moses is commanded to ascend Mount Nebo to "see" the land	32:48–52
b	First stanza of an ancient hymn	33:1–5
x	Moses blesses the twelve tribes	33:6–25
b′	Second stanza of an ancient hymn	33:26–29
a′	Moses ascends Mount Nebo, where he sees the land	34:1–4
A′	*Transition of Leadership from Moses to Joshua*	*34:5–12*
a	Death and burial of Moses; Moses is 120 years old	34:5–7
b	The Israelites mourn Moses' death for thirty days	34:8
x	Joshua is full of the spirit of wisdom	34:9a
b′	The Israelites obey Joshua as Moses commanded	34:9b
a′	There has never been another prophet like Moses	34:10–12

The essential message of the second half of the outer frame of Deuteronomy is highlighted in this structure. In the middle we find the central theme of Deuteronomy—to observe all the words of the Torah (32:46–47). The Song of Moses (Deut 32) and the Testamentary Blessing of Moses (Deut 33) take their place as witnesses to future generations of the covenant commitment they have made and to the blessings on the part of Moses, the founding father of the nation of Israel. This message is placed within the framework of the transition of leadership from Moses to Joshua and the deposition of the Torah in the hands of the Levites, who are to recite it to the people of Israel every seven years at the Festival of Booths (31:9–13).

Reading 9: From Moses to Joshua—Moses Prepares to Die (31:1–30)

Bibliography

Begg, C. T. "The Tables and the Law Book." *VT* 33 (1983) 96–97. **Carillo Alday, S.** "Contexto redaccional del Cántico de Moisés (Dt 31,1–32,47)." *EstBib* 26 (1967) 383–93. **Ridderbos, N. H.** "Die Theophanie im Ps 50,1–6." In *The Priestly Code and Seven Other Studies.* OTS 15. Leiden: Brill, 1969. 213–16. **Rofé, A.** "The Composition of Deuteronomy 31 in Light of a Conjecture about Inversion in the Order of Columns in the Biblical Text." *Shnaton* 3 (1978/79) 59–76 (Heb., Eng. summary, ix–xi).

Introduction

The final three weekly portions from the reading of the Torah in the lectionary cycle (31:1–34:12), which take place in the month of Tishri from Rosh Hashanah (1 Tishri) to Simchat Torah (23 Tishri), are shorter than the others as the community begins the high holy days in the Jewish calendar. The Ten Days of Repentance (*teshuvah,* "the return") extend from Rosh Hashanah (1 Tishri) to Yom Kippur (Day of Atonement; 10 Tishri), followed by the Festival of Sukkoth ("Booths"; 15–22 Tishri), which prepares for Simchat Torah (23 Tishri)—the end of the cycle of readings from the Torah and the beginning of the next cycle.

The ninth of the eleven weekly portions in the lectionary cycle of Torah readings from Deuteronomy (31:1–30), which is relatively brief in length, was outlined above in a five-part concentric structure:

A	Moses announces his departure and Joshua as his successor	31:1–8
B	Deposition of the Torah to teach future generations in Israel	31:9–13
X	Theophany in the tent of meeting with Moses and Joshua	31:14–15
B′	The Song of Moses as a witness to future generations	31:16–22
A′	Joshua succeeds Moses—Torah and song given as a witness	31:23–30

In this reading Moses and Joshua appear together in both halves of the outer frame (vv 1–8 and vv 23–30), and in the structural center (vv 14–15). The inner frame moves from the writing and deposition of the Torah for recitation every seven years in a covenant renewal ceremony at the Festival of Booths (vv 9–13) to the writing of the Song of Moses as a witness to future generations (vv 16–22).

The shift from direct speech to narrative in Deut 31 and the disparate nature of its subunits led von Rad to conclude "that the material from ch. 31 onwards does not in any way belong to Deuteronomy any longer, but belongs instead to the great historical work into which Deuteronomy itself was aborted as a literary unit" ([1966] 188). It was von Rad's failure to observe the concentric structure of the text that led to his negative assessment that "the whole chapter contains debris of traditions rather than a real advance in the narrative" (p. 190). On the contrary, the chapter is closely connected to 3:23–28, as discussed above, and plays a foundational role in the structure of all that follows in Deut 32–34.

A different conclusion from that of von Rad in regard to the unity of this text is suggested by the following outline of the concentric structure of the chapter as a whole, which is based on careful prosodic analysis:

A	Moses announces his departure and replacement by Joshua	31:1–6
B	Moses appoints Joshua as his successor	31:7–8
C	The writing and the reading of the Torah at the Feast of Booths	31:9–12
D	Future generations shall learn to fear YHWH	31:13
X	Theophany in the tent of meeting with Moses and Joshua	31:14–15
D′	Israel's future apostasy and its consequences	31:16–18
C′	The writing of the song as a witness to future generations	31:19–22
B′	YHWH appoints Joshua to succeed Moses	31:23
A′	The Torah and song are given as witnesses to future generations	31:24–30

The structure outlined here is similar to what we have observed elsewhere throughout the whole of Deuteronomy. The focus of attention in the center of this structure is the appearance of YHWH to Moses and Joshua together in the tent of meeting, within a larger context that deals with the impending death of Moses, the transfer of leadership to Joshua, and the function of both the Torah itself and the Song of Moses for future generations in Israel. The framework (A, X, A′) in this structure moves from the announcement of Moses' imminent departure and replacement by Joshua as leader (vv 1–6) to Moses' legacy in the giving of the Torah to the Levites and the recitation of the song to the people of Israel (vv 24–30), with the mysterious theophany to Moses and Joshua in the tent of meeting at the center (vv 14–15). The innermost frame (D, D′) moves from a single verse on teaching future generations to fear YHWH (v 13) to a larger unit on Israel's future apostasy and its consequences (vv 16–18). The next frame (C, C′) moves from the writing of the Torah for recitation at the Festival of Booths every seven years (vv 9–12) to the writing of the Song of Moses as a witness to future generations (vv 19–22). The outermost frame (B, B′) presents parallel accounts of the appointment of Joshua as Moses' successor, by Moses (vv 7–8) and by God himself (v 23).

At the same time, it should be noted that von Rad was correct in his assessment that Deut 31–34 is closely connected to the book of Joshua that follows. It should also be noted, however, how closely the center of the concentric structure here (31:14–15) is related to a more distant text in Exod 33:11, which also places Moses and Joshua together in the tent of meeting—adding the note that Moses' servant Joshua "did not depart from the tent." The larger concentric design of the whole of the Torah plus the Former Prophets, with this verse in the structural center of Exod 33, may be outlined as follows (adapted from J. Milgrom, *Numbers* [1990] xviii; the original source is E. Newing, "A Rhetorical & Theological Analysis of the Hexateuch," *SEAJT* 22.2 [1981] 1–15):

A	Primal history: from Adam to Abram (covenant of Noah)	Gen 1–11
B	Land promised	Gen 12–50
C	Egypt judged	Exod 1:1–12:36
D	Exodus from Egypt	Exod 12:37–14:31
E	Song of Moses	Exod 15:1–21
F	Wilderness wandering	Exod 15:22–18:27
G	Covenant ratified and regulated	Exod 19–24

H	Sanctuary planned	Exod 25–31
I	Covenant broken (golden calf incident)	Exod 32
X	Theophany on Sinai: the promised presence	Exod 33
I′	Covenant renewed (ritual decalogue)	Exod 34
H′	Sanctuary built	Exod 35–40
G′	Regulations	Lev 1:1–Num 10:10
F′	Wilderness wandering and transfer of leadership	Num 10:11–Deut 31
E′	Song of Moses (Deut 32); blessing and death of Moses	Deut 32–34
D′	Eisodus into Canaan	Josh 1–4
C′	Canaan judged	Josh 5–12
B′	Land promise fulfilled	Josh 13–24
A′	Special history: Israel as covenant people in the land	Judges–2 Kings

Within this macrostructure, it is interesting to note that Num 10:11 refers to a cloud being taken up from over the משכן העדת, "tabernacle of the testimony," which parallels the text of Deut 31:14–15 and its reference to the appearance of the pillar of cloud at the door of the tent of meeting. These two references to God's mysterious presence in the form of a cloud, in conjunction with the portable sanctuary in pre-Davidic times, function as an envelope around the larger section on the theme of wilderness wandering and the transfer of leadership in the larger units; this larger section extends from Num 10:11 through Deut 31 in the above outline.

One way of looking at the overall structure of Deut 31 was given above in a detailed outline of the whole of Deut 31–34 in a five-part concentric structural outline. Another way of looking at the structural detail is to divide the chapter into two parts:

A	Moses announces his departure and replacement by Joshua	31:1–6
B	Moses commissions Joshua: "Do not fear!"	31:7–8
X	Writing of the Torah and its recitation by the Levites	31:9–12
B′	Later generations will learn "to fear YHWH"	31:13
A′	Preparations for God's appointment of Joshua	31:14–15

A	Israel's future apostasy and its consequences	31:16–18
B	The writing of the Song of Moses *as a witness*	31:19–22
X	God appoints Joshua to succeed Moses	31:23
B′	The writing of the Torah of Moses *as a witness*	31:24–27
A′	The song is there as a witness in the face of future apostasy	31:28–30

In this reading two major themes of Deut 31–34 are highlighted: the writing of the Torah, which is placed in the hands of the Levites (31:9–12); and the appointment of Joshua to succeed Moses (31:23). The outer frame of the first structure picks up the same theme as the center of the second: the appointment of Joshua to succeed Moses. In the inner frame of the first of the above structures, two different meanings of the verb "to fear" are set against each other: Joshua is commanded by Moses not "to fear," in the language of Holy War (31:8); whereas later generations in Israel will learn "to fear YHWH" (31:13), in the sense of worshiping him (cf. 10:12–13).

The inner frame in the second of the above structures puts the Song of Moses (31:19–22) over against the writing of the Torah (31:24–27), both of which are established as witnesses against future generations who violate the terms of the covenant. That theme of future apostasy is elaborated further in both halves of the outer frame of this unit (31:16–18 and 28–30).

A. Moses' Final Provisions in View of His Impending Death (31:1–13)

1. Moses Hands over Leadership to Joshua as His Successor (31:1–8)

Bibliography

Christensen, D. L. "Janus Parallelism in Genesis 6:3." *HS* 27 (1986) 20–24. **Cross, F. M.** "The Divine Warrior." In *CMHE*. 91–111. **Daube, D.** *Studies in Biblical Law.* 1947. 28–31. **Evans, G.** "'Coming' and 'Going' at the City Gate: A Discussion of Prof. Speiser's Paper." *BASOR* 150 (1958) 28–35. **Grossfeld, B.** "Neofiti to Dt 31:7—The Problem Re-analyzed." *ABR* 24 (1976) 30–34. ———. "Targum Neofiti 1 to Deut 31:7." *JBL* 9 (1972) 533–34. **Hulst, A. R.** *Old Testament Translation Problems.* Helps for Translators 1. Leiden: Brill, 1960. 17. **Klein, M.** "Deut 31:7: תבוא or תביא?" *JBL* 92 (1973) 584–85. **Longman, T.**, and **Reid, D. G.** *God Is a Warrior.* Grand Rapids: Zondervan, 1995. 31–88. **Nelson, R. D.** "Josiah in the Book of Joshua." *JBL* 100 (1981) 531–40 (531). **Rad, G. von.** *Holy War in Ancient Israel.* Tr. M. Dawn. Grand Rapids: Eerdmans, 1991 (Ger. ed. 1958). **Speiser, E. A.** "'Coming' and 'Going' at the City Gate." *BASOR* 144 (1956) 20–23. **Tigay, J. H.** "Excursus 3: The Concept of War in Deuteronomy." In *Deuteronomy.* 1996. 430. **Weinfeld, M.** "Divine Intervention in War." In *History, Historiography, and Interpretation.* Ed. H. Tadmor and M. Weinfeld. Jerusalem: Magnes, 1983. 121–47.

Translation and Prosodic Analysis

Moses Announces a Change in Leadership [(7:6):(5:5):(5:5)]

1 [a]*And Moses / went //*	7	2
and he spoke[a] */ *[b]*these words / to all *[c]*Israel //*	24	3
2 *And he said to them /*	8	1
"a hundred and twenty years old am I /	19	1_
Today / I am no longer able / to go out and to come in //	19	3
and YHWH\[a] *said to me /*	10	1
'You shall not cross over / this Jordan' //	13	2_
3 *YHWH your God / he / *[a]*is crossing over*[a] *before you /*	21	3
he will destroy / these nations /	15	2_
From before you\[b] *and you shall dispossess them //*	12	1
[c]*Joshua / he is*\[d] [e]*crossing over before you /*	18	2
just as / YHWH spoke //	8	2_

4 *So YHWH will do / to them /* 11 2
just as he did / to Sihon and Og[a] */* 17 2
kings of the Amorites[b] */* 11 1_
And to their land // when he destroyed / them // 15 3
5 *and YHWH will set them /* before you[a] // 13 2_

Moses Encourages Joshua in His New Role [6:7]

And you shall do to them / 8 1
[b]according to the all the commandment[b] /
I have commanded / you // 14 3
6 Be strong and be courageous / do not fear / 13 2_
and do not tremble / because of them // 11 2
For / YHWH is *your God / he*\[a] *is going with you*[b] */* 20 3
he will not fail you / and he will not forsake you" // פ 13 2_

Moses Commissions Joshua as His Successor [(6:5):(5:6)]

7 *And Moses summoned / Joshua / and he said to him /* 21 3
in the eyes of all Israel / "Be strong and be courageous / 17 2
for it is you / 5 1_
You shall go[a] \[b] [c]*with this people / into the land /* 17 2
that YHWH swore / to your fathers / to give to them // 20 3_
And as for you / you shall apportion it to them // 14 2
8 *and YHWH / he*[a] */ is the one going before you /* 17 3_
[b]*He / will be*[b] *with you / he will not fail you /* 12 3
and he will not forsake you // 7 1
Do not fear / and do not be afraid" // 13 2_

Notes

1.a-a. DSS and LXX read ויכל משה לדבר, "and Moses finished speaking," for MT וילך משה וידבר, "and Moses went and he spoke." MT is retained as *lectio difficilior.* See *Excursus:* "Travel Notices in Deut 1–3 and 31–34."

1.b. A number of Heb. MSS, DSS, Cairo Geniza fragments, LXX, Syr., and Vg. insert כל, "all." Prosodic analysis supports MT, and the addition of a word here would disturb the patterns in the numerical composition.

1.c. LXX adds υἱούς, "sons of" (= בני). Prosodic analysis supports MT.

2.a. Reading *pašṭāʾ* followed by *zāqēp̄ qāṭôn* as conj.

3.a-a. DSS read עובר for MT עבר, "he is crossing over," with no change in meaning; SP and LXX read העבר, "the one who is crossing over." From a prosodic point of view, either reading is possible.

3.b. Reading *ṭip̄ḥāʾ* as conj. because of misplaced *ʾatnāḥ.*

3.c. SP, LXX ,and Vg. add *waw*-conj.

3.d. Reading *yĕtîb* as conj. *mahpāk.*

3.e. Two Heb. MSS and LXX read העבר, "the one who is crossing over" (see *Note* 3.a).

4.a. Some LXX witnesses add τοῖς δυσί, "to the two (kings)" (= לשני). Prosodic analysis supports MT.

4.b. Some LXX witnesses add οἳ ἦσαν πέραν τοῦ Ιορδανου, "which were beyond the Jordan" (= אשר בעבר הירדן). Prosodic analysis supports MT.

5.a. DSS read 2 sg. MT is retained as *lectio difficilior.*

5.b-b. The text is emended to read כאשר המצוה, "according to the commandment," with most

LXX witnesses, which read καθότι, "just as" (= כאשר). It is easy to understand the change in MT as an attempt to clarify the use of המצוה, "the commandment," in the sg. to refer to the whole of the commandments contained in Deuteronomy. The emendation eliminates one word after *ʾatnāḥ* here, resulting in a total of 130 (= 5 × 26) words in 31:1–8 and a perfectly balanced pattern in terms of the numerical composition of 31:1–30 as a whole, with 322 (= 2 × 7 × 23) + 230 (= 10 × 23) = 552 (= 2 × 12 × 23) words. See discussion at the end of *Form/Structure/Setting*.

6.a. Reading conj. *mahpāk* in place of *yĕtîb* on הוא, "he."

6.b. LXX and *Tg. Ps.-J.* read 2 pl.; some LXX witnesses add ἐν ὑμῖν, "in the midst of you."

7.a. Reading תבוא, "you shall go," with MT, LXX, *Tg. Ps.-J.*, and the parallel text in 1:38. A number of Heb. MSS read תבא and a few read תביא, "you shall bring," with the support of Tg. Neofiti, SP, Syr., and Vg. See the discussion of Klein in *JBL* 92 (1973) 584–85.

7.b. Reading *paštāʾ* followed by *zāqēp qāṭôn* as conj.

7.c. LXX reads πρὸ προσώπου, "before (the face of)" (= לפני). Prosodic analysis supports MT.

8.a. LXX omits; prosodic analysis supports MT.

8.b-b. Omitted in most LXX witnesses. Prosodic analysis supports MT.

Form/Structure/Setting

From a prosodic point of view, 31:1–8 is in three parts: vv 1–5a, 5b–6, and 7–8. The internal boundaries are marked by the *pĕtûḥāʾ* layout marker at the end of v 6 and the *Numeruswechsel* in vv 5 and 6. Prosodic analysis indicates that vv 1–6 constitute a literary unit, which may be outlined as follows:

A	Moses announces he is no longer the military leader	31:1–2a
B	YHWH will dispossess these nations before you	31:2b–3b
X	Joshua is the one who will cross over the Jordan	31:3c
B′	YHWH will do there what he did to Sihon and Og	31:3d–5
A′	Moses encourages Joshua: "Be strong and . . . do not fear!"	31:6

The center of this structure (v 3c) focuses on the fact that Joshua is the one chosen by God to lead the people of Israel into the promised land. The inner frame highlights that it is YHWH who will dispossess nations before them (vv 2b–3c), just as he has already done to the Amorite kingdoms of Sihon and Og (vv 4–5). The outer frame moves from Moses' announcement that he is no longer the military leader in Israel (vv 1–2a) to a verse in which Moses encourages Joshua in his role as leader (v 6). This verse is separated from what precedes by the *Numeruswechsel* at the beginning of v 5 (from second-person sg. to pl.) and in the middle of v 6 (from second-person pl. to sg.).

In 31:6 Moses reports the words of YHWH, who told him to encourage Joshua in his new role of leadership. This content is expanded in 31:7–8 as Moses summons Joshua and relates to him what YHWH told him to say. The structure of this unit may be outlined as follows:

A	Words of encouragement: "Be strong and be courageous!"	31:7a
B	Announcement: "It is you" (whom YHWH has chosen)	31:7b
X	"You shall go with this people into the land . . ."	31:7c
B′	Announcement: "YHWH is the one going before you"	31:7d–8a
A′	Words of encouragement: "Do not fear and do not be afraid!"	31:8b

On the relationship of 31:1–8 to the structure of the chapter as a whole, see the outline of Deut 31–34 above. This particular literary unit is set over against

31:23–30, which begins with YHWH himself appointing Joshua to his new role; in these verses the same words of encouragement are repeated (v 23).

When vv 1–8 are outlined as a whole, the transfer of leadership from Moses to Joshua is highlighted in a somewhat different manner:

A	Moses speaks: YHWH is crossing over before you—not me	31:1–3a
B	Joshua announced as Moses' successor to dispossess the nations	31:3b–5
X	Joshua encouraged: "Be strong and be courageous"	31:6–7a
B′	Joshua appointed to lead the people into the land	31:7b
A′	"YHWH is the one going before you; he will be with you"	31:8

The outer frame here is made up of parallel announcements by Moses: to all Israel (vv 1–3a), and to Joshua in the eyes of all Israel (v 8). Within this framework, Moses announces Joshua as his successor (vv 3b–5), encourages him (vv 6–7a), and appoints him as leader (v 7b). The words of encouragement at the center of this structure may be outlined in the same manner:

A	"Be strong and be courageous, do not fear . . . because of them"	31:6a
B	"For YHWH is your God"	31:6b
X	"He is going with you"	31:6c
B′	"He will not fail you, and he will not forsake you"	31:6d
A′	"Be strong and be courageous"	31:7a

The specific words of encouragement, "be strong and be courageous," are repeated verbatim as a frame around this unit (vv 6a and 7a). Within this frame is a threefold declaration concerning YHWH: he is your God; he is going with you; and he will not fail you or forsake you (v 6b).

The data from Labuschagne on the numerical composition of 31:1–8 (modified by a correction in v 5b) may be summarized as follows:

Words:	before *ʾatnāḥ*		after *ʾatnāḥ*		
31:6	7	+	10	=	17
31:1–8	82	+	49 (= 7 × 7)	=	130 (= 5 × 26)
31:9–13	49 (= 7 × 7)	+	49 (= 7 × 7)	=	98
31:14–15	20	+	12	=	32
31:16–23	102 (= 4 × 26)	+	75	=	177
31:24–28	46 (= 2 × 23)	+	30	=	76
31:29–30	23	+	16	=	39
31:1–30	322 (= 14 × 23)	+	230 (= 10 × 23)	=	552 (= 24 × 23)
32:1–43	244	+	224	=	468 (= 18 × 26)
32:44–34:12	389	+	274	=	663 (= 39 × 17)
31:1–34:12	955	+	728 (= 7 × 32)	=	1,683 (= 99 × 17)

The key verse in this section (v 6), in which Moses encourages Joshua in his new role as leader of the people of Israel, has exactly 17 words: 7 before *ʾatnāḥ* and 10 after *ʾatnāḥ*. Moreover, 31:1–8 as a whole has a total of 130 (= 5 × 26) words. Thus once again both of the divine-name numbers are woven into the fabric of the

Hebrew text. At this point the primary efforts in the numerical composition of this passage appear to be focused on the task of achieving exact figures on a more macrolevel—a task that was done to the glory of YHWH. Thus the number 23, which is associated with the word כבוד, "glory," factors in all three totals for 31:1–30 as a whole: 322 (= 14 × 23) words before *'atnāḥ*, 230 (= 10 × 23) words after *'atnāḥ*, and a total of 552 (= 24 × 23) words. Moreover, in 31:1–34:12 (Readings 9–11) there is a grand total of 1,683 (= 99 × 17) words. The number 32 is present as well, for there are 224 (= 7 × 32) words after *'atnāḥ* in 32:1–43. On the numerical value of כבוד as both 23 and 32, see *Excursus:* "Deuteronomy as a Numerical Composition." The evidence bears witness that these scribes carried out their laborious task of numerical composition with the glory of YHWH in mind.

Comment

1 The statement that "Moses went" (וילך) is part of a system of travel notices in Deut 1–3 and 31–34 (see *Excursus:* "Travel Notices in Deut 1–3 and 31–34"). The verb used here and the verb ויבא, "and he came," in 32:44 were both introduced in 1:19 (in first pl. forms), where they set the stage for what I call "Israel's Unholy War": the aborted command to enter the promised land from Kadesh-barnea. The context here is a second entry into the promised land, this time led by Joshua, coming from Moab across the Jordan Valley, which is aptly designated as the second phase of YHWH's Holy War. The first phase is the exodus from Egypt under Moses and the conquest of the two Amorite kingdoms in Transjordan; and the second the eisodus into the promised land in Cisjordan under Joshua. The clause וידבר את־הדברים האלה, "and he spoke these words," forms an inclusion with the opening words of Deuteronomy, where they appear in reverse order, אלה הדברים אשר דבר משה, "these are the words that Moses spoke." The phrase "all Israel" forms an inclusion with both the first and last verses in Deuteronomy (as the final two words of the book).

2 The statement that Moses was "a hundred and twenty years old" at the time of his death in 31:2 and 34:7 functions as a frame around Deut 31–34. The prosodic analysis reveals that 31:2 is commonly mistranslated, since the major break in this verse is after אנכי, "I," and before היום, "today." The point is that Moses has reached the limit God has set for him. As one of my students put it, he is simply saying: "My meter has run out!" This is the moment God ordained for him to "pass the torch" of leadership to Joshua. The text here is connected with the enigmatic statement in Gen 6:3, where that limit is first imposed: "his days shall be a hundred and twenty years" (see Christensen, *HS* 27 [1986] 20–24). One should remember that in the cycle of Torah readings in Judaism, the recitations of Deut 31–34 and Gen 6:1–4 were never far apart (see *Excursus:* "The Triennial Cycle of Torah Readings in Palestinian Judaism"; and the discussion in D. L. Christensen, *Bible 101: God's Story in Human History* [N. Richland Hills, TX: BIBAL Press, 1996] 55–60).

The phrase "to go out and to come in" is used of Joshua (Josh 14:11), David (1 Sam 18:13), and Solomon (1 Kgs 3:7; 2 Chr 1:10) to refer to the military leadership of a ruler in ancient Israel. That is clearly the context here as well, for Moses is transferring his authority as leader in Israel to Joshua, who will lead Israel in the military encounters often called the "conquest." The statement "YHWH said to me" is a reference to 3:27, where YHWH granted Moses permission to "see" the promised land, but not in the manner he wished. He was allowed to see it with his eyes only, in a marvelous vision of the whole of the land from the top of Mount Nebo; but he was not permitted to "cross over this Jordan."

3–5 According to the Masoretic notes, 31:3 is one of three verses that begin and end with the tetragrammaton. The prosodic analysis suggests that the boundaries of the verse include v 2b as well, which means the verse still begins and ends with the divine name יהוה in a concentric sentence:

A "And YHWH said to me, 'You shall not cross over this Jordan
ויהוה אמר אלי לא תעבר את־הירדן הזה 31:2b
B YHWH your God he is crossing over before you
יהוה אלהיך הוא עבר לפניך 31:3aα
X He will destroy these nations . . . and you shall dispossess them
הוא־ישמיד את־הגוים האלה מלפניך וירשתם 31:3aβ
B′ Joshua he is crossing over before you'
,יהושע הוא עבר לפניך 31:3bα
A′ Just as YHWH said"
כאשר דבר יהוה 31:3bβ

The inner frame in this structure has parallel clauses in which YHWH and Joshua are "crossing over before you" (vv 2b and 3bα). The outer frame moves from YHWH's statement to Moses, "you shall not cross over this Jordan" (v 2b), to the summary remark that all this is just as YHWH said it would be (v 3bβ). The center summarizes the eisodus as YHWH's Holy War: "he will destroy these nations from before you, and you shall dispossess them" (v 3aα). The concept of God as the Divine Warrior who will "destroy these nations from before you" is foundational in the belief system of ancient Israel (see Cross, *CMHE,* 91–111). Joshua will lead the forces of Israel in conquering the nations and dispossessing their lands; but it is God himself who does the fighting. As the Israelites sang at the crossing of the sea when the forces of Pharaoh drowned, "The LORD is a warrior; / the LORD is his name!" (Exod 15:3 NRSV; cf. 14:14, 25). On the conquest of "Sihon and Og kings of the Amorites," see *Excursus:* "Holy War as Celebrated Event in Ancient Israel." On the phrase "all the commandment" in reference to the destruction of the Canaanites in the land, see 7:1–11 and cf. 12:1–3; 20:16–17.

6 In the language of Holy War, Joshua is commanded to "Be strong and courageous. Do not fear . . . for YHWH is your God; he is going with you" (cf. also v 7 below). See the discussion above for 1:21 and *Excursus:* "Holy War as Celebrated Event in Ancient Israel." The promise that God will be with someone is a familiar one throughout the Bible, as witnessed by the meaning of the name Immanuel ("God is with us") in Matt 1:23 (quoting Isa 7:14; cf. Gen 21:22; 26:3, 28; 28:15, 20; 39:2–3; Exod 3:12; Josh 1:5–9; Judg 6:12–13; Isa 8:10; Jer 1:19).

7 The phrase "in the eyes of all Israel" indicates that Joshua is singled out publicly as Israel's leader. At the same time, the true leader of Israel is YHWH himself, as Gideon argued when he was asked to rule as king in Israel: "I will not rule over you. . . . The LORD will rule over you" (Judg 8:23). In the parallel passage of 31:23, where God is speaking privately to Joshua, the theological distinction made here is less obvious. The reading תבוא, "you shall go with," is read תביא, "you shall bring," in Tg. Neofiti, in some medieval Hebrew manuscripts, and in the ancient versions other than the LXX (as in v 23). Tigay supports the MT as it stands here: "Moses, speaking to Joshua in the hearing of the people, may want to emphasize that Joshua is one of them so as to avoid any implication that Joshua rather than God is the real leader. God, speaking privately to Joshua in verse 23, is at less pains to avoid the implication" ([1996] 291; see the discussions of B. Grossfeld in *JBL* 91 [1972] 533–34 and *ABR* 24 [1976] 30–34; and Klein in *JBL* 92 [1973] 584–85).

"You shall apportion it to them." Joshua will assign each of the tribes and clans in Israel their allotment (see Josh 14–21). Milgrom notes that the apportionment of the land is based on what seems at first glance to be two mutually exclusive principles: the lot and the need (*Numbers* [1990] 480). Following the arguments of Abravanel (1437–1508 C.E.), Milgrom concluded that the *location* of each tribe in the land was determined by lot; but the actual *size* of each tribal allotment was determined according to population. Joshua administered the process of distributing the land.

8 "Do not fear and do not be afraid." Once again, this is the language of Holy War (see *Comment* on 1:21 and *Note* 6.b.).

Explanation

When Moses reached the end of his life journey on Mount Nebo, he was still strong and able; for his eye was not dim and he was fully virile as a man (cf. 34:7). He died because he reached the end of his allotted time. Though he had earlier begged God to allow him to cross over into the promised land (3:23–25), he is now resigned to his fate; for he knows that it is YHWH himself who is "crossing over before you. He will destroy these nations from before you; and you shall dispossess them" (31:3).

Joshua is the human agent through whom YHWH will take the land, and Moses has trained him carefully. In his discussion of this text, J. Maxwell cites a study by Warren Bennis, professor of management at the School of Business Administration at the University of Southern California, which merits repetition (*Deuteronomy* [1987] 323). In this four-year study of outstanding leaders, Bennis found what he believes are five strengths common to all "superleaders," like Moses:

1. *Vision*—the capacity to create compelling vision of a desired state of affairs.
2. *Communication*—the capacity to maintain that vision in a way that gains the support of others.
3. *Persistence*—the capacity to maintain the organization's direction, especially when the going gets rough.
4. *Empowerment*—the capacity to create a social structure that harnesses the energies and abilities of others to get the best results.
5. *Organizational learning*—the capacity to monitor an organization's performance, learn from past actions, and use the resulting knowledge to forge a course for the future.

Moses demonstrates all five of these categories, especially empowerment. He empowers the people with words of encouragement: "be strong and courageous;

do not fear . . . for YHWH is your God" (v 6). Those same words of encouragement are addressed to Joshua as well (vv 7–8).

It is important to note that the commissioning of Joshua by Moses was not done in private. Lay leadership in the church today needs to be empowered and publicly commissioned. Pastors and other professional leaders in the church today should recognize those whom God has gifted as leaders, and honor them in public in the same manner that Moses honored Joshua: "Moses summoned Joshua, and he said to him in the eyes of all Israel . . ." (v 7).

2. *Moses Deposits the Torah for Recitation at the Festival of Booths (31:9–13)*

Bibliography

Alt, A. *Essays on Old Testament History and Religion.* 1966. 126–29. **Cazelles, H.** "The Bible and the Liturgical Times: Eschatology and Anamnesis." *Studia liturgica* 14 (1982) 23–33. **Cullen, J.** "Das Deuteronomium: Eine Erwiderung." *ZWT* 48 (1905) 181–93, esp. 182. **Fischer, G.**, and **Lohfink, N.** "'Diese Worte sollst du summen.' Dtn 6,7 *wĕdibbartā bām*—Ein verlorener Schlüssel zur meditativen Kultur in Israel." In *Studien zum Deuteronomium III.* 1995. 181–203, esp. 197–99. **Friedman, M. A.** "Publication of a Book by Depositing It in a Sanctuary." *Leš* 48–49 (1983–85) 49–52 (Heb.). **Haag, H.** "Das 'Buch des Bundes' (Ex 24,7)." In *FS K. H. Schelkle.* 1973. 22–30, esp. 29. **Kumaki, F. K.** "The Deuteronomistic Theology of the Temple—As Crystallized in 2 Sam 7, 1 Kgs 8." *AJBI* 7 (1981) 16–52, esp. 37–39. **Kutsch, E.** "'Bund' und Fest: Zu Gegenstand und Terminologie einer Forschungsrichtung." *TQ* 150 (1970) 299–320. **Lang, B.** "Der tanzende Leser: Die frühjüdische Buchreligion." *BK* 36 (1981) 279–85. **McCarthy, C.** *Tiqqune Sopherim and Other Theological Corrections in the Masoretic Text of the Old Testament.* OBO 36. Göttingen: Vandenhoeck & Ruprecht, 1981. 197–204. **Milgrom, J.** "Excursus 34: The 'Ger.'" In *Numbers.* 1990. 398–402. **Mölle, H.** *Das "Erscheinen" Gottes im Pentateuch: Ein literaturwissenschaftlicher Beitrag zur alttestamentlichen Exegese.* EHS 23.18. Bern: Lang, 1973. 131–41, esp. 138–41. **Perlitt, L.** *Bundestheologie.* 1970. 123–24. **Watts, J. W.** *Reading Law: The Rhetorical Shaping of the Pentateuch.* Biblical Seminar 59. Sheffield: Sheffield Academic Press, 1999. **Weinfeld, M.** *Justice and Righteousness in Israel.* 1985. 505.

Translation and Prosodic Analysis

The Writing and Recitation of the Torah at the Festival of Booths
[(5:5):(4:4):(4:4):(5:5)]

9 *And Moses wrote / this Torah / and he gave it / to the priests /* 28 4
the sons of Levi / 7 1
The ones bearing / the ark / of the covenant of YHWH // [18 3
and to all the elders / of Israel // 11 2
10 *And Moses commanded / them saying //* [14 2
Every / seventh year / 9 2

At the set time /	5	1
the year of release / at the Festival of Booths //	13	2
11 *when all Israel comes /*	9	1
To appear[a] */ before*[b] *YHWH your God /*	16	2
in the place / that [c]*he will choose //*	10	2
You[d] *shall recite*[c] */ this Torah /*	12	2
in front of all Israel / in their hearing //	13	2
12 *Assemble the people / men and women*[a] *and little ones /*	24	2
and your resident alien[b] *who is in your towns //*	10	1
so that they will hear /	7	1
and so that they will learn /	8	1
And they will fear / YHWH your[c] God /	18	2
and they will be careful to do /	10	1
all the words / of this Torah //	13	2

Future Generations Shall Learn to Fear YHWH [6:6]

13 And their children / who have not known it / they will hear /	19	3
and they will learn / to fear / YHWH your[a] God //	20	3
All the days / that you[b] are alive \\[c] in the land /	20	2
when you / cross the Jordan / there / to possess it // פ	21	4

Notes

11.a. SP reads להראות. The word is repointed לְרָאוֹת, "to appear."

11.b. Reading *paštā'* followed by *zāqēp qāṭôn* as conj.

11.c-c. SP reads בחר יקרא, "he chose, he will recite," for MT יבחר תקרא, "he will choose, you shall recite."

11.d. LXX reads 2 pl. ἀναγνώσεσθε, "you [pl.] shall read" (= תִּקְרְאוּ). I follow the 2 sg. reading of MT here.

12.a. Reading *paštā'* followed by *zāqēp qāṭôn* as conj.

12.b. Reading *ṭipḥā'* as conj. because of misplaced *'atnāḥ*.

12.c. A number of Heb. MSS, SP, and some LXX witnesses read 3 pl. rather than 2 pl. The *Numeruswechsel* of MT is read here.

13.a. A few Heb. MSS, SP, Syr., and Vg. read 3 pl.; LXX[B] reads 2 sg.; and some LXX witnesses read 1 pl. MT is followed here as *lectio difficilior.*

13.b. SP, LXX, and Vg. read הֵם, "they."

13.c. Reading *paštā'* followed by *zāqēp qāṭôn* as conj.

Form/Structure/Setting

On the place of 31:9–12 within larger patterns in Deut 31–34 and Deut 31, see the discussions above on Readings 9–11, and Reading 9 in particular. It is useful to examine the content of Deut 31 in terms of a menorah pattern:

A	Moses announces his departure and Joshua as his successor	31:1–8
B	The writing and reading of the Torah at the Feast of Booths	31:9–12
C	Future generations will learn to fear YHWH	31:13
X	Theophany in the tent of meeting with Moses and Joshua	31:14–15
C′	Israel's future apostasy and its consequences	31:16–18
B′	The writing of the song as a witness / God commissions Joshua	31:19–23
A′	The Torah and song given as witnesses to future generations	31:24–30

In this reading, the writing down of the Torah, which is entrusted to the Levites for recitation at the Festival of Booths every seven years (vv 9–12), is set over against the writing and teaching of the Song of Moses as a witness to future generations (vv 19–22), to which a brief note on the commissioning of Joshua by God himself is appended (v 23). The framework in this reading moves from the transfer of leadership from Moses to Joshua (vv 1–8) to the legacy left by Moses for future generations in the Torah and the Song of Moses (vv 24–30), with the mysterious theophany when God revealed himself to Moses and Joshua in the tent of meeting (vv 14–15) at the structural center of the above outline.

The boundaries of subunits in 31:9–23 are marked with the *Numeruswechsel* in vv 12, 14, 19, and 23 (the change between second-person sg. and second-person pl. forms), the *pĕtûḥā'* layout marker after v 13, and the *sĕtûmā'* layout marker after v 15. The prosodic analysis suggests that the verse division between vv 10 and 11 is incorrect, and that the phrase "when all Israel comes" concludes the thought of v 10 and announces the structural center of the prosodic unit, namely the appearance of all Israel at the central sanctuary to hear the recitation of Deuteronomy. The concentric structure of 31:9–12 may be outlined as follows:

A	Moses writes the Torah and entrusts it to the Levites	31:9
B	The Levites are to recite the Torah every seven years	31:10–11aα
X	When all Israel appears before YHWH at the central sanctuary	31:11aβ
B′	The Levites are to recite it in front of all Israel	31:11b
A′	Moses commands the reading of the Torah in the future	31:12

The setting for the public recitation of the Torah is the autumn Festival of Booths, "when all Israel comes to appear before YHWH your God in the place that he will choose" (v 11). Moses writes the Torah and gives it to the Levites, who are commanded to recite it to future generations in Israel, every seven years—to the entire populace in ancient Israel, so that future generations ("their children") will learn to "fear YHWH" in the promised land (v 13).

The boundaries of this brief prosodic unit are marked by the *Numeruswechsel* at the end of v 12 and the *pĕtûḥā'* layout marker at the end of v 13. In terms of the menorah pattern presented in the previous section of this commentary, 31:13 is to be read over against 31:16–18 as the inner frame of a menorah pattern. That 31:13 constitutes a prosodic subunit within the concentric structural design of Deut 31 as a whole has been overlooked by virtually all commentators. In the Hebrew text, emphasis is placed on the words "their children," who will need to learn the experiences and lessons of Deuteronomy. The content moves from a statement about "their children" learning to fear YHWH "all the days that you are alive in the land when you cross over the Jordan there to possess it" (v 13) to an account of Israel's future apostasy when "this people will rise, and they will play the harlot, going after the strange gods of the land" (v 16). YHWH declares, "my anger will be kindled against them in that day, and I will forsake them. . . . I will surely hide my face in that day" (vv 17–18).

The data from Labuschagne on the numerical composition of 31:9–13 as a whole are included in the previous section on 31:1–8. There is no evidence for the use of the divine-name numbers 17 and 26 here, other than the fact that this passage is an integral part of larger contexts in which multiples of these numbers are used in an impressive manner.

Comment

9 By "this Torah" the text is referring to Deuteronomy, which Moses has been expounding, including Deut 31–34. These concluding chapters function as a bridge to connect Deuteronomy with the Former Prophets (Joshua through 2 Kings) as a canonical category. In short, the writing down of Deuteronomy, as the essence of the larger "Torah" (i.e., Genesis through Deuteronomy or what is called the Pentateuch) that was to emerge in due course, was the initial step in what we call the canonical process. In giving the Torah "to the priests, the sons of Levi . . . and to all the elders," Moses delegates responsibility for the transmission of the teaching to future generations. For the Chronicler, who wrote after the Babylonian exile, "the Levites were appointed for all the service of the tabernacle of the house of God" by David (1 Chr 6:48); and the temple musicians in Jerusalem were Levites (1 Chr 25). Still later, in the records of Ezra and Nehemiah we read that the priests and the Levites were assembled together in Jerusalem "to praise and to give thanks, according to the commandment of David the man of God" (Neh 12:24). It is reasonable to assume that this tradition preserves ancient memory, and that the Levites were associated with the transmission of the biblical text in musical form in preexilic Israel. To say that Moses entrusted the Torah "to the priests the sons of Levi" (v 9) and that he commanded them to "recite this Torah in front of all Israel" (v 11) at the covenant ceremony during the Festival of Booths is another way of saying that the teaching of the Torah was literally "in the hands of the Levites." They are the ones who preserved both the consonantal text of the Hebrew Bible and a system of hand signs by which the canting of the Torah was transmitted and taught from one generation to the next in ancient Israel. On the meaning of the phrase "the ones bearing the ark of the covenant of YHWH," see the *Comment* on 10:8–11 and on 18:1.

10–11 The Torah (i.e., Deuteronomy) was to be recited "every seventh year . . . at the Festival of Booths." On the Festival of Booths, see 16:13–15. Though the translation "to appear before YHWH" conveys the meaning of the text, it lacks the force of the Hebrew. The verb may have originally been in the qal rather than niphal, which would read: "to see the face of YHWH your God." The idiom here does not mean literally to see God, but to visit him and to worship him at his sanctuary—"the place that he will choose." It is interesting to note that the vocalization that requires the translation "appear" rather than "see" "is found only in passages that refer to a sanctuary. . . . [T]he intention is to avoid giving the impression that God is physically visible there in the form of a statue" (Tigay [1996] 372 n. 46). On the fact that God is visible in certain circumstances, see Exod 24:10–11; 33:11; 34:23; Num 12:8. Because תקרא, "you shall recite (this Torah)," is in the second singular, some interpreters in times past have assumed that it refers to a single person, perhaps Joshua, and later the king or the high priest (Tigay [1996] 292). It is better to note the function of the *Numeruswechsel* as presented in this commentary, and to realize that we are dealing with a stylistic feature of Deuteronomy.

12 The command to assemble "men and women and little ones and your resident alien" suggests that the Festival of Booths in the sabbatical year was different from the other festivals, where only adult male Israelites were obligated to appear. It is important to note with Tigay that "the verse makes no distinction between the need for men and women to learn the Teaching." Tigay adds that, contrary to common practice in many segments of Judaism through the ages, the sage Simeon ben Azzai insisted that a man is obligated to teach his daughter Torah ([1996] 292; *y. Ḥag.* 1:1, 75d; see also M. Greenberg, *Studies in the Bible and Jewish Thought* [Philadelphia: Jewish Publication Society, 1995] 434–35). The "resident alien who is in your towns" is the non-Israelite living among Israelites. The reference to the "mixed multitude" (Exod 12:38) that participated in the exodus from Egypt suggests that such "aliens" were present from the start. Resident aliens did not normally own land and were often exploited and reduced to poverty. Consequently the Torah groups them with the widows and orphans in appeals to protect vulnerable groups. Since they are thus subject to the civil law and certain religious prohibitions, the resident aliens were permitted to participate in some of the religious celebrations. For this reason they too must learn the Torah by hearing it recited at the Festival of Booths (cf. Josh 8:35).

13 The reference to "their children who have not known it" refers to those in the future who do not know firsthand the experiences of the people of Israel under the leadership of Moses and Joshua. The function of the *waw* attached to the word "children" (ובניהם) at the beginning of this verse is disjunctive, separating v 13 from what precedes it and placing emphasis on the words "their children."

Explanation

The Festival of Booths in the sabbatical year was selected for this great educational event, when the people were more exempt than usual from the concerns of employment so that greater numbers would assemble at the central sanctuary to participate. Two instances of such observations are recorded: in the reign of King Josiah (2 Kgs 23:1–3; though the actual festival is not specified) and in the time of Ezra (Neh 7:73b–9:37). The neglect of this practice appears to be one of the reasons the nation of Israel was carried away into idolatry and ruin. As the prophet Hosea put it, "My people are destroyed for lack of knowledge" (Hos 4:6).

According to the text, the "study" of the Bible is the task of "men and women and little ones" (v 12). The tradition that religious study was reserved for men only is simply false teaching, according to Deuteronomy. The image is vividly portrayed in Barbra Streisand's delightful film *Yentl*, in which the old bookseller had two different displays in his book cart. On one side were the sacred books for the men; and on the other, the simpler books with pictures for the women. Paul once said that "there is no longer male and female; for all of you are one in Christ Jesus" (Gal 3:28 NRSV). Moreover, from the beginning the task of learning the Torah is assigned to all of us—men, women, and children.

Though the public reading of the Scriptures is a time-honored principle within Judaism and Christianity, that practice is sadly lacking in many evangelical settings today. Apart from short texts, which are read in conjunction with the sermon preached, the systematic public reading of the biblical text is virtually unknown in large segments of the church. In Judaism, ancient and modern, the Torah (and much of the Prophets) is read systematically in the worship experience each Sabbath. We would do well to study this ancient practice and emulate it by training lectors and cantors to recite the sacred text more effectively in public worship, "as this would give probable ground to expect far more extensively beneficial effects, to result from so laudable an institution" (Scott, *Holy Bible,* 1:567).

Moses intended Deuteronomy to be understood by children within the context of their own family gatherings at the regular celebration of a major festival in ancient Israel. But teaching Scripture to children was not limited to such a special moment. As Moses put it earlier in this book, "you shall teach [these words] diligently to your children; and you shall speak of them—when you sit in your house, and when you walk by the way, and when you lie down, and when you get up" (6:7). The teaching of the Bible to our children is a matter of primary importance.

Beginning in 1956 on the book of Romans, Kenneth Taylor set out to produce a rendering of the Scriptures in modern speech that grew out of his frustration with his reading of the classic KJV to his own children. His attempts to explain the passages of the Bible in simple, everyday English they could understand culminated in *The Living Bible* (1971), which has sold millions of copies and launched a movement—the growing number of translations of the Bible designed expressly for children.

The best way to teach our children is by example. Memories of my own father faithfully reading his Bible did more to encourage me in my own love affair with this book than anything he could ever have said. John Maxwell's quotation from the writing of George Mueller is worth repeating: "The vigor of our spiritual life will be in exact proportion to the place held by the Word in our life and thoughts. I solemnly state this from experience of fifty-four years. I have read the Bible a hundred times and always with increasing delight. Each time it seems like a new book to me. Great has been the blessing from consecutive, diligent, daily study" (Maxwell [1987] 326). Moses was of the same mind.

B. YHWH's Charge to Moses and Joshua in the Tent of Meeting (31:14–23)

1. Theophany in the Tent of Meeting with Moses and Joshua (31:14–15)

Bibliography

Aharoni, Y. "The Solomonic Temple, the Tabernacle, and the Arad Sanctuary." In *FS C. H. Gordon.* 1973. **Cross, F. M.** "The Priestly Tabernacle." In *BA Reader.* Ed. G. E. Wright and D. N. Freedman. Garden City, NY: Doubleday Anchor Books, 1961. 1:201–28. **Friedman, R. E.** "Tabernacle." *ABD* 6:292–300. ———. "The Tabernacle in the Temple." *BA* 43

(1980) 241–48. ———. *Who Wrote the Bible?* Englewood Cliffs, NJ: Prentice-Hall, 1987. **Haran, M.** "The Ark in Deuteronomy." *IEJ* 9 (1959) 30–38, 89–94. ———. "The Nature of the '*ʾOhel Môʿēdh*' in Pentateuchal Sources." *JSS* 5 (1960) 50–65. ———. "The Priestly Image of the Tabernacle." *HUCA* 36 (1965) 191–226. ———. "Shiloh and Jerusalem: The Origin of the Priestly Tradition in the Pentateuch." *JBL* 81 (1962) 14–24. ———. *Temples and Temple-Service in Ancient Israel.* Oxford: Clarendon, 1978. 260–75. **Milgrom, J.** "Excursus 28: The Tent of Meeting: Two Traditions." In *Numbers.* 1990. 386–87. **Rabe, V.** "The Identity of the Priestly Tabernacle." *JNES* 25 (1966) 132–34. ———. "The Temple as Tabernacle." Diss., Harvard, 1963. **Rad, G. von.** *Das Gottesvolk im Deuteronomium.* 1929. 70–71. ———. "The Tent and the Ark." In *Problem of the Hexateuch.* 1966. 103–24. **Rodríguez Carmona, A.** "Los Anuncios de la Muerte de Moises en el Targum Palestinense." In *FS L. Alonso Schökel.* 1983. 267–79. **Rofé, A.** "Textual Criticism in the Light of Historical-Literary Criticism: Deut. 31:14–15." *EI* 16 (1982) 171–76 (Heb.). **Schutenhaus, F.** "Das Kommen und Erscheinen Gottes im Alten Testament." *ZAW* 76 (1964) 1–22. **Vaux, R. de.** "Ark of the Covenant and Tent of Reunion." In *The Bible and the Ancient Near East.* Tr. D. McHugh. Garden City, NY: Doubleday, 1971. 136–51. **Weinfeld, M.** "The Concept of God and the Divine Abode." In *DDS.* 191–209. **Wilson, I.** *Out of the Midst of the Fire.* 1995.

Translation and Prosodic Analysis

Theophany in the Tent of Meeting with Moses and Joshua [(5:4):(4:5)]

14 And YHWH said / to Moses /	14	2
"Behold the days / approach |[a] for *you to die* /	15	3_
Call Joshua /	10	1
and present yourselves / [b]*at the tent of meeting*[b] */*	14	2
and I will commission him" //	6	1_
And Moses and Joshua / went /	14	2
and they stationed themselves / [b]*at the tent of meeting*[b] *//*	20	2_
15 *And YHWH appeared*[a] */*	10	1
in the tent[b] \\[c] *in a pillar*[d] *of cloud //*	13	1
and a pillar of cloud / stood / by the door of the tent[e] *//* ס	21	3_

Notes

14.a. The *mûnāḥ* under קרבו is read as disj. It should be noted that the Letteris edition places a *metheg* under קרבו, "they approach," which lends some support to this reading.

14.b-b. LXX παρὰ τὰς θύρας τῆς σκηνῆς, "by the doors of the tabernacle" (= על פתח האהל).

15.a. LXX reads καὶ κατέβη, "and he descended" (= וירד).

15.b. The word באהל, "in the tent," is omitted in LXX; Origen marked it with asterisk; Syr. reads באהל מועד, "in the tent of meeting." Prosodic analysis supports MT.

15.c. Reading *ṭipḥāʾ* as conj. because of misplaced *ʾatnāḥ*.

15.d. Some important LXX witnesses and OL omit עמוד, "pillar." Prosodic analysis supports MT.

15.e. One Heb. MS, major LXX witnesses, and Syr. read אהל מועד, "tent of meeting." Prosodic analysis supports MT.

Form/Structure/Setting

The boundaries of the four major subunits in 31:14–23 are marked with the *Numeruswechsel* in vv 14, 19, and 23; and with the *sĕtûmāʾ* layout marker after v 15.

The conclusion of G. E. Wright that the order of material in 31:14–23 "seems rather badly mixed" (*IB* 2:513) is typical of scholars who have failed to see the concentric structural design here. For indeed, as Wright observed, "Vss. 14–15, 23 have to do with the formal commissioning of Joshua by God at the tabernacle. These verses are thus a continuation of or a parallel to vss. 2–8." And so they are—within a carefully crafted concentric structure.

In terms of content, the concentric structural design of this passage may be outlined as follows:

A	YHWH appears to Moses and Joshua at the tent of meeting	31:14–15
B	Israel's future apostasy and its consequences	31:16–18
X	Moses commanded to teach the song as a witness in Israel	31:19
B′	Israel's future apostasy and the Song of Moses as a witness	31:20–22
A′	YHWH appoints Joshua to succeed Moses	31:23

The commissioning of Joshua as Moses' successor functions as the outer frame in this structure (vv 14–15 and 23), with the statement in the center that the Song of Moses is intended as a witness to future generations, so as to provide a means of dealing with apostasy in Israel when it occurs (v 19). The inner frame deals with the matter of future apostasy in terms of its consequences (vv 16–18), and with the role of the Song of Moses as witness against them in that day (vv 20–22).

Within 31:14–23, a series of three concentric structures are found, the first of which (vv 14–16) may be outlined as follows:

A	The days approach for you to die—bring Joshua to the tent	31:14a
B	They stationed themselves at the tent of meeting	31:14b
X	YHWH appeared in the tent in a pillar of cloud	31:15a
B′	And a pillar of cloud stood by the door of the tent	31:15b
A′	You are about to sleep with your fathers	31:16a

The outer frame in this structure reiterates that Moses is about to die (vv 14a and 16a). The inner frame moves from the stationing of Moses and Joshua at the tent of meeting (v 14b) to the appearance of a pillar of cloud that stood by the door of the tent (v 15b). In the center YHWH appears in a pillar of cloud, which "stood at the entrance to the tent" (v 15a).

The structure and content of 31:14–15 should be compared with that of Exod 33:7–11, which may be outlined as follows:

A	Moses used to pitch the tent of meeting outside the camp	33:7
B	When Moses went to the tent, the people watched him enter	33:8
X	The pillar of cloud stood at the entrance to the tent	33:9–10
B′	YHWH spoke to Moses face to face in the tent	33:11a
A′	When Moses returned to the camp Joshua remained at the tent	33:11b

In both texts the appearance of YHWH at the tent of meeting in a pillar of cloud is the focus of interest (cf. Deut 31:15a and Exod 33:9–10). Moreover, both Moses and Joshua are present at the tent in each instance (Deut 31:14 and Exod 33:11).

Labuschagne notes that there are a total of 32 words in 31:14–15, which is one of the two numbers associated with the word כבוד, "glory." On the numerical composition of the larger context of Deut 31 and Deut 31–34, see the discussion above under 31:1–8.

Comment

14 As Milgrom shows, there are two different conceptions of the אהל מועד, "tent of meeting," in the Torah (*Numbers*, 386–87): the משכן, "tabernacle," in the middle of the camp; and the אהל מועד, "tent of meeting," outside the camp.

15 God comes to the tent of meeting "in a pillar of cloud," from which he communicates with the people from the entrance to the tent.

Explanation

Joshua was a member of the tribe of Ephraim (Josh 19:49–50), and thus was not a Levitical priest like Moses (Exod 2:1). Because Joshua was not a priest, he did not enter the tent of meeting (as Moses did in Exod 33:8), where YHWH himself "would speak to Moses face to face, as a man speaks to his neighbor" (Exod 33:11, author's translation). Joshua and Moses stood *before* the door of it at this time, and the pillar of cloud, which generally rested on top of the tent, appeared there at the entrance, and the glory of YHWH appeared in the cloud.

The repeated words of encouragement given to Joshua (Deut 31:7–8, 14–15, 23) stand as a lesson to all. If even the best of us need repeated encouragements and charges to keep steadfast in the work of God, how much more for the rest of us? At the same time, we do well to remember that God will never fail nor forsake those who place their trust in him. We may therefore be strong and of good courage, however numerous, malicious, and powerful our enemies may be. For in such circumstances, and with such a helper, we too will ultimately triumph over any opposition as long as we remain faithful to God and obedient to his commandments.

2. Israel's Future Apostasy and Its Consequences (31:16–18)

Bibliography

Balentine, S. E. "A Description of the Semantic Field of Hebrew Words for 'Hide.'" *VT* 30 (1980) 137–53. ———. *The Hidden God: The Hiding of the Face of God in the Old Testament.* Oxford Theological Monographs. New York; Oxford: Oxford UP, 1983. **Cazelles, H.** "La rupture de la *berît* selon les Prophètes." *JJS* 33 (1982) 133–44, esp. 137–39. **Friedman, R. E.** "The Biblical Expression *mastîr pānîm.*" *HAR* 1 (1977) 139–47. ———. *The Hidden Face of God.* San Francisco: HarperCollins, 1995. **Lloret, V. J. A.** "El Pecado en el Deuteronomio." *EstBib* 29 (1970) 267–85. **Soleh, M. Z.** "Understanding in the Bible." *BMik* 32 (1986/87) 285–87 (Heb.). **Thiel, W.** "*Hēfēr bĕrît*: Zum Bundbrechen im Alten Testament." *VT* 20 (1970) 214–29.

Translation and Prosodic Analysis

Israel's Future Apostasy and Its Consequences [(7:7):(4:4):(7:7)]

16 *And YHWH said\[a] to Moses /*	11	1
"Behold you are about to sleep / with your fathers //	14	2
And this people will rise / and they will play the harlot /	14	2
going after / the strange gods of [b]the land /	17	2_
That are in their midst / where[c] they are going[b] /	13	2
and they[d] will forsake me /	7	1
And they will break / my covenant /	11	2
that I have made / with them //	10	2_
17 *And my anger will be kindled against them IN THAT DAY /*	15	1
and I will forsake them /	5	1
and I will hide my face |[a] from them /	11	2_
[b]*And they shall be ready prey*[b] /	9	1
and there shall come upon them / many evils / and troubles //	21	3_
And they will say / IN THAT DAY /	10	2
'Is it not / because my god is not / in my midst /	16	3
that these evils / have come upon me?' //	18	2_
18 *But it is I myself /*	7	1
[a]*I will surely hide*[a] *my face*[b] */ IN THAT DAY /*	15	2
Because of all the evil\[c] that they[d] have done //	14	1
for they[d] have turned / to other / gods" //	17	3_

Notes

16.a. Reading *pašṭā'* followed by *zāqēp̄ qāṭôn* as conj.

16.b-b. Omitted in some LXX witnesses; one Heb. MS reads only הארץ, "the land" (omitting the next five words in the Hebrew text). The prosodic analysis supports MT.

16.c. SP and *Tg. Ps.-J.* read שם, "there." Prosodic analysis tends to support MT.

16.d. SP, LXX, and Tg. read 3 pl. It is possible to read MT without emendation as *lectio difficilior,* the more difficult reading to explain, by taking the sg. form in a collective sense to render the same meaning: "he [i.e., this people, which is translated 'they' in English] will forsake me."

17.a. Reading the sequence *'azlā* followed by *mahpāk* here as disj.

17.b-b. SP and Syr. read והיו לאכלה, "and they shall be for devouring" (i.e., "ready prey"). As a collective, the subject העם הזה, "this people," takes the sg. verbal forms in MT, but with a pl. meaning.

18.a-a. Some MSS of SP read אסתר הסתיר for MT הסתר אסתיר, "I will surely hide (my face)."

18.b. Some Heb. MSS, SP, LXX, Syr., and Tg. add מהם, "from them." Prosodic analysis supports MT.

18.c. Reading *ṭip̄ḥā'* as conj. because of misplaced *'atnāḥ*.

18.d. 3 pl. verbal forms are read in SP and LXX, but this does not require emendation of MT. See *Notes* 16.d. and 17.b-b. The singular grammatical forms are read in a collective sense.

Form/Structure/Setting

A second concentric structure (vv 16b–18b), which picks up where the previous one in vv 14a–16a left off, may be outlined as follows:

A	After your death, these people will turn to strange gods	31:16b
B	I will forsake them and hide my face from them	31:17a

X	There shall come upon them many evils and troubles	31:17b
B′	I will surely hide my face from them in that day	31:18a
A′	For they have turned to other gods	31:18b

This structure, which is found within a speech by YHWH (31:16–21), focuses on the predicted apostasy in times to come. The outer frame states the situation: the people will turn to other gods (vv 16b and 18b); whereas the inner frame spells out YHWH's reaction: "I will hide my face from them . . . in that day" (vv 17a and 18a). The center indicates the consequences as the people experience "many evils and troubles" (v 17b)

Comment

16 The idiom "to sleep with your fathers" means to die. As Milgrom demonstrates, the "idiom is found only in the Pentateuch—in connection with the deaths of Abraham (Gen. 25:8), Ishmael (Gen. 25:17), Isaac (Gen. 35:29), Jacob (Gen. 49:29, 33), Moses (Num. 27:13; 31:2; Deut. 32:50), and Aaron (Num. 20:24; Deut. 32:50). . . . Its meaning becomes clear in the stories of the patriarchs: It is the act that takes place after dying but before burial. Thus it can neither mean to die nor to be buried in the family tomb. Rather, it means 'be reunited with one's ancestors' and refers to the afterlife in Sheol. Hence, the opposite term *ve-nikhrat me-ʿammav,* 'be cut off from one's ancestors,' means to be denied any afterlife" (*Numbers* [1990] 169–70). The reference to "strange gods" anticipates the use of terminology in the Song of Moses (32:12), which is being introduced here. Elsewhere in Deuteronomy it is "other gods."

17–18 In response to Israel's unfaithfulness, YHWH declares: "I will forsake them, and I will hide my face from them." The same words are repeated in v 18, but this time with the emphatic and disjunctive use of the word ואנכי, "but I": "But as for me, I will surely hide my face in." The "face" of God is his attentive presence and favor, his blessing. Once again, the language anticipates what follows in the Song of Moses: "I will hide my face from them / I will see what their end will be" (32:20). The statement that "my god is not in my midst" is ambiguous in the Hebrew text. Tigay notes that references to God's presence or absence "in our midst" usually include God's name, and adds it when the word אלהי, "my God," is used ([1996] 294–95). In the present text the word אלהי appears without the proper name YHWH and thus should be translated "my god." Note that the prosodic analysis reveals a major break in the middle of v 17, with vv 17b–18 as a subunit of vv 16–18.

Explanation

God is warning Joshua to be prepared for difficult days ahead; for the coming apostasy is not a mere possibility. It is certain. Joshua chooses to remain faithful to the task God has assigned him, regardless.

It is important to note how subtle apostasy may be. The people of Israel did not forsake the worship of YHWH; they merely worshiped other gods as well. In our present circumstances these other "gods" appear in subtle forms. Anything that takes the place of God at the center of our lives is "another god." Thus we, like the people of Israel long ago, are guilty of violating the covenant, which clearly stipulates: "You shall have no other gods beside my presence" (5:7). Punishment for apostasy is certain. Thus it is necessary for God to correct those he loves best. In a sense, then, we should fear prosperity more than affliction, for suffering is often God's means of correction. Moreover, suffering is almost always an opportunity for growth on our part.

3–4. God Commands Moses to Write the Song, and God Commissions Joshua (31:19–23)

Bibliography

Casetti, P. "Funktion der Musik in der Bibel." *FZPhTh* 24 (1977) 366–89. **Christensen, D. L.** "The Aural Tradition Behind the Bible." In *Bible 101: God's Story in Human History.* N. Richland Hills, TX: BIBAL Press, 1996. 109–13. **Ewald, H.** "Das grosse Lied in Deuteronomium 32." In *Jahrbücher der biblischen Wissenschaft* 8 (1856) 63–65. **Friedman, R. E.** "From Egypt to Egypt: Dtr^1 and Dtr^2." In *FS F. M. Cross.* 1981. 178–80. **Lohfink, N.** "The Deuteronomic Picture of the Transfer of Authority from Moses to Joshua." In *Theology of the Pentateuch.* 1994. 243–47. **Tsumura, D. T.** "Hab 2,2 in the Light of the Old Testament." *ZAW* 94 (1982) 294–95. **Waterhouse, S. D.** "A Land Flowing with Milk and Honey." *AUSS* 1 (1963) 152–66. **Watts, J. W.** "'This Song': Conspicuous Poetry in Hebrew Prose." In *Verse in Ancient Near Eastern Prose.* Ed. J. C. de Moor and W. G. E. Watson. AOAT 42. Neukirchen-Vluyn: Neukirchener Verlag, 1993. 345–58.

Translation and Prosodic Analysis

The Writing of the Song as a Witness to Future Generations
[(4:5):(5:6):(5:5):(6:5)]

19 "*And now* / [a]write for yourselves / this song /	19	3
[b]and teach it to the children of Israel /	14	1
Put it[b] in their mouths //	8	1
in order that this song[b] / shall be my / witness /	18	3
against the children of Israel //	8	1
20 When I bring them[a] / to[b] the land /	16	2
that I promised to their fathers[c] /	12	1
flowing with milk / and honey /	11	2
And they will eat and be sated \\[d] and they will grow fat //	13	1
and they will turn / to other gods \\[e] and serve them /	23	2
and they will spurn me / and they will break / my covenant //	18	3
21 [a]And it will be / when there shall come upon them /	14	2
many evils / and troubles[a] / and it will bear witness /	18	3
This song will be [b]before them[b] / as a witness /	16	2
for / it will not be lost / in the mouth of their offspring //	14	3

For I know their intention / that they are devising / TODAY / [21 3
before I bring them / to the land[c] / [15 2
that I have promised"[d] // 7 1_
[22]And Moses wrote / this song / IN THAT DAY // [22 3
and he taught it / to the children of Israel // [15 2_

YHWH Commissions Joshua to Succeed Moses [5:4]

[23]And he commanded / Joshua son of Nun / [13 2
and he said / "Be strong and be courageous / for it is *you* / [15 3_
You shall bring\[a] *the children of Israel* / 13 1
into the land\[b] [c]*that I have promised to them* // [15 1
and as for me / I will be with you"[c] // [12 2_

Notes

19.a. Syr. reads *ktwb lhwn* (= כתב להם, "he wrote for them"). The *Numeruswechsel* here marks the initial boundary of the subunit (vv 19–22).

19.b-b. Omitted in Syr. ([London Polyglot, 1654). Prosodic analysis supports MT.

20.a. The *Sebir* (Aram. notes in Heb. MSS), Syr., and Tg. read 3 pl. In MT YHWH is the speaker (1 sg.).

20.b. LXX adds τὴν ἀγαθήν, "the good" (= הטובה).

20.c. The *Sebir,* LXX[B], and Lucianic recension of LXX add לתת להם, "to give to them." The prosodic analysis supports MT.

20.d. Reading *ṭiphā'* as conj. because of misplaced *'atnāḥ.*

20.e. Reading *pašṭā'* followed immediately by *zāqēp qāṭôn* as conj.

21.a-a. Omitted in LXX; Origen inserts with asterisk. Prosodic analysis supports MT.

21.b-b. Omitted in two Heb. MSS and Vg.; LXX reads κατὰ πρόσωπον (αὐτοῦ), "against (him)," for MT לפניו, "before him." Prosodic analysis supports MT.

21.c. SP reads האדמה, "the land," for הארץ, "the land." Prosodic analysis supports MT.

21.d. SP adds לאבתיו, "to his fathers"; one Heb. MS, LXX, and Syr. add לאבתם, "to their fathers"; cf. also v 20 above, which is parallel in terms of prosodic structure.

23.a. Reading *pašṭā'* followed immediately by *zāqēp qāṭôn* as conj.

23.b. Reading *ṭiphā'* as conj. because of misplaced *'atnāḥ.*

23.c-c. Omitted in one Heb. MS. LXX reads 3 sg. report rather than 1 sg. speech by YHWH. Prosodic analysis supports MT.

Form/Structure/Setting

God's commandment to "write for yourselves this song" (v 19) is followed by the statement that "Moses wrote this song in that day, and he taught it to the children of Israel" (v 22). The verses within this framework spell out what will happen in times to come when the people "will grow fat, and they will turn to other gods and serve them" (v 20). When the consequent "evils and troubles" of the covenant curses come upon them, the words of this song will bear witness against them that God knew "their intention" in advance. At that point the subject shifts abruptly to that of YHWH commissioning Joshua in his new office as leader in Israel and encouraging him in that position with the promise, "I will be with you" (v 23).

The section on the writing of the Song of Moses in vv 19–22 may be outlined in concentric fashion:

A	Moses is commanded to write the song and to teach it	31:19a
B	The song is to be a witness against the people of Israel	31:19b
X	In the future Israel will break the covenant with YHWH	31:20
B′	The song will be a witness to the people of Israel	31:21
A′	Moses writes the song and teaches it to the people	31:22

The opening and closing verses in this unit are virtually identical in content with Moses' receiving of the command to write the song and teach it to the people (v 19), and the statement that he in fact did so (v 22). The function of the Song of Moses is to call the people to faithfulness in keeping their covenant with YHWH, the terms of which they will violate in times to come.

From a prosodic perspective, the brief note in which YHWH commissions Joshua as leader in Israel (v 23) is appended to the unit on writing the song in vv 19–22 as an afterthought. Deut 31:19–23 scans (4:5):(5:6):(5:5):(6:5):(4:5) in syntactic accentual stress units. The boundaries of this larger unit are marked with the *Numeruswechsel.* Though v 23 is also part of a more elaborate nesting of parallel elements, as suggested in the nine-part concentric structure presented above in the introduction to Deut 31 as a whole, prosodic analysis suggests a seven-part menorah pattern as the primary structure here:

A	Moses announces his departure and Joshua as his successor	31:1–8
B	The writing and recitation of the Torah at the Feast of Booths	31:9–12
C	Future generations shall learn to fear YHWH	31:13
X	Theophany in the tent of meeting with Moses and Joshua	31:14–15
C′	Israel's future apostasy and its consequences	31:16–18
B′	The writing of the song as a witness	31:19–22
A′	God commissions Joshua as Moses' successor	31:23

The framework here (A, X, A′) focuses on the transfer of leadership from Moses to Joshua (vv 1–8, 14–15, and 23). The second frame (B, B′) moves from the writing and deposition of the Torah with the Levites for presentation every seventh year in the Festival of Booths (vv 9–12) to the writing and teaching of the Song of Moses as a witness to future generations (vv 19–22). The innermost frame (C, C′) raises the issue of future generations who are called to "fear" YHWH (v 13), but who will turn to idols instead (vv 16–18). The Song of Moses functions as a witness against them on the consequences of their apostasy.

The data from Labuschagne on the numerical composition of 31:19–23 may be summarized as follows:

Words:	before *ʾatnāḥ*		after *ʾatnāḥ*		
31:19–23	68 (= 4 × 17)	+	38	=	106
31:16–23	102 (= 6 × 17)	+	75	=	177
31:16–21	76	+	68 (= 4 × 17)	=	144 (= 12 × 12)
31:19–20	25	+	17	=	42
31:21	17	+	14	=	31
31:22–23	26	+	7	=	33
31:1–30	322 (= 14 × 23)	+	230 (= 10 × 23)	=	552 (= 24 × 23)
31:1–34:12	955	+	728 (= 28 × 26)	=	1,683 (= 99 × 17)

In 31:19–23 there are 68 (= 4 × 17) words before *'atnāḥ.* The divine-name number 17 seems to be the primary building block within this passage, appearing at least four times. The divine-name number 26 appears as well in the concluding subsection 31:22–23. At the same time, it is important to remember that 31:19–23 is part of a larger whole in which the number 23 has a dominant role. The number 23 is associated with the word כבוד, "glory"; hence once again we have evidence that the scribes of ancient Israel carried out this laborious task of numerical composition to the glory of YHWH.

Comment

19 Though the phrase "write for yourselves" may refer to both Moses and Joshua (see 32:44), the abrupt change from second plural to second singular verbal forms is best explained as the means of marking the boundary of a new prosodic unit by means of the *Numeruswechsel.* The song is written down in order to preserve it for future generations; but it is taught orally. Tigay draws attention to an instructive parallel situation in the singing and oral recitation of written Akkadian poems (see J. Tigay, *The Evolution of the Gilgamesh Epic* [Philadelphia: Univ. of Pennsylvania Press, 1982] 107 n. 72). The idiom "put in the mouth" means "teach by heart" in Akkadian and Sumerian as well as in Hebrew, as Tigay notes (see A. Hurowitz, *Inu Anum sirum: Literary Structures in the Non-Juridical Sections of the Code of Hammurabi* [Philadelphia: University Museum, 1994] 27–29). The Song of Moses is intended to be a "witness against the children of Israel" in the sense that it states in advance God's kindness and Israel's betrayal (see 32:1–18).

20 The description of the land of Israel as "flowing with milk and honey" appears frequently in the Bible as a proverbial expression of the fertility of the land (6:3; 11:9; 26:9, 15; 27:3; 31:20; Exod 20:5–6; 34:6–7; Num 14:18; Jer 32:18). "They will eat and be sated, . . . and they will turn to other gods," believing them to be the source of their prosperity. Once again the language anticipates that of the Song of Moses to follow in 32:13–18.

21–22 "This song will be before them as a witness . . . it will not be lost." The words of the song will be "in the mouth of their offspring" and testify to their guilt (cf. 32:15–18). "Moses wrote this song, . . . and he taught it to the children of Israel." This verse forms an inclusion with both v 19 and vv 28–30 at the end of this chapter.

23 God speaks directly to Joshua for the first time: "Be strong and be courageous, for . . . you shall bring the children of Israel into the land." These words form an inclusion with v 8, where Moses used them to promise Joshua that YHWH would be with him. YHWH himself now confirms that promise.

Explanation

The Song of Moses, which follows in 32:1–43, is here delivered to Moses and Joshua, who are instructed to write it down and teach it to the people of Israel. It is intended as a witness to testify beforehand that God has treated the people of Israel with justice and mercy, but they betrayed him. The hope is that when disaster comes the song will prevent the people from thinking it is accidental, so they may see that it is caused by their own behavior. In short, the intention of the song is to elicit true repentance.

The written word attests that YHWH predicted the events, thus proving that he alone controls the events of time and history. The words of a song are not easily forgotten. Time and again I have been able to recall the words of songs I sang as a child. Moses is instructed to put the words "in their mouths in order that this song shall be [God's] witness against the children of Israel" (v 19). The words of the song will be continually "before them as a witness; for it will not be lost in the mouth of their offspring" (v 21). Putting a text to music is the most effective means of writing that text indelibly in our hearts and minds.

C. Moses' Provisions regarding the Torah and the Song (31:24–30)

Bibliography

Aharoni, Y. "Three Hebrew Ostraca from Arad." *BASOR* 197 (1970) 16–18. **Bruston, C.** "Le Deutéronome primitif et ce qu'il suppose." *RTQR* 5 (1896) 247–57, esp. 249–50. **Buchanan, G. W.** "Eschatology and the 'End of Days.'" *JNES* 20 (1961) 188–93, esp. 189–90. **Carroll, R. P.** "Rebellion and Dissent in Ancient Israelite Society." *ZAW* 89 (1977) 176–204, esp. 181. **Černý, J.** *Paper and Books in Ancient Egypt.* London: H. K. Lewis, 1952. 30. **Christensen, D. L.** "Num 21:14–15 and the Book of the Wars of Yahweh." *CBQ* 36 (1974) 359–60. **Fishbane, M.** "Varia Deuteronomica." *ZAW* 84 (1972) 349–52. **Foresti, F.** "Characteristic Literary Expressions in the Arad Inscriptions Compared with the Language of the Hebrew Bible." *EphC* 32 (1981) 327–41, esp. 336–37. **Friedman, R. E.** "From Egypt to Egypt: Dtr^1 and Dtr^2." In *FS F. M. Cross.* 1981. 173, 178–80. **Haran, M.** "Scribal Workmanship in Biblical Times." *Tarbiz* 50 (1980–81) 71–72 (Heb.). **Herrmann, J.** "Ägyptische Analogien zum Fund des Deuteronomium." *ZAW* 28 (1908) 291–302. **Kenyon, F. G.** *Books and Readers in Ancient Greece and Rome.* Oxford: Clarendon, 1932. 59–60, 129–30. **Kritzinger, J. D. W.** *Qehal Jahwe, Wat dit is en wiedaaraan mag behoort.* Kampen: Kok, 1957. **Lichtheim, M.** *Ancient Egyptian Literature.* 3 vols. Berkeley: Univ. of California Press, 1973–80. 2:129–31. **Lohfink, N.** "Die Bundesurkunde des Königs Josias (Eine Frage an die Deuteronomiumsforschung)." In *Studien zum Deuteronomium I.* 1990. 99–165, esp. 133–34 n. 64. **Malamat, A.** "Doctrines of Causality in Hittite and Biblical Historiography: A Parallel." *VT* 5 (1955) 1–12. **Moriya, A.** "The Functions of the Gods in the Aramaic Inscriptions of Sefire." *Oriento* 25.2 (1982) 38–54 (Japanese). **Scott, J. M.** "A New Approach to Habakkuk ii 4–5a." *VT* 35 (1985) 330–40. **Stec, D. M.** "The Use of *hēn* in Conditional Sentences." *VT* 37 (1987) 478–86. **Williams, R. J.** "Scribal Training in Ancient Egypt." *JAOS* 92 (1972) 216.

Translation and Prosodic Analysis

Moses Gives the Torah to the Priests [(7:8):(8:7)]

24 *And it was / when Moses finished /* 11 2
writing / [a]the words of this Torah[b] / on a scroll // 19 3
to / their completion // 4 2_

25 *That Moses commanded / the Levites /* 13 2
bearing / the ark of the covenant of YHWH / saying // 18 3
26 *"Take[a] / this[b] / scroll of the Torah[c] /* 17 3_
And put it / 7 1
beside / the ark of the covenant of YHWH / your God // 17 3
And it shall be there *with you / as a witness //* 11 2
27 *that I indeed know well / your rebellion /* 17 2_
And your stiffness \[a] of neck // 10 1
since even while I am yet alive with you / TODAY / 16 2
You have been rebelling / against YHWH[b] / 11 2
and how much more then / after my death // 12 2_

Moses Gathers the Leaders to Hear the Song [(6:6):(6:6)]

28 Gather to me / all the elders[a] of your tribes / 17 2
and your officers[b] // 7 1
and I will speak in their ears / [c]these / words / 24 3_
And let me call as witness against them / heaven / and earth // 22 3
29 for I know / that after my death / 15 2
indeed you will surely act corruptly / 10 1_
And you will turn from the way / that I commanded \[a] you // 17 2
and the evil [b]will befall[b] you / IN THE LATTER DAYS / 24 2
For you will do what is evil / 10 1
in the eyes of YHWH[c] / 8 1_
to provoke him \[d] by the works of your hands" // 15 1
30 And Moses spoke / in the ears \[a] of all the assembly of Israel / 20 2
the words of this \[b] song // to / their completion // פ 16 3_

Notes

24.a. A few Heb. MSS and LXX[-MS] add כל, "all." Adding a word here would disturb the carefully crafted numerical composition of 31:24–30 and of Deut 31 (Reading 9) taken as a whole.
24.b. Two Heb. MSS read השירה, "the song," for MT התורה, "the Torah."
26.a. SP and LXX read pl.
26.b. Vg. omits הזה, "this."
26.c. The word התורה, "the Torah," is omitted in Vg. Prosodic analysis supports MT.
27.a. Reading *ṭipḥāʾ* as conj. because of misplaced *ʾatnāḥ*.
27.b. LXX reads τὸν θεόν, "God."
28.a. Two Heb. MSS omit זקני, "elders"; a few Heb. MSS and LXX[-Bmin] read ראשי, "heads of"; LXX[-Bmin] adds καὶ τοὺς πρεσβυτέρους ὑμῶν, "and your [pl.] elders" (= וזקניכם).
28.b. LXX[-O] reads καὶ τοὺς κριτὰς ὑμῶν, "and your judges" (= ושפטיכם).
28.c. Some Heb. MSS, LXX, and *Tg. Ps.-J.* add כל, "all." See *Note* 24.a.
29.a. Reading *ṭipḥāʾ* as conj. because of misplaced *ʾatnāḥ*.
29.b-b. SP reads וקרתה for MT וקראת, "will befall," with no change in meaning; the two Heb. roots הרה and קרא can be used interchangeably.
29.c. LXX[Lmin] add τοῦ θεοῦ (ὑμῶν or ἡμῶν), "('your' or 'our') God" (= אלהיכם or אלהינו).
29.d. Reading *ṭipḥāʾ* as conj. because of misplaced *sillûq*.
30.a. Reading *pašṭāʾ* followed by *zāqēp qāṭôn* as conj.
30.b. Reading *ṭipḥāʾ* as conj. because of misplaced *ʾatnāḥ*.

Form/Structure/Setting

When Deut 31 is divided into two equal parts, the resulting structure may be outlined in two parallel prosodic units:

A	Moses announces his departure and replacement by Joshua	31:1–6
B	Moses commissions Joshua as his successor	31:7–8
X	The writing and reading of the Torah at the Feast of Booths	31:9–12
B′	Future generations shall learn to fear YHWH	31:13
A′	Theophany in the tent of meeting with Moses and Joshua	31:14–15

A	Israel's future apostasy and its consequences	31:16–18
B	Moses commanded to teach the song as a witness in Israel	31:19
X	Israel's future apostasy and the Song of Moses as witness	31:20–22
B′	Joshua commanded to be Moses' successor	31:23
A′	The Torah and the song are given as witnesses	31:24–30

In this reading the two foci of interest are the Torah (vv 9–12) and the Song of Moses (vv 20–22), both of which are written to be witnesses for the people of Israel to encourage them in the matter of covenant loyalty.

The boundaries of 31:24–30 are marked by inclusion with the words עד תמם, "to their completion," and the *pĕtûḥāʾ* layout marker at the end of v 30. The *Numeruswechsel* appears at the beginning and the end of v 26 as an indication of boundaries in terms of internal structure in 31:24–27, as the reader moves from third-person report about Moses (vv 24–25) to first-person command on the lips of Moses (v 26ab), and then to first-person report where Moses predicts future apostasy after his death (vv 26c–27). The *Numeruswechsel* appears again in v 27 to signal the division between the two major parts from a prosodic point of view: vv 24–27 and 28–30.

Verse 30 not only functions as the immediate introduction to the Song of Moses in 32:1–43 but also forms an inclusion with 32:44 in which Moses and Joshua are said to have spoken "all the words of this song in the ears of the people." The two verses form a chiastic framework around the Song of Moses:

A	Moses spoke *in the ears of all the assembly* of Israel	31:30a
B	*the words of this song* to their completion	31:30b
X	The Song of Moses	32:1–43
B′	Moses spoke all *the words of this song*	32:44a
A′	*in the ears of the people*, he and Joshua son of Nun	32:44b

The peculiar function of 31:30 as part of the framework around the Song of Moses in 32:1–43 and the conclusion to 31:24–30 is evident in the prosodic analysis in terms of mora count that connects v 30 closely with the last three words in the Hebrew text of v 29. The place of v 30 within the structure of vv 24–30 is shown in the following outline:

A	Report: Moses finished writing the words of the Torah	31:24–25
B	Command: Put this scroll beside the ark for a witness	31:26ab
X	"You have rebelled; how much more so after my death?"	31:26c–27
B′	Command: Assemble the leaders to hear "these words"	31:28–29
A′	Report: Moses spoke the words of the song to completion	31:30

The outer frame in this structure consists of narrative speech in the third person that reports what Moses did: he "finished writing the words of this Torah on a scroll" (v 24), and he "spoke . . . the words of this song" to all the people (v 30). Within this framework, we have a speech by Moses in the first person (vv 26–29) about the role of the Torah and the Song of Moses in the future, when the terms of the covenant are broken. The scroll of Deuteronomy is to be placed beside the ark of the covenant for a witness to the people. The content of that scroll is to be taught to the people by public recitation on a regular basis, at the Festival of Booths in the central sanctuary every seven years (see vv 10–13).

The concluding section in this outline (vv 24–30), which is in two parts from a prosodic point of view (vv 24–27 and 28–30), also functions as the introduction to the Song of Moses (Deut 32). Once again, the resultant structure is in a menorah pattern:

A	Moses gives the Torah to the Levitical priests	31:24–27
B	Moses gathers the leaders to hear the song	31:28–30
C	Recital of YHWH's saving deeds in days of old	32:1–14
X	Israel's future rebellion and YHWH's indignation	32:15–25
C′	YHWH will restore Israel and punish her enemies	32:26–43
B′	Moses spoke all the words of this song to the people	32:44–45
A′	Summary command to observe all the words of the Torah	32:46–47

The two outer frames in this structure focus on the Torah (31:24–27 and 32:46–47) and the Song of Moses (31:28–30 and 32:44–45), respectively, with the Song of Moses itself as a three-part center (32:1–14, 15–25, and 26–43). More on this below in the next section of this commentary.

In the data assembled by Labuschagne on the numerical composition of 31:24–30, the only significant number on the use of the divine-name numbers is the total number of words in this passage, which is 78 (= 3 × 26). At the same time, the number of words in 31:14–30 is such as to produce several other significant figures: 322 (= 14 × 23) words before *'atnāḥ* and 230 (= 10 × 23) words after *'atnāḥ* in Deut 31 (Reading 9); and 728 (= 28 × 26) words after *'atnāḥ* in Deut 31–34 (Readings 10 and 11). Moreover, there is a total of 552 (= 14 × 23) words in Deut 31 (Reading 9) and a total of 1683 (= 99 × 17) words in Deut 31–34 (Readings 10 and 11). In short, the scribes of ancient Israel completed their laborious task in the numerical composition of Deuteronomy in a most impressive manner—as they wove the two divine-name numbers 17 and 26, along with the numbers 23 and 32 (for כבוד, "glory"), into the fabric of the Hebrew text, at all levels, to the glory of YHWH.

Comment

24 The phrase "to their completion" (עד תמם) functions as an envelope around this section (vv 24–30). At the beginning "Moses finished writing the words of this Torah on a scroll to their completion"; and at the end "Moses spoke . . . the words of this song to their completion." The Torah and the Song of Moses are thus parallel exemplars of God's revelation to the people of ancient Israel. The term ספר, translated "scroll" here, refers to any kind of written document, or inscription, or perhaps even to a well-known story or tradition that was not actually written down (cf. ספר מלחמות יהוה, the "Book of the Wars of YHWH," in Num 21:14; see Christensen, *CBQ* 36 [1974] 359–60). The material on which Moses wrote "the words of this Torah" was almost certainly a leather scroll.

25–26 The "scroll of the Torah" was to be placed "beside the ark of the covenant of YHWH," which contained the two tablets of stone on which the Ten Commandments were written (4:13; 10:1–5). As Tigay puts it, "Keeping the Teaching next to the Ark of the Covenant indicates that it embodies the principles of the Covenant and is as binding as the Decalogue itself because it comes from the same Divine source" ([1996] 297).

27 The translation "I indeed know well your rebellion" attempts to render the meaning of the emphatic personal pronoun אנכי, "I." No one is in a better position to know of their "rebellion," for Moses experienced their "stiffness of neck" in times past. The construction "even while I am alive with you today . . . how much more, then," is a biblical formula for what Tigay calls "an *a fortiori* proposition": "Since Moses, despite his authority, could not restrain Israel while alive, the people are even more likely to rebel after his death" ([1996] 297).

28–30 In light of the carefully balanced concentric design of Deut 31 as a whole, in which the Torah and the song are set against each other in parallel structures, it seems best to interpret "these words" as referring to the Torah (cf. 1:1) in the form of an inclusion with the concluding reference to "the words of this song." Though the expression "elders of your tribes" does not occur elsewhere, it does appear to be a preferable reading to the longer text of the LXX and 4QDeut^{b}: "the heads of your tribes, your elders, judges, and officials." From a text-critical point of view, it is easier to explain the additions than it is the shorter text of MT. Moreover, the additional words disturb the patterns of the numerical composition of the text. The elders and the officers are summoned first to hear the words of the Torah and the song. They would then assist in the instruction of "all the assembly of Israel." Moses summons "heaven and earth" as another "witness against them," in keeping with the parallel texts of 4:26 and 30:19. Such references to summoning "heaven and earth" as witnesses against the people are characteristic of covenant treaty texts in the ancient Near East. The phrase translated "in the latter days" is part of the system of temporal terms that play a rhetorical function in the larger structure of Deuteronomy as a whole. The phrase "all the assembly of Israel" probably functions as an inclusion with the phrase "all Israel" (כל ישראל) of 1:1 and 34:12, which forms an inclusion around Deuteronomy as a whole.

Explanation

Moses wrote "the words of this Torah on a scroll to their completion" and gave the scroll to the Levites, who were instructed to place it "beside the ark of the covenant of YHWH your God . . . as a witness" (vv 24–26), thus inaugurating the tradition of granting a book final religious authority.

The Torah was subsequently augmented with the addition of the Former Prophets (Joshua, Judges, 1–2 Samuel, and 1–2 Kings) and the Latter Prophets (Isaiah, Jeremiah, Ezekiel, and the Scroll of the Twelve [Minor Prophets]) to form "the Law and the Prophets" as canonical Scripture. Meanwhile, a fourth segment of the canon took shape in what is called the Writings, referred to in the

"Prologue" to Sirach (Ecclesiasticus) as "the others that followed [the Law and the Prophets]." These books include: Psalms, Proverbs, Job, five Festal Scrolls (Ruth, Song of Songs, Ecclesiastes, Lamentations, and Esther), Daniel, and the so-called Work of the Chronicler (Ezra, Nehemiah, and 1–2 Chronicles). Prior to the writings of Jerome (ca. 400 C.E.), this canon is almost always referred to as a twenty-two-book body of sacred literature. Josephus describes this canon as follows (*Ag. Ap.* 1.8 §§38–40):

> We have not a countless number of books, discordant and arrayed against each other; but only two and twenty, . . . and of these five belong to Moses, which contain both the laws and the history of the generations of men until his death. . . . From the death of Moses, moreover, until the reign of Artaxerxes king of the Persians after Xerxes, the prophets who followed Moses have described the things which were done during the age of each one respectively, in thirteen books. The remaining four contain hymns to God, and rules of life for men.

The four "hagiographa" to which Josephus refers are probably Psalms, Proverbs, Job, and the five Festal Scrolls taken together as a single canonical category, much like the Book of the Twelve (Minor Prophets) in the Latter Prophets (see D. L. Christensen, "Josephus and the Twenty-Two-Book Canon of Sacred Scripture," *JETS* 29 [1986] 37–46). All of these works were written on leather scrolls, like the tradition of the scroll of Deuteronomy of 31:26, which is described as "this scroll of the Torah."

The twenty-seven books of the NT were initially conceived in the early Christian church as a fifth segment of the *Tanakh* (Torah + Prophets + Writings = the Hebrew Bible). Since the purpose of this fifth segment of the canon of sacred Scripture was primarily didactic and apologetic in nature, it soon became evident that the form of the scroll was no longer adequate. Scrolls are ideal for reading the text in public worship in a lectionary cycle that moves from the beginning to the end of that text. Scrolls are much too ponderous to use if the reader wants to locate specific texts to prove a point in an apologetic argument. Thus scrolls were replaced in early Christianity with the newly invented concept of a codex, in which parchment leaves written on both sides were sewn together between two covers to form the first "books" in the modern sense of that word. It is no coincidence that every single fragment of the NT recovered from antiquity is from a codex. Moreover, it was the Christians who first assembled the *Tanakh* itself in the form of a codex, which was bound together with the NT in the great uncial codices of the third and fourth centuries C.E. The entire canonical process that ultimately produced the Bible as we now have it began with the placing of the "scroll of the Torah" (i.e., the "book" of Deuteronomy) "beside the ark of the covenant of YHWH" in 31:26. For a detailed discussion of the canonical process, see D. L. Christensen, *The Completed Tanakh: The Unity of the Bible within the Canonical Process*, 2nd ed. (Columbus, GA: TEC Publications, 2001).

Reading 10: The Song of Moses within Its Narrative Framework (32:1–52)

Bibliography

Albright, W. F. "Some Remarks on the Song of Moses in Deuteronomy 32." *VT* 9 (1959) 339–46. **Alday Carrillo, S.** "El Cántico de Moisés (Dt 32)." *EstBib* 26 (1967) 143–85, 227–48, 327–52, 383–93. ———. "Genero literario de Cántico de Moisés (Dt 32)." *EstBib* 26 (1967) 69–75. **Basser, H.** *Midrash Interpretation of the Song of Moses.* American University Studies, Series VII, Theology and Religion, 2. New York; Frankfurt; Bern: Peter Lang, 1984. ———. "Sifre Deuteronomy to HA'AZINU: Rabbinic Interpretations of Deuteronomy 32, Especially the Song of Moses." Ph.D. diss., Toronto, 1983. **Baumann, E.** "Das Lied des Moses (Dt 32,1–43) auf seine Gedankliche Geschlossenheit Untersucht." *VT* 6 (1956) 414–24. **Bodenheimer, L.** *Das Lied Mosis: Eine wissenschaftliche Vergleichung der auf diesen Pentateuch-Abschnitt in der Walton'schen Polyglotte enthaltenen Uebertragunen mit Bezugnahme auf einige neuere Übersetzungen.* Crefeld: Selbstverlag, 1856. **Boston, A. J. R.** "The Song of Moses: Deuteronomy 32:1–43." Diss., Union Seminary, 1966. DA 28 (1967–68) 284–A. ———. "The Wisdom Influence upon the Song of Moses." *JBL* 87 (1968) 198–202. **Budde, K.** *Das Lied Moses Deut. 32 erläutert und übersetzt.* Tübingen: Mohr, 1920. **Cassuto, U.** "The Prophet Hosea and the Books of the Pentateuch." In *Biblical and Oriental Studies.* 2 vols. Jerusalem: Magnes, 1973–75. 1:79–100, esp. 95–100. ———. "The Song of Moses (Deuteronomy Chapter xxxii 1–43)." In *Biblical and Oriental Studies.* 2 vols. Jerusalem: Magnes, 1973–75. 1:41–46. **Cecchetti, P. I.** "'Audite Caeli': Il Cantico di Mose' nel Deuteronomio e il suo Uso Liturgico." *Lat* 33 (1967) 161–69. **Duhaime, J. L.** "El Elogio de los Padres de Ben Sira y el Cántico de Moisés." *EstBib* 35 (1976) 223–28. **Eichhorn, D.** *Gott als Fels, Burg und Zuflucht: Eine Untersuchung zum Gebet des Mittlers in den Psalmen.* Frankfurt: Lang, 1972. **Eissfeldt, O.** *Das Lied Moses Deuteronomiun 32. 1–43 und das Lehrgedicht Asaphs Psalm 78 samt einer Analyse der Umgebung des Mose-Leides.* Berichte über die Verhandlungen der sächsischen Akademie der Wissenschaften zu Leipzig 104.5. Berlin: Akademie-Verlag, 1958. **Ewald, H.** "Das grosse Lied in Deuteronomium 32." *Jahrbücher der biblischen Wissenschaft* 8 (1856) 41–65. **Fisch, H.** "The Song of Moses: Pastoral in Reverse." In *Poetry with a Purpose: Biblical Poetics and Interpretation.* Indiana Studies in Biblical Literature. Bloomington; Indianapolis: Indiana UP, 1988. 55–79. **Frank, M.** "The Song of Moses Dt XXXII." *Tarbiz* 18 (1946/47) 129–38 (Heb.). **Freedman, D. N.** "Divine Names and Titles in Early Hebrew Poetry." In *FS G. E. Wright.* 1976. 55–107. **Gunkel, H.** "Das Lied des Moses." *RGG.* 1913. 4:534–35. **Harris, J. R.** "Irenaeus and the Song of Moses." *ExpTim* 37 (1925) 333–34. **Harvey, J.** *Le Plaidoyer prophétique contre Israël après la rupture de l'alliance: Etude d'une formule littéraire de l'Ancien Testament.* Paris; Montreal: Desclée de Brouwer, 1967. ———. "Le 'Rib-Pattern,' requisitoire prophétique sur la rupture de l'Alliance." *Bib* 43 (1962) 172–96. **Hauri, R.** "Das Moseslied Dt 32: Ein Beitrag zur israelitischen Literatur- und Religionsgeschichte." Diss., Zurich, 1917. **Henschke, E.** "Konjekturen zu Dt 32." *ZAW* 52 (1934) 279–82. **Hidal, S.** "Some Reflections on Deuteronomy 32." *ASTI* 11 (1977/78) 15–21. **Junker, H.** "Die Entstehungszeit des Ps 78 und des Deuteronomiums." *Bib* 34 (1953) 487–500. **Kamphausen, A. H. H.** *Das Lied Moses: Dt 32,1–43.* Leipzig: Brockhaus, 1862. **Klostermann, A.** "Das Lied Moses." *TSK* 44 (1871) 249–94; 45 (1872) 230–80, 450–502. **Knowles, M.** "'The Rock, His Work Is Perfect': Unusual Imagery for God in Deuteronomy xxxii." *VT* 39 (1989) 307–22. **Kölichen, J.-C. von.** "Die Zitate aus dem Moselied Deut. 32 im Römerbrief des Paulus." *ThVers* 5 (1975) 53–70. **Levy, A. J.** *The Song of Moses: Deuteronomy 32.* Scientific Series of "Oriens—The Oriental Review." Baltimore, 1931. **Linder, J.**

"Das Lied des Moses Dt 32." *ZKT* 49 (1924) 374–406. **Lundbom, J. R.** "The Lawbook of the Josianic Reform." *CBQ* 38 (1976) 293–302. **Luyten, J.** "Primeval and Eschatological Overtones in the Song of Moses (Dt 32,1–43)." In *Das Deuteronomium.* Ed. N. Lohfink. 1985. 341–47. **Mayer, L.** "Le Cantique de Moise: Deutéronome XXXII." *Revue des études juives* 36 (1898) 47–52. **Mendenhall, G. E.** "Samuel's 'Broken *Rîb*': Deuteronomy 32." In *FS J. L. McKenzie.* 1975. 63–74. **Moran, W. L.** "Some Remarks on the Song of Moses." *Bib* 43 (1962) 317–27. **Nielsen, E.** *Yahweh as Prosecutor and Judge: An Investigation of the Prophetic Lawsuit (Rîb) Pattern.* JSOTSup 9. Sheffield: Univ. of Sheffield P, 1978. **O'Connor, M.** *Hebrew Verse Structure.* Winona Lake, IN: Eisenbrauns, 1980. 194–207. **Propp, W.** *Water in the Wilderness: A Biblical Motif and Its Mythological Background.* HSM 40. Atlanta: Scholars Press, 1987. 21–28. **Rafel, D.** "Das Moseslied." *BMik* 12 (1966–67) 3–26; 13 (1967–68) 14–23 (Heb.). **Ramsey, G. W.** "Speech-Forms in Hebrew Law and Prophetic Oracles." *JBL* 96 (1977) 45–58. **Reichert, A.** "The Song of Moses and the Quest for Early Deuteronomic Psalmody." In *Proceedings of the Ninth World Congress of Jewish Studies.* Jerusalem: Magnes, 1986. 53–60. **Riessler, P.** "Das Moseslied und der Mosessegen." *BZ* 11 (1913) 119–28. **Rignell, L. G.** "Isaiah Chapter I: Some Exegetical Remarks with Special Reference to the Relationship between the Text and the Book of Deuteronomy." *ST* 11 (1957) 140–58. **Robertson, D. A.** *Linguistic Evidence in Dating Early Hebrew Poetry.* SBLDS 3. Missoula, MT: SBL, 1972. 154–55, 230–31. **Rohling, A.** *Das Abschiedslied des Moses: Inaugural-Dissertation.* Jena: W. Ratz, 1867. **Sack, K. H.** *Die Lieder in den historischen Büchern des Alten neu übersetzt und erläutert.* Barmen: W. Langewiesche's Verlagshandlung, 1864. 65–101. **Schildenberger, J.** "Ps 78 (77) und die Pentateuchquellen." In *FS H. Junker.* 1961. 231–56. **Schlögl, N.** "Canticum Mosis Dt 32." *BZ* 2 (1904) 1–14. **Segal, M. H.** "The Poem *ha'ăzînû* Dtn 32." *BMik* 2/1 (1957) 56–63 (Heb.). **Segert, S.** "Rendering of Parallelistic Structures in the Targum Neofiti: The Song of Moses (Deuteronomy 32:1–43)." In *Salvacion en la Palabra. Targum—Derash—Berith: En memoria del profesor Alejandro Díez Macho.* Ed. M. L. Domingo. Madrid: Cristiandad, 1986. 515–32. **Sellin, E.** "Wann wurde das Moselied Dt 32 gedichtet?" *ZAW* 43 (1925) 161–73. **Sheppard, G. T.** *Wisdom as a Hermeneutical Construct: A Study in the Sapientializing of the Old Testament.* BZAW 151. Berlin: de Gruyter, 1980. 62–71. **Shields, B. J.** "A Song to Remember: The Setting, Structure and Genre of Dt 32 in Recent Research." *Bulletin of the Catholic Research Institute (of the) China Academy, T'aipei, T'aiwan* 3 (1971) 1–26. **Skehan, P. W.** "The Structure of the Song of Moses in Deuteronomy (Dt 32:1–43)." *CBQ* 13 (1951) 153–63. **Stade, B.** "Aus welcher Zeit stammt das Lied Dt 32?" *ZAW* 5 (1885) 297–300. **Tigay, J. H.** "Excursus 30: The Poem Ha'azinu." In *Deuteronomy.* 1996. 508–13. **Tov, E.** "Special Layouts of Poetical Units in the Texts from the Judean Desert." In *Give Ear to My Words: Psalms and Other Poetry in and around the Hebrew Bible.* Ed. J. Dyk. Amsterdam: Societas Hebraica, 1996. 115–28. **Trapp, T.** "Dispute and Display: The Song of Moses in Deuteronomy 32,1–43." Diss., Heidelberg, 1980. **Volck, W.** *Mosis Canticum Cygneum (Dt XXXII) denuo Illustratum.* Erlangen: Deichert, 1861. **Volkwein, B.** "Textkritische Untersuchungen zu Dtn 32,1–43." Diss., Pontifical Biblical Institute, Rome, 1973. **Westhuizen, P. van der.** "Literary Device in Exodus 15:1–18 and Deut 32:1–43 as a Criterion for Determining Their Literary Standards." *OTWSA* 17/18 (1974/75) 57–73. **Wright, G. E.** "The Lawsuit of God: A Form-Critical Study of Deuteronomy 32." In *FS J. Muilenburg.* 1962. 26–67. **Würthwein, E.** "Der Ursprung der prophetischen Gerichtsrede." *ZTK* 49 (1952) 1–16. **Zorrell, F.** "Magnum Canticum Mosis." *VD* 7 (1927) 197–203.

Form/Structure/Setting

In Jewish tradition, the tenth of the eleven weekly portions in the lectionary cycle of Torah readings from Deuteronomy (32:1–52) is called האזינו, "let us give ear," from its opening word. This text includes what is more commonly known as the "Song of Moses" (32:1–43).

No text within Deuteronomy has received more attention through the years than the Song of Moses (32:1–43), from ancient scribes who copied it to modern critical scholars who ponder its structure and meaning. The text is hauntingly beautiful, even in translation; and it touches on familiar themes found elsewhere throughout the whole Hebrew Bible.

Talmudic rules require that two songs in the Pentateuch (Exod 15; Deut 32) be written in a distinctive manner (*b. Meg.* 16b). Up to this point in L, the text is in three narrow columns of twenty-seven lines each per page—until we reach the words הדברים האלה, "these words," in 31:28, which mirror the opening words of the book in 1:1, אלה הדברים, "these are the words." On the next page of the codex, the first six lines extend across the full width of the page with numerous spaces and large dots between the words of 31:28c–30. A large space follows, separating this introduction from the text of the Song of Moses in 32:1–43, which follows in two columns, as stipulated by the Talmud, for twenty more lines on that page and seventeen on the next page, a total of thirty-seven lines. A smaller space separates the poem from the text of 32:52a, ending with the word הארץ, "the land," so as to make twenty-seven lines of Hebrew text on each page. The following page resumes the standard three narrow columns of Hebrew text per page to the end of the book. Such special treatment is anticipated in the Dead Sea Scrolls containing Deut 32, though in different ways (see Tov, "Special Layouts").

Perhaps the most intriguing study of the structure of the Song of Moses is that of Skehan (*CBQ* 13 [1951] 153–63; followed by Wright, "Lawsuit of God," 33), who argues persuasively that the poem as a whole divides naturally into three major parts (vv 1–14, 15–29, and 30–43), each of which contains precisely twenty-three versets, representing the number of letters in the Hebrew alphabet with an extra *pe* verset added at the close of each cycle.

One should also note, in light of the numerical composition of Deuteronomy, that the number 23 is associated with Hebrew כבוד, "glory." Written without the vowel letter *waw*, כבד has two numerical values depending on whether the initial letter כ is taken as the number 11 (its place value in the order of the Hebrew alphabet) or the traditional value of 20 in the numerical system still in common use in Jewish circles. The number can be taken as either 17 (= כ [11] + ב [2] + ד [4]) or 26 (= כ [20] + ב [2] + ד [4]). Written with the vowel letter *waw*, the numerical value of כבוד is either 23 (= כ [11] + ב [2] + ו [6] + ד [4]) or 32 (= כ [20] + ב [2] + ו [6] + ד [4]). The numbers 17 and 26 are also associated with the tetragrammaton, the personal divine name יהוה, "YHWH," which is explained in Exod 3:14 in terms of the verb אהיה, "I am" or "I cause to be," which suggests an alternate name אהוה. The numerical value of יהוה is 26 (= י [10] + ה [5] + ו [6] + ה [5]). The numerical value of אהוה is 17 (= א [1] + ה [5] + ו [6] + ה [5]. Another way of getting the number 17 from יהוה is to count the sum of the digits in the numerical value of the four letters: 17 = 1 + 0 + 5 + 6 + 5.

Skehan notes the identification of the poem as אמרי־פי, "the words of my mouth," at the outset in v 1. The pattern *'aleph-pe* throughout the macrostructure and the fact that in the resulting list of twenty-three letters the first, middle (i.e., twelfth), and last letters—*'aleph, lamed,* and *pe,* spell out the word *'aleph* (אלף) in Hebrew. For Skehan, sixty-nine versets is the author's way of writing a "seventy-line" poem. According to tradition, the sons of Israel who went down to Egypt were seventy in number (Exod 1:5). The MT reading of בני ישראל, "sons of Israel," in v 8 may also recall that number as well, for the number seventy is actually inserted in the text of *Tg. Ps.-Jonathan* at this point. The Table of Nations in Gen 10 originally had seventy names, and later tradition (see *1 Enoch* 89:59) supports the conclusion that there were thought to be just seventy nations, and therefore seventy angels over them.

The structure first observed by Skehan is confirmed in the prosodic analysis presented here. But the structure is more complex than Skehan, and others who have followed his arguments, realize. The structure of the whole may be outlined in a five-part concentric design:

A	God's justice and Israel's disloyalty	32:1–6
B	God's blessing on Israel in times past	32:7–14
X	Israel's sin provokes God's punishment	32:15–29
B′	God's decision to punish his enemies	32:30–35
A′	God's "vengeance"—Israel delivered	32:36–43

It should be noted that there are twenty-three versets in the center section of this structure (vv 15–29), and there are twenty-three versets in each of the two frames around that center: the outer frame (vv 1–6 + 36–43), and the inner frame (vv 7–14 + 30–35).

Another way of looking at the structure of the poem as a whole is to divide it in half and to outline each half in the same manner:

A	God's justice and Israel's disloyalty	32:1–6
B	God's benefactions to Israel in times past	32:7–14
X	Israel's disloyalty: they forsook the God who made them	32:15–18
B′	God's decision to punish Israel	32:19–25
A′	God's mercy—he chooses to limit Israel's punishment	32:26–29

A	God's decision to punish Israel's enemies	32:30–33
B	YHWH declares: "To me belongs 'vengeance' and recompense"	32:34–35
X	God's loyalty: his plan to deliver Israel	32:36
B′	YHWH will take "vengeance" on his enemies	32:37–42
A′	Celebration of God's grace—the deliverance of Israel	32:43

In this reading, the focus of attention is on the contrast between Israel's disloyalty to the covenant agreement and God's "loyalty" to Israel, which embodies what is elsewhere conveyed in Hebrew חסד, "covenant love" or "lovingkindness." In each of the above five-part structures, the movement in the outer frame (vv 1–6 and 26–29; and vv 30–33 and 43) is from aspects of God's justice to his mercy. The inner frame of the first structure (vv 1–29) contrasts God's blessings on "his allotted inheritance," the people of Israel (vv 7–14), with his decision to punish them for their sin in breaking the terms of the covenant (vv 19–25). The inner frame of the second structure (vv 30–43) explores the meaning of the term "vengeance," as God decides to deliver Israel by punishing their enemies (vv 34–35 and 37–42). In this analysis of the content of the poem, the first half (vv 1–29) contains the first two cycles of twenty-three versets, which are set over against the third such cycle (vv 30–43).

The structure of the Song of Moses may be expanded in similar fashion with each of the five major sections arranged in five-part concentric structures:

A	*God's Justice and Israel's Disloyalty*	*32:1–6*
a	Moses addresses the heavens and the earth	v 1
b	Request: "May my teaching drop like rain" on ready soil	v 2
x	Praise to "the name of YHWH"	vv 3–4
b′	Has God dealt corruptly? No, Israel is without discernment.	vv 5–6a
a′	Moses addresses the people: Is not God the one who made you?	v 6b
B	*The Past: God Blessed Israel in the Exodus/Eisodus*	*32:7–14*
a	Remember what God did in times past	v 7
b	YHWH received Israel as his allotment at the beginning	vv 8–9
x	YHWH birthed you and watched over you (in the exodus)	vv 10–11
b′	YHWH provided for you as he guided you to	vv 12–13
a′	the land of milk and honey (the eisodus—part one)	v 14
X	*Israel's Sin Provokes God's Punishment*	*32:15–29*
a	Israel became "fat" and forgot "the God who birthed you"	vv 15–18
b	God's response: "I will hide my face from them"	vv 19–21
x	The fire of my anger will consume the earth	v 22
b′	God's judgment: bereavement and terror—for everyone	vv 23–25
a′	God's mercy: he chooses to limit Israel's punishment	vv 26–29
B′	*The Present: God's Decision to Punish His Enemies*	*32:30–36*
a	Our God is not like other gods—he "sold them" (Israel)	v 30
b	Their vineyard produces "grapes of wrath"	vv 32–33
x	YHWH says: "To me belongs 'vengeance' and recompense!"	vv 34–35a
b′	The day of their calamity is at hand	v 35b
a′	God will "plead the cause of his people" (buy them back)	v 36
A′	*The "Vengeance" of God—Israel Delivered*	*32:36–43*
a	God's covenant loyalty: his plan to deliver Israel	v 36
b	Where are their gods? Let them rise up and help you!	vv 37–38
x	There is no god beside me—none can deliver from my hand	v 39
b′	My hand returns "vengeance" on my adversaries	vv 40–42
a′	Celebration of God's deliverance of Israel	v 43

The detail in these structures is discussed below. Here it is sufficient to note what is highlighted at the center of each section. The outer frame focuses attention on the praiseworthiness of the God of Israel (vv 3–4), who is beyond comparison (v 39). The inner frame explores the nature of God in relation to his chosen people Israel. On the one hand, he "birthed" them and watched over them in the exodus journey (vv 10–11). On the other hand, he is a god of "vengeance" who will punish evil (vv 34–35a). The fire of his anger will consume the whole of the earth itself (v 22). The seeds of subsequent eschatological theology within the biblical tradition were sown at the outset.

A. The Song of Moses (32:1–43)

1. First Cycle: God's Blessing of Israel in Times Past (32:1–14)

Bibliography for 32:1–5

Castelli, D. "Una Congettura sopra Dt 32,5." *ZAW* 15 (1897) 337–38. **Cecchetti, P. I.** "'Audite Caeli': Il Cantico di Mose' nel Deuteronomio e il suo Uso Liturgico." *Lat* 33 (1967) 161–69 (168). **Dahood, M.** "Ugaritic and the Old Testament." *ETL* 44 (1968) 35–54, esp. 50–51. **Delcor, M.** "Les attaches littéraires, l'origine et la signification de l'expression biblique 'Prendre à témoin le ciel et la terre.'" *VT* 16 (1966) 8–25. **Driver, G. R.** "Three Notes." *VT* 2 (1952) 356–57. **Fisch, H.** "The Analogy of Nature, a Note on the Structure of Old Testament Imagery." *JTS* 6 (1955/56) 161–73, esp. 165–67. **Foresti, F.** "Composizione e redazione deuteronomistica in Ex 15,1–18." *Lat* 48 (1982) 41–69, esp. 57. **Goldman, M. D.** "Lexicographical Notes on Exegesis." *ABR* 1 (1951) 135–42, esp. 141–42. **Lemke, W. E.** "The Near and the Distant God: A Study of Jer 23:23–24 in Its Biblical Theological Context." *JBL* 100 (1981) 541–55. **Loewenstamm, S. E.** "The Address 'Listen' in the Ugaritic Epic and the Bible." In *FS C. H. Gordon*. 1980. 123–31. **Snaith, N. H.** "The Meaning of *śe'îrîm*." *VT* 25 (1975) 115–18, esp. 116.

Bibliography for 32:6–14

Ahlström, G. W. *Aspects of Syncretism in Israelite Religion*. Horae Soederblomianae 5. Lund: Gleerup, 1963. 71–74. **Boer, P. A. H. de.** "The Son of God in the Old Testament." *OTS* 18 (1973) 188–207. **Cohen, A.** "'Ask Your Father and He Will Show You; Your Elders, and They Will Tell You.'" *BMik* 26,84 (1980) 90–92 (Heb.). **Cooke, G.** "The Sons of (the) God(s)." *ZAW* 76 (1964) 22–47. **Cunchillos Ylarri, J. L.** "Los *běnê hā'elōhîm* en Gen 6,1–4." *EstBib* 28 (1969) 5–31. **Dahood, M.** "Hebrew-Ugaritic Lexicography II." *Bib* 45 (1964) 393–412, esp. 408. ———. "Punic *hkkbm 'l* and Isa 14,13." *Or* 34 (1965) 170–72, esp. 171. **Driver, G. R.** "Once Again: Birds in the Bible." *PEQ* 90 (1958) 56–57. **Dussaud, R.** "Jahwe, fils de El; Ugaritica; Dt 32,8." *Syria* 34 (1957) 232–42. **Eissfeldt, O.** "El and YHWH." *JSS* 1 (1956) 25–37. **Eitam, D.** "And Oil out of the Flinty Rock." *Qadmoniot* 16 (1983) 23–27 (Heb.). **Farbridge, M. H.** *Studies in Biblical and Semitic Symbolism*. Repr. New York: Ktav, 1970. 82–84. **Fensham, F. C.** "An Ancient Tradition of the Fertility of Palestine." *PEQ* 98 (1966) 166–67, esp. 167. ———. "Father and Son as Terminology for Treaty and Covenant." In *FS W. F. Albright*. 1971. 121–35, esp. 129. **Fowler, M. D.** "The Israelite *bāmâ:* A Question of Interpretation." *ZAW* 94 (1982) 203–13. **Galling, K.** "Die Ausrufung des Namens als Rechtsakt in Israel." *TLZ* 81 (1956) 65–70. **Gaster, T. H.** *Thespis*. Garden City, NY: Doubleday, 1961. 450. **Geller, S.** "The Dynamics of Parallel Verse: A Poetic Analysis of Deut 32:6–12." *HTR* 75 (1982) 35–56. **Ginsberg, H. L.** *The Israelian Heritage of Judaism*. New York: Jewish Theological Seminary, 1982. 93–94, 101 n. 131, 104 n. 135, 108 n. 136. **Grintz, J. M.** "Between Ugarit and Qumran." In *Studies in Early Biblical Ethnology and History*. Jerusalem: Hakibbutz Hameuchad Publishing House, 1969. 242–57(Heb.). ———. "Some Observations on the 'High-Place' in the History of Israel." *VT* 27 (1977) 111–13, esp. 112. **Habel, N. C.** "Appeal to Ancient Tradition as a Literary Form." *ZAW* 88 (1976) 253–72, esp. 256–57. ———. "'YHWH, Maker of Heaven and Earth': A Study in Tradition Criticism." *JBL* 91 (1972) 321–37, esp. 324–25. **Hartmann, B.** "Mögen die Götter dich behüten und unversehrt bewahren." In *FS W. Baumgartner.* 1967. 102–5. **Hempel, J.** "Zu IV Q Deut 32,8." *ZAW* 74 (1962) 70. **Hermisson, H.-J.** "Zur Erwählung Israels: Alttestamentliche Gedanken zum Amt der Gemeinde." In *FS G. Krause.* 1982. 37–82. **Herrmann, W.** "Die Frage nach Göttergruppen in der Religiösen Vorstellungswelt der Kanaanäer." *UF* 14 (1982) 93–104. **Horst, F.** "Zwei Begiffe für Eigentum (Besitz)." In *FS W. Rudolph.* 1961. 135–56, esp. 151. **Howe, F. R.,** and **Howe, G. F.** "Moses and the Eagle." *Journal of the American Scientific Affiliation* 20.1 (1968) 22–24. **Humbert, P.** "*Qânâ* en hébreu biblique." In *FS A. Bertholet.* 1950. 259–66. **Huonder, V.** *Israel Sohn Gottes: Zur Deutung eines alttestamentlichen Themas in der jüdischen Exegese des Mittelalters.* OBO 6. Freiburg: Universitätsverlag, 1975. **Katz, P.** "The Meaning of the Root קנה." *JJS* 5 (1954) 126–31. **Lach, R.** "Les Origines de Elyon, le Très-Haut, dans la Tradition Cultuelle d'Israël." *CBQ* 24 (1962) 44–64. **Lana, M.** "Deuteronomio e Angelologia alla Luce di una Variante Qumranica (4QDt 32,8)." *Hen* 5 (1983) 179–207. **Loewenstamm, E.** "Ugaritic Formulas of Greeting." *BASOR* 194 (1969) 52–54. **Loretz, O.** "Die Vorgeschichte von Deuteronomium 32,8f.43." *UF* 9 (1977) 355–57. **Marti, K.** "Miscellen 3: Zu Dt 32,10." *ZAW* 39 (1921) 315–16. **Mercer, S. A. B.** "The Little Man of His Eye." *AngTR* 3 (1920/21) 151–52. **Meyer, R.** "The Apple of the Eye." In *FS D. Barthélemy.* 1981. 289–307. ———. "Die Bedeutung von Deuteronomium 32 8f, 43 (4Q) für die Auslegung des Moses Liedes." In *FS W. Rudolph.* 1961. 197–209. **Mihaly, E.** "A Rabbinic Defense of the Election of Israel: An Analysis of Sifre Deuteronomy 32:9, Pisqa 312." *HUCA* 35 (1964) 103–43. **Perlitt, L.** "Der Vater im Alten Testament." In *Das Vaterbild in Mythos und Geschichte.* Ed. H. Tellenbach. Stuttgart: Kohlhammer, 1976. 50–101, esp. 98–99. **Rendtorff, R.** "The Background of the Title *ʾl ʿlywn* in Gen XIV." In *Fourth World Congress of Jewish Studies: Opening Session: Jerusalem July 25th 1965.* Jerusalem: World Union of Jewish Studies, 1965. 167–70. ———. "El, Baal und Jahwe." *ZAW* 78 (1966) 277–91, esp. 280, 287–90. **Richter, G.** "Zum Text von Dt 32,10." *ZAW* 52 (1934) 77–78. **Robertson, E.** "The Apple of the Eye in the Masoretic Text." *JTS* 38 (1937) 56–59. **Schenker, A.** "Gott als Vater—Söhne Gottes." *FZPhTh* 25 (1978) 3–55. **Schlisske, W.** *Gottessöhne und Gottessohn im Alten Testament: Phasen der Entmythisierung im Alten Testament.* BWANT 97. Stuttgart: Kohlhammer, 1973. **Skehan, P. W.** "Qumran and the Present State of Old Testament Text Studies: The Masoretic Text." *JBL* 78 (1959) 21–25. **Soggin, J. A.** "Jeremias XII 10a: Eine Parallelstelle zu Dt XXXII 8/LXX?" *VT* 8 (1958) 304–5. **Usener, H. C.** "Milch und Honig." *Rheinisches Museum für Philologie* 57 (1902) 177–95. **Vaughan, P. H.** *The Meaning of Bāmâ* in the Old Testament. SOTSMS 3. London: Cambridge UP, 1974. **Vincent, L.** "La notion biblique du haut-lieu." *RB* 55 (1948) 245–78, 438–45. **Wilcke, C.** *Das Lugalbandaepos.* Wiesbaden: Harrassowitz, 1969. 9–11, 61–64, 94–97. **Winter, P.** "Der Begriff 'Söhne Gottes' im Moselied Dt 32,1–43." *ZAW* 67 (1955) 40–48. ———. "Dt 32,8b: Gn 1,26." *ZAW* 67 (1955) 292. ———. "Nochmals zu Dt 32,8." *ZAW* 75 (1963) 218–23. **Zenger, E.** "Jahwe und die Götter." *TP* 43 (1968) 338–59, esp. 354. **Zimmermann, F.** "Some Studies in Biblical Etymology." *JQR* 29 (1938/39) 241–46, esp. 241.

Translation and Prosodic Analysis

God's Justice and Israel's Disloyalty [(4:7):(4:4:4):(4:7)] 9 versets

1 Give ear O heavens / and let me speak // 18 2
   let the earth hear / the words of my mouth[a] // 13 2
2 May my teaching / drop like rain / 12 2
   [a]may my speech / descend like dew // 9 2
 Like gentle rain on tender grass / 10 1
   and like showers / on new growth // 12 2
3 For / [a]the name[a] of YHWH \[b] I will proclaim // 10 2
   ascribe[c] greatness / to our God // 15 2

4 The Rock[a] / perfect is his work / 12 2
for all his ways / are just // 11 2_
A faithful God / and never false / 13 2
the Just and Upright One / is he[b] // 10 2_
5 [a]Has he dealt corruptly with them? / 5 1
No \[b] as for his children it is their blemish[a] // 10 1
they are a crooked / and perverse generation // 11 2
6 [a]Is this[a] how you repay \[b] YHWH / 11 1
O foolish people / and without wisdom? // 12 2_
Is not he / *your father who created you* / 13 2_
who made you / and brought you into existence? // 13 2_

Past Blessing: God's Benefactions in the Exodus and Eisodus
[(4:4):(4:4:4):(8:8):(4:4:4):(4:4)] 14 versets

7 [a]*Remember / the days[a] of yore /* 11 2
consider[b] / the years generation by generation // 13 2
Ask your father / and he will inform you / 12 2
your elders / they will tell you // 13 2_
8 *When the Most High gave nations / their inheritance[a] /* 10 2
when he set the divisions / of the children of Adam // 13 2_
He fixed[b] / boundaries for peoples / 11 2
according to the number[c] / of the sons <of God>[d] // 11 2_
9 [a]*And lo / YHWH's portion[a] \[b] is his people //* 11 2
Jacob / his allotted inheritance[c] // 12 2_
10 [a]*He found him[a] / in a[b] desert land /* 13 2
[c]*in a wasteland / a howling wilderness[c] //* 15 2
He encircled him / [d]he took care of him / 15 2
[d]*he guarded him / as the pupil of his eye //* 14 2_
11 *Like an eagle / [a]he rouses[a] his nestlings /* 10 2
[b]*over his fledglings / he hovers //* 11 2
He spreads out his wings / 8 1
[c]<and> *he takes one[c] / he bears him aloft / on his pinions //* 20 3_
12 *YHWH / alone guided him //* 11 2
and there was not with him / a foreign god // 12 2_
13 *He made him ride / on the heights[a] of the earth /* 16 2
and he ate[b] / fruit of the field // 13 2_
And he made him suck[c] honey / from a crag / 14 2
and oil / from flinty rock / 10 2_
14 *Curds[a] of kine / and milk of flocks /* 12 2
with the fat[b] of lambs / 8 1
and rams of the "offspring" of Bashan \[c] and he-goats / 18 1
With the fat / of kidneys of wheat // 10 2
and blood of grapes / you will drink as wine[d] // 11 2_

Notes

1.a. SP reads פיי for MT פי, "my mouth," with no change in meaning.

2.a. SP, LXX, Syr., and *Tg. Ps.-J.* add *waw*-conj.; some SP MSS read ותזאל (meaning uncertain) for MT תזל, "it will condense."

3.a-a. SP and Tg. read בשם, "in the name," for MT שם, "name." Prosodic analysis supports MT.

3.b. Reading *ṭip̱ḥāʾ* as conj. because of misplaced *ʾatnāḥ*.

3.c. SP reads והבו, "and let us (ascribe)," for MT הבו, "let us (ascribe)." Prosodic analysis supports MT.

4.a. B has צ maj; LXX reads θεός, "God," here and in vv 15, 18, and 30, which appears to be an interpretive gloss.

4.b. LXX reads (ὁ) κύριος, "the Lord," for MT הוא, "he."

5.a-a. SP reads שחתו לו לא בני מום, "they have dealt corruptly with him, not (with) the children of defection" (?), for MT שחת לו לא בניו מומם, "has he dealt corruptly with them? No! As for his children, (it is) their blemish." LXX reads לא לו, "not to him," for MT לו לא, "to him, not"; Syr. reads ולא לו בני מום. Prosodic analysis supports MT. The 3 sg. suff. on לו is taken as collective for עם, "people" (= בניו), in v 6, and thus rendered in English as "them."

5.b. Reading *ṭip̱ḥāʾ* as conj. because of misplaced *ʾatnāḥ*.

6.a-a. As Tigay notes, "the interrogative prefix *ha* ('Is it . . . ?') is written in larger script and, anomalously, as a separate word" ([1996] 301–2). The reason may be the need for an additional word in the numerical composition of the text. Cf. 33:28 and the summary discussion of the numerical composition of 29:9–34:12 under 34:1–12 below.

6.b. Reading *pašṭāʾ* followed by *zāqēp̱ qāṭôn* as conj.

7.a-a. SP reads זכרו יומת for "remember [2 pl.] the days (of yore)" for MT זכר ימות, "remember [2 sg.] the days (of yore)"; two Heb. MSS read זכ(ו)ר ימת.

7.b. Syr., Tg., and Vg. read sg., perhaps בִּינָה or בִּין for MT בינו, "consider!"

8.a. Two Heb. MSS read בהנחיל for MT בהנחל, "when he caused (nations) to inherit," with no change in meaning.

8.b. One SP MS reads יַצִּיב for MT יַצֵּב, "he fixes/sets," with no change in meaning.

8.c. *Tg. Ps.-J.* adds the number seventy (see *Comment* on 32:8).

8.d. Reading בני אלהים, "sons of God," in place of MT בני ישראל, "sons of Israel," as *lectio difficilior.* DSS read בני אל, "sons of God," and LXX ἀγγέλων θεοῦ, "angels of God" (so also σʹ and some OL witnesses).

9.a-a. LXX reads καὶ ἐγενήθη μερίς, "and he became the (Lord's) portion" (= ויהי חלק). Prosodic analysis tends to support MT. The כי here is taken as emphatic, with Tigay ([1996] 303; see A. Schoors, "The Particle *ki*," *OTS* 21 [1981] 243–53).

9.b. Reading *ṭip̱ḥāʾ* as conj. because of misplaced *ʾatnāḥ*.

10.a-a. SP reads יאמצהו, "he encouraged him," for MT ימצאהו, "he found him" (cf. LXX αὐτάρκησεν αὐτόν, "he maintained him").

10.b. SP reads המדבר, "the desert," for MT מדבר, "a desert."

10.c-c. SP reads ובתהללות יש(י)מנהו for MT ובתהו ילל ישמן, "in a wasteland, a howling wilderness" (cf. Neh 9:25).

10.d. SP and LXX add *waw*-conj. before both verbs. Prosodic analysis supports MT.

11.a-a. Two Heb. MSS read יער for MT יעיר, "he rouses." Prosodic analysis supports MT.

11.b. Two Heb. MSS, SP, LXX, Syr., *Tg. Ps.-J.*, and Vg. add *waw*-conj., which is best explained as scribal dittography. Prosodic analysis supports MT.

11.c-c. SP adds *waw*-conj., which is possible from a prosodic point of view. The reading taken here is that of a shared consonant; i.e., a single consonant is used to end one word and to begin the next word as well. On this phenomenon, see W. Watson, "Shared Consonants in Northwest Semitic," *Bib* 50 (1969) 525–33; and idem, "More on Shared Consonants," *Bib* 52 (1971) 44–50. See also D. L. Christensen, "The March of Conquest in Isaiah x 27c–34," *VT* 26 (1976) 390–92.

13.a. Reading Q בָּמֳתֵי, "on the heights," rather than K בָּמוֹתֵי (meaning uncertain). This reading is found in DSS, a number of Heb. MSS, and Cairo Geniza fragments.

13.b. SP and LXX read יַאֲכ(י)לֵהוּ, "he fed him"; Tg. *(Tg. Ps.-J.)* reads וַיַּאֲכִילֵם, "and he fed them," for MT ויאכל, "and he ate." Prosodic analysis supports MT.

13.c. SP and Syr. read יינקהו, "he will make him suck," for MT וינקהו, "and he made him suck"; LXX reads ἐθήλασαν, "they sucked" (= יִינְקוּ); Tg. and *Tg. Ps.-J.* have 3 pl. suffs. Prosodic analysis supports MT.

14.a. SP reads חמת, "waterskin" (?), for MT חמאת, "curds."

14.b. Relocating כליון, "kidneys," as a "nomistic correction" in MT as suggested by Tigay ([1996] 403 n. 79).

14.c. The *pašṭā'* followed by *zāqēp qāṭôn* is read as conj.

14.d. SP and LXX insert (ו)יאכל יעקב וישבע, "(and) Jacob ate and was filled." Prosodic analysis supports MT.

Form/Structure/Setting

The first cycle of twenty-three versets in the Song of Moses (32:1–14) is divided into two parts by the *Numeruswechsel* at the end of v 6. In terms of the prosodic analysis presented here, there are nine versets in vv 1–6 and fourteen versets in vv 7–14 for a total of twenty-three versets.

On the basis of the prosodic analysis presented here, the Song of Moses (32:1–43), within its literary framework, may be outlined as follows:

A	Moses speaks the words of this song to all the assembly	31:30
B	Exordium: God's faithfulness and Israel's disloyalty	32:1–6
C	Past: God's benefactions to Israel in times past	32:7–14
D	Israel's disloyalty: they forsook the God who made them	32:15–18
E	God's decision to punish Israel	32:19–25
X	God's mercy and Israel's lack of discernment	32:26–29
E′	God's decision to punish Israel's enemies	32:30–35
D′	God's loyalty: his plan to deliver Israel	32:36
C′	Future: YHWH will take "vengeance" on his enemies	32:37–42
B′	Coda: Celebration of God's deliverance of Israel	32:43
A′	Moses speaks all the words of this song—he and Joshua	32:44–45

The poem begins with what Tigay calls an "exordium" (vv 1–6), in the form of a summons to heaven and earth to pay attention to "the words of my mouth" (v 1). Those words focus on the righteousness of God (vv 3–4) and the disloyalty of his people Israel, who are described as "a crooked and perverse generation" (v 5). The poem ends on a note of celebration in which the heavens are summoned once again to praise God's people and to worship God, together with the (seventy) "sons of God" (v 43). In the center we find the theme of God's mercy in which he chooses to limit the punishment meted out to his people Israel (vv 26–27), in spite of the fact that they are "a nation void of sense" and without understanding (vv 28–29). They do not deserve God's mercy.

The inner frame in this structure presents God's decision to punish Israel (vv 19–25), set over against God's decision to punish Israel's enemies (vv 30–35). The second frame from the center presents a description of Israel's disloyalty in which they choose to forsake the God who made them (vv 15–18), set over against a description of God's loyalty to his covenant agreement, in which he determines to plead the cause of his people and to deliver "his servants" (v 36). The third frame from the center presents a contrast between the past, in which God's blessings bestowed on his people are delineated (vv 7–14), and a glimpse into the future, when God will take "vengeance" on his enemies as he delivers his own people from their oppression (vv 37–42).

The internal structure of 32:1–6 is marked with a change from first-person singular to first-person plural forms in v 3, and a shift to third-person forms in v 4 that marks the center of the unit, which may be outlined as follows:

A	Give ear, O heavens, and let the earth hear the words of my mouth	32:1
B	May my teaching drop like gentle rain	32:2
C	The name of YHWH I proclaim, I ascribe greatness to our God	32:3
X	The Rock—perfect is his work, his ways are just	32:4
C′	Has YHWH dealt corruptly with his people?	32:5a
B′	No, his children are a crooked and perverse generation	32:5b
A′	Is this how you repay the father who created and established you?	32:6

Within this menorah pattern, the outer frame (A, A′) moves from an appeal to heaven and earth to hear the words of the song (v 1) to a rhetorical question in v 6b, which is addressed to Israel (marked by the *Numeruswechsel*), focusing attention on God's creative powers in regard to his people Israel. The original creation event in Gen 1:1 began with the creation of the heavens and the earth, which is where the Song of Moses begins as well. The praise of YHWH in terms of his work in creation and his ways in history is the central focus of the opening section (vv 3–4). The second frame (B, B′) moves from a prayer that Moses' teaching may fall on receptive ears, like the gentle rain on new growth in the fields (v 2), to an indictment on God's "children" for acting corruptly (vv 5–6a). The three-part center in this structure focuses on the person of YHWH, who is presented in the image of the Rock who is faithful and true (v 4). The innermost frame (C, C′) moves from praise ascribing greatness to "our God" (v 3) to a rhetorical question in regard to God's actions in relation to his faithless people (v 5a).

According to the prosodic analysis, the second major section in the song (vv 7–14) falls into a series of five structural units:

A	Remember the days of yore; ask your elders they will tell you	32:7
B	When God allotted the nations, he chose Israel as his own	32:8–9
X	He cared for him and taught him "to fly" in the wilderness	32:10–11
B′	YHWH alone is the one who provided you with food on the way	32:12–13
A′	You will experience future blessings in the promised land	32:14

In this reading the outer frame moves from a look backward in time to "the days of yore" (v 7) to a glimpse into the future blessings in the promised land (v 14). The inner frame moves from the distant past in the days before the time of Abraham in Gen 10–11, when God allotted the nations "according to the number of the sons of God" (vv 8–9), to a look at the immediate past when he alone provided the people of Israel the food they needed from the least likely sources (vv 12–13); for God cares for his "nestlings," whom he has gently taught the lessons they need to know in order "to fly like an eagle" (vv 10–11).

The data from Labuschagne on the numerical composition of 32:1–14 may be summarized as follows:

Words:	before *ʾatnāḥ*		after ʾ atnāḥ		
32:1–3	13	+	13	=	26
32:4–6	20	+	17	=	37
32:5–6	13	+	10	=	23
32:7–9	17	+	15	=	32
32:7–10	23	+	20	=	43 (= 17 + 26)
32:7–11	29	+	26	=	55
32:7–12	32	+	30	=	62
32:10–11	12	+	11	=	23
32:11–14	31	+	20	=	51 (= 3 × 17)
32:13–14	22	+	10	=	32
32:1–43	247	+	221 (= 13 × 17)	=	468 (= 18 × 26)

The divine-name numbers 17 and 26 are woven into the fabric of 32:1–14 in a variety of ways: with 26 words in vv 1–3, 43 (= 17 + 26) words in vv 7–10, and 51 (= 3 × 17) words in vv 11–14. There are also 17 words before *ʾatnāḥ* in vv 7–9, 17 words after *ʾatnāḥ* in vv 4–6, and 26 words after *ʾatnāḥ* in vv 7–11. The two numbers associated with Hebrew כבוד, "glory," 23 and 32, occur on five occasions. Though the figures for 32:1–14 as a whole are not multiples of these numbers, the figures for 32:1–43 (the Song of Moses) are: with a total of 468 (= 18 × 26) words and 221 (13 × 17) words after *ʾatnāḥ*.

Comment

1 Mayes interprets the appeal to heaven and earth "in the light of their regular appearance as witnesses in extra-biblical treaty texts" ([1981] 382), following Huffmon (*JBL* 78 [1959] 285–95) and Moran (*Bib* 43 [1962] 317–27), among others. "The heavens" and "the earth" are addressed in prophetic speeches in contexts where Israel is judged for failure to keep their covenant commitment to YHWH (Isa 1:2–3; Mic 6:1–2; Jer 2:4–13; Ps 50:4). "According to the Midrash Tanḥuma, Moses summoned them [the heavens and the earth] to punish Israel with drought and crop failure if it should violate the covenant, on the principle that the hand of the witnesses should be the first to act against the violator (17:7)" (Tigay [1996] 299). As Tigay himself acknowledges, however, the song never mentions the covenant, and the relationship and moral responsibilities assumed in it are those between father and child, not suzerain and vassal. The Hebrew expression אמרי־פי, translated "words of my mouth," led Skehan to his conclusions on the *ʾaleph-pe* structure of the Song of Moses as a whole (see introductory remarks to 32:1–43 above). The invocation to "give ear" and to "hear" are the normal words a teacher uses to address his student in wisdom literature, as Mayes observes ([1981] 382; cf. Prov 7:24 and the Instruction of Amenemope [*ANET,* 421, ll. 9–10]).

2 Four similes are used here ("rain," "dew," "gentle rain," "showers"), all of which speak to the potential of the song's teaching for the lives of the covenant people by penetrating and saturating their hearts and minds so as to make them grow in the "fear" and strength of YHWH. The context suggests rendering שעירם as "gentle rain." Snaith translates it as "storm rain" (*VT* 25 [1975] 115–18), from the root סער, "to storm, rage." Moran points to Ugaritic *šrʿ* in a context of dew and rain: "no dew, no rain, no welling-up [*šrʿ*] of the deep" (*Bib* 43 [1962] 321–22). On the translation "may my speech descend like dew," which I accept here, see Goldman (*ABR* 1 [1958] 141–42). The word טל, "dew," is also used for moisture from the skies/clouds in what would normally be described as rain (see Isa 18:4; Hag 1:10; Zech 8:12; Prov 3:20).

3 The שם יהוה, "name of YHWH," speaks of his attributes, as in Exod 34:5–6, "The LORD descended in the cloud and stood with him there, and proclaimed the name . . . 'The LORD, a God merciful and gracious, slow to anger, and abounding in steadfast love and faithfulness.'" The word גדל, "greatness," is common in Deuteronomy, though rare in other biblical books—except for the book of Jonah, where it is used as the key word in the literary structure of that book (see D. L. Christensen, "Andrzej Panufnik and the Structure of the Book of Jonah: Icons, Music and Literary Art," *JETS* 28 [1985] 140).

4 Albright argues that Hebrew צור, "rock," corresponds to Ugaritic *ġr*, "mountain" (*VT* 9 [1959] 345), one of the Canaanite god Baal's appellations. The archaic meaning "mountain" appears in the OT as well in Num 23:9 and Isa 44:8. On the word תמים, here translated "perfect" in the sense of "whole" or "without flaw," see J. Tigay ("Psalm 7:5 and Ancient Near Eastern Treaties," *JBL* 89 [1970] 185 n. 39) and M. Weinfeld ("The Covenant Grant in the Old Testament and in the Ancient Near East," *JAOS* 90 [1970] 184–85, nn. 12, 15; following Y. Muffs; see Tigay [1996] 402 n. 20). "His ways are just [משפט]," for he is "a faithful God and never false [ואין עול]"—dependable and trustworthy. The translation "the Just and Upright One is he," as a composite divine title, is that of Dahood (*ETL* 44 [1968] 50; cf. Ps 11:7). Tigay calls attention to the fact that derivatives from the root צדק in Aramaic "are used of loyalty and devotion to an ally, and in Arabic they often have the nuance of true and loyal friendship, for fulfilling a covenant with God" ([1996] 402 n. 23). The term ישר, "upright," conveys a similar meaning, that of unswervingly trustworthy, reliable (with Tigay [1996] 301).

5 For the first part of v 5, I follow the reading of the old JPS translation (1917) with close attention to the disjunctive accents. The first two words, שחת לו, are taken as a question (as in both halves of v 6), "Has he dealt corruptly with him?" The question is answered immediately with לא, "No." The next two words, בניו מומם, are taken as another clause: "his children, it is their blemish"—they are the ones who have acted corruptly; for they "are a crooked and a perverse generation" (עקש ופתלתל)—the opposite of God, who is "true and upright" (v 4). The pattern of "a direct accusation . . . in verse 5, followed by questions in verse 6. . . . is the normal sequence in [the *rîb*, or covenant lawsuit] form. . . . The interrogation was put by the king's messenger, who transmitted the accusation. The same person made the opening appeal to the heavens and the earth and recalled the past benefits of the great king. The parallel is very close in these verses, where Yahweh is King and Moses is His messenger" (Thompson [1974] 298–99).

6 At this point the song addresses the people of Israel: "Is this how you repay YHWH, O foolish people [עם נבל]?" In Torah scrolls (but not in L), the *he*-interrogative at the beginning of this verse is written in larger script and as a separate word. Though the reason for this practice is no longer known, it certainly "has the effect of heightening the shock expressed by the rhetorical question," as Tigay notes ([1996] 302). It may simply be the means of drawing attention to the fact that we have here an additional word so far as the numerical composition of the text is concerned. God is described as Israel's "father," a designation that continues the relational father-child metaphor introduced in v 5; but something new is added in that he is now presented as the one "who created you, who made you, and established you." The verb קנה, "to create," here, also with the same meaning in the other Song of Moses (Exod 15:16), goes with the verbs עשה, "to make," and כנן, "to bring into existence." As Tigay shows ([1996] 402 n. 38), "the meaning of *konen* is clear from Ps. 119:73, where it is used alongside 'make,' and from Ugaritic, which uses *k-n-n* in parallelism with both 'father' and *k-n-h* (*q-n-h*), 'creator' (*UT* 51, iv,47–48; 76, iii,6–7" (on the meaning of קנה see also Humbert in *FS A. Bertholet,* 259–66; Katz in *JJS* 5 [1954] 126–31). A fourth verb to describe God as Israel's parent and creator is used in v 18 below, חול, "to give birth to."

7 The call to "remember the days of yore" recalls the period of Israel's formation in the exodus from Egypt, the making of the covenant with YHWH at Mount Sinai, and what I have called the first phase of YHWH's Holy War under Moses' leadership in the conquest of the two Amorite kingdoms in Transjordan; and to inquire about its meaning: "ask your father and . . . your elders." The phrase דור־ודור, "generation by generation," may also be translated "every generation," as in Ps 90:1. As Tigay observes, "The challenge to consult the elders was apparently a traditional element in ancient rhetoric; examples appear in the Book of Job [Job 8:8–10] and in a Mesopotamian royal inscription" ([1996] 302, citing A. Cavigneaux and B. K. Ismail, "Die Statthalter von Suhᵉu und Mari im 8. Jh. v. Chr.," *Baghdader Mitteilungen* 21 [1990] 400, 403–4).

8 G. R. Driver argues that the verb הנחל here should be rendered "he strewed the nations (as) through a sieve," that is, he "disposed of them as units about the world" (*VT* 2 [1952] 357), from the root נחל, "sifted, pass through a sieve." He reads the verb הפרידו as he "scattered" or "sowed" them like grains of sand or seed upon the earth. According to MT, God divided the nations in relation to Israel's numbers; though Zimmermann suggested translating the word מספר (usually "number") as "boundary" (*JQR* 29 [1938–39] 242), to make better sense of the present text, I emend the text here following the reading בני אלהים, "sons of God," found in 4QDeutʲ and LXX ἀγγέλων [or υἱῶν] θεοῦ, "angels [or sons] of God," to read "according to the number of the sons of God." The Tg. adds "seventy" after "the number," connecting the text with the seventy nations of the Table of Nations in Gen 10 and the song of Jacob in Gen 46:27 (cf. 10:22). It is easy to understand the change that was made in MT to remove a text that seems to suggest the existence of other gods. For a somewhat similar "nomistic correction," see the discussion of v 14 below. These "divine beings" are also mentioned in a variant reading of v 43 below. For a useful discussion of the idea of subordinate divine beings with whom God holds council, see Ps 82 and the study by G. E. Wright (*The OT against Its Environment,* SBT 1.2 [London: SCM, 1950] 30–41). The idea here anticipates the later doctrine of guardian angels watching over the nations in Dan 10:13, 20–21; 12:1.

9 The particle כי, here translated "and lo," carries an emphatic meaning that highlights the magnitude of what God did in choosing Israel as "his allotted inheritance." As Tigay notes, the term חבל נחלתו, "lit. 'His rope-allotment,' . . . is based on the practice of measuring land allotments by rope (*ḥevel;* see Amos 7:17; Mic. 2:5; Zech. 2:5–6; Ps 78:55)" ([1996] 403 n. 56). See Driver at 3:4 ([1895] 48).

10 The Hebrew ימצאהו בארץ מדבר, "he found him in a desert land," refers to the Sinai, where Israel traveled before entering the promised land. LXX and Tg. Onqelos vocalize the verb יְמַצְּאֵהוּ, "provided for" or "maintained," rather than MT יִמְצָאֵהוּ, "found." SP reads יְאַמְּצֵהוּ, "strengthened." MT is retained as the *lectio difficilior.*" See similar uses in Hos 9:10 and Ezek 16:3–6. The word translated "wasteland" here is תהו, which Gen 1:2 and Jer 4:23 use to describe the primordial and ultimate state of the world. The word ישמן, "wilderness," took on a special meaning in subsequent biblical tradition as the wilderness of Judah bordering on the Dead Sea in the vicinity of Jericho, the end point of the wilderness wandering and the site of the encampment of Israel in the region of the Jordan Valley north of Moab, which can be seen from the top of Pisgah and Peor (see D. L. Christensen, "The March of Conquest in Isaiah X 27c–34," *VT* 26 [1976] 389). On יסבבנהו, "he encircled him," and יצרנהו, "he guarded him," Ginsberg (*Israelian Heritage,* 101 n. 131) argues that the pronominal suffixes *-énhu* for standard *-énnu* is an archaism, which occurs again only in the Song of the Sea (Exod 15:2). The presence of these old grammatical forms is further evidence of the premonarchic age of the Songs of Moses here and in Exod 15. The word אישון means "little man," referring to one's reflection as seen in the pupil of another person's eye (Tigay [1996] 403 n. 63).

11 The imagery of "an eagle" (נשר) teaching its young to fly, catching them on its wings when they tire, appears also in Exod 19:4 (cf. also Hos 11:3). G. R. Driver has given us two useful illustrations, in addition to the earlier observations of S. R. Driver ([1895] 358), of what is meant (*PEQ* 90 [1958] 56–57). The instance recorded by A. C. Bent merits quotation:

> The mother started from the nest in the crags and, roughly handling the youngster, she allowed him to drop, I should say, about ninety feet; then she would swoop down under him, wings spread, and he would alight on her back. She would soar to the top of the range with him and repeat the process. Once perhaps she waited fifteen minutes between flights. I should say the farthest she let him fall was a hundred and fifty feet. My father and I watched him, spellbound, for over an hour.

Craigie ([1976] 381 n. 30) calls attention to parallel imagery in lines 38–46 of the Epic of Lugalbanda (see Wilcke, *Das Lugalbandaepos,* 94–95).

12 "YHWH alone guided him" through the desert en route to the promised land (cf. Exod 15:13), with no help from any "foreign god" (אל נכר). There is no reason to turn to the worship of other gods.

13 Though expressed in metaphorical language, במותי ארץ, "the heights of the earth," refers to the central highlands of Israel. On the wide range of meanings in the term במות, "high places," see Vaughan, *Meaning of Bāmâ.* G. E. Wright translates the text as "he made him ride on the back of *Arṣ,*" where *Arṣ* was taken as another name for the Canaanite god *Môt,* Death ("The Lawsuit of God: A Form-Critical Study of Deuteronomy 32," in *FS J. Muilenburg* [1962] 29). God provides food from the places one would least expect to find sustenance: "honey from a crag and oil from flinty rock," though Mayes sees this as "an accurate description of the land where wild honey may be found among rocks, and oil from the olives growing in stony soil" ([1981] 386). Craigie suggests that the honey is from "honeycombs located in the fissures of the cliff-faces" ([1976] 381).

14 "Curds of kine" refers to milk products such as butter, cream, or yogurt. The NEB appears to have relocated the word כליון, "kidneys," from later in the verse as a "nomistic correction," that is, one that makes the reading consistent with biblical law (see A. Rofé, "The Nomistic Correction in Biblical Manuscripts and Its Occurrence in 4QSam[a]," *RevQ* 14 [1989] 247–54). If so, according to Tigay, the scribal correction was "an intentional revision to avoid the implication that God fed Israel kidney fat, which is forbidden as food (Lev. 3:17; 7:23–25)" ([1996] 403 n. 79). I follow the MT here. The words חלב כרים, translated "fat of lambs," means literally the "best" in the idiom "the fat of the land" (see Gen 45:18). "Bashan" was the mountain range in northern Transjordan with good pastureland and herds that were renowned for their quality—the "'offspring' of Bashan" (בני־בשן), or perhaps "Bashan-breed" (with Craigie [1976] 380). The words translated here "fat of kidneys of wheat" (חלב כליות חטה) is an idiom that means "the best of choice wheat."

Explanation

As G. E. Wright puts it, the Song of Moses "is a strong composition, didactic in intent, suffused with a warmth and fire of faith that sustains it throughout its considerable length. As an interpretation of Israel's history in poetry it can be compared only with Pss. 78; 105; 106, though in many respects it is superior to them" (*IB* 2:517).

After a brief introduction in the first person singular (vv 1–3), the theme is stated in an affirmation of God's faithfulness and goodness (v 4), followed by two rhetorical questions that focus attention on Israel's perverse foolishness (vv 5–6). The poem then turns to a five-part description of God's redemptive acts in the exodus from Egypt and the trek through the wilderness that brought them to the promised land (vv 7–14).

The song begins with a summons to the whole of the created order (the heavens and the earth) to attend to the words Moses is about to speak, and to judge between YHWH and his people. The teaching that follows is likened to the rain, which softens the earth and produces a beautiful verdure of fertility; for that is Moses' intention. His words are intended to bring the people to repentance. Implicit here is the conviction that no one can sink to where the word of God cannot reach them.

To ascribe greatness to God (v 3) is to acknowledge his eternity, his matchless power, and his absolute authority. The prayer of David in 1 Chr 29:10–14, when the offerings were brought for the building of the temple in Jerusalem, stands as a moving example of the power of praise (cf. also Dan 4:31–34 [Eng. 34–37], in a prayer of Nebuchadnezzar(!) and Rom 11:33–36):

> Blessed are you, O LORD, the God of our ancestor Israel, forever and ever. Yours, O LORD, are the greatness, the power, the glory, the victory, and the majesty; for all that is in the heavens and on the earth is yours; yours is the kingdom, O LORD, and you are exalted as head above all. . . . In your hand are power and might; and it is in your hand to make great and to give strength to all. And now, our God, we give thanks to you and praise your glorious name. (NRSV)

The metaphor of a Rock is used to speak of God here (v 4) for the first time in Scripture (see also vv 18, 30, 31). It appears frequently in the Psalms, and it has made its way into the hymnology of the Christian church in such songs as "Rock of Ages" and "On Christ the Solid Rock I Stand." The expression denotes the unchangeable power, faithfulness, and love that constitute the secure and immovable foundation on which we build our hopes. The Rock is a source of refuge from human foes, from the burning heat of the sun, and from the destructive storms of life.

The text here describes the Rock by "perfect is his work" (v 4). Absolute perfection is found in God alone. In the Sermon on the Mount, Jesus commanded us: "Be perfect, therefore, as your heavenly Father is perfect" (Matt 5:48 NRSV). Earlier in that same sermon Jesus declared, "For I tell you, unless your righteousness exceeds that of the scribes and Pharisees, you will never enter the kingdom of heaven" (Matt 5:20 NRSV). The essence of the gospel message is that we are accepted by God, as we are, but clothed in the perfection of the Rock (Christ Jesus), whose righteousness is imputed to us as our own.

Stephen described the "blemish" of the people of Israel (that "crooked and perverse generation") in the conclusion of his sermon at the time of his martyrdom: "You stiff-necked people, uncircumcised in heart and ears, you are forever opposing the Holy Spirit, just as your ancestors used to do. Which of the prophets did your ancestors not persecute? They killed those who foretold the coming of the Righteous One, and now you have become his betrayers and murderers. You are the ones that received the law as ordained by angels, and yet you have not kept it" (Acts 7:51–53 NRSV).

The portrayal of God's benefactions to Israel in "days of yore" (v 7) contains powerful images (vv 7–14). When God established the territories of the seventy nations, the descendants of Noah in Gen 10, he chose Israel as his own inheritance (vv 8–9). He found Israel in "a desert land in . . . a howling wilderness" and drew close to them. After all, how close must one get to see the "little man" of God's eye (v 10)? The metaphor of the eagle in v 11 is particularly rich in its portrayal of God's loving parental care. And his blessing continued as the people began their entry (eisodus) into the promised land (vv 12–14). The reference to making Israel "suck honey from a crag" (v 13) suggests that even the most barren places were the source of God's supernatural bounty.

2. Second Cycle: Israel's Sin Provokes God's Anger (32:15–29)

Bibliography

Balentine, S. E. "A Description of the Semantic Field of Hebrew Words for 'Hide.'" *VT* 30 (1980) 137–53. **Barstad, H. M.** "En bemerkning til Deuteronomium 32,15." *NorTT* 76 (1975) 103–6. **Berg, W.** "Die Eifersucht Gottes—Ein problematischer Zug des alttestamentlichen Gottesbildes?" *BZ* 23 (1979) 197–211, esp. 202–4. **Branden, A. van den.** "'Reseph' nella Bibbia." *BeO* 13 (1971) 211–25. **Buchanan, G. W.** "Eschatology and the 'End of Days.'" *JNES* 20 (1961) 188–93, esp. 189. **Caquot, A.** "Sur quelques démons de l'Ancien Testament (*Reshep, Qeteb, Deber*)." *Sem* 6 (1956) 53–68, esp. 57–59, 65–66. **Dahood, M.** "Hebrew-Ugaritic Lexicography XI." *Bib* 54 (1973) 356. ———. "Northwest Semitic Notes on Dt 32,20." *Bib* 54 (1973) 405–6. ———. *Proverbs and Northwest Semitic Philology.* Rome: Pontifical Biblical Institute, 1963. 47. ———. *Psalms III.* AB 17A. Garden City, NY: Doubleday, 1970. 74. ———. "Review of *The Torah.*" *Bib* 45 (1964) 281–83, esp. 283. **Eissfeldt, O.** "Gott und Götzen im Alten Testament." In *KlSchr* 1:266–73, esp. 271. **Friedman, D. N.** "The Biblical Expression *mastîr pānûm.*" *HAR* 1 (1977) 139–47, esp. 145. **Fulco, W. J.** *The Canaanite God Rešep.* American Oriental Series Essay 8. New Haven: AOS, 1976. 56–57. **Fullerton, K.** "On Deuteronomy 32:26–34." *ZAW* 46 (1928) 138–55. **Gaster, T. H.** "Deuteronomy XXXII,25." *ExpTim* 49 (1937/38) 525. **Gerleman, G.** "Der Nicht-Mensch: Erwägungen zur hebräischen Wurzel *NBL.*" *VT* 24 (1974) 147–58, esp. 149, 152–53. **Greenfield, J.** "Smitten by Famine, Battered by Plague." In *FS M. Pope.* 1987. 151–52. **Hackett, J.** "Some Observations on the Balaam Tradition at Deir 'Alla." *BA* 49 (1986) 216–22, esp. 219. **Koch, K.** "*Šaddaj:* Zum Verhältnis zwischen israelitischer Monolatrie und nordwest-semitischem Polytheismus." *VT* 26 (1976) 299–332. ———. *Die Schrift als Zeuge des Evangeliums.* BHT 69. Tübingen: Mohr, 1986. 110. **Köhler, L.** "Hebräische Vokabeln I,5 שדים." *ZAW* 13 (1936) 287–93, esp. 291–92. **Lemke, W. E.** "The Near and the Distant God: A Study of Jer 23:23–24 in Its Biblical Theological Context." *JBL* 100 (1981) 541–55, esp. 546, 551, 554. **Matthiae, P.** "Note sul dio siriano *Rešef.*" *OrAnt* 2 (1963) 27–43. **Rabin, C.** "Three Hebrew Terms from the Realm of Social Psychology." In *FS W. Baumgartner.* 1967. 219–30, esp. 228–30. **Rinaldi, G.** "Nota." *BeO* 13 (1971) 26. **Rupprecht, F.** "'Den Felsen, der dich gebar, täuschtest du . . .' *KuI* 3 (1988) 53–61. **Simpson, W. K.** "Reshep in Egypt." *Or* 29 (1960) 63–74. **Spina, F. A.** "The Concept of Social Rage in the Old Testament and the Ancient Near East." Diss., Univ. of Michigan, 1977. 209. **Vattioni, F.** "Il Dio Resheph." *Annali dell' Instituto Universitario Orientali di Napoli* 15 (1965–66) 39–74. **Wächter, L.** "Israel und Jeschurun." In *FS A. Jepsen.* 1971. 58–64. **Walker, N.** "Elohim and Eloah." *VT* 6 (1956) 214–15. **Wenham, G. J.** "*bĕûlāh*—A Girl of Marriageable Age." *VT* 22 (1972) 326–48. **Wohlstein, H.** "Zur Tier-Dämonologie in der Bibel." *ZDMG* 113 (1963) 491–92. **Yahuda, A. S.** *The Language of the Pentateuch in Its Relation to Egyptian.* London: Oxford UP, 1933. 68. .

Translation and Prosodic Analysis

Israel's Disloyalty: They Forsook the God Who Made Them
[4:(4:4:4):4] 5 versets

15 *And*[a] *Jeshurun became fat / and he kicked*[b] / 12 2
you[c] *became fat / you*[c] *became gross you*[c] *became gorged //* 14 2_
And he forsook / the God[d] *who made him /* 14 2
and he[e] *treated like a fool / the Rock of his salvation /* 14 2_
16 [a]*They made him jealous*[a] / *with strangers*[b] // 12 2
[c]*with abominations / they provoked him*[d] // 14 2_
17 *They sacrificed / to demons*\\[a] *pseudo-gods*[b] / 15 2
gods / whom they did not know // 12 2_
New ones / from nearby came / 14 2
of whom your[c] fathers / were not cognizant // 13 2_

God's Decision to Punish Israel [(4:4):(4:5):(4:4):(4:4):(5:4):(4:4)]	13 versets	
18 The Rock that begot *you / you neglected*[a] //	10	2
and you forgot / the God who birthed you[b] //	11	2_
19 *And YHWH saw / and he spurned (them) //*	9	2
because of vexation by his sons / and his daughters //	14	2_
20 *And he said / "I will hide my face*[a] *from them /*	14	2
[b]*I will see / what their end will be //*	10	2_
For a [c]*turnabout / generation / they are*[c] /	13	3
children / in whom there is no faithfulness[d] //	12	2_
21 *They / made me jealous with no-gods /*	12	2
they have provoked me / with their idols[b] //	11	2
And as for me / I will make them jealous with a no-people /	14	2
with a nation of fools / I will provoke them //	12	2_
22 *For a fire / is kindled by my nostrils /*	13	2
and[a] *it burns / to the depths of Sheol //*	11	2_
[And][b] *it devours the earth / and its increase /*	11	2
and[c] *it sets ablaze / the foundations of the mountains //*	14	2_
23 *And I will gather*[a] *evils*[b] *against them //*	15	1
<and>[c] *my arrows*[d] *I will spend on them //*	8	1
24 *Wasting*[a] *famine /* [b]*and ravaging plague /*	15	2
[c]*and deadly*[d] *pestilence*[e] //	8	1_
And fanged beasts / I will send on them /	12	2
with venomous / creepers[f] *in the dust //*	12	2_
25 *Outside / a sword bereaves /*	8	2
and from rooms within[a] */ terror //*	13	2_
For young man / and virgin alike /	11	2
[b]*from suckling / to gray-haired man //*	11	2_

God's Mercy: He Chooses to Limit Israel's Punishment [4:(4:4:4):4]	5 versets	
26 *I would have said /* [a]*'I will cleave them in pieces'*[a] //	11	2
I would remove[b] *from humankind / their remembrance //*	13	2_
27 [a]*Were it not that*[a] */ I feared*[b] *vexation from the enemy*[c] /	14	2
lest their[d] *adversaries / misconstrue //*	12	2_
Lest they should say / 'Our hand[e] *is triumphant /*	16	2
YHWH[f] *has not / wrought all this' //*	12	2_
28 *For a nation / void* [a]*of sense*[b] *are they*[a] //	15	2
and they have no / understanding" //	11	2_
29 *If*[a] *they were wise / they would comprehend* [b]*this //*	14	2
[c]*they would understood / what their end would be //*	13	2_

Notes

15.a. SP, Tg., and Vg. omit *waw*-conj.

15.b. B reads וַיִּבְעַט for MT וַיִּבְעָט, "and he kicked," with no change in meaning.

15.c. LXX reads 3 sg.

15.d. Many Heb. MSS and printed editions read אֱלוֹהַּ for MT אֱלוֹהַ, "God," with no change in meaning.

15.e. SP has 3 pl.

16.a-a. Some MSS of SP read ויקניאהו for MT יקנאהו, "they made him jealous," with no change meaning; LXX reads παρώξυνάν με, "they provoked me to anger" (= יקנאני).

16.b. Vg. reads *in diis alienis,* "by strange gods," which is probably an interpretation of MT זרים, "strangers."

16.c. SP, OL, Syr., and Vg. add *waw*-conj.

16.d. LXX (except for LXX[B]) reads ἐξεπίκρανάν με, "they bitterly angered me" (= יַכְעִסֻנִי), for MT יכעיסהו, "they provoked him."

17.a. The *paštā'* followed by *zāqēp qāṭôn* is read as conj.

17.b. Many Heb. MSS and printed editions read אלוֹה (see *Note* 15.d).

17.c. LXX, Tg., and Vg. read 3 pl.

18.a. Reading תֶּשַׁה, "you forgot, neglected," for MT תֶּשִׁי from the root שיה, which is otherwise unattested in MT. Many Heb. MSS have י min; SP reads תִּשָּׁא, "you forgot" (from the root נשא, a by-form of נשה).

18.b. SP reads מהללך, "shown upon you," for MT מחללך, "birthed you." The root חול is read here as a poel ptcp. with the meaning "to writhe" in travail with child, "to (give) birth."

20.a. The *paštā'* followed by *zāqēp qāṭôn* is read as conj.

20.b. Two Heb. MSS, SP, Syr., and Vg. add *waw*-conj. (cf. LXX καὶ δείξω, "and I will show").

20.c-c. SP reads הפ(י)כות הם for MT תהפכת המה, "turnabout (generation) they are" (cf. Gen 19:29).

20.d. SP reads האמן, "the faithfulness," for MT אמן, "faithfulness."

21.a. SP reads באבליהם, "with their mourning" (?), for MT בהבליהם, "with their idols."

22.a. LXX omits *waw*-conj.; one Heb. MS and SP read ותוקד for MT ותיקד, "and it consumes," with no change in meaning.

22.b. Omitting *waw*-conj. with SP, LXX, Syr., and Tg.

22.c. SP, LXX, and Tg. omit *waw*-conj.

23.a. Reading אֹסְפָה, "I will gather" (from the root אסף), with LXX, Vg., and Syr., for MT אַסְפֶּה, "I will sweep away" (from the root ספה; cf. Mic 4:6). It is also possible to read it as אֹסְפָה, "I will add" (from the root יסף).

23.b. Reading *ṭiphā'* as conj. because of misplaced *'atnāḥ.*

23.c. Adding *waw*-conj. with SP, LXX, and Tg. to read וחצי, "and my arrows," for MT חצי, "my arrows."

23.d. Reading *ṭiphā'* as conj. because of misplaced *sillûq.*

24.a. One Heb. MS, Cairo Geniza fragments, and SP read מזה, "sucked out, empty," for MT מזי, "wasting" (famine).

24.b. DSS omit *waw*-conj.; SP reads לחמו, "ravaging plague," for MT ולחמי, "and ravaging plague."

24.c. SP and Vg. omit *waw*-conj.

24.d. SP reads מררים, "bitter things" (?), for MT מרירי, "deadly."

24.e. A few Heb. MSS read וקטף, "and plucked off" (?), for MT וקטב, "and pestilence."

24.f. Some SP MSS read זהלי (meaning uncertain) for MT זחלי, "creepers."

25.a. One SP MS reads ומהדרים (meaning uncertain) for MT ומחדרים, "and chambers."

25.b. SP reads וינק (= וְיֹנֵק, "and suckling"), for MT יונק, "suckling."

26.a-a. α', Syr., and Vg. read אֵיֹּה הֵם, "where are they," for MT אפאיהם, "I will cleave them in pieces"; SP reads אפיהם, "their anger[?]"; one SP MS reads אפי הם (meaning uncertain).

26.b. DSS and SP read אשבית for MT אשביתה, "I would remove," with no change in meaning.

27.a-a. Two Heb. MSS read לולא for MT לולי, "if not, unless," with no change in meaning; LXX reads εἰ μή, "were it not"; SP reads לו לא (meaning uncertain).

27.b. The *paštā'* followed by *zāqēp qāṭôn* is read as conj.

27.c. SP reads אֹיְבִי, "my enemy," for MT אוֹיֵב, "enemy"; LXX and Vg. read pl.

27.d. SP reads צרינו, "our adversaries," for MT צרימו, "his adversaries."

27.e. Many Heb. MSS, Cairo Geniza fragments, LXX, Syr., and Vg. read יָדֵנוּ, "our hand," for MT יָדֵינוּ, "our hands."

27.f. DSS read אדני, "Lord," for MT יהוה, "YHWH."

28.a-a. SP reads עצותם, "their counsel[?]," for MT עצות המה, "(void) of sense are they"; one SP MS reads עצותיהם, "their counsel[?]."

28.b. Reading *ṭiphā'* as conj. because of misplaced *'atnāḥ.*

29.a. A few Heb. MSS, some SP MSS, and LXX read לא, "not," for MT לו, "if only, O that, would that"; SP reads ולא, "and not."

29.b. Most LXX witnesses add πάντα, "all" (= כל). Prosodic analysis supports MT.

29.c. SP, Syr., and Vg. add *waw*-conj.

Form/Structure/Setting

In the second cycle of twenty-three versets in the Song of Moses, the focus shifts from God's blessing to Israel's sin, which provokes God's punishment (vv 15–29). Israel provoked God's wrath by worshiping false gods (vv 15–17). The people forgot their "Rock," the God who birthed them (v 18). In anger, God decided to hide his face from them (vv 19–21), and to consume them by gathering great evils against them (vv 22–24), which will bring bereavement and terror on everyone (v 25).

From a prosodic point of view, the second cycle of twenty-three versets (32:15–29) in the Song of Moses is in three parts: vv 15–17, 18–25, and 26–29. The three sections are carefully arranged in a balanced concentric design in terms of the distribution of the twenty-three versets. The first and third sections (vv 15–17, 26–29) are identical in structure, each made up of five versets. The central section (vv 18–25) is made up of thirteen versets, which are arranged in a balanced symmetrical pattern by combining the two versets in vv 23–24 into a single prosodic unit made up of five accentual stress units, which are set over against the five accentual stress units of v 20b.

The *Numeruswechsel* (change between second-person sg. and pl. forms) in vv 17 and 18 marks the boundary between the first and second sections. A similar phenomenon marks the initial boundary in v 15, with the change from third singular forms to second singular and back. The change to first person singular forms occurs in v 20 for the speech of YHWH in vv 20–27a. In terms of speaker, the opening section (vv 15–17) has Moses as narrator describing the apostasy of Israel. That narration continues through v 19 in the second section (v 19). The speech of YHWH includes most of the second section (vv 20–25) and extends through v 28 of the third section (vv 26–29), giving way to a resumption of Moses as narrator again in v 29. The transition from the end of YHWH's speech in v 27 to the beginning of Moses' concluding narration in v 29 appears to be deliberately ambiguous, as the words of v 28 make sense in reference to the enemy nation as well as to Israel.

The structure of the first section (32:15–17) may be outlined in concentric fashion:

A	Israel became "fat" and "kicked"	32:15a
B	He "forsook the God who made him"	32:15b
X	Israel made God jealous with strange gods	32:16
B′	They provoked God's wrath by worshiping "pseudo-gods"	32:17a
A′	They turned to gods "of whom your fathers were not cognizant"	32:17b

The outer frame in this structure presents the situation of Israel's rebellion as "Jeshurun became fat and he kicked" against YHWH (v 15a); for Israel turned to gods "of whom your fathers were not cognizant" (v 17b). The inner frame states the matter more explicitly: Israel "forsook the God who made him" (v 15b), by worshiping false gods (v 17a). In short, Israel provoked God's jealous wrath with strange gods (v 16).

The major part of YHWH's speech in vv 18–25, within a narrative framework, may be outlined in similar fashion:

A Israel forgot their Rock—"the god who birthed you" 32:18a
B In anger YHWH decided to hide his face from them 32:18b–20
X As they provoked me, so I will provoke them in fiery wrath 32:21–22
B′ YHWH decided to "gather evils against them" 32:23–24
A′ Bereavement and terror will come upon everyone 32:25

The outer frame in this structure moves from the narrator's description of Israel's sin against YHWH (v 18a) to a description of the coming devastation with its "bereavement" and "terror" that will be experienced by everyone (v 25). The inner frame moves from YHWH's decision, "I will hide my face from them; I will see what their end will be" (vv 18b–20a), to the sevenfold depiction of the curses YHWH is sending against them (vv 23–24). In the center is a statement justifying YHWH's fierce anger, portrayed in the metaphor of fire, which portends the imagery of subsequent apocalyptic literature: consuming the earth itself, setting ablaze "the foundations of the mountains" (v 22).

The seven-part list of destructive forces that God has gathered against his people in vv 23–24 may also be arranged in a concentric pattern:

A Evils gathered against them / YHWH's arrows 32:23
B Wasting famine 32:24aα
X Ravaging plague (רשף) 32:24aβ
B′ Deadly pestilence 32:24aγ
A′ Fanged beasts and venom of creepers 32:24b

In the outer frame the evils that YHWH has gathered against Israel are likened to his arrows that he will spend on them. The second half of the outer frame opens with the word "fanged" (ושן), which is associated with the piercing arrows of v 23. The inner frame consists of another pair in the "wasting famine" (מזי רעב) and "deadly pestilence" (קעב מרירי), where all but one of the six consonants in the first expression appears in the second, which suggests that the pairing of these terms is an example of poetic assonance. The center of this structure is "ravaging plague" (לחמי רשף), in which the curses are personified in an allusion to Resheph, the god of pestilence, who is clearly under YHWH's control when all these evils are gathered against Israel.

The third subsection of this section of the Song of Moses concludes the speech of YHWH and resumes and concludes the narration on the part of Moses; it may be outlined as follows:

A I could have just exterminated them 32:26
B But their enemies would misconstrue this 32:27a
X Saying "our hand has done this!" 32:27b
B′ For they [and Israel too] are a nation void of understanding 32:28
A′ If they were wise, they would know what their end would be 32:29

The outer frame in this structure moves from the musing of YHWH on whether simply to blot out the remembrance of Israel from humankind (v 26) to a concluding note of warning on the part of Moses: "If they were wise, . . . they would understand what their end would be" (v 29). The three versets within this frame conclude the speech of YHWH: his decision not to obliterate Israel was made so that Israel's enemy would not misconstrue events and conclude that they had destroyed Israel in their own power (v 27); for they are a nation without common sense (v 28). YHWH's concluding remark in v 28 is ambiguous in that the words fit when applied to Israel as well as to the enemy nation that destroys them. The closing verse picks up the language of vv 6 and 20 to make clear that the subunit of vv 26–29 ends where it began, with Moses' reflection on YHWH's determination to judge his own people Israel for their apostasy.

The data from Labuschagne on the numerical composition of 32:15–29 may be summarized as follows:

Words:	before *ʾatnāḥ*		after *ʾatnāḥ*		
32:15–18	18	+	17	=	35
32:15–21	34 (= 2 × 17)	+	35	=	69
32:15–24	51	+	52 (= 2 × 26)	=	103
32:16–17	9	+	8	=	17
32:16–18	12	+	11	=	23
32:16–29	68 (= 4 × 17)	+	71	=	139
32:19–21	16	+	18	=	34 (= 2 × 17)
32:19–24	33	+	35	=	68 (= 4 × 17)
32:19–27	47	+	55 (= 23 + 32)	=	102 (= 6 × 17)
32:19–31	67	+	69	=	136 (= 8 × 17)
32:22–24	17	+	17	=	34 (= 2 × 17)
32:22–27	31	+	37	=	68 (= 4 × 17)
32:25–27	14	+	20	=	34 (= 2 × 17)
32:25–29	23	+	25	=	48

The divine-name number 17 is woven into the fabric of 32:15–29 in numerous ways: vv 16–17 have a total of 17 words; vv 22–24 have 17 words before *ʾatnāḥ* and 17 words after *ʾatnāḥ*, and several multiples of 17 appear, including 34 (four times), 68 (three times), and 102. The divine-name number 26 appears as well, with vv 15–24 having 52 (= 2 × 26) words after *ʾatnāḥ*. The number 23, which is associated with Hebrew כבוד, "glory," appears twice: in the total words of vv 19–21, and in the words before *ʾatnāḥ* in vv 25–29. Once again, the scribes of ancient Israel have taken great pains in the numerical composition of 32:15–29 to glorify YHWH by weaving his name into the fabric of the Hebrew text.

Comment

15 The subject of the Song of Moses shifts sharply here from God's past blessing exhibited in the "mighty acts" of YHWH's Holy War to an indictment on the people of Israel for their disloyalty. Craigie calls "Jeshurun" (ישרון) a hypocoristicon ([1976] 382). It derives from the root ישר, "upright," and may be related in some way to the Book of Jashar (ספר הישר) of Josh 10:13, which appears to be a poetic epic story of Israel from the time before the present written text was arranged in the form we now have it in the Hebrew Bible (see D. L. Christensen, "The Lost Books of the Bible," *BRev* 14.5 [1998] 24–31). The title "Jeshurun" is used positively in 33:5, but here is an ironic emphasis on Israel's ingratitude to God. Cazelles thinks it alludes to the word שור, "ox," especially in the context of the verb "kicked" (ויבעט; see Mayes [1981] 386–87). Rabin, however, suggests the meaning "despise" for the verb בעט, from an Arabic cognate (*FS Baumgartner,* 228–30). Following this are three successive verbs in the second-person singular that directly address Israel: שמנת, "you became fat"; עבית, "you became gross"; and כשית, "you became gorged." The meaning of the third verb, כשית, is uncertain because the root כשה appears nowhere else in the Bible. Ben-Yehudah relates it to the Arabic root *kš'*, "be gorged with food" (Tigay [1996] 403 n. 84). Israel "forsook [ויטש] the God who made him, and he treated like a fool [וינבל] the Rock of his salvation." On the usage of the word צור, "rock," see the *Comment* on 32:4. In short, Israel behaved like a spoiled ox fattened on rich pasture. The phenomenon of enallage, the use of one grammatical form for another, in vv 15–16 is striking, as the grammatical forms move from third singular to second singular to third singular and then third plural forms in v 16. These changes are an extension of the so-called *Numeruswechsel,* which occurs in vv 17–18, and appear to establish the boundaries between the first three versets in vv 15–16.

16–17 The parallel terms זרים, "strangers," and תועבת, "abominations," refer to foreign gods and idols, which provoked YHWH to anger. "They sacrificed to demons [לשדים], pseudo-gods [לא אלה], gods whom they did not know." The word שדים, "demons," is an Akkadian loanword that appears also in Ps 106:37 and possibly in Amos 2:1 (see Dahood, *Psalms III,* 74; W. F. Albright, *Yahweh and the Gods of Canaan* [1968] 240; cf. 1 Cor 10:20: "I do not want you to be partners with demons"). Some scholars read the text here as referring to a cult of "Shadday gods," which included child sacrifice (see J. Hackett, "Religious Traditions in Israelite Transjordan," in *FS F. M. Cross* [1987] 133–34). Neither the Israelites nor their ancestral fathers knew the "demons," these false gods, in the way that they knew by experience the living YHWH. The reference to "new ones from nearby came," is another way of saying "deities-come-lately" (so Tigay [1996] 306). In sharp contrast, YHWH is described as "the ancient God" (33:27). The "olden gods," as Frank Cross puts it, are the ones who carry the hallmark of authority in the world of antiquity. The meaning of the verb שערום, translated here as "they were not cognizant," is not certain. Though שער in Jer 2:12; Ezek 27:35; and 32:10 means "bristle with horror," LXX renders the text here as "whom your fathers did not *know.*" According to Tigay, this reading is supported by Arabic *ša'ara,* "know, be cognizant"([1996] 306). The *Numeruswechsel* appears twice in vv 17–18 to mark the boundary between the two literary subunits in this section of the Song of Moses.

18 Once again the poet addresses Israel with an indictment using maternal imagery: "you forgot the God who birthed you [מחללך]." Together with v 6, God is presented in the image of both father and mother. Tigay calls attention to the fact that "a similar combination of metaphors appears in ancient Syrian inscriptions that describe kings as father and mother to their people" ([1996] 307, citing *ANET,* 653, 654; cf. *ANET,* 397, referring to a Hittite god). The emendation of תשי to תשה is supported by the parallelism with ותשכח, "and you forgot."

19 "And YHWH saw" the apostasy described in vv 15–19 and announces his decision to punish Israel (vv 19–25). The translation of וינאץ as "spurned" is a bit awkward because the direct object is missing (for a parallel usage see Jer 14:21). 4QPhyl^{n} (and LXX) reads "was incensed" (ויקנא); but this root requires an object too (Tigay [1996] 404 n. 102). The term מכעס, "because of vexation," refers to the "strange gods" and the "abominations" with which the people vexed God in v 16. The phrase "sons and daughters" refers to the idolatry of both men and women (cf. 17:2; 29:17).

20 Dahood (*Bib* 54 [1974] 405) reads אסתירה, "I will hide," as an infixed-*t* conjugation of סור, "turn away," paralleling the root הפך, "turn," in תהפכת, "turn-about." As Mayes notes ([1981] 38), however, there remains some doubt of the existence of this conjugation in biblical Hebrew. "A turnabout generation" (דור תהפכת) is defined in the words that follow: "in whom there is no faithfulness."

The root הפך, "turn, overturn," carries a double meaning in the Hebrew Bible, as evidenced by Jonah's message that Nineveh "will be overturned" (נהפכת, Jonah 3:4). To Jonah the word meant that Nineveh would be "overturned" in the sense of being destroyed; but to God the same word meant that Nineveh would be "overturned" in the sense of being turned around or converted (see D. L. Christensen, "Narrative Poetics and the Interpretation of the Book of Jonah," in *Directions in Biblical Hebrew Poetry,* ed. E. R. Follis, JSOTSup 40 [Sheffield: JSOT Press, 1987] 29–48). That same double meaning may be anticipated here in that Israel is presented as a "turnabout generation" that broke faith with YHWH. The hope is that God's punishment will lead to another "turnabout" that will ultimately produce a cleansing of the land of God's people, in which God will one day wipe away his people's tears (32:43).

21 The word for "idols" here is הבלים, literally "puffs of breath, vapor." Numerous attempts have been made to identify the לא־עם, "no-people," as a historical allusion to Canaanites (Cassuto), Philistines (Eissfeldt), or some nomadic invader such as the Midianites and the Amalekites (Tigay; cf. Judg 6:2–6) who threaten Israel's existence; but it is not possible to identify with any certainty this "nation of fools" (גוי נבל) whom God uses to vex his people Israel. The terms used here are poetic in nature, used in analogy with "no-god," with no specific nation in mind (Mayes [1981] 388).

22 The fire of God's anger, once kindled, knows no limits: "a fire is kindled by [YHWH's] nostrils" that "burns to the depths of Sheol" (the netherworld); "it devours the earth, . . . and it sets ablaze the foundations of the mountains" (cf. Jer 15:14; 17:4). On the translation "by my nostrils" (באפי), see Dahood in *Bib* 45 (1964) 283. As Craigie puts it, "The anger of God is like the love of God, knowing no limits in the places to which it extends (see Rom. 8:38); but the anger of God is an awesome and terrible thing exactly because it follows from a rejection of the equally pervasive love of God" ([1976] 384).

23–24 The list of seven רעות, "evils," should be compared to the list of seven disasters in 28:22, 27–28. The verb אַסְפֶּה, "I will sweep up," appears in this form only here in MT. I repoint it to read אֹסְפָה, "I will gather," with LXX, Vg., and Syr., thereby improving the balance of the two versets in 32:23–24a in terms of mora count from (12:8):(15:8) to (15:8):(15:8). The word translated "my arrows" (חצי) appears again in v 42 as a metaphor for devastation in war. The לחמי רשף, "ravaging plague," includes an allusion to the Syro-Canaanite deity Resheph, god of pestilence, who is also associated with arrows in some texts (so Tigay [1996] 404 n. 115). The reference to קטב מרירי, "deadly pestilence," is probably to smallpox, which is known as *ketev* in some Arabic dialects to the present time (see J. Blau, "Über Homonyme und angeblich Homonyme Wurzeln II," *VT* 7 [1957] 98;

Tigay [1996] 404 n. 117). The "fanged beasts" (שֶׁן־בְּהֵמוֹת) include lions, bears, and poisonous snakes or perhaps insects of some kind—"venomous creepers in the dust."

25 War will affect everyone, from "suckling to gray-haired man." There will be no escape.

26–27 I reject the proposed emendation of אַפְאֵיהֶם to read אֵיפֹה הֵם, "where are they?" (with Aquila, Syr., and Vg.). The emendation adds a word, which disturbs the patterns of the numerical composition of the text as a whole. God decided in advance that he would not "remove from humankind their remembrance," because "their adversaries" would "misconstrue" (ינכרו) things and claim for themselves the honor of the victory, saying "our hand is triumphant; YHWH has not wrought all this." On כעס, "vexation," see the use of the same Hebrew root in vv 16, 18, and 21. The phrase "our hand is triumphant" (ידינו רמה, lit. "our hand is high") is a metaphor for "military arrogance," according to Craigie, who calls attention to the fact that the Egyptian god Min is described as "he with uplifted arm" ([1976] 385 n. 48; citing P. Montet, *Eternal Egypt,* tr. D. Weightman [New York: New American Library, 1964] 223).

28–29 Though the reference to "a nation void of sense" applies to the enemy cited in v 27, it also includes the people of Israel, to whom the poet now turns his attention by way of summary. God raised the possibility of obliterating them in v 26; but that was not his intention from the outset. "If they were wise they would comprehend this; they would understand what their end would be," and they would take steps to change the course of those events. The ambiguity here as to whether vv 28–29 refer to Israel or to Israel's enemies is probably intentional. The next section (vv 30–43) focuses attention specifically on Israel, whereas v 27 contains the very words of the enemy nation. Both that enemy nation and the people of Israel are "void of sense" and with "no understanding." The reason for God's judgment is Israel's lack of discernment. The beginning of that judgment is not a hidden thing; the signs are there for all to see. Unfortunately, however, the people "keep listening, but do not comprehend; keep looking, but do not understand" (Isa 6:9 NRSV). "If they were wise" and would look with their eyes, and listen with their ears, and "comprehend this" with their minds, "they would understand what their end would be," and they could choose to turn and be healed.

Explanation

The theme announced in vv 4–6 is in two contrasting parts: the goodness and stability of God, and the faithlessness of Israel. The second part of that theme is expanded in the indictment of vv 15–18, which describe Israel's disloyalty in forsaking the God who made them into a people in the first place. When Israel became well fed, indeed fat and gorged, the people abandoned their true Rock and turned to idolatry. YHWH's sentence against them is introduced by the statement that he saw what Israel did (v 19) and decided to act (v 20). YHWH determined to punish them "with a no-people, with a nation of fools" (v 21), and with fire, warfare, pestilence, and "beasts" (vv 22–24)—the unruly forces of nature and history that make up the covenant curses of Deut 28. The only reason God gives for not destroying Israel outright, as they deserve, is that the enemy people who bring this terror and destruction would think that they had brought all this to pass by their own power (vv 26–29).

The situation in our own time is no different. Our national riches and successes have produced the same effect: like Jeshurun, we have become fat and have kicked; and the glaring infidelity, which abounds on every side, proves that we too have forsaken God and provoked his anger, as ancient Israel did centuries ago. Indeed, both then and now, many who behave well in adversity or low circumstances change markedly as they become prosperous and wealthy. As Martin Luther once put it, "A full stomach does not promote piety, for it stands secure and neglects God" (quoted by Thompson [1974] 300). It is as though they seem to say to God, "We are in control now; we don't need you anymore." They turn to the worship of the gods of this world, "pseudo-gods, gods whom they did not know; new ones from nearby came, of whom your fathers were not cognizant" (v 17). Many a faithful minister in the church today finds occasion to lament that some who continue to think of themselves as faithful Christians bear fruit in their lives that proclaims another message: "For from the vine of Sodom is their vine, and from the terraces of Gomorrah; their grapes are grapes of poison, their clusters are venomous. The venom of asps is their wine" (vv 32–33).

3. Third Cycle: God's Punishment and Salvation (32:30–43)

Bibliography

Albright, W. F. "Some Remarks on the Song of Moses in Deuteronomy." *VT* 9 (1959) 339–46, esp. 340–41. **Ap-Thomas, D. R.** "Notes on Some Terms Relating to Prayer." *VT* 6 (1956) 225–41. **Artom, E. S.** "Sul testo de Deuteronomio XXXII, 37–43." *RSO* 32 (1957) 285–91. **Bogaert, P.-M.** "Les trois rédactions conservées et la forme originale de l'envoi du Cantique de Moise (Dt 32,43)." In *Das Deuteronomium.* Ed. N. Lohfink. 1985. 329–40. **Budde, K.** "Zu Dt 32,43." *JBL* 40 (1921) 38–39. **Caquot, A.** "Remarques sur la tablette alphabétique." In *FS S. E. Loewenstamm.* 1978. 1–6. ———. "Les rephaim ougaritiques." *Syria* 37 (1960) 75–93. **Cecchetti, P. I.** "'Aidote Caeli': Il Cantico di Mose' nel Deuteronomio e il suo Uso liturgico." *Lat* 33 (1967) 161–69, esp. 168. **Christensen, D. L.** "Janus Parallelism in Genesis 6:3." *HS* 27 (1986) 20–24. ———. "Jeremiah and the 'Cup of YHWH's Wrath.'" In *Prophecy and War in Ancient Israel.* Berkeley: BIBAL Press, 1989. 193–207. **Craigie, P. C.** "A Note on Judges v 2." *VT* 18 (1968) 397–99. **Croatto, J. S.,** and **Soggin, J. A.** "Die Bedeutung von *šdmwt* im Alten Testament." *ZAW* 74 (1962) 46–50. **Cross, F. M.** *The Ancient Library of Qumran.* 3rd ed. Minneapolis: Fortress, 1995. 182–83. **Cunchillas Ylarri, J. L.** "Los *běnê hā'elohîm* en Gen 6,1–4." *EstBib* 28 (1969) 5–31, esp. 20–21. **Dahood, M.** "The Divine Designation *hû'* in Eblaite and the Old Testament." *AION* 43 (1983) 193–99, esp. 197. ———. "Ugaritic-Hebrew Parallel Pairs." In *RSP* 1:374–75. **Dietrich, M., Loretz, O.,** and **Sanmartín, J.** "Die ugaritischen Totengeister RPU(M) und die biblischen Rephaim." *UF* 8 (1976) 45–52. **Driver, G. R.** "Mythical Monsters in the Old Testament." In *Studi Orientalistici in onore de Giorgio Levi della Vida.* Istituto per l'Oriente (Italy) Pubblicazioni 52. Rome: Istituto per l'Oriente, 1956. 234–49, esp. 243. **Efros, I.**

"Textual Notes on the Hebrew Bible." *JAOS* 45 (1925) 152–53. **Gees, F.** "Hebräische Wortstudien: כמס in Dt 32,34." *BZ* 9 (1911) 1–2. **Ginsberg, H. L.** "The Conclusion of *Ha'azinu*: Dt 32:34–43." *Tarbiz* 24 (1954) 1–3 (Heb.). **Goldman, M. D.** "The Root *pll* and Its Connotation with Prayer (Attempted Exploration of Dt 32:31)." *ABR* 3 (1953) 1–6. **Greenberg, M.** "The Hebrew Oath Particle *ḤAY/ḤE*." *JBL* 76 (1957) 34–39. **Grintz, Y. M.** "Between Ugarit and Qumran." In *Studies in Early Biblical Ethnology and History.* Jerusalem: Hakibbutz Hameuchad Publishing House, 1969. 242–57. **Hallo, W. W.** "The Origins of the Sacrificial Cult: New Evidence from Mesopotamia and Israel." In *FS F. M. Cross.* 1987. 3–13. **Held, M.** "MḪ^{e}Ṣ / *MḪ^{e}Š in Ugaritic and Other Semitic Languages." *JAOS* 79 (1959) 169–76. **Hoffmann, Y.** "The Root QRB as a Legal Term." *JNSL* 10 (1982) 67–73, esp. 71. **Israel, F.** "Un nuovo sigillo ammonita? (Vattioni, *Sigilli Ebraici,* n. 126)." *BeO* 19 (1977) 167–70. **Janowski, B.** *Sühne als Heilsgeschehen.* WMANT 55. Neukirchen-Vluyn: Neukirchener Verlag, 1982. **Jeremias, J.** *Die Reue Gottes.* Biblische Studien 65. Neukirchen-Vluyn: Neukirchener Verlag, 1975. **Johnson, A. R.** *The Vitality of the Individual in the Thought of Ancient Israel.* Cardiff: Univ. of Wales Press, 1949. 108–9. **Kuntzmann, R.** *Le symbolisme des jummeaux au Proche-Orient ancien: Naissance, fonction et évolution d'un symbole.* Beauchesne Religions 12. Paris: Beauchesne, 1983. **Kutsch, E.** "Die Wurzel *'ṣr* im Hebräischen." *VT* 2 (1952) 57–69, esp. 61–65. **Lehmann, M. R.** "Biblical Oaths." *ZAW* 81 (1969) 74–92. ———. "A New Interpretation of the Term *Shedamoth.*" *VT* 3 (1953) 360–71. **Lemaire, A.** "Vengeance et justice dans l'ancien Israel." In *La Vengeance.* Vol. 3: *Vengeance, pouvoirs et idéologies dans quelques civilisations de l'Antiquité.* Ed. R. Verdier and J.-P. Poly. Paris: Cujas, 1984. 13–33. **Lewy, J.** "Lexicographical Notes." *HUCA* 12/13 (1937/38) 91–101. **Lindström, F.** *God and the Origin of Evil: A Contextual Analysis of Alleged Monistic Evidence in the Old Testament.* ConBOT 21. Lund: Gleerup, 1983. **Lipiński, E.** "Sale, Transfer and Delivery in Ancient Semitic Terminology." In *Gessellschaft und Kultur im alten Vorderasien.* Ed. H. Klengel. SGKAO 15. Berlin: Akademie-Verlag, 1982. 173–85. **McCarthy, D. J.** "Some Holy War Vocabulary in Joshua 2." *CBQ* 33 (1971) 228–30. **McKane, W.** "Poison, Trial by Ordeal and the Cup of Wrath." *VT* 30 (1980) 474–92, esp. 478–84. **Mendenhall, G. E.** "The 'Vengeance' of Yahweh." In *The Tenth Generation: The Origins of the Biblical Tradition.* Baltimore: Johns Hopkins UP, 1973. 69–104, esp. 77, 84. **Moor, J. C. de.** "*Rāpi'ūma*—Rephaim." *ZAW* 88 (1976) 323–45. **Otto, E.** "Geschichte einer religiösen Formel (Du erhältst am Leben, wen du willst und du tötest, wen du willst)." *Zeitschrift für ägyptische Sprache und Altertumskunde* 87 (1962) 150–54. **Pitard, W. T.** "Amarna *ekēmu* and Hebrew *nāqam.*" *MAARAV* 3 (1982) 5–25. **Rabin, C.** "The 'Ideology' of Deborah's War." *JJS* 6 (1955) 125–34, esp. 130–32. ———. "Three Hebrew Terms from the Realm of Social Psychology." In *FS W. Baumgartner.* 1967. 219–30, esp. 219–25. **Robert, P. de.** "La Fin de Moïse: Les traditions Samaritaines." *MDB* 44 (1986) 24. **Saydon, P. P.** "The Meaning of the Expression *'āṣûr wᵉ'āzûb.*" *VT* 2 (1952) 371–74. **Schenker, A.** "*Kōper* et Expiation." *Bib* 63 (1982) 32–46. **Schnutenhaus, F.** "Das Kommen und Erscheinen Gottes im Alten Testament." *ZAW* 76 (1964) 1–22, esp. 8. **Seybold, K.** *Das Gebet der Kranken im Alten Testament.* BWANT 99. Stuttgart: Kohlhammer, 1973. 17–29, 39–55, 169. **Skehan, P. W.** "A Fragment of the 'Song of Moses' (Deut. 32) from Qumran." *BASOR* 136 (1954) 12–15. ———. "Qumran and the Present State of Old Testament Text Studies: The Masoretic Text." *JBL* 78 (1959) 21–25. ———. "The Structure of the Song of Moses in Deuteronomy (Deut. 32:1–43)." *CBQ* 12 (1951) 156. **Speiser, E. A.** "Pālil and Congeners: A Sampling of Apotropaic Symbols." In *Studies in Honor of B. Landsberger.* AS 16. Chicago: Oriental Institute, 1965. 389. ———. "The Stem *PLL* in Hebrew." *JBL* 82 (1963) 301–6. **Stager, L.** "The Archaeology of the East Slope of Jerusalem and the Terraces of the Kidron." *JNES* 41 (1982) 111–21. **Talmon, S.,** and **Fields, W. W.** "The Collocation *mashtin bakir ve'atsur ve'azuv* and Its Meaning." *ZAW* 101 (1989) 85–112. **Tigay, J. H.** "Excursus 31: Text and Theology in Deuteronomy 32:8 and 43." In *Deuteronomy.* 1996. 513–18. ———. "Some Archaeological Notes on Deuteronomy." In *FS J. Milgrom.* 1995. 377–80. **Toll, C.** "Ausdrücke für 'Kraft' im Alten Testament mit besonderer Rücksicht auf die Wurzel BRK."

ZAW 94 (1982) 111–23, esp. 120. **Tur-Sinai, N. H.** "Note on Dt XXXII 43." *Tarbiz* 24 (1955) 232 (Heb., Eng. summary). **Vinnikov, I. N.** "L'énigme de '*'āṣūr et 'āzūb*' (Dt 32,36 etc.)." In *FS A. Dupont-Sommer.* 1971. 343–45. **Waard, J. de.** *A Comparative Study of the Old Testament Text in the Dead Sea Scrolls and in the New Testament.* Studies in the Texts of the Desert of Judah 4. Leiden: Brill, 1965. 13–16, 81. **Walker, N.** "Concerning *hû'* and *'anî hû'*." *ZAW* 74 (1962) 205–6. **Westbrook, R.** "Lex Talionis and Exodus 21,22–25." *RB* 93 (1986) 52–69, esp. 58. **Williamson, H. G. M.** "A Reconsideration of *'zb* II in Biblical Hebrew." *ZAW* 97 (1985) 74–85.

Translation and Prosodic Analysis

God's "Vengeance"—Punishment and Salvation
[(4:4:4):(4:4:4):(4:4:4)] 9 versets

30 *How*[a] / *can one chase*\[b] *a thousand?* /	12	2
and two / put ten thousand to flight? //	16	2_
Unless / [c]*their rock had sold them* /	14	2
indeed YHWH / had given them up //	9	2_
31 *For / their rock is not / like our Rock* //	15	3
as even our enemies concede[a] //	<u>13</u>	1_
32 *For from the vine of Sodom / is their vine* /	11	2
and from the terraces / of Gomorrah //	11	2_
[a]*Their grapes*[a] / *are grapes*[b] *of poison*[c] /	13	2
their clusters / are venomous //	13	2_
33 *The venom of asps / is their wine* //	11	2
and deadly / poison of vipers //	<u>11</u>	2_
34 *Is that not /* [a]*laid up in store*[a] *with me* //	13	2
sealed up / in my treasuries? //	11	2_
35 *To me*[a] *belongs "vengeance" / and recompense* /	10	2
at the time / when their foot shall slip //	10	2_
For the day of their calamity / is near /	12	2
and impending doom / hastens upon them //	<u>12</u>	2_

God's Plan to Deliver Israel [(4:4):(4:4):(4:4):(5:5):(4:4):(4:4):(4:4)] 14 versets

36 *For YHWH will justify / his people* /	12	2
and on his servants / he will show compassion //	11	2
When he sees / that their power is gone /	11	2
and neither / ruler nor helper remains //	<u>12</u>	2_
37 *Then <YHWH>*[a] *will say / "Where*[b] *are their gods* //	16	2
the rock / [c]*in whom they sought refuge?"*[c] //	10	2
38 *Who ate*[a] / *the fat*[b] *of their sacrificial offerings?* /	18	2
[c]*They drank*[d] / *the wine of their libations*[e] //	<u>10</u>	2_
Let them rise up / [f]*and let them help* you[f] /	12	2
Let them be[g] a shelter / over you //	10	2_
39 See \[a] now /	6	1
that I alone \[b] am he / and there is no god / beside me //	<u>23</u>	3_
I myself deal death and I give life /	11	1
I wound / and indeed I heal /	12	2

and from my hand there is no / rescuing // 11 2_
40 For I raise to heaven[a] / my hand // 14 2
and I say / as I live / forever // 18 3_
41 When I whet[a] / my flashing sword / 10 2
and my hand lays hold / on judgment // 13 2
I will return "vengeance" / on my adversaries / 13 2
and as for those who hate me / I will repay them // 8 2_
42 [a]I will make my arrows drunk[a] / with blood / 9 2
and my sword / will devour flesh // 11 2
With blood of the slain / and the captive / 10 2
from the head / of the "longhaired leaders"[b] of the enemy // 11 2_
43 Make glad, O <heavens>[a] / [b]his people[b] / 13 2
[c]<and worship him | all you sons of God ||>[c] 13 2_
For the blood of [d]his servants[d] \[e] he will avenge /[f] 10 1
indeed "vengeance" \[g] he will return on his[h] adversaries[i] / 14 1
[j]and make atonement[j] for his[k] land / <and>[l] his people // פ 11 2_

Notes

30.a. SP reads איך for MT איכה, "how," with no change in meaning.
30.b. The *paštā'* followed by *zāqēp qāṭôn* is read as conj.
30.c. The phrase אם־לא כי is translated as "unless." The word כי, "that," is omitted in two Heb. MSS and SP (cf. LXX).
31.a. LXX reads ἀνόητοι, "fools" (= אוילים), for MT פלילים, "judges." On the usage of פלילים, see Exod 21:22. BDB, 813b, translates ואיבינו פלילים as "our enemies being judges."
32.a-a. SP and Syr. read ענביהם, "their grapes," for the more archaic form of the pronominal suffix in MT ענבמו, "their grapes."
32.b. B reads עִנְבֵי for MT עִנְּבֵי, "grapes," with no change in meaning.
32.c. A few Heb. MSS and SP read ראש, "bitter and poisonous herb," for MT רוש, "poison."
34.a-a. SP reads כָּנוּס, "gathered," for MT כָּמֻס, "sealed up"; cf. LXX συνῆκται, "stored up."
35.a. SP and LXX read ליום, "in the day," for MT לי, "to me."
37.a. Adding יהוה with 4QDeut[q] and LXX; SP reads pl. ואמרו, "and they will say."
37.b. SP, Tg., and *Tg. Ps.-J.* read איה for MT אי, "where," with no change in meaning.
37.c-c. LXX reads ἐφ' οἷς ἐπεποίθεισαν ἐπ' αὐτοῖς, "in whom they trusted," for MT חסיו בו, "in whom they sought refuge" (cf. Syr. and Vg.).
38.a. LXX reads 2 pl. for MT יאכלו, "they ate."
38.b. Cairo Geniza fragments read חלבי, "my fat," for MT חלב, "fat" (cf. Vg.).
38.c. SP, LXX, Syr., and Vg. add *waw*-conj. Prosodic analysis favors MT.
38.d. LXX reads 2 pl.
38.e. One Heb. MS and SP read נִסְכָּם, "their drink offerings," for MT נְסִיכָם, "their libations."
38.f-f. A few Heb. MSS, SP, Syr., and Vg. read (ו)יעזרוכם for MT ויעזרכם, "and let them help you," with no change in meaning.
38.g. Interpreting יהי, "let them be," in a pl. sense with SP and the ancient versions.
39.a. Reading *lĕgarmēh* (*mûnāḥ* plus *pāsēq*) as conj.
39.b. The *paštā'* followed immediately by *zāqēp parvum* is read as conj.
40.a. SP, Syr., Tg., and *Tg. Ps.-J.* read השמים, "the heavens," for MT שמים, "heavens." Prosodic analysis supports MT.
41.a. Some Heb. MSS and SP read שנתי for MT שנותי, "I whet," with no change in meaning.
42.a-a. DSS read אשכירה, "let me make drunk," for MT אשכיר, "I will make drunk."
42.b. The translation "longhaired leaders" attempts to convey the double meaning of the word פרעות (see *Comment* on 32:42). The root פרע appears elsewhere only in Num 6:5; Judg 5:2; and Ezek 44:20, where it seems to mean "uncut hair" or perhaps "leader(s)" or "soldier(s)."
43.a. Reading שמים, "heavens," with 4QDeut[q] and LXX for MT גוים, "nations."
43.b-b. One Heb. MS inserts אֶת before עמו, "his people." LXX reads ἅμα αὐτῷ, "with him" (= עִמּוֹ). In *BHS,* Hemple suggests the reading עַם עִמּוֹ, "with his people."

43.c-c. Adding והשתחוו לו כל בני אל, "and worship him all you sons of God" (cf. 4QDeut[q] and LXX καὶ ἐνισχυσάτωσαν αὐτῷ πάντες υἱοὶ Θεοῦ, "and let all the sons of God strengthen themselves in him"; and cf. the use of בני אל, "sons of God," in v 8). This colon was probably omitted in MT as a "nomistic correction" to prevent an angelological or polytheistic interpretation. Adding the line improves the prosodic balance and restores the larger structural design in terms of the numerical composition of Readings 9–11 (Deut 31–34). See the discussion at the end of the section on *Form/Structure/Setting.*

43.d-d. 4QDeut[q] and LXX read בניו, "his sons," for MT עבדיו, "his servants."

43.e. Reading *ṭip̄ḥā'* as conj. because of misplaced *'atnāḥ.*

14,f. Reading *ṭip̄ḥā'* as conj. because of misplaced *'atnāḥ.*

43.g. Reading *pašṭā'* followed by *zāqēp̄ qāṭôn* as conj.

43.h. Vg. reads *in hostes eorum,* "to their enemies" (= לצרימו), for MT לצריו, "to his enemies."

43.i. 4QDeut[q] and LXX add ולשנאיו ישלם, "and as for those who hate him, he will repay them" (from v 41).

43j-j. 4QDeut[q] reads ויכפר, "and he will make atonement," for MT וכפר, "and make atonement"; LXX adds κύριος, "Lord" (= יהוה).

43.k. 4QDeut[q], SP, LXX, and Vg. read אדמת, "the land (of his people)," for MT אדמתו, "his land."

43.l. Adding *waw*-conj. with Syr., Tg., and *Tg. Ps.-J.* This may be another example of the phenomenon of a shared consonant (see *Note* 32:11.c-c.).

Form/Structure/Setting

The focus of attention in the third cycle of twenty-three versets in the Song of Moses is on God's continued covenant loyalty in the face of Israel's perfidy as he plans to deliver them once again (v 36). God's "vengeance" has two sides, for it includes both punishment and salvation (vv 30–35). Moreover, the punishment includes the enemies God used to humble his people in the first place. YHWH will "show compassion" on his people "when he sees that their power is gone" (v 36). He will make clear that this was not accomplished by the gods of Israel's enemies, for he alone is God (vv 37–40). He will deliver Israel by returning "vengeance" on his adversaries (vv 41–42). The Song concludes, as it began, with a summons to praise and worship God—for avenging "the blood of his servants" and making "atonement for his land and his people" (v 43).

The third cycle in 32:30–43 is arranged in two parts, vv 30–35 and 36–43, which complete the larger menorah pattern of the Song of Moses as a whole:

A	In praise of YHWH, who is faithful and just	32:1–6
B	God's benefactions to Israel in the exodus/eisodus	32:7–14
C	Israel's apostasy: they forsook the God who made them	32:15–18
X	God's decision to punish Israel	32:19–25
C′	God's mercy: he chooses to limit Israel's punishment	32:26–29
B′	God's "vengeance"—punishment and salvation	32:30–35
A′	God's plan to deliver Israel and punish his enemies / praise	32:36–43

In terms of the prosodic structure of the three cycles of twenty-three versets in the Song of Moses, the first and third cycle are similar in that each is in two parts made up of nine versets (32:1–6 and 30–35) plus fourteen versets (32:7–14 and 36–43). The first cycle (vv 1–14) focuses primarily on the past, in praise of YHWH for creating Israel and caring for his people through the events of the exodus from Egypt and the journeys through the wilderness that brought them to the promised land. The third cycle (vv 30–43) focuses on the future, after God has used enemy nations to punish the people of Israel for their apostasy. God's "vengeance" means both punishment and salvation: punishment for Israel's enemies and salvation for his people, who have already received their deserved punishment at the hand of enemy nations. The second cycle (vv 15–29), which is in three parts, focuses on God's decision to punish Israel for their apostasy (vv 15–25), but not to destroy them utterly as they deserve (vv 26–29).

The internal structure of 32:30–35, which is marked by the change from plural to first-person plural forms in v 31 and the use of first-person singular forms as YHWH speaks in vv 34–35, may be outlined as follows:

A	Israel's defeat is a divinely determined rout	32:30
B	For our Rock is not like theirs (Who is like YHWH?)	32:31
X	The enemy will drink the cup of YHWH's wrath	32:32–33
B′	The matter is sealed up awaiting God's timing	32:34
A′	YHWH brings "vengeance" on his enemies	32:35

The outer frame in this structure moves from an account of YHWH's decision to deliver his people Israel into the hands of their enemies (v 30), to an announcement that YHWH has prepared his recompense on those enemies (v 35). The inner frame moves from a first-person plural account of the uniqueness of YHWH as Israel's "Rock" in relation to the gods of the enemies (v 31), to a first-person singular statement in regard to YHWH storing up the poisoned wine (v 34), which he will use in the cup of wrath that will be proffered to them (vv 32–33). Their end will be that of Sodom and Gomorrah.

The structure of vv 32–33, which occupies the center of the concentric design of 32:30–35, may be outlined in a similar manner:

A	"From the vine of Sodom is their vine"	32:32aα
B	"and from the terraces of Gomorrah"	32:32aβ
X	The grapes of YHWH's wrath / their grapes are poison	32:32b
B′	"The venom of asps is their wine"	32:33a
A′	"and deadly poison of vipers"	32:33b

In this structure we see more clearly the nature of YHWH's "vengeance" in the metaphor of the vine and the terraces of grapes that are linked with the image of the destruction of Sodom and Gomorrah (cf. Gen 19). YHWH's grapes of wrath will produce a wine as deadly as the venom of vipers, which those enemies are obliged to drink.

In v 36 a brief announcement of YHWH's plan to deliver Israel functions as the introduction to YHWH's speech in vv 37–42, in which he promises to return "vengeance" on his adversaries:

A	God's plan to deliver Israel when "their power is gone"	32:36
B	YHWH speaks: Where are your gods? Let them help you.	32:37–38
X	"I myself deal death and I give life"	32:39
B′	I swear that "I will return 'vengeance' on my adversaries"	32:40–42
A′	Celebration of God's deliverance of Israel	32:43

The outer frame in this structure moves from the announcement of YHWH's plan to plead the cause of his people "when he sees that their power is gone" and deliver them (v 36) to a joyous note of celebration for avenging the blood of his servants (v 43). In the inner frame, YHWH speaks. On the one hand, he ridicules Israel's enemies: "Where are their gods, the rock in whom they took refuge? . . . Let them help you" (vv 37–38). On the other hand, he swears a solemn oath: "I will return 'vengeance' on my adversaries" (vv 41). The boundary that separates v 39 from vv 37–38, in the center of this structure, is marked with the *Numeruswechsel.* YHWH declares his uniqueness, "There is no god beside me," and the nature of his "vengeance": "I myself deal death, and I give life; I wound, and indeed I heal; and from my hand there is no rescuing."

God's promise to return "vengeance" on his foes in vv 41–42 may be outlined in the form of a circular sentence:

A	When I whet *my flashing sword*	אם־שנותי ברק חרבי	32:41aα
B	and my hand lays hold on judgment	ותאחז במשפט ידי	32:41aβ
X	I will return "vengeance" on my adversaries . . .	אשיב נקם לצרי	32:41b
B′	I will make my arrows drunk with blood	אשכיר חצי מדם	32:42aα
A′	and *my sword* will devour flesh	וחרבי תאכל בשר	32:42aβ

The repetition of the word חרבי, "my sword," functions as an envelope in which the inner frame presents the pairing of ידי, "my hand," and חצי, "my arrows." The focus of attention in this structure is God's decision to "return 'vengeance' on my adversaries; and as for those who hate me, I will repay them" (v 41b). The concluding coda in v 43, which celebrates God's deliverance of Israel, has a similar structure with repetition of the word עמו, "his people," which becomes עבדיו, "his servants," in the center. The verse begins with a summons to the heavens to rejoice with YHWH's people and to worship YHWH; for he will "avenge" the blood of his sons, by punishing his adversaries and making "atonement for his land and his people."

The double meaning of the word פֶּרַע as "long hair" and "leader" in v 42, along with the parallel text in the opening verse of the Song of Deborah in Judg 5:2, was used to shape the telling of the story of Samson in Judg 13–16 in "protomidrashic" form along the lines of what we have already seen for 21:10–25:19 and narratives in the Torah and Former Prophets, and Genesis in particular. Samson appears as the last of the twelve "judges." The story in Judg 13–16 presents him as a "longhaired leader" who is neither a warlord in the normal sense of leading troops into battle—as is the case with Othniel, Ehud, Deborah (with Barak), Gideon, and Jephthah—nor a judge like Deborah, who "used to sit under the palm of Deborah; . . . and the people came up to her for judgment" (Judg 4:5). Samson is a leader who "delivered" Israel from the hand of the Philistines by killing them, as long as his hair remained uncut on his head. The influence of the words מראש פרעות, "from the head of the . . . leaders," of Deut 32:42 in shaping the structure of the book of Judges is shown by the following outline in a menorah pattern:

A	From Joshua to the period of the judges	Judg 1:1–3:6
B	Othniel, Ehud, Shamgar, and Deborah—בפרע פרעות (Judg 5:2)	3:7–5:31
C	Gideon and his son Abimelech in Ephraim—a מלך in Israel	6:1–9:57
X	Tola and Jair in Ephraim and Gilead	10:1–6
C′	Jephthah and his daughter in Gilead—ראש vs. קצין	10:7–12:7
B′	Ibzan, Elon, Abdon, and Samson—"no razor on his head"	12:8–16:31
A′	From the judges to Samuel—"there was no king in Israel"	17:1–21:25

The framework (A, X, A′) in this structure moves from a transitional section that connects the period of the twelve judges with the book of Joshua (Josh 1:1–3:6) to a parallel transitional section that connects the period of the twelve judges with the story of the prophet Samuel (1 Sam 1–8), with the curious "riddle at the middle" about Tola and Jair (Judg 10:1–5). In the inner frame of this menorah pattern, we find the key words for leadership so far as kingship is concerned. On the one hand (Judg 6–9), we learn that Gideon was asked by the people of Israel to "rule over us, you and your son and your grandson also" (Judg 8:22). That the institution of kingship is in mind is clear by the name of Gideon's son Abimelech ("my father is king") and by Jotham's fable (Judg 9:7–15), which speaks directly of Israel's first experience with "kingship" under Gideon's son, who ruled as "king" in Shechem for three years. On the other hand (Judg 10:7–12:7), the story of Jephthah explores two primary aspects of kingship in the usage of the key words for "leadership" in ancient Israel: ראש, "head," and קצין, "chief, ruler" (see Judg 11:6–11). The word ראש, which appears in Deut 32:42, is primarily a term for military leadership (as in 1:13–15; see J. R. Bartlett, "Use of the Word ראש as a Title in the Old Testament," *VT* 19 [1969] 1–10). On the other hand, the קצין is primarily a judicial figure, as witnessed by the village *qaḍi'* in Arabic, who is an elder, to whom civil cases are taken in matters of legal dispute. The *qaḍi'* is selected for his legal acumen and is seldom, if ever, a military figure. The second of the key words in Deut 32:42, פרעות, "longhaired leader," plays a central role in both halves of the second frame in the above concentric structural pattern for the book of Judges. The word appears twice in the opening verse of the Song of Deborah (Judg 5:2), and its dual meaning applies throughout in the story of Samson—the "longhaired leader" in Israel—and the last of the twelve judges, who delivered the people of Israel and ruled in the days when "there was no king in Israel" (Judg 17:6; 18:1; 19:1; 21:25).

The data from Labuschagne on the numerical composition of 32:30–43 may be summarized as follows:

Words:	before *'atnāḥ*			after *'atnāḥ*				
32:19–31	67		+	69	(= 3 × 23)	=	136	(= 8 × 17)
32:25–31	34	(= 2 × 17)	+	34	(= 2 × 17)	=	68	(= 4 × 17)
32:25–33	43	(= 17 + 26)	+	43	(= 17 + 26)	=	86	(= 2 × 43)
32:28–31	20		+	14		=	34	(= 2 × 17)
32:28–32	26		+	20		=	46	(= 2 × 23)
32:28–33	29		+	23		=	52	(= 2 × 26)
32:29–31	15		+	11		=	26	
32:32–36	26		+	26		=	52	(= 2 × 26)
32:34–36	17		+	17		=	34	(= 2 × 17)
32:36–39	26		+	25		=	51	(= 3 × 17)
32:37–39	20		+	17		=	37	
32:37–42	38		+	32		=	70	
32:39–42	27		+	24		=	51	(= 3 × 17)
32:39–43	35		+	34	(= 2 × 17)	=	69	(= 3 × 23)
32:1–18	105		+	87		=	192	
32:19–31	67		+	69	(= 3 × 23)	=	136	(= 8 × 17)
32:32–36	26		+	26		=	52	(= 2 × 26)

32:37–42	38		+	32		= 70	
32:43	8		+	10		= 18	
32:1–43	244		+	224	(= 7 × 32)	= 468	(= 18 × 26)
32:44–52	88		+	65		= 153	(= 9 × 17)
33:1–29	194		+	142		= 336	
34:1–12	107		+	67		= 174	
31:1–30	322	(= 14 × 23)	+	230	(=10 × 23)	= 552	(= 24 × 23)
32:1–52	332		+	289	(= 17 × 17)	= 621	
33:1–34:12	301		+	209		= 510	(= 30 × 17)
31:1–34:12	955		+	728	(= 28 × 26)	= 1,683	(= 99 × 17)

The first conclusion to be drawn from this data is the close manner in which this section of the Song of Moses is tied to what precedes, for a series of structures built on the two divine-name numbers 17 and 26 starts as early as 32:19, 25, 28, and 29. In addition to frequent use of these two numbers and multiples of them, there is also evidence for the use of both of the numbers associated with Hebrew כבוד, "glory," namely, 23 and 32.

When the data for the numerical composition of 32:30–43 are placed in their larger context, the results are remarkable. In Readings 9–11 (31:1–34:12) there is a grand total of 1,683 (= 99 × 17) words, and 728 (= 4 × 7 × 26) words after *'atnāḥ*. In the Song of Moses (32:1–43) there are 224 (= 7 × 32) words after *'atnāḥ* and a total of 468 (= 3 × 6 × 26). In Reading 10 (32:1–52) there are 289 (= 17 × 17) words. Numerous other examples of exact multiples of the two divine-name numbers 17 and 26, and of the two numbers associated with כבוד, "glory" (23 and 32), are also present in what is clearly a carefully crafted numerical composition, which was done to the glory of YHWH.

Comment

30 "One person chasing a thousand or two putting ten thousand to flight" is a proverbial motif (1 Sam 18:7; Isa 30:17). God fought in behalf of Israel's enemy, reversing Holy War ideology (see *Excursus:* "Holy War as Celebrated Event in Ancient Israel"). On the use of the word "Rock" see the *Comment* on 32:4.

31 The translation of ואיבינו פלילים as "even our enemies so assess it" follows E. Fox (*FBM,* 1005) in a paraphrastic attempt to render the sense of a difficult text. The NRSV reads "our enemies are fools," following LXX. Speiser's identification of the root פלל as "assess" is uncertain. G. E. Wright ("The Lawsuit of God," in *FS J. Muilenburg* [1962] 31 n. 17), following a suggestion of W. F. Albright, emends MT כי לא to הלא, "Are not our enemies themselves the judges?" In a somewhat similar manner, basing his arguments on the traditional interpretation of פלילים in Exod 21:22 as "judges," Craigie ([1976] 385) renders it "even our enemies may be judges!" Taking פלילים as cognate to Akkadian *palilu,* "meaning something like 'guardian,' 'leader,' used as an epithet of deities," Tigay suggests, "nor are our enemies' guardians [equal to our Rock]" ([1996] 310–11).

32–33 On the metaphor of an enemy nation drinking a poisonous drink for a disastrous fate, see D. L. Christensen, "Jeremiah and the 'Cup of YHWH's Wrath,'" in *Prophecy and War in Ancient Israel* (Berkeley: BIBAL Press, 1989) 193–207. The translation "terraces of Gomorrah" is problematic because the meaning of שדמת is uncertain. The JPS *Tanakh* renders it "vineyards," though "terraces" or "fields" is possible (see Stager, *JNES* 41 [1982] 111–21). The word שדמת was apparently chosen to be assonant with סדם, "Sodom." For a detailed interpretation of this word as a technical term associated with the cult of the god Mot, see Lehmann (*VT* 3 [1953] 361–71). Sodom and Gomorrah are referred to here as places of corruption and perversion, not as examples of utter destruction. The translation of אשכלת מררת, "their clusters are venomous," is based on Tigay's arguments for the meaning of מרירי (32:24) as "poisonous" ([1996] 311 and 404 n. 116). The translation "deadly poison of vipers" takes אכזר, "deadly," as an adjective of ראש, "poison," rather than of פתנים, "vipers" with the Targums: "poison of pitiless vipers" (Tigay [1996] 311). On the pairing of the words "serpents" and "asps" in Ugaritic, see Dahood, *RSP*, 1:374–75.

34 The word הוא, "that," refers to the "latter end" of Israel's enemies in v 29, or perhaps their calamity as announced in vv 32–33. The word כמס, "laid up in store," appears only here in the Hebrew Bible, and Mayes suggests emending it to read כנס, "gathered up, collected," with SP. As Tigay observes, "Describing the wine as 'sealed up' is based on the practice of sealing the latches to storerooms with clay, stamped with the signet of the king or the official in charge of them, so as to detect whether an unauthorized person had opened the room" ([1996] 311; see also idem, in *FS J. Milgrom*, 377–80).

35 "To me belongs 'vengeance' [נקם]." The verb נקם does not mean "to avenge," as in the primitive desert institution of the blood feud. The words from this root occur almost exclusively in contexts of mythology and international politics with the meaning of defensive vindication (as in Latin *vindicatio*). The familiar translation as "vengeance" is retained, but it is placed in quotation marks to alert the reader to this specialized meaning: "the executive exercise of power by the highest legitimate authority for the protection of his own subject" (Mendenhall, *Tenth Generation*, 69–104). The term לי, "is mine," was read as ליום, "for the day of," in LXX, which appears to be influenced by the thought of what follows: "at the time [לעת] . . . for the day of their calamity [יום אידם]." The expression יום אידם, "the day of their calamity," refers to that day when YHWH's storehouse is opened and the wicked enemy is forced to drink the cup of YHWH's wrath—and that day "is near, and impending doom [עתדת] hastens upon them." The word עתיד is normally an adjective with the meaning "ready" or "prepared." Here it is used substantively with the sense "the impending things are hastening [חש]." Paul quoted this verse in Rom 12:19 to support his contention that Christians ought to live at peace with others and under no circumstances seek revenge.

36 "YHWH will justify [ידין] his people"—literally he will "judge (in favor of)" Israel and "show compassion [יתנחם] upon his servants." There is overlap with the meaning of נקם, "to vindicate," of the previous verse, as Mayes notes ([1981] 391). YHWH will satisfy his anger by punishing the guilty. Tigay notes another possible translation, "change one's mind," "meaning that God will relent from punishing Israel after all that it has suffered" ([1996] 312). The translation of עצור ועזוב, "neither ruler nor helper," is that of Tigay ([1996] 312). The commonly accepted reading "neither bond nor free" (NRSV) is doubtful, since this would imply that neither slaves nor freemen remain and thus no one is left for God to deliver. Other suggestions include: "kept in by legal impurity or at large," "under taboo and free," and "under parental restraint and free from it." For other occurrences of the idiom, see 1 Kgs 14:10; 21:21; 2 Kgs 9:8; and 14:26 (where it appears in a similar context). Reasoning from a careful examination of each of these texts, Tigay concludes, "The verse would then mean that God will act when he, or Israel, sees that Israel is without a ruler and helper to deliver it."

37–38 The reference to "the rock" is ironic, as it is in v 31 above—these false gods are nothing in comparison with YHWH, the true "Rock." The question "Who ate?" is sarcastic. The false gods are presented as eating and drinking the offerings, but they are powerless to "be a shelter over you." The reference to "the fat of their sacrificial offerings" is to the fat parts or pieces, which in Levitical legislation were reserved for God or here for strange gods (see Hallo, in *FS F. M. Cross: Ancient Israelite Religion* [1987] 3–13.

39 The powerlessness of foreign gods (vv 37–38) is contrasted with the efficacy of YHWH (v 39). On similar use of repeated words such as אני אני הוא, "I alone am he" (lit. "I, I am he"), see 2:27 and 16:20. The expression "there is no god beside me" (עמדי, "with me") does not deny the existence of other gods, as in 4:35, 39. It merely focuses attention on the uniqueness of YHWH: "I myself deal death and I give life, I wound and indeed I heal." It is YHWH alone who determines the welfare of human beings. The false gods are powerless before YHWH: "from my hand there is no rescuing." As Mayes observes ([1981] 392), the closest parallels to v 39 are Isa 41:4; 43:10, 13; 44:6; 45:6–7, 22; 48:12.

40–41 The expression "I raise to heaven my hand" refers to the making of a solemn oath, which continues in the expression "as I live forever." On the structure of this oath formula, see the discussion of Lehmann in *ZAW* 81 (1969) 74–92. The reference to YHWH's "flashing sword" is the language of Holy War, and the image of the Divine Warrior in particular (see Exod 15:3; the "Song of the Sword" in Isa 34:5–6; and the "sword of YHWH" in Jer 47:6). The word משפט, "judgment," here refers to a "weapon of judgment" in the hand of YHWH—the "flashing sword" of the parallel line in this verset. On the meaning of נקם, "vengeance," see the *Comment* on v 35.

42 The expression "blood of . . . the captive" alludes to the custom of slaughtering prisoners after the victory (Driver [1895] 380). The meaning of ראש פרעות, translated here as "the head of the 'longhaired leaders,'" is uncertain. Of the four passages where the word פרע appears, it refers to locks of hair in Num 6:5 and Ezek 44:20; the meaning in Judg 5:2 and here is less certain. The word פרע has therefore been taken to mean longhaired (probably uncut or disheveled), referring to the practice of warriors like Samson letting their hair grow long, either out of a belief that strength resides in their hair or as a mark of the Nazirite vow (see Num 6:1–21; Judg 13:1–5). Since "there is little evidence that warriors normally did this in the ancient Near East," Tigay suggests the meaning "leaders" or "soldiers" for פרעות in Judg 5:1, where it parallels עם, "people, army" ([1996] 314).

A seal cut from white opal found in Samaria has the inscription לפרע alongside the portrayal of a bearded human figure with long hair, dressed only in an apron, walking to the right and holding a rod or staff in his left hand (for photo see *BeO* 19 [1977] 169). In his analysis of this seal, A. Reifenberg concludes, "If

פרע in our case is not a proper name it may simply point to the fact that it is the 'leader's' seal." In short, as Reifenberg puts it, "there existed seals giving only the official capacity of its owner, but not his proper name" (*PEQ* [1939] 197), which he substantiated with another seal published by E. L. Sukenik (*Palestine Exploration Fund Quarterly Statement* [1928] 51) with the inscription לשר, "for the governor," and the portrayal of the transport of a prisoner by a man carrying a similar rod or staff in his left hand (cf. 1 Kgs 24:26–27). Tigay goes further to suggest the emendation of ראש, "head," to שאר, "flesh," with the original meaning of the phrase here as "flesh of the enemy troops" ([1996] 314 and 405 n. 169; cf. C. Rabin, *JJS* 6 [1955] 131). A simpler solution is to read פַּרְעוֹת here as a poetic allusion to פַּרְעֹה, "Pharaoh," the title of Egyptian kings. The meaning would then be something like "from the head of the *pharaohs* [using the term loosely] of your enemies," which is what I am attempting to express in the translation "from the head of the 'longhaired leaders' of the enemy." The word שְׁבִיָּה, "captive," in the preceding phrase, along with images of YHWH's Holy War as originally expressed in the earlier Song of Moses preserved in Exod 15, led the poet to a metaphoric use of the word פרעות in the sense of "pharaohs" (i.e., leaders), which may have influenced the subsequent use of the newly coined word for "leaders" in the Song of Deborah (Judg 5:1) as well.

43 The text of this verse in LXX and DSS is considerably longer and has produced much comment (see Skehan, *CBQ* 12 [1951] 156; idem, *BASOR* 136 [1954] 12–15; Albright, *VT* 9 [1959] 340–41; and *Comment* on 32:8). The translation "make glad, O heavens" is based on an emendation of the text, with 4QDeut^q and LXX, to read הרנינו השמים in place of MT הרנינו גוים. The usual translation "Praise his people, O you nations," is in tension with its larger context; and it is unjustified in light of the textual evidence from DSS and LXX. The subsequent clause, "and worship him all you sons of God," is restored from 4QDeut^q and LXX. On the meaning of בני אלהים, "sons of God;" see the *Comment* on 32:8. In place of "the blood of his servants [עבדיו]," 4QDeut^q and LXX read τὸ αἷμα τῶν υἱῶν αὐτοῦ, "the blood of his sons [בניו]." In this part of the poem, Israel is no longer described as God's children but as his servants (see v 36), whom God "will avenge" (יקום, from the root נקם).

Explanation

Israel's trouble at the hands of their adversaries is the result of YHWH's giving them up (v 30). It is not the gods of the enemy who have done this, for everything belonging to them is vile and poisonous (vv 31–33). The time for YHWH's just and punishing action against his enemies is coming; for "the day of their calamity is near, and impending doom hastens upon them" (vv 34–35).

Unless the people of Israel had provoked God by their sins to deliver them into the hands of their enemies, no power would have prevailed against them; for God would have continued to be their protector and helper. The corruption of Israel is described in the metaphor of a vineyard that yields "grapes of poison"—where their iniquity surpasses that of Sodom and Gomorrah in ages past (cf. the "Song of the Unfruitful Vineyard" in Isa 5:1–7). All their wickedness was noticed and "laid up in store" (v 34), until the appointed time of YHWH's "vengeance" (v 35). Paul quotes the words of this text in Rom 12:19 to emphasize the biblical position that vengeance is God's portion and not an option for an individual to exercise. The word "vengeance" in English almost always means requital out of an angry and vengeful spirit; but this is not what the word נקם means in Hebrew. As shown in the *Comment* on vv 35–36, the word carries the meaning of defensive vindication, in what may be either punishment or salvation in a given situation. In this instance, God has chosen to limit the nature of Israel's justly deserved punishment (vv 26–29) by turning his attention to the punishment of Israel's enemies—"for the day of their calamity is near, and impending doom hastens upon them" (v 35). God's plan is to deliver Israel, by showing compassion on them, "when he sees that their power is gone and neither ruler nor helper remain" (v 36). YHWH will make a mockery of the foreign gods to which the people have turned, for none can deliver from his hand (vv 37–39). "'Vengeance' he will return on his adversaries, and make atonement for his land and his people" (v 43). When the cup of God's wrath goes round and all the nations drink it, "They shall drink and stagger and be crazed because of the sword which I am sending among them" (Jer 25:16). As the apostle Peter put it, "the time has come for judgment to begin with the household of God; and if it begins with us, what will be the end of those who do not obey the gospel of God?" (1 Pet 4:17).

The concept of God's "vengeance" as both punishment and salvation is a primary theme in shaping the book of Judges. The theme is stated explicitly in Judg 2:11–12 (NRSV):

> Then the Israelites did what was evil in the sight of the LORD and worshiped the Baals; and they abandoned the LORD, the God of their ancestors, who brought them out of the land of Egypt; they followed other gods, from among the gods of the peoples who were all around them, and bowed down to them; and they provoked the LORD to anger. . . . So the anger of the LORD was kindled against Israel, and he gave them over to plunderers who plundered them, and he sold them into the power of their enemies all around, so that they could no longer withstand their enemies. . . . Then the LORD raised up judges, who delivered them out of the power of those who plundered them. Yet they did not listen even to their judges; for they lusted after other gods and bowed down to them.

And the cycle began again, and is repeated over and over again. When the people of Israel were sore oppressed, "they put away the foreign gods from among them and worshiped the LORD; and he could no longer bear to see Israel suffer" (Judg 10:16 NRSV). In short, when they were reduced to the last extremity, when "their power was gone, and neither ruler nor helper remained" (Deut 32:36), then God stepped in to help them. God's time to deliver his people is when things are at their worst for them. God tries our faith by knocking out all the props, as it were, so that we stand helpless, so as to magnify his own power and glory in snatching the brands out of the fire (Zech 3:2).

B. Moses' Final Charge to "All Israel" (32:44–47)

Bibliography

Aharoni, Y. "Three Hebrew Ostraca from Arad." *BASOR* 197 (1970) 25. **Gross, W.** "Bundeszeichen und Bundesschluß in der Priesterschrift." *TTZ* 87 (1978) 98–115, esp. 107 n. 25. **Kutsch, E.** "Menschliche Weisung—Gesetz Gottes: Beobachtungen zu einem aktuellen Thema." In *Gott ohne Eigenschaften?* Ed. S. Heine and E. Heintel. Vienna: Evangelischer Presseverband, 1983. 77–106, esp. 83. **Laberge, L.** "Le texte de Deutéronome 31 (Dt 31,1–29; 32,44–47)." In *Pentateuchal and Deuteronomic Studies.* Ed. C. Brekelmans and J. Lust. BETL 94. Leuven: Leuven UP, 1990. 143–60. **McCarthy, D. J.** "Covenant and Law in Chronicles-Nehemiah." *CBQ* 44 (1982) 25–44, esp. 38. **Perlitt, L.** "Priesterschrift im Deuteronomium?" *ZAW* Sup 100 (1988) 65–88.

Translation and Prosodic Analysis

Moses' Final Charge to "All Israel" [(6:5):(5:5):(5:6)]

44 And Moses came / and he spoke / all the words of this song /	26	3
in the ears of the people //	8	1
he / and Hoshea the son of Nun //	11	2_
45 And when Moses finished / speaking / [a]all[b] these words[a] /	23	3
to all Israel // 46 he said to them /	15	2_
Set your hearts / toward all[a] the words /	16	2
that I / am giving in witness against you / TODAY //	18	3_
That you may command them / to your children /	11	2
to take care <and>[b] to do / all the words / of this Torah //	21	3_
47 For / this is not a trifling matter / for you /	14	3
for it / is your life //	8	2_
And through this word / you shall long endure \[a] on the land /	27	2
that you / are crossing the Jordan /	14	2
(to go) there / to possess it // ס	8	2_

Notes

45.a-a. Omitted in LXX[Bmin]. Prosodic analysis favors MT.

45.b. The word כל, "all," is omitted in a few Heb. MSS, SP, LXX[-LO], and Syr. The omission improves the balance in terms of mora count, but I reject it here because it disturbs the pattern in the numerical composition, i.e., the total of 68 (= 4 × 17) words.

46.a. SP reads על כל, "according to all," for MT כל, "all." Prosodic analysis favors MT.

46.b. Adding *waw*-conj. with some Heb. MSS, SP, LXX, Syr., and Vg. (cf. 28:1).

47.a. Reading *pašṭā'* followed by *zāqēp qāṭôn* as conj.

Form/Structure/Setting

The two-part paragraph in 32:44–47, which serves as an editorial conclusion to the Song of Moses, corresponds to 31:16–22, 28–29. Driver ([1906] 381) suggests that 31:16–22 and 32:44 belong together, as do 31:28–29 and 32:45–47.

The three-part Song of Moses (32:1–43), within its narrative framework, may be outlined in a menorah pattern:

A	Moses gives *the Torah* to the Levitical priests	31:24–27
B	Moses gathers the leaders to hear *the song*	31:28–30
C	God's blessing of Israel in times past	32:1–14
X	Israel's sin provokes God's anger	32:15–29
C′	God's punishment and salvation	32:30–43
B′	Moses spoke all the words of *this song* to the people	32:44–45
A′	Moses commands them to observe all the words of *the Torah*	32:46–47

The outer frame in this structure focuses on the Torah that Moses gave to the Levitical priests (31:24–27), and which he commanded all Israel to observe (32:44–45). The second frame concerns the Song of Moses that Moses assembled the leaders to hear (31:28–30), and that he recited to the people (32:44–45). Another way of showing the nested nature of this double frame is to note the repetition of words:

A	"the words of this Torah"	את־דברי התורה־הזאת	31:24
B	"the words of this song"	את־דברי השירה הזאת	31:30
X	the Song of Moses		32:1–43
B′	"all the words of this song"	את־כל־דברי השירה־הזאת	32:44
A′	"all the words of this Torah"	את־כל־דברי התורה הזאת	32:46

The phrase "the words of this Torah" occur at the beginning of the first half of the outer frame (31:24–27) and the end of the second half (32:46–47). The phrase "the words of this song" appears immediately before the Song of Moses (31:30) and immediately afterward (32:44).

On the use of the data from Labuschagne in regard to the numerical composition of 32:44–47 within its larger literary context, see the discussion at the end of the section on *Form/Structure/Setting* for 32:30–43. The passage here has a total of 68 (= 4 × 17) words, with 40 words before *ʾatnāḥ* and 28 words after *ʾatnāḥ*.

Comment

44 The words "Moses came" refer back to 31:22, where "Moses wrote this song in that day, and he taught it to the children of Israel." The LXX repeats 31:22 at this point in the text to make the recapitulation explicit. The name "Hoshea" refers to Joshua, who was renamed by Moses in Num 13:16 (see also Num 13:8, where his name appears as "Hoshea son of Nun").

45–46 The reference to "all these words" here refers to the whole book of Deuteronomy, including the Song of Moses. This is also what is meant by the statement "all the words that I am giving in witness against you [מעיד בכם]." The same verb appears in 31:28, which I translate "let me call as witness against them [ואעידה בם]." That the people are instructed to "command them to your children" indicates that "the words" here refer to Deuteronomy as a whole and not just the Song, for there are no commands in the Song as such. The instruction of the younger generation is an important theme that runs through the whole of Deuteronomy (cf. 4:9; 6:7; 11:19; 31:13).

47 The teaching "is not a trifling matter" (דבר רק); cf. Isa 55:11, "So shall my word be that goes from my mouth; it shall not return to me empty [ריקם]." Tigay calls attention to the fact that Hammurabi uses the same term regarding his own laws ([1996] 316): "My words are choice, my deeds have no equal; it is only to the fool that they are *empty;* to the wise they stand forth as an object of wonder" (Code of Hammurabi, Epilogue, rev., xxv, ll. 100–104; see *ANET,* 178). The unusual use of the Hebrew preposition מן here, "literally 'for it is not an empty thing *from* you' . . . prompted a midrashic explanation: there is nothing empty in the Torah, and if it is empty (unclear, meaningless)—(it is) from you; it is due to your own failure to study it thoroughly" (Tigay [1996] 316).

Explanation

As a final charge to the people of Israel, Moses and Joshua together remind them to take to heart all the words of this Torah and the Song of Moses and to see that this teaching is handed on to their children in generations to come. Nothing is more important.

The words of Moses here could not be more emphatic: "Set your hearts toward all the words that I am giving in witness against you today. . . . For this is not a trifling matter for you; for it is your life" (vv 46–47). If people were fully persuaded of this, that our religion is our life, how differently we would order our conduct.

C. YHWH's Command to Moses to Climb Mount Nebo to "See" the Land (32:48–52)

Bibliography

Alfrink, L. "L'Expression *ne'eśaph 'el 'ammāw.*" *OTS* 5 (1948) 118–31. **Horst, F.** "Zwei Begiffe für Eigentum (Besitz)." In *FS W. Rudolph.* 1961. 135–56, esp. 153–56. **Hurvitz, A.** "Dating the Priestly Source in Light of the Historical Study of Biblical Hebrew." *ZAW* Sup 100 (1988) 33. **Lux, R.** "Der Tod des Mose als 'besprochene und erzählte Welt': Überlegungen zu einer literaturwissenschaftlichen und theologischen Interpretation von Deuteronomium 32,48–55 und 34,1." *ZTK* 84 (1987) 395–425. **Milgrom, J.** "The Concept of *Ma'al* in the Bible and the Ancient Near East." *JAOS* 96 (1976) 236–47. **Rodriguez Carmona, A.** "Los Anuncios de la Muerte de Moises en el Targum Palestinense." In *FS L. Alonso Schökel.* 1983. 267–79, esp. 272–75. **Seebass, H.** "Josua." *BN* 28 (1985) 53–65. **Vaux, R. de.** "Le pays de Canaan." *JAOS* 88 (1968) 23–30.

See also *Bibliography* for 34:1–8.

Translation and Prosodic Analysis

YHWH's Command to Moses to Climb Mount Nebo to "See" the Land
[(7:9):(5:5):(9:7)]

48 And YHWH spoke / to Moses / on THIS / SAME DAY\[a] saying //	24	4
49 "Go up / on this mountain of the Abarim / Mount Nebo[a] /	18	3_
Which / is in the land of Moab /	9	2
which / is opposite Jericho //	11	2
And see / the land of Canaan /	11	2
which I am giving / to the Israelites / for a possession //	22	3_
50 And die / on the mountain / where you \[a] are going up there /	19	3
and be gathered / unto [b]your people[b] //	12	2_
Just as Aaron your brother / died / on Mount Hor /	21	3
and he was gathered / unto [c]his people[c] //	10	2_
51 Because you broke faith / with me[a] / among \[b] the Israelites /	19	3
by the waters of Meribath-kadesh / in the wilderness of Zin //	14	2
Because you did not revere / me /	12	2
among / the Israelites //	11	2_
52 At a distance / you shall see the land //	13	2
but there / you shall not enter / [a]the land /	15	3
which I am giving / to the children of Israel[a] // פ	17	2_

Notes

48.a. Reading *ṭip̱ḥāʾ* as conj. because of misplaced *sillûq*.

49.a. SP reads נבא for MT נבו, "Nebo," with no change in meaning; LXX reads Ναβαυ.

50.a. Reading *pašṭāʾ* followed by *zāqēp̱ qāṭôn* as conj.

50.b-b. Reading עַמְּךָ, "your people [sg.]," for MT עַמֶּיךָ, "your people [pl.]," with a number of Heb. MSS, SP, LXX, Syr., and Tg.

50.c-c. Reading עַמּוֹ, "his people [sg.]," for MT עמיו, "his people [pl.]," with SP, LXX, Syr., and Tg.

51.a. LXX reads τῷ ῥήματί μου, "my word" (= בִּדְבָרִי) for MT בִּי, "with me." Prosodic analysis supports MT.

51.b. Reading *pašṭāʾ* followed by *zāqēp̱ qāṭôn* as conj.

52.a-a. Omitted in LXX; prosodic analysis supports MT.

Form/Structure/Setting

This transitional passage looks back to 3:27, and even further back to Num 27:12–14, where the same words appear. Though Deut 32:48–52 plays an introductory role in relation to what follows on the death of Moses, it also plays a significant role in relation to what precedes it from the beginning of Reading 9 (31:1–30), as the following outline indicates:

A	Moses' final provisions in view of his nearing death	31:1–13
B	YHWH's charge to Moses and Joshua in the tent of meeting	31:14–23
C	Moses' provisions regarding the song	31:24–30
X	The Song of Moses	32:1–43
C′	Moses' last charge to "all Israel"	32:44–47
B′	YHWH's command to Moses to climb the mountain	32:48–52
A′	Moses' blessing, death, funeral, and necrology	33:1–34:12

This particular outline is adapted from that of Labuschagne, who describes it as an example of the "menorah pattern" (see "The Setting of the Song of Moses in Deuteronomy," in *FS C. H. W. Brekelmans* [1997] 115). In this reading the Song of Moses (32:1–43) is the structural center of the second half of what I have called the outer frame (Deut 31–34).

The passage also anticipates what is yet to come in 34:1–4, as the following outline indicates:

A	Moses is commanded to ascend Mount Nebo to "see" the land	32:48–52
B	First stanza of an ancient hymn	33:1–5
X	Moses' testamentary blessing on the twelve tribes of Israel	33:6–25
B′	Second stanza of an ancient hymn	33:26–29
A′	Moses ascends Mount Nebo, where he sees the land	34:1–4

The last will and testament of Moses, which is addressed to the twelve tribes of Israel (33:6–25), is framed with parallel passages on Moses' ascent of Mount Nebo to see the promised land from a distance (32:48–52 and 34:1–4). The testamentary blessing itself is further framed by placing it between two parallel sections of an ancient theophanic hymn (33:1–5 and 26–29).

The boundaries of 32:48–52 are marked with *pĕtûḥāʾ* layout markers at the beginning and end. No indications are given on matters of internal structure, other than the content itself, which may be outlined as follows:

A	Moses is told to go up on Mount Nebo and see the land	32:48–49
B	God's judgment: Moses is to die on the mountain	32:50a
X	Just as his brother Aaron died on Mount Hor	32:50b
B′	Reason for judgment: Moses "sinned" at Meribath-kadesh	32:51
A′	Moses is permitted to see the land from a distance	32:52

Moses has reached that point in his personal journey where he must follow his brother Aaron in death, leaving behind his successor Joshua to take the people of Israel into the promised land.

The data from Labuschagne on the numerical composition of 32:48–52 within the larger literary context of Readings 9–11 (Deut 31–34, the outer frame) may be summarized as follows:

Words:	before *ʾatnāḥ*		after *ʾatnāḥ*		
32:44–47	40	+	28		= 68 (= 4 × 17)
32:48–52	48	+	37		= 85 (= 5 × 17)
32:44–52	88	+	65		= 153 (= 9 × 17)
32:1–52	332	+	289	(= 17 × 17)	= 621
31:1–34:12	955	+	728	(= 28 × 26)	= 1,683 (= 99 × 17)

Both of the divine-name numbers 17 and 26 have been carefully woven into the fabric of the Hebrew text of Deut 31–34, of which 32:48–52 is an essential part.

Comment

48 Though the phrase "on this same day" is part of the series of temporal expressions discussed earlier (see *Note* 1:9.a), it also looks back to 1:3, when Moses began to expound the Torah on the first day of the eleventh month (Sebat) in the fortieth year after the exodus from Egypt. That task is now completed and the day in question is the day of Moses' death (see 34:5), which according to Josephus occurred on the first day of the twelfth month (i.e., in Adar; see Josephus *Ant.* 4.8.49 §327). As there was exactly one month between the completion of the building of the tabernacle at Mount Sinai in Exod 40:33 and the departure of the people of Israel from Mount Sinai in Num 10:11, so there was only one month between the arrival of Moses and the people of Israel on the plains of Moab in Num 36:13 and the death of Moses in Deut 34:5.

49 The traditional location of Mount Nebo is Ras es-Siyaghah (3,586 ft.), which is located above the northeast corner of the Dead Sea, "opposite Jericho," which is visible in the Jordan Valley below. Though the site provides a spectacular view of the promised land, as so many tourists and pilgrims through the years know by experience, it is not possible to see from there all that God showed Moses, namely the whole of the land—"as far as Dan . . . and the Negev," including "the Western [Mediterranean] Sea" (34:1–3). As the Arabic name suggests, Jebel Neba (3,935 ft.) is also a candidate for this honor. The "land of Canaan" here refers to the whole of the promised land as envisioned by Moses; this expression corresponds in meaning to the use of the term in Egyptian sources as the region under their control (see de Vaux, *JAOS* 88 [1968] 23–30).

50 Milgrom says (*Numbers* [1990] 169–70) that the idiom "be gathered unto your people" refers to a specific ancient idea in which the spirit of the deceased is united with those of one's ancestors in the afterlife of Sheol (the grave). See the *Comment* on 31:16. According to Num 33:38, the death of "Aaron your brother" on Mount Hor occurred exactly six months earlier (on the first day of the fifth month). See also Num 20:23–28. The statement in Deut 10:6 that Aaron died at Moserah on the journey from Beeroth Bene-jaakan suggests that Mount Hor is to be located near the border of ancient Edom as one journeys east from Kadesh-barnea to the rift valley of the Arabah. The most likely site is Jebel Madurah, 15 miles northeast of Kadesh, at the extreme northwestern boundary of Edom.

51–52 Milgrom discusses ten explanations given by medieval Jewish commentators for what Moses did wrong (see his "Excursus 50: Magic, Monotheism, and the Sin of Moses," in *Numbers,* 448–56) and concludes that the sin of Moses "may not have been in what he said but in the bare fact that he spoke at all" (p. 454). The "wilderness of Zin" is the desert region in the Negev that is elsewhere referred to as the wilderness of Kadesh (Ps 29:8). It is thus part of "that great and terrible wilderness" of Deut 1:19 and 8:15. The translation "at a distance" (מנגד) is that of E. Fox (*FBM,* 1008). The same expression appears in 2 Kgs 2:15.

Explanation

As Matthew Henry put it long ago, Moses "did not carry himself with a due decorum, in executing the orders he had then received" (*Exposition of the Old and New Testament* [1828] 706).

As a good many other pilgrims have done through the years, I remember well standing on top of Mount Nebo at the traditional sight where Moses looked across reflecting on these events. I tried to imagine what Moses might have thought and felt at that moment—a mixture of joy and sadness. It was a joy to know that the long journey through the wilderness had come to an end, for they had reached their destination. But at the same time, there was sadness to know the lasting consequences of those acts at the waters of Meribah.

There is a practical lesson here about the price of sins we commit, however provoked we may be at the moment. But there is also a deeper lesson in that a visionary leader who is called to take a people to a "new land" often takes them only to the edge of his or her dream. Martin Luther King (1929–68) knew this, as did Mahatma Gandhi (1869–1948) and so many others in times past.

Happy are they who die with the promised inheritance in full view, and with clear assurance of eternal life. At the same time, let us remember to walk circumspectly, lest some false step we have taken be remembered against us on a deathbed and render that final scene less comfortable.

Reading 11: Moses' Blessing, Death, Funeral, and Necrology (33:1–34:12)

Bibliography for 33:1–29

Albright, W. F. *Yahweh and the Gods of Canaan.* 1968. 17. **Armerding, C.** "The Last Words of Moses: Deuteronomy 33." *BSac* 114 (1957) 225–34. **Budde, K.** *Der Segen Mose Dt 33 erläutert und übersetzt.* Tübingen, 1922. **Burkitt, F. C.** "On the Blessing of Moses." *JTS* 35 (1934) 68. **Caquot, A.** "Les bénédictions de Moise (Deutéronome 33,6–25): I—Ruben, Juda, Lévi, Benjamin." *Sem* 32 (1982) 67–81. ———. "Les bénédictiones de Moise (Deutéronome 33,6–25): II—De Joseph à Asher." *Sem* 33 (1983) 59–76. **Cassuto, U.** "Deuteronomy Chapter xxxiii and the New Year in Ancient Israel." In *Biblical and Oriental Studies.* Tr. I. Abrahams. 2 vols. Jerusalem: Magnes, 1973–75. 1:47–70. **Christensen, D. L.** "Two Stanzas of a Hymn in Deuteronomy 33." *Bib* 65 (1984) 382–89. **Clements, R.** *In Spirit and in Truth: Insights from Biblical Prayers.* Atlanta: John Knox, 1985. **Collins, T.** *Line-Forms in Hebrew Poetry: A Grammatical Approach to the Stylistic Study of the Hebrew Prophets.* Studia Pohl, Series Maior. Rome: Biblical Institute Press, 1978. **Craigie, P. C.** "The Conquest and Early Hebrew Poetry." *TynBul* 20 (1969) 76–94. **Cross, F. M.,** and **Freedman, D. N.** "The Blessing of Moses." *JBL* 67 (1948) 191–210. ———. *Studies in Ancient Yahwistic Poetry.* SBLDS 21. Missoula, MT: Scholars Press, 1975. 97–124 (2nd ed. Grand Rapids: Eerdmans, 1997). **Fensham, C. F.** "The Use of the Suffix Conjugation and the Prefix Conjugation in a Few Old Hebrew Poems." *JNSL* 6 (1978) 9–18. **Freedman, D. N.** "Divine Names and Titles in Early Hebrew Poetry." In *FS G. E. Wright.* 1976. 55–107, esp. 68–70. ———. "The Poetic Structure of the Framework of Deuteronomy 33." In *FS C. H. Gordon.* 1980. 25–46. ———. *Pottery, Poetry, and Prophecy: Studies in Early Hebrew Poetry.* Winona Lake: Eisenbrauns, 1980. ———. "'Who Is Like Thee among the Gods?': The Religion of Early Israel." In *FS F. M. Cross.* 1987. 315–35, esp. 318–23. **Garsiel, M.** *Biblical Names: A Literary Study of Midrashic Derivations and Puns.* Ramat Gan: Bar Ilan UP, 1981. 104–5, 115, 143, 172, 178. **Gaster, T. H.** "An Ancient Eulogy on Israel: Deuteronomy 33:3–5, 26–29." *JBL* 66 (1947) 53–62. **Geus, C. H. J. de.** *The Tribes of Israel: An Investigation of Some of the Presuppositions of Martin Noth's Amphictyony Hypothesis.* Assen; Amsterdam: Van Gorcum, 1976. **Graf, K. H.** *Der Segen Moses.* Leipzig: Dyk, 1857. 9–10. **Gunneweg, A. H. J.** "Über den Sitz im Leben der sogenannten Stammessprüche." *ZAW* 76 (1964) 245–55. **Halpern, B.** *The Emergence of Israel in Canaan.* SBLMS 29. Chico, CA: Scholars Press, 1983. 149–56. **Hoonacker, A. Van.** "Notes sur le texte de la 'Bénédiction de Moïse' (Deut. XXXIII)." *Mus* 42 (1929) 42–60. **Kaufmann, Y.** *The Religion of Israel.* Tr. M. Greenberg. Chicago: Univ. of Chicago Press, 1960. 242–44. **Kittel, H. J.** "Die Stammessprüche Israels: Gen 49 und Dt 33 traditionsgeschichtlich untersucht." Diss., Berlin, 1959. **Labuschagne, C. J.** "The Tribes in the Blessing of Moses." *OTS* 19 (1974) 97–112. **Mowinckel, S.** *Der actungsechzigste Psalm.* Avhandlinger utgitt av det Norske videnskaps-akademi i Oslo II. Historisk-filosofisk klasse 1. Oslo: Dybwad, 1953. **Nielsen, E.** "Historical Perspectives and Geographical Horizons: On the Question of North-Israelite Elements in Deuteronomy." In *Law, History, and Tradition.* 1983. 82–92, esp. 81–82. **Nordheim, E. von.** *Die Lehre der Alten: I. Das Testament als literarische Gattung im Judentum der hellenistisch-römischen Zeit.* ALGHJ 13. Leiden: Brill, 1980. **O'Connor, M.** *Hebrew Verse Structure.* Winona Lake, IN: Eisenbrauns, 1980. 207–18, 433–43, 550–52. **Phythian-Adams, W. J.** "On the Date of the 'Blessing of Moses' (Deut XXXIII)." *JPOS* 3 (1923) 158–66. **Riessler, P.** "Das Moseslied und der Mosessegen." *BZ* 11 (1913) 119–28. **Robertson, D. A.** *Linguistic Evidence in Dating Early Hebrew Poetry.* SBLDS 3. Missoula, MT: Scholars Press, 1972. 49–56, 68. **Rofé, A.** "Moses' Blessing, the Sanctuary at Nebo and the Origin of the Levites." In *FS E. Loewenstamm.* 1978. 409–24 (Heb.; Eng. summary, 207–9). **Sanmartín, J.** "Erwägungen zum altisraelitischen System der zwölf Stämme." *ZAW* 90 (1978) 196–220. ———. "Problemas de textología en las 'Bendiciones' de Moisés (Dt 33) y de Jacob (Gn 49)." In *FS L. Alonso Schökel.* 1983. 75–96. **Seebass, H.** "Die Stämmeliste von Dtn xxxiii." *VT* 27 (1977) 158–69. **Seeligmann, I. L.** "A Psalm from Pre-Regal Times." *VT* 14 (1964) 75–93. **Tellerus, G. A.** *Notae Criticae et Exegeticae in Gen XLIX, Dt XXXIII.* Halle, 1766. ———. *Übersetzungen des Segens Jakobs und Mosis etc mit beygefügten praktischen Anmerkungen.* Halle, 1766. **Tigay, J. H.** "Excursus 33: The Blessing of Moses (Deuteronomy 33)." In *Deuteronomy.* 1996. 519–25. **Tournay, R.** "Le Psaume et les Bénédictions de Moise (Dt XXXIII)." *RB* 65 (1958) 181–213. **Volck, W.** *Der Segen Moses: Deut. Kap. XXXIII.* Erlangen: Deichert, 1873. **Weippert, H.** "Das geographische System der Stämme Israels." *VT* 23 (1973) 76–89. **Zobel, H.-J.** *Stammesspruch und Geschichte: Die Angaben der Stammessprüche von Gen 49, Dtn 33 und Jdc 5 über die politischen und kultischen Zustände in damaligen "Israel."* BZAW 95. Berlin: Töpelmann, 1965.

Introduction

The eleventh and final weekly portion in the lectionary cycle of Torah readings from Deuteronomy (33:1–34:12), known in Jewish tradition as וזאת הברכה, "and this is the blessing," from its opening words, may be outlined as follows:

A	YHWH's protection and provision for his people	33:1–5
B	Moses' testamentary blessing on the twelve tribes of Israel	33:6–25
X	Israel's security and blessing "a people delivered by YHWH"	33:26–29
B′	Moses ascends Mount Nebo to see the whole land of Israel	34:1–4
A′	Transition of leadership from Moses to Joshua	34:5–12

In this reading the focus at the center is on Israel's security and blessing as "a people delivered by YHWH" (33:26–29). The outer frame moves from the description of YHWH's protection and provision for his people as their "king" in the days of yore (33:1–5), to the transfer of leadership to Joshua in anticipation of the second phase of YHWH's Holy War (34:5–12). The inner frame moves from Moses' testamentary blessing of the twelve tribes, in which he anticipates their subsequent life in the promised land (33:6–25), to the description of the whole of the promised land that will be allotted to the nine and a half tribes in Canaan, as seen from the top of Mount Nebo (34:1–4).

We have already seen that Deut 31–34 constitutes a single literary structure that may be outlined in different ways. When the testamentary blessing is the central focus, the material may be outlined in a menorah pattern:

A	Moses' final charges to Joshua and to all Israel (plus the song)	31:1–32:47
B	Moses commanded to ascend Mount Nebo to "see" the land	32:48–52
C	First stanza of ancient hymn: YHWH's protection and provision	33:1–5
X	Moses' testamentary blessing on the twelve tribes of Israel	33:6–25
C′	Second stanza of ancient hymn: Israel's security and blessing	33:26–29
B′	Moses ascends Mount Nebo, where he sees the promised land	34:1–4
A′	Transition of leadership from Moses to Joshua	34:5–12

This outline should be compared with the complementary one given in the discussion of 32:48–52, in which the Song of Moses (32:1–43) is placed at the center of a similar menorah structure embracing the whole of Deut 31–34.

A. First Stanza of an Ancient Hymn: YHWH's Protection and Provision (33:1–5)

Bibliography

Ahituv, S. *Canaanite Toponyms in Ancient Egyptian Documents.* Jerusalem: Magnes, 1984. 122 n. 295, 169 n. 491. **Ahlström, G. W.** "Where Did the Israelites Live?" *JNES* 41 (1982) 133–38, esp. 134. **Axelsson, L.** *The Lord Rose Up from Seir: Studies in the History and Traditions of the Negev and Southern Judah.* ConBOT 25. Stockholm: Almqvist & Wiksell, 1987. **Bartlett, J. R.** "The Land of Seir and the Brotherhood of Edom." *JTS* 20 (1969) 1–20, esp. 8. **Beeston, A. F. L.** "Angels in Deut. 33:2." *JTS* 2 (1951) 30–31. **Blau, L.** "Zwei Dunkel Stellen im Segen Moses (Dt. 33 2–3, 24–25)." In *FS G. A. Kohut.* 1935. 95–96. **Boling, R.** *The Early Biblical Community in Transjordan.* SWBA 6. Sheffield: Almond Press, 1988. **Buber, M.** *The Kingship of God.* Tr. R. Scheimann. New York: Harper & Row, 1967. 131. **Cassin, E.** *La Splendeur Divine.* Paris; The Hague: Mouton, 1968. **Christensen, D. L.** *Prophecy and War in Ancient Israel.* Berkeley: BIBAL Press, 1989. 52. ———. "Two Stanzas of a Hymn in Deuteronomy 33." *Bib* 65 (1984) 382–89. **Clifford, R.** *The Cosmic Mountain in Canaan and the Old Testament.* HSM 4. Cambridge: Harvard UP, 1972. **Cross, F. M.** *CMHE.* 70, 99–105. **Dahood, M.** "Philological Notes on Jer 18,14–15." *ZAW* 74 (1962) 207–9, esp. 207. ———. "Qohelet and Northwest Semitic Philology." *Bib* 43 (1962) 349–65, esp. 352–53. ———. *Ugaritic-Hebrew Philology: Marginal Notes to Recent Publications.* BibOr 17. Rome: Pontifical Biblical Institute, 1965. ———. "Ugaritic Lexicography." In *Mélanges E. Tisserant.* 7 vols. Studi e Testi 231–37. Citta del Vaticano: Biblioteca Apostolica Vaticana, 1964. 1:81–104, esp. 87. **Driver, G. R.** "Hebrew Homonyms." In *FS W. Baumgartner.* 1967. 50–64. **Emerton, J. A.** "New Light on Israelite Religion: The Implications of the Inscriptions of Kuntillet ʿAjrud." *ZAW* 94 (1982) 2–20, esp. 10. **Freedman, D. N.** "The Poetic Structure of the Framework of Deuteronomy 33." In *FS C. H. Gordon.* 1980. 25–46. **Gaster, T. H.** "An Ancient Eulogy on Israel: Deuteronomy 33:3–5, 26–29." *JBL* 66 (1947) 53–62. **Hiebert, T.** *God of My Victory: The Ancient Hymn in Habakkuk 3.* HSM 38. Atlanta: Scholars Press, 1986. **Jeremias, J.** *Das Königtum Gottes in den Psalmen.* FRLANT 141. Göttingen: Vandenhoeck & Ruprecht, 1987. 82–92. **Kaufmann, Y.** *The Religion of Israel.* Tr. M. Greenberg. Chicago: Univ. of Chicago Press, 1960. 242–44. **Komlós, O.** " תֻּכּוּ לְרַגְלֶךָ (Deut 33,3)." *VT* 6 (1956) 435–36. **Labuschagne, C. J.** "The Tribes in the Blessing of Moses." *OTS* 19 (1974) 97–112, esp. 99–100. **Maier, J.** "Zum Begriff *jd* in den Texten von Qumran." *ZAW* 72 (1960) 148–66. **Mann, T. W.** *Divine Presence and Guidance in Israelite Tradition.* Baltimore: Johns Hopkins UP, 1977. 178–89. **Marcus, R.** "Philo, Josephus and the Dead Sea *Yaḥad.*" *JBL* 71 (1952) 207–9. **Margulis, B.** "Gen. XLIX, 10 / Deut XXXIII, 2–3." *VT* 19 (1969) 202–10. **Mazar, B.** "Yahweh Came out from Sinai." In *Temples and High Places in Biblical Times.* Jerusalem: HUC-JIR, 1981. 5–7 (= *Beer Sheva* 2 [1985] 111–14). **Milik, J. T.** "Deux documents inédits du désert de Juda." *Bib* 38 (1957) 245–68, esp. 254 n. 2. **Miller, P. D.** "Animal Names as Designations in Ugaritic and Hebrew." *UF* 2 (1970) 177–86. ———. "Aspects of the Religion of Ugarit." In *FS F. M. Cross.* 1987. 53–66, esp. 59–60. ———. "A Critical Note on Deut. 33:2b–3a." *HTR* 57 (1964) 241–43. ———. *The Divine Warrior in Early Israel.* HSM 5. 2nd ed. Cambridge: Harvard UP, 1975. 76–78. **Nyberg, H.S.** "Deuteronomium 33:2–3." *ZDMG* 92 (1938) 320–44. **Perlitt, L.** "Sinai und Horeb." In *FS W. Zimmerli.* 1977. 302–22. **Porter, J. R.** *Moses and Monarchy.* Oxford: Blackwell, 1963. 14 n. 35. **Rendsburg, G.** "Hebrew *ʾšdt* and Ugaritic *išdym.*" *JNSL* 8 (1980) 81–84. ———. "Late Biblical Hebrew and the Date of 'P.'" *JANESCU* 12 (1980) 65–80, esp. 80. **Ringgren, H.** "Behold Your King Comes." *VT* 24 (1974) 207–11. **Rowley, H. H.** *From Joseph to Joshua.* London: Oxford UP,

1964. 149–55. **Schultz, J. P.** "Angelic Opposition to the Ascension of Moses and the Revelation of the Law." *JQR* 61 (1970/71) 282–307. **Sheppard, G. T.** *Wisdom as a Hermeneutical Construct: A Study in the Sapientializing of the Old Testament.* BZAW 151. Berlin: de Gruyter, 1980. 62–71. **Soleh, M. Z.** "Revelation—Not Only at Sinai." *BMik* 29 (1983/84) 285–86 (Heb.). **Steiner, R. C.** "דָּת and עֵין: Two Verbs Masquerading as Nouns in Moses' Blessing (Deuteronomy 33:2, 28)." *JBL* 115 (1996) 693–98. **Stummer, F.** "תכו = Adpropinquant: Ein Beitrag zur Klärung der Vulgata zu Dt 33,3." In *Alttestamentliche Studien: FS T. Nötscher.* Ed. H. Junker. Bonn: P. Hanstein, 1950. 265–70. **Talmon, S.** *King, Cult, and Calendar in Ancient Israel.* Jerusalem: Magnes, 1986. 48–49. **Vaux, R. de.** *The Early History of Israel.* Tr. D. Smith. Philadelphia: Westminster, 1978. 333–37. **Wächter, L.** "Israel und Jeschurun." In *FS A. Jepsen.* 1971. 58–64. **Weinfeld, M.** "'Justice and Righteousness' in Ancient Israel against the Background of 'Social Reforms' in the Ancient Near East." In *Mesopotamien und seine Nachbarn.* Ed. H.-J. Nissen and J. Renger. Berlin: Reimer, 1982. 491–519, esp. 508. ———. "The Tribal League at Sinai." In *FS F. M. Cross.* 1987. 303–14. ———. "Kuntillet 'Ajrud Inscriptions and Their Significance." *Studi epigrafici e lingistici* 1 (1984) 121–30, esp. 124. **Zimmermann, F.** "The Root *Kahal* in Some Scriptural Passages." *JBL* 50 (1931) 311–12.

Translation and Prosodic Analysis

First Stanza of an Ancient Hymn: God's Protection and Guidance
[(4:6):(6:6):(4:6)]

1 And this is the blessing /	9	1
with which Moses / the man of God blessed / the Israelites //	26	3
It was before \[a] his death // 2 and he said /	11	2
"YHWH / from Sinai he came /	11	2
and he shone forth from Seir / for them[a] /	13	2
He burst forth / from Mount Paran /	12	2
[b]He marched / from Ribeboth-kodesh[b] //	14	2
from his southland / [c]to the mountain slopes for them[c] //	13	2
3 Indeed \[a] (he is) the lover of peoples /	8	1
[b]all his[c] holy ones \[d] are at your hand[e] //	11	1
Indeed[f] they / place themselves at your feet[g] /	10	2
[h]they carry out[h] / your pronouncements //	12	2
4 Instruction (Torah) / Moses commanded us (to do) //	14	2
as the heritage[a] / of the assembly of Jacob //	13	2
5 And in Jeshurun he became / king //	12	2
when the chiefs of the[a] people / assembled /	11	2
in conclave / the tribes of Israel" //	10	2

Notes

1.a. Reading *tipḥā'* as conj. because of misplaced *sillûq.*

2.a. LXX reads ἡμῖν, "to us" (= לָנוּ or perhaps לְעַמּוֹ) here, but not in the second instance of the term לָמוֹ at the end of the verse, where μετ' αὐτοῦ, "with him," was read. The translation of לָמוֹ here as "for them" follows that of Freedman (*FS C. H. Gordon* [1980] 32) and E. Fox (*FBM,* 1008). O'Connor reads the enigmatic לָמוֹ as a periphrastic genitive, modifying a proper noun that cannot take a suff.; the sense being "the Seir which belongs to, is proper to, Yahweh" (*Hebrew Verse Structure,* 208). In my earliest treatment of this text (*Transformations of the War Oracle in Old Testament Prophecy,* Harvard Dissertations in Religion 3 [Missoula, MT: Scholars Press, 1975] 52), I followed Cross (*CMHE,* 101), reading the first לָמוֹ as "upon us" (with LXX) and emending the second to read ל<א>ם, "the peoples." In a subsequent study I read it as "for them" (*Bib* 65 [1984] 386), as is also the case here.

2.b-b. LXX reads σὺν μυριάσιν Καδες, "with the ten thousands of Kadesh" (= אֶת רִבְבֹת קָדֵשׁ); Syr. reads *wʿmh mn rbwtʾ dqdyš* (= ואתו רבבת קדש). I follow MT here, reading the archaic use of the root אתה, "to march."

2.c-c. The reading accepted here, "from his southland to the mountain slopes for them," is that of Freedman (*FS C. H. Gordon* [1980] 30, 32), who repoints MT אֵשְׁדָּת as אֲשֵׁדֹת, "mountain slopes" (cf. Deut 3:17; 4:49). Four MSS of SP read אשדות. In a much earlier study Cross and Freedman emended the text to read אשר אֵלִם, "proceeded the mighty ones" (*JBL* 67 [1948] 193, 199). The word מימינו, which JPS *Tanakh* translates as "from his right," is interpreted to mean "from his south (land)," i.e., Mount Seir and Mount Paran in Edom and southern Judah (cf. 1:1–2). The translation in *Tanakh* follows the marginal Q reading אש ד(א)ת, "fire flew" or "lightning flashed," from the verbal root דאה (cf. 28:49); see also Steiner (*JBL* 115 [1996] 693–96). Labuschagne's "logotechnische analyse," however, presents strong evidence against the introduction of an additional word at this point in the Hebrew text, for it would disturb the carefully worked out patterns of the numerical composition. Another possibility is to emend the text to read אָשַׁדְתָּ למו, "you marched to them," for MT אֵשְׁדָּת למו, but this requires altering the consonantal text as well as repointing the word. LXX reads ἄγγελοι μετ' αὐτοῦ, "his angels with him" (= אֲשֵׁרוּ אֵלִים). The archaic verbs אתה, "to come, march," and אשר, "to march, tread," appear in parallel in Num 21:14 (see my remarks in *Prophecy and War,* 52; and my earlier article in *CBQ* 36 [1974] 359–60). See v 29 below, where the verb אשר was also misread.

3.a. Reading *yĕtîb* as conj.

3.b. SP, LXX, and Syr. add *waw*-conj.

3.c. LXX reads οἱ ἡγιασμένοι, "the sanctified ones" (= קדשים).

3.d. Reading *ṭip̄ḥāʾ* as conj. because of misplaced *ʾatnāḥ*.

3.e. LXX reads ὑπὸ τὰς χεῖράς αὐτοῦ, "under his hands" (= בידיו).

3.f. Some LXX witnesses omit *waw*-conj. I take the *waw* here as emphatic.

3.g. Reading לרגליך, "your [pl.] feet," for MT לרגלך, "your [sg.] feet," with a number of Heb. MSS, Cairo Geniza fragments, SP, and α΄.

3.h-h. Reading ישא<ו>ם דברתיך, "they carry out your pronouncements," as Hempel suggests in *BHS* for MT ישא, "he carries out." LXX adds *waw*-conj.; SP and Vg. add *waw*-conj. and read the verb ישא as pl., "they carry out." Cross and Freedman (*JBL* 67 [1948] 193, 201), followed by others, read a *t*-infix verbal form (see *Comment* below). It is also possible to interpret the sg. form in MT with a pl. meaning, with the change from pl. to sg. here as an extension of the *Numeruswechsel* to mark a boundary that is reinforced by the introduction of a 1 pl. form at the beginning of v 4.

4.a. Reading the archaic 3 sg. suff., מוֹרָשׁה, "his heritage," for MT מוֹרָשָׁה, "possession, heritage."

5.a. SP, Syr., and Tg. read העם, "the people," for MT עם, "people"; LXX reads pl. Though the def. art. was apparently not written frequently in archaic Hebrew poetry, it is often required in translation to other languages ancient and modern.

Form/Structure/Setting

The blessings of Moses are placed within a framework of two stanzas of an ancient hymn (vv 1–5, 26–29; see Christensen, *Bib* 65 [1984] 382–89).

The three markers of internal structure within 33:1–5 are the shift from third-person narrative (v 1) to direct speech in v 2, the shift to second-person singular forms in v 3, and the change to the first-person plural form at the beginning of v 4, which is a form of enallage, the use of one grammatical form for another, like the *Numeruswechsel* (change between second-person sg. and pl. forms elsewhere in Deuteronomy). The separation of vv 4–5 from what precedes is also suggested by the prosodic analysis, with vv 1–3 forming a two-part prosodic structural entity different from that of vv 4–5.

In his 1980 study on the framework of the Blessing of Moses in Deut 33, Freedman demonstrated a degree of symmetry between the proem (vv 2–5) and the closing (vv 26–29) that is too elegant in its detail to be dismissed as mere reading of a theory into the evidence (*FS C. H. Gordon* [1980] 25–46). My own studies (1984 and 1989), which carried the discussion further, are expanded here in matters of detail. Freedman cites a number of rhetorical features in support of his case for structural chiasm and symmetry. The word *YHWH,* which appears at the beginning of the poem (v 2), appears only once again, at the end (v 29), forming an inclusion. The unusual term for Israel, Jeshurun, occurs at the end of the "first stanza" (v 5) and in the beginning of the "second stanza" (v 26), and only two other times in the Hebrew Bible (Deut 32:15; Isa 44:2). The end of each of these two stanzas is marked by the repetition of the terms עם, "people," and ישראל, "Israel," in reverse order (vv 5, 26). Moreover, the beginning and end of the conclusion (vv 26–29) are marked by repetition of the words בעזרך ובגאותו, "for your help and in his splendor" (v 26), and עזרך . . . גאות<ו>, "of your help . . . of <his> splendor" (v 29). The structure of the larger whole may be outlined in a menorah pattern:

A	YHWH's march of conquest from the southland	33:2
B	YHWH's protection and provision for his people	33:3–4
C	YHWH is king in Jeshurun	33:5
X	The Blessing of Moses	33:6–25
C′	"There is none like God, O Jeshurun"	33:26
B′	Israel's security and blessing	33:27–28
A′	Israel, a people delivered by YHWH	33:29

This outline should be compared with that of 31:1–34:12 in the previous section of this commentary, in which the Song of Moses (32:1–43) is in the center of a similar structure that includes this one within it. The phenomenon of placing "wheels within wheels" in this manner has been shown to be a characteristic feature in the literary structure of Deuteronomy, and the rest of the canon of the Tanakh as well (see D. L. Christensen, *Study Guides on the Torah, Former Prophets, Latter Prophets, and the Writings* [N. Richland Hills, TX: BIBAL Press, 1996–2001]). In short, the two sections of the framework are virtually identical from a prosodic point of view. The proem (vv 2–5) may be outlined in a five-part concentric structure:

A	YHWH's march of conquest from the southland	33:2–3c
B	He upholds the pronouncements entrusted to you	33:3d
X	Moses is the one who charged us with the Torah	33:4a
B′	As his heritage to the assembly of Jacob	33:4b
A′	YHWH's reign in Jeshurun	33:5

Here the outside frame focuses on YHWH's traditional march of conquest, which is related to YHWH's kingship in Jeshurun (Israel). The inner frame focuses on pronouncements of YHWH in the Torah as the heritage entrusted to Jacob/Israel. In the center we find the simple statement that it was Moses who charged us with the Torah—to keep it.

The closing of this archaic hymn in vv 26–29 has a similar five-part concentric structure:

A	There is no god like God ("El")	33:26
B	He is a refuge for his people	33:27a
X	He drove out the enemy before you / he said "Destroy!"	33:27b
B′	Israel settled in untroubled safety	33:28
A′	There is no people like Israel, a people delivered by YHWH	33:29a

Here the outer frame focuses on the uniqueness of God and of Israel, as a people delivered by YHWH from their enemies. The inner frame focuses on God as refuge and source of security in the promised land; and the center summarizes the eisodus from the perspective of YHWH's Holy War: God drove the enemies from before the people of Israel when they entered the land. When taken as a whole, the two halves of this poem take on a different focus, as suggested in the following menorah pattern:

A	YHWH's march of conquest from the southland	33:2
B	YHWH's protection and provision for his people	33:3–4
C	YHWH is king in Jeshurun	33:5a
X	The chiefs gathered in conclave the tribes of Israel	33:5b
C′	"There is none like God, O Jeshurun!"	33:26
B′	Israel's security and blessing	33:27–28
A′	Israel, a people delivered by YHWH	33:29

.Here YHWH's march of conquest is an act of salvation for Israel (vv 2, 29a); and YHWH's protection and provision (vv 3–4) are the source of Israel's security and blessing (vv 27–28). The central frame presents YHWH himself, who is Israel's king and beyond comparison (vv 5, 26); and in the very center we find a single poetic statement that takes on fresh meaning: "The chiefs of the people assembled in conclave [unity] the tribes of Israel" under the rulership of YHWH their king (v 5c).

The data from Labuschagne on the numerical composition of 33:1–5 may be summarized as follows:

Words:	before *ʾatnāḥ*		after *ʾatnāḥ*		
33:1–11	80	+	52 (= 2 × 26)	=	132
33:1–7	50	+	28	=	78 (= 3 × 26)
33:1–5	36	+	19	=	55 (= 23 + 32)
33:1	10	+	2	=	12
33:2–25	153 (= 9 × 17)	+	119 (= 7 × 17)	=	272 (= 16 × 17)
33:2–5	26	+	17	=	43 (= 17 + 26)
33:2–4	23	+	11	=	34 (= 2 × 17)
33:3–6	17	+	17	=	34 (= 2 × 17)
33:4–6	11	+	12	=	23
33:5–7	17	+	15	=	32
31:1–34:12	955	+	728 (= 28 × 26)	=	1,683 (= 99 × 17)
33:1–34:12	301	+	209	=	510 (= 30 × 17)

A number of conclusions can be drawn from this data, beyond the fact that 33:1–5 itself is a numerical composition based on the two divine-name numbers 17 and 26, and the number 23 (associated with Heb. כבוד, "glory"). In this brief passage (33:1–5), the author manages to incorporate both of the divine-name numbers 17 and 26 into the numerical composition, as well as the two numbers associated with כבוד, "glory" (23 and 32). At the same time, the passage is an integral part of a larger numerical composition that embraces the whole of Deut

31–34. In particular, 33:1–5 is carefully tied to its immediate context, with building blocks that extend well into the rest of chap. 33, particularly vv 2–25.

Comment

1 Though this chapter is titled "The Blessing," many interpreters give it the title "The Testament of Moses." I call the poem a "Testamentary Blessing" to bring out its character as a final pronouncement on the part of Moses within the literary genre of "blessings" (cf. Gen 48:21 in relation to 49:1–28).

2 The phrase "from Sinai he came" refers to the coming of YHWH as a Divine Warrior to the people of Israel, marching in the vanguard of his troops on their journey to the promised land. O'Connor explains למו as "a periphrastic genitive, modifying a proper noun that cannot take a suffix; the sense is 'the Seir that belongs to, is proper to, Yahweh'" (*Hebrew Verse Structure,* 208). The words "he shone forth" refer to his brilliant radiance—"wrapped in light as with a garment" (Ps 104:2 NRSV)—as he set out "from Seir" (the southern wilderness of Edom) to "Mount Paran" (in southern Judah, southwest of Edom). Following Clifford (*Cosmic Mountain,* 115 n. 16), O'Connor reads הר פארן as "the Paran hills" or "the mountain country of Paran" rather than a specific mountain. From there YHWH's "march of conquest" continued on to "Ribeboth-kodesh," which is probably to be interpreted with the LXX as Kadesh-barnea (i.e., "Ribeboth at, or near, Kadesh"). Though possible, the emendation proposed by O'Connor (*Hebrew Verse Structure,* 208; cf. BDB, 872) to read מרבת קדש, "Meribat-Qadesh," is not necessary. The translation "from his southland to the mountain slopes for them" is that of D. N. Freedman, who repoints MT אֵשְׁדָּת as אֲשֵׁדֹת, "mountain slopes" (cf. the phrase "slopes of Pisgah" in 3:17; 4:49). Traditional midrashic interpretation of Hebrew אשדת renders it as two words, אֵשׁ דָּת, "a law of [or from] fire" (cf. 4:33); but the Persian word דת as "law" did not enter the Hebrew language before the fifth century B.C.E. Steiner argues in favor of the traditional Q reading אש דת (for MT אשדת), which he interprets as אש ד(א)ת, "fire flew forth" (cf. 28:49; *JBL* 115 [1996] 695). Though the translation "lightning flashing" of the JPS *Tanakh* was apparently based on an emendation to read אש דלקת (see Tigay [1996] 320), it renders the same sense. The numerical composition of the text, however, does not allow for the addition of a word here. LXX (ἄγγελοι μετ' αὐτοῦ, "angels with him") may be reading אשרו אלים, as Hempel suggests in *BHS.*

3 With some hesitation I follow the traditional reading "lover of peoples" here. Freedman renders it "protector of peoples" (*FS C. H. Gordon* [1980] 32). Though Mendenhall's interpretation of חבב as "to be pure" from Akk. *ebēbu* is possible and was accepted by Miller (*HTR* 57 [1964] 241–43), Dahood ("Ugaritic-Hebrew Syntax and Style," *UF* 1 [1969] 15–36), Cross (*CMHE,* 101–2 n. 38), Craigie ([1976] 392), and O'Connor (*Hebrew Verse Structure,* 209), that reading is usually accompanied by other changes as well in order to make sense of a difficult text. Tigay, who notes that this statement is "a surprisingly universalistic one for a poem about [God's] protection of Israel," goes on to cite a number of interesting parallels in Egyptian ("Ptah who loves his people"), Akkadian ("lover of his subjects"), and Nabatean (king described as "lover of his people") ([1996] 320–21 and 407 n. 32). YHWH's "holy ones" are angelic beings (cf. Zech 14:5 and Ps 103:20). The emendation of MT והם תכו, "indeed, they place themselves (at your hand)," to read המתכו, "they bow down (at your hand)," is possible but not necessary. Cross and Freedman take it as an infixed-*t* verbal form from מוך or מכך, "to bend" (*Studies in Ancient Yahwistic Poetry,* 108 n. 16), which Hempel follows in *BHS.* Milik (*Bib* 38 [1957] 252–54) preserves the consonants of MT and derives תכו from תכך, "to fall to one's feet." On the root מכך, see Dahood ("Hebrew-Ugaritic Lexicography V," *Bib* 48 [1967] 425–26; see O'Connor, *Hebrew Verse Structure,* 208). Following Cross and Freedman, who read an emphatic *mem,* O'Connor reads ישא־ם דברתיך, "they honor your commands," for MT ישא מדברתיך, "he carries out your . . . (?)." The same meaning is achieved with the reading יִשָּׂא<ו>ם דברתיך, "they carry out your pronouncements"—"they carry them out, (namely) your pronouncements" (cf. the use of יִשָּׂאֻנוּ [DSS have ישאונו], "they take us away," in Isa 64:5 [Eng. 6]; and Gen 29:1: וישא יעקב רגליו, "then Jacob went on his journey").

4 The "instruction" (תורה, "Torah") that "Moses commanded us (to do)" is described as "the heritage [מורשה] of the assembly of Jacob." "Because this verse is such a pithy expression of fundamental Jewish beliefs—that the Teaching was commanded by Moses, that it is a heritage, and that it belongs to the entire people, not just to an elite group—the rabbis selected it and the first verse of the Shema (Deut. 6:4) as the first biblical verses to be taught to a child when it is able to speak" (Tigay [1996] 321–22).

5 The epithet "Jeshurun" (יְשֻׁרוּן, "the Upright") refers to Israel (cf. 32:15 and the *Comment* there, especially on the possible connection of this term with the Book of Jashar (ספר הישר). On the premonarchic date for Israel's recognition of YHWH as king, see the comments of J. J. M. Roberts, "In Defense of the Monarchy: The Contribution of Israelite Kingship to Biblical Theology," in *FS F. M. Cross* (1987), 395 n. 41.

Explanation

The poem in vv 1–5 and 26–29, which makes up the framework around the blessing itself (vv 6–25), "reflects a rare tranquility and sustained optimism" that stands in sharp contrast with what precedes it in Deut 31–32. "As in the great prophetic books, where the record of unrelieved defection was mitigated by a happier editorial addition at the close, so Deuteronomy now comes out from the storms of sin, ingratitude, and apostasy into the still waters of hope. . . . While the human spirit needs the discipline of facing up to its shortcomings, it also needs encouragement to call forth its best efforts" (H. H. Shires and P. Parker, *IB* 2:528).

Moses is described at the outset as "the man of God" (v 1). The same title appears in the superscription to Ps 90, which is also attributed to Moses. The title appears elsewhere in the Hebrew Bible in reference to a prophet (see 1 Sam 9:6; 1 Kgs 13:1–3; 2 Kgs 4:7, 16). It should be noted that Moses is presented as the paradigm of a prophet in Deuteronomy (18:15; 34:10). Here Moses gives a blessing that itself functions as prophecy. The scene of Moses blessing the twelve tribes of Israel evokes the image of another scene of the "prophet like Moses" who spoke with his twelve disciples the night before his crucifixion to encourage them, concluding with an affectionate prayer for them (John 14–17), and blessed them when he parted from them on the Mount of Olives to ascend into heaven (see Luke 24:50–53).

The blessings uttered by Moses are introduced with a brief recitation of YHWH's actions in Israel's behalf in times past (v 2). When YHWH made himself known at Mount Sinai, he marched on through the wilderness with his people to their temporary stopping place at Kadesh-barnea ("Ribeboth-kodesh" here, but cf. 1:2). As God's "holy ones," the people of Israel place themselves at his feet and they choose to carry out his instructions (v 3b). The Torah came from God through Moses "as the heritage of the assembly of Jacob" (v 4). In giving the Torah, Moses functions as a prophet; but he also takes on much of the functions of "a king" in his capacity as leader in ancient Israel. At the same time, it is important to note that Moses never takes upon himself the name or the position of royalty. Like Gideon in another day, Moses would have declared: "I will not rule over you, and my son will not rule over you; the LORD will rule over you" (Judg 8:23). It is YHWH himself who is declared king in Jeshurun, "when the chiefs of the people [including Moses] assembled in conclave the tribes of Israel" (v 5).

We may put "In God we trust" on our coins and currency, but Israel went much further—they made God their king. At least that is what it was at the outset, in the teaching of Moses. The ideal continued through the days of Gideon. It was Gideon's son Abimelech whose action foreshadowed fundamental changes in the life of ancient Israel in the establishment of a monarchy. Abimelech slew his seventy brothers, except for Jotham the youngest, and established himself as king in Shechem (Judg 9:1–6). The principle that God alone is in reality king in Israel means that God's official spokesperson, the prophet like Moses, must share political authority alongside the designated king, who was originally known as a נָגִיד, "leader" in the sense of being a permanent warlord, rather than a מֶלֶךְ, "king." The נָבִיא, "prophet," was the spokesperson of YHWH, with the responsibility of keeping both the king and the people faithful to the covenant as mediated through Moses. As S. Dean McBride has shown ("Polity of the Covenant People," in SBTS 3:62–77), Deuteronomy preserves in essence the national "constitution" of ancient Israel, in which God was king. The impact of this ideology in shaping modern Western constitutionalism through the centuries is profound, for the very idea of "separation of powers" in the U.S. Constitution appears to have its ultimate origin in the distinction made in the religion of ancient Israel between these separate locations of power in human society, more than it does in the political systems of ancient Greece and Rome.

B. Moses' Testamentary Blessing on the Twelve Tribes (33:6–25)

Bibliography for 33:6–12

Albright, W. F. "The Old Testament and Canaanite Language and Literature." *CBQ* 7 (1945) 5–31, esp. 23–24 n. 64. **Baisas, B. Q.** "Ugaritic *ʿdr* and Hebrew *ʿzr* I." *UF* 5 (1973)

41–52, esp. 44–45. **Berlin, A.** "On the Meaning of *rb*." *JBL* 100 (1981) 90–93. **Buis, P.** "Qadesh, un lieu maudit?" *VT* 24 (1974) 268–85. **Christensen, D. L.** "Dtn 33,11—A Curse in the 'Blessing of Moses'?" *ZAW* 101 (1989) 278–82. **Cody, A.** *A History of Old Testament Priesthood.* AnBib 35. Rome: Pontifical Biblical Institute, 1969. 114–23. **Cross, F. M.** "The Ammonite Oppression of the Tribes of Gad and Reuben: Missing Verses from 1 Samuel 11 Found in 4QSamuel[a]." In *History, Historiography, and Interpretation.* Ed. H. Tadmor and M. Weinfeld. Jerusalem: Magnes, 1983. 148–58. ———. *CMHE.* 195–215. ———. "Reuben, First-Born of Jacob." *ZAW* 100 (1988) 46–65. ———. "Ugaritic *db'at* and Hebrew Cognates." *VT* 2 (1952) 162–64. **Curtis, J. B.** "Some Suggestions concerning the History of the Tribe of Reuben." *JBR* 33 (1965) 247–49. **Dahood, M.** "Hebrew-Ugaritic Lexicography V." *Bib* 48 (1967) 421–38, esp. 428–29. ———. *Psalms I: 1–50.* AB 16. Garden City, NY: Doubleday, 1966. 45. ———. "Ugaritic-Hebrew Parallel Pairs." In *RSP.* 2:26. ———. "Ugaritic Lexicography." In *Mélanges Eugéne Tisserant.* Studi e Testi 231. Città del Vaticano: Biblioteca Apostolica Vaticana, 1964. 81–104, esp. 94. **Daube, D.** "Rechtsgedanken in den Erzahlungen des Pentateuchs." In *FS O. Eissfeldt.* 1961. 32–41, esp. 34. **Dummermuth, F.** "Zur deuteronomischen Kulttheologie." *ZAW* 70 (1958) 59–98, esp. 91–95. **Eissfeldt, O.** "Zwei verkannte militärtechnische Termini im Alten Testament." *VT* 5 (1955) 232–38, esp. 235–36. **Fitzmyer, J. A.** "4QTestimonia and the New Testament." *TS* 18 (1957) 513–37, esp. 530–35. **Gaster, T. H.** "Deuteronomy 33:12." *ExpTim* 46 (1934/35) 334. ———. "A Qumran Reading of Deut. 33:10." *VT* 8 (1958) 217–19. **Gevirtz, S.** "The Reprimand of Reuben." *JNES* 30 (1971) 87–98. **Goldfarb, S. D.** "Was Simeon Not Included in Moses' Blessing?" *DD* 4 (1975) 51–55. **Greenberg, M.** "Urim and Thummim." *EncJud.* 16:9–10. **Grimme, H.** "Der Südarabische Levitismus und sein Verhältnis zum Levitismus in Israel." *Mus* 37 (1924) 169–99. **Gunneweg, A. H. J.** *Leviten und Priester.* FRLANT 89. Göttingen: Vandenhoeck & Ruprecht, 1965. 37–44. **Halpern, B.** *The Emergence of Israel in Canaan.* SBLMS 29. Chico, CA: Scholars Press, 1983. 149–56. **Haran, M.** "Incense of the Court and of the Temple Interior." In *Temples and Temple Service in Ancient Israel.* Winona Lake, IN: Eisenbrauns, 1985. 233–35. **Heck, J. D.** "The Missing Sanctuary of Deut 33:12." *JBL* 103 (1984) 523–29. **Jepsen, A.** "Mose und die Leviten: Ein Beitrag zur Frühgeschichte Israels und zur Sammlung des alttestamentlichen Schrifttums." *VT* 31 (1981) 318–23. **Lehming, S.** "Massa und Meriba." *ZAW* 73 (1961) 71–77. **Lindblom, J.** "Lot-Casting in the Old Testament." *VT* 14 (1964) 67–74. **Lipiński, A.** "Urim and Thummim." *VT* 20 (1970) 495–96. **Loewenstamm, S. E.** *From Babylon to Canaan.* Jerusalem: Magnes, 1992. 55–65. ———. "The Investiture of Levi." *EI* 10 (1971) 169–72 (Heb.; Eng. summary, xiv–xv). **Mendelsohn, I.** "Urim and Thummim." *IDB.* 4:739–40. **Milgrom, J.** "Excursus 64: The Urim and Thummim." In *Numbers.* 1990. 484–86. **Nyberg, H. S.** "Studien zum Religionskampf im Alten Testament." *ARw* 35 (1938) 329–87, esp. 372–73. **O'Callaghan, R. T.** "The Word *ktp* in Ugaritic and Egypto-Semitic Mythology." *Or* 21 (1952) 37–46. **O'Connor, M.** *Hebrew Verse Structure.* Winona Lake, IN: Eisenbrauns, 1980. **Oded, B.** "The Settlement of the Tribe of Reuben in Transjordania." In *Studies in the History of the Jewish People and the Land of Israel in Memory of Zvi Avneri.* Ed. A. Gilbo'a et al. Haifa: Univ. of Haifa Press, 1970. 11–36, esp. 20–21. **Propp, W. H.** *Water in the Wilderness: A Biblical Motif and Its Mythological Background.* HSM 40. Atlanta: Scholars Press, 1987. 53–55. **Qimron, E.** "*ḥopep* 'Fluttering': Dt 33,12 'He Covered Him all the Day." *BMik* 24 (1979) 140–41 (Heb.; Eng. summary, 242). **Robertson, E.** "The ʾŪrīm and Tummīm; What Were They?" *VT* 14 (1964) 67–74. **Ruppert, L.** "Das Motiv der Versuchung durch Gott in vordeuteronomischer Tradition." *VT* 22 (1972) 55–63, esp. 56–59. **Schaller, B.** "Targum Jeruschalmi I zu Deuteronomium 33,11: Ein Relikt aus Hasmonäischer Zeit?" *JSJ* 3 (1972) 52–60. **Sellin, E.** "Zu dem Judaspruch im Jaqobsegen Gen 49,8–12 und im Mosesegen Deut 33,7." *ZAW* 60 (1959) 47–57. **Thompson, J. A.** "Israel's 'Haters.'" *VT* 29 (1979) 200–205.

Bibliography for 33:13–25

Baeck, L. "*ś-n-h* and *ś-y-n-y*." *MGWJ* 46 (1902) 299–301. **Bartlett, J. R.** "Use of the Term ראש as a Title in the Old Testament." *VT* 19 (969) 4. **Beek, M. A.** "Der Dornbusch als Mohnsitz Gottes." *OTS* 14 (1965) 155–61. **Blau, L.** "Zwei dunkle Stellen im Segen Moses." In *FS G. A. Kohut.* 1935. 91–108, esp. 105–8. **Boehmer, O.** "Der Gottesberg Tabor." *BZ* 23 (1935/36) 333–41. **Botterweck, G. J.** "Gott und Mensch in den alttestamentlichen Löwenbildern." In *FS J. Ziegler.* 1972. 117–28, esp. 122. **Buit, M. du.** "La Tabor: Limite des trois tribus." *MDB* 23 (1982) 11. **Burkitt, F. C.** "On the Blessing of Moses." *JTS* 35 (1934) 68. **Clark, B.** "The Biblical Oryx—a New Name for an Ancient Animal." *BARev* 10 (1984) 66–70. **Cross, F. M.** "Ugaritic *db'at* and Hebrew Cognates." *VT* 2 (1952) 162–64. **Dahood, M.** "Ancient Semitic Deities in Syria and Palestine." In *Le antiche divinità semitiche.* Ed. S. Moscatti. Studi Semitici 1. Rome: Center of Semitic Studies, 1958. 65–94, esp. 66. ———. "Deuteronomy 33:19 and UT 52:61–63." *Or* 47 (1978) 263–64. ———. "Hebrew-Ugaritic Lexicography II." *Bib* 45 (1964) 393–412, esp. 407, 412. ———. "Review: *The Torah.*" *Bib* 45 (1964) 281–83. **Eissfeldt, O.** "Der Gott Tabor." *ARw* 31 (1934) 14–41 (repr. in *KlSchr* 2:29–54). **Gevirtz, S.** "Adumbrations of Dan in Jacob's Blessing on Judah." *ZAW* 93 (1981) 21–37. **Giesebrecht, F.** "Zwei Cruces Interpretum Ps. 45:7 und Deut 33:21." *ZAW* 7 (1887) 291–93. **Gordis, R.** "Critical Notes on the Blessing of Moses." In *The Word and the Book.* New York: Ktav, 1976. 337–39 (repr. from *JTS* 34 [1933] 390–92). **Gray, J.** *Joshua, Judges and Ruth.* NCBC. London: Marshall, Morgan & Scott, 1977. 283. **Grintz, J. M.** "Some Observations on the 'High Place' in the History of Israel." *VT* 27 (1977) 111–13. **Koch, K.** "Wesen und Ursprung der 'Gemeinschaftstreue' im Israel der Königszeit." *ZEE* 5 (1961) 72–90. **Levine, B. A.** *In the Presence of the Lord.* SJLA 5. Leiden: Brill, 1974. 135–37. **Lohfink, N.** "Textkritisches zu *jrš* im Alten Testament." In *FS D. Barthélemy.* 1981. 273–88, esp. 277. **Mazar, B.** "They Shall Call Peoples to Their Mountains." *EI* 14 (1978) 39–41 (Heb.; Eng. summary, 123). **Miller, P. D.** "El the Warrior." *HTR* 60 (1967) 411–31, esp. 422–23. **Motzki, H.** "Ein Beitrag zum Problem des Stierkultes in der Religionsgeschichte Israels." *VT* 25 (1975) 470–85, esp. 484. **Na'aman, N.** *Borders and Districts in Biblical Historiography.* Jerusalem: Simor, 1986. 192–94. **Niemann, H.** *Die Daniten: Studien zur Geschichte eines altisraelitischen Stammes.* FRLANT 135. Göttingen: Vandenhoeck & Ruprecht, 1985. 212–13. **Nyberg, H. S.** "Studien zum Religionskampf im Alten Testament." *ARw* 35 (1938) 329–87, esp. 370. **Porat, E.** "'*ywny mqr.*'" *Leš* 21 (1957) 239–43, esp. 240–41. **Pritchard, J. B.** "Ships and Sailing in the OT." *IDB.* 4:333–35. **Rupprecht, F.** "'Den Felsen, der dich gebar, täuschest du. . . .'" *KuI* 3 (1988) 53–61. **Scharbert, J.** "Die Geschichte der *bārûk*-Formel." *BZ* 17 (1973) 1–28, esp. 15–16. **Täubler, E.** *Biblische Studien: Die Epoche der Richter.* Ed. H.-J. Zobel. Tübingen: Mohr, 1958. 96–97, 112–15, 124–28. **Tournay, R.** "Le nom du 'Buisson ardent.' *VT* 7 (1957) 410–13. **Waldman, N. M.** "The Wealth of Mountain and Sea: The Background of a Biblical Image." *JQR* 71 (1980) 176–80. **Weinfeld, M.** *Justice and Righteousness in Israel and in the Nations.* Jerusalem: Magnes, 1985. 107–8 (Heb.). **Weisman, Z.** "A Connecting Link in an Old Hymn: Deut xxxiii 19a; 21b." *VT* 28 (1978) 365–68. **Zakovitch, Y.** "The Synonymous Word and Synonymous Name in Name-Midrashim." *Shnaton* 2 (1977) 100–115, xxx (Heb.). **Zobel, H.-J.** *Stammesspruch und Geschichte.* BZAW 95. Berlin: Töpelmann, 1965. 38–39, 64–65, 82–83.

Translation and Prosodic Analysis

Reuben and Judah [3] [3:6] or [6:6]

6 "Let Reuben live \ [a] and[b] not die // 14 1
and may his men be / [c]beyond counting"[c] // ס 11 2

7 And this is for Judah /	9	1
and he said / "Hearken O YHWH \[a] to the voice of Judah /	16	2_
And to his people / restore him //	11	2
his hands / [b]<may they> contend[b] for him /	12	2
and a help against his adversaries / may you be" // ס	11	2_

Levi, with the First Apostrophe [7:7:4:7:7]

8 And for Levi he said /	10	1
[a]"Let your Thummim and your Urim[b] / be with your pious one[c]//	18	2
Whom you tested[d] / at Massah /	11	2
[e]with whom you contended / at the waters of Meribah //	15	2_
9 The one who says / of his father and his mother /	16	2
[a]'I consider them not'[a] /	7	1
And his brothers / he disregards /	10	2
and his (own) child[b] / he does not know //	12	2_
For they[c] have observed / your precepts[d] /	12	2
and your covenant / they[e] have kept //	12	2_
10 They shall teach[a] your judgments \[b] to Jacob /	15	1
and [c]your Torah[c] / to Israel //	12	2
They shall set incense / in your nostrils /	15	2
and whole burnt offerings / on your altar //	10	2_
11 Curse[a] O YHWH / his strength /	11	2
but the work of his hands[b] / you shall accept favorably /	11	2
Smash the loins[c] of his opponents[d] /	9	1
[e]and of those who hate him[e] / [f]that they rise no more"[f] // ס	12	2_

Benjamin [4:4]

12 [a]For Benjamin he said /	8	1
"The beloved of YHWH / tents securely / [b]by him[b] //	17	3
[c]He enfolds him / all the day long /	12	2
indeed between his shoulders[d] / he tents" // ס	13	2_

Joseph (Ephraim and Manasseh) [7:7:4:7:7]

13 And for Joseph he said / "Blessed of YHWH / be his land //	21	3
with the bounty of moisture[a] / from heaven /	10	2
and of the deep / lying beneath //	13	2_
14 And with the bounteous \[a] yield of the sun //	13	1
and with the bounteous / crop[b] of the months[c] //	12	2_
15 And with the 'best' / from the ancient mountains[a] //	11	2
and with the bounty / of the everlasting hills[b] //	12	2_
16 And with the bounty / of earth \[a] and[b] its fullness /	14	2
and the favor of the one dwelling[c] / in a bush[d] //	12	2_
May it come \[e] upon the head of Joseph /	13	1
and upon the pate / of his brothers' prince //	12	2

[17] His[a] firstling bull / is majestic / 13 2
indeed the horns of a wild ox / are his horns / 10 2_
With them / peoples / are gored together[b] / 12 3
the ends of the[c] earth // 6 1
And[d] they \[e] are the ten thousands of Ephraim / 10 1
[f]and they[f] / are the thousands of Manasseh" // ס 10 2_

Zebulun and Issachar [5:5]

[18] And for Zebulun he said / 9 1
"Rejoice, O Zebulun / in your journeys // 12 2
and[a] O Issachar / in your tents // 14 2_
[19] Peoples \[a] are summoned to the mountain / 9 1
[b]there \[c] they offer sacrifices of success // 11 1
For from the riches of the seas \[d] they draw / 13 1
and the hidden treasures[e] / of the sand" // ס 13 2_

Gad, with the Second Apostrophe [(4:4):(4:4)]

[20] And for Gad he said / "Blessed / be he who enlarges Gad // 17 3
like a lion he couches / 9 1
And[a] he tears the arm / and scalp // 12 2
[21] and he provided[a] the first / for him / 8 2_

Indeed he assigned[b] / the commander's portion // 11 2
and the chiefs of the people / [c]gathered together[c] / 12 2
The righteousness of YHWH / he executed / 9 2
and his judgments / with Israel" // ס 13 2_

Dan, Napthali, and Asher [4:7] [7:4]

[22] And for Dan he said / "Dan / is a lion's whelp // 14 2
[a]he shies away / from the viper" // 9 2_
[23] And for Naphtali he said / 11 1
"Naphtali / is satisfied with favor / 11 2
And he is full / of the blessing of YHWH // 11 2
the sea[a] and to the south / he will possess"[b] // ס 12 2_

[24] And for Asher he said / 10 1
"Blessed above sons / be Asher // 13 2
<And>[a] may he be the favorite / of his brothers / 10 2
and[b] may he dip his foot[c] / in oil // 11 2_
[25] Of iron and brass / are your gate bolts[a] // 13 2
and as your days /[b] so shall your strength[c] be" // 11 2_

Notes

6.a. Reading *ṭipḥā'* as conj. because of misplaced *'atnāḥ*.
6.b. SP[MSS] omits *waw*-conj. Prosodic analysis tends to support MT.

6.c-c. Emending MT מִסְפָּר to read מִסְּפָר, "beyond counting," with Dahood (*Bib* 48 [1967] 429) and O'Connor (*Hebrew Verse Structure,* 210), which seems to be how the phrase was read in LXX: καὶ ἔστω πολὺς ἐν ἀριθμῷ, "and let him be many in number" (cf. Ps 40:6 [Eng. 5]).

7.a. Reading *paštā'* followed by *zāqēp qāṭôn* as conj.

7.b-b. Reading inf. abs. רֹב, used here for a finite verb, from the root ריב, "to contend," with O'Connor (*Hebrew Verse Structure,* 210). The line has posed difficulties for most translators, ancient and modern. The same sense is achieved if MT רָב, "he contended," is emended to read יָרִיבוּ, "let them contend."

8.a. DSS and LXX (δότε Λευι) add הבו ללוי, "give to Levi." Prosodic analysis supports MT.

8.b. DSS read ואורך for MT ואוריך, "your Urim," with no change in meaning; Tg. reads והאורים, "and the Urim."

8.c. A number of Heb. MSS and Cairo Geniza fragments read חסידיך, "your pious ones," for MT חסידך, "your pious one." Prosodic analysis supports MT.

8.d. SP reads נסיתהו for MT נסיתו, "you tested him," which is possible from a prosodic point of view.

8.e. DSS and SP add *waw*-conj.

9.a-a. DSS read לי רעתיכהו for MT לא ראיתיו, "I did not see him"; LXX has 2 sg. suff.

9.b. Q reads בניו, "his children," along with numerous Heb. MSS, Cairo Geniza fragments, LXX, Syr., and Vg. MT בנו, "his child," is retained in light of the similar text in Exod 32:29, which is dependent on the text here (see *Comment* on v 9 below).

9.c. DSS and LXX read 3 sg. Prosodic analysis supports MT.

9.d. Cairo Geniza fragments and LXX (τὰ λόγιά σου, "your words") read אמרתיך, "your precepts," for MT אמרתך, with no change in meaning. Prosodic analysis tends to support MT.

9.e. DSS and LXX read 3 sg. Prosodic analysis supports MT.

10.a. DSS read ויאירו (hiph. of אור) for MT יורו, "they shall teach"; the word is omitted in Vg.

10.b. Reading *paštā'* followed by *zāqēp qāṭôn* as conj.

10.c-c. DSS read תורתכה, "your Torah," for MT ותורתך, "and your Torah"; some SP witnesses and Syr. read pl.

11.a. Reading בָּרֵךְ, "to curse," as an amphibolous usage. See Christensen, *ZAW* 101 (1989) 278–82.

11.b. Two Heb. MSS, DSS, and SP read ידו, "his hand," for MT ידיו, "his hands." Prosodic analysis supports MT.

11.c. SP reads מתני for MT מתנים, "loins."

11.d. DSS read קמו, "his opponent," for MT קמיו, "his opponents."

11.e-e. DSS read משנאו, "of those who hate him," for MT ומשנאיו, "and of those who hate him." Prosodic analysis supports MT. The conj. probably carries an emphatic sense, which is difficult to render in English translation here.

11.f-f. DSS read בל יקומו, "they shall not rise," for MT מן־יקומון, "from arising (again)." Cf. SP^{W} and מי יקימנו in the blessing of Judah in Gen 49:9.

12.a. A few Heb. MSS, Cairo Geniza fragments, SP, LXX, Syr., and Vg. add *waw*-conj. Prosodic analysis supports MT.

12.b-b. Omitted in SP and Syr.; 4QDeut reads אל, "God," and takes it as the first word in the next clause, which thus reads "God protects him ever"; LXX reads ὁ θεός, perhaps for עליון, "the Most High."

12.c. SP adds *waw*-conj.

12.d. SP reads כתפתיו for MT כתיפיו, "his shoulders/shoulder blades."

13.a. Some Heb. MSS and Gen 49:25 read מֵעָל, "from above," for MT מטל, "from dew, moisture."

14.a. Reading *ṭiphā'* as conj. because of misplaced *'atnāḥ*.

14.b. SP reads גרושי, "crops of [constr. state]," for MT גרש, "thing thrust or put forth, yield."

14.c. The word ירחים means both "months" and "moons." The second meaning parallels "sun" in the previous colon (see Craigie [1976] 397).

15.a. SP reads הרי, "mountains," for MT הררי, "mountains." Prosodic analysis supports MT.

15.b. Some Heb. MSS and SP read גבעת, "(everlasting) hill," for MT גבעות, "hills." Prosodic analysis supports MT.

16.a. Reading *yĕtîb* followed by *zāqēp qāṭôn* as conj.

16.b. DSS and LXX omit *waw*-conj.

16.c. A few Heb. MSS and Cairo Geniza fragments read שוכני for MT שכני, "the one dwelling (in a bush)," with no change in meaning; SP reads שכן, "dweller," or "living (in)."

16.d. The term סנה, "thorny bush," seems to be a wordplay on סיני, "Sinai." Cf. Beek, *OTS* 14 (1965) 155–61.

16.e. Reading *paštā'* followed by *zāqēp qāṭôn* as conj.

17.a. 1QDeut[b], SP, LXX, Syr., and Vg. read שור, "bull," for MT שורו, "his bull." Prosodic analysis favors MT.

17.b. A few Heb. MSS and Cairo Geniza fragments read יחדיו for MT יחדו, "together," with no change in meaning. Prosodic analysis tends to support MT. O'Connor reads a finite verb form from a cognate of Arab. *ḥadā,* "to urge, spur on, instigate," translating: "He incites the peoples of the earth's ends" (*Hebrew Verse Structure,* 214).

17.c. SP, LXX, Syr., and Tg. add def. art. Prosodic analysis supports MT, with the context requiring that it be interpreted in a definite sense. The def. art. is not common in archaic Hebrew poetry.

17.d. Some Heb. MSS, LXX, Syr., and Vg. omit *waw*-conj.

17.e. Reading *pašṭā'* followed by *zāqēp̄ qāṭôn* as conj.

17.f-f. Omitted in some Heb. MSS and in some LXX witnesses.

18.a. Hempel's suggestion of reading ושיש יששכר, "and exult, O Issachar," is rejected because adding an additional word disturbs the patterns of the numerical composition.

19.a. Reading *pašṭā'* followed by *zāqēp̄ qāṭôn* as conj.

19.b. SP and Syr. add *waw*-conj.

19.c. Reading *ṭip̄ḥā'* here as conj.

19.d. Reading *pašṭā'* followed by *zāqēp̄ qāṭôn* as conj.

19.e. The suggestion to emend MT ספני, "hidden things," to read צפני, "treasures," is unnecessary. The two words are close enough in sound and meaning to communicate the idea of "hidden treasures."

20.a. SP reads טרף, "he tears," for MT וטרף, "and he tears"; other SP witnesses read טרוף, "torn."

21.a. On the translation of וירא, "provide," see Gen 22:14.

21.b. Reading שׁם in place of שׂם with Freedman in *FS C. H. Gordon* (1980), 34–35.

21.c-c. Combining ספון and ויתא to form ויתאספון with Freedman in *FS C. H. Gordon* (1980) 33. Cf. בהתאסף in v 5 and LXX συνηγμένων. Freedman calls attention to the fact that the hithp. of אסף appears only in 33:5 in the Hebrew Bible and that both verses have the words ראשי עם, "chiefs of the people," which supports the emendation here.

22.a. SP reads ויזנק, "and he shies away," for MT יזנק, "he shies away."

23.a. SP reads ימה, "to(ward) the sea," for MT ים, "sea," which is here interpreted as the Sea of Galilee (cf. Isa 8:23 [Eng. 9:1]).

23.b. SP and ancient versions read יִירָשׁ, "let him be filled," for MT ירשה, "he shall possess."

24.a. Reading ויהי, "and may he be," with SP and LXX καὶ ἔσται for MT יהי, "let him be."

24.b. Some LXX witnesses omit *waw*-conj.

24.c. SP and *Tg. Ps.-J.* read רגליו, "his feet," for MT רגלו, "his foot."

25.a. A number of Heb. MSS, B, Cairo Geniza fragments, and Syr. read מנעלך, "your gate bolt," for MT מנעליך, "your gate bolts."

25.b. The *'atnāḥ* under וכימיך in *BHS* is an error and should be replaced with *ṭip̄ḥā'* as in *BHK* and Letteris.

25.c. SP reads רביך, "your greatness[?]," for MT דבאך, "your strength."

Form/Structure/Setting

The date of Deut 33 has been debated extensively. G. E. Wright argued that the problem of the tribe of Judah as inferred from v 7 makes it difficult to date the poem in the monarchy; thus he dated it to the eleventh century, from the latter part of the period of the judges (*IB* 2:527). Tigay discusses the full range of the evidence and concludes that "the poem was composed prior to the exile of the northern tribes ca. 720 B.C.E., possibly during the time of Solomon or (perhaps excepting part of the blessing of the Levites) earlier in the United Monarchy, or conceivably in the pre-monarchic period" ([1996] 524). In other words, the precise date remains uncertain.

Prosodic analysis suggests that the poem has been carefully edited to fit into the larger structural design of the second half of the outer frame of Deuteronomy (31:1–34:12). The "Testamentary Blessing of Moses" in 33:6–25 has been deliberately framed by placing it between two stanzas of an archaic Yahwistic hymn (33:1–5, 26–29). That the resultant poem contains two "apostrophes" (vv 11, 21), one of which is closely connected with the hymnic framework, and that the grouping of the tribes appears to have shaped the corresponding narrative of the birth of Jacob's twelve sons in Gen 29:31–30:24 and 35:16–18 suggest an early date, as W. F. Albright, F. M. Cross, and D. N. Freedman have argued through the years. The first apostrophe (v 11) helps to explain the absence of Simeon from the list (or perhaps better, its inclusion by way of allusion). The second apostrophe (v 21), which was first identified by Freedman, is closely related to both the proem (vv 2–5) and the closing (vv 26–29). Moreover, it establishes the centrality of Moses within the tribal assembly of ancient Israel.

There are different ways to look at the structure of the blessings of the twelve tribes in 33:6–25. In terms of the above prosodic analysis, the blessings are arranged in a menorah pattern of seven subunits of varying length:

	Tribe / Son of Jacob (Israel)	*Mother in Genesis*	
A	Reuben and Judah	Leah	33:6–7
B	Levi, with first apostrophe (and Simeon?)	Leah	33:8–11
C	Benjamin	Rachel	33:12
X	Joseph (Ephraim and Manasseh)	Rachel	33:13–17
C′	Zebulun and Issachar	Leah	33:18–19
B′	Gad and second apostrophe (Moses as leader)	Zilpah	33:20–21
A′	Dan, Naphtali, and Asher	Bilhah and Zilpah	33:22–25

The first observation of note is that the tribe of Simeon is missing and that the tribe of Joseph has been divided into Ephraim and Manasseh (vv 13–17) to maintain the number twelve in the structure of the whole. If the structure is condensed to the familiar five-part concentric structural pattern, the grouping of the tribes is clearer:

A	Reuben, Judah, Levi, and Simeon (?)	Leah	33:6–11
B	Benjamin	Rachel	33:12
X	Joseph (Ephraim and Manasseh)	Rachel	33:13–17
B′	Zebulun and Issachar	Leah	33:18–19
A′	Gad, Dan, Naphtali, and Asher	Zilpah and Bilhah	33:20–25

The outer frame moves from the first four sons of Leah (vv 6–11) to the four sons of the two handmaids, with the sons of Leah's handmaid Zilpah (Gad and Asher) framing the two sons of Rachel's handmaid Bilhah (Dan and Naphtali). In the center is a third group of four sons: two sons of Rachel (Benjamin and Joseph) and the remaining two sons of Leah (Zebulun and Issachar). In the structural center we find the tribe of Joseph.

It is interesting to note the order of this listing of the individual tribes in terms of the Genesis account of the birth of Jacob's twelve sons (Gen 29:31–30:24; 35:16–18). In the center of this structure we find the "tribe of Joseph" (i.e., Ephraim and Manasseh—the two sons of Joseph), who was the firstborn son of Rachel and Jacob's favorite son in the stories of Gen 37–50 that focus specifically on Joseph and Judah. Though Reuben is mentioned in v 6, the prosodic analysis makes clear that the opening unit (vv 6–7) is primarily concerned with Judah, the fourth son of Leah. As we move toward the center of the above structure we move from the four primary sons of Leah (Reuben, Levi, Simeon, and Judah) to the sons of Rachel (Joseph and Benjamin). As we move from the center to the end of the structure, we move from two secondary sons of Leah (Issachar and Zebulun) to four sons of the two handmaids, Zilpah and Bilhah. The two sons of Rachel's handmaid, Bilhah (Dan and Napthali), are framed by the two sons of Leah's handmaid, Zilpah (Gad and Asher).

The blessings of the twelve tribes in 33:6–25 may also be arranged in two major parts, each of which includes six tribes as follows:

A	Reuben and Judah	33:6–7
B	Levi	33:8–10
X	Apostrophe: curse on Simeon and Levi (cf. Gen 49:7)	33:11
B′	Benjamin	33:12
A′	Ephraim and Manasseh (Joseph)	33:13–17

A	Zebulun and Issachar	33:18–19
B	Gad	33:20
X	Apostrophe: Moses and the tribal assembly (cf. 33:4–5)	33:21
B′	Dan and Naphtali	33:22–23
A′	Asher	33:24–25

This reading is based on Freedman's observation that v 21, which has nothing to do with the blessing of Gad, is an apostrophe that is closely related to vv 4–5 in the proem of the testamentary blessing of Moses. The focus of attention in v 21 is Moses; and YHWH is the subject of the verbs. The action is that of YHWH appointing Moses as leader in Israel and awarding him the victor's share. Moses in turn executes the judgments of YHWH within and on behalf of the people of Israel. Freedman called attention to the fact that v 21 is structurally tied to other verses in both the opening proem (vv 2–5) and the closing (vv 26–29). Its content confirms and amplifies what is said in the former, as it establishes the centrality of Moses in the tribal assembly. It shares the key words "YHWH" and "Israel" that appear in vv 2 and 5, and again in vv 28 and 29.

A somewhat similar structure appears in v 11, which functions as an apostrophe of a different sort. Here the verse in question is both the conclusion to the blessing of Levi (vv 8–11) and the structural center of the larger concentric design in 33:6–17, as I showed in my earlier study (*ZAW* 101 [1989] 278–82), where I argued that we have here an instance of amphibology. Of the known instances of amphibolous usage involving the root ברך, the most familiar example is on the lips of Job's wife after the series of catastrophes that poor Job suffered. As Job sat in the ashes, scraping himself with a potsherd, her advice was "Curse [בָּרֵךְ] God, and die" (Job 2:9). Similar uses of ברך appear in the words of Job himself (1:5) and twice on the part of Satan (1:11; 2:5). Another interesting example appears twice in the story of Naboth's vineyard (1 Kgs 21:10–13). The two scoundrels hired by Jezebel follow her advice and accuse Naboth in court of having "cursed [בֵּרַךְ] God and the king." The text of Ps 10:3 speaks similarly of the man who is greedy for gain who "curses [בֵּרֵךְ] and renounces the LORD."

With seven clear examples of the use of the verb ברך meaning "to curse" rather than "to bless" when associated with God as the subject or object, a similar reading is possible in Deut 33:11, which the RSV renders: "Bless [בָּרֵךְ], O LORD, his substance, and accept the work of his hands" (see Christensen, *ZAW* 101 [1989] 90–93). Though YHWH is not the object of the verb, the phrase ברך יהוה חילו is so similar in form to ברך אלהים ומת (Job 2:9) that it may be a euphemism here as well. These two occurrences are perhaps the only instances of the infinitive absolute of ברך used in the imperative sense in the Hebrew Bible. Moreover, the parallel blessing of the tribe of Levi in Gen 49:7 contains the term אָרוּר, "curse," which is applied to both Levi and Simeon: "Cursed be their anger, for it is fierce; / and their wrath, for it is cruel!" If the verse is translated in a similar manner here in Deut 33:11 ("Curse, O YHWH, his strength, but the works of his hands you shall accept"), it refers to the tradition of Levi and Simeon taking matters into their own hands as related in Gen 34:25–31. Levi's "strength" in military matters is cursed, whereas the "work" of his hands is accepted. It is interesting to note that the term for "work" here is פֹּעַל, which in the Hebrew Bible almost always has God as subject. As G. Östborn puts it, "The specific designation of Yahweh's activity in the OT seems to be the term פעל" (*Tōrā* in the Old Testament [Lund: H. Ohlssons, 1945] 74). The language thus suggests, in poetic fashion, that Levi's work is none other than the work of YHWH himself, done on behalf of the tribal assembly.

In terms of prosodic structure, the content of the blessing of Levi in 33:8–11 is also arranged in five parts:

A	Thummim and Urim are entrusted to Levi, who was tested at Massah	33:8
B	He (Levi) is set apart from his brothers	33:9a
X	For they have observed your precepts and kept your covenant	33:9b
B′	They shall teach YHWH's Torah and perform ritual ceremony	33:10
A′	Cursed be his "strength" but accept the work of his hands	33:11

The outer frame in this structure moves from a historical allusion to the testing of Levi "at the waters of Meribah" (v 8) to another allusion to still earlier events in the story of Levi and Simeon and the violence perpetrated against the men of Shechem (v 11; cf. Gen 34:25–31). Within this framework we see that the tribe of Levi is set apart from the other tribes ("his brothers," v 9a) as a reward for observing YHWH's Torah (v 9b), which they are entrusted to teach, along with their other priestly duties in matters relating to the offering of incense and sacrificial offerings (v 10).

The tribes listed in the first half of the concentric structure of 33:6–7 include the other three sons of Leah by name, and Simeon by allusion in the "curse" of v 11. The tribes listed in the second half of this structure (vv 12–17) include both the sons of Rachel, Joseph and Benjamin. The pairing of Judah and Joseph in this structure parallels the central role these two brothers play in the concluding stories of Genesis (chaps. 37–50), which may be outlined as follows:

A	Joseph and his dreams that he will rule	Gen 37
B	Judah and Tamar—birth of Perez, ancestor of David	Gen 38
X	Joseph in Egypt—rise to power by interpreting dreams	Gen 39:1–44:17
B′	Judah's speech: "Keep me in place of Benjamin!"	Gen 44:18–34
A′	Joseph's dreams fulfilled—Jacob's family in Egypt	Gen 45–50

The tribe of Levi is the tribe of Moses (cf. Exod 2:1); and together with the tribes of Judah, Joseph (Ephraim and Manasseh), and Benjamin—which appear in this structure—we have the four primary sons of Leah and the two sons of Rachel of the Genesis stories. The six tribes in the second half of the testamentary blessing of Moses include two secondary sons of Leah (Zebulun and Issachar) and four sons of the two handmaids, Bilhah (Dan and Naphtali) and Zilpah (Gad and Asher).

The data from Labuschagne on the numerical composition of 33:6–25 may be summarized as follows:

Words:	before *ʾatnāḥ*			after *ʾatnāḥ*				
33:1–11	80		+	52	(= 2 × 26)	=	132	
33:1–7	50		+	28		=	78	(= 3 × 26)
33:2–25	153	(= 9 × 17)	+	119	(= 7 × 17)	=	272	(= 16 × 17)
33:3–6	17		+	17		=	34	(= 2 × 17)
33:4–6	11		+	12		=	23	
33:6–7	14		+	9		=	23	
33:6–12	51	(= 3 × 17)	+	40		=	91	
33:6–17	81		+	64	(= 2 × 32)	=	145	
33:7–21	102	(= 6 × 17)	+	85	(= 5 × 17)	=	187	(= 11 × 17)
33:8–12	37		+	31		=	68	(= 4 × 17)
33:11–12	13		+	13		=	26	
33:12–17	37		+	31		=	68	(= 4 × 17)
33:13–16	17		+	18		=	35	
33:18–23	38		+	30		=	68	(= 4 × 17)
33:20–25	34	(= 2 × 17)	+	29		=	63	
33:21	8		+	9		=	17	

The conclusions to be drawn from this data are much the same as that of the previous section on 33:1–5. The text is structured in terms of the divine-name numbers 17 and 26 with occasional use of the numbers 23 and 32 (associated with Heb. כבוד, "glory").

Comment

6 On the traditional meaning of the phrase מתיו מספר as "few in number," see Gen 34:30; Deut 4:27; Jer 44:28; Ps 105:12 (= 1 Chr 16:19). It should be noted, however, that in each instance the two words are bound together in a single syntactic accentual stress unit with the conjunctive accent *mûnāḥ* under מתיו. The situation here is more like that of Ps 40:6 (Eng. 5) in which the word מספר is separated from what precedes it by a disjunctive accent. Dahood emends MT מִסְפָּר to read מִסַּפֵּר, "(may his men be) beyond counting," to agree with Ps 40:6 (*Bib* 48 [1967] 429), which seems to be how the LXX read the phrase מתיו מספר: καὶ ἔστω πολὺς ἐν ἀριθμῷ, "and let him be many in number."

7 Moses prays that God will "hearken . . . to the voice of Judah" and "restore him," by bringing "help against his adversaries." Tigay notes: "Targum Onkelos aptly paraphrases: 'Accept, O Lord, the prayer of Judah when he goes forth in battle . . . bring him back safely to his people'" ([1996] 323). The translation of the words ידיו רב לו as "his hands <may they> contend for him" stands with or without the proposed emendation to read יריבו for MT רב (see Christensen, *ZAW* [1989] 279 n. 5). It is more important to note, with Tigay ([1996] 323), the wordplay on the name of Judah in the word ידיו, "his hands," probably pronounced *yadayu* "in biblical times." Dahood emends רָב, "he contended," to read רַבֵּ<ה>, "increase" (cf. Judg 9:29), with the result: "increase his forces [lit. 'his hands'] for him" (*RSP*, 2:26). O'Connor reads רב here as an infinitive used for a finite verb, which requires no emendation in the consonantal text of MT, with the resultant meaning: "may you fight for him at his enemies' hands" (*Hebrew Verse Structure*, 210). For a detailed discussion of the meaning of עזר, "a help," see Baisas, *UF* 5 (1973) 44–45.

8 The text here, which is the fourth of seven occurrences of "Thummim" and "Urim" (Exod 28:30; Lev 8:8; Num 27:21; Deut 33:8; 1 Sam 28:6; Ezra 2:63; Neh 7:65), is the only place in the Bible that the terms appear in reverse order. According to Exod 28:30 and Lev 8:8, the chief priest carried the lots in a pouch of some sort attached to "the breastpiece of decision" (NIV) worn on the linen ephod, a sacred vestment. The expanded text of LXX in 1 Sam 14:41 merits quotation, "Why have you not responded to your servant today? If this iniquity was due to my son Jonathan or to me, O Lord, God of Israel, show Urim, and if you say it was due to your people [Israel] show Thummim." This text suggests that the two objects could only give a yes or no answer. In some instances when the high priest "inquired of YHWH," an uncertain response emerged, or a specific answer that moves well beyond a yes or no as such. The recently discovered Hebrew word אורתום (1QH 4:6, 23; 18:29), which, according to context, means "perfect illumination," appears to be a combination of the singular of אורים, "Urim," and the singular of תומים, "Thummim." Some have suggested that the names Urim and Thummim refer to the first and last letters of the Hebrew alphabet, א and ת, and that the lots consisted of all twenty-two letters of the alphabet. Three letters were withdrawn from the pouch and interpreted by the high priest: "As the basis of the Hebrew language is the triliteral root, it follows that any three letters would provide meaningful words from which the High Priest could extract a message" (Robertson, *VT* 14 [1964] 72).

The references to those whom YHWH נסיתו במסה, "tested at Massah" (lit. "you tested at Testing Place"), and תריבהו . . . מריבה, "with whom you contended at the waters of Meribah" (lit. "you challenged at Challenge-Place"—so Tigay [1996] 324) are more of a play on words than specific references to historical incidents that can be identified elsewhere in the biblical text. The Massah-Meribah incident is alluded to in Pss 81:8 (Eng. 7) and 95:8–9, and related in Exod 17:1–7 and Num 20:1–13, where the people of Israel put YHWH to the test (cf. Deut 32:51 and Ps 106:32, where Moses and Aaron put YHWH to the test "at the waters of Meribah"); but here it is YHWH who put Levi to the test. Mayes argues that the background to the verse here is Exod 15:25, "where those whom Yahweh 'proved' were probably the Levites" ([1981] 403). It seems likely that the words of the blessing on Levi in Deut 33:8 played a role in shaping subsequent tradition on the subject of being "tested at the waters of Meribah" along the lines of what eventually became midrashic exegesis in Jewish tradition.

9–10 Of Levi it is written that "his brothers [אחיו] he disregards, and his (own) child [בנו] he does not know." The episode of the golden calf in Exod

32:26–29 appears to be shaped, at least in part, by the text here; for the Levites there rallied to punish the calf worshipers, including their own relatives, and were rewarded with priesthood. The account in Exod 32:29 concludes with "Today you have ordained yourselves for the service of YHWH, each one at the cost of his (own) child and his brothers" (author's translation). The terms appear in reverse order from that of 33:9, forming a chiasm: אחיו / בנו // בנו / אחיו. The episode with the Levites in Exod 32:29 concludes with the word ברכה, "blessing," which should be compared with the title of the concluding weekly portion of Torah readings in the lectionary cycle and the opening words of Deut 33:1: וזאת הברכה, "and this is the blessing."

11 On the translation "Curse, O YHWH, his strength," see Christensen (*ZAW* 101 [1989] 278–82) and discussion under *Form/Structure/Setting* above. This verse is read as an apostrophe attached to the blessing of Levi, within a larger concentric structure that sets this verse over against another apostrophe in v 21, which makes allusion to the Genesis story of Simeon and Levi and their vengeance on the men of Shechem for the rape of their sister Dinah (Gen 34:25–31; 49:5–7). The clause ברך יהוה חילו carries two very different meanings in this text. When read in relation to the story in Gen 34, it means "Curse, O YHWH, his strength"; but when read in isolation, it also conveys the sense of "Bless, O YHWH, his substance (wealth)"—the more traditional reading. As Tigay notes in his quotation from *Sifre* 352 ([1996] 408 n. 70), "From this verse it is said 'Most priests are wealthy.'" The "work [פעל] of his hands" refers in poetic fashion to the work of YHWH himself that is entrusted to the Levites. Craigie translates the phrase מן־יקומון, "whoever opposes," taking the *mem* as an indefinite interrogative, similar to Ugaritic ([1976] 395; see W. F. Albright, *CBQ* 7 [1945] 23 n. 64). O'Connor emends the text to read מחץ מתני־מ־קמיו, "strike the loins of his enemies," interpreting the *mem* as emphatic (*Hebrew Verse Structure,* 212). Fox (*FBM,* 1009) translates the phrase as "from rising up," which is essentially the same as what is given here—"that they rise no more" (cf. NRSV).

12 The reference here to Benjamin as "the beloved of YHWH" may have played a role in shaping the story in Genesis in which Jacob dotes over his son Benjamin after the presumed death of Joseph (Gen 42). Compare also the favoritism that Joseph showed at the banquet he prepared for his brothers in Egypt in which "Benjamin's portion was five times as much as any of theirs" (Gen 43:34).

The reading "YHWH tents securely" attempts to call attention to the usage of שכן, "to dwell," from which the word משכן, "tabernacle," derives. Rather than reading עליו in the first clause as "by him," Craigie reads it as a divine name with what follows: "'Eli surrounds him all the day long" ([1976] 396). See M. Dahood, "The Divine Name ʿEli in the Psalms," *TS* 14 (1953) 452–57. The problem with this reading is that it ignores the *ʾatnāḥ* and destroys the balance in terms of mora count between the two halves of v 12. Though the LXX reading ὁ θεὸς, "the god," for MT עליו does support the emendation proposed by Dahood, Craigie, O'Connor, and others, it is easier to explain how this text derived from the MT than the reverse. The *lectio difficilior* is read with the sense of "by him," or alongside YHWH, who "enfolds him all the day." The verb חפף, "enfolds," which appears nowhere else in the Bible, is probably related to חוּפָּה, "canopy," and thus the verb would mean "form a protective canopy," as Tigay suggests ([1996] 326);

he cites the parallel text in Isa 4:5–6: "The Lord will create over . . . Mount Zion cloud by day and smoke . . . by night . . . a canopy [חֻפָּה], which shall serve as a cover for shade from heat by day and as a shelter for protection against drenching rain."

The statement "between his shoulders he tents" is here interpreted as Benjamin resting in security between God's shoulders, much as that of a child being carried on its parent's shoulders. Tigay prefers to see God as the subject "so that it is he who rests between Benjamin's 'shoulders'" ([1996] 326). "Shoulders" is taken topographically, meaning that God's sanctuary is within Benjamin's borders. Craigie reads the text in a different sense altogether: "And between his weapons he dwells" ([1976] 396). He takes כתיף, normally "shoulders, shoulder blades," in the sense of "weapons, blades," from Ugaritic *ktp* (see *CTA* 6.V.2 = *UT* 49.V.2).

13 The tribe of Joseph is divided into two tribes, Ephraim and Manasseh (v 17b), the sons of Joseph in the Genesis narrative (Gen 48). The tribe of Ephraim was located in the central highlands north of the tribe of Benjamin. Manasseh occupied the section of central highlands to the north of Ephraim and also on the other side of the valley of the Jordan River, in Bashan and Gilead of Transjordan. As Tigay observes, the very names of two of these tribes suggest fertility ([1996] 327). יוסף, "Joseph," means "may he increase," and Gen 41:52 explains Ephraim's name as meaning "God has made me fruitful," from the root פרה, "be fertile."

The term מגד, "bounty," appears five times in vv 13–16, with what Tigay takes as double entendre with the sense of "gift," "blessing," like Hebrew מגדנות, "presents," "precious objects"; and of מגדים, "choice fruits." The double meaning is that "the rain and water are both the 'fruit' of heaven and earth and their 'gifts'" (Tigay [1996] 327). "The deep lying beneath" refers to waters beneath the earth that produce springs and wells. The word תהום, "the deep," has overtones from the world of ancient mythology, for the name of the Babylonian god Tiamat is an Akkadian cognate of תהום.

14–15 O'Connor reads the *mem* on ירחים, "months," as emphatic, rather than deleting it with Cross and Freedman (*Studies in Ancient Yahwistic Poetry,* SBLDS 21 [Missoula, MT: Scholars Press, 1975] 116 n. 49), translating the phrase: "From the favor of Moon's yield" (*Hebrew Verse Structure,* 212–13). The word ראש, translated "best," normally means "head," or in this instance "(mountain) top"—hence another case of double entendre. Craigie interprets it as "wealth" of "the ancient mountains" in the sense of forests growing densely on the top of Mount Carmel ([1976] 398). The reference to "ancient mountains" and "everlasting hills" may simply be to the physical topography of the hills of Joseph's territory. Tigay suggests an allusion to the role of mountains in mythology, "such as the mountains where the Sumerians believed that the gods of cattle and grain were located. The point would be that Joseph enjoys fertility like that of those ancient mountains" ([1996] 328 and 409 n. 111, where he cites T. Jacobsen, "Sumerian Mythology: A Review Article," *JNES* 5 [1946] 141).

16 The reference to "the favor of the one dwelling in סנה [a bush]" points to the source of all the blessings: the God who first appeared to Moses at הַסְּנֶה "the burning bush," which sounds like and calls our attention back to סִינַי, "Sinai," the mountain where God revealed himself to Moses (Exod 3:1–6). Tigay notes that the reference to "the bush" here forms an inclusion around the whole story of Moses in terms of his relationship with YHWH, for he is now approaching the moment of his own death ([1996] 328). It appears that the reference to the סנה, "bush," is also a wordplay on מנשה, "Manasseh," as numerous scholars have suggested. O'Connor reads the *-t(h)* termination on the verb תבואתה, "may it come," as an emphatic particle, with C. Krahmalkov ("The Amorite Enclitic Particle *TA/I*," *JSS* 14 [1969] 201–4; idem, "The Enclitic Particle *TA/I* in Hebrew," *JBL* 89 [1970] 218–19), translating the line as follows: "May [blessings] come on the head of Joseph, Nazir of his Brothers" (*Hebrew Verse Structure,* 213). The term נזיר is used of Joseph in the Blessing of Jacob in Gen 49:26. Note that Joshua, Deborah, and Jeroboam I were Ephraimites; and Gideon was from the tribe of Manasseh. The central sanctuary at Shechem was in Manasseh, and subsequently moved to Shiloh in Ephraim. The Northern Kingdom itself was sometimes called "(the house of) Joseph" (Ezek 37:16; Amos 5:6; Ps 77:16), as is the entire nation in Pss 80:2 (Eng. 1); 81:6 (Eng. 5). The term נזיר, "prince," calls to mind the Nazirite, who was distinguished by his uncut hair, and the context here speaks of the head (ראש) and the pate (קדקד), where hair is found.

17 Joseph is likened to a בכור שור, "firstling bull," with "the horns of a wild ox" to connote his great strength (Ibn Ezra), or perhaps to denote his role in terms of leadership as he exercised the birthright of the firstborn (see 1 Chr 5:1–2).

The interpretation of the word יחדו, "together," in this line is uncertain. *BHS* and most English translations ignore the accents that link it closely with the preceding word in the phrase ינגח יחדו, "(they) are gored altogether." The normal order of "ten thousands" appearing after reference to "the thousands" is reversed here, because the first tribe mentioned (Ephraim) is the more influential of the two, hence the larger number. In the narrative in Gen 48:8–20, the episode with Jacob as "he put Ephraim ahead of Manasseh," against the wishes of their father Joseph (Gen 48:20), corresponds with this reversal in the normal order of things.

18 The prosodic analysis indicates that Zebulun and Issachar are the subjects of parallel poetic lines and that the *sillûq* (and thus the verse division) is misplaced. In the story of Gen 30:17–20, the order is reversed with Issachar and Zebulun, respectively, as the fifth and sixth sons of Leah. The two brothers are mentioned together in the Blessing of Jacob (Gen 49:13–14) and the Song of Deborah (Judg 5:14–15) with Zebulun appearing before Issachar. Moreover, in the allotment of territory in Josh 19, the territory of Zebulun is presented before that of Issachar. If this is an indication of priority, the unnamed "mountain" (הר) to which "peoples are summoned" (יקראו) may be Mount Carmel rather than Mount Tabor. Zebulun's territory included at least part of Mount Carmel, immediately south of Haifa (see Mazar's discussion in *EI* 14 [1978] 40). Josh 21:34 locates Jokneam (northwest of Megiddo) in the tribe of Zebulun, and Josh 12:22 mentions "the king of Jokneam in Carmel."

The ambiguity of these verses is probably to be explained, at least in part, with Tigay in terms of wordplay on the sound of the names: "The sounds *z-b* of Zebulun may have inspired *yiZBeḥu ZiVeḥei* (originally pronounced *ZiBeḥei*), 'offer sacrifices,' while the sounds *s-s* or *sas* in 'Issachar' (*yiSSakhar* or *yiSaSkhar*) may have inspired 'rejoice' (*semaḥ,* a synonym of *sas,* 'rejoice'" ([1996] 329). בצאתך, "your

[Zebulun's] journeys," are probably maritime trade ventures as Driver ([1906] 408) suggests, or perhaps fishing excursions with M. Greenberg (see Tigay [1996] 329 and 409 n. 130). Craigie translates בצאתך as "your going forth," and calls attention to the Hebrew idiom "going out / coming in" of 28:6 and 31:2 ([1976] 399; see also Driver [1895] 408). Though Driver interprets this as a poetical variation of that common phrase, "used to designate a man's whole activity and enterprise" (cf. also Ps 121:8), this is not likely. The second of the two verbs is missing here; moreover, the meaning of the phrase is often quite different from what Driver assumes. See the *Comment* on 31:2 and the articles by Speiser (*BASOR* 144 [1956] 20–23) and Evans (*BASOR* 150 [1958] 28–35). Issachar's tents are probably to be explained as the dwellings of herdsmen, in light of the parallel text in Gen 49:14 (NRSV), "Issachar . . . lying down between the sheepfolds." Tigay's suggestion that "in your tents" is addressed to Zebulun as well as Issachar is intriguing, for "this would imply that Issachar lives in Zebulun's territory (like Simeon in Judah's), under its protection or in its service, and is too insignificant to rate a blessing in its own right" ([1996] 330).

19 Of the two possibilities for the unnamed "mountain," Mount Tabor is suggested as the more likely by Mayes ([1981] 407), though Tigay leaves the matter open ([1996] 330). I follow Craigie's suggestion here: "the initial expression of the blessing indicates that no particular place is intended" ([1976] 399 n. 33). The "mountain" is where one anticipates meeting God. The "peoples . . . summoned to the mountain" are probably fellow Israelites, as J. B. Herder argues (*The Spirit of Hebrew Poetry,* tr. J. Marsh [1833; repr. Naperville, IL: Aleph Press, 1971] 160), where they offer "sacrifices of צדק," which normally means "righteousness," here translated "success." Tigay suggests that the reference is "to a thanksgiving offering, in which case the verse could mean that Zebulun and Issachar will invite other tribes and peoples to join them in thanking God for their maritime wealth" ([1996] 330). Mayes, however, suggests that the reference to the "hidden treasures of the sand" "may be to caravan trade as a source of wealth" ([1981] 407), which would form a merism of sorts with wealth in v 19b coming by commerce at sea and by land (i.e., from all sources).

20 The statement about "he who enlarges Gad" probably refers to increasing the population rather than extending the territory, as Tigay argues; "for the tribe itself is the direct object of 'enlarge.' Enlarging someone's territory is expressed with the owner as the indirect object and the territory as the direct object. See 12:20; 19:8; Gen. 26:22; Exod. 3:8; 34:24; Amos 1:13" ([1996] 410 n. 154). The blessing of Gad is the only one in the series that is a blessing of God for helping the tribe. The term ברוך, "blessed," appears only here and in the blessing of Asher in v 24, which Tigay connects with the meaning of the names of these two tribes as given in the narrative of Gen 30:11–13, where Gad is explained as meaning "good luck" and Asher as "good fortune."

21 The clause "he provided the first for him" is ambiguous. On the translation of וירא as "provided," see Gen 22:8, where Abraham answers Isaac's question with the words, "God himself will provide [יראה־לו] the lamb for a burnt offering" (NRSV). Gad received the "first" allotment of territory to the tribes, in both time and quality (i.e., "prime," or "best"). Since the term ראשית, "first," appears also in Jacob's blessing of Reuben in Gen 49:3, Mayes suggests "that what is hinted at here is Gad's absorption of the tribe of Reuben and its land, and so also its assumption of, or claim to, leadership" ([1981] 408). Though I accept in principle the interpretation of Freedman that v 21 is an apostrophe, which "has nothing to do with the Blessing of Gad" (*FS C. H. Gordon* [1980] 34), the prosodic analysis presented here results in the separation of the first segment of the verse from what follows. YHWH has "assigned the commander's portion" to Moses and "the righteousness of YHWH he [Moses] executed." As Freedman puts it, "The action of YHWH in appointing Moses as leader, and awarding him the victor's share, is matched by that of Moses in executing the judgments of YHWH both within and behalf of his people Israel" (*FS C. H. Gordon* [1980] 35). O'Connor reads כי יְשׁם, "he pants after," from the root נשם, "to pant after," with Cross and Freedman and *BHS* (*Hebrew Verse Structure,* 215). The traditional reading שׂם, "assigned," is followed here, which indicates the centrality of Moses in the tribal configuration, to whom is assigned חלקת מחקק, "the commander's portion." In further support of this reading, Tigay notes that several ancient translations and medieval commentaries interpreted מחקק, "commander," as referring to Moses, and they "understood the *meḥokek* as Moses, the 'scribe' or lawgiver, and 'the *meḥokek*'s portion' as his burial plot in Transjordan" ([1996] 331 and 410 n. 161—where he cites Tg., Syr., Vg., *Sifre* 355, *b. Sot.* 13b, *b. B. Bat.* 15a, *Yal.* 962, Saadia, Rashi, Shadal). The role of Moses is also the point of reference in what follows—"the chiefs of the people gathered together" (inverting ספון ויתא of MT as ויאספון, as in v 5, where the phrase בהתאסף ראשי עם is rendered "when the chiefs of the people gathered together").

22 The expression "Dan is a גור אריה [lion's whelp]" is also used to describe the tribe of Judah in Gen 49:9 of Jacob's blessing. The image is that of a powerful young lion. The use of the metaphor here may have been inspired by the former name of the city of Dan, *Laish,* since that is another term for lion in Hebrew, as Tigay notes ([1996] 332). The tribe of Gad is also blessed with lionlike strength in v 20 above. The translation of the word יזנק, "leaps forth," is problematic, since the root is used nowhere else in the Bible. "The translation seems to assume that it is a metathesized cognate of Arabic *nazaka* (*nazaqa*), 'be swift, rush forth,' used of horses" (Tigay [1996] 411 n. 174). The translation of יזנק מן־הבשן, "he shies away from the viper," follows the suggestion of Cross and Freedman, who take הבשן as cognate with Ugaritic *bṯn,* "viper" (*JBL* 67 [1948] 191–201). As Craigie observes ([1976] 401), "the words may be a play on the saying addressed to Dan by Jacob (Gen. 49:17), where the metaphor describes Dan as a serpent or viper. Dan now has the potential for greater strength [as 'a lion's whelp'], but is still nervous in the presence of a viper." Historically the "viper" may refer to whatever caused the tribe to relocate from the Shephelah and the coastal plain, near Philistia, to the northern extremity of the land of Israel. On the other hand, it may be that we are dealing with "a traditional saying on Dan of uncertain provenance and significance" (Mayes [1981] 409), which may never be explained. "The geographic order of the tribes in this poem indicates that it pictures the tribe of Dan in its northern location. . . . Contrast Numbers 34:22, where Dan is listed in accordance with its earlier southern location" (Tigay [1996] 332). The tribe of Dan never controlled Bashan, nor did they attack Laish from there.

23 The description of Naphtali as "satisfied with favor" and "full of the blessing of YHWH" is apropos, for its territory in Upper Galilee was well watered and rich in fruit trees, and a wide variety of vegetation. As Tigay notes ([1996] 411 n.

175), "Josephus is unrestrained in his praise of the region's fertility and the Talmud describes its fruits as extraordinarily sweet (Josephus, War 3:516–521; Ber. 44a; cf. Targ. Jon.)." The reference to Naphtali's possession extending to "the sea and to the south" refers to the Sea of Galilee and its western and southern shores (see Dahood, *Le antiche divinità semitiche,* 66 n. 2).

24–25 Asher's "blessedness" (ברוך) plays on the meaning of its name in Gen 30:13, which is related to the term בְּאָשְׁרִי, "in my happiness" (cf. also אֶשֶׁר or אֹשֶׁר, "happiness, blessedness"). The statement "may he dip his foot [רגלו] in oil" probably refers to the abundance of olive oil from the highlands of Galilee; though, once again, the clause may be another play on the name of Asher (אָשֵׁר), since the word אָשׁוּר means "foot," as Tigay notes ([1996] 333; cf. Pss 37:31; 40:3 [Eng 2]). On "gate bolts" see Neh 3:3, 6.

Explanation

In the Blessing of Moses (33:6–25) each tribe is singled out for blessing, with the exception of Simeon. From the perspective of history, the tribe of Simeon was absorbed into that of Judah. By mentioning each tribe, all members of the assembly were included.

The first apostrophe (v 11) alludes to the tribes of Simeon and Levi and their violent vengeance against the men of Shechem for the rape of their sister Dinah. In this instance the blessing is mixed, for it includes a curse on Levi's "strength" in military matters, with a prayer that the divine service of Levi (the "work" of his hands) be accepted.

The more lengthy blessing of Joseph (vv 13–17) shows that we have here the most prominent of the twelve tribes. The fivefold repetition of the word ממגד, translated "with the bounty" or "with the bounteous" in vv 13–16, speaks of prosperity. The blessing includes a prayer for military strength as well, in the metaphor of a bull or wild ox goring the nations (v 17). The two tribes of Ephraim and Manasseh, the two sons of Joseph, are given in reverse order of their birth, with the younger given the greater blessing ("ten thousands" as opposed to "thousands").

The blessing of Gad (v 20), which had received its allotment of land in Transjordan under Moses, calls attention to their military strength and introduces the second apostrophe (v 21), with its focus on the person of Moses. YHWH has appointed Moses as the leader, giving him "the commander's portion." Moses in turn exercises the judgments of YHWH in behalf of the people of Israel.

Deut 33–34 are the traditional readings in the synagogue liturgy for Simchat Torah, the "Celebration of Torah" (see Tigay [1996] 525). Christians would do well to recover some of this "joy of the Torah" in public worship. Many have misread the teaching of Jesus in his Sermon on the Mount. When Jesus said, "you have heard that it was said to those of ancient times, . . . but I say to you" (Matt 5:21–22 NRSV), he was not replacing the Torah. He was merely challenging the manner in which the Torah was being interpreted in rabbinic circles of his day. Jesus was interpreting the text as it was written, for when properly interpreted, there is nothing there that is contrary to his own gospel message. The Torah is a way of life, and a source of meaning and joy to Jew and Christian alike. The Torah was not intended to be something external to us, which only the highly trained specialists could truly understand. The Torah was to be learned by every member of the community; and its message is exceedingly practical. Jesus summed up the matter well when he was asked, "Which commandment in the law [Torah] is the greatest? He said to him, 'You shall love the Lord your God with all your heart, and with all your soul, and with all your mind.' This is the greatest and first commandment. And a second is like it: 'You shall love your neighbor as yourself.' On these two commandments hang all the law and the prophets" (Matt 22:36–39 NRSV). The law (Torah) and the prophets (Former Prophets plus the Latter Prophets), to which Jesus referred on this occasion, make up one half of the Christian Bible as we know it. And all of it is built on these two primary teachings of Deuteronomy. We would do well to become more familiar with the words of the Torah, as a guide to proper living in the very manner in which Jesus lived and taught his disciples. What better way to do this than to include once again the systematic public reading of the Torah within the context of Christian worship?

C. Second Stanza of an Ancient Hymn: Israel's Security and Blessing (33:26–29)

Bibliography

Bar-Magen, M. "וישכן ישראל בטח בדד עין יעקב." *BMik* 18 (1972–73) 48–50, 136 (Heb.). **Ben-Zvi, I.** "A Lamp with a Samaritan Inscription: *'There is none like unto the God of Jeshurun.'*" *IEJ* 11 (1961) 139–42. **Brin, G.** "The Roots *'zr—'zz* in the Bible." *Leš* 24 (1960) 8–14 (Heb.). **Cassuto, U.** "Deuteronomy xxxiii and the New Year in Ancient Israel." In *Biblical and Oriental Studies.* Tr. I. Abrahams. 2 vols. Jerusalem: Magnes, 1973–75. 1:47–91. **Christensen, D. L.** *Prophecy and War in Ancient Israel.* N. Richland Hills, TX: BIBAL Press, 1988. ———. "Two Stanzas of a Hymn in Deuteronomy 33." *Bib* 65 (1984) 382–89. **Craigie, P. C.** "Psalm XXIX in the Hebrew Poetic Tradition." *VT* 22 (1972) 143–51, esp. 145–46. **Cross, F. M.** *CMHE.* 15–19. ———. "The 'Olden Gods' in Ancient Near Eastern Creation Myths." In *FS G. E. Wright.* 1976. 329–38. ——— and **Freedman, D. N.** "A Note on Deuteronomy 33:26." *BASOR* 108 (1947) 6–7. **Dahood, M.** "Hebrew-Ugaritic Lexicography II." *Bib* 45 (1964) 393–412, esp. 396, 399. ———. "Hebrew-Ugaritic Lexicography III." *Bib* 46 (1965) 311–32, esp. 319. ———. "Hebrew-Ugaritic Lexicography VI." *Bib* 49 (1968) 355–69, esp. 360. ———. *Proverbs and Northwest Semitic Philology.* Rome: Pontifical Biblical Institute, 1963. 45–46. ———. "Ugaritic *DRKT* and Biblical *DEREK.*" *TS* 15 (1954) 627–31. ———. "Ugaritic Lexicography." In *Mélanges Eugéne Tisserant.* Studi e Testi 231. Citta del Vaticano: Biblioteca Apostolica Vaticana, 1964. 96. **Driver, G. R.** "Misreadings in the Old Testament." *WO* 1 (1947) 234–38. **Fowler, M. D.** "The Israelite *bāmâ:* A Question of Interpretation." *ZAW* 94 (1982) 203–13. **Freedman, D. N.** "The Original Name of Jacob." *IEJ* 13 (1963) 125–26. **Gaster, T. H.** "An Ancient Eulogy on Israel: Deuteronomy 33:3–5, 26–29." *JBL* 66 (1947) 53–62. **Ginsberg, H. L.** "On Bulletin 108 (Dec. 1947): 6–7." *BASOR* 110 (1948) 26. **Gordis, R.** "Critical Notes on the Blessing of Moses" and "Additional Note on Dt 33,27." In *The Word and the Book.* New York: Ktav, 1976. 337–39 and 340–41, respectively. ———. "The Text and Meaning of Deuteronomy 33:27." *JBL* 67 (1948) 69–72. **Gray, J.**

Legacy of Canaan. 2nd ed. 1965. 259. **Habel, N. C.** "'YHWH, Maker of Heaven and Earth': A Study in Tradition Criticism." *JBL* 91 (1972) 321–37, esp. 323. **Hiebert, T.** *God of My Victory: The Ancient Hymn in Habakkuk 3.* HSM 38. Atlanta: Scholars Press, 1986. **Hoonacker, A. van.** "Notes sur le texte de la 'Bénédiction de Moïse' (*Deut.* XXXIII)." *Mus* 42 (1929) 42–60, esp. 59. **Loewenstamm, S. E.** "עין יעקב (Deut 33:28)." *BMik* 21 (1975) 152–53 (Heb.). **Lozachmeur, H.,** and **Margain, J.** "Une amulette samaritaine provenant de Tyr." *Sem* 32 (1982) 117–20. **Malamat, A.** "'AMM L[e]BAḎAḎ YIŠKON: A Report from Mari and an Oracle of Balaam." *JQR* 76 (1985) 47–50. **Mann, T. W.** *Divine Presence and Guidance in Israelite Traditions: The Typology of Exaltation.* Johns Hopkins Near Eastern Studies 9. Baltimore: Johns Hopkins UP, 1977. 178–82. **Miller, P. D.** "Ugaritic *ǴZR* and Hebrew *ʿZR* II." *UF* 2 (1970) 159–75. **Seeligmann, I. L.** "A Psalm from Pre-Regal Times." *VT* 14 (1964) 75–92. **Steiner, R. C.** "דָּת and עַיִן: Two Verbs Masquerading as Nouns in Moses' Blessing (Deuteronomy 33:2, 28)." *JBL* 115 (1996) 696–98. **Vaughan, P. H.** *The Meaning of "bāmâ" in* the Old Testament: A Study of Etymological, Textual and Archaeological Evidence. SOTSMS 3. London; New York: Cambridge UP, 1974. **Wächter, L.** "Israel und Jeschurun." In *FS A. Jepsen.* 1971. 58–64. **Weinfeld, M.** "'Rider of the Clouds' and 'Gatherer of the Clouds.'" *JANESCU* 5 (1973) 421–26. **Zenger, E.** "Jahwe und die Götter." *TP* 43 (1968) 338–59, esp. 347–48. **Zijl, P. J. van.** *Baal: A Study of Texts in Connexion with Baal in the Ugaritic Epics.* AOAT 10. Kevelaer: Butzon & Bercker; Neukirchen-Vluyn: Neukirchener Verlag, 1972. 329–31. **Zobel, H.-J.** "Das Selbstverständnis Israels nach dem Alten Testament." *ZAW* 85 (1973) 281–94, esp. 290–92.

See also *Bibliography* for 33:1–5.

Translation and Prosodic Analysis

Second Stanza of an Ancient Hymn: Israel's Security and Blessing
[(6:4):(5:5):(4:6)]

26 There is none [a]like God[a] / O Jeshurun //	11	2
riding the heavens / for your help /	12	2
and in his splendor / the clouds //	14	2_
27 A refuge / is the ancient God /	12	2
[a]and the outstretching[a] / of the[b] arms of the Eternal One[c] //	13	2_
And he drove out from before you / the enemy /	14	2
and he said "Destroy!" //	7	1
28 so Israel tents / securely |[a]	11	2_
Alone \\[b] dwells[c] Jacob / in[d] a land / of grain and must //	22	3
[e]indeed his heavens[e] / drip down dew //	11	2_
29 Happy are you Israel! / Who is like you? /	15	2
[a]a people delivered[a] by YHWH / shield of your help /	15	2_
And the sword [b]of <his> splendor[b] / marches[c] on //	14	2
and your enemies come cringing / to you /	14	2
and you / on [d]their backs[d] you shall tread // ס	16	2_

Notes

26.a-a. Reading כְּאֵל, "like God (= El), (O Jeshurun)" of MT, with D. N. Freedman (*FS C. H. Gordon* [1980] 33) rather than כָּאֵל, "like the God (of Jeshurun)," as proposed by Driver ([1895] 415), Craigie ([1976] 402), Mayes ([1981] 409), and others. The meaning remains essentially the same, for

YHWH is the God of Jeshurun (Israel). MT is retained as *lectio difficilior.* LXX reads ὥσπερ ὁ θεός, "like the god," which may be a translation of MT כָּאֵל; cf. also Vg., Syr. Prosodic analysis favors MT.

27.a-a. Repointing MT וּמִתַּחַת, "and an undergirding," to read וּמְתַחַת, "and the outstretching," from the verb מתח, "to stretch, extend," with Gordis (*The Word and the Book,* 338–41). Prosodic analysis supports the emendation.

27.b. Some SP witnesses read זרועתו, "his arms."

27.c. Reading עולם, "Eternal One," as a divine epithet with Freedman (*FS C. H. Gordon* [1980] 33).

28.a. Reading *'azlā* followed immediately by *mĕhuppāk* as disj.

28.b. Reading *pašṭā'* followed by *zāqēp qāṭôn* as conj.

28.c. Reading the verb עָן from the root עון, "to dwell," with Freedman, who suggests the possiblity that MT represents a piel form of the same root, with intensive force (*FS C. H. Gordon* [1980] 45).

28.d. SP reads על, "on"; one Heb. MS omits the prep. In an earlier study Freedman proposed that the prep. אל be detached to the preceding noun יעקב, to produce the original full form of the name: Jacob-El (*IEJ* 13 [1963] 125–26; cf. the comments of M. Dahood, *Psalms I: 1–50,* AB 16 [Garden City, NY: Doubleday, 1966] 242, 273). More recently Freedman opted to retain the MT reading, interpreting the prep. אל to mean "in" (*FS C. H. Gordon* [1980] 33). The reason for the unusual use of the pronoun may be the need for an additional word here in terms of the numerical composition of the text (cf. the unusual detachment of the *he*-interrogative as a separate word in 32:6, which may have the same explanation). On the numerical composition of 29:9–34:12, see the summary explanation under 34:1–12 below.

28.e-e. SP reads ואף שמיך, "and indeed, your heavens"; Syr. reads *w'p šmy'* (= ואף שמים).

29.a-a. SP and Tg. read העם הנושע, "the people, the ones delivered," for MT עם נושע, "a people delivered."

29.b-b. Emending to read גאותו, "his splendor," as in v 26. The misreading of the archaic verb אשר, "to march, tread upon," as the relative pronoun led to the addition of the 2 sg. suff. to read גאותך, "your splendor," in parallel with עזרך, "your help," in this poetic line.

29.c. Reading the archaic verb אשר, "he marched" (cf. 33:2; Num 21:14). It should be noted that the archaic verb אתה, "to come," appears in 33:2. These verbs also appear in Num 21:14, where both were misread (see Christensen, *Prophecy and War,* 52; idem, *CBQ* 36 [1974] 359–60). Here in Deut 33 the verb אתה, "to come, march," was correctly read in v 2 but the verb אשר, "to come, proceed, march," was read as the relative pronoun ואשר, "and who," which is omitted in most English translations as "awkward and superfluous" (so Tigay [1996] 411 n. 208). Tigay proposes three other possibilities: (1) a partial dittography of the earlier אשריך; (2) a misreading of שַׁדַּי, "the Almighty," in which case the clause originally meant "and (by) Shaddai, your sword triumphant"; (3) אשר as an epithet of God with the meaning, "and (by) the Bestower of Good Fortune, your sword triumphant" ([1996] 411 n. 208). Tigay suggests that "*'-sh-r* seems to be the theophoric element in some Hebrew names, synonymous with *gad,* 'good fortune'" (see Gen 30:11–13).

29.d-d. SP reads במתם for MT במותימו, "on their backs." The reading taken here follows MT with archaic 3 pl. pronominal suff.

Form/Structure/Setting

See the discussion of 33:1–5 above, where 33:26–29 is discussed as well, since the two passages function together as two stanzas of an ancient hymn used as a frame around the blessings of Moses on the twelve tribes of Israel (vv 6–25). When examined in terms of its place within the final weekly portion in the lectionary cycle of Torah readings (הברכה, Deut 33–34), the central role of 33:26–29 is evident in the following outline:

A	YHWH's protection and provision for his people	33:1–5
B	Moses blesses the twelve tribes of Israel	33:6–25
X	Israel's security and blessing a people delivered by YHWH	33:26–29
B′	Moses sees the land promised to the twelve tribes of Israel	34:1–4
A′	Transition of leadership from Moses to Joshua	34:5–12

The opening stanza of the hymn in 33:1–5 moved from an account of YHWH's march of conquest from the southland to his reign as king in Jeshurun (Israel) with a specific focus on the Torah, transmitted through Moses, which constitutes "the heritage of the assembly of Jacob" (v 4). In the above structure, this unit on the kingship of YHWH is set over against the account of the transition of leadership in Israel from Moses to Joshua. The inner frame here moves from the blessing of Moses on the twelve tribes of Israel (33:6–25), to an account of Moses' remarkable vision from the top of Mount Nebo: a bird's-eye view of the whole promised land (34:1–4). The center of this structure consists of the final words of Moses in 33:26–29.

The second stanza of that ancient hymn in 33:26–29 may be outlined in a similar concentric structure:

A	Who is like God, O Jeshurun?	33:26
B	God is a refuge and undergirding presence	33:27a
X	He drove out the enemy before you	33:27b
B′	Israel settled securely in a land of plenty	33:28
A′	"Who is like you? A people delivered by YHWH"	33:29

The outer frame in this structure moves from a brief account of the incomparability of YHWH (v 26) to that of the uniqueness of the people of Israel whom YHWH has delivered from their enemies (v 29). YHWH is a refuge for his people in time of danger and opportunity (v 27a), one who establishes his people securely in a fertile and prosperous land (v 28). In the center of this structure stands a brief summation of the second half of YHWH's Holy War, the eisodus: it was YHWH himself who destroyed the enemy nations whom Israel has dispossessed.

The data from Labuschagne on the numerical composition of 33:26–29 within its larger literary context may be summarized as follows:

Words:	before *'atnāḥ*		after *'atnāḥ*		
33:1	10	+	2	=	12 ("tribes")
33:2–5	26	+	17	=	43 (= 17 + 26)
33:6–25	127	+	102 (= 6 × 17)	=	229
33:26–29	31	+	21	=	52 (= 3 × 17)
33:2–25	153 (= 9 × 17)	+	119 (= 7 × 17)	=	272 (= 16 × 17)
33:2–29	184 (= 8 × 23)	+	140	=	324 (= 19 × 17)
33:20–25	34 (= 2 × 17)	+	29	=	63
33:1–34:12	301	+	209	=	510 (= 30 × 17)
31:1–34:12	955	+	728 (= 28 × 26)	=	1,683 (= 99 × 17)

The opening verse (33:1), which is a prose introduction to the series of blessings on the twelve tribes of Israel, is made up of a total of 12 words. The blessings of the twelve tribes in 33:2–29 have a total of 324 (= 19 × 17) words, with 184 (= 8 × 23) words before *'atnāḥ*. The most impressive subsection in terms of its numerical composition is 33:2–25, with 272 (= 16 × 17) total words, 153 (= 9 × 17) words before *'atnāḥ*, and 119 (= 7 × 17) after *'atnāḥ*. On 17 and 26 as divine-name numbers and 23 and 32 as the numbers for כבוד, "glory," see *Excursus:* "Deuteronomy as a Numerical Composition." The numerical composition of 33:1–29 as a whole is such that vv 26–29 are clearly set off from the rest as a discrete unit. This very unit is the climax of the lectionary cycle, which reaches its culmination in Jewish worship on Simchat Torah ("the joy of the Torah").

Comment

26 On the term ישרון, "Jeshurun" (= Israel), see the *Comment* on 33:5, for the verse here picks up where that one left off. Following the arguments of Driver ([1895] 415), many scholars emend MT כָּאֵל ישרון, "like El, O Jeshurun," to read כְּאֵל ישרון, "like the God of Jeshurun [Israel]." It is better to retain the MT without change. (See Lozachmeur and Margain, who translate the phrase אין כאל ישרון on a Samaritan amulet as "no one is like God, Jeshurun," *Sem* 32 [1982] 117 n. 4.) On the relationship between the names YHWH and El for God in the Bible, see Cross (*CMHE,* 44–75). The image of God as one "riding the heavens/clouds" appears particularly in archaic poetry (see esp. Ps 68:5 [Eng. 4]; see also 2 Sam 22:11; Isa 19:1; Hab 3:8; Pss 18:11 [Eng. 10]; 68:34 [Eng. 33]; 104:3). Cassuto notes that all of these have to do with God punishing evildoers and delivering his people (*Biblical and Oriental Studies* 1:244; see Tigay [1996] 411 n. 190). The imagery of a deity described as a sky-rider ("rider of the clouds") appears in Babylonian and Canaanite literature (see, e.g., *ANET,* 66, 84, 132, 134, 138; see Tigay [1996] 411 n. 191).

27 The reading of ומתחת as "and the outstretching," which Gordis proposed (*JBL* 67 [1948] 69–72), is supported by parallel usage in Isa 40:22 and medieval Hebrew texts. Gordis interprets the following phrase, זרעת עולם, "of the Everlasting Arms," as a subjective genitive in the sense that "the Everlasting Arms stretched out the heavens as a tent" (p. 341). The reading עולם, "the Eternal One," here as a divine epithet, with Freedman (in *FS C. H. Gordon* [1980] 33, 45), is in keeping with that of Gordis as evidenced by his decision to capitalize "Everlasting Arms." The descriptive phrase זרעת עולם, "the arms of the Eternal," is that of a parent who carries Israel protectively in his/her arms. The epithet "El the eternal one" (*'l ḏ-ʿlm*) is found in a Canaanite inscription of the fifteenth century B.C.E. from Sinai (see Cross, *CMHE,* 15–19, 46–50). The command השמד, "Destroy!" is addressed to Israel, whereas the previous clause presents God's role as "he drove out from before you the enemy." The verb גרש, "he drove out," is used elsewhere for YHWH's activity in the battles of the eisodus (cf. Exod 23:28–30; 33:2; 34:11; Josh 24:12, 18; Judg 2:3; 6:9).

28 The description of the land here is reminiscent of the blessing of Joseph in vv 13–16 and that of Isaac's blessing of Jacob, "May God give you of the dew of heaven, and of the fatness of the earth, and plenty of grain and wine" (Gen 27:28). The translation "alone dwells Jacob" interprets עֵין as a stative verb from the root עון, "to dwell," with Steiner (*JBL* 115 [1996] 696), who traces this interpretation back to Menahem b. Saruq (tenth century). Cross and Freedman reach much the same conclusion in *Studies in Ancient Yahwistic Poetry,* SBLDS 21 (Missoula, MT: Scholars Press, 1975) 121 n. 87 (see also Freedman's essay in *FS C. H. Gordon* [1980] 45). The language of this verse resembles that of Gen 27:28.

Malamat says that Hebrew בדד, "alone," carries the nuance of strength (both here and in the parallel text of Num 23:9): Israel dwelling securely and peacefully in self-reliance, in the sense of "independent, unaligned" from a political point of view (*JQR* 76 [1985] 49).

29 The "sword of (YHWH's) splendor" is personified as in Isa 34:5–6, where YHWH's sword "has drunk its fill" and "is sated with blood" (cf. also the "Song of YHWH's Sword" in Jer 50:35–38). The translation "marches on" (ואשר) interprets the relative pronoun as the misreading of an archaic verbal root found also in Num 21:14 (see Christensen, *Prophecy and War,* 50–51).

Explanation

The words of 33:26–29 are the final words of Moses, for what follows in 34:1–12 is written about him in the third person. The figure of God riding on a chariot through the heavens, though common in the Bible (cf. Pss 18:11 [Eng. 10]; 68:34 [Eng. 33]; Isa 19:1; Ezek 1), derived ultimately from Canaanite descriptions of their god Baal. Nonetheless, there is no comparison.

It is not only the God of Israel who is incomparable; the same is true of the Israel of God. No words can adequately express the excellence of the God of Jeshurun, or the privileges and blessing of his people (v 26). The righteousness with which they are clothed is everlasting. The eternal God is their dwelling place and his undergirding arms form their unfailing support (v 27). He is the one who defeats the enemy so that Israel may settle securely in a fertile land, whose "skies drip moisture" (v 28). Israel is "a people delivered by YHWH," whose "enemies come cringing to you" as you tread upon their backs (v 29). God help us to know the happiness of Israel as portrayed here, so that we too may find our dwelling place in the everlasting arms of the God of Jeshurun.

D. Death of Moses and Transfer of Leadership to Joshua (34:1–12)

Bibliography

Barth, C. "Moses, Knecht Gottes." In *FS K. Barth.* 1966. 68–81. **Benedetti, P.** *La Morte di Mose.* Milan: Bompiani Tascabili, 1979. **Blenkinsopp, J.** "The Structure of P." *CBQ* 38 (1976) 276–92. **Braulik, G.** "Die Tora als Bahnlesung: Zur Hermeneutik einer zukünftigen Auswahl der Sonntagsperikopen." In *Bewahren und Erneuern: FS H. B. Meyer.* Ed. R. Meßnerr et al. Innsbruck: Tyrolia-Verlag, 1995. 50–76. **Brueggemann, W.** "Unresolved Openness of the Pentateuch." In *Theology of the Old Testament.* Minneapolis: Fortress, 1997. 209–12. **Coats, G. W.** "Legendary Motifs in the Moses Death Report." *CBQ* 39 (1977) 34–44. **Daube, D.** "Rechtsgedanken in den Erzählungen des Pentateuch." In *FS O. Eissfeldt.* 1958. 32–41. ———. *Studies in Biblical Law.* 1947. 25–39. **Friedman, T.** "The Origin and Transformation of a Biblical Image." *BMik* 33 (1987/88) 135–38 (Heb.). **Goldin, J.** "The Death of Moses: An Exercise in Midrashic Transposition." In *FS M. Pope.* 1987.

219–25. **Haaker, K.**, and **Schäfer, P.** "Nachbiblische Traditionen vom Tod des Mose." In *Josephus Studien: Untersuchungen zu Josephus, dem antiken Judentum und dem Neuen Testament: FS Otto Michel.* Ed. O. Betz, K. Haacker, and M. Hengel. Göttingen: Vandenhoeck & Ruprecht, 1974. 147–74. **Hänsler, H.** "Mosis letzte Verfügungen und Abschied." *Das Heilige Land* 73 (1929) 9–22. **Houtman, C.** "De dood van Mozes, de knecht des Heren: Notities over an naar aanleiding van Deuteronomium 34:1–8." In *De Knecht: FS J. L. Koole.* Kampen: Kok, 1978. 72–82. **Kasher, R.** "Two 'Targum Tosephtas' on the Death of Moses." *Tarbiz* 54 (1984) 217–24 (Heb.; Eng. summary, ii–iii). **Liptzin, S.** "The Death of Moses." *DD* 6 (1978) 180–90. **Loewenstamm, S. E.** "The Death of Moses." *Tarbiz* 27 (1957/58) 142–57 (Heb.). **Lohfink, N.** "Moses Tod, die Torah und die alttestamentliche Sonntagslesung." *TP* 71 (1996) 481–94. **Lux, R.** "Der Tod des Mose als 'besprochene und erzählte Welt'; Ûberlegungen zu einer literaturwissenschaftlichen und theologischen Interpretation von Deuteronomium 32,48–55." *ZTK* 84 (1987) 395–425. **Robert, P. de.** "La fin de Moïse: Les traditions Samaritaines." *MDB* 44 (1986) 24. **Rodriguez Carmona, A.** "Los Anuncios de la Muerte de Moíses en el Targum Palestinense." In *FS L. Alonso Schökel.* 1983. 267–79. **Sanders, J. A.** *Torah and Canon.* Philadelphia: Fortress, 1972. 9–53. **Tabor, J. D.** "'Returning to the Divinity': Josephus's Portrayal of the Disappearances of Enoch, Elijah, and Moses." *JBL* 108 (1989) 225–38. **Zenger, E.** "Das alttestamentliche Israel und seine Toten." In *Der Umgang mit den Toten: Tod und Bestattung in der christlichen Gemeinde.* Ed. K. Richter. QD 123. Freiburg: Herder, 1990. 132–52.

Bibliography for 34:1–8

Albright, W. F. "The 'Natural Force' of Moses in the Light of Ugaritic." *BASOR* 94 (1944) 32–35. **Avi-Yonah, M.** *The Madaba Mosaic Map.* Jerusalem: Israel Exploration Society, 1954. **Bartlett, J. R.** "Sihon and Og, Kings of the Amorites." *VT* 20 (1970) 257–77. **Baumstark, A.** "Ps.-Jonathan zu Dtn 34,6 und die Pentateuchzitate Afrahats." *ZAW* 59 (1942–43) 99–111. **Christensen, D. L.** "Biblical Genealogies and Eschatological Speculation." *PRS* 14 (1987) 59–65. ———. "Did People Live to be Hundreds of Years Old before the Flood?" In *The Genesis Debate.* Ed. R. Youngblood. New York: Nelson, 1986. 166–83. ———. "Janus Parallelism in Genesis 6:3." *HS* 27 (1986) 20–24. **Dayagi-Mendels, M.** *Inscribed Seals: First Temple Period.* Jerusalem: Israel Museum, 1979, nos. 3–5. **Gemser, B.** "*Beʿēber hayyardēn:* In Jordan's Borderland." *VT* 2 (1952) 349–55. **Goldin, J.** *Studies in Midrash and Related Literature.* Philadelphia: Jewish Publication Society, 1988. 180–85. **Greenfield, J. C.** "A Touch of Eden." In *Orientalia J. Duchesne-Guillemin Emerito Oblata.* Acta Iranica 23. Leiden: Brill, 1984. 223–24. **Halkin, A. S.** "The Scholia to Numbers and Deuteronomy in the Samaritan-Arabic Pentateuch." *JQR* 34 (1943/44) 41–59. **Haran, M.** "Priestertum, Tempeldienst und Gebet." In *Das Land.* Ed. G. Strecker. 1983. 141–53. **Klein, J.** "The 'Bane' of Humanity: A Lifespan of One Hundred and Twenty Years." *Acta Sumerologica* 12 (1990) 57–70, 271–318. **Loewenstamm, S. E.** *From Babylon to Canaan.* Jerusalem: Magnes, 1992. 136–66. **Lubetski, M.** "New Light on Old Seals." *JQR* 68 (1977) 65–77. **Noth, M.** "Israelitische Stämme zwischen Ammon und Moab." *ZAW* 60 (1944) 11–57. **Riesener, I.** *Der Stamm* עבר *im Alten Testament: Eine Wortuntersuchung unter Berücksichtigung neuerer sprachwissenschaftlicher Methoden.* BZAW 159. Berlin: de Gruyter, 1979. 186–88. **Ringgren, H.** *Word and Wisdom: Studies in the Hypostatization of Divine Qualities and Functions in the Ancient Near East.* Lund: H. Ohlsson, 1947. **Roscher, W. H.** *Die Zahl 40 im Glauben, Brauch und Schriften der Semiten.* Abhandlungen der Sächsischen Akademie der Wissenschaften zu Leipzig, Philologisch-Historische Klasse 27. Leipzig: Teubner, 1909. 93–128, esp. 109. **Sansom, M. C.** "Laying on of Hands in the Old Testament." *ExpTim* 94 (1983) 323–26. **Schwertner, S.** "Erwägungen zu Moses Tod und Grab in Dtn 34,5.6." *ZAW* 84 (1972) 25–46. **Speier, S.** "The Jerusalem Targum to Num. 18:12 and Deut. 34:3." *JBL* 65 (1946) 315–18. **Tigay, J. H.** "לא־נס לחה, 'He had not become wrinkled' (Deuteronomy 34:7)." In *Solving Riddles and Untying Knots: FS J. C.*

Greenfield. Ed. Z. Zevit et al. Winona Lake, IN: Eisenbrauns, 1995. 345–50. **Vellas, I. B. M.** "Eine Berichtigung au Dt 34,7." Θεολογια 24 (1953) 29–32 (Greek).

See also *Bibliography* for 32:48–52.

Bibliography for 34:9–12

Eissfeldt, O. "Israels Führer in der Zeit vom Auszug aus Ägypten bis zur Landnahme." In *KlSchr* 4:297–304. **Goetschel, R.** "Les traditions juives sur la fin de Moise." *MDB* 44 (1986) 24–26. **Klein, C. A.** "Moses and Josiah: A Rabbi's Experience with His Congregation." *DD* 15 (1986/87) 199–201. **Knoppers, G. N.** "'There Was None Like Him': Incomparability in the Book of Kings." *CBQ* 54 (1992) 411–31. **Perlitt, L.** "Mose als Prophet." *EvT* 31 (1971) 588–608. ———. "Priesterschrift im Deuteronomium?" *ZAW*Sup 100 (1988) 65–88. **Peter, R.** "L'imposition des mains dans l'Ancien Testament." *VT* 27 (1977) 48–55. **Seebass, H.** "Josua." *BN* 28 (1985) 53–65. **Tigay, J.** "The Significance of the End of Deuteronomy (Deut. 34:10–12)." In *FS M. Haran.* 1996. 345–50. **Vogels, W.** "The Spirit in Joshua and the Laying on of Hands by Moses." *Lavan théologique et philosophique* 38 (1982) 3–7. **Weisman, Z.** "The Personal Spirit as Imparting Authority." *ZAW* 93 (1981) 225–34. **Wright, D. P.** "The Gesture of Hand Placement in the Hebrew Bible and in Hittite Literature." *JAOS* 106 (1986) 433–46.

Translation and Prosodic Analysis

Moses Ascends Mount Nebo to "See" the Whole of the Land [(7:4):(6:6):(6:6)]

1 And Moses went up / from the plains of Moab /	15	2
to Mount Nebo / summit / of the Pisgah (range) /	11	3
which / is opposite Jericho //	11	2_
And YHWH let him see |[a] all the land /	16	2
[b]the Gilead / as far as Dan[b] //	8	2_
2 [a]And / all of [b]Naphtali /	9	2
and [c]the land of Ephraim / and Manasseh //	12	2
and / all the land of Judah[a] /	11	2_
[d]as far as \\[e] the Western Sea //	10	1
3 [a]And the Negev / and the plain /	11	2
the valley of Jericho / city of palm trees /	15	2
as far as Zoar[a] //	4	1_
4 [a]And YHWH said / to him[a] / "This is the land /	18	3
that I promised[b] / to Abraham to Isaac |[c] and to Jacob /	22	3_
Saying / 'To your[d] descendants / I will give it' //	13	3
I have let you see it with your eyes /	12	1
but there / you shall not cross over" //	11	2_

Death and Burial of Moses [4:7]

5 And Moses the servant of YHWH / died there[a] /	14	2
in the land of Moab / as decreed by YHWH //	13	2_
6 [a]And he buried[a] him in a valley[b] /	10	1
[c]in the land of Moab[c] / opposite / Beth-peor //	14	3
and no one knows \\[d] his burial site / to / THIS DAY //	22	3_

Moses Is One Hundred and Twenty Years Old When He Dies [6:6]

7 And Moses / was one hundred and twenty / years old /	18	3
at his death //	5	1
<And>[a] his eye was not dim[b] /	12	1
and his virility[c] had not departed //	9	1_
8 And the children of Israel wept for Moses /	16	1
in the plains of Moab / thirty days //	15	2
and the days of weeping / the mourning for Moses / ended //	17	3_

Joshua Replaces Moses as Leader [5:5]

9 And Joshua son of Nun / was filled / with a spirit of wisdom /	20	3
for Moses had laid his hands[a] / upon him //	17	2_
And the children of Israel hearkened to him /	17	1
and they did / just as / YHWH commanded / Moses //	19	4_

Epitaph: "There Has Never Been Another Prophet Like Moses" [7:(7:7)]

10 And there has not risen [a]a prophet since[a] /	11	1
in Israel / like Moses //	10	2
whom / YHWH knew / face / to face //	21	4_
11 For all the signs / and the wonders /	15	2
that YHWH \[a] sent him / to do / in the land of Egypt //	21	3
to Pharaoh [and to all his servants][b] / and to all his land //	10	2_
12 And for all / the strong hand /	13	2
and for all / the great awesome deeds //	14	2
that \[a] Moses did / [b]before the eyes / of all Israel //	20	3_

Notes

1.a. Reading *ʿazlā* followed by *dargā* as disj.

1.b-b. SP reads מנהר מצרים עד הנהר הגדול נהר פרת, "from the river of Egypt as far as the great river, the River Euphrates," for MT אֶת־הַגִּלְעָד עַד־דָּן, "the Gilead as far as Dan." Prosodic analysis supports MT.

2.a-a. Omitted in SP.

2.b. One Heb. MS and LXX add ארץ, "the land of (Naphtali)." Prosodic analysis supports MT.

2.c. One Heb. MS, Cairo Geniza fragments, LXX, and Syr. add כל, "all."

2.d. SP adds *waw*-conj.

2.e. Reading *ṭiphā'* as conj. because of misplaced *sillûq*.

3.a-a. Omitted in SP.

4.a-a. Omitted in SP.

4.b. LXX adds πρὸς Μωυσην, "to Moses" (= למשה).

4.c. Reading *ʿazlā* followed by *mahpāk* as disj.

4.d. LXX and Syr. read 2 pl.

5.a. The term שם, "there," is omitted in some LXX witnesses.

6.a-a. SP[MSS] and LXX read 3 pl. MT is retained as *lectio difficilior*.

6.b. Reading בגיא, "in a valley," with some Heb. MSS, Cairo Geniza fragments, and SP (cf. 3:29 and 4:46), for MT בגי, "in a valley[?]."

6.c-c. LXX and some SP[MSS] omit. Prosodic analysis supports MT.

6.d. Reading *pašṭā'* followed by *zāqēp qāṭôn* as conj.

7.a. Adding *waw*-conj. with one Heb. MS, Cairo Geniza fragments, and some LXX witnesses.
7.b. One SP MS reads כחחה, "it was (not) strong" (?), for MT כהתה, "it was (not) dim."
7.c. Some LXX witnesses omit; Vg. reads *dentes*, "teeth."
9.a. Two Heb. MSS and SP read ידו, "his hand."
10.a-a. SP reverses order, reading עוד נביא, "yet a prophet."
11.a. Reading *paštā'* followed by *zāqēp qāṭôn* as conj.
11.b. The phrase ולכל־עבדיו, "and to all his servants," is omitted here with Cairo Geniza fragments. The deletion of two words here completes the architectural design of Deut 31–34 in terms of its numerical composition. See discussion below at the end of the section on *Form/Structure/Setting.*
12.a. Reading *paštā'* followed by *zāqēp qāṭôn* as conj.
12.b. Many Heb. MSS read ל maj. (written larger).

Form/Structure/Setting

At this point, it is useful to examine the structure of the Torah readings in Genesis in the lectionary cycle for the two weeks following Simchat Torah, the 23rd of Tishri and the ninth day of the Festival of Booths, that marks the annual completion of the lectionary cycle and the beginning of another year. The first weekly portion (Gen 1:1–6:8) is known as בראשית ("in the beginning"); and the second (Gen 6:9–11:32) is called נח, "Noah." The concentric structure of Gen 1:1–11:32 may be outlined in a menorah pattern:

A	Story of creation/dispersion (ending with three sons of Adam)	Gen 1–4
B	Enoch ("walked with God")	Gen 5
C	Sons of God take daughters of האדם as wives	Gen 6:1–2
X	YHWH said: "he is flesh and his days shall be 120 years"	Gen 6:3
C′	Sons of God and daughters of האדם breed giants	Gen 6:4
B′	Noah ("walked with God")	Gen 6:5–9:29
A′	Story of dispersion (beginning with three sons of Noah)	Gen 10–11

The structure opens with an account of the story of creation (Gen 1–4), which includes the "dispersion" of Adam and Eve from the garden of Eden. That story includes the account of Adam and his three sons: Cain, Abel, and Seth. The structure concludes with the story of the tower of Babel and the dispersion of human beings (האדם) among the people groups of antiquity, which is preceded by the account of Noah and his three sons: Shem, Ham, and Japheth (Gen 10–11). Within this framework we find a brief reference to Enoch, a man who "walked with God" (Gen 5:22), and the elaborate story of Noah, who also "walked with God" (Gen 6:9). These are the only two individuals in Genesis whose relationship with God is described in this terminology.

The center of the above structure poses a problem to many readers, who are startled by the sudden reference to what looks at first glance like what is normally called mythology. The "sons of God" marry the "daughters of Adam" to produce the giants of old (the *Nephilim;* Gen 6:1–4). In the middle of this enigmatic episode YHWH himself speaks in the form of a riddle: "My spirit shall not remain in האדם forever, בשגם he is flesh; and his days shall be 120 years" (6:3, author's translation). In the center of this sentence stands a single word in the Hebrew text, בשגם, which appears nowhere else in the Hebrew Bible. That the Hebrew consonants in this word appear with a different vowel in some manuscripts led to an important discovery: namely, that both readings are to be heard here, at the level of a literary pun (see Christensen, *HS* 27 [1986] 20–24). On the one hand, we have reached a turning point in the narrative. God's patience has run out "because of their going astray" (בְּשַׁגָּם; reading the word as the Hebrew verb שׁגג, "to go astray," with third-person plural pronominal suffix). The great flood, which follows in Gen 6–9, is a necessary consequence because of human sin. At the same time, another message is carried on this same word, which may be rendered as a connecting phrase—"*in that also* [בְּשַׁגָּם] he is flesh, and his days shall be 120 years." But the question then almost leaps off the page: of whom is the writer speaking? None of the ancestors to follow on the pages of Genesis is limited to a life span of 120 years. The only person in the entire Bible to die at that age is Moses, a fact that is highlighted in the framing of the final section of Deuteronomy (chaps. 31–34), at the conclusion of the Pentateuch (see 31:2 and 34:7).

A third meaning is also possible, as noted by A. Geiger more than a hundred years ago (*ZDMG* 28 [1874] 489–91), who suggested that the term בשגם here refers to Moses. He cited both Josephus and Jerome in his arguments, noting that in terms of gematria the terms משה, "Moses," and בשגם are identical.

The content of Deut 34:1–12 may be outlined in similar fashion, by focusing on the nesting of repeated vocabulary items, where the concentric structure highlights the limit in life span of one hundred and twenty years:

A	Moses saw the whole of the land "with *[his] eyes*"	34:1–4
B	Death and burial of Moses—"no one *knows*" where	34:5–6
X	Moses was 120 years old—"*his eye* was not dim"	34:7–8
B′	Incomparability of Moses—"whom YHWH *knew* face to face"	34:9–10
A′	Moses did great wonders "before *the eyes* of all Israel"	34:11–12

At the conclusion of the account of Moses ascending Mount Nebo "to see" the promised land, as YHWH had commanded him (cf. 3:27 and 32:49–52), YHWH reminds Moses that this is the land that he promised in times past to give to the descendants of the ancestral fathers (Abraham, Isaac, and Jacob). He then adds: "I have let you see it *with your eyes.*" The Hebrew עינים, "eyes," does not appear in 32:49–52, though it is used twice in 3:27 and twice more in this final chapter: in 34:7 and 34:12, where it functions as a structural feature around which the concentric design of the chapter as a whole is shaped. The opening section concludes with the note that God allowed Moses to see the promised land "*with [his] eyes*" (v 4). The center of the structure highlights that "*his eye was not dim*" at the time of death (v 7); and Deuteronomy itself closes with a reference to "*the eyes of all Israel*" (v 12).

Daube says transfer of ownership in Roman and biblical law was implemented by "showing" the object to be transferred to the new owner (*Studies in Biblical Law*, 28–31; cf. Mayes [1981] 411–12). In this act of legal fiction, Moses receives ownership of the land in behalf of the people, for indeed God himself "showed" Moses the entire land—he saw it all, with his own eyes.

The inner frame in the concentric design of 34:1–12 focuses attention on the verb "to know." Moses dies and is buried by God somewhere in the vicinity of Mount Nebo; but "no one *knows* the place of his burial to this day" (v 6). In the concluding remarks about the uniqueness of Moses as a prophet, the text highlights that Moses was one "whom YHWH *knew* face to face" (34:10; cf. Exod 33:18–23, where Moses is told that "you cannot see my face, for no one may see me and live . . . my face shall not be seen" [NRSV]). The chapter concludes with a brief necrology that focuses attention on the uniqueness of this man whom God "*knew face to face*" (v 10) and through whom God did such "great awesome deeds" when he brought the people of Israel from the land of Egypt to the promised land (vv 11–12).

Once again, it should be noted that the common verb "to know" in the language of ancient Israel carries legal overtones. To say that YHWH "knew" Moses (34:10) implies that Moses also "knew" YHWH. To "know" is a technical term for mutual legal recognition of sovereign and vassal (Botterweck, *TDOT* 5:478). Huffmon points out that it is said of both Suppiluliumas (in Hittite literature) and Ashurbanipal (in Assyrian records) that the gods "know" them, which is a way of saying that the gods recognize them as legitimate rulers (*BASOR* 181 [1966] 31). It is also possible to interpret "knowing" within the context of marriage and a relationship of marital fidelity (so W. Eichrodt, "'The Holy One in Your Midst': The Theology of Hosea," tr. L. Gaston, *Int* 15 (1961) 259–73, esp. 264). In either case Moses enjoys a peculiar relationship with YHWH in which he is granted the promised land as a legal inheritance that he in turn entrusts to his successor Joshua.

The opening section on the ascent of Mount Nebo (vv 1–4) is closely connected with the command Moses receives to do that very thing in 32:48–52, immediately before he delivers the testamentary blessing in 33:1–29. The concentric structural design of Deut 33–34 may be outlined as follows:

A	Testamentary blessing of Moses	33:1–29
B	Moses ascends Mount Nebo to see the whole land	34:1–4
X	Death and burial of Moses at 120 years of age	34:5–8
B′	Joshua assumes command to take the people into the land	34:9
A′	Necrology of Moses—never another prophet like him	34:10–12

This outline should be compared to the one given in the discussion of Deut 33, where the focus was on the blessing as such. Here in this reading of the eleventh weekly portion of Torah readings from Deuteronomy, and the final reading in the annual lectionary cycle, the focus is on Moses' death and burial, which occurs when he is one hundred and twenty years of age. The outer frame moves from the extended testamentary blessing on the twelve tribes of Israel (33:1–29) to the brief necrology of Moses, the man "whom YHWH knew face to face"—for "there has not risen a prophet since in Israel" (34:10–12). The inner frame moves from Moses' bird's-eye vision of the whole promised land on Mount Nebo (34:1–4) to Joshua being "filled with a spirit of wisdom" as he assumes leadership to bring the people of Israel across the Jordan to possess the land Moses "saw" (34:9). In the middle we find the description of the death and burial of Moses at the age of one hundred and twenty years (34:5–8).

When examined in light of the structure of Deut 31–34 as a whole, the primary structure of chap. 34 focuses attention on observing the Torah under the leadership of Joshua, as the following menorah pattern suggests:

A	In view of his impending death, Moses commissions Joshua	31:1–15
B	Moses' final works: Torah and song as witnesses	31:16–30
C	The Song of Moses as a witness for future generations	32:1–43
X	Moses' final charge: observe all the words of the Torah	32:44–47
C′	The testamentary blessing of Moses	33:1–25
B′	Moses' final words: on Israel's security and blessing	33:26–29
A′	Death of Moses and transition of leadership to Joshua	34:1–12

Though this is certainly a valid way of reading Deut 34 within its larger literary context, it is also instructive to examine 34:1–12 as a literary unit in its own right, as shown above in the introduction to this section of the commentary.

It is useful to divide 34:1–12 in two equal parts and to observe that each half may be outlined in similar fashion:

A	Moses ascends Mount Nebo in the land of Moab	34:1a
B	YHWH shows him the whole of the promised land	34:1b–3
X	YHWH says: "This is the land I promised your fathers"	34:4a
B′	YHWH lets Moses see it but does not let him enter it	34:4b
A′	Moses dies on Mount Nebo and is buried in the land of Moab	34:5–6

A	Moses is 120 years old when he dies	34:7
B	Israel mourns his death for 30 days	34:8
X	Joshua takes Moses' place as leader in Israel	34:9
B′	There has not risen a prophet since in Israel like Moses	34:10
A′	Moses did awesome things in the eyes of all Israel	34:11–12

This particular reading highlights that what YHWH shows Moses from the top of Mount Nebo is the very land that was "promised to Abraham, to Isaac, and to Jacob, saying: 'To your descendants I will give it'" (v 4); and that Joshua is designated as the leader to take the people there (v 9). The outer frame in the first of the above concentric structures moves from the account of Moses ascending Mount Nebo in the land of Moab (v 1a) to the report of Moses' death on that mountain and his burial in the land of Moab (vv 5–6). The inner frame moves from the vision of the whole of the promised land that YHWH shows Moses (vv 1b–3) to YHWH's statement that he is allowing Moses to see the land but not to enter it himself (v 4b).

The center of the concluding unit (vv 7–12) focuses on the person of Joshua, on whom "Moses had laid his hands" in the final transference of authority (v 9). On one side of this summary statement we find another mystery: though Moses dies at 120 years, he is at the height of his physical strength and virility (v 7–8). On the other side, we are reminded that there has never been another "prophet" in Israel like this man Moses (v 10), who did such marvelous things "before the eyes of all Israel" (vv 11–12).

It is also possible to divide vv 1–6 into two parts that are structured in the same manner:

A	YHWH lets Moses see all the land	34:1a-d
B	To the north: Gilead, Napthali, Ephraim, and Manasseh	34:1d–2a
X	All the land of Judah its boundaries	34:2b–3
B′	This is the land promised to Abraham, Isaac, and Jacob	34:4a
A′	YHWH says: "I have let you see it with your eyes"	34:4b

A	"Moses the servant of YHWH died there"	וימת שם משה עבד־יהוה	34:5a
B	"*in the land of Moab* as decreed by YHWH"	בארץ מואב על־פי יהוה	34:5b
X	"and he buried him in a valley"	ויקבר אתו בגי	34:6a
B′	"*in the land of Moab* opposite Beth-peor"	בארץ מואב מול בית פעור	34:6b
A′	"and no one knows his burial site"	ולא־ידע איש את־קברתו	34:6c

The first subsection here (vv 1–4) is framed by references to the fact that YHWH permits Moses to see the promised land. The extent of that land is described from north to south (vv 1d–3), concluding with a simple summary: "This is the land that I promised [to give] to Abraham, to Isaac, and to Jacob" (v 4a).

The account of Moses' death and burial in vv 5–6 is arranged in a circular sentence in which the repeated phrase "in the land of Moab" functions as the inner frame. The center of this structure presents the mystery of the death of Moses: since YHWH himself is responsible for his death and burial, no one knows the actual site of Moses' final resting place.

The concluding eulogy on Moses in vv 10–12 is placed within a concentric structure that focuses on the actual transfer of leadership to Joshua:

A	Joshua is filled with a spirit of wisdom	34:9aα
B	Moses had laid his hands upon him	34:9aβ
X	The people obey Joshua as Moses commanded	34:9b
B′	There has not risen a prophet since in Israel like Moses	34:10
A′	Moses performed awesome signs and wonders	34:11–12

The outer frame of this structure presents the two leaders in sharp contrast: Joshua is filled with a spirit of wisdom (v 9aα); but Moses performed awesome signs and wonders "before the eyes of all Israel" (vv 11–12). The contrast continues in the inner frame as well, for the very endowment of wisdom on Joshua came through the hands of Moses (v 9aβ); and Moses, like YHWH himself, is incomparable (v 10). The conclusion of the matter is clear: the people of God are to submit themselves to the leader God raises up in their midst, in this instance Joshua, as Moses commanded (v 9b).

Lohfink explores the account of the death of Moses as a connecting link with each of the major divisions of the canon of sacred Scripture, including the NT (*TP* 71 [1996] 481–94). The connection with the Former Prophets in the opening verses of the book of Joshua is obvious. That connection led von Rad to disregard the limit of the Pentateuch as such and to speak of the Hexateuch instead: six books, including Joshua. In this way he found a fulfillment of the promise of the land in the conquest of Joshua.

Lohfink sees the account of the death of Moses, including the Song of Moses (32:1–43), as a literary boundary marker within the structure of the canon as a whole. The opening verses of Isaiah (1:2) are structurally tied to the Song of Moses, and Isa 1:10 with its reference to Sodom and Gomorrah reflects Deut 29:22. The connection between the ending of Deuteronomy and the beginning and the ending of the Psalter is the worshiper whose "delight is in the law of the Lord" in which "he meditates day and night" (Ps 1:2; cf. Josh 1:8). In short, the death of Moses is located in a key position for reading the canon of sacred Scripture as a whole, which is not arranged in a linear fashion. Lohfink goes even further to include the NT, which he sees as essentially the definitive commentary on the Torah. Moreover, he and his colleague G. Braulik argue that recent liturgical reforms within the Roman Catholic Church do not go far enough, and that regular readings of the Torah in Christian worship should be restored. Braulik suggests a three-year cycle of readings, each of which begins with a prescribed reading from the Torah and ends with a reading from the Gospels, with two alternative readings in between, one from the rest of the books of the OT and one from elsewhere in the NT (Braulik, in *FS H. B. Meyer,* 50–76; idem, "Kanon und liturgische Schriftlesung," *BLit* 68 [1995] 181–86).

The data from Labuschagne on the numerical composition of 34:1–12 may be summarized as follows:

Words:	before *'atnāḥ*		after *'atnāḥ*		
34:1–4	43 (= 17 + 26)	+	21	=	64 (= 2 × 32)
34:5–8	33	+	19	=	52 (= 2 × 26)
34:5–12	64 (= 2 × 32)	+	46	=	110 (= 2 × 55)
34:9–12	31	+	27	=	58 (= 26 + 32)
29:9–34:12	1,312 (= 41 × 32)	+	1,034	=	2,346 (= 138 × 17)
29:9–32:52	1,011	+	825	=	1,836 (= 108 × 17)
29:9–30:20	357 (= 21 × 17)	+	306 (= 18 × 17)	=	663 (= 39 × 17)
31:1–34:12	955	+	728 (= 28 × 26)	=	1,683 (= 99 × 17)
31:1–30	322 (= 14 × 23)	+	230 (= 10 × 23)	=	552 (= 24 × 23)
32:1–52	332	+	289 (= 17 × 17)	=	621
33:1–34:12	301	+	209	=	510 (= 30 × 17)

There is clear evidence that the author(s) of this text used the two divine-name numbers 17 and 26 in the numerical composition of 34:1–12, but it is more important to observe how this text is used to complete the larger design of Readings 8–11 (29:9–34:12) as a whole. There is a total of 2,346 (= 6 × 23 × 17) words in this macrosection of Deuteronomy. What better way to say that "these words" are written to the glory of YHWH, for the number 23 stands for כבוד, "glory," and the number 17 for YHWH. This fact is reinforced by the total number of words before *'atnāḥ,* 1,312 (= 41 × 32). Both of the numbers for Hebrew כבוד, "glory" (23 and 32), appear in this structure.

In Readings 8–10 (29:9–32:52) there is a total of 1,836 (= 108 × 17) words, and in Readings 9–11 (31:1–34:12) there is a total of 1,683 (= 99 × 17) words, with 728 (= 4 × 7 × 26) words after *'atnāḥ.*

In Reading 8 (29:9–30:20) there is a total of 663 (= 39 × 17) words, with 357 (= 3 × 7 × 17) words before *'atnāḥ* and 306 (= 18 × 17) words after *'atnāḥ.* In Reading 9 (31:1–30) there is a total of 552 (= 2 × 12 × 23) words, with 322 (= 2 × 7 × 23) words before *'atnāḥ* and 230 (= 10 × 23) words after *'atnāḥ.* In Reading 10 (32:1–52) there is a total of 289 (= 17 × 17) words after *'atnāḥ.* Finally, in reading 11 (33:1–34:12) there is a total of 510 (= 3 × 10 × 17) words. It is difficult to imagine the labor that went into achieving these impressive totals on the part of an author or authors in antiquity who labored long and hard to the glory of YHWH. In so doing, they left us a legacy of enormous worth, particularly in the matter of textual criticism. Not a single word can be added or subtracted without disturbing the system.

Comment

1 The summit of the Pisgah was one of the places to which Balak, king of Moab, took the prophet Balaam in his attempt to get him to curse the hosts of Israel (Num 21:20). In that context we learn that the Pisgah range overlooks the Jeshimon (see *Comment* on 32:10). The summit of Pisgah refers to a promontory of a particular mountain, the Ras es-Siyaghah, which is slightly lower than the summit of Mount Nebo and separated from it by a saddle. It is an ideal place from which to view the Rift valley and points beyond in the promised land—and the wilderness region known as the Jeshimon (cf. Num 21:20), in the "plains of Jericho" (cf. Josh 4:13), where Joshua subsequently set up battle camp to take possession of the land YHWH showed Moses. YHWH "let him see all the land"—beginning with Gilead, the Transjordanian hill country extending from the Arnon River northward beyond the Yarmuk River into what is elsewhere called Bashan.

2–4 See the *Comment* on 33:23. "Ephraim and Manasseh" include the central hill country in the land of Canaan, which extends from Judah in the south to the Esdraelon Valley in the region of Galilee. The reference to "the plain" here probably refers to the Jordan Valley immediately north of the Dead Sea (cf. "the great plain" in Josephus *J.W.* 4.8.2 §§452–56), which includes "the valley of Jericho city of palm trees." Here the phrase "as far as Zoar" refers to the southern end of the Dead Sea, which is not visible from the summit of Mount Nebo, because of the mountain range extending to the viewer's left that blocks the view such that only the northern part of the Dead Sea is visible. Moses was given a vision of the promised land in its entirety that no tourist today can see without ascending into the skies. Perhaps this fact helps to explain the subsequent tradition known as *The Assumption of Moses,* with its account of Moses being taken directly to heaven rather than dying a natural death. Jude 9 appears to refer to such a tradition, which was apparently well known in early Jewish circles. At any rate, it would require such an airborne experience for Moses to actually see all that the biblical text says he saw in his vision from the summit of Mount Nebo. At this point Moses is once again told that he "shall not cross over" into the promised land (cf. 3:27; 4:21–22; 32:42; and Num 20:12).

5 "Moses the servant of YHWH died there." According to Josephus (*Ant.* 4.8.49 §327), Moses died on the first of Adar, the twelfth month—exactly six months after the death of Aaron. Moses died "as decreed by YHWH," that is, at YHWH's command (lit. "at the mouth of"). The midrashic interpretation that Moses died at a kiss from God (see *b. B. Bat.* 17a) is the source of the Jewish idiom "death by a kiss," which refers to "sudden, painless death in old age" (Tigay [1996] 338).

6 Though the subject of the clause ויקבר אתו, "he buried him," is ambiguous, the context makes clear that it is God who "buried him in a valley" in the vicinity of Mount Nebo and Beth-peor. "Many commentators have conjectured that Moses' gravesite was kept secret to prevent people from making it a shrine, . . . the statement . . . could be polemical, intended to undermine claims that a particular site *is* Moses' grave" (Tigay [1996] 338, citing F. M. Cross, "Reuben, First-Born of Jacob," *ZAW* Sup 100 [1988] 50–52).

7 "Moses was one hundred and twenty years old at his death." Gen 6:3 refers to 120 as a limit imposed by God on the life span of human beings, a limit that applies specifically only to Moses in the Bible (see *Comment* on 31:2). The number 120 may have been "based on a combination of empirical observation and ancient Near Eastern mathematics," as Tigay suggests ([1996] 338). At the same time, however, it should be noted that the scribes of ancient Israel had their own system of "biblical mathematics" (see Christensen, *PSR* 14 [1987] 59–65; and C. J. Labuschagne, *Numerical Secrets of the Bible: Rediscovering the Bible Codes* [N. Richland Hills, TX: BIBAL Press, 2000]).

The statement that "his eye was not dim" makes clear that Moses was not feeble. Indeed, "his virility had not departed"—all his juices were still there; he had not "dried up." The noun לחה, translated "virility," appears only here in the Hebrew Bible, though two occurrences in Ugaritic are known, from which Albright concludes that it means "sexual power" (*BASOR* 94 [1944] 32–35). Though Tigay interprets this verse, with Ibn Ezra and others, to mean "he had not become wrinkled," in the sense that despite his years he did not look aged, this does not do justice to the Hebrew idiom (see Albright's arguments). Moreover, his claim that "Moses' *vigor* had, in fact abated (31:2)" is incorrect (see *Comment* on 31:2 above). Moses died because he reached the limit God had set for him, namely 120 years. Unlike the senile David at the time of his death at a later point in time (1 Kgs 2), Moses died at the height of his physical strength shortly after he had commanded the tribes of Israel in battle against the Canaanite kings, Sihon and Og, and immediately after he had climbed to the summit of Mount Nebo alone. He died forty years after the exodus from Egypt, which took place when he was eighty (Exod 7:7; cf. Deut 1:3). Though forty more years had passed, he had not aged.

8 The people mourned Moses' death for "thirty days," which is the normal period in ancient Israel to mourn for the dead (cf. 21:13 and Num 20:29 for the death of Aaron).

9 The "spirit of wisdom" that rested on Joshua was a divine gift to enable him to govern justly, like that which Solomon received in 1 Kgs 3:7–12. The act of Moses laying "his hands" on Joshua is connected with the idea of a transference of authority in a rite of investiture. Daube has challenged Robertson Smith's assertion that only in the case of the scapegoat was the laying on of hands to be interpreted as indicating transference; elsewhere, in the case of sin and burnt offerings, the idea was the same as in acts of blessing and consecration, namely, a general identification, by means of physical contact, of the person imposing his hands with the person or animal on whose head he imposed them. Sansom has explored five contexts for the use of Hebrew סמך, "leaning on (of hands)," and concludes as follows: "Some, but not all, of Moses' authority is given to Joshua. He is to be dependent upon Eleazar, who is to enquire of the Lord. Yet he is appointed to lead the people. We may therefore take the laying-on of hands as the official investiture to that task, and we may confidently accept that the hand-laying is connected with the idea of a transference—although this time of authority rather than of guilt" (*ExpTim* 94 [1983] 325). It should be noted, however, that there is no "apostolic authority" here; for Joshua does not appoint a successor. Indeed, he is the only one on whom hands are laid. Hands are not laid on priests or on the elders (Exod 18:13–27), even though it is sometimes assumed that in the case of the elders they were. As Tigay notes ([1996] 339), the gesture of סמכה, "laying (of hands)," became part of the ceremony of rabbinic ordination. From this point on, the people of Israel "hearkened to him"—they began to obey Joshua as their leader.

10 The statement that "there has not risen a prophet since in Israel like Moses" makes a sharp contrast between Joshua and Moses. Although Joshua succeeded Moses, neither he nor any other prophet after him is to be compared with Moses (on the concept of incomparability in the Bible, see C. Labuschagne, *The Incomparability of Yahweh in the Old Testament* [Leiden: Brill, 1966]; and Knoppers, *CBQ* 54 [1992] 411–31). See also the *Comment* on 18:18. In subsequent tradition, this promise that God would "raise up a prophet like (Moses)" was fulfilled in the succession of canonical prophets in ancient Israel, and culminated in the person of Jesus Christ, to whom the words of 31:10 apply in a more complete sense—there has not risen a prophet since.

By saying "YHWH knew" Moses, the Hebrew means that YHWH "chose" Moses by singling him out to speak with him "face to face." This statement, however, poses somewhat of a puzzle, as Tigay's discussion suggests ([1996] 380). Exod 33:11 affirms that God spoke to Moses "face to face, as one speaks to a friend" (NRSV); but at the same time, God spoke different words a few verses later in Exod 33:20, when he declared: "you cannot see my face; for no one shall see me and live" (NRSV). According to Num 12:8 Moses did see God, who spoke with him "mouth to mouth," that is, plainly and not in riddles. The phrase is used differently in Deuteronomy (cf. 4:12–15 and 5:4), where it has become an idiom that indicates "in person," or "directly," "without mediation." As Tigay puts it ([1996] 340), "The point of the text is that Moses had the most direct contact with God of any prophet, and hence had the clearest knowledge of Him and His will." As the "Word of God" incarnate, and the ultimate fulfillment of the promise of a "prophet like (Moses)" at some future point in time (Deut 18:15, 18), Jesus had even deeper personal contact with God and God's will for his people.

The statement that "there has not risen a prophet since in Israel" has an interesting parallel in the Mari documents, as A. Malamat notes ("A Forerunner of Biblical Prophecy: The Mari Documents," in *FS F. M. Cross* [1987] 44). In the case of the professional prophets noted there, the actual message given is preceded by the verb "to arise" (*tebû*), "which alludes to the stimulation of the prophets in the temple (perhaps getting up from a sitting or crouching position)" (p. 44; cf. *CTA* 4.1.23; 4.3.30; 4.4.32; etc.). Mayes finds the presentation of Moses here to be in conflict with 18:18 ([1981] 413). It is better to see these two verses as forming an inclusion around Deut 18–34, which anticipates the whole of the Former Prophets, where indeed there is no prophet "in Israel like Moses." In the Latter Prophets we find the expectation of the appearance of the prophet like Moses, which becomes an essential part of eschatological speculation within apocalyptic literature—and in the NT, where Jesus is seen as the fulfillment of this hope.

11–12 "The signs and the wonders" that God performed through Moses in the exodus from Egypt demonstrate that the words of Moses really do come from God. These same signs and wonders are invoked in 4:32–40 to show God's uniqueness and his incomparability. "The great awesome deeds that Moses did" refer to what my teacher G. E. Wright often described as "the *Magnalia Dei*" (the title of his *Festschrift* [1976]). Deuteronomy concludes with the phrase "before the eyes of all Israel." In the phrase "all Israel" we find an envelope around the book as a whole (see 1:1) that tells the reader we have reached the end of a long journey, which is also the beginning of another even longer journey for God's people, one that extends from Joshua to another "Joshua" in times to come, for "Jesus" is simply the Greek form of "Joshua."

Explanation

Anyone who stands atop Mount Nebo and looks across the great Rift valley toward the land of Israel knows full well that Moses saw much more than the normal human eye can see, for God enabled him to "see" the whole promised land. Today we see the northern end of the Dead Sea, the green of the palm trees in the oasis of Jericho down in the valley below, and dimly on top of a distant ridge on the horizon there in front of us, beyond the valley, is the tiny speck of the Tower of the Ascension (of the Russian Orthodox monastery) on top of the Mount of Olives. That very building calls attention to the fact that the "prophet like Moses," who is described as being greater than Moses (Heb 3:3), also looked out on the whole promised land as he ascended into heaven (Acts 1:9). The city of Jerusalem is on the other side of that mountain. There is no way from that spot for us to see with Moses "all the land of Judah as far as the Western Sea" (v 2).

At the "burning bush" on Mount Sinai, God revealed his presence to Moses and called him to lead the people of Israel out of slavery in Egypt, and to take them "home" to the promised land. Moses now gazed on that very land, which he himself was not permitted to enter. "And Moses the servant of YHWH died there in the land of Moab, according to the mouth of YHWH" (v 5). According to rabbinic tradition, he died "with a kiss from the mouth of God," which is a midrashic rendering of the Hebrew text, as Tigay notes ([1996] 338, 412 n. 7). God arranged a private burial; for Moses was buried "in a valley in the land of Moab opposite Beth-peor, and no one knows his burial site to this day" (v 6). Moses needs no grave or funerary monument to preserve his memory. His name is engraved in history by virtue of his work, which is far more enduring than any granite sarcophagus.

Joshua was praised as being "filled with a spirit of wisdom" (v 9). The prophet Isaiah envisioned that same "spirit of wisdom and understanding" resting on "a shoot from the stump of Jesse" (Isa 11:1–2), whose name was also "Joshua," or Jesus, as a Greek version of that Hebrew name has come to us. It is an honor reserved for this second Joshua to do "what the law [Torah], weakened by the flesh, could not do" (Rom 8:3). For God sent "his own Son in the likeness of sinful flesh, and to deal with sin, he condemned sin in the flesh, so that the just requirement of the law might be fulfilled in us, who walk not according to the flesh, but according to the Spirit" (Rom 8:3–4 NRSV).

The greatness of Moses lies not in his character or even in his astounding achievements. It is true that he took a self-willed and stiff-necked people of disparate backgrounds and forged them into a nation. With a profound love for his people, which burned like a consuming fire, he was willing to have his own name blotted out in their behalf. His enthusiasm, his compassion, and his sound judgment inspired the people of Israel to dream the impossible dream and see it come to pass. Nonetheless, all this does not explain his unique greatness, for God used him as he did no other until the time of Jesus, as an instrument of revelation. The Torah of Moses was the foundation on which all subsequent leaders in Israel and the early Christian church would build. Jesus did not come to do away with that marvelous edifice, but to complete it. On the Mount of Transfiguration, one of the figures with Jesus was none other than Moses himself (Matt 17:3; Mark 9:4; Luke 9:30).

Index of Modern Authors

Index of Biblical and Other Ancient Sources

The Old Testament

The New Testament

Apocrypha

Dead Sea Scrolls

Josephus

Rabbinic Literature

Rabbinic and Medieval Jewish Authors

Other Ancient Sources

Church Fathers

Christian Medieval Authors

Index of Principal Topics